THE
COLD
WAR
1945-1991

Leaders and Other

Important Figures in

the Soviet Union,

Eastern Europe, China,

and the Third World

Edited by
Benjamin Frankel

A MANLY, INC. BOOK

 **Gale Research Inc.**

DETROIT • WASHINGTON, D.C. • LONDON

PLANNING BOARD
William Emerson
Paul A. Jureidini
Ronald D. McLaurin

Matthew J. Bruccoli and Richard Layman, *Editorial Directors*
Karen L. Rood, *Senior Editor*

Printed in the United States of America

Cover Photo/Bettman Archives

Library of Congress Catalog Card Number 92-30486
ISBN 0-8103-8928-2

10 9 8 7 6 5 4

Table of Contents

Preface

The purpose of *The Cold War, 1945-1991* is to provide the reader with an accessible source of information on the events that dominated and defined the second half of the twentieth century. The central theme of the period was the tense, grim rivalry between the United States and the Soviet Union. The Cold War was not merely a political conflict between the two states, although the competition over spheres of influence was a central part of it. Two aspects made the Cold War unique. The first was that is was also a competition between two rival social systems, two incompatible views of man and society. The second was the introduction of nuclear weapons. These two elements combined to endow the Cold War with an apocalyptic air and messianic fervor absent from the usual, and more mundane, competition between states for power and influence. There were many other important developments in the post–World War II world, but all of them, to a greater or lesser degree, were shaped or influenced by the U.S.–Soviet rivalry. The encyclopedia describes, explains, and analyzes the major events of this anxious time.

It does so by examining the careers of the important individuals who played major roles and made unique contributions during the period: they participated in the events, made the decisions, fought the wars, passed the laws, coined the terms of policy and debate, wrote important analyses, mobilized public opinion, or anchored the events of the Cold War in the larger historical sweep. It is no coincidence that very different participants in the Cold War chose similar titles for their memoirs of the period: Dean Acheson's *Witness at the Creation*, Charles Bohlen's *Witness to History*, Whittaker Chambers's *Witness*. The individuals studied in the first two volumes of the encyclopedia were all intimate and active witnesses to the Cold War as it unfolded.

The biographical entries are not full–scale biographical studies. Rather, they concentrate on these individuals' participation in and contribution to the events we call the Cold War. The first volume offers biographical entries on 149 personalities from the United States and Europe. The second volume consists of biographical entires of 134 important figures from the Soviet Union, China, the communist countries of East Europe and Asia, and the Third World.

The encyclopedia also offers, in volume 3, a detailed examination of the major events, concepts, terms, and themes that dominated the Cold War.

It should be remembered that editing an encyclopedia begins with the act of selection, winnowing the thousands of relevant biographies and pertinent nonbiographical entries to a manageable number of a few hundreds. This encyclopedia, like others, is therefore suggestive and representative, not exhaustive or comprehensive.

This reference work serves the reader as a first and a full resource for information on the Cold War. It is organized so that each entry is self contained: terms are explained each time they appear; every entry is accompanied by a detailed bibliography for further research and a list of other entries in which additional pertinent information may be found; the third volume contains a chronology and analytical history of the Cold War, allowing the reader to place individual entries into the larger picture.

The main features of *The Cold War, 1945-1991* are:

— a close study of the careers and contributions of 149 individuals who played an important role in shaping the Cold War. Each entry is followed by a detailed bibliography for further research

— a detailed chronology of the Cold War, listing the major events, conferences, wars, agreements, laws, and more. Each entry is followed by a detailed bibliography for further research

— a narrative analytical history of the period, offering a comprehensive history of the Cold War and analysis of its major events

— a comprehensive thematic bibliography, broken into categories and sub–categories

— a research guide to the archival material, including private papers, public documents, and oral histories relevant to the Cold War

Benjamin Frankel is a specialist in the areas of U.S. national security, defense, and foreign policy; military strategy; and international relations theory. He completed undergraduate work at the University of Tel Aviv and graduate work in political science at the University of Chicago. He is founder and editor of the journal Security Studies.

Mr. Frankel is editor of the books In the National Interest: A National Interest Reader *(Lanham, Md.: University Press of America, 1990);* Opaque Nuclear Proliferation: Methodological and Policy Implications *(Frank Cass, 1991); and* The Nuclear Proliferation Fact-book *(Washington, D. C.: Congressional Research Service, 1992).*

Acknowledgments

This book was produced by Manly, Inc. Karen L. Rood is senior editor. James W. Hipp and Dennis Lynch were the in-house editors.

Projects manager is Charles D. Brower. Photography editors are Edward Scott and Timothy C. Lundy. Layout and graphics supervisor is Penney L. Haughton. Copyediting supervisor is Bill Adams. Typesetting supervisor is Kathleen M. Flanagan. Mary Scott Dye is editorial associate. Systems manager is George F. Dodge. The production staff includes Rowena Betts, Steve Borsanyi, Teresa Chaney, Patricia Coate, Rebecca Crawford, Margaret McGinty Cureton, Denise Edwards, Sarah A. Estes, Robert Fowler, Brenda A. Gillie, Bonita Graham, Jolyon M. Helterman, Ellen McCracken, Kathy Lawler Merlette, John Myrick, Pamela D. Norton, Thomas J. Pickett, Maxine K. Smalls, Deborah P. Stokes, and Wilma Weant.

Walter W. Ross and Samuel Bruce did library research. They were assisted by the following librarians at the Thomas Cooper Library of the University of South Carolina: Jens Holley and the interlibrary-loan staff; reference librarians Gwen Baxter, Daniel Boice, Faye Chadwell, Cathy Eckman, Rhonda Felder, Gary Geer, Jackie Kinder, Laurie Preston, Jean Rhyne, Carol Tobin, Virginia Weathers, and Connie Widney; circulation-department head Thomas Marcil; and acquisitions-searching supervisor David Haggard.

T H E
COLD
WAR
1945-1991

Michel Aflaq

Founder, Syrian Ba'th Party, 1947
Born Damascus, Syria, 1910
Died Paris, France, 23 June 1989

Michel Aflaq was a Syrian writer and political leader who played a major role in the Arab nationalist movement during and following World War II. Aflaq, along with Salah al-Din Bitar, founded the Ba'th (Renaissance) party, which fashioned the leading political ideology of Syria and Iraq. More a theorist and organizer than a politician, Aflaq held public office only once, in 1949 as Syrian minister of education, a position he held for only three months. His Pan-Arabist ideology converged around three concepts: unity, freedom, and socialism, which became the slogans of the Ba'th party. To Aflaq unity of the Arab world was the most important. He believed if unity could be achieved, freedom and social reform would naturally follow. Aflaq got closest to realizing his dreams in 1958 when Syria and Egypt merged to form the United Arab Republic (UAR), a process Aflaq had initiated. With the disintegration of that union three years later, and the ensuing split within the Ba'th party in 1966, Aflaq ceased to play an important role in Syrian politics.

Founding of the Ba'th Party

Aflaq was the son of Greek Orthodox Christian parents, and his father was a politically active grain merchant who opposed French rule, which Syria had been placed under after World War I. After completing his secondary school education in Damascus, Aflaq studied history at the Sorbonne in Paris from 1928 to 1932, where he developed many of his ideas of Arab unity. He spent the next ten years teaching school in Damascus, along with Salah al-Din Bitar, a fellow Syrian who had studied in France with him. In 1942 the two men gave up teaching to concentrate on political activity. In 1947 they formally established the Ba'th party, and Aflaq became general secretary.

Arab Socialist Resurrection Party

Beginning in 1949 the military became involved in Syrian politics. Over the next few years Aflaq was imprisoned twice and exiled for a year in Beirut, Lebanon. While there he and Akram Hourani, head of Syria's Arab Socialist party, agreed to merge their two parties. The merger was accomplished in 1953, and the resulting party was given the name of Arab Socialist Resurrection party. The merger united the opposition in Syria and began to affect parliamentary elections.

Michel Aflaq

United Arab Republic

As the Left gained power in Syria, Egypt was experiencing a surge of Pan-Arabist feeling following President Gamal Abdel Nasser's success in the 1956 Suez Crisis. The politically charged atmosphere in Syria facilitated the way for Aflaq to initiate moves that led to the union of Syria and Egypt in the UAR. As a price, however, Nasser insisted that all political parties in Syria be disbanded, and soon the Ba'th found itself politically impotent in Syria. In 1961 Syria's military took over the country, and Syria seceded from the UAR.

In February 1963 the Ba'th took power in Syria, after Ba'thist military officers overthrew the government. But the party was split between Aflaq and Bitar's old guard on the one hand and the new generation of military party members on the other. In 1966, when the military element seized control of both party and government, Aflaq went into exile to Beirut. Later he took up residence in Iraq, where he became general secretary of Iraq's Ba'th party. Aflaq's position was largely ceremonial, as real power lay in the hands of Assistant Secretary-General Saddam Hussein, who later became Iraq's president and commander of its armed forces.

Aflaq died on 23 June 1989 in Paris, where he had undergone heart surgery two weeks earlier.

Books by Aflaq

The Ba'ath and the Heritage (New Dehli, India: Rajendra Ravindra, 1976);

Choice of Texts from the Ba'th Party Founder's Thought (Florence, Italy: Cooperative Laboratory, 1977).

Article about Aflaq

Norma Salem-Babikian, "Michel Aflaq: A Biographic Outline," *Arab Studies Quarterly,* 2 (1980): 162–169.

General References

Richard T. Antoun and Donald Quataert, eds., *Syria: Society, Culture, and Polity* (Albany, N.Y.: State University of New York Press, 1991);

Kamel S. Abu Jaber, *The Arab Ba'th Socialist Party* (Syracuse, N.Y.: Syracuse University Press, 1966);

John F. Devlin, *The Ba'th Party: A History from Its Origins to 1966* (Stanford, Cal.: Hoover Institution Press, 1976);

John F. Devlin, *Syria: Modern State in an Ancient Land* (Boulder, Colo.: Westview, 1983);

Tabitha Petran, *Syria* (New York: Praeger, 1972);

Itmar Rabinovitch, *Syria under the Ba'th 1963–1966: The Army-Party Symbiosis* (Jerusalem: Israel Universities Press, 1972);

Patrick Seale, *The Struggle for Syria: A Study of Post-War Arab Politics, 1945–1958*, second edition (New Haven, Conn.: Yale University Press, 1986).

– V. A.

SEE ALSO THESE RELATED ENTRIES

Hafiz al-Assad, 2; Saddam Hussein, 2; Gamal Abdul Nasser 2.

Ramiz Alia

First Secretary, Albanian Communist Party, 1985–1991
Born Shkodër, Albania, 18 October 1925

Ramiz Alia was the leader of Albania and the first secretary of the Albanian Communist party. Alia was born into a poor Muslim family. In his youth he took part in the patriotic youth movement organized by supporters of King Zog I, the country's first monarch since it gained independence in 1912. Alia joined the insurgent National Liberation Movement (NLM) during the Italian occupation of Albania in World War II. The NLM was formed in 1942 by the communists, including the orthodox Stalinist Enver Hoxha, and was under the direct control of the fledgling Albanian Communist party and received sponsorship and assistance from the Yugoslav communists, the Partisans. The Albanian Communist party and Hoxha seized power at the close of the war when Italian and German forces retreated from the Balkans. In November 1948 the ruling party was renamed the Albanian Party of Labor (APL).

Early Career

In the late 1940s Alia was dispatched to Moscow for ideological studies and political training. He remained extremely loyal to Hoxha, and their close relationship ensured Alia a fast climb through Communist party ranks. He was elected to the party's Central Committee in 1948 and to the People's Legislative Assembly in 1950. By 1961, when Albania formally split with the Soviet Union in protest over the latter's de-Stalinization program, Alia was a member of the APL Secretariat and a full member of the ruling politburo. During the 1960s and 1970s Albania established a close relationship with the People's Republic of China, the political and economic support of which proved valuable as a counterweight to potential Soviet pressure. But relations were severed in the early 1980s, after the death of Mao Zedong, when Beijing veered away from the tenets of Marxism-Leninism and was accused by Albania of adopting a "revisionist" position. Afterward the Albanian regime maintained its distance from the two Communist giants, as well as from the Western capitalist states, and did not play an important role in the Third World.

The Death of Hoxha

Alia was chosen to replace Haxhi Leshi as chairman of the Albanian People's Assembly in November 1982. From 1984, as Hoxha's health failed, Alia's responsibilities for state and party affairs greatly increased. On 13

Ramiz Alia

April 1985, after Hoxha's death on 11 April, Alia became chairman of the Presidium of the People's Assembly and was also appointed first secretary of the APL. Alia committed himself to preserving one-party rule and maintaining Albania's hard-line brand of Marxism-Leninism. However, some gestures were made to open the country economically and politically to the outside world and end its extreme isolation. Relations were reestablished with some Western countries as well as with the Soviet Union, and in 1990 Albania applied for observer status with the Committee for Security and Cooperation in Europe (CSCE). Domestic repression was somewhat lifted, particularly in religious life, but communist controls over the political and economic systems remained intact.

With democratic revolutions sweeping across Eastern Europe during the fall and winter of 1989, Albania found itself increasingly isolated, ideologically and politically, as the last bastion of traditional Marxism-Leninism in Europe. In late June and early July 1990 Albania entered a crisis period when several hundred citizens stormed Western embassies in an attempt to flee the country. Several dozen were eventually allowed to leave, but new restrictions were subsequently imposed to prevent a mass exodus and a major political crisis. The regime came under mounting internal and international pressure to implement democratic reforms, while social unrest showed signs of increasing in the wake of the democratic transformations witnessed in the rest of Eastern Europe.

The Unrest of 1990

There was evidence of factional conflicts between dogmatic and reformist forces in the ruling party that heralded some important political changes at the close of 1990, when a multiparty system was officially sanctioned and National Assembly elections were scheduled for the spring of 1991. Demonstrations and riots in several Albanian cities were violently suppressed in December 1990, but a new political party, the Albanian Democratic party, was allowed to operate by the authorities in preparation for national elections. Several other noncommunist parties were formed in early 1991 and were allowed to compete in the country's first multiparty elections in the spring of 1991. The elections in March 1991 were won by the ruling communists, and Alia was reappointed president. But amid increasing economic decline and social unrest, the government collapsed in preparation for a new ballot. General elections were won comfortably by the Democratic party, and Alia retired from political life.

In September 1992 Alia was placed under house arrest. As of early 1993 charges had not yet been filed against him.

Books by Alia

Albania Will Always Advance on the Road of Socialism (Toronto: Marx, Engels, Lenin, Stalin Institute, 1985);

The Correct Line of the Party, The Source of Our Victories (Toronto: Marx, Engels, Lenin, Stalin Institute, 1985);

Enver Hoxha and His Work Lives and Will Live Forever (Toronto: Marx, Engels, Lenin, Stalin Institute, 1985).

General References

Elez Biberaj, *Albania: A Socialist Maverick* (Boulder, Colo.: Westview Press, 1990);

Nicholas C. Pano, *The People's Republic of Albania* (Baltimore: Johns Hopkins University Press, 1968);

Stephanaq Pollo, *The History of Albania* (London: Routledge & Kegan Paul, 1981);

Peter R. Prifti, *Socialist Albania since 1944: Domestic and Foreign Developments* (Cambridge, Mass.: MIT Press, 1978);

Tom Winnifrith, ed., *Perspectives on Albania* (New York: St. Martin's Press, 1992).

— J. B. and A. B.

SEE ALSO THESE RELATED ENTRIES

Enver Hoxha, 2; Joseph Stalin, 2; Josip Broz Tito, 2.

Salvador Allende Gossens

President of Chile, 1970–1973

Born Valparaiso, Chile, 26 July 1908
Died Santiago, Chile, 11 September 1973

Salvador Allende Gossens was the only Marxist president in Chile's history and the second democratically elected Marxist leader in Latin America. Elected in 1970, he sought to initiate a transition to socialism while maintaining the nation's democratic and constitutional structure. In September 1973 a military coup overthrew Allende, ending Chile's experiment in democratic socialism and marking a dramatic end to Chile's relatively peaceful democratic history.

Allende, born into an upper-middle-class Chilean family, had a long political career. While a student of medicine, he was a Marxist activist and participated in the founding of the Chilean Socialist party in 1934. After serving as a representative in the Chamber of Deputies in 1937, minister of health in 1939, and secretary-general of the Socialist party in 1943, Allende won a seat in the senate in 1945 and continued to serve there until he was elected president in 1970.

Early Runs for the Presidency

In 1952 Allende made his first of three unsuccessful bids for the presidency of Chile. Despite the backing of the Communist party (some argue because of it), Allende placed last of four candidates. His performance improved considerably in 1958 when, as the candidate of a coalition of socialists, communists, and other small groups, he was narrowly defeated by the rightist candidate Jorge Alessandri Rodriguez. Allende was again defeated in the 1964 presidential campaign by Christian Democrat Eduardo Frei Montalva, who won an absolute majority.

The 1970 Election

By 1970 Allende's political base had expanded. As the leader of the Popular Unity coalition, which comprised not only socialists and communists but also radicals and certain Christian Democrats, Allende won a plurality of the vote with 36.3 percent. In the ensuing runoff, required since no candidate had received an absolute majority, Allende defeated former president Alessandri. Much to the chagrin of the United States, Allende became the second elected Marxist president in Latin America. The election further confirmed the suspicions of many U.S. officials that the Soviet Union was attempting to ally itself with the nations of the Western Hemisphere, one by one, with the goal of expanding its ideology across the globe.

Salvador Allende Gossens

The Marxist Agenda for Change

In the three years that Allende served as president, Chile's economy underwent major changes. To redistribute the wealth, Allende ordered wage increases, particularly for the lowest-paid workers, while freezing prices and printing large amounts of currency. Allende also expropriated U.S.-owned copper companies in Chile without compensation, pushed for the organization of collective farms, and "temporarily" seized control of hundreds of small and medium-sized enterprises. At first the reforms seemed successful. By increasing demand, they stimulated economic growth, which in 1971 was the highest in decades. After about a year, however, inflation soared to 164 percent, exports fell, and production stagnated. Strikes and shortages of food became widespread. Under these conditions, foreign investors lost confidence in Chile and international lines of credit dried up. The

7

United States tried to isolate Chile politically and economically. As Chile's relationship with the United States rapidly deteriorated, Chile opened new ties with Cuba and the People's Republic of China. Although Allende maintained support from Chile's peasant population, he lost the support of the increasingly dissatisfied middle class.

The 1973 Coup

On 11 September 1973 the Chilean military, led by General Augusto Pinochet Ugarte and funded by the Central Intelligence Agency (CIA), launched a successful coup. In the course of the bombings of the presidential palace, Allende was killed. Several recent studies say that he killed himself during the attack.

The forces that led to Allende's overthrow were complex and cannot be reduced to a single explanation. Scholars agree, however, that the extreme polarization that came to characterize Chilean politics in the early 1970s, along with the absence of moderating forces, made governing nearly impossible. And when Allende incorporated the "neutral" military into his cabinet to maintain institutional order in an atmosphere of heightened crisis in October 1972, the military itself became part of the political process.

General References

Genaro Arriagada, *Pinochet: The Politics of Power* (Boulder, Colo.: Westview Press, 1991);

Pamela Constable, *By Reason or by Force: The Pinochet Years in Chile* (New York: Norton, 1991);

Jack Hopkins, *Latin America: Perspectives on a Region* (New York: Holmes & Meier, 1987);

Jennie K. Lincoln and Elizabeth G. Ferris, *The Dynamics of Latin American Foreign Policies: Challenges for the 1980s* (Boulder, Colo.: Westview Press, 1984);

Heraldo Muñoz and Joseph S. Tulchin, *Latin American Nations in World Politics* (Boulder, Colo.: Westview Press, 1984);

Ernest Rossi and Jack C. Plano, *The Latin American Political Dictionary* (Santa Barbara, Cal.: ABC–Clio, 1980);

Howard J. Wiarda and Harvey F. Kline, *Latin American Politics and Development* (Boulder, Colo.: Westview Press, 1979).

– B. D.

SEE ALSO THESE RELATED ENTRIES

Fidel Castro Ruz, 2; Central Intelligence Agency, 2; Eduardo Frei Montalva, 2; Richard M. Nixon, 1; Augusto Pinochet Ugarte, 2.

Idi Dada Amin Oumee

President of Uganda, 1971–1979
Born Koboko, Uganda, 1925

Idi Dada Amin Oumee was president of Uganda from 1971 to 1979. Amin became one of the most notorious Third World leaders as a result of the institutionalized, random violence and often bizarre brutality that marked his tumultuous tenure in power.

While very little is known about his early life, Amin was born sometime around 1925 into a small, poor Muslim peasant family in the village of Koboko in the West Nile Province in the British colony of Uganda. After his intermittent primary education at a local mission school, he worked on the family farm. In 1946 he enlisted in the King's African Rifles, the Ugandan unit of the British army in Africa, and quickly rose through the ranks. Promoted to platoon commander in 1948, Amin served under British officers during the Mau Mau rebellion in Kenya in 1948–1949, and was implicated in committing atrocities. For his exemplary service both in Kenya and later in Somalia, he was promoted to corporal in 1949. A large man, Amin won the heavyweight boxing championship of Uganda in 1951, holding the title for nine years. In 1961 he became the first Ugandan commissioned officer with the rank of lieutenant, and by 9 October 1962, when Uganda became independent with Milton Obote serving as prime minister, Amin had risen to the rank of major. He was later sent to Britain and Israel for officer training courses.

Idi Dada Amin Oumee

The Overthrow of Obote

Amin rose from political obscurity as a result of his participation in resolving the 1964 army mutiny against British officers, and he consequently began a close working relationship with Obote. Although he cooperated with contrabandists smuggling gold into Uganda, Amin was promoted to chief of staff in 1966. By 1968, however, relations with Obote were strained after he was suspected of being involved in an attempted assassination of the prime minister. In 1970 Amin was promoted to chief of the general staff, thus gaining control of the army. Amidst deteriorating relations with the unpopular and repressive Obote, Amin staged a coup d'état on 25 January 1971 against Obote, who was out of the country. Amin's seizure of power reportedly came at the urging of Great Britain and Israel.

Massacres and Repression

The initial phases of Amin's rule gave little indication of the radical changes to come. His coup was cheered by Ugandans who expected that he would restore order and democratic rule to strife-ridden Uganda. Amin's overthrow of Obote was also well received by the Buganda ethnic group, who had been repressed under Obote. Immediately after assuming power Amin made a series of populist gestures, including the release of political prisoners, and vowed to restore civilian rule within five years. His personal rule quickly turned chaotic as he moved to consolidate his yet tenuous hold on power through a series of assassinations and massacres of the members of rival ethnic groups in the army and police. He organized death squads to eliminate Obote supporters in the country, many of whom, including members of the military, fled to neighboring Tanzania where they began to organize an anti-Amin exile force. Between May 1971 and

January 1972 Amin's factions massacred troops in the armed forces who belonged to the Langi and Acholi ethnic groups. Amin began to turn the army into a coterie of regional warlords who plundered the state, and the rule of law was quickly replaced with arbitrary and draconian edicts.

Foreign Relations

Amin's domestic and foreign policies were erratic, guided more by Amin's own impulses than by other, more coherent, considerations. In August 1972 Amin expelled all of Uganda's large and economically important Asian population, an action which had adverse effects on the economy. Relations were ruptured with Britain, which responded to Amin's actions by imposing an economic embargo. The arbitrary expulsion of foreigners and their physical harassment by Amin's forces produced a negative international image. In December he ordered the nationalization of British-owned companies in Uganda without compensation. After he expelled Israeli advisers from Uganda, Amin established cordial relations with the Soviet Union and Libyan head of state Muammar Qaddafi, and took a pro-Arab stance in his foreign policy. Relations with Tanzania, which had been tense, erupted into violent border clashes after a pro-Obote exile force launched a small-scale invasion from Tanzania in September 1972 to topple Amin. The invasion failed but prompted Libya's Qaddafi to send combat troops and military aid to assist Amin. In June 1976 Palestinian terrorists with the collaboration of Amin and the army hijacked an Air France jet en route to Tel Aviv and forced it to land in Entebbe, Uganda. An Israeli commando raid freed the hostages, killed the terrorists and numerous Ugandan soldiers, and destroyed a large number of Ugandan military aircraft. Despite his growing infamy and the wave of repression and violence inside Uganda, Amin was elected chairman of the Organization of African Unity (OAU) in 1975.

Aside from an erratic foreign policy, domestically the period of Amin's rule was marked by decentralized violence and institutional collapse. Whatever semblance of stability there was during his first few months in power had quickly dissipated. To remain in power, Amin ruled by thuggery and terror, and in the process destroyed the organization of both the army and the state. In addition to decapacitating Uganda's leaders and managers in the public and private sectors, Amin's Mafia-like regime seized private property with impunity. Amin and his top lieutenants appropriated the choice properties for themselves, with the rest distributed to loyal soldiers as booty. In 1976, amidst student demonstrations and mounting violence, Amin declared himself president-for-life. Factional infighting within the army resulted in the large-scale massacre of soldiers both loyal to and against Amin,

who responded by using extremely brutal methods to suppress opposition. By early 1978 an estimated two hundred thousand people had been killed in interethnic and political violence, with thousands of others who simply "disappeared." Gripped by general lawlessness and indiscriminant violence, the situation in Uganda, once considered the "jewel of East Africa," neared anarchy.

Invasion of Tanzania

In October 1978 Amin ordered an invasion of Tanzania, and after occupying and devastating Tanzanian territory near the Kagera salient, his army withdrew into Uganda in late November. In January the Tanzanian president, Julius Nyerere, who had been an ardent critic of Amin and his brutality, launched an invasion into Uganda. The estimated twenty thousand Tanzanian troops, accompanied by exile Ugandan forces, met little resistance from Amin's disintegrating forces despite the airlift of fifteen hundred Libyan troops to support Amin. By April the anti-Amin forces had captured the capital, Kampala, and Amin fled to Libya later in the month, subsequently moving to Jidda, Saudi Arabia, in 1980.

Amin's violent rule precipitated the collapse of the administrative and economic infrastructure of Uganda, which was plunged into further interethnic, factional violence. Amin's bizarre and arbitrary rule proved to be a lasting stigma on postcolonial African political leadership.

Books about Amin

Tony Avirgan and Martha Honey, *War in Uganda: The Legacy of Idi Amin* (Westport, Conn.: L. Hill, 1982);

Francis A. W. Bwengye, *The Agony of Uganda, from Idi Amin to Obote: Repressive Rule and Bloodshed* (New York: Regency Press, 1985);

Samuel Decalo, *Psychoses of Power: African Personal Dictatorships* (Boulder, Colo.: Westview Press, 1989).

David Gwyn, *Idi Amin: Death-Light of Africa* (Boston: Little, Brown, 1977);

Martin Jamison, comp., *Idi Amin and Uganda: An Annotated Bibliography* (Westport, Conn.: Greenwood Press, 1992);

Henry Kyemba, *A State of Blood: The Inside Story of Idi Amin* (New York: Grosset & Dunlap, 1977);

Judith Listowel, *Amin* (London: I.U.P. Books, 1973);

David Martin, *General Amin* rev. ed. (London: Sphere, 1978);

George Ivan Smith, *Ghosts of Kampala* (London: Weidenfeld and Nicolson, 1980; New York: St. Martin's Press, 1980).

General References

Dan Jacobs, *The Brutality of Nations* (New York: Knopf, 1987);

James Mittelman, *Ideology and Politics in Uganda: From Abote to Amin* (Ithaca, N.Y.: Cornell University Press, 1975.

—J. R.-S.

SEE ALSO THESE RELATED ENTRIES

Julius Nyerere, 2; Mu'ammar Qadaffi, 2

Yuri Andropov

General Secretary, Soviet Communist Party, 1982–1984

Born Stavropol, Russia, 15 June 1914
Died Moscow, Soviet Union, 9 February 1984

Yuri Vladimirovich Andropov, general secretary of the Communist party of the Soviet Union (CPSU) between 1982 and 1984, was born of partly Greek ancestry near the Caucasian city of Stavropol. His father was an employee of the rail yards at Nagutskoye. At the age of sixteen Andropov quit school and worked a variety of jobs —as a telegraph operator, a crewman on Volga riverboats, and a film projectionist — before entering a technical institute to study inland water transportation. After graduating in 1936 he went to work for the Communist Youth League (Komsomol) as an organizer of shipyard workers, marking the beginning of his political career. By 1938 he had become first secretary of the Komsomol branch in Yaroslavl, northeast of Moscow, and the following year he joined the Communist party.

Early Political Career

In 1940 Andropov was put in charge of the Komsomol in the Karelo-Finnish Republic, a newly formed Soviet state composed of territory taken from Finland after the Winter War of 1939–1940. During World War II he remained in Karelia, operating the Komsomol as a guerrilla unit behind German lines. His activities brought Andropov to the attention of Otto Kuusinen, head of the Finnish party and at that time highly influential in the Moscow-dominated Communist International (Comintern). Before being called back to Moscow in 1951 to work for the Central Committee, Andropov, under Kuusinen's patronage, rose to become a party secretary in Karelia in 1947, a move that put him close to the center of power in the Soviet Union.

Yuri Andropov

Ambassador to Hungary

Two years later Andropov was assigned to the foreign service and sent as counselor to the Soviet embassy in Hungary. Promoted to ambassador in 1954, he continued serving in Budapest during Imre Nagy's reform movement of 1953–1956, and the relatively young Andropov found himself on a political center stage as

Moscow's deputy during the first major postwar challenge to Soviet rule in Eastern Europe.

In a moment of duplicity, Andropov assured Nagy that the Soviet Union would not intervene in Hungary's affairs. On 31 October 1956, however, Soviet troops poured across the border to crush the Hungarian resistance. Nagy took refuge in the Yugoslav embassy, only leaving after Andropov and other Soviet emissaries gave him guarantees of safety. But Nagy was abducted and in 1958 tried and executed for treason. Afterward Andropov convinced General Secretary Nikita S. Khrushchev to appoint János Kádár as chairman of the Hungarian Communist party.

Department of Relations with Communist Parties

Andropov returned to Moscow in March 1957 to take charge of the Department of Relations with Communist Parties in Power, an organ of the Central Committee that had been set up by Khrushchev in part to restore the Soviet Union's image after the uprising in Hungary and largely to prevent a similar occurrence elsewhere. Andropov remained with this department until 1967, taking part in Soviet attempts to improve relations with China, efforts which bore little result.

He continued to maintain cordial relations with Kádár, even after Kádár introduced into Hungary a series of limited political and economic reforms. That the Soviet Union did not interfere with Kádár is largely to the credit of Andropov, who had by 1967 earned the reputation of being one of the members of the Central Committee most tolerant of at least limited reform.

KGB

In 1967 General Secretary Leonid I. Brezhnev named Andropov to head the Soviet Union's all-pervasive secret police and intelligence agency, the Committee for State Security (KGB). During Andropov's fifteen-year tenure as KGB chief, his reputation for tolerance extended more into the economic than the political realm. He was part of the conservative group that urged Brezhnev to invade Czechoslovakia in 1968 to reassert Soviet control over Alexander Dubcek's growing reform movement. Within the Soviet Union he clamped down on dissident intellectuals, overseeing writer Aleksandr Solzhenitzyn's deportation to the West and physicist Andrei Sakharov's exile to the closed city of Gorki.

Relations between Brezhnev and Andropov were fairly close. Andropov and his wife, Tanya, lived on the floor directly above the Brezhnevs in a large apartment building on Kutuzoski Prospekt. In 1973 Brezhnev made Andropov a full voting member of the Politburo, the executive body of the Central Committee. He simultaneously granted Foreign Minister Andrei Gromyko and

Defense Minister Andrei Grechko full membership in the Politburo. When Grechko died in 1976 his successor, Dmitri Ustinov, also became a member of the Politburo. This trio – Andropov, Gromyko, and Ustinov – would come to rule after Brezhnev's death in 1982.

After party ideologue Mikhail Suslov died on 25 January 1982 Andropov returned to the Secretariat of the Central Committee to resume a position he had had to surrender when he went to the KGB. Suslov's death and Andropov's subsequent political advancement were probably more than coincidental: relations between the two had been cool, and it has been suggested that Suslov wanted Andropov at the KGB to keep him out of any future power struggle.

General Secretary

In May 1982 Andropov stepped down from the KGB and immediately became a contender to succeed Brezhnev, who was by then quite ill. By the time Brezhnev died on 10 November, Andropov had apparently secured his position and defeated his principal rival, Konstantin Chernenko. Andropov's ascendance was determined to a great extent by the support of Ustinov and Gromyko, who both saw a greater potential for leadership in Andropov than in Chernenko, Brezhnev's longtime aide and party apparatchik.

Domestic Policy

The situation that Andropov inherited from Brezhnev was one of political and economic stagnation at home and rising tensions with the United States. To counter the lethargy of the Soviet economy Andropov immediately announced his intention to impose discipline and order on all levels of society. He bluntly denounced complacency and profiteering and instituted an antialcohol campaign. Additionally, he tried to reorganize economic planning by assigning greater powers to the Central Committee. To some extent he was successful: absenteeism from work declined, and industrial productivity saw a brief spurt. But Andropov lacked a solid base of support within the bureaucracy, a reflection of his long tenure at the KGB, and ultimately his efforts at reform were thwarted by the large number of traditionalists left over from the Brezhnev era. Andropov's espousal of discipline and initiative, however, struck a responsive chord in the average Soviet citizen, who had come to dismiss exhortations from the Kremlin with a certain measure of cynicism.

Relations with the West

In relations with the West, Andropov was not as successful. When he came to power he assumed a generally conciliatory stance toward the United States and expressed a renewed Soviet desire for détente. The American president, Ronald Reagan, however, was not amena-

ble to these Soviet overtures. In March 1983 Reagan unveiled the Strategic Defense Initiative (SDI), an ambitious program to develop a space-based, anti-ballistic-missile system, which, when operational, would in theory render the Soviet nuclear arsenal useless.

On 1 September 1983 the Soviet Air Force shot down a Korean airliner, apparently thinking that it was a military aircraft. This incident badly damaged the Soviet Union's standing in the world and came at a time when Andropov was out of public view and suffering from the kidney disease that would ultimately kill him.

When it became apparent that the United States would go ahead with the 1979 decision by the North Atlantic Treaty Organization (NATO) to upgrade its nuclear arsenal in Europe, the Soviet negotiators walked out of the Intermediate Range Nuclear Force (INF) talks in protest. Two weeks later, on 8 December 1983, the Soviets broke off the Strategic Arms Reduction Talks (START) for the same reason

Andropov had been seriously ill since at least February 1983, and he had to a large extent disappeared from sight for the six months preceding his death on 9 February 1984. It would be difficult to say how successful he would have been in overcoming the Soviet Union's internal stagnation had he remained alive longer to consolidate his power and institute more radical reforms. Similarly, in foreign affairs, he simply was not in office long enough to effect any long-term changes.

Book by Andropov

Speeches and Writings (New York: Pergamon Press, 1982; enlarged, 1983).

Books about Andropov

Arnold Beichman and Mikhail S. Bernstam, *Andropov, New Challenge to the West, A Political Biography* (New York: Stein & Day, 1983);

Seweryn Bialer, *The Soviet Paradox: External Expansion, Internal Decline* (New York: Knopf, 1986);

Martin Ebon, *The Andropov File: The Life and Ideas of Yuri V. Andropov, General Secretary of the Communist Party of the Soviet Union* (New York: McGraw-Hill, 1983);

Zhores A. Medvedev, *Andropov* (Oxford: Blackwell, 1983; revised, 1984);

Vladimir Solov'ev, *Yuri Andropov, A Secret Passage into the Kremlin* (New York: Macmillan / London: Collier, Macmillan, 1983);

Jonathan Steele and Eric Abraham, *Andropov in Power: From Komsomol to Kremlin* (Oxford: Martin Robinson, 1983; Garden City: Doubleday/Anchor, 1984).

General Reference:

John W. Parker, *Kremlin in Transition* (Boston: Unwin Hyman, 1991).

– M. B.

SEE ALSO THESE RELATED ENTRIES
Konstantin Chernenko, 2; János Kádár, 2; Imre Nagy, 2; Refuseniks, 3.

Yassir Arafat

Chairman, Palestine Liberation Organization, 1969–

Born Cairo, Egypt, 24 August 1929

Yassir Arafat is chairman of the Palestine Liberation Organization (PLO) and the leading international spokesperson for the Palestine national movement. He consolidated his power through Fatah, a Palestinian guerrilla group that he cofounded, becoming PLO chairman in the late 1960s. Unlike that of some other Palestinian leaders, Arafat's ideology has been a simple call for Palestinian statehood. His views toward accommodation with Israel, however, have changed over the years in response to changing historical circumstances.

Abd al-Rahman Abd al-Raouf Arafat al-Qudwa al-Husseini was born to a well-to-do trading family. His mother, Hamida, belonged to one of Jerusalem's most prominent Arab families, the Husseinis; his father, Abd al-Raouf al-Qudwa, was a prominent member of the Ikhwan (Muslim Brotherhood), which was sometimes allied with the Husseinis and sometimes not. Although Arafat himself was likely born in Cairo, he spent his youth in Jerusalem and Gaza, where he saw the Palestinian Arab revolt of 1936–1939 and the Arab-Jewish fighting that marked the creation of the state of Israel in 1948. Arafat learned to fight alongside his older cousin, Abd al-Qader al-Husseini, who was the Palestinian forces' military leader until his death in battle in 1948, and took the name Yassir as his nom de guerre after a 1930s guerrilla, Yassir al-Bira.

After the Arab defeat in the 1948 war, Arafat studied engineering at Cairo University (then called Fuad al-Awal University), where he became one of the founders and prime organizers of the Palestinian Students' Union in 1952. The main themes of that group, and of Arafat's later politics, were self-reliance and Palestinian unity. Unlike other Palestinian leaders, Arafat has always distanced himself from both Marxist ideology and Islamic fundamentalism, allowing him to garner support from Palestinians of a variety of ideological biases and from the gamut of Arab regimes.

Fatah

During the 1956 war at the Suez Canal, Arafat joined an engineering corps at Port Said as a reserve officer with the Egyptian army. In 1957 he left for

Yassir Arafat

Kuwait, where many Palestinians then worked as expatriates in the oil industry, and again began organizing a Palestinian nationalist movement. In the late 1950s and early 1960s nascent Palestinian nationalist networks came together to form Fatah. Its first leadership included, on a more or less equal basis, Arafat, Salah Khalaf, and Khalil Wazir, who had also been organizers in the Palestinian Students' Union, and several other activists. These men set up Fatah as a series of overlapping networks, each responsible to one leader, and that structure has remained in effect throughout the 1980s and early 1990s. Arafat, also called Abu Ammar, reportedly rarely spends two nights in one place.

The Palestine Liberation Organization

In May 1964 the Arab states set up their own shell Palestinian organization, the Palestine Liberation Organization, which the Fatah leaders origi-

nally viewed as a threat but later came to dominate. While Fatah had spread its word through the fiery journalism of the periodical *Our Palestine* in the late 1950s, after the formation of the regime-sponsored PLO, it launched its first sabotage operation against Israel, an unsuccessful attack on 1 January 1965 on Israel's national water carrier.

The 1967 War

After the June 1967 Arab-Israeli war, in which Israel captured the West Bank from Jordan and the Gaza Strip from Egypt, Palestinian nationalism grew at a rapid rate. Fatah's organization and military operations against Israel also increased. In the weeks after the cease-fire, Fatah operatives went to the West Bank and Gaza Strip to stir up a popular revolt against Israeli occupation. But after the Israeli Defense Forces (IDF) had killed two hundred suspected members of his resistance movement and imprisoned and deported scores more, Arafat fled across the river to Jordan. After that, Fatah turned to mobilizing Palestinians in refugee camps of Jordan and Lebanon and mounting cross-border attacks against Israel.

Under an agreement negotiated in 1968 and 1969, brokered by Egyptian president Gamal Abdel Nasser, Fatah took over the PLO in coordination with other guerrilla groups. At a February 1969 meeting of the Palestine National Council (PNC), the PLO's governing body, Fatah, installed its candidate, Arafat, as PLO chairman. With this the PLO completed its transformation into a genuinely independent Palestinian liberation organization, which at the Arab League meeting of 1974 was recognized as "the sole legitimate representative of the Palestinian people." But the PLO became more than a political umbrella and was seen by many Palestinians as "the organizational expression and symbolic repository of Palestinian nationalism as a whole."

Within the PLO itself, however, divisions remained. In political terms, and in budgetary allocations, Arafat's Fatah stabilized at about two-thirds of the PLO's total weight. Among the myriad other groups within the PLO were George Habash's Popular Front for the Liberation of Palestine (PFLP), Nayif Hawatmeh's Democratic Front for the Liberation of Palestine (DFLP), and a few groups with ties to Arab regimes, such as the Syrian-backed Saiqa. Although these groups retained importance as counterweights within the Palestinian movement, Fatah was able to promote itself as the representative of the masses.

However, the activities of these smaller guerrilla groups also affected Fatah. In September 1970, for example, a PFLP hijacking of three civilian planes provided a pretext for Jordan's King Hussein ibn Talal to expel to Lebanon all Palestinian armed resistance, including less radical groups within the PLO, amid widespread bloodshed. This expulsion became known as "Black September."

Although the PLO played little role in the October 1973 Arab-Israeli war, the question of PLO participation in the postwar talks gained importance. In spring 1974 Fatah leaders garnered PLO backing for the goal of creating a "Palestinian national authority" in any territory from which Israel might withdraw. On the one hand, then, the PLO accepted a "two-state solution" in the 1970s, but, on the other, the PNC still said that formation of a ministate would be only a first step in the creation of a Palestine-wide "democratic secular state." At the October 1974 Arab summit Arafat won support for his new program and was awarded head-of-state status, and the following month he brought his "gun and olive branch" message to the United Nations General Assembly in New York.

After Jimmy Carter became U.S. president in 1977, Arafat tried to capitalize on his interest in the Middle East. Through the summer the two engaged in indirect contacts to discuss Palestinian representation at a reconvened peace conference. That fall, however, Egyptian president Anwar al-Sadat jettisoned those hopes for an all-Arab approach with his pursual of bilateral peace with Israel that culminated in the Camp David Accords.

Israeli Invasion of Lebanon

In 1981 Israeli prime minister Menachem Begin began a clampdown on the Palestinian movement with the appointment of hard-liner Ariel Sharon as defense minister. Begin's government attempted to counter PLO influence within the Israeli-occupied territories by building up alternative groups called "village leagues" and to quash Palestinian cross-border raids from Lebanon with reprisals, which escalated the original violence. In June 1982, on the pretense of stopping Palestinian cross-border raids, Israel invaded Lebanon, forced the PLO to evacuate, and then became bogged down in a bloody war over the future of that country.

In the years after the Lebanon war, Arafat continued to bid for inclusion in any Arab-Israeli peace process and to build up clandestine networks in the West Bank and Gaza Strip. In September 1982 U.S. president Ronald Reagan announced a peace plan that called for Palestinian participation in a Jordanian negotiating team. Arafat began a dialogue with King Hussein but broke off talks in 1986 and abro-

gated the agreement. This led to a reconciliation between Arafat and Habash, who reversed his previous Rejectionist Front stance at the PNC's eighteenth session and accepted resolutions calling for the creation of an independent West Bank–Gaza state and the convening of an international peace conference.

Arafat's political agenda was boosted with the eruption of the Palestinian *intifada* (uprising) in the West Bank and Gaza Strip in December 1987. Although the revolt was not led by Arafat, its unified leadership is generally assumed to be composed of supporters of Fatah, the PFLP, the DFLP, and other groups. Arafat has maintained political staying power in the international arena.

On 13 December 1988 in Geneva, Arafat said that the PLO accepted "the right of all parties concerned in the Middle East conflict to live in peace and security, including the state of Palestine, Israel, and other neighbors, according to the [United Nations] Resolutions 242 and 338." U.S. secretary of state George Shultz deemed those statements fulfillment of the United States conditions for dialogue with the PLO, and political contacts immediately commenced. In 1990, however, the United States broke off its talks with Arafat because of his refusal to denounce an attempted raid on Israel. In 1990 and 1991 the United States and Arafat found themselves at odds on the occupation of Kuwait by Iraq, with the PLO supporting Iraq's Saddam Hussein in his occupation of Kuwait and the United States sending forces to Saudi Arabia to oppose the violation of sovereignty and to prepare for war. After the war the United States brokered peace negotiations among the Middle East parties. Following the 1993 Oslo Accords between Israel and the PLO, the Palestinian Authority was created to control the Gaza Strip and major Palestinian population centers in the West Bank. Arafat has been the president of the Palestinian Authority since its inception.

Books about Arafat

Jillian Becker, *The PLO: The Rise and Fall of the Palestinian Liberation Organization* (London: Weidenfeld & Nicolson, 1984);

Andrew Gowers and Tony Walker, *Behind the Myth: Yasser Arafat and the Palestinian Revolution* (New York: Olive Branch Press, 1992);

Alan Hart, *Arafat, A Political Biography* (Bloomington: Indiana University Press, 1989);

Alan Hart, *Arafat, Terrorist or Peacemaker?* (London: Sidgwick & Jackson, 1984);

Thomas Kiernan, *Arafat, the Man and the Myth* (New York: Norton, 1976);

Shaul Mishal, *The PLO under Arafat: Between Gun and Olive Branch* (New Haven: Yale University Press, 1986);

Diana L. Reische, *Arafat and the Palestine Liberation Organization* (New York: F. Watts, 1991);

Emile F. Sahliyeh, *The PLO after the Lebanon War* (Boulder, Colo.: Westview Press, 1986).

General References

Abu Iyad (Salah Khalaf) and Eric Rouleau, *My Home, My Land* (New York: Times Books, 1981);

Jillian Becker, *The PLO: The Rise and Fall of the Palestine Liberation Organization* (New York: St. Martin's Press, 1984);

Rex Brynen, *Sanctuary and Survival: The PLO in Lebanon* (Boulder, Colo.: Westview Press, 1990);

Helena Cobban, *The Palestinian Liberation Organization: People, Power and Politics* (Cambridge: Cambridge University Press, 1984);

David McDowell, *Palestine and Israel: The Uprising and Beyond* (Berkeley: University of California Press, 1989);

Emile Sanliyeh, *The PLO After the Lebanon War* (Boulder, Colo.: Westview Press, 1986).

– A. F.

SEE ALSO THESE RELATED ENTRIES
George Habash, 2; Gamal Abdul Nasser, 2; Ronald Reagan, 1; George Shultz, 1.

Jacobo Arbenz Guzmán

President of Guatemala, 1950–1954
Born Quetzaltenango, Guatemala, 14 September 1913
Died Mexico City, Mexico, 27 January 1971

Jacobo Arbenz Guzmán was a Guatemalan leftist political leader who was elected president of the country in 1950 and overthrown in 1954 by an invasion force organized by the U.S. Central Intelligence Agency (CIA).

Arbenz was born to Jacobo Arbenz, who was a Swiss druggist, and Octavia Guzmán de Arbenz, who was Salvadoran. He attended Guatemala's national military academy, where he graduated first in his class. After graduation he remained at the academy as an instructor.

The 1944 Coup and the Elections of 1950

In 1944 Arbenz, by then a military captain, resigned his post to protest continuing political repression by Guatemala's military government. He joined forces with Major Francisco Javier Arana and Jorge Toriello, a businessman, to force the regime out of power. The three then supervised the December 1944 elections, which brought José Arévalo Bermejo to the presidency of Guatemala's first democratic government.

Under Arévalo, Arbenz and Arana became the country's most important political figures. Arévalo and the left wing supported Arbenz, while conservative factions endorsed Arana. After Arana was assassinated, just four months prior to the 1950 elections, Arbenz won easily, with 65 percent of the vote.

Jacobo Arbenz Guzmán

Agrarian Reform Law

Arbenz's Agrarian Reform Law of 1952 was central to his legislative program, but the question of compensation for expropriated land provoked sharp conflict among the propertied classes. The United Fruit Company demanded the full market value of its lands, but the government offered only the amount that the company itself had declared for tax purposes. Land-reform opponents soon began calling the program "Marxist," citing also the increased influence of the Communist party under Arbenz. Washington politicians, as well, labeled the country a satellite of the Soviet Union. U.S. secretary of state John Foster Dulles, repudiating Marxist ideology at an Inter-American Conference in Caracas, Venezuela, promoted a resolution to isolate Arbenz.

The last straw was Arbenz's attempts to organize a militia. The Guatemalan army refused to supply arms to the civilians, so Arbenz obtained from Czechoslovakia small arms for the militia. The United States denounced the move as an impermissible step on the road to communism.

The 1954 Coup

The CIA organized, trained, and equipped a small group of Guatemalan exiles in Honduras and Nicaragua to invade under the command of Carlos Castillo Armas, a former colonel in the Guatemalan army. The invaders crossed the border in May 1954, without opposition from the Guatemalan armed forces. Arbenz resigned and fled the country. A military regime was organized to replace the Arbenz government, which had included several communists.

Arbenz's defeat evoked anti-American sentiment among many Latin Americans, who believed the United States government had improperly intervened in Central American affairs. The involvement of the CIA in the overthrow of Arbenz illustrated the extent to which the

U.S. government has been willing to go in order to curtail communism or procommunist penetrations in the region. These events also stand with the Bay of Pigs invasion of 1961 and the U.S. military intervention in the Dominican Republic in 1965 as aberrations from President Herbert Hoover's Good Neighbor Policy, first initiated in the early 1930s.

Following the coup Arbenz lived in Czechoslovakia, the Soviet Union, and other European countries. He later moved to Uruguay and Cuba. He died in Mexico City on 27 January 1971 of natural causes.

General References

Jonathan L. Fried, ed., *Guatemala in Rebellion: Unfinished History* (New York: Grove, 1983);

Eduardo H. Galeano, *Guatemala: Occupied Country* (New York: Monthly Review Press, 1969);

Piero Gleijeses, *Shattered Hope: The Guatemalan Revolution and the United States* (Princeton, N.J.: Princeton University Press, 1991);

Mario Rosenthal, *Guatemala, the Story of an Emergent Latin American Democracy* (New York: Twayne, 1962).

– L. H.

SEE ALSO THESE RELATED ENTRIES

Central Intelligence Agency, 3; John Foster Dulles, 1.

Hafez al-Assad

President of Syria, 1971–
Born Qurdaha, Syria, 6 October 1930

Hafez al-Assad was born on 6 October 1930 into a poor, large peasant family named Wahsh of the Alawite ethnic group, a non-Muslim, heterodox sect comprising about 12 percent of Syria's population, in the rural village of Qurdaha, located near the port city of Latakia. He later changed his name to Assad (meaning "lion" in Arabic). After attending primary and secondary schools, Assad enrolled in the Homs Military Academy in 1952. He then attended the Air Force Academy in Aleppo, from which he graduated as a combat pilot officer in 1955. He was one of the first Alawites to join the Syrian air force. Three years later he was sent to the Soviet Union for training and study in military science as a member of the armed forces of the newly formed United Arab Republic (UAR), a national confederation between Syria and Gamal Nasser's Egypt. Assad was based in Cairo, Egypt, as a squadron leader in the UAR Air Force. It was during this period that he became one of the leaders of a secret group of Syrian officers that came to be known as the "Military Committee." The Military Committee opposed the Syrian-Egyptian union and resented Egyptian dominance in the UAR and was linked to Syria's Ba'ath (Resurrection) party, a secularist, nationalist political party that embraced Pan-Arabism.

Hafez al-Assad

The 1963 Coup

After the 1961 breakup of the Syrian-Egyptian confederation, which was precipitated by a military seizure of power in Syria on 28 September, and the ensuing political turmoil in the country, Assad was dismissed from his military duties and assigned to a civilian post. He then worked briefly for the Ministry of Sea Transport. Assad did, however, maintain close contacts with the members of the Military Committee, which at this time was plotting an overthrow of the government. After the 8 March 1963 coup d'état that brought the military wing of the Ba'ath party to power, Assad, who had been a member of the party since 1947, was appointed commander of the Syrian air force and promoted to general. On 23 February 1966 Assad joined Major General Salah al-Jadid and other radical members of the Ba'ath party in a counter-coup. Assad, named minister of defense, became the number two man in the regime.

Following the Arab defeat in the June 1967 Six-Day War against Israel, in which Syrian units suffered heavy losses, Assad concentrated on rebuilding Syrian military force and strengthening ties with other Arab states. Political stability, however, was undermined by factional infighting within the Ba'ath party between the dominant, pro-Soviet, Marxist faction and the opposing nationalist faction headed by Assad, which had grown increasingly critical of the heavy Soviet influence in Syria. For the nationalists, the level of Soviet presence in the country was tantamount to colonialism. As a result of growing disagreements with the other members of the regime, Assad engineered an attempted coup in February 1969 but was forced to back down under pressures from Syria's principal superpower sponsor, the Soviet Union, which threatened to cut off military aid.

Elected President

Personal and ideological differences within the leadership, however, went unresolved. Tensions came to a head in late 1970, when a civil war broke out in neighboring

Jordan when King Hussein ibn-Talal I sought to expel the Palestine Liberation Organization (PLO) and other Palestinian guerrillas from Jordan. In September 1970 Syrian leader Jadid ordered Syrian forces into Jordan to assist the Palestinian guerrillas. Assad, who disagreed with Jadid's decision, refused to provide air cover for the Syrians. In the ensuing power struggle Assad, with the full backing of the armed forces, finally overthrew Jadid on 13 November 1970, in a bloodless coup. Assad ordered the arrest and execution of leaders and delegates of the Ba'ath party in late 1970 and created a new party, the Ba'ath Regional Command, which quickly nominated him secretary-general. The only candidate in the presidential elections, he was subsequently "elected" president in March 1971.

Assad, who created the first centralized presidential system in Syria's history, concentrated absolute power in his own hands. While using brute force to gain control of Syrian political life, Assad introduced economic and social reforms that brought significant improvements in agriculture, industry, and the living standards of the population. His secular rule and the Alawite dominance of the party and regime have generated resentment among Syria's Sunni (orthodox) Muslim population, which he has sought both to suppress and placate. Although he assembled a formidable internal security and intelligence apparatus, Assad was unwilling to dispense with the facade of democratic rule in Syria.

Assad's early foreign policy was marked by some flexibility and moderation, and since assuming power in 1970 he has emerged as a powerful figure in Middle Eastern politics. In addition to strengthening ties with the Soviet Union, his early foreign relations were guided by Nasserist, Pan-Arabic aims of solidifying the Arab bloc and included renewed attempts at another political union with Egypt, with Nasser's successor, Anwar el-Sadat. In 1972 Syria joined Egypt and Mu'ammar Qaddafi's Libya to form the short-lived Federation of Arab Republics. Politics in the Arab world, however, were fraught with rivalry and acrimony, and as such the prospects of Arab unity largely remained a function of the vagaries of inter-Arab relations and the shifting sands of Middle Eastern politics. Syria's relations with pro-Soviet Iraq, which had been ruled by a rival Ba'ath party since 1963, were historically poor as a result of the animosity between the competing Ba'athist parties, and after the succession of Saddam Hussein to power in 1979, uneasy relations gave way to open hostility and mutual attempts at destabilization. Even though Syria's relations with Jordan (which had been severed after King Hussein's forceful expulsion of Palestinian guerrillas from Jordan) and with neighboring Iraq were strained and marked by mutual suspicion, Assad strongly continued to advocate the unification of Arab states into a single Arab nation.

1973 Arab-Israeli War

Assad joined Egypt and Jordan in the 1973 Arab-Israeli war, motivated primarily by the desire to regain Syrian territory lost in the 1967 war. Syrian forces again suffered heavy losses, however, with Israeli forces reaching within artillery range of Damascus, the capital of Syria. Under the negotiated truce agreements, brokered by American secretary of state Henry Kissinger during his 1974 "shuttle diplomacy" in the Middle East, Syria was able to recover only part of the Golan Heights, but Assad continued his hopes of regaining all of the lost territory. He sought to improve relations with the United States in an attempt to get American support on the Golan Heights issue, and in March 1974 President Richard M. Nixon visited Syria. Although American support for Israel remained a source of tension in Syrian-American relations, Assad did not cut off diplomatic channels to the United States, and in 1977 he met with President Jimmy Carter for talks regarding a peace plan that included the return of the Golan Heights. The plan, however, proved abortive when Israel refused to accept the terms of the agreement.

Syria's relations with Israel remained poor, with Assad opposing any Arab accommodation with the Jewish state. While he saw the military destruction of Israel as the only viable option to regional peace, Assad urged Arab states to attain a "strategic balance" with Israel before engaging in another armed conflict. During the period after Syria's costly defeat in the 1973 war, Assad pursued the policy of strategic balance through the accelerated buildup and modernization of Syria's military. For Assad the national-historic struggle against Israel was zero-sum, and there could be no compromises or a separate peace.

During the second half of the 1970s the Assad regime, while careful to avoid a military confrontation with Israel until Syrian and Arab forces were prepared, turned to a more interventionist regional policy, primarily in neighboring Lebanon. Syria's ambitions for regional hegemony were coupled with its long-standing aspirations for a "Greater Syria" encompassing Lebanon and parts of Jordan, Israel, and Iraq. Assad had shown considerable interest in the Lebanese civil war since it started in early 1975. His intervention in the civil war was also motivated by his other ambition of controlling the Palestinian nationalist groups based there following their expulsion from Jordan. In January 1976 Assad sent Syrian-equipped forces into Lebanon, but after the fighting intensified he finally intervened overtly on 9 April, ostensibly to restore order at the invitation of the Lebanese government. Relying on astute diplomacy, he strengthened his hand in Lebanon with an Arab-mediated ceasefire agreement in October, which established a thirty-thousand-strong peacekeeping force made up largely of

Syrian troops. His goal of dominating Lebanon remained elusive, however, as Syrian forces became embroiled in the country's drawn-out, bloody civil war and sectarian warfare.

Although "reelected" by more than 99 percent of the vote in February 1978 to another seven-year term, Assad essentially turned his country into a tightly controlled military dictatorship once he assumed power. Signs of internal dissent and opposition to his secular rule mounted in the late 1970s and early 1980s, but Assad responded to internal disturbances and challenges to his power swiftly and brutally. In February 1982 he ordered the army to put down antigovernment demonstrations in the city of Hama by the Muslim Brotherhood, a politicoreligious fundamentalist group. The action caused an estimated twenty thousand deaths.

Events in Hama, however, were overshadowed by problems elsewhere. Largely confined to northern and eastern Lebanon (where an estimated thirty thousand Syrian forces had been deployed since 1975, still under the guise of a peacekeeping force), Syria's entanglement in Lebanon was further aggravated by renewed hostilities with Israel. In early 1981 Israel made a series of raids into Lebanon, in part to prevent Lebanese Christian Phalangist militia groups from being overrun by Syrian and Syrian-backed forces. Assad responded by introducing Soviet-made surface-to-air missiles (SAMs) into the Bekáa valley. A limited but costly engagement with Israeli forces ensued following the 6 June 1982 Israeli invasion of Lebanon, which saw the early destruction of Syrian missile installations in the Bekáa. While Assad's Soviet-equipped ground forces prevented Israeli forces from reaching the important Damascus-Beirut highway, his air forces sustained heavy losses as Israeli's American-equipped air force established its dominance throughout the conflict.

Despite the embarrassing defeats at the hands of the invading Israeli forces, Assad moved steadfastly to secure Syria's position in Lebanon. An August 1982 agreement provided for the withdrawal of the PLO and Syrian forces from Beirut, the Lebanese capital, under the supervision of a multinational force comprised of American, French, and Italian troops that arrived in Lebanon on August 25. Yet events in Beirut and in other parts of Lebanon remained in a state of flux as Syria, which was reportedly behind the 14 September 1982 assassination of the pro-Israeli Lebanese president Bashir Gemayel, and the multinational forces were unable to contain the sectarian fighting.

Shortly after negotiations on the withdrawal of foreign troops from Lebanon got under way in January 1983, Assad deployed newly acquired SAM-5 missiles as well as the Soviet-made Scud surface-to-surface rockets — which had never before been deployed outside of the Soviet-bloc countries. Aware that international opinion would force Israel to withdraw from Lebanon, Assad rejected the American-sponsored withdrawal agreement, the so-called Reagan Plan sponsored by the administration of President Ronald Reagan on 17 May 1983, which called for the withdrawal of foreign troops from Lebanon. He refused to withdraw the estimated forty thousand Syrian troops from Lebanon, arguing that they did not fall under the same category as the invading Israeli forces. With the collapse of the Reagan Plan, against which Assad had sought to mobilize Arab opposition, Syria accelerated its buildup in Lebanon and sought to undermine the Lebanese government by uniting Druze and Shiite militia factions into a "national front." In addition, the Assad regime renewed efforts to split the PLO by strengthening pro-Syria, rebel PLO factions led by Abu Musa in their struggle against Chairman Yassir Arafat and the main Fatah faction. Fighting had erupted in May between the rival Palestinian factions in the Bekáa valley.

Despite the presence of the multinational force and opposition from various armed factions, by late 1983 Syria had reemerged with an effective veto power over questions relating to the future of Lebanon. Syrian refusal to withdraw from Lebanon proved to be the major stumbling block to a negotiated settlement in Lebanon, frustrating the diplomatic initiatives of the Reagan administration, which had dispatched fourteen hundred U.S. Marines to Lebanon as part of the multinational force. After the simultaneous suicide bombing of American and French military compounds on 23 October, resulting in the deaths of 241 American marines and 58 French soldiers, the multinational force began pulling out of war-torn Beirut on 7 February 1984. Although pro-Iranian Shiite extremists claimed responsibility for the bombing, Syria was also implicated. On 5 March, Assad, who opposed any Lebanese-Israeli accommodation, pressured the Lebanese president, Amin Gemayel, to abrogate the 17 May agreement with Israel, which had withdrawn its troops to southern Lebanon. Although Assad attempted to restrain pro-Syrian forces and to broker a coalition government, interfactional fighting intensified in and around Beirut. While his involvement in the Lebanese imbroglio was proving to be costly, Assad had emerged as the pivotal player in Lebanon and had forced the splintering of the PLO and the withdrawal of the multinational force. In December 1984 Syrian and American forces clashed briefly in Lebanon, with American battleships shelling Syrian positions around Beirut and attacking Syrian antiaircraft missile installations in the Bekáa valley.

By the mid 1980s Assad had shown himself undeterred by international pressure to disengage from Lebanon, even though he was unable to put an end to the factional, internecine warfare that threatened to precipitate the partitioning of Lebanon into warring ministates along Syria's border. Disturbed by the reemergence of pro-Arafat PLO forces in Lebanon following the early 1985 Israeli phased withdrawal, Assad backed the Amal militia, one of the main Shiite militia groups, in its war against the PLO during May and June. With the help of Shiite factions in the Lebanese army, Syrian-backed militias lay siege to the Palestinian refugee camps of Sabra, Chatila, and Bourj el-Barajneh in Beirut, where the PLO forces were based, resulting in several hundred deaths. Even though he mediated a fragile cease-fire around the camps, Assad's attempt to prevent the resurgence of the PLO in Lebanon had the unforeseen consequence of uniting pro- and anti-Arafat Palestinian factions. In a demonstration of his formidable position in Lebanon, Assad secured the release of thirty-nine American hostages, taken captive in Beirut by the Iranian-backed Hezbollah ("Party of God"), a Shiite extremist group that had hijacked an American airliner. Under pressure from Assad, the hostages were released by the Hezbollah on 30 June 1985 and taken to Damascus.

Syrian forces were drawn into the widening vortex of internecine fighting in and around Beirut, and during September and October 1985 heavy fighting broke out between the three main rival militia groups, the Christian Phalangists, Druze, and Shiite Amal, in the city of Tripoli. Assad brokered another truce agreement, signed on 28 December in Damascus, in an unsuccessful attempt to put an end to the civil war within a year.

In addition to its intervention and unbending stance in Lebanon, the Assad regime's alleged support for international terrorism became a source of tension in its relations with Western countries. The United States implicated Syria, Libya, and Palestinian terrorists in the bombings of the Rome and Vienna airports in December 1985 and a discotheque in West Berlin in April 1986. On 24 October 1986 Great Britain severed relations with Syria after evidence of Syrian complicity in an attempted bombing attack on an Israeli airliner in London was uncovered. Members of the European Economic Community, joined by the United States and Canada, imposed diplomatic and economic sanctions against Syria, but, mindful of Syria's importance in Middle Eastern negotiations and the release of Western hostages held in Lebanon, the sanctions remained limited.

Although the Soviet Union was its principal backer, the Assad regime, which had signed a treaty of friendship with the Soviets in January 1980, displayed a large measure of independence in its foreign policy, often straining relations with Moscow. Despite its heavy dependence on Soviet military assistance, Assad skillfully steered Syria away from a client relationship with the Soviet Union. After Soviet leader Mikhail S. Gorbachev came to power in March 1985, relations between Syria and the Soviet Union cooled somewhat as a result of Moscow's general reduction in assistance to its Third World clients.

Israeli Invasion of Lebanon

Even though his position and role in Middle Eastern politics were strengthened by the 1982 Israeli invasion of Lebanon and his confrontation with the United States, Assad remained isolated in the Arab world during the first half of the 1980s as a result of his support for non-Arab, revolutionary Iran during the Persian Gulf war between Iran and Iraq. The radical, fundamentalist regime in Iran, whose 1979 revolution had sparked Shiite fundamentalism across the Muslim world, was perceived by most Arab states, especially the more conservative regimes, as a threat and source of instability for the region. Assad's pro-Iranian stance, which also drew Western censure, put him at odds with the Soviet Union, a principal backer of Iraq. Beginning in 1986, however, he began to modify his support for revolutionary Iran as he moved to repair relations with Jordon and Iraq as well as expel Palestinian terrorist groups based in Syria. His rapprochement with Jordan and Iraq, and the consequent distancing from Iran, was motivated by a growing concern to regain favor with Western and Arab countries and to play a major role in Middle Eastern peace initiatives. Relations between Syria and Iran were further strained as a result of their divergent interests in Lebanon, where Hezbollah and Iranian Revolutionary Guard forces were operating. Assad viewed the growing strength of the Iranian-backed Hezbollah as a challenge to his position and ambitions in that country. In May 1988 he imposed a cease-fire between the Syrian-backed Amal and the Hezbollah, which had been fighting for two months.

Events in Lebanon continued to distract Assad's attention throughout the latter half of the 1980s. Fighting between Amal and Druze militias, both of whom were Syria's erstwhile allies, had compelled the intervention of some four thousand Syrian troops, which were deployed in West Beirut in February 1987 to impose a cease-fire and lift another siege of Palestinian refugee camps. An apparent reunification of the rival PLO factions in mid April weakened Assad's goal of maintaining a split in the movement. Beginning in March 1989 a more serious challenge to his position erupted when his forces were drawn into a self-described "war of liberation" launched by interim Lebanese president General Michel Aoun and his Iraqi-backed, Christian rebel army. Vowing to fight until Syria withdrew its occupation forces from Lebanon, General Aoun was unable to enlist international support, however, and in September 1989 consented to an Arab League agreement that put a temporary end to the fighting. After renewed fighting broke out the following year, the pro-Syrian Lebanese government of President Elias Hrawi asked for Syrian intervention to quell the renegade Aoun in early October 1990. From 9 October to 11 October, Assad responded with a decisive air and ground offensive against the strongholds of Aoun's fifteen-thousand-strong rebel group in Beirut, leaving more than seven hundred people dead. With the surrender of Aoun's forces days later, it appeared that Assad had finally emerged with control over Lebanon.

Iraq's Invasion of Kuwait

Aside from his victory in Lebanon, the shifting sands of Middle Eastern politics once again brought Assad into the mainstream of Arab and international affairs following the 2 August 1990 invasion of Kuwait by Syria's long-standing rival, Iraq. The Iraqi invasion of Kuwait drew immediate international response, spearheaded by the United States, which assembled a multinational force to defend Saudi Arabia and force the withdrawal of Iraqi troops from Kuwait. Syria, which committed an estimated nineteen thousand troops, and Egypt were the largest contributors in the Arab component of the multinational force in the Gulf region, where more than four hundred thousand combat troops and support personnel from more than twenty countries had been deployed by mid October. Assad, who remained in close contact with American president George Bush and other foreign leaders, emerged as a crucial link in the coalition. Despite signs of domestic opposition to his tactical alliance with the United States, the principal backer of Israel, Syria's archenemy, Assad became a leading advocate for the use of force to dislodge Iraq from Kuwait and to weaken the strength of Iraq's military, which had been a source of growing security concern for Syria and other Arab countries.

Assad appeared to be the biggest winner in the aftermath of the Iraqi invasion. His participation in the multilateral coalition resulted in improved relations with the West, in particular the United States, which had condemned Syria, a sworn enemy of its most important ally in the Middle East, Israel, for sponsoring international terrorism and the kidnapping of Westerners held hostage in Lebanon. Relations with other Arab countries, Egypt and Saudi Arabia in particular, also went through a remarkable transformation. The short-run effect of the Gulf crisis, whose outcome held out the possibility of eliminating Iraq as Syria's principal Arab rival, appeared to allow Assad to consolidate his position in Lebanon and to restore him as a key player in Middle Eastern politics.

Hafez al-Assad has been described by observers as a man with no permanent friends but only permanent interests, constantly shifting alliances to achieve his objectives. His regional political-military policies have been largely shaped within the context of his paramount, linked goals of Arab unity and the destruction of Israel. Skillful, ambitious, and an astute hard-liner, Assad has single-handedly transformed Syria from a weak, vulnerable country into a regional power.

Books and Articles about Assad

Malcom Kerr, "Hafiz Assad and the Changing Patterns of Syrian Politics," *International Journal*, 28 (1975): 689–706;

Moshe Ma'oz, *Asad: The Sphinx of Damascus: A Political Biography* (London: Weidenfeld & Nicolson, 1988);

Ma'oz, "Profile: Hafiz al-Assad of Syria," *Orbis*, 31 (Summer 1987): 207–217;

Patrick Seale, *Asad of Syria: The Struggle for the Middle East* (Berkeley: University of California Press, 1989).

General References

E. Karsh, *The Soviet Union and Syria: The Assad Years* (London: Royal Institute for International Affairs, 1988);

Daniels Pipes, *Greater Syria: The History of an Ambition* (New York: Oxford University Press, 1990).

– J. R.-S.

SEE ALSO THESE RELATED ENTRIES

Yassir Arafat, 2; George Bush, 1; Jimmy Carter, 1; Bashir Gemayel, 2; Mikhail S. Gorbachev, 2; Saddam Hussein, 2; Henry Kissinger, 1; Gamal Abdul Nasser, 2; Richard M. Nixon, 1; Ronald Reagan, 1.

Fulgencio Batista y Zaldívar

President of Cuba, 1940–1944, 1954–1958

Military Leader of Cuba, 1933–1958

Born Banes, Cuba, 16 January 1901
Died Estoril, Portugal, 6 August 1973

Fulgencio Batista y Zaldívar was the dominant political and military leader of Cuba from 1933 to 1959. The son of Belisario Batista Palermo and the former Carmela Zaldívar Gonzales, impoverished mulatto farmers, Batista received little formal education. In 1921 he began his career in the army where he gained popularity among the enlisted rank. He emerged as an important political figure in 1933 when he led a coup on 12 August overthrowing the repressive regime of General Machado y Morales and established a revolutionary government led first by Dr. Carlos Manuel de Céspedes y Quesada and later by Ramón Grau San Martín. In January 1934, apparently encouraged by a U.S. government uncomfortable with Grau's radical support, Batista, then a colonel, led a coup against Grau.

Military Power Broker

As colonel, Batista remained the power behind the three presidents (Carlos Mendieta Monteflur, 1934–1936; Miguel Mariano Gomez, 1936; and Federico Laredo Brú, 1937–1940) who served between 1933 and 1940. During this period Batista implemented the Three-Year Plan of social and economic reforms, including the establishment of workers' pensions, workmen's compensation, and minimum wages. The Confederation of Cuban Workers was formed and union membership was encouraged. Gains were made in health, sanitation, and public education, while tenant farmers were granted the security of tenure. Social reforms continued from 1940 to 1944, during which time Batista himself served as president for the first time. During his term Cuba prospered as a supplier of sugar to the United States and its allies in World War II.

Election to the Senate

Because the 1940 constitution (regarded as one of the most progressive in Latin America for the time) restricted Batista from reelection, he attempted to wield power through a handpicked successor, Carlos Saladrigas. However, Saladrigas lost the election to former leader Grau, who, as leader of the Party of the Cuban Revolution (Autenticos), campaigned for greater social and economic reform. Following the loss, Batista went into self-imposed exile in Daytona Beach, Florida, for six years. However, he was elected in

Fulgencio Batista y Zaldívar

1948 to the Cuban senate, in absentia, thereby maintaining his ties to his political supporters.

The 1952 Coup

Batista returned to power by overthrowing then-president Carlos Prío Soccarrás on 10 March 1952 in a bloodless coup. After taking power, Batista suspended the constitution, closed the Cuban congress, and outlawed all political parties. Originally the coup was welcomed by many as a solution to the problems of corruption and government inefficiency. However, Batista's own corruption and use of repression quickly created resentment, though Batista maintained steadfast support among the conservative politicians, the armed forces, and the U.S. business community in Cuba. His government was formally recognized by the United States on 27 March 1952.

Rigged Elections of 1954

In November 1954, under pressure from the United States, Batista held elections in an attempt to legitimize his rule. The elections were rigged, and Batista's only real opponent, Grau San Martín, pulled out of the race. It was during Batista's second term that a young revolutionary, Fidel Castro, after preparing for revolution while in Mexico, first landed in Cuba with a group of eighty-two revolutionaries. By 1958 Castro's guerrilla struggle had gained support and forced Batista to become more ruthless in treatment of all dissenters, alienating much of the middle class and thus allowing Castro to win their support. A weakened administration, faced with assassinations, bombing, and widespread burning of sugar planta-

tions, finally collapsed, and Batista fled to the Dominican Republic on 31 December 1958. Later Batista went into exile on the Portuguese island of Madeira and finally to Estoril, near Lisbon, where he died on 6 August 1973.

General References

Jack Hopkins, *Latin America: Perspectives on a Region* (New York: Holmes & Meier, 1987);

Ernest Rossi and Jack C. Plano, *The Latin American Political Dictionary* (Santa Barbara, Cal.: ABC-Clio, 1980);

Howard J. Wiarda and Harvey F. Kline, *Latin American Politics and Development* (Boulder, Colo.: Westview Press, 1979).

– B. D.

SEE ALSO THESE RELATED ENTRIES

Fidel Castro Ruz, 2; Raul Castro Ruz, 2; Ernesto "Che" Guevara de la Serna, 2.

Ahmed Ben Bella

President of Algeria, 1963–1965
Born Maghnia, Algeria, 25 December 1918

Ahmed Ben Bella, Algerian nationalist leader and president from 1963 to 1965, was the leading member of the small group of Algerian nationalists, the so-called historic chiefs, who planned and launched the Algerian revolution of 1954–1962.

Ben Bella, the youngest child of a large, modest peasant family, was born in the small town of Maghnia near the Algerian frontier with Morocco. After local primary school he attended high school in the city of Tlemcen but dropped out after a few years. Drafted into the French army in 1937 as a member of the Algerian Sharpshooters, he later served with distinction in the Italian campaign during World War II. He was decorated with the *Medaille militaire* by Charles de Gaulle, the French leader. Ben Bella returned to colonial Algeria in 1945 at a time of growing anticolonial unrest, which eventually erupted into the spring 1945 Sétif uprisings.

The Sétif Uprisings

The Sétif demonstrations and riots, and the subsequent French repression that followed, became a turning point in the Algerian independence struggle. Ben Bella joined the newly created Movement for the Triumph of Democratic Liberties (MTLD), a popular and militant

Ahmed Ben Bella (left) and Houari Boumédienne, 1962

party, and served on the municipal council in Maghnia as the MTLD representative. Convinced that revolutionary action was the only recourse in the face of French colonial intransigence toward political reforms, he and other radical nationalists in 1947 founded the clandestine Organisation Speciale (OS), a paramilitary organization designed to conduct terrorist operations against the French colonial administration. In 1950 Ben Bella, already the national chief of the OS, was captured and imprisoned by the French but managed to escape two years later and fled to Cairo, Egypt, where he and other Algerian nationalists convinced President Gamal Abdul Nasser to support the Algerian revolutionary movement.

The FLN

In the meantime the French had managed to break up the OS, the MTLD disintegrated into factionalism, and Ben Bella created a new underground organization, the Revolutionary Committee of Unity and Action (CRUA). Ben Bella became one of the nine original leaders of the CRUA, the historic chiefs, considered the founding fathers of the Algerian revolution which they launched in November 1954. The CRUA was renamed the National Liberation Front (FLN), which became the political arm of the independence movement, with the National Liberation Army (ALN) as its military arm. Martinique-born Frantz Fanon became the leading political theorist of the FLN, providing arguments for the use of violence and armed struggle in the revolution. Ben Bella performed a variety of diplomatic and military liaison functions, including arranging arms shipments to the guerrillas. On 22 October 1956 a plane carrying Ben Bella was forced down by the French military in Algeria. He had been flying to Tunisia, and he was imprisoned for six years until he was released after the March 1962 French-Algerian cease-fire negotiations.

While in prison Ben Bella had been named, in September 1958, deputy premier of the Provisional Government of the Republic of Algeria (GPRA), formed in exile. However, Ben Bella's preeminence in the newly established provisional government was not recognized by some nationalist leaders, as long-standing personal and ideological differences among the leadership aggravated tensions and rivalry between the political and military wings. The Algerian nationalist leadership was marked by deep internal divisions and fractious infighting, and a split developed between the two wings after the political wing tried to assert control over the Morocco-based ALN. With the signing of the Evian Accords between France and Algeria, which scheduled a national referendum in September 1962, the various nationalist groups jockeyed for position to dominate the revolutionary government. Backed by the taciturn ALN commander, Houari Boumédienne, Ben Bella and the army crossed the border from Morocco into western Algeria in July 1962, and set up the Political Bureau as an alternative to the GPRA. In September 1962 Ben Bella and Boumédienne's forces reached Algiers as the country verged on civil war. After elections for a national assembly, Ben Bella was named premier of the newly declared Democratic and Popular Republic of Algeria.

Differences over the direction of the government and party and an intense power struggle in the de facto triumvirate leadership quickly emerged during the government's first turbulent year. Ben Bella consolidated his power after he was elected president and thereafter sought to weaken the military's influence in the government as well as to eliminate political opponents. Relations between Ben Bella and Boumédienne, the defense minister, also deteriorated as a result of disagreements over domestic and foreign policies, Ben Bella's dictatorial tendencies, and his attempts to create a national militia to counterweight the national army. Ben Bella's flamboyant, radical leadership style, and his impulsive, unpredictable nature, clashed with Boumédienne's reserved, reticent style and preference for discipline and planning. Ben Bella further attempted to undermine Boumédienne by appointing Colonel Tahar Zbiri as chief of staff of the army. The other historic chiefs considered Ben Bella a usurper of power, which they believed should have been shared collectively. Boumédienne, who preferred a collegial style of decision making, became concerned not only with the weakening of the military's role in decision making, but also over Ben Bella's alliances with labor unions and Algerian communists. Boumédienne wanted to give the Algerian revolution an Islamic-Arab character, while Ben Bella, a more secular, doctrinaire ideologue, advocated a one-party socialist state with its concomitant radical land reform programs.

Throughout his tenure in power Ben Bella gave Algeria a revolutionary image. Algeria became a vigorous supporter of liberation movements in Africa and in other parts of the Third World. Ben Bella envisioned an international role for Algeria, with him being a leading spokesman for national liberation movements in the Third World. Developing close ties to the Soviet Union, Ben Bella won the Lenin Peace Prize in 1964. Algeria's international activism, however, concealed deepening political instability in Ben Bella's regime as well as his own domestic isolation. By early 1965 a serious breach had developed between Ben Bella and his opponents when he tried to remove Boumédienne's supporters in the government. On 19 June 1965 Boumédienne led a coup d'état that ousted Ben Bella from power. Ironically, the unit that arrested Ben Bella and took him to prison was led by Tahar Zbiri, the chief of staff who was appointed to weaken Boumédienne. Ben Bella was arrested and imprisoned until 1980, when he was released and went into voluntary exile in France. In 1983 he moved to Switzerland and continued to involve himself in exile politics, and in May 1984 he founded the Movement for Democracy in Algeria. Ben Bella, who married the leftist journalist Zobra Sellami in 1971 while under house arrest in Douera, was allowed to return to Algeria on 27 September 1990.

Book about Ben Bella
Robert Merle, *Ahmed Ben Bella* (Paris: Gallimard, 1965).

General References
John P. Entelis, *Algeria: The Revolution Institutionalized* (Boulder, Colo.: Westview, 1986);

David C. Gordon, *The Passing of Algeria* (London: Oxford University Press, 1966);

Arslan Humbarati, *Algeria: The Revolution That Failed* (New York: Praeger, 1966);

David Ottaway and Marina Ottaway, *Algeria: The Politics of a Socialist Revolution* (Berkeley: University of California Press, 1970);

William Quandt, *Revolution and Political Leadership: Algeria 1954–1968* (Cambridge, Mass.: MIT Press, 1969);

John Talbott, *The War Without a Name: France in Algeria, 1954–1962* (New York: Knopf, 1980).

—J. R.-S.

SEE ALSO THESE RELATED ENTRIES
Houari Boumédienne, 2; Gamal Abdul Nasser.

David Ben-Gurion
Prime Minister of Israel, 1949–1953, 1955–1963
Born Plonsk, Poland, 16 October 1886
Died Jerusalem, Israel, 1 December 1973

David Ben-Gurion was a major force in the founding of the state of Israel in 1948 and its first prime minister. His view of Zionism became dominant during the early years of the Jewish state's existence and, despite some internal contradictions, remains its guiding force today.

David Gruen was born in Plonsk, Poland, about thirty-five miles from Warsaw, while that area was under Czarist Russian control. He was the sixth of eleven children of Avigdor and Sheindal Gruen. His father was a cofounder in 1890 of the Love of Zion Society, which was a precursor to Theodor Herzl's political Zionism. David learned Hebrew from his grandfather and received his early education in his father's one-room Hebrew school. Although he gave up religion after his bar mitzvah at age thirteen, Ben-Gurion (who took that name only after his arrival in Palestine) became increasingly active in socialist Zionist circles. In 1906, after having been arrested for Zionist political activity as editor of a socialist Zionist newspaper, Ben-Gurion joined a group of two thousand Plonsk Jews who immigrated to Palestine. He planned to become a labor organizer and found work as a farmhand, first on the coastal plain and later in Galilee.

At the time there were many different ideas about what Zionism meant and might mean in the future. Herzl, one of the earliest Zionist thinkers and without doubt the most prominent, wrote the first tract of political Zionism, *Der Judenstadt* (The Jewish State, 1896). Others, however, such as Ahad Ha'am, viewed Zionism in cultural rather than nationalist terms, and still other then-prominent Jewish leaders rejected the philosophy outright. Ben-Gurion's Zionist vision was premised on the building of a new Hebrew nation through Jewish capital and labor.

In 1910 Ben-Gurion moved to Jerusalem and became one of the leading organizers and propagandists of Poalei Zion (Workers of Zion), the first labor Zionist party, joining the editorial staff of its paper, *Ahdut* (Unity). In 1911 he was elected to the Eleventh Zionist Congress. At about that time he also joined a group of young socialist Zionists to study at Turkish universities with the hope of establishing ties with the ruling Ottoman Empire circles and through them gain a Jewish homeland in Palestine; while there, he taught himself Turkish and earned a law degree from the University of Constantinople. When Ben-Gurion returned to Palestine in 1914, he resumed his work as a labor organizer. Despite his absence, in 1913 he had been elected to the central committee of Poalei Zion and began organizing Jewish workers into labor unions.

Gale International Portrait Gallery

David Ben-Gurion

In 1915, despite his openly pro-Ottoman stance, Ben-Gurion was exiled by the commander of the Turkish forces in Palestine. He made his way to Alexandria, Egypt, where he met the then-obscure militant Vladimir Jabotinsky (leader of the Revisionist movement and Menachem Begin's ideological mentor). He then traveled to New York, where he set up an organization to recruit new immigrants from among left-wing Jewish trade union activists. While there, he married Paula Munweiss, a Brooklyn nurse. Like other Zionist leaders, Ben-Gurion welcomed the Balfour Declaration of 2 November 1917, in which Great Britain called for the creation of a Jewish homeland in Palestine.

Formation of Histadrut

When he returned to Palestine, Ben-Gurion provided the impetus that led to the 1920 formation of the Histadrut, the general federation of labor, which became dominant in all economic affairs. Ben-Gurion opposed those who argued for a labor union open to all workers and adamantly called for it to limit its membership to Jewish workers, thus placing Jewish nationalist interests before class-based goals. In 1921 Ben-Gurion became general secretary of the Histadrut, the activities of which

were designed to create the infrastructure for a Jewish state. He remained in that position for fourteen years. In 1919 Ben-Gurion founded the Ahdut Ha'avodah (Unity of Labor) movement from a coalition of Poalei Zion and other affiliated socialist groups. This new movement eventually merged with a former rival into Mapai (Workers' Party of Israel), the socialist Zionist party that became the core of the present Labor party. By 1935 Mapai dominated the agencies of the World Zionist Organization, its purposes becoming almost indistinguishable from Zionism itself. Through the Histadrut, trade unions, labor exchanges, workers' kitchens, schools, a bureau of public works, and a sick fund were set up.

Chairman of the Jewish Agency

In 1935 Ben-Gurion became chairman of the Jewish Agency, the executive body of Zionism, a position he retained until the state's formation. As chairman, Ben-Gurion favored partition of the region into Jewish and Palestinian homelands as recommended by the British Peel Commission in 1936. The partition plan was publicly denounced by the Arabs and dropped by the British, who three years later issued the White Paper, which limited Jewish immigration to and land purchases in Palestine. By June 1939 Ben-Gurion had authorized illegal immigration under the auspices of the Haganah, the pre-independence army, which was soon made impossible by the outbreak of World War II in September. By 1942 Ben-Gurion had flip-flopped on his desire for partition; at the New York Biltmore Hotel conference, just two years after Jabotinsky's death, Ben-Gurion endorsed what had been his rival's political program: a Jewish state in all of Palestine. It was only in 1947, after a British crackdown and the response of militant Jews by blowing up Jerusalem's King David hotel, that Ben-Gurion decided to again moderate his stance and accept partition.

Founding the State of Israel

When Britain gave up the Palestine mandate on 14 May 1948, it was Ben-Gurion who proclaimed the state of Israel. The sixty-two-year-old "B. G.," as he was called, announced a provisional government with himself as prime minister. During the war that ensued with the Arabs, he also adopted the position of de facto defense minister. Although Ben-Gurion gained credit for the military victory, he sowed the seeds for the ongoing Israeli-Palestinian conflict. And he alarmed the newly formed United Nations by adopting a policy of swift and ruthless retaliation for raids against Israel, which he termed "self defense," a policy that remains central to Israel's military doctrine today.

While prime minister from 1948 until 1953, Ben-Gurion confronted the task of consolidating the prestate bodies, from the Histadrut to the Jewish Agency, and establishing a civilian army, the Israeli Defense Forces (IDF), from the array of military groups. He was also responsible for integrating into the new state Jewish immigrants, seven hundred thousand of whom arrived during his five-year tenure, more than doubling the country's Jewish population. In 1950, he persuaded the Knesset (parliament) to enact the Law of Return, which gave every Jew the right to immigrate to Israel and to claim citizenship immediately. Such a law was possible only in the absence of a written constitution, which, though attempted, has never been instituted. Also in 1950 Ben-Gurion moved the capital from Tel Aviv to Jerusalem, the western half of which was then in Israeli jurisdiction.

Resignation and Return

In November 1953 Ben-Gurion resigned as prime minister and moved to Sde Boker, an obscure kibbutz (collective farm) deep in Israel's southern Negev desert. But a scandal that came close to causing his successor's government to collapse – the so-called Lavon affair, in which Israeli agents, who were believed to have been authorized by the defense minister Pin.has Lavon to place bombs in U.S. institutions in the Egyptian cities of Alexandria and Cairo – pulled him back from retirement. The plan was discovered, some of the agents executed, and Lavon forced out of office on the basis of a report that established his culpability and of Ben-Gurion's recommendation. Not surprisingly, Ben-Gurion took Lavon's spot in the defense ministry in December 1955, and became the government's strongman. Within a very short time he had returned to the prime ministership.

During those years in office Ben-Gurion oversaw many events of crucial importance, and his popularity and his stature within the international community increased. In 1956, when Egyptian president Gamal Abdul Nasser nationalized the Suez Canal, Ben-Gurion prepared plans for a secret attack on Egypt with Britain and France and struck in October. Three years later Ben-Gurion gained politically for the kidnapping from Argentina and trial in Jerusalem of Adolf Eichmann, the Nazi bureaucrat who had organized the killing of millions of Jews during World War II.

Ben-Gurion's foreign policy emphasized Israel's relations with France and a tacit alliance with Germany. Israel's relationship with France also allowed Ben-Gurion to initiate Israel's nuclear weapons. Ben-Gurion concluded a reparation agreement with the West German government and was an ardent proponent of the idea that West Germany was a "new" Germany.

But Ben-Gurion's political fortunes changed when the Lavon scandal came back to the forefront. When a new inquiry into the defense minister's role exonerated Lavon (finding that the earlier indictment had been made on falsified evidence), Ben-Gurion resigned the government in anger in January 1961. In an attempt to keep the government together again, the party dismissed Lavon and pleaded with Ben-Gurion to return. When the fiery, white-haired Ben-Gurion resigned again in June 1963, no one implored him to return. While the 1965 elections again sent Ben-Gurion to the Knesset, his new party, Rafi (Israeli Workers), did poorly. The "Old Man" resigned from government in 1970 and died, at age eighty-seven, on 1 December 1973.

Books by Ben-Gurion

Recollections, edited by Thomas H. Bernstein (Tel Aviv: Bitan, 1970);

Israel: A Personal History (New York: Funk & Wagnall's, 1971);

My Talks with Arab Leaders (Jerusalem: Keter, 1972).

Books about Ben-Gurion

Michael Bar-Zohar, *Ben-Gurion: A Biography* (New York: Delacorte, 1978);

Shabtai Teveth, *Ben-Gurion and the Palestinian Arabs: From Peace to War* (Oxford: Oxford University Press, 1985);

Shabtai Teveth, *David Ben-Gurion: The Burning Ground, 1886–1948* (Boston: Houghton Mifflin, 1987).

General References

Hannah Arendt, *Eichmann in Jerusalem: A Report on the Banality of Evil* (New York: Viking, 1963);

Bernard Avishai, *The Tragedy of Zionism: Revolution and Democracy in the Land of Israel* (New York: Farrar, Straus & Giroux, 1985);

Uri Bialer, *Between East and West: Israel's Foreign Policy Orientation 1948–1956* (Cambridge: Cambridge University Press, 1990);

Simhal Flapan, *The Birth of Israel: Myths and Realities* (New York: Pantheon, 1987);

Itamar Rabinovich and Yehuda Reinharz, eds., *Israel in the Middle East: Documents and Readings on Society, Politics and Foreign Relations 1948–Present* (New York: Oxford University Press, 1984).

– Q. I.

SEE ALSO THESE RELATED ENTRIES
Levi Eshkol, 2; Golda Meir, 2; Yitzhak Rabin, 2.

Zulfikar Ali Bhutto

Prime Minister of Pakistan, 1973–1977

President of Pakistan, 1971–1973

Born Larkarna, India, 5 January 1928
Died Islamabad, Pakistan, 4 April 1979

Zulfikar Ali Bhutto, served as president of Pakistan from 1971 to 1973 and as prime minister from 1973 to 1977.

Born in Larkarna, India, Bhutto received most of his early education in Bombay. He then attended the University of California, Berkeley, and subsequently earned a law degree at Christ Church, Oxford.

Bhutto's political career began in 1958, when he was appointed energy minister by President Ayub Khan. Bhutto rose quickly to prominence in national politics and became an influential figure in the military government despite his youth. In 1961 he engineered an oil-exploration agreement with the Soviet Union, which also agreed to provide economic and technical aid. Bhutto soon became the de facto chief foreign-policy spokesman in the government, and in 1963 he was finally appointed foreign minister.

As foreign minister, Bhutto set out to transform and diversify Pakistan's foreign policy, which had hitherto been strongly pro-Western. Pakistan, a member of the United States–led Southeast Asian Treaty Organization (SEATO) and the Central Asian Treaty Organization (CENTO), had become an important element in U.S. regional-security policy and an important regional client in its efforts to contain the neighboring Soviet Union and People's Republic of China. Although he sought to avoid a rupture in relations with Pakistan's Western backers, Bhutto moved to establish close relations with China, Indonesia, and other Muslim countries. Despite U.S. displeasure, he built close relations with communist China, which agreed to finance a large military-industrial complex in Pakistan. Bhutto guided Pakistani foreign policy toward a nationalist, nonaligned orientation, which stressed Third World as well as Muslim world unity and cooperation. He developed close ties with Indonesia's Bung Sukarno, one of the prominent leaders of the Non-Aligned Movement, and became active in Third World political forums.

Zulfikar Ali Bhutto

The 1965 Kashmir War

In mid 1965 Bhutto, considered to be a "hawk" on relations with India, Pakistan's traditional rival and primary security threat, convinced the government to undertake a military operation in the Indian state of Kashmir, over which the two countries had a long-standing dispute. The military action quickly escalated into a full-scale war when India launched a massive attack on Pakistan on 6 September. Two weeks later the two countries agreed to a United Nations–sponsored cease-fire.

Bhutto subsequently took part in the Soviet-sponsored negotiations to reach a more durable peace agreement with India. Bhutto resigned from the government in 1966, apparently in disagreement with the final Indo-Pakistani settlement.

The People's Party of Pakistan

Remaining active in national politics, Bhutto founded the People's Party of Pakistan (PPP) in 1967. The PPP reflected much of Bhutto's own political thinking and combined elements of nationalism, socialism, Islamic revival, and populism. Bhutto and the party emerged victorious in the 1970 national elections. In addition to a political impasse caused by the PPP's refusal to join negotiations for a new constitution, the country was plunged into a bloody civil war in 1970 and 1971, when East Pakistan (present-day Bangladesh) attempted to secede. The civil war turned into a full-blown armed confrontation with Soviet-backed India, which launched an invasion into East Pakistan on 4 December 1971 after repeated cross-border, armed incursions by Pakistani forces.

After the war, which ended in defeat and territorial diminution for Pakistan, Bhutto assumed power on 20 December 1971. His first priority was to repair Pakistan's image abroad and its relations with neighboring countries. Domestically he launched the country on a socialist path of development, with major sectors of the economy, including international trade, placed under state control. Economic success was limited, however, as a result of ineffective policies and economic mismanagement. Bhutto also moved to concentrate power and decision making in his own hands. He undercut the power and influence of the military by purging its top ranks and created a paramilitary force which essentially served as his personal bodyguard. In addition to banning leading opposition parties, he also sought to undermine the power of his political opponents and powerful political families. In April 1972 he lifted martial law and arranged a constitutional convention in 1973. Despite trappings of democratic rule, Bhutto's dictatorial tendencies and authoritarian style did not subside.

Bhutto, who had withdrawn Pakistan from the moribund SEATO and the Commonwealth of Nations, resumed an avowedly nonaligned foreign policy. As part of an effort to heal Indo-Pakistani relations, he signed an agreement with India's Indira Gandhi in 1972. While he continued to focus on the Middle East, he also moved to improve relations with the Soviet Union, which provided economic aid. Relations with China, which had strongly backed Pakistan in the 1971 war, remained good, as did relations with the United States, which finally lifted its arms embargo in 1975. Even though Bhutto's foreign policy remained a source of discomfort for the United States, Pakistan continued to enjoy the U.S. military umbrella in the event of a superpower attack. For Pakistan, close relations with the United States were based on its strategic needs, given its security situation and need for military and technical assistance. The tension and rivalry produced by the regional balance of power, and the dynamics produced by the global superpower competition, dictated a continued reliance on the United States for military assistance.

Bhutto's rule came to a bloody end following the March 1977 elections. The country was hurled into another political crisis as violent clashes erupted between the military and the opposition, which claimed that the elections were fraudulent. After the military intervened and declared martial law, Bhutto was ousted by General Mohammad Zia ul-Haq on 5 July 1977. The new military regime brought a series of charges against Bhutto, including conspiracy to commit murder, and he was sentenced to death in 1976. Bhutto was executed on 4 April 1979.

Books by Bhutto

The Myth of Independence (London: Oxford University Press, 1969);

The Third World: New Directions (London: Quartet Books, 1977).

Books about Bhutto

Shahid J. Burki, *Pakistan Under Bhutto, 1971–1977* (London: Macmillan, 1988);

Anwar H. Syed, *The Discourse and Politics of Zulfikar Ali Bhutto* (London: Macmillan, 1991);

Salmaan Tasser, *Bhutto: A Political Biography* (New Delhi: Vikas, 1980).

–J. R.-S.

SEE ALSO THESE RELATED ENTRIES
Indira Gandhi, 2; Bung Sukarno, 2; Mohammad Zia ul-Haq, 2.

Boleslaw Bierut

Prime Minister of Poland, 1952–1953

Chairman, Polish United Workers Party, 1948–1952

Born Rury Jezuickie, Poland, 18 April 1892
Died Moscow, Soviet Union, 12 March 1956

Boleslaw Bierut, Polish leader and Communist party official, was born Boleslaw Krasnodebski in Rury Jezuickie, near Lublin, Poland. In his youth he was greatly influenced by leftist and socialist ideas and joined the newly formed Polish Communist party after Poland gained its independence in 1918. As an agent of the Bolshevik-directed Communist International (Comintern), Bierut spent much of his time organizing communist cells and agitating for communist influence in Poland, Bulgaria, Czechoslovakia, and Austria. For his activities in Poland, he was arrested and imprisoned several times during the 1920s and 1930s, as the right-of-center Polish government cracked down on communist subversion. Throughout the interwar period the communists, who since the Polish-Soviet war of 1918–1920 were widely viewed as Soviet agents, remained a small and uninfluential force. In 1938, after being released from jail, Bierut went to the Soviet Union and was based there during most of World War II.

Polish Workers Party

In June 1943 the Kremlin set up the Union of Polish Patriots with a view to transforming it into a future communist government of Poland. Its core leaders, including Bierut, were communists who had survived Joseph Stalin's mass purges of suspected Trotskyists and "national deviationists." They formed the Polish Workers party (PWP) in an attempt to disguise their communist program and to give the impression that they were a homegrown socialist movement. Bierut returned to Poland during 1943 as the Soviet Red Army pushed back the Nazi German forces and captured Polish territory. The Stalin-sponsored Polish Committee of National Liberation was formed in July 1944 as a provisional communist-controlled administration for Poland. In September of that same year, Bierut became head of the National Council of the Homeland, established as a quasi-parliamentary body under communist direction. He was also a member of the PWP politburo, in which the Moscow-trained communists, or "Muscovite" faction, predominated over the "native" faction which had remained in Poland during the German occupation.

Boleslaw Bierut

Postwar Partition of Poland

As a result of agreement between the United States, Great Britain, and the Soviet Union, Poland lost one-third of its prewar territories to the Soviet Union, areas from which nearly two million Poles had been deported by Stalin at the outset of the war. In compensation the former German territories of Pomerania and Silesia and parts of East Prussia were incorporated into Poland, and Polish settlement in these areas was encouraged. About five million Germans from these "reclaimed territories" either fled westward or were forcibly expelled by the Soviet and Polish security forces. Thousands died during the exodus, and only a small German minority remained in parts of western Poland after the war. The new Polish-German border on the Oder and Neisse rivers became a source of tension between the two states as the West German government formally accepted the location of the frontier only at the close of 1990. The new Polish government, with Bierut as president, was proclaimed on 28 June 1945.

Elimination of Opposition

The Bierut regime in Poland set about stamping out all armed resistance by destroying the remnants of the noncommunist Polish Home Army. It also emasculated the political opposition by eliminating or restricting rival parties, such as the popular Peasant and Socialist parties, while extending its own controls over the state and society. Throughout Eastern Europe the local Communist parties under Soviet supervision imposed their monopoly on power in stages. First, each party entered into temporary coalition governments with noncommunist political organizations while excluding those parties that were denounced as "undemocratic" or "reactionary." Second, the coalitions were replaced with bogus alliances in which the communists dominated, a few token noncommunists were retained, and important political rivals were banned or eliminated. Third, absolute one-party rule was established with the abolition of all opposition groups or through forced mergers with the ruling party. The length of the first two stages varied between states, depending on the strategic importance of the country for Moscow, the urgency of establishing firm Communist party control, and the degree of threat posed by rival parties.

In Poland the first period was practically bypassed, while in Czechoslovakia stage three was only completed by early 1948. A rigged referendum in Poland in June 1946 was followed by a fraudulent general election in January 1947 – an election won overwhelmingly by the communist-controlled bloc of parties. Bierut was able to consolidate his power in the party as the "native" faction was attacked by Muscovites for their alleged resistance to Stalinization. Bierut then became instrumental in the Sovietization of all aspects of Polish political, economic, and social life during the late 1940s and early 1950s. He was appointed first secretary of the PWP in 1948, after the removal of local communists who were charged with "national deviations and other political offences." The "natives" were accused of delaying the imposition of essential Stalinist tenets such as the collectivization of agriculture, the centralization of economic planning, the focus on heavy industry, and the banning of organized religion.

Reorganization of Party

After replacing the disgraced Wladyslaw Gomulka in August 1948, Bierut proceeded to reorganize the party. He oversaw the merger of the PWP with the truncated left wing of the Polish Socialist party to form the Polish United Workers party (PUWP) and was elected chairman of the new organization. Under his direction an agricultural collectivization program was launched in 1949. Thousands of peasant families were forced to surrender their land to the state-appointed managers of newly formed cooperative farms. Bierut also staged a crackdown against the Roman Catholic church in an attempt to eliminate religious influence from the country. Because of his faithfulness to Moscow, his hardline policies, and his imitative "personality cult" he became known as Poland's "little Stalin." In 1952 Bierut vacated the PUWP chairmanship to become the country's prime minister. Under the Stalinist Bierut leadership Poland became a stalwart Soviet satellite and followed all of Moscow's foreign-policy initiatives in the escalating Cold War conflict. Like other Eastern European states, Poland refused to accept Western economic aid under the U.S. Marshall Plan, which had helped to reconstruct the economies of Western Europe but which Stalin feared would undermine Soviet influence in the region and increase ties with the Western democracies.

After Stalin's death in 1953, Bierut's dogmatic Stalinist followers were ousted from the leadership of the PUWP. Bierut himself was forced to resign from the party as well as from the premiership during the process of gradual de-Stalinization. He traveled to Moscow, where he died on 12 March 1956 while attending the Soviet Communist party's Twentieth Congress, during which Soviet leader Nikita S. Khrushchev admitted the extent and brutality of the Stalinist terror.

General References

J. F. Brown, *Eastern Europe and Communist Rule* (Durham, N.C.: Duke University Press, 1988);

M. K. Dziewanowski, *The Communist Party of Poland*, second edition (Cambridge, Mass.: Harvard University Press, 1976);

Christopher D. Jones, *Soviet Influence in Eastern Europe: Political Autonomy and the Warsaw Pact* (New York: Praeger, 1981);

Krystyna Kersten, *The Establishment of Communist Rule in Poland, 1943–1948* (Berkeley: University of California Press, 1991);

Joseph Rothschild, *Return to Diversity: A Political History of East Central Europe since World War II* (New York: Oxford University Press, 1989);

Richard Felix Staar, *Poland 1944–1962: The Sovietization of a Captive People* (Baton Rouge: Louisiana State University Press, 1962);

Sarah M. Terry, ed., *Soviet Policy in Eastern Europe* (New Haven: Yale University Press, 1984);

Teresa Toranska, *"Them": Stalin's Polish Puppets* (New York: Harper & Row, 1987).

Adam Ulam, *Expansion and Coexistence: The History of Soviet Foreign Policy, 1917-1967* (New York: Praeger, 1968).

– J. B. and A. B.

SEE ALSO THESE RELATED ENTRIES

Wladyslaw Gomulka, 2; Nikita S. Khrushchev, 2; Joseph Stalin, 2.

Maurice Bishop

Prime Minister of Grenada, 1979–1983
Born Aruba, 29 May 1944
Died Saint George, Grenada, 19 October 1983

Maurice Rupert Bishop served as prime minister of Grenada from 13 March 1979 until his death in 1983. Four years after leading an armed rebellion that overthrew Prime Minister Eric Matthew Gairy, Bishop himself fell victim to a coup led by members of his own government.

After completing high school in Grenada, Bishop earned a law degree from the University of London, where he became active in the civil rights movement. As a member of the Campaign Against Racial Discrimination, Bishop worked to secure civil and political rights for Great Britain's migrant population, especially those of West Indian origin.

Return to Grenada

In 1970 Bishop returned to Grenada, where he quickly took advantage of the skills he had learned as a student activist to mobilize and organize grass-roots support against racial discrimination. In May 1970 Bishop and his peers founded a discussion group called Forum, which attracted young radical intellectuals and professionals. Eventually this group evolved into the Movement for the Advancement of Community Effort (MACE), the objective of which was the political education of the urban poor. Through these organizations, Bishop staged protests against the government of Prime Minister Gairy. As support for his groups grew, Bishop came to serve as a spokesman for Grenada's poor.

The New Jewel Movement

Bishop later formed the Movement for Assemblies of the People (MAP), a union of MACE and the Committee of Concerned Citizens whose members were drawn from Grenada's young entrepreneurial population. In March 1973 Bishop merged MAP with the Joint Endeavour for

Maurice Bishop

the Welfare, Education and Liberation of the People (JEWEL), a movement which had made inroads among agricultural laborers, who traditionally sided with Gairy. This new group, the New Jewel Movement (NJM), was the institution which Bishop used to advance his causes in the 1970s. Soon after its formation, the NJM became active in inciting strikes and sending petitions to London opposing Gairy's attempt to free the island from British rule without free elections.

In 1973, despite petitions and apparent widespread opposition, Great Britain decided to grant Grenada independence and allow Gairy to maintain his power. To protest the decision, Bishop and the NJM organized a demonstration in November 1973 which was reportedly attended by more than ten thousand. (The total population of Grenada was less than one hundred thousand.) In retaliation for their involvement in the demonstrations, government authorities had Bishop and other NJM members apprehended and tortured. After being released, Bishop and others called for a general strike, which lasted for three months. On the day that Grenada officially received its independence (7 February 1976), all of the NJM's leaders were jailed. Several NJM members, including Bishop's father, Rupert, were killed by government troops during this period.

Leader of the Opposition

In 1976 Bishop became the official leader of the opposition in Grenada's house of representatives after a coalition to which the NJM belonged won six of fifteen seats. Bishop used his position to promote the NJM's programs and to condemn and expose certain actions taken by Gairy and his supporters. At this point the NJM's ideology became more radical, causing rifts in the leadership of the opposition alliance. This infighting, combined with attempts by Gairy to weaken or possibly eliminate the NJM, led Bishop and other NJM leaders to form a secret revolutionary wing, the People's Army.

The 1979 Coup

When the People's Army took advantage of Gairy's absence from Grenada to seize power on 13 March 1979, the response from the people was overwhelmingly supportive. The New People's Revolutionary Government replaced the old Westminster form of government. Bishop's government attempted to establish voluntary mass organizations which were declared to be democratic thereby eliminating, according to Bishop, the need for free and open elections. In this new government Bishop served as prime minister and also as ministers of information, defense, health, and interior. Although Bishop maintained a moderate economic policy and kept trade relations open with the West, his government was Marxist-oriented. A personal friend of Fidel Castro of Cuba

and Daniel Ortega Saavedra of Nicaragua, Bishop attempted to incorporate aspects of the Cuban and Nicaraguan economic model into Grenada's economy. Bishop declared his government to be "anti-imperialist, non-aligned and pro-socialist" and developed close ties with Cuba, the Soviet Union, and Eastern Europe. The most controversial support was the assistance of 250 Cuban technicians along with Soviet advisers in the building of a large airport runway on the southwestern end of the island and the stockpiling of a large quantity of military equipment. Many observers, including the U.S. government and some Caribbean nations, saw this as an attempt to foster another Soviet puppet in the Caribbean.

U.S. Invasion of Grenada

Troubled by this activity, U.S. president Ronald Reagan ordered economic and political action against the island nation in 1983. At the same time, a serious internal conflict emerged between Bishop (and his supporters) and the supporters of Vice-minister Bernard Coard. Bishop refused to share political power with Coard, who apparently favored closer ties with the Soviet Union. When Coard had Bishop arrested on 12 October 1983, there was a public outcry for Bishop's release. On 19 October after Bishop was set free by a crowd of supporters, government troops shot and killed Bishop, three government ministers, and about one hundred demonstrators. The army, under the control of Coard, then seized control.

The Organization of Eastern Caribbean States, an organization founded in 1981 of five nations, called for U.S. intervention in Grenada in order to restore peace, order, and democracy on the island. Considering these concerns, and to protect the U.S. citizens living on the island (many were studying medicine there), President Reagan ordered the 25 October 1983 landing of approximately nineteen hundred U.S. Marines and Army Rangers on the island, along with hundreds of troops from the neighboring islands. After one week of considerable resistance from the Cuban and the Grenadian military forces, leaders of the coup were arrested and control was handed over to the governor-general, Sir Paul Scoon. Scoon established a nonpolitical interim government paving the way for the return to democratic elections.

Books by Bishop

Forward Ever: Three Years of the Grenadian Revolution (Sydney: Pathfinder Press, 1982);

Maurice Bishop Speaks: The Grenada Revolution, 1979–1983 (Sydney: Pathfinder Press, 1984).

General References

Jacqueline Ann Braveboy-Wagner, "Grenada," in *Latin American and Caribbean Contemporary Record*, edited by

Jack W. Hopkins, volume one (New York: Holmes & Meier, 1983);

Reynold A. Burrowes, *Revolution and Rescue in Grenada: An Account of the U.S.-Caribbean Invasion* (New York: Greenwood, 1988);

Chris Searle, *Grenada: The Struggle Against Destabilization* (London: Writers and Readers Publishing Cooperative Society, 1983);

Anthony Thorndike, *Grenada* (Boulder, Colo.: Lynne Reiner Press, 1985).

– B. D.

SEE ALSO THESE RELATED ENTRIES

Fidel Castro Ruz, 2; Daniel Ortega Saavedra, 2; Ronald Reagan, 1.

Tomás Borge Martínez

Nicaraguan Minister of the Interior, 1979–1990
Born Matagalpa, Nicaragua, 12 August 1930

Tomás Borge Martínez was the only surviving founder of Nicaragua's Sandinista National Liberation Front (FSLN) at the time of the overthrow of the Somoza dynasty in July 1979. He went on to become Nicaragua's minister of the interior and overseer of intelligence operations during the Sandinista regime.

Borge is the son of middle-class parents; his father was a pharmacist who had resisted U.S. intervention in Nicaragua's internal affairs in 1912, and his mother was a devout Catholic.

Opposition to Somoza

Borge first asserted his opposition to the dictatorship of Anastasio Somoza García at the age of thirteen, when he refused to shake hands with the dictator, who was on a visit to Borge's secondary school. His revolutionary fervor was further awakened when he came across the writings of Augusto Sandino, the Nicaraguan guerrilla leader who fought the government and the U.S. Marines from 1927 to 1930.

The FSLN

In 1951 Borge enrolled in law school at the National University in Léon, where he quickly distinguished himself as a natural orator and leader. Just a few months before Borge was to graduate, however, Anastasio Somoza García was assassinated, and Borge was taken into custody as a suspected accomplice. A military tribunal sentenced him to eight years in prison, but he managed to escape to Honduras in 1959. Two years later he

had returned to Nicaragua and banded together with Carlos Fonseca Amador and other revolutionaries to form the FSLN (named after Sandino) in opposition to Luis Somoza Debayle, who had succeeded his father to the presidency.

Until the early 1970s the FSLN was made up of only a few hundred men, and its sporadic actions in opposition to the Somoza government did not garner much support. The group did, however, receive support from progressive priests in Nicaragua, supporters of liberation theology who were committed to the idea of a preferential option for the poor.

Finally, in January 1978, Pedro Joaquin Chamorro, editor of the conservative anti-Somoza newspaper, *La prensa*, was assassinated, and public opinion solidified against Anastasio Somoza Debayle, who had succeeded his brother as president in 1967. The ranks of the Sandinistas quickly expanded to seven thousand men. Supported and supplied by several Latin American nations, including Panama and Cuba, and undaunted by the torture, rape, and murder of Borge's wife at the hands of Somoza's National Guard, the Sandinistas launched a major offensive in June 1979. Under pressure from the United States, Somoza resigned the presidency and fled Nicaragua the following month, leaving the country in the hands of the Sandinistas.

Of the nine Sandinistas who formed the national directorate, the leadership body of the Sandinista regime, Borge was the most charismatic and engaging. A small, nearsighted man, he charmed foreign visitors to Nicara-

Margaret Randall

Tomás Borge Martínez

gua yet also moved freely among common Nicaraguans. He was largely regarded as the leader of the Sandinista "ideologues," who were committed to a radicalization of the revolution. His speeches often explained or applied some principle of Karl Marx or Vladimir I. Lenin, though he used simple language and quoted more from the Bible than from Marxist volumes.

Support for Anti-Americanism

During their decade in power, from 1979 to 1990, the Sandinistas collaborated closely with the Cubans, the East Germans, and the secret services of several other communist countries to train guerrillas and anti-Western subversives. They supported Muammar Qaddafi's Libya and Ayatollah Khomeini's Iran, both nations openly hostile to the United States.

Domestic Control

At home the Sandinistas imposed a strict system on Nicaragua which was far less politically open than even the corrupt Somoza regime had been. The opposition was oppressed and denied its means of expression. Church leaders withdrew their support for the regime. The Sandinistas' proposed transformation of Nicaragua was hindered significantly by the Nicaraguan counterrevolutionaries known as the contras, supported by the United States in an effort to prevent the consolidation of the second socialist regime, after Cuba, in the Western hemisphere.

Despite intense indoctrination at every level of society, in the 1990 presidential elections the Nicaraguans, weary of armed conflict and economic chaos, elected Violeta Barrios de Chamorro, wife of the late Pedro Joaquin Chamorro, over the incumbent Sandinista Daniel Ortega Saavedra. The Sandinistas accepted their defeat at the polls, and Borge is now serving in the political opposition to the Chamorro regime.

Books by Borge

and others, *Sandinistas Speak* (New York: Pathfinders Press, 1982);

The Patient Impatience: From Boyhood to Guerrilla: A Personal Narrative of Nicaragua's Struggle for Liberation (New York: Curbside Press, 1992).

Book about Borge

Andrew Reding, ed., *Christianity and Revolution: Tomás Borge's Theology of Life* (Maryknoll, N.Y.: Orbis Books, 1987).

General Reference

Dennis Gilbert, *Sandinistas, the Party and the Revolution* (Oxford, U.K.: Blackwell, 1988)

– L. H.

SEE ALSO THESE RELATED ENTRIES

Violeta Barrios de Chamorro, 2; Manuel Antonio Noriega, 2; Daniel Ortega Saavedra, 2; Anastasio Somoza Debayle, 2.

Juan Bosch Gavino

President of the Dominican Republic, 1962–1963
Born La Vega, Dominican Republic, 30 June 1909

Juan Bosch Gavino is a Dominican essayist and short-story writer who emerged in the 1940s and 1950s as the major leader of the opposition to the Dominican dictator Rafael Leónidas Trujillo Molina. Bosch was born to lower-middle-class parents. He completed a degree in literature at the University of Santo Domingo. He has gained considerable fame in Latin America as a novelist, journalist, poet, and historian.

Early Years in Exile

Bosch went into self-imposed exile in 1937 to protest the killing of ten thousand Haitian squatters on Dominican land at the order of then-dictator Trujillo. Living in Cuba for the next twenty-four years, Bosch lectured throughout Latin America, making contact with other Latin American intellectuals and democrats.

Dominican Revolutionary Party

In 1939, with other exiled Dominicans, Bosch founded the Dominican Revolutionary party (PRD), a leftist socialist party which became the major opposition party to the Trujillo regime. When Trujillo was assassinated in May 1961, Bosch and other leaders of the PRD returned to the Dominican Republic to organize the party on their own soil and to field candidates in the 1962 elections. Bosch, a striking man with blue eyes and white hair, quickly gained wide popular support in the presidential race through a series of television and radio appearances. Although denounced as a Marxist-Leninist and almost forced from the race, Bosch was overwhelmingly elected president on 20 December 1962. His was the first democratic government in the Dominican Republic in more than thirty years, but after only seven months the army overthrew him, largely the result of his political incom-

Juan Bosch Gavino

petence and alleged communist sympathies. Bosch was forced into exile again, this time in Puerto Rico.

The U.S. Invasion

In April 1965 his followers tried to bring him back to the Dominican Republic by staging a coup. The ensuing unrest pitted the army and other right-wing elements against a faction of the military and the civilian center and leftist groups headed by Bosch. President Lyndon B. Johnson sent large U.S. military forces to end the civil war and restore stability to the country. Bosch vehemently opposed the intervention.

President Johnson initially justified the intervention on the grounds that U.S. citizens needed protection, although he later indicated that his decision had been influenced by Fidel Castro's communist Cuba; Johnson was determined to prevent another communist state in the Western Hemisphere. The Dominican intervention highlighted the conflict facing U.S. presidents when Latin American civil wars and revolutions set rebel forces against forces defending the established order.

Dominican Liberation Party

Within a year the two factions had reached a settlement and all American troops were withdrawn. In the presidential elections called in 1966, Bosch was defeated by Joaquín Balaguer. Bosch continued to lead the PRD, but his advocacy of the concept of a dictatorship supported by the people cost him many of his backers. He later formed the Dominican Liberation party (PLD). He was a candidate for president on the PLD ticket in the 1982, 1986, and 1990 elections but did not win.

General References

James Ferguson, *The Dominican Republic: Beyond the Lighthouse* (New York: Monthly Review Press, 1992);

Howard J. Wiarda, *The Aftermath of the Trujillo Dictatorship: The Emergence of a Pluralist Political System in the Dominican Republic* (Gainesville: University of Florida Press, 1965).

—J. R.-S.

SEE ALSO THESE RELATED ENTRIES
Lyndon B. Johnson, 1; Rafael Leónidas Trujillo Molina, 2.

Houari Boumédienne

President of Algeria, 1965–1978
Born Clauzel, Algeria, 23 August 1927
Died Algiers, Algeria, 27 December 1978

Houari Boumédienne was an Algerian military officer, statesman, and Algerian president from 1965 to 1978.

Named Mohamed Ben Brahim Boukharouba at birth, Boumédienne was born into a poor farming family in the small village of Clauzel in eastern Algeria. While not much is known about his early life, he was sent to French and Koranic primary schools and in 1940 began secondary school at a conservative Muslim school near the city of Constantine. After he completed his Islamic secondary education, Boumédienne fled Algeria in 1952 in order to avoid being drafted into the French army and went to Tunisia and Egypt, where he continued his studies at Al-Azhar. He met Algerian nationalist leader Ahmed Ben Bella in Cairo and decided to abandon university studies for revolutionary politics, joining the Algerian National Liberation Front (FLN). When the Algerian revolutionary war began in November 1954, Boumédienne received military training in Egypt provided by President Gamal Abdul Nasser. Adopting the nom de guerre of Houari Boumédienne, he spent the large part of his revolutionary military career with the external Algerian nationalist army based in Morocco. Boumédienne rose quickly through the ranks of the nationalist army to become head of the General Staff West, commanding three military districts.

The GPRA

When the Provisional Government of the Republic of Algeria (GPRA) was formed in exile in Cairo in September 1958, Boumédienne, a protégé of Ben Bella, was appointed to the National Council of the Algerian Revolution. In 1960 he became head of the FLN General Staff headquartered in Tunisia, but remained detached from infighting and factionalism between the FLN and the GPRA (which sought to establish its control over the external army). Boumédienne rose out of political obscurity within the divided nationalist movement during 1961 when he resisted attempts by the provisional president of the GPRA, Ben Youssef Ben Khedda, to disband the General Staff and bring the military under the control of the provisional government.

The 1962 Elections

The March 1962 French–Algerian Evian accords that established a transitional period to independence did not resolve long-standing personal and ideological differences within the nationalist leadership or the rift between the political and military wings of the Algerian nationalist movement. With Algeria on the verge of a civil war during the first half of 1962, Boumédienne aligned himself with Ben Bella, who set up a rival provisional government to the GPRA. Having marshaled army support behind Ben Bella, Boumédienne's forces had established control over most of the country by September. After the national elections of 22 September 1962 Ben Bella became prime minister and named Boumédienne as minister of national defense. Even though he held a powerful position within the revolutionary government, he remained in the background initially, concentrating on organizing an efficient and autonomous military.

Relations between the reserved, disciplined, and puritanical Boumédienne and the flamboyant Ben Bella were strained as a result of both ideological differences and Ben Bella's moves to undermine the military as an independent force. After the 1963 elections Boumédienne – the only holdover from the first cabinet – was named first deputy premier in the Ben Bella government, but insisted on retaining the post of minister of defense and army commander. In contrast to Ben Bella's dictatorial tendencies, Boumédienne favored collegial rule and an autonomous military. He also became concerned over the former's alliances with labor unions and Algerian communists. Relations between the two men deteriorated following Ben Bella's attempts to create a people's militia which could counterweight the national army. Boumedienne's emphasis on Arab-Islamic themes as part of the Algerian political culture were anathema to Ben Bella and his eclectic brand of scientific socialism. Finally, after several attempts to undermine him and remove his supporters in the government, Boumédienne preempted further moves to oust him by staging a bloodless coup d'état on 19 June 1965. He justified his actions as a corrective coup and not a rejection of the socialism upon which Algeria had embarked.

Head of State

Having suspended the national assembly and replaced it with the military Council of the Revolution, Bou-

Houari Boumédienne (smoking cigarette), with two aides

medienne – who assumed the offices of the president, head of the party, and minister of defense – concentrated on consolidating his power over the next few years. Boumédienne's international stature grew after the Arab defeat in the 1967 war with Israel. A militant anti-Zionist, many looked to him as the successor to Nasser, the Egyptian revolutionary leader, as leader of the Arab world. Boumédienne continued the socialist economic programs of the previous government, including nationalizing the oil industry in February 1971, agrarian reforms, and ambitious plans for rapid industrialization and modernization. Under Boumédienne, Algeria took control of its national economy and natural resources. He placed much emphasis on improving the living standards of the people, especially the peasantry.

Foreign Policy

Boumédienne had an activist foreign policy, playing a leading role in the Non-Aligned Movement, a loose grouping of Third World states that espouse a neutral foreign policy; the Arab League; and the Organization of African Unity. He became chairman of the Non-Aligned Movement in 1973 and successfully persuaded member countries to sever relations with Israel following the October 1973 Arab-Israeli War. Boumédienne urged Third

World countries to wrest control of their natural resources from foreigners. Soviet-Algerian relations expanded under Boumédienne, although he sought to avoid a dependent client relationship with the Soviet Union. For example, he refused to allow the Soviet Union to use the naval base at Mers al-Kabir or the use of other formerly French military facilities. Algeria was also a leading active supporter of liberation movements in the Third World, especially in Africa. Since 1975 Algeria has been the principal backer of the POLISARIO guerrilla movement in the Western Sahara. As a consequence relations with Morocco, which claims sovereignty over the disputed territory, and many other Arab states were strained. Boumédienne died on 27 December 1978 of a rare blood disease and was succeeded by Chadli Bendjedid.

General References

John Entelis, *Algeria: The Revolution Institutionalized* (Boulder, Colo.: Westview Press, 1986);

Arslan Humbarati, *Algeria: The Revolution That Failed* (New York: Praeger, 1966);

David Ottaway and Marina Ottaway, *Algeria: The Politics of a Socialist Revolution* (Berkeley: University of California Press, 1970);

William Quandt, *Revolution and Political Leadership: Algeria 1954–1968* (Cambridge, Mass.: MIT Press, 1969).

–J. R.-S.

┌──┐
│ SEE ALSO THESE RELATED ENTRIES   │
│ Ahmed Ben Bella, 2; The Non-Aligned Move- │
│ ment, 3.   │
└──┘

Habib Ben Ali Bourguiba

President of Tunisia, 1956–1987
Born Monastir, Tunisia, 1903

Habib Bourguiba is a Tunisian nationalist leader and was the country's president from 1956 to 1987. A charismatic and popular leader, Bourguiba is considered the father of Tunisian independence and responsible for turning Tunisia into the most modernized and Westernized of the Arab countries.

While his exact date of birth is unclear, Bourguiba was born into a modest family in Monastir. He received his secondary education at the prestigious Sadiki school in Tunis, the capital of the French protectorate. After he graduated from the Lycée Carnot in 1924, he received a scholarship to study law at the University of Paris, returning to Tunisia in 1927. Upon his return Bourguiba joined the Destour (Constitutionalist) party, the moderate nationalist party, and plunged himself into the nationalist-movement politics. However, he became dissatisfied with the conservative leadership of the party and in early 1932 founded the *Tunisian Action*, a nationalist newspaper that expressed the radical, proindependence views of the younger, French-educated members of the party. His political journalism brought him national prominence as a result of his controversial views and advocacy of independence. Ideological differences with party leadership finally led to his expulsion together with his followers.

The Neo-Destour Party

In March 1934, a year after the Destour party was banned, Bourguiba formed the Neo-Destour party as a younger, more radical nationalist organization. He and the rest of the party's leadership were arrested in September 1934 and internally exiled for their political activities, but were released in 1936. Bourguiba was arrested again in 1938 following Neo-Destour-led violent demonstrations and sent to prison in France. He was freed in November 1942 by the German forces entering France, but he declined to cooperate with the Axis. In April 1943 he was permitted to return to Tunisia where he urged his followers to cooperate with the approaching

Gale International Portrait Gallery

Habib Ben Ali Bourguiba

Allied forces. In 1945 Bourguiba traveled throughout the Middle East and the United States and to the United Nations on an international diplomatic mission to win support for Tunisian independence.

Working for Independence

Recognized as the most popular and prominent nationalist leader in Tunisia, Bourguiba returned in 1950, amid a mild rift in the Neo-Destour party, and began a grass-roots campaign to solidify his popular backing. After failed negotiations with the French, he left Tunisia in 1951 on a trip to Asia, Europe, and the United States to push for Tunisian independence. Upon his return he organized mass protests that led to his arrest and imprisonment in early 1952. Unable to resolve the Tunisian crisis, French officials released him in the spring of 1954 to conduct negotiations leading to internal autonomy. After the April 1955 agreements were reached, Bourguiba returned to Tunisia on 1 June to a hero's welcome, and he continued to press for full independence, which was finally granted on 3 March 1956.

President
Bourguiba's Neo-Destour party easily won the 1956 elections for a constituent assembly, which elected him as the first prime minister. His first official act was to introduce the Code of Personal Status, which abolished polygamy and enfranchised women. After Tunisia became a republic in 1957, the widely popular Bourguiba was elected president with extensive powers. Bourguiba used his national prestige and popularity to implement far-reaching social and economic reforms with the aim of modernizing Tunisia. In addition to policies that sought to break the influence of traditional Islamic values and practices, he launched policies for a free-market economy with liberal investment codes to attract foreign investors. While he maintained a close relationship with France, Bourguiba pursued a nonaligned, neutralist foreign policy even though most postcolonial states became entangled in the superpower ideological and political competition.

Foreign Policies
Bourguiba's foreign policies, like his domestic policies, were characterized by moderation accompanied by sudden and always consistent initiatives. A moderate on the Arab-Israeli conflict, he was the first Arab head of state to call for a recognition of the state of Israel and a peace agreement with it. He toured Middle Eastern countries in 1970 to win support for his idea but failed. In 1982, after the Israeli invasion of Lebanon, he allowed the Palestine Liberation Organization (PLO), the Palestinian nationalist organization, to use Tunisia as its new base. In 1986 the Israeli air force attacked PLO facilities in Tunisia.

With no challenges to his power, Bourguiba was continuously reelected until 1974, when the National Assembly confirmed him president for life. Bourguiba erected a centralized political system that functioned around his own personal power. Poor economic performances and a rigid political system led to the "Black Thursday" violent demonstrations in 1978. Again in 1984 Bourguiba faced violent demonstrations and riots over price rises in basic commodities. Throughout, Bourguiba skillfully manipulated his cabinet to deflect direct blame for the deteriorating conditions and unpopular policies, while cracking down on political opponents. On 7 November 1987 Bourguiba was finally removed from office because of deteriorating health and mounting questions regarding his mental condition. He was replaced by Zine el-Abidine Ben Ali.

Book about Bourguiba
Norma Salem, *Habib Bourguiba, Islam, and the Creation of Tunisia* (London: Croom Helm, 1984).

General References
Charles Micaud, *Tunisia: The Politics of Modernization* (New York: Praeger, 1964);

Kenneth J. Perkins, *Tunisia: Crossroads of the Islamic and European Worlds* (Boulder, Colo.: Westview Press, 1986).

–J. R.-S.

SEE ALSO THESE RELATED ENTRIES

Yassir Arafat, 2.

Leonid Brezhnev

General Secretary, Soviet Communist Party, 1964-1982
Born Kamensk, Ukraine, 19 December 1906
Died Moscow, Soviet Union, 10 November 1982

Leonid Ilyich Brezhnev led the Soviet Communist party between 1964 and 1982. His policies as general secretary were marked by striking dualities: détente – the pursuit of relaxed tensions with the West – served as the centerpiece of his foreign policy, yet Brezhnev began a massive military buildup that eventually forced the United States again to look at the ascending Soviet Union as a rival superpower. In the 1970s Brezhnev's foreign policy became increasingly adventurous, as the Soviet Union flexed its newly developed muscle in Africa and the Middle East and sought to translate its nuclear-weapons parity with the United States into worldwide political equality. But this adventurism abroad was matched by a domestic conservatism that produced a repressive sense of stagnation in Soviet life, most apparent in the miserable performance of the economy.

Brezhnev was born in the village of Kamensk in the eastern Ukraine. The village – since renamed Dneprodzerzhinsk – lies on the Dnieper River in a region rich in iron ore. The ore deposits were mined and shipped east to be processed in Dnepropetrovsk.

Little is known of Brezhnev's childhood or adolescence, except that his father, a Russian, was a worker in the nearby steel mill and that at the age of fifteen he too went to work in the mill. At the age of seventeen he joined the Komsomol (Communist Youth League). He received his secondary education at a land-surveying technical school in Kursk. Following graduation in 1927, he moved to the Ural, where he briefly worked as a surveyor. Afterward he held several administrative posts during the first years of General Secretary Joseph Stalin's drive to collectivize the Soviet peasantry.

In 1930 he attended the Moscow Agricultural Academy, but left the same year. The year 1931 seemed to mark a transition in his life: he joined the Communist party; he married Viktoria Petrovna, a nurse; and he switched the focus of his studies to metallurgy. In 1935 he entered the Red Army and most probably worked as a political officer.

Early Career in the Soviet Communist Party

Quitting the military in 1937, Brezhnev returned to the Ukraine, where he was elected deputy mayor of Dneprodzerzhinsk in May. About this time he first met Nikita S. Khrushchev, who had been sent by Stalin, along

Leonid Brezhnev

with Vyacheslav M. Molotov, the future foreign minister, to purge the top Ukrainian party leadership. It is difficult to assess the extent of Brezhnev's role in the purges, but that he survived the Great Terror of 1936–1938, when Stalin had millions of party members and Soviet citizens executed and imprisoned, is testament to some combination of skill and chance. The German invasion on 22 June 1941 interrupted Brezhnev's career in the party, but he had achieved a position far advanced for his relatively young age and limited experience.

World War II

During World War II Brezhnev was a political officer in the Red Army, attaining the rank of major general in charge of propaganda and party affairs. He served for a while directly under Khrushchev, who by then was most likely his mentor.

44

After the war Khrushchev secured Brezhnev a position with the Zaporozh'ye oblast party committee at a time of near famine in the Ukraine. Brezhnev's performance in dealing with the crisis contributed to his promotion to first secretary of the Dnepropetrovsk oblast party committee in November 1947.

The Central Committee

In 1950 he followed Khrushchev to Moscow, where for a while he worked in the Central Committee, the administrative body of the Communist party of the Soviet Union (CPSU). In July 1950 he was appointed first secretary of the Moldavian Communist party. His activities were taken up with collectivizing agriculture and Russifying the ethnic nationalities of this formerly Romanian territory.

Brezhnev was elected to the Central Committee in 1952 and attained candidate membership in the Presidium, the Central Committee's executive body and the center of power in the Soviet Union. With Stalin's death in March 1953, however, Brezhnev lost both positions and was demoted to a job in the ministry of defense, looking after political affairs in the navy.

By early 1954 Khrushchev had become first secretary of the CPSU – in fact if not name – making him the leader of the Soviet Union. In February he unveiled a scheme to cultivate ninety million acres of virgin land in western Siberia and Kazakhstan. The success of this program would require the active cooperation of the Kazakhstan party leadership. To this end, he sent Brezhnev to the republic to purge the followers of the party's previous first secretary, who had opposed Khrushchev's plan. Brezhnev was apparently successful: in August 1954 he was promoted to first secretary.

The first harvests from the area were part of a record thirty-three-million-ton harvest in 1956, and Brezhnev, now with a reputation as an outstanding administrator, was rewarded by regaining the party positions he had lost in 1953.

On 4 July 1957, in a shake-up at the Kremlin, Khrushchev replaced five members of the Presidium with nine new faces, most of whom were his protégés. Brezhnev was among this group of new members. He remained a secretary in the Central Committee for three years, at a time when Khrushchev's foreign and domestic policies saw their greatest successes.

Chairman of the Presidium

In July 1960 Brezhnev, for reasons still unclear, was appointed chairman of the Presidium of the Supreme Soviet, making him the Soviet head of state. This was, at first glance, a demotion: he traded a position with administrative power in the Central Committee for one which was largely ceremonial. But the new position did give him

his first extensive exposure to international affairs. He traveled frequently, representing the Soviet Union in Africa, India, and Czechoslovakia in 1961.

Khrushchev's Ouster

In June 1963 Brezhnev reassumed his old post in the Secretariat, apparently having been chosen to succeed Khrushchev as first secretary. Khrushchev, as a precaution, simultaneously named another member of his circle, Nikolay Podgorny, to the Secretariat to prevent any hasty move by Brezhnev. But in a palace coup on 14 October 1964, Khrushchev was ousted as first secretary of the CPSU and replaced by Brezhnez, his protégé. Alexei Kosygin became chairman of the Council of Ministers and Anastas Mikoyan, head of state. In December 1966 Mikoyan was replaced by Podgorny, who had been unable or unwilling to prevent Khrushchev's overthrow.

Khrushchev's ouster was largely the result of his anti-Stalinist campaign and his attempts at administrative reforms. The reforms, by no means extensive, and his growing disdain for the party apparatus threatened Soviet bureaucrats, many of whom had come to power under Stalin.

General Secretary

Brezhnev was elected in order to bring a measure of stability to the Soviet system. His eighteen-year rule was marked by a corporate and faceless style that contrasted with his predecessor's brash unpredictability. It has been said that after Stalin's terror Khrushchev gave Soviet officials personal security and Brezhnev gave them job security. He put a premium on compromise and consensus, so that no single group or individual dominated. He was, indeed, the "true representative of a bureaucracy that had grown tired of strong leaders."

This new collegial style of management obscured the actual extent of Brezhnev's role and influence in the Soviet leadership. During his first years in power, he apparently concentrated his efforts on party affairs and the world communist movement, while Kosygin came to be identified with economic planning and relations with the noncommunist world. But by 29 March 1966, when he adopted Stalin's old title of general secretary at the 23rd Party Congress, Brezhnev had emerged as *primus inter pares* within the ruling triumvirate. Even so, he spent more than a decade consolidating his power: it was only with the forced retirement of Podgorny in May 1977 that Brezhnev had finally eliminated his last rival.

Domestic Policy

The Soviet Union remained a highly repressive police state under Brezhnev. Although he avoided the worst excesses of Stalin's mass terror – the arbitrary arrests, executions, and imprisonments – nonconformity and dissidence continued to be punished. The infamous KGB, the all-pervasive secret police – its organization merely purged, never dismantled – regained much of the status and power that it had lost in Khrushchev's zealous attack on Stalinism.

The use of repression was Brezhnev's most direct way of maintaining control over the Soviet population in the absence of terror. Another less apparent means was through an increase in the average Soviet citizen's standard of living. Consumer durables, such as television sets and household appliances, finally began to appear in the homes of the middle and working classes. Although these products were not luxuries in the Western sense, having them meant much to the average Soviet citizen and reassured him that his lot in life had dramatically improved.

In September 1965 the Brezhnev-Kosygin team instituted a series of economic reforms in an effort to reverse Khrushchev's "hare brained" schemes and to devote more resources to the production of consumer goods.

Military Buildup

Simultaneously, Brezhnev unveiled an ambitious plan to build up the Soviet military in an effort to attain strategic equality with – if not superiority to – the United States. Beginning in 1965 spending for the military grew by an average of about 4 percent a year – a trend that continued throughout the rest of Brezhnev's rule. The buildup of strategic nuclear forces, started in 1960 under Khrushchev, took on even greater urgency following the Soviet humiliation during the 1962 Cuban missile crisis. The Strategic Rocket Forces (SRF) tripled its number of intercontinental ballistic missiles (ICBMs), and the navy greatly expanded its inventory of submarine launched ballistic missiles (SLBMS), so that by the end of the 1960s the Soviet Union possessed more of both weapons than the United States. It was Brezhnev's greatest achievement to ensure Soviet nuclear parity with the United States by 1970.

The military buildup was broad as well as deep. The evolving Soviet doctrine called for the ability to fight not just a general nuclear war but local wars as well. To this end, Brezhnev strengthened conventional capabilities, particularly the ability to deploy forces overseas. The development of long-range air transport and the construction of a blue-water navy ensured that client states could receive direct and rapid Soviet military assistance.

Foreign Policy

An abiding Soviet foreign policy goal since the mid 1950s was relaxed tensions with the United States. This desire for improved relations – called "peaceful co-existence" in the 1950s and "détente" under Brezhnev – derived from various motives, one being formal Western recognition of the postwar political and territorial status quo. A second was economic: The reforms undertaken in 1965 had not been drastic enough to achieve the desired increases in productivity and technological development. In March 1971, at the 24th Congress of the CPSU, Kosygin announced that the Soviet Union would seek better relations with the United States in order to gain access to advanced technology and cooperative economic projects.

The Sino-Soviet rift that Brezhnev inherited, combined with China's determination to upgrade its nuclear forces and the periodic skirmishes on the Soviet Union's eastern border, convinced him that an accommodation with the West was necessary to keep China in check. A constant fear of the Soviet leadership was that the United States would play its "China card" and join with the Chinese at Moscow's expense. Furthermore, the Soviets had suspected for some time that the Chinese wanted to provoke a war between the United States and the USSR.

In seeking détente, Brezhnev was not renouncing competition with the West. Rather he hoped to implement a political strategy whereby the Soviet Union would lessen the risk of nuclear war with the United States and maneuver around the Chinese, while it would simultaneously gain the technological and economic assistance that could be used to improve its industrial base. Competition with the West would continue, but in the 1970s it would increasingly take place in the Third World.

Improving relations with the West did not proceed smoothly during the 1960s, largely because of Soviet policies in the Middle East and Czechoslovakia. The Soviets fueled tensions between Israel and Egypt in 1967, tensions which led to the June war between the Israelis on one side and the Egyptians, Syrians, and Jordanians on the other. Following Israel's victory, Moscow rearmed the Egyptians and the Syrians, much to the consternation of the United States.

Soviet Invasion of Czechoslovakia

In 1968 political events in Czechoslovakia seemed to require a Soviet response. In January, Alexander Dubcek replaced Antonín Novotny as first secretary of the Czechoslovak Communist party. A wave of expectation overtook the country with the promise of sweeping political and cultural reforms – the so-called Prague Spring. On the night of 20 August, however, Soviet and other Warsaw Pact forces invaded to reassert Soviet control.

On 12 November 1968 Brezhnev offered his clearest explanation for the Soviet invasion of Czechoslovakia. Speaking in Poland, he warned that "when internal and external forces, hostile to socialism, seek to reverse the development of any socialist country whatsoever in the direction of the restoration of the capitalist order, [this becomes] the concern of all socialist countries." This proclamation soon became known in the West as the

Brezhnev Doctrine – the Soviet Union's unambiguous threat to use force to maintain control over its satellites.

That it took so long for the military to enter Czechoslovakia was a reflection of the indecision operating at the highest levels of the Kremlin. What must have finally convinced the Soviets to quash the incipient rebellion was fear that their other satellites might follow suit. Piotr Shelest, at that time first secretary of the Ukrainian Communist party and always a thorn in Brezhnev's side, feared that the Ukraine would be swift to follow the Czech example, and he led the hard-line group that urged intervention.

SALT

The Soviet invasion of Czechoslovakia temporarily delayed the beginning of talks between the United States and the Soviet Union on controlling nuclear weapons. President Lyndon B. Johnson had proposed talks in January 1967, but it was not until 17 November 1969 that the Strategic Arms Limitation Talks (SALT) began in Helsinki.

Soviet support for Hanoi during the Vietnam War presented a dilemma to SALT's successful conclusion. American congressional and public opinion would not accept a treaty with North Vietnam's main supplier of military equipment. The Soviet Union, for its part, feared that a treaty with the "imperialist" United States might poison relations it was cultivating with the Third World nations and that China would be quick to exploit such an opportunity.

Brezhnev ultimately pressured the Vietnamese to facilitate an American withdrawal from Vietnam. In a televised address to the American people during his June 1973 visit to the United States he spoke of U.S.–Soviet cooperation in ending the war. The American decision to leave Vietnam, coupled with the announcement in August 1971 that Secretary of State Henry A. Kissinger had traveled secretly to Beijing to arrange a visit by President Richard M. Nixon for the following year, acted to ensure that the talks would continue.

The thrust of the SALT treaty that was signed on 26 May 1972 was a five-year freeze on an increase in numbers of U.S. and Soviet strategic launchers, as well as a virtual ban on antiballistic missile (ABM) systems. While hardly a model of disarmament, SALT was an admission that the U.S.-Soviet competition had its bounds.

The Final Act

The Soviet Union achieved one of its central postwar political goals: Western recognition of the territorial and political status quo in Europe, with the conclusion of the Conference on Security and Cooperation in Europe, which began on 22 November 1972 in Helsinki. The Final Act, signed on 1 August 1975, effectively ratified

the existing frontiers in Europe and recognized Soviet hegemony over Eastern Europe. What the Soviets traded in return was the inclusion in the act of several political principles on the free flow of ideas, people, and information. These were cited frequently by President Jimmy Carter in the 1970s when criticizing Soviet human rights violations.

The pursuit of improved relations with Western Europe was part of a Soviet strategy to detach Europe, and especially West Germany, from the United States in an effort to weaken the North Atlantic Treaty Organization (NATO). On 12 August 1970 the Federal Republic of Germany (FRG) and the Soviet Union signed a treaty in Moscow by which the FRG essentially accepted the postwar division of Germany and agreed to renounce the possession of nuclear weapons.

New Prestige

The successes of détente raised Brezhnev's stature within the Soviet leadership. By 1971–1972 he had come to be personally credited with the Soviet Union's new prestige. He was no longer seen as merely the Politburo's spokesman, but rather as the dominant figure in Soviet politics.

Brezhnev's private life, however, remained generally modest despite his political successes: he and his family continued to occupy a five-room apartment in Kutuzovski Prospekt, living directly below Yuri Andropov, Brezhnev's successor.

His most obvious vice, other than a strong addiction to tobacco and a fondness for attractive young women was a passion for fast luxury cars, and in this he indulged himself. He owned one of the few Rolls Royces in the Soviet Union, and foreign dignitaries would often add to his collection: a Lincoln Continental from President Nixon and a Mercedes coupe from West German chancellor Willy Brandt.

Soviet Third-World Policy

The 1970s witnessed growing Soviet adventurism in the Third World in pursuit of strategic and political leverage against the United States. Following Portugal's decision to end its colonial presence in Africa in 1974, the Soviet Union provided equipment to the Popular Movement for the Liberation of Angola (MPLA) in the ensuing civil war. This equipment, operated by Soviet advisers and some twenty thousand Cuban troops, was crucial to the MPLA victory. What inspired the Soviet action was Angola's strategic position near the sea route around the Cape of Good Hope.

In the Horn of Africa the Soviets courted Somalia with military and economic aid, which was followed by the signing of a friendship treaty in 1974. Somalia's location at the entrance to the Red Sea and the northwest coast of the Indian Ocean coincided neatly with the Soviet desire for leverage in the Middle East and a heightened naval presence in the Indian Ocean.

Events in Ethiopia, however, set the Soviets back. The Marxist regime that came to power in 1974 after the overthrow of Emperor Haile Selassie had appealed for Soviet military assistance. Brezhnev reluctantly yielded to the Ethiopian request, thinking he might turn it to his advantage and gain an even stronger foothold in the Horn. By 1977 Soviet advisers and Cuban troops were in Ethiopia along with advanced military equipment. Soviet designs were undermined, however, when Somalia invaded Ethiopia in July 1977 in order to seize the desert province of Ogaden. Somalia's president, Siad Barre, broke with the Soviets and expelled them from the country. In a major political realignment, the Soviets intervened to force the Somalians from Ethiopia. This was followed by a twenty-year friendship treaty between Ethiopia and the USSR, signed on 20 November 1978.

Deteriorating Relations with the United States

These efforts by Brezhnev to project Soviet power and influence abroad aggravated already deteriorating relations between the United States and the Soviet Union. Soviet support of Egypt and Syria during the fifth Arab-Israeli war, begun on 6 October 1973, had brought the United States and the USSR closer to armed conflict than at any time since the Cuban Missile Crisis. Brezhnev was on the brink of sending troops to the Middle East to prevent a total Egyptian and Syrian defeat. President Nixon, however, to keep the Soviet Union from directly intervening, put U.S. nuclear forces on the highest stage of readiness since the beginning of the Cold War.

In the late 1970s the Soviets chafed at President Carter's emphasis on human rights and his support of Soviet dissidents such as Andrei Sakharov, a physicist and the leader of the first civil rights organization in the Soviet Union, and Anatoly Shcharansky, a mathematical engineer, who after seeking to emigrate from the Soviet Union had been accused of spying for the United States.

Another area of contention between the United States and the Soviet Union was the Middle East. On 26 March 1979 a peace treaty between Egypt and Israel was signed, following an historic meeting between Anwar Sadat and Menachem Begin at the U.S. presidential retreat in Camp David, Maryland, in September 1978. Brezhnev, who had long coveted a more influential Soviet role in the Middle East, had been left out of the negotiations; yet he was certain, in any case, that they would fail. The exclusion of the Soviets brought them closer to the more radical factions of the Arab world, especially Syria and the Palestine Liberation Organization (PLO).

On 27 December 1979 the Soviet Union invaded Afghanistan to install its puppet, Babrak Karmal, in Kabul

and destroy the Afghan resistance fighters, the mujahedin. The invasion effectively ended the chances of U.S. congressional ratification of SALT II, much to Brezhnev's disappointment. The first SALT treaty had formally expired on 3 October 1977, although both parties had agreed to respect its provisions for the time being. Following two years of negotiation, SALT II was signed in Vienna by Brezhnev and Carter on 18 June 1979. On 2 January 1980 Carter requested the U.S. Senate to delay consideration of SALT II indefinitely.

In Poland increases in food prices in 1980 led to strikes which highlighted the impotence of the Polish Communist party. A new political force appeared: the independent trade union Solidarity, led by Lech Walesa. It soon seemed likely that Soviet troops would enter Poland to reassert communist control – reminiscent of Czechoslovakia in 1968 – but instead martial law was declared on 13 December 1981. The imposition of martial law led the U.S. government to cancel almost all its trade agreements with the Soviet Union by June 1982.

When Ronald W. Reagan entered the White House in January 1981, U.S.-Soviet relations were chilly, and prospects for any further arms control agreements looked bleak. Indeed, Reagan accelerated the buildup in conventional and nuclear forces that Carter had begun and was determined to press forward with the 1979 decision by NATO to deploy nuclear-armed Pershing II and cruise missiles in Europe.

Domestic Stagnation

Brezhnev continued to consolidate his power during 1977: in May he was made a marshal of the Soviet Union, in June he assumed the presidency following Podgorny's resignation, and in November he became commander in chief of the armed forces.

But he had been seriously ill since December 1974, when he suffered a heart attack. In an attempt to stop smoking, he had taken to keeping his cigarettes in a case set to release them at regular intervals. However, he admitted to having a "reserve pack in the other pocket." An American intelligence report from 1978 speculated that he was suffering from gout, leukemia, and emphysema. His vacations became longer, and his absences from public view more frequent.

The absence of a strong leader was noticeable: Mikhail Gorbachev, the future first secretary, commented on the "stagnation among the leadership" during the late 1970s when the Soviet Union "began to lose momentum."

The Soviet economy in particular lost momentum during Brezhnev's last years. Economic growth slowed from an estimated 3 percent a year in the early 1970s to less than 2 percent in the 1980s. Four disastrous agricultural harvests in a row between 1979 and 1982 forced the average citizen to endure even longer queues for basic necessities. The Eleventh Five-Year Plan, approved in May 1982, emphasized agriculture and light industry and deferred increases in military spending. Speaking to the Central Committee on 24 May 1982, Brezhnev warned that securing a steady supply of foodstuffs for the rest of the decade remained an "urgent socio-political task." Despite his awareness of the crisis, Brezhnev was unwilling and probably unable to undertake the basic structural reforms necessary to make the economy operate more efficiently.

The entire society seemed to suffer from a spiritual malaise during this time. The young, educated middle class resented the stability of tenure that Brezhnev had given his apparatchiks, a stability that when combined with repression of dissent and disregard for public opinion led to patronage, inefficiency, and corruption within the party. A mood of apathy and cynicism pervaded the factories, and productivity among the workers declined along with the country's standard of living. The cultural landscape remained a desert as prominent writers and artists were exiled or deported. Lesser known dissident intellectuals were shunted off to the labor camps or to psychiatric wards to undergo long-term "observation and treatment."

In 1982 Moscow was rife with rumors: Brezhnev would step down voluntarily by the end of the year, certainly the first such transition of power in the Soviet Union. There was also a scandal in February linking Brezhnev's daughter, Galina, with a flamboyant circus performer, Boris the Gypsy, who had been arrested for possession of a large number of diamonds.

Speaking to military officers and defense officials at the Kremlin in October, Brezhnev dwelt on two themes that had dominated his foreign policy. He saw a continuing need for efforts to lessen the "threat of nuclear war hanging over mankind" and called for a "constant strengthening of the country's defense." He promised the military that they would have everything they needed.

On 10 November 1982 Brezhnev died. His rule had been marked by a stability unprecedented in the sixty-year history of the Soviet Union. Gone were the days of Stalin's terror or Khrushchev's brash unpredictability. This stability, however, came at the price of economic and political stagnation – a stagnation that would in turn inspire the reforms of Yuri Andropov and Mikhail Gorbachev.

Book by Brezhnev (Selected)
Memoirs (Oxford: Pergamon Press, 1982).

Books about Brezhnev
George W. Breslauer, *Khrushchev and Brezhnev as Leaders: Building Authority in Soviet Politics* (London: Allen & Unwin, 1981);

Robin Edmonds, *Soviet Foreign Policy – The Brezhnev Years* (Oxford: Oxford University Press, 1983);

Harry Gelman, *The Brezhnev Politburo and the Decline of Détente* (Ithaca, N.Y.: Cornell University Press, 1984);

Donald Kelley, ed., *Soviet Politics in the Brezhnev Era* (New York: Praeger, 1980).

General Reference
Carl A. Linden, *Khrushchev and the Soviet leadership, 1957-1964* (Baltimore, Md.: Johns Hopkins University Press, 1966; updated, 1990).

– M. B.

SEE ALSO THESE RELATED ENTRIES

Brezhnev Doctrine, 3; Détente, 3; Alexander Dubcek, 2; Nikita S. Khruschev, 2; Richard M. Nixon, 1; Refuseniks, 3; Strategic Arms Limitation Talks, 3.

Nikolai Bulganin

Prime Minister, Soviet Union, 1955–1958
Born Nizhni Novgorod, Russia, 1895
Died Moscow, Soviet Union, 24 February 1975

Nikolai Aleksandrovich Bulganin, prime minister of the Soviet Union from 1955 to 1958, was born in the Volga river town of Nizhni Novgorod, renamed by the Soviets as Gorky. Little is known of his childhood, other than that he might have received his early education at a modern language school.

Early Career

He joined the Bolshevik faction, which later became the Communist party of the Soviet Union (CPSU), during the Russian Revolution of 1917. He soon entered the *Cheka*, the secret police agency, and worked with it until 1922 to root out and execute anti-Bolsheviks. The next five years Bulganin spent as an economic planner with the Supreme Economic Council.

Between 1927 and 1931 he directed Moscow's *Electrovazod*, the largest electrical equipment factory in the Soviet Union. Under his management the plant fulfilled its five-year quota in half the time, a showpiece in General Secretary Joseph Stalin's drive to industrialize the Soviet Union.

Mayor of Moscow

In 1931 Bulganin was named mayor of Moscow, a post he held for six years. He supervised efforts to transform Moscow into a modern capital city and model for the communist world, overseeing, for example, the initial construction of Moscow's subway system.

The CPSU's Central Committee, from which the ruling Politburo took its members, elected him a candidate-member in 1934. He continued his ascent during Stalin's purge of the party in the late 1930s, filling several positions as they emptied. In 1937 he became premier of the Russian Republic; the next year he took over the State Bank and became a deputy premier of the Soviet Union.

World War II

When the Soviet Union entered World War II in June 1941, Bulganin volunteered for frontline duty, the first high official to do so. His request to fight, of questionable sincerity, was denied, and in-

Nikolai Bulganin

stead he served as a political officer during the war, rising to the rank of general by November 1944. As a "political general," Bulganin was not highly appreciated by those officers from the army's more traditional combat branches.

Bulganin represented the Soviet Union at a meeting in July 1944 to organize the "Lublin Poles," pro-Soviet, anti-German leaders who later dominated Poland's postwar government and ensured Soviet control. They opposed the "London Poles," the pro-Western Polish government in exile, which had taken refuge in England during the war.

In 1947 Bulganin succeeded Stalin as defense minister. That same year he was appointed a Marshal of the Soviet Union, the country's highest military rank, as well as vice-president of the Council of Ministers, the executive and administrative organ of the Soviet government. By 1948 he had attained full membership in the Politburo.

Power Struggle

Stalin died on 5 March 1953, and Bulganin became a key player in the ensuing struggle for leadership. Nikita S. Khrushchev, Georgi Malenkov, the party first secretary, and Vyacheslav Molotov, the former foreign minister, pitted themselves against Lavrenti Beria, Stalin's chief of the secret police. Bulganin, putting his early training with the *Cheka* to good use, contrived to neutralize the military and ensnare Beria, who was later secretly executed. As a reward, Khrushchev nominated him in February 1955 to succeed Malenkov as prime minister in the ongoing power struggle. For the next three years Bulganin and Khrushchev ruled jointly, although Khrushchev clearly was the more politically powerful of the two.

Four-Power Conference

One of Bulganin's first official duties was to lead the Soviet delegation to the Four-Power Conference in Geneva, Switzerland, in July 1955, where U.S. president Dwight D. Eisenhower presented his "Open Skies" proposal, which would permit the United States and the Soviet Union to conduct aerial photography over each other's territory. The Soviets rejected this idea, but Bulganin and Eisenhower drank martinis together, and Bulganin toasted the "martini road to peace and friendship."

Khrushchev and Bulganin

At the Twentieth Party Congress, held in February 1956, Khrushchev announced the new Soviet desire for "peaceful coexistence" with the West and better relations with the recently decolonized, nonaligned countries of the Third World. In pursuit of these policies, Bulganin and Khrushchev — "B and K" to the Western press — carried out a series of foreign visits between 1955 and 1957, the first Soviet leaders to travel abroad since Stalin had met with U.S. president Harry S Truman and British prime minister Winston Churchill at Potsdam in July 1945. The two — ebullient, ruddy Khrushchev and charming, well-dressed Bulganin — in marked contrast to the intransigent hostility of the Stalin era, heralded a new Soviet desire for friendship and peace and signaled a willingness to discuss world affairs in an open, cordial fashion.

Foreign Affairs

In 1955 they visited Yugoslavia, China, Burma, Afghanistan and India; in 1956, England; and in 1957, Finland. The trip to Belgrade in May resulted in a tenuous reconciliation with President Josip Broz Tito, who, by leading Yugoslavia on an independent path to socialism after World War II, had rejected Soviet hegemony.

The December 1955 trip to India came after the Soviet Union had agreed to finance and construct a huge steel plant in central India. The Soviet Union courted India, the most important power in Southern Asia, to offset American influence in the region and to make India a showcase for Soviet economic assistance.

Relations with the West

These trips coincided with the removal of Soviet occupation troops from Austria and the recognition of West Germany in 1955, and the return of a naval base to Finland in 1956 — each a gesture by the Soviet Union designed to improve their relations with the West.

In October 1956 Bulganin wrote to President Eisenhower proposing an agreement to end all nuclear testing. This proposal became an issue in the 1956 American election campaign, with Eisenhower publicly insulted at the tone of the letter and some Democrats interested in examining the Soviet offer.

On 5 November 1956, during the Suez Crisis, Bulganin, in another message to Eisenhower, proposed a joint U.S.-Soviet force to intervene in Egypt following the invasion by France, Great Britain, and Israel. Eisenhower dismissed the proposal as "unthinkable."

Soviet Crackdown

Bulganin also represented the darker side of Soviet diplomacy during this period. In 1956, following civil unrest in the city of Poznan, he went to Poland twice to demand that the press be silenced and that Wladyslaw Gomulka, the newly elected head of the Polish party, maintain control over the incipient popular rebellion.

In October 1956 Soviet troops invaded Hungary to remove Imre Nagy from the head of the new multiparty government that was supported by students, intellectuals, and the military.

Domestic Affairs

Continuing to show an interest in economic planning, Bulganin was active in domestic affairs during the fifties. In a report to the Central Committee, reprinted on 14 July 1955 in *Pravda*, the party newspaper, he called for the elimination of waste and inefficiency and urged that Soviet managers copy Western industrial techniques.

By 1957 dissatisfaction with Khrushchev was growing in the Soviet leadership. It was felt that his "de-Stalinization" speech to the Twentieth Party Congress in February 1956, which criticized many of the former leader's policies, had encouraged the Polish and Hungarian revolts that year. Furthermore, Khrushchev's economic reforms of 1957, by trying to decentralize decision making, threatened the control of party bureaucrats.

In June 1957, when Khrushchev was away in Finland, the Presidium, the Central Committee's executive body, voted 7–4 to remove him as general secretary. Bulganin voted with the conspirators. Khrushchev returned to Moscow, however, to announce that he would not resign unless the entire Central Committee voted to ratify the Presidium's decision. The resulting vote went unanimously in his favor, and Khrushchev remained in power.

Bulganin, having been implicated as a member of the "Anti-Party Group," was forced to resign as prime minister on 27 March 1958. On 5 September he was forced from the Presidium. His last official position was chairman of the Stavropol Economic Council in the northern Caucasus. He retired to a small cottage outside Moscow in February 1960, where he lived until his death on 24 February 1975. The government announcement was a one-line statement: "The Council of Ministers announces with regret the death of Pensioner Bulganin."

General References

Nikita S. Khrushchev, *Khrushchev Remembers,* edited by Strobe Talbott (Boston: Little, Brown, 1970);

Carl A. Linden, *Khrushchev and the Soviet leadership, 1957–1964* (Baltimore, Md.: Johns Hopkins University Press, 1966);

Myron Rush, *Political Succession in the USSR* (New York: Columbia University Press, 1965);

Michel Tatu, *Power in the Kremlin, from Khrushchev to Kosygin* (New York: Viking, 1969).

–M. B.

SEE ALSO THESE ENTRIES
Nikita S. Khrushchev, 2; Suez Crisis, 3.

Amílcar Lopes Cabral

Founder, Partido Africano da Independência da Guiné e Cabo Verde
Born Bafatá, Portuguese Guinea, 12 September 1924
Died Conakry, Portuguese Guinea, 20 January 1973

An African revolutionary leader and political thinker, Amílcar Lopes Cabral was the founder and leader of the Partido Africano da Independência da Guiné e Cabo Verde (African Party for the Liberation of Guinea and Cape Verde [PAIGC]), one of the most successful African liberation movements during the decolonization period. Cabral's theories on political mobilization and guerrilla military organization became respected internationally.

Cabral grew up with his father on the islands of Cape Verde, located off the coast of Senegal and which at that time was attached administratively to Guinea. Cabral's father, Juvenal, a Cape Verdean poet and teacher, was a major influence on Cabral's political thinking. Juvenal Cabral, who traveled and worked in many parts of the mainland colony, often discussed with his son the socio-economic and political conditions in the colony. After completing his primary and secondary education in Cape Verde at the prestigious Liceu Gil Eanes during a time of increasing cultural and political ferment, Cabral was awarded a scholarship in 1945 to study agronomy at the Instituto Superior da Agronomia in Lisbon, Portugal.

During his university years Cabral became politically active, devoting most of his time to student political and cultural organizations. He came into association with other African students from Portuguese colonies studying in Lisbon. Yet, unlike Agostinho Neto, the future Angolan independence leader, or other students, Cabral did not join any political party. Neither did he have problems with the Portuguese authorities. A popular and intelligent student, he organized various cultural and literary activities with the other African students and was influenced by the literature of black consciousness and liberation, which affirmed the authenticity and heritage of black and African culture. He came to believe that the success of colonialism rested on its domination of local culture and that therefore culture was the key to liberation. This view of liberation was grounded in the rejection of colonial culture and reassertion of African culture.

The PAIGC

After graduating with honors in 1952, Cabral chose to work at an agronomy research center in Guinea, where

Amílcar Lopes Cabral

he compiled a comprehensive agricultural survey of the country. He founded the PAIGC in 1956 with Aristides Pereira, Abilio Duarte, and brother Luis Cabral, all future leaders of the party. The name of the party reflected Cabral's agreement with Ghanaian nationalist and revolutionary leader Kwame Nkrumah on the need for continental political unification, even though Cabral's own Pan-Africanism revolved around a parochial preoccupation with unification of Cape Verde and Guinea. The party's original strategy focused on clandestine political activities among urban trade unions, students, and intellectuals in Guinea, where the PAIGC carried out nearly all of its activities. The barren landscape, geographical fragmentation, and small population of Cape Verde precluded political mobilization.

Mobilization of the Countryside

After the violent 1959 dock riots in Guinea, in which the PAIGC was implicated, the party leadership decided to shift to a strategy of political mobilization in the countryside and guerrilla struggle. By 1964, with material support from president Sekou Toure in neighboring Guinea-Conakry, where the party was headquartered, the PAIGC had liberated the southern half of the country. An administrative apparatus was set up in liberated areas, providing social services such as education and health care. While fighters were sent abroad to Guinea-Conakry, China, Morocco, and Algeria for military training, Cabral took personal charge of political training of the thinly experienced and educated cadre. Cabral's approach to mobilizing the peasantry was nondoctrinaire and pragmatic. His earlier work as a researcher took him all over the country, giving him an intimate knowledge of the peasantry and socioeconomic conditions in the countryside. He understood how to communicate with the villagers and their chiefs.

Efforts to Isolate Portugal

Cabral had concluded that national liberation was a political, not military, struggle. Beginning with a speech to the United Nations on 12 December 1962, Cabral set out not only to win support for the PAIGC but also to isolate Portugal internationally. Although other Third World liberation movements had been drawn into the widening vortex of the Cold War between the superpowers, the PAIGC not only avoided entanglement in East-West politics but skillfully exploited the international media to turn its remote struggle into an international campaign against Portuguese colonialism. Cabral believed that the national liberation struggle in the colonies would hasten the end of Fascist dictatorship in Portugal, and he continuously appealed to the Portuguese public on the basis of this common interest. Grounded in his Pan-Africanist thinking, Cabral argued that the liberation struggle had to be continentwide in order to weaken the colonial power on all fronts. He cofounded the Popular Movement for the Liberation of Angola (MPLA) with Agostinho Neto in 1956 and was the leading organizer of the Conference of the Nationalist Movements of the Portuguese Colonies (CONCP), an umbrella organization of the liberation movements in the Portuguese colonies founded in 1961 in Rabat, Morocco. Cabral urged African liberation movements to steer clear of ideological and political entanglement with outside powers, and he advocated nonalignment in their relations with other countries.

Under Cabral's leadership and organizational skills, the PAIGC, which received support from Western countries such as Canada and Sweden, became an effective, disciplined, and well-organized party. While Cabral's leadership was never challenged or questioned, the party was characterized by a collegial leadership style. The party's military conduct reflected Cabral's adherence to his moral and humane principles: captured Portuguese soldiers were immediately turned over to the International Red Cross. The party's psychological campaign against the Portuguese armed forces was as successful as their military campaigns. It was no accident that the officers who led the 24 April 1974 military coup d'état that overthrew the civilian Fascist regime in Portugal were the same officers who were influenced and persuaded by Cabral's writings while serving in Guinea. These officers, including the coup leader General Antonio de Spinola, who had served in Guinea, pushed for the independence of Guinea and Cape Verde, which came the following year.

By the early 1970s internal friction surfaced within the party between two factions split along Guinean–Cape Verdean lines. The Guinean faction favored continued adherence to the original strategy of guerrilla struggle and political mobilization among the peasantry. The Cape Verdean faction favored escalating the war to secure a quick victory. These factional disagreements, however, were less over strategy than over Guinean concerns that a quick victory would mean a postcolonial state and party dominated by Cape Verdeans. It was within this context that Cabral was assassinated on 20 January 1973 by members of the Portuguese secret service, who had infiltrated the party. While the assassination did not spawn violence, the intraparty strains were never resolved. Cabral's hope of union between Guinea and Cape Verde, which had joined in a loose political federation under the PAIGC, disappeared with the 14 November 1980 military coup in Guinea that overthrew Luis Cabral.

Cabral, the party leader and teacher, made significant contributions to revolutionary thinking. While his writing and thinking reflected a Marxist perspective, he did not see himself as a Marxist nor did he have any affiliation with communist groups. Like the party he founded, Cabral was a pragmatist whose thinking and actions were grounded in his practical idealism. He saw Marxism-Leninism as being of limited practical and theoretical value to colonial countries, where principles of guerrilla warfare and ideological prescriptions had to be adapted to local conditions. His approach to revolution and socialism was influenced by his personal concerns and local conditions rather than theoretical abstractions. Furthermore, revolution and socialism were moral questions, not ideological formulas; the human and moral attributes of the people fighting for independence were more important than adherence to a particular ideology. Cabral's political thinking attracted considerable influence in the Third World, but less for its ideological precepts than its practical prescriptions. His reputation as a revolutionary leader is one of a practitioner and not a theoretician of revolution.

Books by Cabral

Revolution in Guinea (New York: Monthly Review Press, 1969);

National Liberation and Culture (Syracuse, N.Y.: Syracuse University Press, 1970);

Return to the Source: Selected Speeches (New York: Monthly Review Press, 1973);

Unity and Struggle: Speeches and Writings (London: Heinemann, 1980).

Books about Cabral

Patrick Chabal, *Amílcar Cabral: Revolutionary Leadership and People's War* (Cambridge: Cambridge University Press, 1983);

Ronald H. Chilicote, *Amílcar Cabral's Revolutionary Theory and Practice: A Critical Guide* (Boulder, Colo.: L. Rienner, 1991);

Jock McCulloch, *In the Twilight of the Revolution: The Political Thought of Amílcar Cabral* (London: Routledge & Kegan Paul, 1983).

General Reference

Basil Davidson, *No Fist Is Big Enough to Hide the Sky: The Liberation of Guinea-Bissau and Cape Verde* (London: Zed Press, 1981).

–J. R.-S.

SEE ALSO THESE RELATED ENTRIES
Kwame Nkrumah, 2; Antonio Agostinho Neto, 2.

Fidel Castro Ruz

President of Cuba, 1967–

Prime Minister of Cuba, 1959–1967

Born Mayarí, Cuba, 13 August 1926

Fidel Castro Ruz is a Cuban revolutionary leader and the current head of state of Cuba. Castro rivals Mao Zedong and Ho Chi Minh as the most prominent and influential Third World revolutionary leader in the twentieth century. "Maximum Leader" of the first Marxist-Leninist regime in the western hemisphere, Castro has attained legendary status.

The fifth of nine children of Angel Castro y Argiz, a Spanish landowner, and Lina Ruz Gonzáles, a Cuban native and Angel's second wife, Castro was born in the family's farmhouse in Oriente Province. He was sent to a local public grammar school, after which he attended a Marist private boys' school in the city of Santiago. At the age of sixteen he was sent to the Colegio de Belén, an exclusive preparatory school in Havana. At Belén he became familiar with the writings of José Martí y Pérez, the legendary Cuban revolutionary leader of the late 1800s. In 1945 Castro enrolled at the University of Havana law school, where he immediately plunged into campus and national politics.

As an autonomous institution, the University of Havana was a breeding ground for militant political activism and political gangsterism, as well as a sanctuary for political agitators and radicals. Student political activism on campus, often violent and marked by extremist ideologies, had always been an influential factor in Cuban national politics. In the violence-ridden rivalry between the two principal campus political organizations, the Insurrectional Revolutionary Union (UIR) and the Revolutionary Socialist Movement (MSR), Castro aligned himself with the UIR, which had long-standing ties to Cuban communist groups. In addition to factional political and revolutionary activities, he took part in protests against the university administration. An active participant in the violent rivalry between the MSR and the UIR, he was implicated in the murder of a rival student leader. In 1947 Castro joined an expedition to topple the dictator of the Dominican Republic, Rafael Leónidas Trujillo Molina, but the expedition never materialized. A year later Castro was arrested in Bogotá, Colombia, where he was attending a Latin American student conference, for participating in the internationally publicized, violent anti-American riots and demonstrations that broke out.

Castro's participation in the events in Bogotá made him a national political figure at the age of twenty-one

Gale International Portrait Gallery

Fidel Castro Ruz

when he returned to Cuba. He married Mirta Diaz Balart, a philosophy student, with whom he had a son, but the marriage later dissolved. Castro's interests in national politics had broadened since his freshman year, even though he remained distrustful of politicians and the corrupt political system. He became a devout follower of Eduardo Chibas, the charismatic leader of the nationalistic, reformist Ortodoxo party, and campaigned for Chibas in his unsuccessful presidential campaign in 1948.

The 1952 Batista Coup

The first half of the 1950s was a time of political and social unrest in Cuba. After graduating in September 1950, Castro opened a law firm in Havana, remaining publicly visible as a result of his criticisms and investigations of corruption in the government. In 1952 he was nominated to run as an Ortodoxo candidate for Congress in the June elections. The election, however, never took place. On 10 March 1952 General Fulgencio Batista y Zaldívar, who had been a dominant figure in Cuban politics since the 1930s, seized power in a bloodless military coup d'état.

Attack on the Moncada Barracks

After his failed attempts to bring constitutional charges against President Batista, Castro decided to organize an urban insurrectional movement to overthrow Batista. He personally planned and launched his first attempt to topple the Batista regime on 26 July 1953, when he led a group of armed rebels in an unsuccessful assault on the Moncada military barracks in Santiago, the country's second largest barracks. The Moncada assault was repelled by Batista's troops, with Castro's rebel force suffering heavy losses. Castro fled into the mountains but was captured days later by government troops. Despite being sentenced to fifteen years in prison for treason, he used the widely publicized 16 October trial to outline a blueprint for revolutionary change in Cuba. In his speech, "History Will Absolve Me," he called for the restoration of the 1940 constitution, free elections, free speech, and an independent judiciary.

Released from prison in May 1955 under a general amnesty issued by Batista, who was under pressure from civil opposition groups, Castro returned to Havana to a large, popular welcome and resumed working for the Ortodoxo party. Faced with an intransigent and repressive military dictatorship, however, he concluded that neither constitutional nor revolutionary change was possible from within the country. Two months after his release, he left Cuba with some of his followers for voluntary exile in Mexico. From Mexico City, Castro maintained contacts with militants back in Cuba as well as other exiled Cubans in the country. In Mexico he organized the 26 of July Movement, and received military training from the Mexican government in preparation for an expedition to topple the Batista regime. He recruited Ernesto "Che" Guevara de la Serna, the young Argentine revolutionary who had recently arrived in Mexico from Guatemala, where he had worked for the deposed Jacobo Arbenz Guzmán's government.

On 2 December 1956 Castro and eighty fellow revolutionaries, including his brother Raul and Che Guevara, landed in Oriente Province to launch a guerrilla campaign against the U.S.-backed Batista regime. The rebels, however, were ambushed by government troops when they landed. Castro regrouped the remaining thirty or so rebels and withdrew into the Sierra Maestra range, where over the next two years his guerrilla force grew to one thousand armed rebels. While Castro concentrated on rebuilding the 26 of July Movement and launching small-scale, hit-and-run operations in the countryside, anti-government urban opposition, and terrorism were on the rise, including an unsuccessful student-led attack on the presidential palace which nearly killed Batista. Castro emerged as the most prominent national leader of the anti-Batista forces in the wake of the American-backed regime's eroding popularity and its isolation.

Castro and his top lieutenants, brother Raul and Che, based the guerrilla war on the Maoist-influenced *foco* strategy, a rural-based guerrilla campaign that initially involved hit-and-run operations against isolated army outposts and ambushes of pursuing troops. Growing in numbers and strength, the guerrillas continued to inflict losses on Batista's forty-thousand-strong, U.S.-backed national army, which began to disintegrate after the guerrillas defeated Batista's elite troops during a 1958 offensive. Once the countryside was effectively under their control, the guerrillas descended from their mountain bases and began to seize large cities.

U.S. Support for Batista

Exposed by the international press, Castro became a national hero in Cuba and a romantic, idealistic figure in foreign public opinion during the Cuban revolutionary war. Even though his guerrilla movement was not avowedly communist (albeit containing committed Marxist-Leninists such as Che Guevara), Castro himself was not outwardly committed to any particular ideology at the time aside from the vague, left-of-center revolutionary nationalism. Orthodox members of the pro-Soviet Cuban Communist party, which played a marginal role in the war, denounced the guerrilla campaign as putschist. The revolution, however, caused some alarm and discomfort in the United States government, which had committed itself to the pro-American Batista regime in Cuba as part of its Cold War global policy. Domestic political support for the Batista regime, which had become increasingly isolated, vanished as a result of its indiscriminant repression and human rights abuses. By 1958 it had lost its political legitimacy and had alienated the large Cuban middle class because of its repressive measures and police brutality. In March 1958 the United States cut off military assistance to the Cuban military, which was gradually disintegrating because of its inefficiency, low morale, and lack of professionalism.

The Ouster of Batista

By late 1958 the Batista regime verged on the brink of collapse as a result of guerrilla advances on the battlefield, growing popular opposition, and its own severe internal weaknesses. Finally, large-scale army defections precipitated its downfall in late December 1958, and, after Batista fled into exile on 1 January 1959, Castro and the 26 of July Movement marched into Havana. He established a provisional government and initiated public trials and executions of the members of the Batista regime. The provisional government appointed by Castro, mostly made up of moderate, middle-class figures, was largely a front for a parallel, hidden government that exercised the real power. After a few months of hesitation, Castro decided to support the Marxist-Leninist program favored by his followers, and assumed formal control of the government in March. To consolidate his power and solidify his popular backing, he introduced several social and economic reforms, including an extensive land-reform program. The revolution became slowly radicalized toward the end of the year with the purges of some leaders and their replacement by more-radical, militant members.

There were few early indications that Castro's overthrow of the Batista regime would turn into a full-fledged revolution. It is often remarked that Cuban history ended and began on 1 January 1959. The Cuban "revolution" became more than simply the overthrow of Batista, but a historical process that began in 1959 and continues to the present under its sole caudillo.

The Break with the United States

Even though during the initial stages of the revolution the Castro regime laid the groundwork for the structural transformation of Cuban society, politics, and economy, the Cuban revolution's greatest impact was in the area of foreign relations. Scholars continue to debate whether the break with the United States was the result of U.S. policies, Castro's policies, or a product of structural inevitability. Evidence of Castro's anti-Americanism dates back to his guerrilla days, and as early as mid October 1959 he had made secret contacts with Soviet officials. After a brief period of mutual uncertainty, relations between the United States and the young regime in Havana gradually worsened throughout 1959 and 1960. In February 1960 the deputy premier of the Soviet Union, Anastas Mikoyan, visited Cuba and signed diplomatic and trade agreements with Castro. The Soviets, wary of the consequences of bilateral relations with the United States, had initially restricted their actions to vocal support for the Cuban revolution. Castro's slow drift toward the Soviet Union and his increasing verbal attacks against the United States escalated into ruptured relations between Cuba and the United States. When Castro confiscated American oil refineries in June 1960, the administration of President Dwight D. Eisenhower responded by withdrawing Cuba's export-sugar quota. Castro retaliated by nationalizing American-owned sugar mills in Cuba; he later expropriated all remaining American investments in the country. In September 1960 he attended the opening session of the United Nations General Assembly in New York City, where he exchanged embraces with Soviet premier Nikita S. Khrushchev. A month later the United States imposed an economic embargo on Cuba, and in January 1961 the Eisenhower administration severed re-

lations with Cuba. The administration gave final approval to a secret plan to topple the Castro regime by training and arming anti-Castro exiles in the United States in preparation for an invasion of the island. The administration left office before it could carry out the plan, which was approved by the incoming president, John F. Kennedy. The April 1961 Bay of Pigs invasion, however, was a total failure and had the unintended effect of helping the shaky new regime consolidate its power. The abortive invasion, which gave Castro the opportunity to suppress remaining opposition groups on the island and to consolidate his power, enhanced his domestic and international stature.

After the Bay of Pigs fiasco, Castro declared Cuba a socialist state and implemented Soviet-style economic central planning, headed by Che Guevara. In December 1961 Castro formally espoused Marxism-Leninism, declaring that "I am a Marxist-Leninist, and shall be one until the end of my life." Political activity was restricted to the embryonic Communist party of Cuba (PCC), which emerged out of the United Party of the Socialist Revolution. Castro remained the sole source of power, and decision making became highly centralized and hierarchical. He ruled with a small circle of trusted advisers (members of the 26 of July Movement and the military) in a government with no formal administrative or political structure during the period of 1959 to 1970. During and long after this period, one of the principal modes of political discourse in the country appeared to be through mass mobilization and popular rallies, where Castro often declared and amended policies. While he gained notoriety for his long-winded speeches, his overbearing oratory became an essential feature of his personal mystique and popularity.

The Cuban revolution had suddenly altered the political and strategic landscape in the United States's traditional sphere of influence. In January 1962 Cuba was expelled from the Organization of American States as a result of its deteriorating relations with neighboring Latin American countries. Immediately after coming to power, the Castro regime had begun actively to support attempts to overthrow the governments of Nicaragua, the Dominican Republic, Haiti, Panama, and Venezuela. In the backdrop of Cuban-U.S. hostility, Castro appealed to the Soviet Union for military assistance. Moving cautiously at first, the Soviet Union increased its military assistance to Cuba, including the introduction of surface-to-air missile installations in August 1962. By this time the Cuban army was among the best equipped in Latin America. Two months later Cuba was at the center of world attention during the "missile crisis" of October 1962.

The Cuban Missile Crisis

As early as September, the Kennedy administration had been issuing stern warnings to the Soviet Union that the United States would not tolerate the introduction of offensive missiles into Cuba, adding that such an action would provoke U.S. action. Even though the motives for the missile placement remain as unclear as the questions concerning whether Castro had asked the Soviet Union to install them in Cuba, on 14 October the United States announced the discovery of Soviet medium- and intermediate-range ballistic missiles in Cuba. On 22 October the United States imposed a naval quarantine of Cuba and requested that the missiles and Soviet military personnel be removed from the island. Finally on 28 October, after six days of nuclear brinkmanship, Khrushchev capitulated to the American demands and removed the missiles from Cuba without asking Castro's consent. Even though the Soviet Union had secured Cuban immunity from American military aggression, Cuban-Soviet relations were strained by the missile crisis, which had been resolved without Cuban input. Yet, despite its secondary role in the superpower standoff, Cuba had suddenly been thrust onto the world center stage.

For the remainder of the decade the Castro regime concentrated on domestic economic affairs while at the same time orienting its foreign policy toward influencing hemispheric affairs. From 1962 to 1968, Cuban-Soviet relations were marked by episodic conflicts and disagreements over Cuba's domestic and foreign policies. The cooling of relations with the Soviet Union was accompanied by a brief experimentation with the Chinese political economy model. Economic performance, however, fell far short of the regime's expectations, as a result of ineffective policies and mismanagement. While the regime made advances in the areas of public health care and education, the economy remained poorly managed, overly centralized, and heavily dependent on the continued infusion of Soviet economic and technical aid and subsidies.

The embryonic stages of Cuba's activist, globalist foreign policy, which the regime labeled "proletarian internationalism," evolved during the 1960s. Members of the regime, particularly Che Guevara, one of Castro's most trusted advisers, were convinced that the survival of the revolution and socialism in Cuba could only be guaranteed by exporting Cuba's revolutionary model throughout Latin America and to the rest of the Third World. Partly to deflect American attention and hostility toward Cuba as well as to create favorable conditions abroad, the Castro regime increased its support for guerrilla movements in many parts of Latin America, and in 1966 Castro founded the Organization of Latin American Solidarity (OLAS), which was to be an alternative to the Organization of American States. Castro's revolutionary initiatives in Latin America and the Caribbean placed him at odds with the Soviet Union, which felt that such initiatives had little chances of success but were politically costly for its bilateral relations with the United States. The Soviet Union regarded his role in the world

revolutionary movement as divisive. Castro's hemispheric initiatives also met with American-sponsored counterinsurgency campaigns and an ambitious foreign aid program to support democratic reforms in the hemisphere, the Alliance for Progress. By the close of the decade Castro's revolutionary campaign in the hemisphere appeared to have failed.

The Tricontinental Congress

Although its proletarian internationalism had failed in Latin America, the Castro regime made significant strides elsewhere. An active supporter of the Algerian National Liberation Front during the Algerian revolution (1954–1962), Castro committed a battalion of Cuban troops to assist Algeria during the Algerian-Moroccan border conflict in 1963. In addition to its military mission in Algeria, Cuba established other missions in Ghana and the Congo-Brazzaville, where an estimated one thousand Cuban military personnel were stationed from 1965 to 1968. Cuba also became an active supporter of African liberation movements, particularly the Popular Movement for the Liberation of Angola (MPLA), whose fighters were being trained in the Congo by Cuban military personnel. In January 1966 Castro hosted the First Conference of Solidarity of the Peoples of Africa, Asia, and Latin America, better known as the Tricontinental Congress, which brought together leaders of guerrilla movements and communist parties in an effort to create a worldwide network of revolutionaries. Toward the end of the decade relations improved with the Soviet Union, whose military and economic commitment to Cuba deepened. The turning point in relations came in 1968 when the Soviet Union pressured Cuba, vulnerable because of its economic and military dependence on the Soviets, to support its invasion of Czechoslovakia.

Angola

Third World–oriented globalism reemerged as the centerpiece of Cuban foreign policy following a brief period of retrenchment in the late 1960s and early 1970s. Throughout the 1970s and 1980s Cuba's impact on international affairs and superpower relations was disproportionate to the country's modest size and meager resources. Although it cannot be discounted that Cuba's actions were the result of a surrogate foreign policy, the principal motives behind Cuban foreign policy appeared to be Castro's unambiguous desire to make Cuba the leader of the Third World. Insofar as differences over strategy were minimal, there was a marked degree of convergence between Cuban and Soviet foreign-policy objectives, with both Havana and Moscow gaining from an activist, expansive Cuban role in the Third World. Cuba's attempts to shape political developments in the Third World through its proletarian internationalist foreign policies reached an unprecedented level during the second half of the 1970s. Sustained by Soviet logistical support and power-projection capabilities, Cuba's overseas military commitments expanded, including Cuban troops assisting the Syrian army during the October 1973 Arab-Israeli War. The turning point in Cuba's overseas military commitment was its bold intervention during the incipient stages of the Angolan civil war in mid 1975. Castro had long supported the Marxist MPLA movement in its war against both the Portuguese colonial system and against rival liberation movements in Angola. He developed a close relationship with the group's leader, António Agostinho Neto, becoming an important link between the MPLA and its main sponsor, the Soviet Union, with whom relations were periodically strained.

Negotiations between Portugal and the three main liberation groups in early 1975 set 11 November as the date of independence following national elections. However, internecine warfare among the three rival groups broke out and by July the Soviet-equipped MPLA controlled most of the country. Shipment of Soviet and Cuban military equipment to the MPLA had accelerated since mid 1974, but it was only after the 23 October 1975 South African invasion of Angola that Cuba and the Soviet Union orchestrated a large-scale military intervention in Angola, including the Soviet airlift of what in early 1976 eventually numbered twelve thousand Cuban combat troops. The Soviet-Cuban intervention on behalf of the MPLA proved decisive both in turning back the invasion and in installing the MPLA in power. Even though there had been an estimated three thousand to five thousand troops and military personnel already in Angola by September 1975, the significance of Cuba's involvement in Angola was its magnitude and international repercussions. While Castro's standing and prestige in the Third World were enhanced by the intervention, the presence of Cuban troops in Angola, numbering over fifty thousand in 1988, was a source of regional tensions and strained superpower relations. Cuba was implicated in the 1977 and 1978 invasions of Zaire by Angola-based Zairian rebels, who allegedly received training and weapons from the Cuban military personnel based in Angola.

The Ethiopian-Somali War

Cuba's second large-scale military involvement in the Third World came in mid 1977 during the Ogaden war between Ethiopia and Somalia. After the 1974 military coup d'état that overthrew the pro-West monarchy, the Marxist regime in Ethiopia moved to establish close ties with the Soviet Union and Cuba, which prior to 1974 had been providing military assistance to secessionist rebels in the Province of Eritrea. Cuba also had established close relations with Ethiopia's historic archrival, the pro-Soviet, Marxist Somalia, but those relations began to unravel as both Cuba and the

Soviet Union strengthened ties with neighboring Ethiopia. When war broke out between the two countries in May 1977, Ethiopia appealed to the Soviet Union and Cuba for help; they responded with a Soviet airlift of weapons and an estimated sixteen thousand Cuban combat troops. Although the Ethiopian counteroffensive turned back the Somali attack, Castro was reluctant to allow the Ethiopians to use Cuban troops against secessionist rebels in Eritrea and Tigre. His initial refusal to commit Cuban troops against the secessionist rebels, who had been supported by Cuba during the prerevolution period, caused a mild strain in Soviet-Cuban relations. Castro unsuccessfully attempted to act as a peace broker between the brutal Mengistu regime and the secessionist rebels.

Nicaragua

The Castro regime intensified its revolutionary efforts in Latin America, primarily in Central America, during the late 1970s and 1980s. Cuban support for the Sandinista National Liberation Front (FSLN), the Nicaraguan revolutionary movement founded in Cuba in 1961, was instrumental in the defeat of the dictator Anastasio Somoza Debayle on 19 July 1979. Castro had not only provided military and ideological training, weapons, and logistical support to the Nicaraguan revolutionaries since the 1960s but was also instrumental in unifying the three Sandinista factions through his personal mediation in the summer of 1978. The top leadership of the FSLN, including the leaders of the pro-Cuban faction, Tomás Borge Martínez and Daniel Ortega Saavedra, were trained in Cuba. After the Sandinistas seized power in July 1979, Cuba became the principal political and military backer of the new regime.

In addition to Nicaragua, Cuba also provided arms to insurgency movements in El Salvador and Guatemala and helped to consolidate a Marxist regime in the Caribbean island of Grenada. After the pro-Soviet New Jewel Movement, led by Maurice Bishop, came to power in Grenada in early 1979, it fostered close ties with the Soviet Union and Cuba, from where it received military and technical assistance, including the construction of a large airport on the island.

Castro's Central American initiatives, motivated by his ideological commitment to export revolution, strained superpower relations throughout the 1980s. The United States, which continued to impose an economic and diplomatic embargo on the island, continued to regard Cuba with suspicion and bitterness. While the United States, whose intervention in Cuban political life since the late 1800s continued to generate so much antipathy and resentment in Cuba, viewed Cuba as a source of subversion and instability in the hemisphere, Castro believed that Cuba had a historical, national duty to oppose the United

States and its interests wherever possible. The varying degrees of hostility and tension between the two countries, however, gave way to President Jimmy Carter's tentative steps toward normalized relations.

The Reagan Administration

By 1979–1980 relations had rapidly deteriorated again as a result both of the domestic political fallout in the United States following the disclosure of the presence of a Soviet brigade in Cuba and of Castro's forced exile of over 125,000 dissidents, some of whom were criminals, who were allowed to sail to the United States from the port of Mariel. The newly elected administration of Ronald Reagan reacted strongly to what it viewed as a coordinated Cuban-Soviet attempt to subvert American interests in a region that it considered important to its national security interests. The Reagan administration reversed the policies of the previous administration, policies which had initially relaxed Cuban-American relations. Unlike Carter, Reagan took an aggressive posture toward leftist movements and states in the Third World, particularly in Central America, and threatened to "go to the source" if Cuba did not stop its flow of arms to Nicaragua and leftist guerrillas in El Salvador and Guatemala. Cuba's deepening involvement with Grenada's radical regime, especially its construction of the large airport on the island, had become a source of growing concern for the American government. With the overthrow of Bishop by a more radical faction of his movement in early 1983, precipitating a period of instability on the island, President Reagan ordered small-scale military action against Grenada, ostensibly to protect American students studying in the country. The American forces briefly encountered disorganized armed resistance by the Cuban military personnel and Grenadan leftists.

In mid 1985 acrimonious verbal exchanges between Castro and the Reagan administration mounted after the opening of Radio Marti, a Miami-based radio station that broadcast to Cuba. The administration also accused Cuba of supporting international terrorism and drug trafficking into the United States. In July 1989 Castro ordered the execution of a top military leader and some government officials who were charged with drug trafficking.

Relations with the Soviet Union

Cuban-Soviet relations remained cordial from the time of their military collaboration in Africa up until the mid 1980s. Even though disagreements exist over the exact nature of Cuba's ties to the Soviet Union, it continued to receive the bulk of Soviet military and economic aid to the Third World until 1990. Cuba continued to depend on the Soviet bloc countries for its economic survival. Soviet assistance to Cuba reached an estimated $3 billion annually by 1979, almost 20 percent of Cuba's gross national product,

and an estimated $5 billion annually during the mid 1980s. Although Cuba was denied membership in the Warsaw Pact and the Council of Mutual Economic Assistance (CEMA), the respective military and economic groupings of the Soviet bloc countries, close to 80 percent of its trade was with the CEMA countries. But, despite being an economic liability, Cuba proved to be the Soviet Union's most important political asset in the Third World. Cuba, which sought to use the Non-Aligned Movement as its primary forum to influence the Third World, became an ideal sponsor of Soviet geopolitical interests.

Cuba's international standing was not based solely on its highly visible military commitments abroad but also on its technical and humanitarian assistance to several developing countries. While Cuban troops and military personnel were present in Africa, the Middle East, the Caribbean, and Latin America, the Castro regime also provided technical assistance to numerous Third World countries, principally in the areas of health care and education. Castro attempted to mobilize Third World support and strengthen his credentials for Cuban leadership of the Non-Aligned Movement, which he finally chaired from 1979 to 1983, through the combination of military and developmental internationalism. Castro's international standing, however, waned as a result of his lonely support for the December 1979 Soviet invasion of Afghanistan. His support of the widely condemned invasion placed him at odds with the bulk of Third World countries that criticized the invasion.

By the second half of the 1980s, however, the international environment had suddenly grown inhospitable for Castro and the Cuban revolution. After the ascension to power of premier Mikhail S. Gorbachev in early March 1985, Cuban-Soviet relations reached their lowest point. Gorbachev's "new thinking," which introduced revolutionary changes in Soviet domestic and foreign policies, called for the overhaul of the Soviet economic and political system, particularly the injection of market-oriented measures in the economy. The new Soviet leadership, both reluctant and unable to finance its Third World clients, became disenchanted with Castro's refusal to undertake economic reforms aimed at restructuring Cuba's overly centralized and inefficient economy. Incapable of sustaining the high levels of aid needed to keep Cuba's economy functioning and strapped by its own internal difficulties, the Soviet government began to scale back its overall military and economic assistance to Cuba, including cutbacks in oil shipments, which Cuba had resold for hard currency.

Sharp disagreements also arose in the area of foreign policy. Castro, who had been dissatisfied with the Soviet Union's measured support for the Sandinista regime in Nicaragua, was unwilling to retreat both from Cuba's internationalist policies and from his strident and repeated denunciations of the United States, with whom Gorbachev was trying to improve relations. During 1986 and 1987 relations between Cuba and the Soviet Union were seriously strained, as Castro turned from his earlier veiled criticisms of the Soviet Union and Gorbachev's reforms to open condemnation of what he saw as capitulation to capitalism and the abandonment of socialist, revolutionary principles. On 22 December 1988 Cuba, incapable of sustaining its costly internationalist commitments abroad and pressured by the Soviet Union, agreed to an American-sponsored tripartite agreement with South Africa and Angola that provided for the phased withdrawal of Cuban combat troops in Angola.

Cuba thus entered the 1990s estranged from an international arena, undergoing structural transformations as a result of the lessening of superpower ideological competition and global political liberalization. The rapid changes in Eastern Europe and the Soviet Union left Cuba isolated. The February 1990 electoral defeat of the Sandinista regime further isolated Cuba, now the only Latin American country espousing socialism.

Although Castro had publicly vowed to pursue "socialism or death," by 1989 there was scattered evidence that his regime was exploring reforms to save the revolution at home. Politically, however, Cuba remained closed, and there were no signs that the aging Castro, who continued to be highly visible and energetic, would lessen his dominance of the decision-making process. Despite its monopoly on power and outside charges that the political system had ossified, the Cuban Communist party, like its leader, still enjoys moral authority and legitimacy among Cubans.

While there are few neutral views on Castro, few other Third World leaders in the twentieth century have had an equivalent impact on postwar international relations. Cuba's high profile and international stature, and its capacity to wield leverage and influence far beyond its borders and disproportionate to its small size, can only be attributed to Castro's political acumen, audacity, and personal leadership of the Cuban revolution since he founded it.

Books by Castro

Fidel Castro Speaks (New York: Grove, 1969);

Speeches: Cuba's Internationalist Foreign Policy (New York: Pathfinder, 1981).

Books about Castro

Sebastian Balfour, *Castro* (New York: Longman, 1990);

Don E. Beyer, *Castro* (New York: Franklin Watts, 1993);

Theodore Draper, *Castroism: Theory and Practice* (New York: Praeger, 1965);

Georgie Anne Geyer, *Guerrilla Prince: The Untold Story of Fidel Castro* (Boston: Little, Brown, 1991);

Edward Gonzalez, *Castro, Cuba, and the World* (Santa Monica, Cal.: RAND Corporation, 1986);

Ernst Halperin, *Fidel Castro's Road to Power* (Cambridge, Mass.: M.I.T. Press, 1970);

Lee Lockwood, *Castro's Cuba, Cuba's Fidel* (Boulder, Colo.: Westview Press, 1990);

Carlos Alberto Montaner, *Fidel Castro and the Cuban Revolution* (New Brunswick: Transaction Publishers, 1989);

Andres Oppenheimer, *Castro's Final Hour: The Secret Story Behind the Coming Downfall of Communist Cuba* (New York: Simon & Schuster, 1992);

Robert E. Quirk, *Fidel Castro* (New York: Norton, 1993);

Wayne S. Smith, *The Closest of Enemies: A Personal and Diplomatic Account of U.S.-Cuban Relations since 1957* (New York: Norton, 1987);

Tad Szulc, *Fidel: A Critical Portrait* (New York: Morrow, 1986).

General References

Jorge I. Dominguez, *To Make the World Safe for Revolution: Cuba's Foreign Policy* (Cambridge: Harvard University Press, 1989);

Jorge I. Dominguez, ed., *Cuba: Internal and International Affairs* (Beverly Hills: Sage Publications, 1982);

Jorge I. Dominguez, ed., *U.S.-Cuban Relations in the 1990s* (Boulder, Colo.: Westview, 1989);

William M. LeoGrande, *Cuba's Policy in Africa, 1959–1980* (Berkeley: University of California Press, 1980);

Peter Shearman, *The Soviet Union and Cuba* (London: Routledge & Kegan Paul, 1987).

–J. R.-S.

SEE ALSO THESE RELATED ENTRIES

Fulgencio Batista y Zaldívar, 2; Tomás Borge Martinez, 2; Raul Castro Ruz, 2; Dwight D. Eisenhower, 1; Mikhail S. Gorbachev, 2; Ernesto Che Guevara, 2; John F. Kennedy, 2; Nikita S. Khrushchev, 2; Mao Zedong, 2; Mengistu Haile Mariam, 2; Anastas Mikoyan, 2; António Agostinho Neto, 2; Daniel Ortega Saavedra, 2; Ronald Reagan, 1; Rafael Leónidas Trujillo Molina, 2.

Raúl Castro Ruz

First Vice-Premier of Cuba, 1972–
Born Birán, Cuba, 3 June 1931

Generally considered the number two man, after his brother Fidel, in the government of Cuba, Raúl Castro is the nation's first vice-premier, minister of the armed forces, and second secretary of the Communist party.

Castro's interest in politics began at the University of Havana, where he became a member of the Communist Youth, a branch of the Popular Socialist party. In the early 1950s, convinced that social change in Cuba could not be brought about by constitutional means, he left the Communist Youth to become one of the main leaders of Fidel Castro's guerrilla movement to overthrow the government of Fulgencio Batista y Zaldívar, the "strong man" of Cuba.

The Ouster of Batista

After a 26 July 1953 aborted attack on the Moncada military barracks, Castro was arrested and convicted of treason, along with his brother and other rebels. As part of a general amnesty in May 1955, the Castros were released. They fled to Mexico, where they, together with other revolutionaries, including Argentine Ernesto Che Guevara, continued to plan and train for the invasion of Cuba and the overthrow of the Batista regime. On 25 November 1956 the Castros, together with eighty-two revolutionaries, boarded the "Granma" yacht from Mexico and sailed to the Oriente province of Cuba. Their landing marked the beginning of a two-year battle against the U.S.-backed forces of the Batista government. Raúl, as chief lieutenant, with the support of impoverished farmers, led the eventual victory over the dictatorship of Batista, who was overthrown at the end of 1958.

After the triumph of the revolution, Raúl married on 26 January 1959 Massachusetts Institute of Technology-educated revolutionary Vilma Espin, whom he had met during the course of the revolution. She later held various posts within the Communist party.

The Turn to Communism

After taking power on February 1959, Fidel Castro staffed his cabinet with moderate, liberal, middle-class politicians, appointing Raúl as armed forces commander and later minister of the armed forces. It was not until December 1961, shortly after the failed Bay of Pigs invasion, that Fidel proclaimed his government as Marxist-Leninist, replacing former officials with those of his new ideological direction. Raúl was instrumental in the organization of a one-party political system along the lines of the Soviet model. To the dismay of the United States, he established diplomatic relations with the Soviet Union.

Relations with the Soviet Union

Cuban-Soviet ties changed the balance of power in the Caribbean. Never before had a communist regime resided so close to the United States. The proximity of Castro's new Soviet-style one-party system was problematic for U.S. national security. In October 1962 this troubled relationship led to a near nuclear disaster when final arrangements were made, reportedly by Raúl, for the deployment of Soviet missiles in Cuba. Although the crisis was resolved favorably for the United States, U.S. officials continued to consider Cuba a security threat in large part because of its attempts to export revolution.

For example, foreign troops from numerous socialist countries, such as Vietnam, Angola, and Syria, were trained in guerrilla warfare tactics on Cuban soil. Cuban troops were also sent overseas to help in the guerrilla struggles of its allies, and Cuba's training of troops in guerrilla warfare brought Castro considerable recognition from important Soviet officials. Castro's strong ties with Soviet officials were also demonstrated when, in 1966, during the Soviet Union's ideological rift with China, Castro openly denounced China for allegedly trying to intervene in Cuban affairs.

General References

Sebastian Balfour, *Castro* (London, New York: Longman, 1990);

Don E. Beyer, *Castro!* (New York: Franklin Watts, 1993);

Rolando Bonachea and Nelson P. Valdés, eds., *Cuba in Revolution* (Garden City, N.Y.: Doubleday, 1971);

Jorge I. Domínguez, *Cuba: Order and Revolution* (Cambridge, Mass.: Harvard University Press, 1978);

Carlos Franqui, *The Twelve* (New York: Lyle Stuart, 1968);

Georgie Anne Geyer, *Guerrilla Prince: The Untold Story of Fidel Castro* (Boston: Little, Brown, 1991);

Lee Lockwood, *Castro's Cuba, Cuba's Fidel* (Boulder, Colo.: Westview Press, 1990);

Carlos Alberto Montaner, *Fidel Castro and the Cuban Revolution* (New Brunswick: Transaction Publishers, 1989);

Miami Herald/*Maurice Cohn Band*

Raúl Castro Ruz

Andres Oppenheimer, *Castro's Final Hour: The Secret Story Behind the Coming Downfall of Communist Cuba* (New York: Simon & Schuster, 1992);

Robert E. Quirk, *Fidel Castro* (New York: Norton, 1993);

Wayne S. Smith, *The Closest of Enemies: A Personal and Diplomatic Account of U.S.-Cuban Relations since 1957* (New York: Norton, 1987);

Tad Szulc, *Fidel: A Critical Portrait* (New York: Morrow, 1986).

– B. D.

SEE ALSO THESE ENTRIES

Fulgencio Batista y Zaldívar, 2; Fidel Castro, 2; Bay of Pigs, 3; Cuban Missile Crisis, 3; Ernesto Che Guevara, 2; John F. Kennedy, 1; Nikita S. Khrushchev, 2.

Nicolae Ceausescu

President of Romania, 1974–1989

General Secretary, Romanian Communist Party, 1965–1989

Born Scornicesti, Romania, 26 January 1918
Died Bucharest, Romania, 25 December 1989

Nicolae Ceausescu, general secretary of the Romanian Communist party and president of Romania, was born into a Romanian peasant family. He joined the small Romanian Union of Communist Youth in 1933 and, in 1936, became a full member of the Romanian Communist party (RCP).

During World War II, Ceausescu was jailed on numerous occasions by the pro-German Romanian authorities for his subversive antigovernment activities. He was able to escape from jail just prior to the multiparty coup d'état against the wartime quasi-Fascist government of General Ion Antonescu in August 1944. After the war, in late 1945, he became secretary of the Romanian communist youth organization. Having spent the war years outside the Soviet Union, Ceausescu belonged to the "native" party faction that was at odds with the postwar "Muscovite" party leadership whose members lived in the Soviet Union during the war and were considered more loyal to Moscow.

Protégé of Gheorghiu-Dej

After the communists assumed full power in the country in 1947, Ceausescu served as the minister of agriculture from 1948 to 1950. From 1950 through 1954 he served with the rank of major general as deputy minister of the Romanian armed forces, and in 1951 he became chief of the army's political administration. Ceausescu was a protégé of Romania's communist dictator Gheorghe Gheorghiu-Dej. In 1954 he became a secretary of the Romanian Workers party Central Committee and, by 1955, a full member of the party's ruling Politburo. Following the death of Gheorghiu-Dej in March 1965, Ceausescu succeeded him to the leadership of the now-renamed Romanian Communist party as its general secretary. Shortly afterward Romania was proclaimed a "socialist republic." In December 1967 Ceausescu also became head of state by assuming the presidency of Romania's state council.

Independence from Moscow

Ceausescu had started his rise to power virtually unknown in the country but achieved some domestic popularity for his relative independence from the Kremlin.

Nicolae Ceausescu

He continued to apply Gheorghiu-Dej's distinct "Romanian road to socialism," in which Soviet direction and supervision were severely curtailed during the 1960s, and the state pursued a more independent foreign policy. For example, Bucharest condemned the Warsaw Treaty Organization's invasion of Czechoslovakia in August 1968, and even though Romania continued to be a member of the Warsaw Pact, it refused to allow Russian troops to be stationed on its soil and did not participate in the pact's military maneuvers. In contrast to all other European leaders, Ceausescu also maintained ties with Israel, undertook mediation efforts in the Arab-Israeli conflict as well as other Middle Eastern hostilities, refused to condemn the Chinese communist regime, and established reasonably friendly ties with several Western European countries. He also formed cordial relations with the United States, as shown by President Richard Nixon's visit to Romania in 1969.

Domestic Corruption and Repression

Although Ceausescu initially drew praise from the West because of his apparent independence from Moscow, his internal policies grew increasingly arbitrary and repressive. His exploitative economic policies resulted in a severe fall in living standards for the mass of the population. While building up a personal fortune and engaging in ostentatious displays of wealth and familial prestige, he created domestic shortages of food, energy, fuel, and other basic needs. He exported these goods throughout the 1980s to pay off a $10 billion foreign debt. He also intensified the collectivization of agriculture, launched a program of "rationalization" or "systematization" of rural life, in the process destroying several thousand traditional Romanian and Hungarian villages, and refused to allow any liberalization or decentralization in the state's economic management.

Ceausescu installed more than thirty of his relatives into leading positions in the party, the government, the military, the police, and other important bureaucracies. He established a vast network of spies and surveillance techniques and crushed all manifestations of political opposition. He promoted his own personality cult through the mass media, the educational system, literature, and all forms of artistic expression. Poets, painters, and writers were expected to glorify his personality, underscore his wisdom, and highlight his historic role in the country's development. Ceausescu also gave immense powers to his wife, Elena, whom he married in 1939. She was a staunch communist and a competent chemist. Because of her scientific background she was made head of numerous scientific organizations, including the Central Chemical Research Institute and the National Council for Science and Technology. In 1980 she was promoted to deputy prime minister and used her authority to ban all birth-control usage in order to help increase Romania's population and thus the country's potential strength in the future. To help enforce a high birthrate she ordered physical examinations for all women of childbearing age to detect and discourage any recourse to abortions.

Overthrow of Ceausescu

Resentment against Ceausescu's personal dictatorship among various sectors of the population grew during the 1980s. A series of army plots to unseat him were uncovered and preempted. But the Ceausescu regime began to crumble on 17 December 1989, when soldiers fired into a group of protesters in the Transylvanian city of Timisoara. The regime then tried to organize a pro-Ceausescu rally in Bucharest, but the crowd turned re-

bellious, and the army staged a mutiny. The Ceausescus fled the capital but were captured by the army, interrogated, summarily tried on television, found guilty of genocide against the Romanian people, and executed on 25 December 1989, somewhere near Bucharest. There is some evidence that the plot to unseat Ceausescu had been drawn up several months in advance by a clandestine group of party reformers and military officers styling themselves as the National Salvation Front. The spontaneous public revolt in December 1989, the regionwide anticommunist revolution in Eastern Europe, and evident approval from Moscow assured the front of success in ousting Ceausescu.

Books about Ceausescu

Mark Almond, *The Rise and Fall of Nicolae and Elena Ceau'sescu* (London: Chapmans, 1992);

Edward Behr, *Kiss the Hand You Cannot Bite: The Rise and Fall of the Ceau'sescus* (New York: Villard, 1991);

Mary Ellen Fischer, *Nicolae Ceau'sescu: A Study in Political Leadership* (Boulder, Colo.: L. Rienner, 1989);

Trond Gilberg, *Nationalism and Communism in Romania: The Rise and Fall of Ceausescu's Personal Dictatorship* (Boulder, Colo.: Westview, 1990);

John Sweeney, *The Life and Evil Times of Nicolae Ceausescu* (London: Hutchinson, 1991).

General References

J. F. Brown, *Eastern Europe and Communist Rule* (Durham, N.C. and London: Duke University Press, 1988);

Lawrence S. Graham, *Romania: A Developing Socialist State* (Boulder, Colo.: Westview, 1982);

Robert L. Hutchings, *Soviet-East European Relations: Consolidation and Conflict, 1968–1980* (Madison: University of Wisconsin Press, 1983);

Robert R. King, *A History of the Romanian Communist Party* (Stanford, Cal.: Hoover Institution Press, 1980);

Daniel N. Nelson, ed., *Romania in the 1980s* (Boulder, Colo.: Westview, 1981);

Martyn C. Rady, *Romania in Turmoil: A Contemporary History* (New York: I. B. Tauris, 1992);

Joseph Rothschild, *Return to Diversity: A Political History of East Central Europe since World War II* (New York: Oxford University Press, 1989);

Sarah M. Terry, ed., *Soviet Policy in Eastern Europe* (New Haven: Yale University Press, 1984);

Adam Ulam, *Expansion and Coexistence* (New York: Praeger, 1968);

Katherine Verdery, *National Ideology under Socialism: Identity and Cultural Politics in Ceau'sescu's Romania* (Berkeley: University of California Press, 1991);

Iv'an V'olgyes, *The Political Reliability of the Warsaw Pact Armies: The Southern Tier* (Durham: Duke University Press, 1982).

– J. B. and A. B.

SEE ALSO THESE RELATED ENTRIES

Gheorghe Gheorghiu-Dej, 2; Josip Broz Tito, 2; Warsaw Pact, 3.

Violeta Barrios de Chamorro

President of Nicaragua, 1990–
Born Rivas, Nicaragua, 18 October 1929

The president of Nicaragua and former publisher of *La prensa*, Nicaragua's leading opposition newspaper, Violeta Barrios de Chamorro represents to the Nicaraguan people the possibility of a democratic solution to their country's prolonged civil war. Facing opposition from right and left, Chamorro sought a compromise between the Sandinistas and their Contra opponents.

Violeta Barrios was born 18 October 1929 in the southern Nicaraguan town of Rivas, close to the Costa Rican border. The daughter of a wealthy ranching family, at the age of twenty-one Violeta married Pedro Joaquin Chamorro, whose family owned and ran the Nicaraguan daily newspaper, *La prensa*. The Chamorros were committed to the overthrow of the Anastasio Somoza dictatorship, and Pedro was jailed several times for his outspoken editorials. In 1978, when he was assassinated, resistance to the Somoza regime escalated. His death sparked countless public demonstrations and a prolonged nationwide strike. The Catholic church disassociated itself from the Somoza regime, citing Pedro Chamorro's death as one of many brutal human rights abuses the government had committed. Violeta Chamorro took up her husband's cause and actively began to support the rebel Sandinista National Liberation Front (FSLN). She loaned the FSLN over fifty thousand dollars, which was vital to their occupation of the National Palace in Managua in August 1978.

The Overthrow of Somoza

After the Somozan government was deposed by the Sandinista army in July 1979, Violeta Chamorro was appointed to the five-member governing junta, which also included Daniel Ortega Saavedra, Sergio Ramirez, Moises Hassan, and Alfonso Robelo. Chamorro and Robelo, a Social Democrat, were the only members of the junta who were not also military leaders of the FSLN.

Violeta Barrios de Chamorro

Chamorro rapidly became disillusioned with the new policies of the Sandinista-controlled government, seeing "an excessive militarism, an exaggerated Cuban presence, and less interest in democratic ideas." In April 1980 the Sandinistas enlarged the thirty-three-member legislative Council of State by fourteen FSLN representatives, gaining a clear majority within the council. For this and other reasons, Chamorro and Robelo resigned their seats on the governing junta.

Opposition to the Sandinistas

Chamorro became one of the harshest critics of the Sandinista government. She turned *La prensa* into the leading opposition newspaper, even though its offices were repeatedly shut down by the Sandinista government. When, as a condition of the 1987 Central American Peace Plan (proposed by Costa Rican president Oscar Arias Sanchez), the Sandinistas needed to prove that the Nicaraguan press was free, they offered to reopen *La prensa*, provided that the newspaper be subject to censorship. Chamorro refused, demanding complete freedom for *La prensa*. The Sandinistas eventually complied.

The 1990 Election

When Ortega, the self-appointed president of the Sandinista government, announced a free presidential election in 1989, Chamorro was suggested as a possible candidate. Twelve small opposition parties merged, forming the National Opposition Union (UNO), and chose Chamorro as their candidate. Despite the fact that popularity polls consistently showed Chamorro in the lead, her victory over Ortega in the 1990 election was a stunning surprise.

As president of Nicaragua, Chamorro was faced with tremendous economic and political unrest. The Sandinista party maintained control over the army and the Interior Ministry. The Contra army initially refused to lay down arms, declaring that an unopposed Sandinista party would quickly oust the newly elected president. Despite these and other obstacles, Chamorro succeeded in reducing the size of the military and the percentage of the national budget apportioned for its support.

General Reference

Dennis Gilbert, *Sandinistas: The Party, and the Revolution* (Oxford, U.K.: Blackwell, 1988).

–J. S.

SEE ALSO THESE RELATED ENTRIES
Daniel Ortega Saavedra, 2; Tomás Borge Martínez, 2.

Konstantin Chernenko

General Secretary, Soviet Communist Party, 1984–1985
Born Bolshaya Tes, Russia, 24 September 1911
Died Moscow, Soviet Union, 10 March 1985

Konstantin Ustinovich Chernenko served a brief thirteen months as general secretary of the Communist party of the Soviet Union (CPSU) in 1984 and 1985.

He was born into a peasant family in the southern Siberian village of Bolshaya Tes. Like many other future Soviet leaders of his generation he received little formal education. At the age of eighteen he began propaganda work for the Komsomol (Communist Youth League) in the county seat of Novoselovo. A year later he volunteered for the army, serving in Kazakhstan on the Chinese border until 1933. He joined the Communist party in 1931. From 1933 on, Chernenko continued his agitation and propaganda activities at increasingly higher levels of the party apparatus, interrupting his work only to attend the Higher School for Party Organizers in Moscow, from which he graduated in 1945. Between 1948 and 1956 he served as party secretary for propaganda in the Republic of Moldavia. He also earned a degree in 1953 for part-time studies at a local teaching institute.

Brezhnev's Chief of Staff

In 1950 Chernenko met Leonid I. Brezhnev, at that time head of the Moldavian party and later general secretary of the CPSU. Brezhnev was to become Chernenko's mentor, ensuring his protégé's rise in the party hierarchy. In 1956, when Brezhnev was renamed to the Presidium, the executive body of the Central Committee of the CPSU, he summoned Chernenko to Moscow to work in the party's central propaganda department. Chernenko remained in this position until 1960, when Brezhnev became chairman of the Presidium of the Supreme Soviet – essentially the president of the Soviet Union – and made him his chief of staff. Chernenko continued to serve as his chief of staff after Brezhnev succeeded Nikita S. Khrushchev as general secretary of the CPSU in 1964.

Full Member of Politburo

As Brezhnev's own power grew during his eighteen years in office, his loyal aide's ascendancy within the party hierarchy continued in step. Chernenko became a candidate member of the Central Committee in 1966 and a full member in 1971. Five years later he was named to the Secretariat – that part of the Central Committee entrusted with running everyday party affairs. In 1977 he

Konstantin Chernenko

became an alternate member of the Politburo – the governing body which replaced the Presidium – and he became a full member in 1978. Belonging to both the Secretariat and the Politburo, which were the two centers of power in the Soviet Union, was normally requisite to becoming party general secretary, and by this time Chernenko, at age sixty-seven the youngest member of both bodies, had emerged as Brezhnev's personal favorite to succeed him.

Despite Chernenko's high rank, he rarely stepped out beyond Brezhnev's shadow to voice his own views. Whatever respect he earned appeared to be the result of his intimate friendship with and easy access to Brezhnev, for other Soviet politicians resented his rapid attainment of full membership in the Politburo. Arkady Shevchenko, a former Soviet diplomat who defected to the West, said Andrei Gromyko, the foreign minister, considered Chernenko a "second-rate opportunist."

With Mikhail Suslov's death in January 1982, Chernenko inherited the mantle of party ideologist and began to assume a higher public profile in anticipation of a post-Brezhnev power struggle. When Andrei Kirilenko, the Central Committee's administrative secretary, became ill, Chernenko took greater control over running the everyday affairs of the party and soon became a prime contender for the position of general secretary.

When Brezhnev died on 10 November 1982, the choice was between Andropov and Chernenko, and the Politburo voted to elect Yuri Andropov to succeed him. By not choosing Chernenko the political leadership signaled that it wanted to end the economic and political stagnation that marked Brezhnev's last years. Chernenko, unimpressive in both style and substance, was viewed as too close to Brezhnev and had little weight beyond his relationship to the former general secretary. He had never held a managerial position running a state enterprise or government agency, and he had not been a party first secretary in any region of the Soviet Union; instead, his career had been spent largely specializing in propaganda and agitation, functions of relatively low prestige in the party.

The older members, most notably Andrei Gromyko and Defense Minister Dmitri Ustinov, appreciated Andropov's background in foreign affairs and reputation as a strong disciplinarian. The younger members, like Mikhail Gorbachev, were especially impatient for change within the Soviet Union and counted on Andropov, who had a reputation as the most reform-minded member of the Politburo, to provide that change.

Andropov's tenure was brief, only fifteen months. He began a campaign against sloth, corruption, and inefficiency and attempted some small reforms of the economy, but chronic illness intervened before he had a chance to consolidate his power and implement stronger reforms. When Andropov became seriously ill around mid 1983, Chernenko increasingly took over his duties.

General Secretary

On 9 February 1984 Andropov died, and Chernenko finally had his turn as general secretary. That he was picked to succeed Andropov can only be attributed to the relative youth and inexperience in party affairs of his potential rivals, Grigori Romanov and Mikhail Gorbachev. Had Andropov lived a few years longer one of these two would more than likely have replaced him. As it was, Chernenko's selection was seen as a temporary expedient: a cautious decision by the Politburo traditionalists which revealed their fear of unexpected risk.

Domestic Affairs

Chernenko's style of leadership essentially reflected the lack of enthusiasm that had attended his selection. He was conservative in domestic affairs, continuing to mouth his predecessor's exhortations against inertia and corruption, but without Andropov's vigor. He promised to continue with Andropov's economic experimentation, but it was soon apparent that Chernenko lacked both the intellect and the conviction to take bolder steps to reform the Soviet system. Shevchenko recounts that Chernenko was "so dull a public figure" that the people did not even make jokes or tell anecdotes about him, an honor usually accorded Soviet politicians.'

Foreign Affairs

In foreign policy Chernenko echoed Brezhnev's support for détente, but his lack of experience forced him to rely largely on Gromyko and Ustinov for advice on foreign and military matters. Their influence on Soviet policy, not coincidentally, reached its highest level under Chernenko and must have played a role in the particularly harsh Soviet line taken against the United States in 1984. The Soviet media attacked the United States with an intensity not seen since the Stalin era. That summer the Soviet Union boycotted the Olympic games in Los Angeles to retaliate for the American boycott of the 1980 Moscow games, ordered by President Jimmy Carter to protest the 1979 invasion of Afghanistan.

Chernenko did preside over some small successes in foreign affairs. In December 1984 the Soviet Union and China held talks that concluded with a trade pact, while ignoring the long-standing political differences between the two countries. And in January 1985 the stalemate with the United States over arms-control discussions appeared to be broken when U.S. secretary of state George Shultz met Gromyko in Moscow to schedule new talks to begin that March.

Chernenko, however, would hold the top position in the Kremlin for only thirteen months. In his last six months in office his health began to fail, and his control over Soviet affairs, tenuous to begin with, showed signs of slipping. Mikhail Gorbachev, who would succeed him, began to preside over meetings of the Politburo even when Chernenko was present. After the announcement of Chernenko's death on 10 March 1985, it took the Politburo four and a half hours to elect Gorbachev and begin a new era in Soviet politics.

Books by Chernenko

Human Rights in Soviet Society (New York: International Publishers, 1981);

Selected Speeches and Writings (Oxford: Pergamon Press, 1982);

Soviet-U.S. Relations (New York: Praeger, 1984);

Soviet Democracy (New York: Vantage Press, 1987).

Books about Chernenko

Seweryn Bialer, *The Soviet Paradox: External Expansion, Internal Decline* (New York: Knopf, 1986);

Vladimir Solovyov and Elena Klepikova, *Behind the High Kremlin Walls* (New York: Dodd, Mead, 1986);

Ilya Zemstov, *Chernenko, the Last Bolshevik: The Soviet Union on the Eve of Perestroika* (New Brunswick: Transaction Books, 1989).

General References

Arnold Beichman and Mikhail S. Bernstam, *Andropov, New Challenge to the West: A Political Biography* (New York: Stein & Day, 1983);

Zhores A. Medvedev, *Andropov* (New York: Penguin Books, 1984);

John W. Parker, *Kremlin in Transition* (Boston: Unwin Hyman, 1991);

Jonathan Steele, *Andropov in Power: From Komsomol to Kremlin* (Garden City, N.Y.: Anchor/Doubleday, 1984);

Mark Zlotnik, "Chernenko Succeeds," *Problems of Communism*, 33 (March–April 1984).

– M. B.

SEE ALSO THESE RELATED ENTRIES

Yuri Andropov, 2; Leonid Brezhnev, 2; Mikhail Gorbachev, 2.

Vulko Chervenkov

Prime Minister of Bulgaria, 1949–1956

General Secretary, Bulgarian Communist Party, 1949–1954

Born Zlatitsa, Bulgaria, 24 August 1900
Died Sofia, Bulgaria, 21 October 1980

Vulko Chervenkov, Bulgarian communist leader, was born to a military family. He joined the communist Bulgarian Workers party in 1919, and from 1920 to 1925 he was a member of the Central Committee of the Communist Youth League. Chervenkov took part in the unsuccessful communist uprising of 1923 in Bulgaria and was forced to flee to Moscow in 1925.

Early Communist Training

The 1917 communist revolution in Russia inspired several other communist takeovers during the early 1920s in Hungary, Bavaria, and Bulgaria, but local Bolsheviks were unable to establish viable regimes there. The Bulgarian authorities outlawed communists and imposed a more authoritarian regime to forestall further coup attempts. During the next decade, Chervenkov received political and ideological training in Moscow and held various positions in the Moscow-directed Communist International (Comintern). He also became closely associated with Soviet leader Joseph Stalin. In 1941 he was appointed director of the Khristo Botev radio station. It broadcast Soviet propaganda into Bulgaria during World War II, when Sofia formed an alliance with the Axis powers in order to regain lost territories in the Balkans.

Postwar Activities

At the close of the war, when the Russians helped to install a communist regime in Bulgaria, Chervenkov was recalled to Bulgaria by Georgi Dimitrov, the country's leading communist activist and Chervenkov's brother-in-law. Recognized as a staunch Stalinist, Chervenkov was elected a member of the Central Committee of the Bulgarian Communist party (BCP).

General Secretary and Prime Minister

After Dimitrov's death in July 1949, Chervenkov became general secretary of the BCP and the country's prime minister. He proceeded to tighten party control in all areas of public life in imitation of the Soviet system and eliminated all remaining vestiges of "national deviationism," in which local officials had differed with Moscow on the tempo of communization. He built up a cult of personality based on Stalin's pattern and became known as Bulgaria's "little Stalin." During Chervenkov's six-year rule, thousands of BCP members were expelled or demoted, and Stalin's economic model was imposed on Bulgaria. This included full-scale nationalization, the promotion of heavy industry, and comprehensive collectivization of the peasantry to root out all vestiges of capitalism and small-scale production.

The Death of Stalin

Chervenkov suffered a serious blow to his power base when Stalin died in March 1953, and Chervenkov's closest supporters were purged from the Soviet party. As in other East European states, local communists benefited from the post-Stalin thaw in Moscow and used the growing uncertainty in Soviet policy to oust their "Muscovite" factional rivals. Chervenkov was replaced as general secretary of the BCP in March 1954. Soviet leader Nikita S. Khrushchev denounced Stalin in 1956, and in April of that year Chervenkov resigned from the premiership. But he remained in the government for the next five years, serving as one of the deputy premiers. He also retained his membership in the BCP Politburo. This was a clear signal that de-Stalinization in Bulgaria had definite limits and that the hard-line BCP faction retained much of its influence. As the minister of education and culture in 1957, Chervenkov helped to silence those intellectuals who were pressing for greater political democratization. But during the late 1950s and early 1960s, the police terror was somewhat relaxed, and pressures on collective farmers were partially loosened.

With the rise to power of Todor Zhivkov, the Chervenkov faction was gradually discredited and removed from all positions of power. In November 1962 Chervenkov himself was expelled from the BCP Politburo and the Central Committee, and removed from the deputy premiership. He was subjected to extensive criticism by the new leadership, who sought to find scapegoats for the Stalinist terror. Chervenkov went into a long retirement and died in the Bulgarian capital, Sofia, on 21 October 1980.

General References

John D. Bell, *The Bulgarian Communist Party from Blagoev to Zhivkov* (Stanford, Cal.: Hoover Institution Press, 1986);

J. F. Brown, *Bulgaria Under Communist Rule* (New York: Praeger, 1970);

J. F. Brown, *Eastern Europe and Communist Rule* (Durham: Duke University Press, 1988);

Christopher D. Jones, *Soviet Influence in Eastern Europe: Political Autonomy and the Warsaw Pact* (New York: Praeger, 1981);

Nissan Oren, *Bulgarian Communism: The Road to Power, 1933–1944* (New York: Columbia University Press, 1971);

Joseph Rothchild, *Return to Diversity: A Political History of East Central Europe since World War II* (New York: Oxford University Press, 1989);

Sarah M. Terry, ed., *Soviet Policy in Eastern Europe* (New Haven: Yale University Press, 1984);

Adam Ulam, *Expansion and Coexistence* (New York: Praeger, 1968).

–J. B. and A. B.

SEE ALSO THESE RELATED ENTRIES

Comintern, 3; Georgi Dimitrov, 2; Joseph Stalin, 2; Todor Zhivkov, 2.

Chiang Kai-shek

President of the Republic of China, 1926–1975
Born Zhejiang Province, China, 31 October 1887
Died Taipei, Taiwan, 5 April 1975

Chiang Kai-shek, the "man who lost China," was the president of the Republic of China. He appeared at many times on the verge of uniting the country but failed because of bad luck, miscalculation, and outright greed. Chiang's efforts cost millions of dollars in U.S. aid, but American politicians felt that the real failure lay in the lost opportunity to create a strong, united China to fill the power vacuum that existed in East Asia following Japan's defeat in World War II. The United States envisioned China as the fourth pillar of the United Nations (UN) structure that would keep Asia at peace. The much glorified images Americans had of Chiang during World War II helped nurture this naive optimism. Chiang was perceived to be a benevolent Christian and a brave commander fighting for democracy. He and his American-educated wife lived a life of glamour. But many of these images were illusory. Beneath Chiang's surface was a cunning, driven man whose fearlessness was matched only by his obstinacy. A corrupt government and the communists' will to prevail eventually defeated him, but, even after fleeing to Taiwan in 1949, he did not give up hope for regaining control of the mainland. His refusal to surrender two strategic islands off China's coast drew the United States into two crises, in 1954–1955 and 1958, which strongly tested America's strategy of containment.

Chiang's father was a salt merchant in Qikou village; his mother was an educated woman from a rich farming family. As a child Chiang already gave signs of his future career when he reveled in playing war games with the neighborhood children. Young Chiang would appoint himself commanding general and give orders to his playmates.

Chiang was given a tutor at age five and was taught in the austere Confucian mode. His personality showed the effects of this teaching. He was disciplined and respectful of his elders. Chiang was also taciturn and passionless. Legend holds that only on three occasions did Chiang ever show emotion in public – when his mother died, when the head of his secret police died, and when he was kidnapped by his own forces in 1936.

In 1901, at the age of fourteen, Chiang's parents arranged a marriage for him. He wed seventeen-year-old Mao Fumei, the first of two wives in his early years. He and Fumei had one child, Chiang Ching-kuo, in 1908.

Gale International Portrait Gallery

Chiang Kai-shek

Chiang's teenage years coincided with the final bitter years of the Manchu dynasty. Like many other Chinese youths of the time, Chiang was angered by the poverty and weakness of his country and sought ways to change it. When he was seventeen Chiang decided to become a revolutionary and, in a gesture which showed his resolve, lopped off his queue – the long pigtail which symbolized compliance to the dynasty.

Chiang received his military education at the Chinese Baoding Academy (1906) and at the Preparatory Academy in Tokyo, Japan (1907–1913). In 1908 he was introduced to Dr. Sun Yat-sen. Sun was American-educated and had long been trying to foment revolution in China. Energetic and always optimistic, Sun launched seven failed attempts at revolution while Chiang was in Japan. Chiang studied in Tokyo until 1913, with a brief break in 1911–1912 when he came back to China to fight in the revolution that toppled the dynasty. In 1913 he returned to China, where Sun was masterminding another revolution to overthrow China's new leader Yüan Shih-k'ai. Yüan had become president of China in 1912 by vowing to support the 1911 revolution with his powerful troops in exchange for the new position. After ascending, however, he dissolved all political parties and ruled as a military dictator until his death in 1916.

KMT

From 1913 to 1925 Chiang was under the Sun Yat-sen–led wing of the Kuomintang (KMT). The KMT, or Nationalist party, was created in 1912 out of a group of political parties which arose during the 1911 revolution. It was generally ineffective as a political body until Sun reorganized it in 1922. As a division commander Chiang's role in the KMT was strictly military. From his base in Fujian province Chiang helped Sun plan his revolution attempts, which, after 1916, were directed at the warlords. These were the military strongmen who had carved China into many sections and, with few exceptions, were oppressively ruling each as an independent kingdom.

During these years Chiang developed a reputation for being impulsive and temperamental in private. On several occasions, when Sun did not heed his advice, Chiang sulked and threatened retirement. Once, in the fall of 1920, Chiang was so fed up he retired to his home in Zhejiang. Three months later, after weeks of Sun's pleading letters, Chiang returned, apologizing for his temper. Sun, known for his extraordinary capacity for forgiveness, mused, "you are extremely self-willed to an almost incorrigible extent."

In January 1923, after failed attempts to get military and financial aid from the West, Sun allied the KMT with the Soviet Union. In August, Sun named Chiang, who was then his chief of staff at the KMT base at Canton, to head a group being sent to Moscow to study military organization and obtain arms. Chiang was suspicious of the communists, and after returning to China he warned Sun about the Soviets' "sinister designs." As was often the case, Sun did not listen to him. The Comintern (Communist International) persuaded Sun to allow members of the nascent Chinese Communist party (CCP) to join the KMT.

In January 1924 the KMT decided to create a military academy to train officers for the next revolution. Chiang was appointed to head it, but, because of frustration over the communists, he retired. Five months later Sun officially opened the Whampoa Academy and appointed a penitent Chiang Kai-shek its commandant.

The Whampoa Academy was the finest institution of its kind. Chiang's staff included many who would become officers in both the nationalist and communist armies. Chiang's abilities as leader of the National Revolution Army (NRA) gave him prestige in the KMT. Although he lacked Sun's personal magnetism, Chiang nevertheless enjoyed the admiration of his soldiers, who responded favorably to his dignified rectitude.

Sun's death in March 1925 was followed by a one-year crisis of succession. Chiang, a military man and considered too young at the age of thirty-seven, was at first not a front-runner in the contest to fill the vacant position as head of the KMT. But in March 1926 he made his move to party chairman by appealing to the anticommunist faction which sought to curtail growing communist strength in the party. Chiang would dominate Chinese politics for the next twenty-three years.

The Northern Expedition

From July 1926 to June 1928 Chiang led his NRA on the Northern Expedition. The objective of the expedition was ambitious – to drive north and defeat the warlord armies, unifying China under KMT rule. His victories were swift and convincing. When he left Canton, the NRA had 100,000 troops; in November 1926 it had 264,000. The NRA was immediately popular with the masses, but the increase in the number of troops had as much to do with warlords who had decided to join Chiang instead of fighting him. Chiang ended the expedition in June 1928 with 700,000 men in control of virtually all the large cities. Pockets of warlord-resistance remained, but Chiang was clearly the leader of China from his new base in Nanking.

Two especially significant events occurred on the Northern Expedition. On 12 April 1927 Chiang used his troops to slaughter about three hundred communist leaders in the Shanghai Working-Class Headquarters, in effect destroying the communists' largest base and officially ending the period of KMT-CCP collaboration. Chiang had temporarily removed the "cancer" of communism.

On 1 December 1927 Chiang married his third wife, Soong Mei-ling. Madame Chiang, as she was called, was a public-relations dream. She came from a wealthy Christian family that was descended from the Sung dynasty. She was pretty, gracious, and charming, and American-educated – a graduate of Wellesley who spoke perfect English. At first, Mei-ling's mother opposed the marriage. Her eldest daughter had married Sun Yat-sen, who was Christian, English-speaking, and exuberant. Chiang began to study the Bible in earnest and Mei-ling's mother relented. Mei-ling played an important role in Chiang's life. She was his confidante and promoter.

From 1928 to 1937 Chiang adopted Germany as a social and political model to emulate. He employed German advisers and even had his own secret gendarmes. His major program, the New Life Movement, was launched in 1934 to instill Confucian and Christian ideals in the Chinese populace. In a tone resembling that of the fascist movements in Europe, he stated that his goals were to "thoroughly militarize the lives of the citizens ... so they will at any time sacrifice for the nation."

The "Xian Incident"

In the mid 1930s, while much of the country, including some of his own men, urged him to fight the Japanese, who had taken over Manchuria, Chiang opted to continue his campaign to rout out the communists. On the morning of 12 December 1936, in what came to be known as the "Xian Incident," a bizarre contretemps unfolded which altered Chiang's fortunes. He was kidnapped by his own forces in the city of Xian. Chiang had traveled to Xian to force a young marshal, Zhang Xueliang, to begin another anticommunist "extermination campaign." Zhang, who believed that engaging the Japanese was more prudent, ordered his men to seize Chiang. Zhang offered Chiang a plan to unite the KMT and CCP in an all-out war against Japan. Chiang challenged Zhang to kill him instead. The standoff continued for the next two weeks while the nation held its breath. Madame Chiang and her brother, Premier Soong Tzuwen, flew into Xian, as did Zhou Enlai, who represented the communists (who, by most accounts, were not involved in the kidnapping). Zhou, the master of diplomacy, argued successfully for Chiang's release. The communists had scored a victory. They were able to demonstrate that they were sincere in their desire for peaceful relations with the KMT. Chiang agreed to a "united front" war against Japan.

The war against Japan (1937–1945) unraveled Chiang's hold on China. The Japanese fighting machine swept through the coastal cities. Although the communists assumed a share of the battles, they used the invasion to their political advantage and infiltrated urban areas overrun by the Japanese. Chiang's forces adopted a strategy of "trading space for time," a calculated retreat which moved them away from their coastal stronghold. When the communists emerged from the war, they clearly had broadened their base of support.

U.S. Support

The U.S. government began to support Chiang in the late 1930s, providing weapons, advisers, and money. Americans had an infatuation with the Chiangs, thanks in large part to the influence of Henry Luce, a staunch Chiang supporter. *Time* magazine, published by Luce, named them Man and Wife of the Year in 1937. In 1942–1943 Madame Chiang mesmerized Americans during a seven-month visit to the United States, raising millions for her cause.

After the start of the Pacific war, Chiang asked for and received a half-billion dollars, only later to ask for one

billion more. The American public did not know of the staggering corruption of the Chiang government. Most notorious was Chiang's brother-in-law, Soong Tsu-wen, the premier. The Harvard graduate diverted much of the American aid into officials' pockets. Soong's own slice of the aid helped to make him one of the world's richest men.

The U.S. government agonized over China. It would not support the communists, who were thought to be puppets of the Soviets, but it found Chiang's government repugnant. The U.S. Foreign Service estimated that if a free election were held, 80 percent of Chinese would vote against Chiang. It recommended to discontinue aid. But the United States continued to support Chiang, guided by the philosophy "the enemy of my enemy is my friend."

The United States tried to mediate between Chiang's government and the communists. In August 1945 U.S. ambassador Patrick Hurley was sent as a mediator, and, when he failed, General George C. Marshall tried to bridge the differences in December 1945. He, too, failed, and Chiang's forces engaged the communists in April 1946. In the early fighting the nationalists' numerical advantage and superior weaponry won them many battles. But by winter 1947 the superior tactical skill exhibited by the communist commanders began to take its toll on the nationalist forces. Chiang's forces lost the war in 1948, despite their two-to-one troop advantage. The communists inaugurated their leaders in October 1949, and Chiang – after futile attempts to continue the fight in several cities – escaped to Taiwan in December, taking with him more than a million followers.

Mainly because of the political pressure applied by anticommunist groups, such as the China Lobby, the United States continued to recognize Chiang's government in Taiwan, an island ninety miles off China's eastern coast.

The Quemoy and Matsu Crises

On 3 September 1954 a test of wills between the People's Republic of China (PRC) and the United States began with the shelling of the Quemoy islands by PRC forces. Quemoy and Matsu were strategic islands just off the mainland. The islands were launching points for assaults against the mainland by Chiang's troops. The United States feared that if the PRC occupied the islands an attack on Taiwan would be imminent. In December 1954 the United States signed the Mutual Defense Treaty with Taiwan which assured Chiang that the United States would defend the island and the nearby Pescadores if they were attacked. The PRC riposte was to invade the Quemoy islands in January 1955. President Dwight D. Eisenhower continued the brinkmanship by persuading Chiang to evacuate his ten thousand troops from the islands in exchange for a joint resolution signed on 28 January 1955. The resolution gave Eisenhower the authority to use force, if necessary, to defend Taiwan. U.S. secretary of state John Foster Dulles then heightened tensions with thinly veiled threats of nuclear attacks against China. The PRC gradually ceased shelling in the summer of 1955.

Starting on 23 August 1958 a similar crisis occurred when the PRC shelled and blockaded Quemoy in response to the commando raids Chiang's air force had been launching from the island. The United States reacted to the daily shelling by suggesting that the 1955 joint resolution could be interpreted to include Quemoy and Matsu under the U.S. umbrella. Dulles was intentionally vague in his statements so as not to encourage Chiang to attack the mainland in the belief that he had U.S. protection. As the shelling and blockade became more severe, the United States again used veiled threats of nuclear attack against China. In October tensions relaxed when the PRC made a peculiar move by announcing it would now shell every other day, which prompted Eisenhower to say, "I wondered if we were in a Gilbert and Sullivan war."

The crises tested the American commitment to the strategy of containment. With accusations concerning the "loss of China" still ringing in their ears, U.S. policymakers were determined not to allow communism to expand any further in Asia. The United States had already fought a war in Korea. Now, it threatened the PRC with another.

The issue of protecting Quemoy and Matsu became controversial. Some questioned U.S. support for Chiang's impotent government in Taiwan. Many more questioned the logic of going to war over two small islands off the coast of China and the liberal use of brinkmanship within the policy of massive retaliation.

The Development of Taiwan

During the next twenty years Chiang built a thriving economy in Taiwan with a combination of political order and economic freedom. The United States assisted Chiang with capital and military hardware, which helped him secure the country and produce double-digit growth rates. Chiang stressed the importance of education, which helped turn Taiwan into a technologically developed country. Along with Hong Kong, South Korea, and Singapore, Taiwan became known as one of the "four little dragons," the newly industrialized economies in Asia that were prospering in the 1970s and 1980s.

Taiwan's relationship with other countries remained mainly positive, as shown by the maintenance of its UN membership until October 1971. This was due to Taiwan's continual recognition by the United States and the excellent relations it enjoyed with the emerging African nations, who voted for Taiwan's membership to the UN in return for substantial technological assistance.

Chiang remained president of the Republic of China until his death in Taipei on 5 April 1975. He was unable to fulfill his dream of regaining the mainland.

Books about Chiang Kai-shek

Brian Crozier, *The Man Who Lost China* (New York: Scribner's, 1976);

Robert Payne, *Chiang Kai-shek* (New York: Weybright and Talley, 1969);

Sterling Seagrave, *The Soong Dynasty* (New York: Harper & Row, 1985).

– K. W. M.

SEE ALSO THESE RELATED ENTRIES
John Foster Dulles, 1; Mao Zedong, 2; Zhou Enlai, 2.

Deng Xiaoping

Leader of the People's Republic of China

Born Xiexing, Sichuan Province, China, 22 August 1904
Died Beijing, PR of China, 19 February 1997

Deng Xiaoping is the principal architect of post-Mao China. The fiery Sichuanese, whose pragmatic politics alienated party ideologues in the 1960s and 1970s, rose from the ashes of the Cultural Revolution to guide the People's Republic of China (PRC) into an era of reform in the 1980s. Deng's style of politics is encapsulated in his famous utterance, "It doesn't matter if a cat is black or white, as long as it catches mice." His broad reform program transformed the PRC, which had been politically and economically isolated under Mao Zedong, into an international player.

His career touched every aspect of the history of the Chinese Communist party (CCP). His most notable participation in international politics came about in the 1960s, when he played a prominent role in the Sino-Soviet breakup. Deng's political reputation, however, has mostly been formed by his near miraculous ability to survive the CCP's often treacherous political waters. He was stripped of power three times in his career, only to be reincarnated with powers even greater than he had had before.

Deng Xiaoping was born Deng Xixian in Xiexing village, located about 150 miles north of the Yangtze River in Sichuan province. Deng's father, Deng Wenming, was a wealthy landowner. His mother was Wenming's first of three concubines. Wenming married her after his first wife was found to be barren.

Deng lived a comfortable, even privileged, childhood. At the age of sixteen, he followed the route of many young, educated Chinese by joining the work-study movement. The purpose of the movement was to allow Chinese to travel overseas to learn in Western institutions. Tuition and board were paid from work salaries. Deng chose to study in France and left China on 11 September 1920 aboard a steamer.

While living in and around Paris, Deng took jobs as an unskilled laborer to pay the food-and-study bills, which always seemed to exceed his earnings. Two years into his stay Deng, having grown disenchanted with his pay and working conditions at a shoe factory, displayed his legendary fire by staging a solo strike. He was dismissed for refusing to work.

While in Paris Deng became active in the Communist party. In 1922 he joined the Communist Youth

Deng Xiaoping

League, the CCP preparatory organization, and soon made a reputation for himself as a skilled organizer and leader. One year later, at the age of nineteen, Deng was elected to its leadership. The league's secretary was future premier Zhou Enlai, who remained Deng's friend throughout his career.

Deng and Zhou belonged to the editorial board of the communist journal *Red Light*, where they disseminated their opinions about the future direction of the Kuomintang party (KMT). The KMT, or Nationalist party, was committed to revolution in order to reunify China. At this time the KMT included the communists among its ranks.

Deng held the second highest position of authority in the CCP in Europe, when on 27 January 1926 he left Paris and his job at Renault to go to school in the Soviet

Union. In Moscow Deng spent eight months at the Sun Yat-sen University of the Working Chinese before returning to China to fight in the Northern Expedition, launched by KMT leader Chiang Kai-shek in July 1926. The purpose of the expedition was to defeat the warlords, the military strongmen dominating China. Deng joined the expedition in the city of Xian as a political commissar.

Chiang, a man who had begrudgingly accepted communist participation in the KMT, declared war on the communists in April 1927. Deng was relieved of his duties and forced to go underground in Shanghai.

In the fall of 1929 the CCP sent Deng from the underground to the southern province of Guangxi to lead an uprising. Deng was named a political commissar in charge of organizing and planning a military offensive to establish a communist base in the south. In the summer of 1930 Deng led a division of twenty thousand local soldiers in a doomed mission. In a succession of battles in Guangxi and Guangdong provinces, his troops were routed by the superior KMT forces. Fourteen thousand men were killed and the remaining six thousand chased from the area. Deng's first party assignment was a humiliating failure.

Deng recovered from the demoralizing losses in Guangxi. In the summer of 1932 he was married (his first wife, Zhang Qianyuan, having died in 1926 following a miscarriage) to a beautiful and ambitious revolutionary, Jin Weiying. He was also given the position of first party secretary of Jiangxi Province – the CCP's base province – where his role was to manage party activity.

The CCP was controlled at this time by the Bolsheviks, those Chinese who had learned communism in Moscow schools. A competing faction within the party was led by Mao Zedong, who, in disagreement with the Bolsheviks, advocated leniency toward middle-class farmers when confiscating property for land reform. In April 1933 Deng publicly declared himself in favor of Mao's policies, and the Bolsheviks retaliated. A party member named Luo Man blasted Deng in a communist newspaper, demanding a "ruthless struggle" against him. Deng was stripped of his position and forced to make a self-criticism. He was jailed when his response to the charges was considered by the Bolsheviks to be insufficiently repentant. Further insult was added when his wife Weiying divorced him to marry his accuser Lo Man. Deng, however, showed his resilience by climbing back to his previous position in about three months.

The Long March
In October 1934 Chiang Kai-shek's forces had a stranglehold on Jiangxi Province. In what was called the Fifth Extermination Campaign, the KMT was preparing to deal the final blow to the communist base, when the CCP leaders decided to retreat. On 16 October 1934, 85,859

Communists abandoned their Jiangxi base and began the Long March, a calculated retreat over an eighty-five-hundred-mile horseshoe-shaped escape route. Thousands died from exposure, disease, starvation, and KMT gunfire. When, after 378 days, they completed the journey in Shanxi Province in central China, only nine thousand had survived. Deng began the march in the second rank as the editor for the army newspaper. One year later he was in the Central Committee secretariat, overseeing the civilian party machine.

Deng befriended Mao Zedong on the Long March. An odd-looking pair, Mao towered over the four-foot eleven-inch Deng. Mao enjoyed Deng's sardonic humor and respected his mettle. He took Deng into his confidence. This was the beginning of a complex forty-two-year relationship which alternated between close and adversarial.

War with Japan
From 1937 to 1945 the KMT and CCP fought on the same side against the Japanese. In January 1938 Deng was named political commissar, in charge of political training, of the 129th Division. The 129th was one of three communist divisions in the KMT-CCP "united front" army. The commander was the master strategist Liu Bocheng, the "one-eyed dragon." Together, they formed the leadership of the "Liu-Deng army," the communists' best unit. From their base in southern Hubei province, Liu and Deng developed their "pinprick" strategy. The 129th separated into guerrilla groups that conducted surprise attacks against Japanese enclaves. Liu and Deng's six-thousand-man division killed or wounded ten thousand Japanese between January and September 1938. With each victory the Liu-Deng army increasingly added to its image of invincibility.

Deng took a ten-day vacation in August 1939 to marry his third wife, Pu Zhuolin. She was a revolutionary from the southern province of Yunan, where her father was a renowned businessman known as the "ham king of Yunan." Deng and Zhuolin had five children.

Chinese Civil War
Even before the Chinese civil war began in April 1946, Chiang Kai-shek wanted to attack the Liu-Deng army. In September 1945 he ordered his Eighth Route Army to surprise the 129th Division in Shanxi Province. Liu and Deng devised a "gunnysack" guerrilla strategy to lure the KMT forces into a trap and then surround them with waves of communist soldiers. The scheme worked to perfection as thirty-five-thousand KMT troops were killed or wounded.

The fighting ceased in October 1949. Deng had been a substantial contributor to one of the greatest upsets in modern military history. The nationalists had outnumbered the communists over three to one and possessed superior weapons. But the communists had superior commanders and morale.

Agrarian Reforms

Deng's first three years after the civil war were spent instituting agrarian reform in Yunan, Guizhou, and Sichuan provinces in southwest China. His tasks included confiscating land, animals, and equipment for equal distribution. He performed well and was called to Beijing in summer 1952 to serve as deputy premier, assisting in the management of China's state apparatus. Premier Zhou Enlai was his superior.

In the mid 1950s Deng solidified his spot among the party's leaders. In September 1956 Deng entered the Standing Committee of the Politburo, making him one of the seven most powerful decision makers in the CCP, alongside the likes of Chairman Mao and Premier Zhou. He also was named general secretary of the 197-member Central Committee, presiding over party congresses.

In the 1950s Deng mainly dealt with domestic affairs. More-experienced leaders – such as Mao, Zhou, and PRC president Liu Shaoqi – controlled foreign relations. In 1958 Deng's responsibilities were broadened following Mao's resignation from active party duties. Mao's self-imposed abdication was due in large part to the failure of his Great Leap Forward (GLF) policy in 1957. The program sought to propel the Chinese directly into communism by introducing larger work units known as communes. The GLF caused famine and widespread hardship in China. Mao handed Deng and Liu dual leadership.

Sino-Soviet Split

Sino-Soviet relations were already deteriorating by the end of the Chinese civil war. Although Mao and the other Chinese leaders continued to extol the greatness of Stalin and the Soviet Union, they were discontent with and mistrustful of Soviet policy concerning China: Stalin had supported Chiang Kai-shek during World War II because he needed the Chinese to occupy the Japanese while he fought the Germans.

After Stalin's death in 1953 and Nikita Khrushchev's rise to power in the Soviet Union, tension between the two countries became increasingly evident. Deng's first trip to Moscow was in February 1956 to attend the Twentieth Party Congress of the Communist Party of the Soviet Union. Deng was stunned as he heard Khrushchev trenchantly denounce Stalin's cult of personality. Upon reflection, however, Deng agreed that a cult of personality was not appropriate for China, either. Mao disagreed with him. He saw Khrushchev's attack as an attempt to succeed Stalin as the patriarch of the world communist movement, a role which Mao believed he himself would

be the best qualified to fill. Sino-Soviet relations entered a stage of mutual suspicion.

Outright belligerence erupted between the two countries in July 1960, when the Soviets withdrew 343 contracts and proposals, 257 scientific and technical projects (including aid for developing nuclear weapons), and 1,390 economic advisers. The Soviet action could not have come at a worse time for China, for millions of Chinese were dying of starvation due to the GLF calamity.

Deng and Liu Shaoqi went to Moscow in November 1960 to speak to Soviet leaders. If placating tensions was the motive, the CCP had sent the wrong man in Deng. Living up to his nickname, the "little cannon," Deng cited Khrushchev's praise for American president Dwight D. Eisenhower as "unforgiveable." He also chastised the Soviets for supporting India, a capitalist country, in its border dispute with China. After having voiced myriad complaints about Soviet "revisionist" and "opportunist" communism, Deng returned to Beijing hailed by the Chinese as the great "anti-revisionist." At the Twenty-Second Soviet Party Congress in October 1961, Khrushchev indirectly struck back at Deng in a speech directed at CCP representative Zhou, proclaiming "to those who wish to know what communism is . . . Read our party program." Zhou walked out in protest.

The public bickering between the two countries ceased until the Cuban Missile Crisis in the fall of 1962. The CCP relentlessly criticized Khrushchev for his role in the crisis, characterizing his delivery of missiles to Cuba as Soviet adventurism and faulting him for having capitulated to the West when he later withdrew the missiles. Then, in October and November, the Sino-Indian border conflict began. The Chinese resented the Soviets for adopting a policy of neutrality during the conflict, even though India was not a communist country.

In July 1963 Deng was sent to Moscow as head of a delegation to discuss the direction of the communist world. The delegation was kept waiting for hours as their plane circled the Moscow airport. Meanwhile, the Soviets entertained British and American delegations, who were in Moscow for separate talks. When the talks began, Deng was condescending toward Soviet ideologist Mikhail Suslov and continually enraged the Soviets with his obstinacy. The atmosphere of the talks was chaotic. As the Deng-Suslov meeting was taking place, other Soviet leaders were having talks with U.S. representative William Averell Harriman and British representative Quintin Hogg, Lord Hailsham, in regard to a nuclear-test ban. In addition to both sets of talks, anti-Chinese demonstrations occupied Red Square with Khrushchev leading a rally. The rallies show the great enmity between the two countries at that time. The talks ended on 20 July without much agreement, and the two parties formally ended their relations in 1966.

The Sino-Soviet breakup grew out of both personality and doctrinal conflicts. The Chinese saw their brand of communism as fitting the unique balance of Chinese industrial and agricultural sectors. The CCP felt that the Soviets had no right to dictate communist policies to China.

The breakup cast doubt on the prevailing notion of a "monolithic" communist movement directed by Moscow. Although Sino-American relations did not improve until the early 1970s, the breakup enabled American policymakers to think in terms of a U.S.-Soviet-China strategic triangle. By forming an alliance with the Chinese, the United States would be befriending a Soviet enemy. It was an enemy which shared a long border with the Soviets and possessed military strength.

Deng's Rise and Fall

From late 1959 through 1962, nineteen million Chinese died from either overexertion or malnutrition as a result of the GLF. In the early 1960s Deng and Liu set Chinese agriculture on a more pragmatic course, with good results.

Mao watched Deng and Liu with an envious eye. Aided by Jiang Qing, his wife, and Politburo member Lin Biao, Mao in 1965 began to orchestrate a scheme to remove Deng and Liu by launching a purge of the bureaucratic element within the CCP. They urged adolescent revolutionaries, called Red Guards, to find and eliminate "bourgeois liberals." The Cultural Revolution had begun.

Deng was ousted in March 1967 and was placed under house arrest shortly thereafter. On 5 August 1967 the Red Guards forced him to kneel and put his head to his knees so he could listen to shouted accusations of his bourgeois crimes. As the story goes, a defiant Deng turned off his hearing aid. In October 1969 Deng was relocated to the southern city of Nanchang with his wife and stepmother. He worked there in a tractor factory until 1973.

Deng's comeback began in April 1973. He was brought to Beijing to help a cancer-stricken Zhou with his state duties. He feverishly worked to set the government back on course after the years of turmoil. On 10 April 1974 Deng was given the honor of publicly presenting the Chinese foreign-policy program to the United Nations (UN) General Assembly in New York. He outlined the "three worlds": the two superpowers, the United States and the Soviet Union, "which exploited and oppressed the world"; countries such as Japan and France, which strove for independence from the superpowers; and China, Asia, Africa, and Latin America, which strug-

gled against imperialism. Deng could not resist singling out the Soviets when he said "in bullying others, the superpower which flaunts the label of socialism is especially vicious." His speech was well received in Beijing, and he returned to a hero's welcome.

Deng's ascent in Chinese politics was quick. By January 1975 he held leading positions in the party, state, and military apparatuses. His success, however, did not last long. Deng was purged for a third time, in April 1976, by party radicals. Backed by a wave of support from the Chinese populace, Deng was reinstated to his positions in July 1977. His popularity with the Chinese masses was such that when his reinstatement was broadcast the staccato clatter of firecrackers broke out from different parts of Beijing. Deng's return to power as a practitioner of moderate party politics symbolized the end of the Cultural Revolution.

By the end of 1978 Deng controlled the direction of the CCP, although Chairman Hua Guofeng was still titular leader. Deng's foreign policy can be divided into four domestically influenced periods. The first began during the initial months of his comeback and lasted until just prior to the Sino-U.S. normalization in December 1978. Deng was constrained in his ability to take risks due to his unstable position within the CCP. Having recently been rehabilitated, Deng stressed a reserved foreign policy to prevent any controversy leading to another purge. Enticements by the Carter administration were set aside until the domestic uncertainty was resolved.

Deng solidified his position at the CCP helm in 1978 after his blueprint for the next generation was accepted by party leaders. His theme was "seek truth from facts," which stressed a reliance on a mixture of pragmatic approaches to domestic and foreign matters rather than on the ideological fervor embraced by Maoist policy.

December 1978 saw Deng's most impressive foreign-policy achievement – the normalization of U.S.-Chinese relations. The Nixon administration made the first conciliatory gestures, but neither country could capitalize on the opportunity because of domestic pressures. Relations between the United States and China had improved in the 1970s to the extent that the Chinese no longer regarded the United States along with the Soviet Union as an international bully. The Soviets were clearly number one on China's enemies list. Deng used his newly acquired party mandate to initiate the formalities of normalization.

For the United States, normalization was long in coming. The recognition of Taiwan as China's government was a relic of the Cold War. By 1978 American perceptions of China had changed enough to facilitate a new relationship. The United States began the discussions in the spring of 1978, and in December that year it normalized relations with full diplomatic, military, and cultural exchanges.

Deng benefited from the new relationship. The United States provided insurance against the Soviets. The presence of Soviet troops on the Sino-Soviet border convinced Deng that the Soviets were expansionists, and Deng played the U.S. card to deter any Soviet adventurism. The United States also helped China's commercial interests. Deng's reform plans required the United States to jump-start China's economy with knowledge, technology, and capital.

Deng went to the United States in January 1979 to attract American business to China. The trip was a success. Deng was portrayed by the American press as a savior, single-handedly guiding China away from isolationism. Deng basked in the glow of his popularity. He was affable and accommodating, even sporting a cowboy hat at a Texas barbeque.

To lead his economic reform, Deng chose two CCP members from outside Beijing. Hu Yaobang, a CCP member respected for his work with communist youth, was installed as general secretary, and Zhao Ziyang, an innovative economic reformer from Sichuan province, was named premier. It is a testament to Deng's strength that his two reformist protégés could be brought to Beijing to manage the PRC.

In 1979 Deng ordered the military to attack Vietnam in order to "teach Vietnam a lesson" for its 1978 invasion of Cambodia, a country China supported. The Chinese army failed abysmally, fighting the Vietnamese army to a standstill at the Vietnamese border. Casualties were heavy on both sides, each losing about thirty thousand men. The war highlighted the deficiencies of the Chinese army, in which weapons and vehicles had not been modernized for years – in some cases not since the Korean War. It sparked a drive to rebuild China's military hardware.

Deng's zest for relations with the United States began to moderate in 1982, although Sino-U.S. business, military, and cultural relations steadily expanded. In that year Hu Yaobang introduced China's "independent foreign policy," which implied that Chinese policy was no longer to be influenced by the U.S.-Soviet relationship. The shift was a reaction to conservative criticism, most notably from Politburo member Li Xiannian. In early 1982 Li had encouraged more-moderate relations with the Soviets and a distancing from the United States. Despite normalization, Deng continued to assert that China would always be in the Third World and would never align itself with a superpower. Furthermore, the United States continued to sell weapons to Taiwan, which was seen as a breach of good faith by Deng.

Relations with both the United States and the Soviet Union did not change noticeably until the last half of the 1980s. Throughout the decade, the Chinese had been selling high quantities of weapons to the Middle East in order to help the country modernize its own defense systems. The PRC sold weapons to Saudi Arabia, Egypt, and Syria, but the largest markets by far were Iran and Iraq, who had been fighting a war since 1980. Seventy percent of all of the PRC weapons exports, including missiles, went to these two countries. The United States became upset when Chinese-made missiles were directed at U.S. ships protecting Kuwaiti oil tankers in the Persian Gulf in the fall of 1986. After a U.S. reproach the Chinese reluctantly stopped selling missiles but not other weapons. The arms sales issue became a source of tension in Sino-U.S. relations.

The Sino-Soviet relationship was slow to develop during the Deng era. Deng had set three stipulations that had to be met before talks could begin: Soviet withdrawal from Afghanistan, Soviet withdrawal from the Sino-Soviet border, and Vietnamese withdrawal from Cambodia. The Soviets gave no hints they would meet any of the requirements in the 1980s, but in a span of a few months in 1988–1989 they met all three, opening a path for the historic meeting between Soviet president Mikhail Gorbachev and Deng in May 1989.

The fourth period of Deng's foreign policy began after the politically disastrous events on 3–4 June 1989 in Beijing's Tiananmen Square. In early May students demonstrating for democracy initiated a hunger strike, which rapidly turned into a protest by more than one million sympathizing Chinese. The occupation of Tiananmen Square became a global event due to its coverage by the Western press, who were in Beijing to document the Gorbachev-Deng summit. Chinese soldiers were ordered to clear the square. In the ensuing violence hundreds, perhaps thousands, perished.

China was universally condemned for human rights violations. Deng's foreign policy was in tatters. His relationship with the United States was especially troubled. The United States suspended military and high-technology sales and extended the visas of visiting Chinese students. The CCP launched a defensive campaign blaming the United States for meddling in China's internal affairs. Even though President George Bush kept communication channels open, the Chinese refused to express regret.

Deng's government turned sharply inward after 4 June to its most isolated state since the Cultural Revolution.

Book about Deng
Uli Franz, *Deng Xiaoping* (San Diego: Harcourt Brace Jovanovich, 1988).

General Reference
King Chen, *China and the Three World's* (White Plains, N.Y.: Sharpe, 1979).

– K. W. M.

SEE ALSO THESE RELATED ENTRIES
Hu Yaobang, 2; Liu Shaoqi, 2; Mao Zedong, 2;

Ngo Dinh Diem

President of the Republic of Vietnam, 1954–1963
Born Hue, Vietnam, 3 January 1901
Died Saigon, South Vietnam, 3 November 1963

Ngo Dinh Diem was born in the capital city of Hue, in central Vietnam, into a Roman Catholic aristocratic family of mandarins linked to the imperial court. His father, Ngo Dinh Kha, was a counselor to Emperor Thanh Thai. After Diem received his secondary education in a French Catholic school, he attended the prestigious National Academy, the Quoc Hoc, founded by his father. In 1921 Diem graduated from the School of Law and Administration in Hanoi, a French institution for training native civil servants.

After serving in the imperial army, he was appointed governor of Phan-Thiet province in 1929, where he engaged in fighting the Communist Revolutionary Youth movement. In 1933 he was appointed the minister of the interior in the government of Emperor Bao Dai but resigned shortly thereafter in protest of French interference in Vietnam's domestic affairs that prevented him from introducing legislative reforms. Diem withdrew from national politics for the next ten years, even though he maintained contacts with other anti-French nationalists. Following the Japanese occupation of Indochina in 1942, Diem unsuccessfully attempted to persuade the Japanese to declare Vietnam independent from the French.

The Division of Vietnam

After defeating the Japanese, the Allied forces agreed at the 1945 Potsdam Conference to divide Vietnam temporarily along the 17th parallel, with China administrating to the North where the communist Vietminh were strongest, and Britain administrating to the South. In August 1945 the Vietminh, led by Ho Chi Minh, called for a general uprising and by the end of the month had taken over Hanoi, Saigon, and various other Vietnamese cities in the wake of the collapse of the French colonial administration. After establishing a provisional government in Hanoi, Ho Chi Minh declared Vietnamese independence and renamed the country the

Ngo Dinh Diem

Democratic Republic of Vietnam (DRV), on 2 September, but factional violence and French attempts to reimpose colonial rule continued. Franco-British cooperation allowed the French to recover control in Saigon and by late 1945 they had restored control over the British zone, apart from a few rural areas under guerrilla control.

While traveling to Hue in September 1945 to warn Bao Dai against collaborating with Ho Chi Minh, Diem was kidnapped by Vietminh agents and offered a position in Ho's provisional government. A devout Catholic who disliked communism as much as he disliked French colonialism, Diem refused to cooperate with the Vietminh, who had assassinated his brother Ngo Dinh Khoi during the August uprisings. Diem was released by the Vietminh six months later. In the meantime the French had retaken most of the provincial capitals and pushed the Vietminh forces out of central and northern Vietnam. In 1948 the French granted nominal independence to Vietnam as an "associated state" within the French Union, with Bao Dai as head of state. The arrangement was widely criticized by nationalists, including Diem, who refused an offer by the emperor to serve as prime minister in the government.

The conflict in Indochina began to take on Cold War dimensions following the October 1949 communist revolution in China. The United States financed the French forces in Indochina as part of its global strategy to contain communist advances in Asia. Diem, already seen by some American officials as a potential leader of Vietnam, visited the United States in 1951–1952. While touring American universities he advocated anticommunist, anti-French nationalism. After the French defeat at Dien Bien Phu by the Vietminh in May 1954, and urged by the administration of U.S. president Dwight D. Eisenhower, Diem finally accepted another offer by Bao Dai in June 1954 to serve as prime minister and assumed office on 7 July.

U.S. Aid

The 1954 Geneva agreements between the French and the Vietnamese provided a temporary division of Vietnam until national reunification elections scheduled for June 1956. Diem, who refused to accept the agreements, nonetheless opted for a permanent partition of Vietnam by consolidating his power in South Vietnam. He centralized power around himself and his family, especially his brother Ngo Dinh Nhu, Diem's top lieutenant. Diem was regarded by the United States as a solid ally in the containment of communism in Southeast Asia. The United States, which had backed the failed French attempt to reimpose colonial rule, began sending direct economic and military aid – including military advisers to train South Vietnamese forces – to the Diem regime. U.S. aid to South Vietnam reached an estimated two billion dollars between 1955 and 1960. While he moved to court American backing, Diem faced opposition from various armed factions operating in the South, principally the Hoa Hao, a millenarian Buddhist movement, and the

Cao Dai, a political-religious movement. During the first half of 1955, Diem moved to eliminate the Cao Dai and Hoa Hao, as well as renegade factions in the national army. After an attempted coup d'état by the army chief of staff, Diem withstood attempts by Bao Dai and General Binh Xuyen to oust him in April 1955. After defeating the forces of Binh Xuyen, Cao Dai, and Hoa Hao (whose men fled to join the Vietminh), Diem defeated Bao Dai in a rigged referendum on 23 October and declared the southern half of Vietnam to be the Republic of Vietnam. He then launched a brutal campaign against the remnants of the Vietminh and by late 1956 had destroyed 90 percent of the Vietminh cells in the South.

The Diem Regime

Widely accused of nepotism and brutality, the Diem regime proved to be a source of political instability in South Vietnam. Diem's anticommunist campaign alienated large segments of the southern population, and by late 1959 social and political unrest had increased. After some ninety thousand Vietminh guerrillas had infiltrated back into South Vietnam, the communist forces in the South became unified under the National Liberation Front (NLF), more widely known as the Vietcong. By the end of 1959 an estimated 80 percent of the countryside was under the control of communist guerrillas and anti-Diem armed factions. With only a narrow base of support among his anticommunist Catholic constituency, and distrustful of anyone outside of his own family, Diem became intransigent to domestic and American appeals for political and economic reforms of his regime, and he responded to growing unrest with increasingly repressive measures. However, he was unable to put an end to Vietcong-instigated political violence and terrorism in the countryside. In early 1962, with the support of the United States, Diem made an effort to bolster his counterinsurgency campaign through the so-called strategic hamlets program, which sought to collectivize the rural population into armed camps in the hopes of depriving the communist forces of recruits and matériel.

A Catholic president in an overwhelmingly Buddhist country, Diem cracked down on Buddhist dissidents and other political opponents. In the spring and summer of 1963 Buddhist uprisings and antigovernment demonstrations led to the collapse of his regime. Unable to deal effectively with internal instability, let alone the growing communist guerrilla threat, Diem had become a liability to the United States. On 1–2 November 1963 he was overthrown in a bloody military coup d'état backed by the United States. Along with his brother Ngo Dinh Nhu, the widely unpopular minister of the interior, Diem was assassinated the following day and replaced by an interim military government.

General References

David Halberstam, *The Best and the Brightest* (New York: Random House, 1972);

George Herring, *America's Longest War: The United States and Vietnam, 1950–1975* (New York: Wiley, 1979);

Anthony Joes, *The War for South Viet Nam, 1954–1975* (New York: Praeger, 1989);

Stanley Karnow, *Vietnam: A History* (New York: Viking, 1983).

—J. R.-S.

SEE ALSO THESE RELATED ENTRIES

Dwight D. Eisenhower, 1; Ho Chi Minh, 2; John F. Kennedy, 1.

Georgi Dimitrov

Prime Minister of Bulgaria, 1946–1949
Born Kovachevtsi, Bulgaria, 18 June 1882
Died Moscow, Soviet Union, 2 July 1949

Georgi Dimitrov, Bulgarian communist leader and prime minister of Bulgaria from 1946 to 1949, was born in Kovachevtsi, Bulgaria. He left school at the age of twelve to start work and continued his education privately. Dimitrov joined the Social Democratic party (SDP) in 1902 and remained in the left wing of the party when the SDP split into socialist and social-democratic factions in 1903. He became a secretary of the SDP left wing and from 1909 was a member of its Central Committee. Dimitrov became active as a printer, journalist, and trade union leader and was elected to parliament in 1913. In 1915 he helped lead the Bulgarian socialist parliamentary group in opposition to national war credits. The socialists were protesting against Bulgarian involvement on the German side during World War I.

Dimitrov played a major role in the formation of the Bulgarian Communist party (BCP) in 1919. He was imprisoned by the Bulgarian authorities for a short time in 1918 for his participation in the antiwar campaign. After his release he traveled to the Soviet Union where he was elected to the executive committee of the Comintern (Communist International) in 1921. In 1923 Dimitrov led an aborted communist uprising in Bulgaria that provoked a fierce reaction from the authoritarian government in Sofia. He fled to Yugoslavia and was sentenced to death in absentia. As a result he was unable to return to Bulgaria until after World War II. Dimitrov gained world attention in 1933, when he was arrested in Berlin by Adolf Hitler's Nazi regime and accused of participating in the burning of the German Reichstag, or parliament. The

Georgi Dimitrov

Nazis staged the arson episode and blamed it on the communists to discredit their political opponents and justify a tightening of party-state controls in Germany. Dimitrov was subsequently acquitted and in 1934 went to the Soviet Union and took Soviet citizenship. While in Moscow he served as the secretary-general of the Comintern's Executive Committee from 1935 until 1943.

Bulgarian Resistance

Dimitrov helped channel assistance to various communist resistance movements against the Nazis before and during World War II, except during the period of the Nazi–Soviet Non-Aggression Pact (1939–1941). During the war he played a major role in the formation of Bulgaria's resistance movement, and in 1945 he returned to Bulgaria to take over the BCP leadership and assume the premiership. The Bulgarian communists had staged a coup in September 1944, soon after the Soviet occupation, and began to neutralize and eliminate their political opponents. With Dimitrov's arrival a few months later, the communization process gathered steam, and in September 1946 Bulgaria was proclaimed a people's republic.

The rigged national elections in October 1946 placed the BCP firmly in control. Following the adoption of the "Dimitrov" constitution in December 1947, modeled on the Soviet Stalinist prototype, the party initiated a reign of terror which liquidated the remaining independent political and labor associations. During the full-scale Stalinization drive in 1948–1949, the "native" faction of the BCP, which had remained in Bulgaria during the war, was purged by the "Muscovites," that is, those leaders of the BCP who spent the war years in Moscow. Under Dimitrov's orders hundreds of Bulgarian communists were imprisoned or executed. But at the height of the Stalinist terror Dimitrov fell ill and returned to Moscow, where he died on 2 July 1949.

Books by Dimitrov

Dimitroff's Letters from Prison (New York: International Publishers, 1935);

The War and the Working Class (New York: Workers Library Publishers, 1939).

General References

John D. Bell, *The Bulgarian Communist Party from Blagoev to Zhivkov* (Stanford, Cal.: Hoover Institutional Press, 1986);

J. F. Brown, *Eastern Europe and Communist Rule* (Durham, N.C. and London: Duke University Press, 1988);

Nissan Oren, *Bulgarian Communism: The Road to Power, 1933-1944* (New York: Columbia University Press, 1971);

Joseph Rothschild, *Return to Diversity: A Political History of East Central Europe since World War II* (New York: Oxford University Press, 1989);

Sarah M. Terry, ed., *Soviet Policy in Eastern Europe* (New Haven: Yale University Press, 1984);

Adam Ulam, *Expansion and Coexistence* (New York: Praeger, 1968);

Iv'an V'olgyes, *The Political Reliability of the Warsaw Pact Armies: The Southern Tier* (Durham, N.C.: Duke University Press, 1982).

– J. B. and A. B.

SEE ALSO THESE RELATED ENTRIES

Vulko Chervenkov, 2; Comintern, 3; Joseph Stalin, 2; Todor Zhivkov, 2.

Milovan Djilas

Yugoslavian Writer and Dissident
Born Podbišce, Montenegro, 12 June 1911
Died Belgrade, Yugoslavia, 20 April 1995

Milovan Djilas was a Yugoslav political writer, dissident, and former communist official. Djilas rose to prominence as a leader of communist Yugoslavia, broke with the regime on principle, and went on to create a body of political writings that stands as one of the most far-reaching indictments of communist rule and ideology. His career spans the history and fortunes of postwar communism. As a young man, he fought for communism; in the prime of his life, he was imprisoned for opposing it; as an aging critic, he watched its collapse.

Djilas was born on 12 June 1911 in the village of Podbišce in Montenegro, a stark, mountainous region of Yugoslavia that borders on the Adriatic Sea and Albania. He was attracted to communism as a boy, not because he understood its complex claims (or, for that matter, knew any real communists), but because it promised escape from the hard life that had always been his family's lot. As he would later write in describing his youthful radicalism, "The rebellion of the hungry mountains against the rich valley has been going on in this country for several generations."

Djilas left home in 1929 to attend the University of Belgrade. There he refined his ideological convictions and became a communist activist. He organized student demonstrations against the royalist regime and began to put his political views into writing. After receiving his law degree in 1933, he was arrested and tortured by the regime for his radical activities. He spent three years in prison, and emerged a committed revolutionary.

In 1937 Djilas met Josip Broz Tito, the general secretary of the Yugoslav Communist party. He rose quickly to the upper ranks of the party, joining the Central Committee in 1938 and the Politburo two years later. His revolutionary ardor and considerable literary talents made him a natural choice to direct the party's propaganda efforts.

The Nazi Occupation

During the Nazi occupation of Yugoslavia in World War II, Djilas served as a top commander in Tito's Partisan resistance. He also served in the civil war that broke out in 1943 between the Partisans and the Chetnik (royalist) resistance forces. In October 1944 the Soviet army entered Belgrade with Tito's

Milovan Djilas with his sister (left) and wife, 1955

Partisans, thereby cementing communist control. Tito assumed the leadership of communist Yugoslavia in 1945, and Djilas took a senior post in his cabinet.

In early 1948 Djilas led a mission to Moscow to meet with Stalin in a vain attempt to avert a break between Yugoslavia and the Soviet Union, whose self-serving behavior as an occupying power and attempts to control the Yugoslav regime had embittered Tito and his loyalists. Later that year Yugoslavia severed its ties with the Soviet Union and was promptly expelled from the Cominform, the Soviet-dominated world organization of Communist parties. As the Yugoslav party's chief publicist, Djilas proceeded to make the case for "national Communism" in postwar Eastern Europe and to develop a critique of the Soviet regime to explain Yugoslavia's break with its erstwhile comrades.

Yugoslav Liberalization

The Soviet Union, he concluded, was not genuinely socialist. It had fallen prey to bureaucratism, "a reactionary antisocialist tendency that appears in the transition from capitalism to Communism." Consequently, it exploited its people for the benefit of its bureaucratic rulers. Djilas was not satisfied simply to use this understanding to denounce the Soviets; he saw its implications for the Yugoslav regime as well. He used the party newspaper *Borba* as a platform for his critique, becoming a force for liberalization within the government and the party. He helped to develop the idea of "workers' self-management" and promoted many of the decentralizing reforms that were adopted with Tito's approval at the Sixth Party Congress in November 1952 – the acme of Yugoslav communist liberalization.

Repression

Within a year Tito had decided to put a halt to reform and to reestablish party discipline. Djilas refused to fall in line. From October 1953 to January 1954 he published in *Borba* what he called a "series of antibureaucratic articles." Here he used terms like "Communist Democrat" and "good Communist" in contrast to those who merely followed the party. He decried the Communist party's monopoly of power and spoke out for democracy, equality before the law, and freedom of thought. "The only obstacle to ... despotic dangers and tendencies," he wrote, "is democratic forms and their permanent reinforcement."

Fall from Power

In January 1954 the Central Committee stripped Djilas – then the third ranking official in the regime – of all his party and government posts. He had gone too far, advocating "democracy at any price," according to Tito. At the time, Djilas was president of the Federal People's Assembly, one of four vice-presidents of Yugoslavia, and widely considered to be Tito's eventual successor. In April 1954 he resigned from the party.

Djilas's precipitous fall from power spurred him to look anew at communism. Whereas before he had seen bureaucratism as a transitional phase in communism's development, he began to see it as the very essence of communism. This insight led him to start work on his most important book, *The New Class* (1957). He also began to denounce his former associates in stronger terms. "The name communism is good," he said in an interview with the *New York Times* in December 1954, "but it has been compromised. It is a synonym for totalitarianism in this country as well as in Russia." For this "hostile propaganda," a crime in the eyes of the regime, he was convicted in 1955, receiving a suspended sentence of three years.

In 1956, in the midst of a thaw between Tito and the Soviet Union, he condemned the Soviet invasion of Hungary in an article that appeared in the American magazine *New Leader*. He paid for his dissent with imprisonment in Sremska Mitrovica, the same prison where he had been held by the royalist dictatorship in the 1930s. When *The New Class* was published in the West (he had completed the manuscript before being arrested), he was brought to trial again and his sentence was extended. *The New Class* carried an authority unmatched by other critiques of communism: Djilas knew Communist rule as few others could, and he still considered himself a true follower of Marx, whose principles had been betrayed, he believed, by those who acted in his name.

The "new class" is the communist bureaucracy, "a class whose power over men is the most complete in history." Like any other class in the Marxist understanding, it is defined by its relationship to the means of production. The new class is a class of owners, ownership being "the use, enjoyment, and disposition of material goods," and it is recognizable because it enjoys "the material and other privileges that ownership brings." The new class does not exercise ownership in the traditional Marxist sense, however, because private property does not exist. Rather it exercises ownership by virtue of the political monopoly of the Communist party: "In practice, the ownership privilege of the new class manifests itself as an exclusive right ... to distribute the national income, to set wages, direct economic development, and dispose of nationalized and other property." In short, "so-called socialist ownership is a disguise for the real ownership of the political bureaucracy."

The new class, unlike other ruling classes (e.g., the bourgeoisie in a capitalist society), does not arise organically, that is, through the slow and steady accumulation of social authority. Instead, it seizes power first and then sets out to create the social circumstances suited to its rule. Political and social coercion are its necessary tools. Thus the new class often implements policies that are unjustifiable except as a means for securing its own power. Communist economic planning is the most obvious example. Though it gives rise to "perhaps the most wasteful economy in the history of human society," it serves to "insure the strengthening of the regime."

Lenin, the founder of the Soviet state, gave political direction to the new class and led it to power. He was the key figure, according to Djilas, in the transition from Marxism to communism. Lenin appropriated Marx's revolutionary ideas, which were "conditional and not universally applicable," and transformed them into the "absolute and universal principles" that justify communist tyranny. In his hands the "dictatorship of the proletariat," which Marx intended to be "democracy within and for the benefit of the proletariat," became "the authority of one party, his own." Most importantly perhaps, in bringing these principles into practice, Lenin presided over the creation of a "stratum of professional revolutionaries," the communist vanguard, that would develop into the new class.

In prison Djilas continued to write, but not on explicitly political subjects. Having served a total of nine years in prison, he was released on the last day of 1966 and told not to make any public statements or publish any of his writings for the next five years.

Djilas immediately began working on *The Unperfect Society: Beyond the New Class*, which he arranged to have published in the West in 1969 (despite the ban by the authorities). In *The Unperfect Society* he continued his analysis of communism, this time looking beyond Lenin and Stalin to Marx himself. He attempted to understand why the humane impulse that had drawn him and others to the thought of Marx resulted in such utter human devastation. As Djilas asked, how can we "fail to notice the blood ties between Lenin and Stalin; and . . . who could deny the relationship between Marx and Lenin?" Djilas argued that the spirit of Marx's work is democratic and humanistic, and that many of his ideas are sound. Marx's contribution to the wrongs committed in his name rested not in the substance of his thought, but in believing that his thought gave a complete account of man: "Having arrived at a truth – man's economic dependence – he turned that into *the* truth about man." "Tyranny," wrote Djilas, "begins with ultimate truths."

Djilas has remained at liberty since his release in 1966, sending his works to Western Europe and the United States for publication and occasionally being allowed to travel. For years, however, he continued to be a favorite target for the Yugoslav regime's harassment and vilification, and his writings remained taboo. As recently as 1985 three scholars were sentenced to prison primarily for having attended a private lecture by the then seventy-three-year-old Djilas. In the late 1980s he was finally given permission to speak out publicly and some of his works were published in Yugoslavia.

Shortly after dismissing Djilas in 1954, Tito told foreign journalists that his onetime confidant was "politically dead; the most terrifying death of all." Djilas lived on, however, if not politically then certainly as a unique figure in the history of communism. Milovan Djilas lives today as a free-lance writer in Belgrade with his wife Stefania.

Books by Djilas
The New Class: An Analysis of the Communist System (New York: Harcourt, Brace, 1957);

Land without Justice (New York: Harcourt, Brace, 1958);

Anatomy of a Moral: The Political Essays of Milovan Djilas (New York: Praeger, 1959);

Conversations with Stalin (New York: Harcourt, Brace & World, 1962);

Montenegro (New York: Harcourt, Brace & World, 1963);

The Unperfect Society: Beyond the New Class (New York: Harcourt, Brace & World, 1969);

The Eve of Battle (New York: Harcourt Brace Jovanovich, 1971);

Parts of a Lifetime (New York: Harcourt Brace Jovanovich, 1971);

The Stone and the Violets (New York: Harcourt Brace Jovanovich, 1972);

Memoir of a Revolutionary (New York: Harcourt Brace Jovanovich, 1973);

Wartime (New York: Harcourt Brace Jovanovich, 1977);

Tito: The Story from the Inside (New York: Harcourt Brace Jovanovich, 1980);

Nomenklatura: The Soviet Ruling Class (Garden City, N.Y.: Doubleday, 1984);

Rise and Fall (San Diego: Harcourt Brace Jovanovich, 1985);

Of Prisons and Ideas (San Diego: Harcourt Brace Jovanovich, 1986).

Book about Djilas
Steven Crissold, *Djilas: The Progress of a Revolutionary* (New York: Universe Books, 1983).

– G. R.

SEE ALSO THESE RELATED ENTRIES
Joseph Stalin, 2; Josip Broz Tito, 2.

Aleksander Dubcek

First Secretary, Czechoslovak Communist Party, 1968–1969
Born Uhrovice, Czechoslovakia, 27 November 1921
Died Prague, Czechoslovakia, 7 November 1992

Aleksander Dubcek, Czechoslovak political leader and first secretary of the Czechoslovak Communist party (CCP) during the Prague Spring of 1968, was born in Uhrovice, Czechoslovakia. His father, Stefan Dubcek, was a CCP bureaucrat. Dubcek attended school and worked in an industrial cooperative that his father and other Czechoslovak communists had first organized after World War I. Dubcek spent much of the 1930s working and studying in Soviet Central Asia because his father, a dedicated Communist, wanted firsthand experience in the "worker's state." His family returned to Czechoslovakia in 1938. When World War II broke out Dubcek reportedly enlisted in the underground movement and fought with the resistance against the Nazi occupation of the Czech lands. In 1939 he joined the then-illegal Communist party and began studying engineering. In 1944 he joined a group of Slovak guerrillas and took part in the uprising against the Nazi puppet regime in Slovakia.

Dubcek started his rise through the ranks of the CCP after the war. He attended the advanced political school of the Soviet Communist party in Moscow from 1955 to 1958. In 1958 he became the first secretary of the party's regional committee in Bratislava and a member of the Central Committees of both the Slovak and Czech Communist parties. In 1962 he was appointed a full member of the CCP Central Committee's Presidium.

Prague Spring

In October 1967, at a Central Committee session in Prague, Dubcek was able to rally the support and confidence of party reformers, economic technocrats, and Slovak nationalists against the repressive leadership of Antonin Novotny. Under growing party pressure, Novotny resigned on 5 January 1968, and Dubcek replaced him as first secretary of the CCP. This ushered in the Prague Spring liberalization, when communist controls over social and political life were significantly loosened and censorship was lifted. Although Dubcek was not an enthusiastic reformer, he was thrust into this role because of considerable pressure from liberal, reformist, and radical factions within the party. Dubcek initially sought to strengthen the party's domestic position and public legitimacy through a closely supervised liberalization program. He did not aim to bring about the CCP's ultimate demise, as Moscow later claimed.

Cultural and Political Reforms

Dubcek's reforms included increased freedom of expression as well as the release and rehabilitation of political prisoners who had been victims of the Stalinist purges. But government reforms also reawakened demands among noncommunist intellectuals, students, and workers calling for a full-fledged democracy and a multiparty system. Many of their demands were subsequently adopted by the reformist CCP leaders. The eight-month-long Prague Spring, during which political repression visibly decreased, witnessed the emergence of substantial political diversity. Dubcek's official liberalization program did not advocate outright political pluralism. It focused instead on the separation of the party apparatus from the state administration and from economic management. The CCP's "Action Program," issued in April 1968, called for greater democratization but stopped short of supporting a full multiparty system. This program and the liberal measures adopted throughout 1968 were styled as "socialism with a human face."

The Soviet Invasion

Moscow grew increasingly anxious about the Dubcek reforms, fearing that the CCP could lose all political control and that the Czechoslovak reforms could serve as a model for other communist states. Dubcek gave in to minor compromises with the Kremlin, but the Soviets became perturbed by the scheduled Extraordinary Party Congress, which was due to ratify far-reaching reforms, such as the sanctioning of political pluralism. Warsaw Pact forces under Soviet command invaded Czechoslovakia 20–21 August 1968, claiming that they were "defending socialism" against "counterrevolutionary forces" and German "revisionists." The pretext for Soviet intervention became known in the West as the "Brezhnev Doctrine." It justified Soviet armed intervention throughout Eastern Europe and placed limitations on the sovereignty of socialist states already in the Soviet orbit, if the "gains of socialism" were believed to be jeopardized by serious domestic instability and purported Western aggression.

The Czechoslovak army was swiftly immobilized by Russian forces, while the unarmed population engaged in strikes, demonstrations, and various other forms of

Aleksander Dubcek, 1968

passive resistance. Dubcek and other CCP leaders were seized and taken to Moscow, where they were coerced to agree to major political concessions to reverse the reform program. Dubcek returned to Prague, and in an emotional address asked his countrymen for patience, support, and cooperation. Aside from condemning Brezhnev's policies, the West reacted passively to the Soviet invasion and did not impose economic or other sanctions on either the Soviet Union or the new Czechoslovak regime.

Aftermath of the Takeover

After the Soviet takeover Dubcek was left in a weak position and was gradually stripped of all power. His more progressive and reformist aides were removed from positions of influence, and in April 1969 he was demoted from first secretary of the party to president of the Federal Assembly. In 1970 Dubcek was expelled from the CCP altogether and served for a time as ambassador to Turkey. He was recalled to Prague in June 1970 and later on that year was made an inspector of the forestry administration in Bratislava. The post-Dubcek leadership reversed the democratization process under a program of "normalization" which reestablished the CCP's monopoly over all social activities and restored inner-party discipline, based on the Leninist principle of "democratic centralism."

The Velvet Revolution

Dubcek remained in the political wilderness until the "velvet revolution" of November 1989, when he returned

to Prague to address the mass demonstrations then taking place which toppled the hard-line communist government. In December he was appointed chairman of the country's Federal Assembly in recognition of his important role in the Prague Spring reform movement. Dubcek maintained this position after the democratic national elections in June 1990 and remained a popular symbol of peaceful reform and resistance to Soviet domination. He died on 7 November 1992 in Prague, from injuries suffered in an automobile accident on 1 September.

Book by Dubcek

Dubcek Speaks (London: I. B. Tavris, 1990).

Books about Dubcek

William Shawcross, *Dubcek*, revised and updated edition (New York: Simon & Schuster, 1990);

Pavel Tigrid, *Why Dubcek Fell* (London: Macdonald, 1971.

General References

J. F. Brown, *Eastern Europe and Communist Rule* (Durham, N.C. and London: Duke University Press, 1988);

Karen Dawisha, *The Kremlin and the Prague Spring* (Berkeley: University of California Press, 1984);

Robert L. Hutchings, *Soviet-East European Relations: Consolidation and Conflict, 1968–1980* (Madison: University of Wisconsin Press, 1983);

Christopher D. Jones, *Soviet Influence in Eastern Europe: Political Autonomy and the Warsaw Pact* (New York: Praeger, 1981);

Karel Kaplan, *Report on the Murder of the General Secretary* (Columbus: Ohio State University Press, 1990);

Jiri Pehe, ed., *The Prague Spring: A Mixed Legacy* (New York: Freedom House, 1988);

Joseph Rothschild, *Return to Diversity: A Political History of East Central Europe since World War II* (New York: Oxford University Press, 1989);

Zdenek Suda, *Zealots and Rebels: A History of the Ruling Communist Party of Czechoslovakia* (Stanford, Cal.: Hoover Institution Press, 1980);

Ivan Svitak, *The Czechoslovak Experiment: 1968–1969* (New York: Columbia University Press, 1971);

Sarah M. Terry, ed., *Soviet Policy in Eastern Europe* (New Haven: Yale University Press, 1984);

Adam Ulam, *Expansion and Coexistence* (New York: Praegre, 1968).

                                                                                 —J. B. and A. B.

SEE ALSO THESE RELATED ENTRIES

Leonid Brezhnev, 2; Václav Havel, 2; Antonìn Novotny, 2; Warsaw Pact, 3.

Levi Eshkol

Prime Minister of Israel, 1963–1969
Born Oratova, Russia, 25 October 1895
Died Jerusalem, Israel, 26 February 1969

A Zionist pioneer who immigrated to Palestine in 1914 when it was still part of the Ottoman Empire, Levi Eshkol helped found Deganya Bet, one of the first kibbutzim in Palestine. Later he was one of the founders of the Histadrut (General Federation of Labor). After Israel became an independent state in 1948 Eshkol held various important government posts, including minister of agriculture, finance, and defense. He became prime minister and defense minister in 1963 after David Ben-Gurion resigned. In 1965, when Ben-Gurion again ran for the premiership, Eshkol easily won reelection.

Born Levi Shkolnik in Oratova, a railway junction in the Kiev district of the Ukraine, Eshkol was educated by the local rabbi until his bar mitzvah, after which he went to a Hebrew school in Lithuania. At the age of nineteen he left Lithuania for Palestine. While living and working in Jewish settlements, he married Rivka Marshak and they had a daughter, Noa, but the marriage ended in divorce a few years later. He married Elisheva Kaplan in 1928, and she gave birth to three children, Dvora, Tama, and Ofra. She died in 1959.

Histadrut, Mapai, and Government Posts

In 1920 Eshkol attended a convention of labor Zionists out of which came the Histadrut. Eshkol joined the executive board and later became involved in the left-of-center political party, Mapai, where he was later to serve as party secretary. It was through Mapai that he met David Ben-Gurion, with whom he worked closely until their split in the 1960s when they both vied for the nation's leadership.

In the 1930s Eshkol was sent to Germany, where he worked with pioneer organizations settling European Jews in Palestine. In the 1940s he worked at Deganya Bet and also held high positions in the paramilitary Haganah and the Jewish Agency. With the establishment of the state of Israel in 1948, Levi Shkolnik changed his name to the Hebraic Levi Eshkol and was appointed director general of the Ministry of Defense. He became minister of agriculture and development in 1951

Gale International Portrait Gallery

Levi Eshkol

and in 1952 minister of finance. A folksy, unbookish man, Eshkol, although a member of the nominally socialist Mapai party, was known as a pragmatic politician, uncomfortable with ideological fervor.

Prime Minister

Eshkol's success as finance minister placed him in position to become the prime minister upon Ben-Gurion's resignation in June 1963. President Zalman Shazar designated Eshkol as premier on 19 June 1963. Upon taking office Eshkol resigned his post as minister of finance and instead took on the defense portfolio, serving as both prime minister and minister of defense.

Struggle with Ben-Gurion

In 1965, after serving as prime minister for two years, Eshkol was reelected in a power struggle with Ben-Gurion, who came back from retirement and, along with Moshe Dayan and Shimon Peres, had split from Mapai and created his own splinter political party, Rafi. But the internal political disputes did not end there. In 1967, as Israel and its Arab neighbors inched toward war, Eshkol found himself under vehement attack from the opposition. Egyptian president Gamul Abdul Nasser closed the Gulf of Aqaba to Israeli shipping, which was viewed as a cause for war by most Israelis. Eshkol's attempt to resolve the matter diplomatically was perceived as indecisive waffling, and it cost him his post as defense minister. Dayan, who succeeded him in the post, became an instant hero in the wake of Israel's war victory. After the war Eshkol enunciated Israel's policy of readiness to give up the territories it had captured in the war. Eshkol died in Jerusalem of a heart attack on 26 February 1969 at the age of seventy-three. He was survived by his widow, Miriam, whom he had married in 1964. Golda Meir was chosen to be his successor as prime minister.

Book by Eshkol

The State Papers of Levi Eshkol, edited by Henry M. Christman (New York: Funk & Wagnalls, 1969).

Book about Eshkol

Terence Prittie, *Eshkol of Israel: The Man and the Nation* (London: Museum Press, 1969).

General References

Michael Bar-Zohar, *Embassies in Crisis: Diplomats and Demagogues Behind the Six-Day War* (Englewood Cliffs, N.J.: Prentice-Hall, 1970);

Michael Brecher, *The Foreign Policy System of Israel: Setting, Images, Process* (New Haven, Conn.: Yale University Press, 1972);

Peter Y. Medding, *Mapai in Israel: Political Organization and Government in a New Society* (London: Cambridge University Press, 1972);

Shimon Peres, *From These Men: Seven Founders of the State of Israel* (New York: Wyndham Books, 1979);

Nadav Safran, *Israel: The Embattled Ally* (Cambridge, Mass.: Belknap Press, 1978).

                                                              – V. A.

SEE ALSO THESE RELATED ENTRIES

David Ben-Gurion, 2; Golda Meir, 2; Gamal Abdul Nasser, 2.

Eduardo Frei Montalva

President of Chile, 1964–1970
Born Santiago, Chile, 16 January 1911
Died Santiago, Chile, 22 January 1982

The Christian Democratic president of Chile from 1964 to 1970, Eduardo Frei Montalva led a centrist movement which attempted to serve as a moderating force in Chile's polarized political system. However, the centrist alternative was never well-enough consolidated to prevent the radicalization and eventual breakdown of Chilean democracy.

The son of Eduardo Frei, a Swiss immigrant, and Victoria Montalva, Frei was educated in the public schools of Santiago. He graduated from the Law School of the Catholic University of Chile in 1933. At the university he became interested in the political philosophy of Jacques Maritain and in the ideas which became associated with the Christian Democracy movement.

The National Falange Party

Frei won his first elected office in 1949 as senator. In 1954 Frei and his colleagues formed the National Falange party, an anti-Fascist Social Christian party, and Frei was nominated to be the presidential candidate for the left-center coalition in the presidential elections. However, the candidacy was rejected, and the National Falange party ended up supporting the radical candidate.

The Christian Democratic Party

In 1957 the National Falange joined with two other small groups to form the centrist Christian Democratic party, and in 1958 Frei became the party's first nominee for president. He placed third, winning over 20 percent of the votes. As the party received increasing support in subsequent congressional elections, Frei became the leading alternative to Chile's other rising politician, Salvador Allende Gossens, leader of the Communist-Socialist coalition. Backed by the Right and certain centrist factions and financed by the Central Intelligence Agency of the United States in an effort to prevent Chile from becoming another Cuba, Frei won an absolute majority in the 1964 presidential elections, receiving 56 percent of the popular vote. This represented a significant turning point in Chilean politics. The emergence of the Christian Democratic party, which claimed to be a cohesive centrist party, seemed to represent a break in the political stalemate of the polarized Chilean politics.

Eduardo Frei Montalva

Program as President

In his six years as president, Frei undertook several major domestic programs to restructure the Chilean political and economic system: an agrarian reform program allowing peasant cooperatives to be set up on land expropriated from large landowners; the passage of a 1967 law legalizing the formation of peasant unions, increasing the political participation of Chile's peasant population; a progressive tax system which redistributed wealth; and a program for the "Chileanization" that ensured 51 percent Chilean ownership of previously U.S.-owned copper interests, thereby strengthening national control over Chile's natural resources.

1970 Elections

Despite these efforts, Frei was not entirely successful. His agrarian reforms did not achieve their stated objective, problems of labor unrest persisted, and inflation, which had started before Frei took office, continued to be a problem. The Right, increasingly disgruntled by increased taxes and expropriations, refused to support Frei in the 1970 elections. The Left criticized Frei's reforms for not going far enough and charged, for example, that his "Chileanization" program was still too favorable to U.S. corporate interests. Without the support of the Right or Left, Frei's party placed a disappointing third in the 1970 presidential elections. The left-wing Popular Unity coalition won a plurality of the votes, and its leader, Salvador Allende, was elected by the congress in a runoff of the two leading candidates.

Frei was elected to the senate again in March 1973 and shortly after became its president. He did not support the military coup of September 1973 and, until his death in 1982, was a prominent opposition leader to the dictatorship of General Augusto Pinochet Ugarte.

General References

Jack Hopkins, *Latin America: Perspectives on a Region* (New York: Holmes & Meier, 1987);

Jennie K. Lincoln and Elizabeth G. Ferris, *The Dynamics of Latin American Foreign Policies: Challenges for the 1980's* (Boulder, Colo.: Westview Press, 1984);

Heraldo Muñoz and Joseph S. Tulchin, *Latin American Nations in World Politics* (Boulder, Colo.: Westview Press, 1984);

Ernest Rossi and Jack C. Plano, *The Latin American Political Dictionary* (Santa Barbara: ABC-Clio, 1980);

Howard J. Wiarda and Harvey F. Kline, *Latin American Politics and Development* (Boulder, Colo.: Westview Press, 1979).

– B. D.

SEE ALSO THESE RELATED ENTRIES

Salvador Allende Gossens, 2; Central Intelligence Agency, 3; Augusto Pinochet Ugarte, 2.

Indira Gandhi

Prime Minister of India, 1966–1977, 1980–1984
Born Anand Bhawan, Allahabad, India, 19 November 1917
Died New Delhi, India, 31 October 1984

Indira Gandhi served as prime minister of India from 1966 to 1977 and from 1980 to 1984. She was a member of a dynasty that had dominated Indian politics since the country's independence and that ruled India until the late 1980s.

The daughter of Jawaharlal Nehru – one of India's most prominent nationalist leaders – she was born Indira Priyadarshini Nehru, into a wealthy family belonging to a high caste among the Hindus in Anand Bhawan, Allahabad. Because of her family's active involvement and leadership in the independence movement, she traveled frequently and received her secondary education in both India and Britain. In 1937 she entered Somerville College, Oxford University, but did not complete her degree. She married Feroze Gandhi in 1942.

Following in the footsteps of her father, she became actively involved in the Indian nationalist movement. After India became independent in 1947, she continued working for the Congress party – India's ruling movement. In 1955 she was promoted to the working committee, the party's policy-making body. Rising rapidly in the party hierarchy, she was elected president of the Congress party in 1959, having run unopposed. After Nehru died in 1964, she was appointed to serve as minister of information and broadcasting in the interim government.

Prime Minister

On 24 January 1966 Gandhi was sworn in as prime minister. In moving decisively to undercut the power and influence of old guard politicians in the party hierarchy, she employed what many considered to be draconian measures. In June 1975 she declared a state of emergency in the midst of social unrest and a campaign waged to force her resignation. During the emergency, which lasted only briefly, many of her political opponents were imprisoned.

India's Role in Third World

India, which had become a pivotal leader of the Nonaligned movement in the Third World, played a major role in regional political affairs. Due to its size and geographic location, India also became caught up in the diplomatic sparring among the United States, the Soviet Union, and the People's

Gale International Portrait Gallery

Indira Gandhi

Republic of China (PRC). Gandhi continued Nehru's policy of friendly relations with the Soviet Union, India's largest supplier of economic aid and military assistance and hardware. She, however, attempted to avoid a cliental relationship with the Soviet Union by emphasizing India's formal nonalignment. Relations with the United States, which had been close in the 1950s, were neither amicable nor hostile during the 1960s and 1970s, despite India's pro-Soviet policies. Close relations and military cooperation between the United States and Pakistan, however, were a source of diplomatic strain, which diminished over the span of Gandhi's rule as relations between India and Pakistan improved. Diplomatic relations with the PRC – another traditional rival, and a country with which India had territorial disputes – however, were never good.

Pakistani Conflict

Gandhi's greatest challenge in foreign policy came in 1971 when East Pakistan (present-day Bangladesh) declared its independence from West Pakistan, from which it was separated by nearly one thousand miles of Indian territory. From the initial stages of the civil war India had declared its support for East Pakistan. Relations between India and Pakistan – which had been fragile due to military conflict between the two countries in 1962 and 1965 – deteriorated rapidly as cross-border tensions mounted. The civil war resulted in a mass exodus of Pakistani refugees into India, and domestic pressures mounted, pressing Gandhi's government to intervene. The United States, however, in support of Pakistan – a member of the Southeast Asia Treaty Organization (SEATO) – sent U.S. secretary of state Henry A. Kissinger to warn Gandhi that India should not expect U.S. assistance if its intervention provoked a counterinvasion of India by China. Mainly as a countermeasure against China, with whom India had poor relations and border disputes, Gandhi reversed India's formal policy of nonalignment in August 1971 and signed a treaty of friendship and cooperation with the Soviet Union. Following a Pakistani air attack on northern India – ostensibly aimed at Eastern rebels – India launched an integrated air, sea, and ground offensive into East Pakistan on 4 December. The Indo-Pakistani War came to an abrupt end when Pakistani forces surrendered on 16 December, despite a show of force by a U.S. carrier group in support of Pakistan.

By 1974 India had established a nuclear arsenal, and Gandhi had begun to reassert a policy of nonalignment. India and Pakistan worked at improving relations, and by the early 1980s both governments had taken steps to establish a mutually reassuring relationship. In March 1977 Gandhi and the Congress party lost the national elections, but both would return to power after winning the January 1980 elections.

Relations with the Superpowers

The December 1979 Soviet invasion of Afghanistan presented a another major challenge to Indian foreign policy. Gandhi's initial reactions to the invasion were measured, and India abstained in a United Nations (UN) vote for a resolution condemning the Soviet action. India's abstention for many observers signaled a rebuke of the Soviet Union, for India had consistently voted in support of Soviet positions. Within months of the invasion, however, Gandhi became openly critical of the Soviet invasion and began calling for a Soviet withdrawal – a watershed in Indo-Soviet relations, which after 1979 were strained. The occupation of Cambodia by Vietnam, a client state of the Soviet Union, further worsened relations. By the early 1980s Gandhi began charting a more independent course in foreign affairs and became critical of both U.S. and Soviet policies in Central America, Africa, and Asia. She called for both superpowers to remove all military bases from the Indian Ocean region.

During this period Gandhi also began an effort to diversify India's arms suppliers, even declaring her interest in purchasing advanced American weaponry. In mid 1982, however, India signed an agreement with the Soviet Union to modernize the Indian military, although it proceeded to acquire weapons in Western Europe as well. The Soviets had engaged in an intense political and diplomatic campaign to maintain Indo-Soviet military cooperation and to keep India within the Soviet orbit. In addition to maintaining a détente with China and Pakistan, Gandhi sought to improve relations with the United States, visiting the United States in July 1982.

By 1983 many parts of the country were engulfed in political and ethnic violence, especially in the Sikh-dominated Punjab. Gandhi's use of force to suppress the violence alienated many segments of the population. She was assassinated on 31 October 1984 by her Sikh bodyguards. Indira was succeeded to office by her son, Rajiv Gandhi.

–J. R.-S.

Book by Indira Gandhi

My Truth (New Delhi: Vision Books, 1981).

Books about Indira Gandhi

Pranay Gupte, *Mother India: A Political Biography of Indira Gandhi* (New York: Scribners, 1992);

Inder Malhotra, *Indira Gandhi: A Personal and Political Biography* (Boston: Northeastern University Press, 1991).

SEE ALSO THESE RELATED ENTRIES
Zulfikar Ali Bhutto, 2.

Bashir Gemayel

First Commander, Lebanese Forces, 1976–1982
Born Bikfaya, Lebanon, 10 November 1947
Died Ashrafieh, Lebanon, 14 September 1982

Bashir Gemayel was the charismatic and ruthless Lebanese Maronite leader who solidified the relationship with Israel that led to that country's invasion of Lebanon in 1982. A paid informant of both the Central Intelligence Agency (CIA) and the Israeli intelligence agency (Mossad), Gemayel was elected to the presidency of Lebanon in 1982 but was assassinated before his inauguration.

Bashir was the youngest of six children of Sheikh Pierre Gemayel, a founder and main leader of the Lebanese Phalange (*al-Kataeb al-Lubnaniah*), the paramilitary youth organization that became that country's most powerful political force. He was born on 10 November 1947 in Bikfaya, Lebanon, a mountain village near Beirut. Because of his position as the youngest of Pierre's children, Bashir was not expected to gain prominence, being five years younger than his brother Amin, but by age thirty-four he had become one of Lebanon's most important and charismatic leaders.

Bob Woodward describes Gemayel as "a baby-faced ruthless warlord." After becoming the first commander of the Lebanese Forces, the combined Maronite militias, in 1976, Gemayel became the most important Maronite leader by defeating or killing his rivals. In June 1978, for example, Gemayel attacked the home of Tony Frangieh, a rival Christian leader and son of former Lebanese president Suleiman Frangieh, slaughtering him, his family, and his servants. In July 1980 Gemayel's militia launched a surprise attack on another rival Christian militia, the Tigers of Danny Chamoun, whose leader was the son of another former president. The attack left eighty militiamen dead; Gemayel then bought off Camille Chamoun, the former president and father of the slain militia leader, with $1 million in reparations.

The National Pact

Because of Lebanon's political system, which favored the Christians despite demographics that increasingly favored the Muslims, Gemayel was able to use his base within the Maronite community to become the most powerful player in this divided country. This political inequality was institutionalized in Lebanon's 1943 National Pact, which set up the modern state as a sectarian democracy with a Christian president and a parliament constituted on a six-to-five ratio in favor of the Christians.

Bashir Gemayel, 1978

The Lebanese Forces

Gemayel rose through the ranks of the rightist Phalange beginning in the early 1970s. He graduated from Saint Joseph University with a degree in law and political science in 1971 and was named political director of the Phalange office in Ashrafieh the next year. During the Maronite siege of the Palestine refugee camp Tel al-Zaater in East Beirut, Gemayel was named deputy commander of the Phalange militia, and on 13 July 1976 he was promoted to chief of its military council. Gemayel was propelled to national prominence when the camp fell. And when, after the battle, the Christian militias decided they needed a unified force, Gemayel became head of the

99

joint command council of the newly united Lebanese Forces.

At this same time Gemayel was establishing contacts with the United States and with Israel. Leaders in both of those countries viewed him as an "asset" in the region, a Christian among Moslems and a strongman bent on modernizing the country at almost any cost. As Gemayel would tell them, "We have not spilled the blood of thousands of young men in order to move backward."

Gemayel was recruited by the CIA while working at a Washington, D.C., law firm in the early 1970s. Initially he worked on the basis of a straight exchange of a few thousand dollars for information. But, after Gemayel took charge of the militia in 1976, the payments and his importance to the CIA grew, and finally, after urgings from Israeli defense minister Ariel Sharon, President Ronald Reagan authorized $10 million in covert aid to Gemayel's Maronite militia.

The Israeli relationship with Gemayel began to solidify during the 1978 lull in Lebanon's civil war. In this period, with Israeli support, Gemayel reorganized and reinforced the Phalange militia, which served as his power base, and the balance of power within Lebanon shifted in his favor. Gemayel began to urge the Israelis to invade Lebanon, a move he believed would give the Maronites the advantage over Syria in their battle to control the country.

The Israeli Invasion

Gemayel's urgings eventually paid off when Israel invaded Lebanon on 6 June 1982 – assuring his ability to become the country's leader. Two months after the Israeli invasion, on 23 August 1982, Gemayel won election as president. But before he could take office, Gemayel was assassinated in a bomb blast detonated by Habbib Tanious Shartouni on 14 September 1982 while making a speech at the Phalange office in Ashrafieh. "The opposition will grow accustomed to the portrait of the new president even though it didn't want him," were Gemayel's words, as Shartouni, a member of the National Syrian Socialist party and an operative for Syrian intelligence,

set off the blast. Gemayel was survived by his wife, Solange Toutounji, and one child; another child had died in a February 1979 attempt on Gemayel's life.

After Gemayel's assassination the Israelis panicked, for he had been the sole foundation of their strategy for altering the balance of power in the region. On 15 September 1982, ignoring an oral promise to the United States, Israeli troops invaded West Beirut; the following day the army's Order Number Six stated that the Phalange would take care of "searching and mopping up" the Sabra and Shatila Palestinian refugee camps, which resulted in the massacre of hundreds of civilians.

The United States, similarly, found itself in a bit of a bind after Gemayel's assassination because of the CIA's secret ties with him. After Gemayel's election Reagan had approved a covert operation that would ally the CIA and the Lebanese intelligence forces more closely at an initial cost of $600,000 and a projected expense of between $2 million and $4 million per year. That money was put into a presidential contingency fund following Gemayel's death.

Amin Gemayel, who virtually inherited the presidency from his younger brother, attempted to step back from Bashir's relationships with the United States and Israel. Amin Gemayel served his term through September 1988 as the head of a more broadly supported but ineffectual administration. When he resigned, he appointed the Maronite army commander to be prime minister, though that had always been a Sunni post. At the end of the Gemayel years, then, Lebanon, already torn by a civil war, was split between two cabinets.

General References

Walid Khalidi, *Conflict and Violence in Lebanon: Confrontation in the Middle East* (Cambridge, Mass.: Center for International Affairs, Harvard University, 1984);

Ze'ev Schiff and Ehud Ya'ari, *Israel's Lebanon War* (London: Allen & Unwin, 1984);

Bob Woodward, *Veil: The Secret Wars of the CIA: 1981–1987* (New York: Simon & Schuster, 1987).

– A. F.

SEE ALSO THESE RELATED ENTRIES
Central Intelligence Agency, 3; Ronald Reagan, 1; Ariel Sharon, 2.

Ernö Gerö

First Secretary, Hungarian Socialist Workers Party, 1956

Deputy Prime Minister of Hungary, 1955–1956

Born Budapest, Hungary, 8 July 1898
Died Budapest, Hungary, 12 March 1980

Ernö Gerö was a Hungarian leader during the revolt of 1956. Originally named Ernö Singer and believed to be of Jewish background, Gerö became a member of the Hungarian Communist party in 1918 but immigrated to Germany in 1919. He returned to Hungary a few years later and became the editor of an illegal Communist party magazine. Gerö was arrested by the Hungarian authorities in the early 1920s during the nationwide crackdown on left-wing groups but was exchanged for non-communist prisoners held in the Soviet Union. Upon his release from prison he settled in the Soviet Union, where he received intensive political training. From 1936 to 1938 he fought with communist contingents in the International Brigade in the Spanish civil war where many East European communists gained combat experience.

Gerö returned to Hungary in 1944 and became a member of the Central Committee of the Hungarian Communist party in 1946. He was appointed minister of transport in 1945, minister of finance in 1948, and minister of state and foreign trade in 1950. He became a driving force for the rapid industrialization of Hungary during the height of Stalinist rule. He was named deputy prime minister in 1955 and was elected first secretary of the renamed Hungarian Socialist Workers party (HSWP) in 1956.

The 1956 Revolt

Popular aspirations for democratic reform and an end to communist rule escalated in Hungary after the death of Joseph Stalin in March 1953. Gerö was appointed HSWP first secretary in July 1956 and replaced the hard-line Stalinist Mátyás Rákosi. But Gerö proved to be an equally doctrinaire communist, unable to forestall rising discontent through relatively minor concessions such as wage increases to industrial workers. During the first part of the Hungarian revolt in October 1956, Gerö held fast to his Stalinist ideals and to the party leadership, and he made a pro-Soviet broadcast on 23 October 1956. Large crowds gathered to protest against the communist system, and when security police opened fire on demonstrators, the armed rebellion was ignited and quickly spread throughout the country. Gerö was unable to subdue the insurgency as the party effectively lost power to the new reformist government of Imre Nagy, installed as a result of growing public pressure, and to the independent workers' councils that were formed in every Hungarian city.

Aftermath of the Revolt

Gerö was replaced as HSWP leader by János Kádár on 25 October 1956. Kádár had proven his unswerving loyalty to Moscow but was not closely associated with Stalinism. The Soviet army invaded Hungary in early November, and the revolution was violently crushed within a few weeks. At first it was thought that Gerö was killed by anticommunist rebels in Budapest, but it was later discovered that he had been evacuated by the Soviet forces, together with other discredited communist loyalists. Gerö disappeared into obscurity but returned to Hungary sometime during the 1960s. He died on 12 March 1980 in Budapest.

General References

J. F Brown, *Eastern Europe and Communist Rule* (Durham, N.C. and London: Duke University Press, 1988);

François Fejto, *Budapest 1956* (Paris: Juillard, 1966);

Charles Gati, *Hungary and the Soviet Bloc* (Durham, N.C.: Duke University Press, 1986);

Robert L. Hutchings, *Soviet-East European Relations: Consolidation and Conflict, 1968–1980* (Madison: University of Wisconsin Press, 1983);

Bennett Kovrig, *Communism in Hungary: From Kun to Kadar* (Stanford, Cal.: Hoover Institution Press, 1979);

Miklos Molnar, *Budapest 1956: A History of the Hungarian Revolution* (London: Allen & Unwin, 1971);

Joseph Rothschild, *Return to Diversity: A Political History of East Central Europe since World War II* (New York: Oxford University Press, 1989);

Mátyás Rákosi, Ernö Gerö, and Imre Nagy

Sarah M. Terry, ed., *Soviet Policy in Eastern Europe* (New Haven: Yale Univeristy Press, 1984);

Adam Ulam, *Expansion and Coexistence* (New York: Praegre, 1968);

Iv'an V'olgyes, *The Political Reliability of the Warsaw Pact Armies: The Southern Tier* (Durham, N.C.: Duke University Press, 1982).

–J. B. and A. B.

Gheorghe Gheorghiu-Dej

First Secretary, Romanian Workers Party, 1955–1965

Prime Minister of Romania, 1952–1955

Born Bîrlad, Romania, 8 November 1901

Died Bucharest, Romania, 19 March 1965

Gheorghe Gheorghiu-Dej, a Romanian Communist party leader, prime minister, and president after World War II, was born to a working-class family. He became involved in radical politics and joined the then-illegal Romanian Communist party (RCP) in 1926. In 1931 he was sent by party superiors to the town of Dej and later added the place-name to his own last name. In 1933 Gheorghiu-Dej took part in the Grivita railwaymen's strike and was elected chairman of the local strike committee. After the strike was broken up he was arrested by the right-wing Romanian regime and sentenced to prison for twelve years.

After serving nearly eleven years in jail, Gheorghiu-Dej escaped in August 1944 and quickly established himself as an RCP leader immediately prior to the multiparty coup of 23 August 1944, which unseated the pro-German government of General Ion Antonescu in Bucharest. After Soviet troops entered and occupied Romania, the RCP occupied a predominant role in the coalition government set up to smooth the transition to a communist system. In March 1945 Gheorghiu-Dej was appointed RCP first secretary. As the party stepped up its drive toward full domination, rival political leaders were neutralized, and the communists captured control over the security organs.

Gheorghiu-Dej served as minister of communications in the coalition government from 1944 to 1946 and played a major role in forcing Prime Minister Nicolae Radescu out of office and establishing a communist-dominated government. Rigged elections in the fall of 1946 sealed the communist victory. King Michael was formally deposed in December 1947, and the largest independent rival party, the National Peasant party, was outlawed by the authorities. A new constitution was adopted in April 1948, and Romania was declared a people's republic. Gheorghiu-Dej served as minister of the economy from 1946 to 1948, and as chairman of the State Planning Commission from 1948 to 1949.

Prime Minister

In February 1948 the RCP was renamed the Romanian Workers party (RWP) after its fusion with the left wing of the dismembered Social Democratic party. Fol-

Gheorghe Gheorghiu-Dej

lowing its consolidation of power, the RWP embarked on a program of enforced Stalinization closely following the Soviet model of "socialist constitution." This included the nationalization of industry, central economic planning, a campaign of rural collectivization, and stringent measures to eliminate the influence of various churches. By 1952 Gheorghiu-Dej had won the factional struggle within the party between the "Muscovites," who had arrived with the Red Army, and the "native communists," who had spent the war years in Romania. Gheorghiu-Dej successfully purged his party rivals, and once he was appointed prime minister, he became the de facto head of both the RWP and the government.

Gheorghiu-Dej maintained a more independent stance toward the Soviet regime than the party's "Muscovite" faction did, and he laid the foundations for Bucharest's semi-autonomous foreign policy after Joseph Stalin's death. For example, the Romanian regime maintained a more neutral position within the Warsaw Treaty Organization by refusing to allow the stationing of Soviet troops on Romanian soil and by refusing to participate in Warsaw Pact military maneuvers. After Gheorghiu-Dej's demise the government also adopted a friendlier posture toward the West and maintained relations with Communist China and other states with which the Soviets had severed diplomatic relations. Moscow tolerated these Romanian foreign policy deviations because it received assurances that Bucharest would not forge alliances with the Western states and would preserve the communist system.

Gheorghiu-Dej resigned as prime minister in 1955 but was elected president of the State Council in 1961. During the late 1950s Gheorghiu-Dej resisted Moscow's efforts to integrate Romania into the Eastern European economic system and supported a more independent economic course for Romania by diversifying its agricultural and industrial production. In November 1958 the RWP formalized its "Romanian road to socialism," and the remaining small contingents of Russian troops were soon withdrawn from the country. The Kremlin acquiesced in the Romanian request. It was reassured that stringent communist controls would be upheld and the country would not deviate from socialist economic planning or form close alliances with the capitalist states.

Friendly relations were established with some non-communist nations and with the People's Republic of China after the Sino-Soviet split. But although Romania issued a "declaration of independence" in April 1964 and officially adopted a posture of international neutrality, its freedom of maneuver was limited by the regime's ultimate dependence on Moscow for its political and economic survival. But Romania's overtly independent posture helped to give the regime some semblance of domestic and international legitimacy. Gheorghiu-Dej died in Bucharest on 19 March 1965 and was replaced as party chief by Nicolae Ceausescu, who followed his mentor's foreign policy direction.

General References

J. F. Brown, *Eastern Europe and Communist Rule* (Durham, N.C.: Duke University Press, 1988);

Stephen Fischer-Galati, ed., *Romania* (New York: Praeger, 1957);

Ghita Ionescu, *Communism in Rumania, 1944–1962* (London: Oxford University Press, 1964);

Robert R. King, *A History of the Romanian Communist Party* (Stanford: Hoover Institution Press, 1980);

Joseph Rothschild, *Return to Diversity: A Political History of East Central Europe since World War II* (New York: Oxford University Press, 1989);

Sarah M. Terry, ed., *Soviet Policy in Eastern Europe* (New Haven: Yale University Press, 1984);

Adam Ulam, *Expansion and Coexistence* (New York: Praeger, 1968);

Ivan V'olgyes, *The Political Reliability of the Warsaw Pact Armies: The Southern Tier* (Durham, N.C.: Duke University Press, 1982).

—J. B. and A. B.

SEE ALSO THESE RELATED ENTRIES
Nicolae Ceausescu, 2; Andrei Vyshinsky, 2; Warsaw Pact, 3.

Vo Nguyen Giap

Minister of Defense, Democratic Republic of Vietnam, 1945–1980
Born An Xa, Vietnam, 1912

Vo Nguyen Giap, Vietnamese military officer and longtime defense minister of the Democratic Republic of Vietnam (DRV), was the principal military leader of the communist forces during the first and second Indochina wars.

The son of a scholar, Giap was born in the village of An Xa in Quang Binh province. In 1924 he attended the National Academy in Hue but was expelled soon afterward as a result of his participation in various protests and demonstrations. During this period he was associated with several revolutionary and communist organizations, including the Revolutionary Youth League of Vietnam (Thanh Nien), a leading nationalist movement founded and led by Ho Chi Minh. Briefly imprisoned by the French in 1930, Giap enrolled in the University of Hanoi, where he also pursued graduate degrees. He joined the Indochina Communist party in 1937.

Giap was forced into exile in 1939 and fled to southern China, which had become a training ground and sanctuary for Vietnamese revolutionaries. There he began his close and long-standing relationship with Ho Chi Minh, with whom he helped organize the Vietminh Front. During 1941–1945 Giap joined Vietminh bands fighting against French and Japanese units in southern China and the northern Tonkin region of Vietnam. Under Giap's leadership, the Vietminh forces grew in size and effectiveness. He was promoted to commander in chief of the Vietminh army by Ho Chi Minh after the communist forces unilaterally declared the Democratic Republic of Vietnam independent in September 1945. Giap also became a member of the ruling politburo of the DRV.

The declaration of independence by the Vietminh proved to be short-lived, however, as France moved quickly to reimpose colonial rule, setting in motion the First Indochina War. By the fall of 1947, the U.S.-backed French forces had succeeded in reestablishing control over most of the country. Giap and the Vietminh remained confined to rural areas in the northern half of the country, where it concentrated on rebuilding its military strength and guerrilla networks.

Dien Bien Phu

In October 1949 the communists came to power in China and began to provide arms and matériel to the Vietminh, enabling Giap to inflict losses on the French forces. Giap's military strategy was influenced by Maoist

Vo Nguyen Giap

guerrilla tactics used during the Chinese civil war, although he also relied on large-scale frontal attacks that often proved very costly for the Vietminh forces, as in the Red River offensive of 1951. By 1953 Giap's forces had established control over most of central and northern Vietnam. The turning point in the war was the stunning defeat of the French at Dien Bien Phu, a village in northwest Vietnam which had been crucial to a French attempt at regaining military control of Vietnam. In orchestrating the French defeat, Giap concentrated on isolating and then overpowering the French forces. After repeated attacks, which had begun in late 1953, the French finally surrendered in early May 1954. The next day peace talks between French and Vietnamese representatives began in Geneva, Switzerland. Despite an agreement aimed at reunifying the country under an elected government, the temporary partition between the DRV and southern Vietnam had become permanent by October 1955, when the South proclaimed itself the Republic of Vietnam.

For the next several years the leadership of the DRV turned its efforts toward domestic rebuilding, and Giap concentrated on reorganizing and training the People's

Army of North Vietnam (PANV). The DRV leadership at first avoided military confrontation with South Vietnam and moved cautiously in supporting communist guerrillas based in the South. By 1960, however, the communist forces in the South had been organized into the National Liberation Front (NLF). The NLF, called the Vietcong by the U.S.-backed South Vietnamese government of Ngo Dinh Diem, was led by Vietminh veterans and remained heavily dependent on the DRV for support. By 1963 North Vietnam was sending thousands of cadres and advisers to the communist guerrillas. After 1964, regular units from Giap's North Vietnamese army were infiltrating into South Vietnam, and by year's end most of the South was under communist control.

U.S. Involvement

As Giap and the Hanoi leadership began to commit regular forces, U.S. commitment in South Vietnam – which had become a centerpiece of its global, anticommunist containment policy – also deepened, and by March 1965 the United States was conducting large-scale deployments of U.S. troops in Vietnam. During the Second Indochina War, Giap increasingly relied on a conventional military strategy that called for direct confrontation with U.S. forces, although Giap never abandoned guerrilla tactics and the hope of forcing his opponent into a political settlement. Giap, who vowed to fight against the United States for "ten, fifteen, twenty, fifty years," was willing to bear heavy casualties in his confrontations with U.S. forces.

Tet Offensive

A turning point in the war came in early 1968, when communist forces began the Tet Offensive – large scale, simultaneous attacks launched from inside South Vietnam. The goal of the operation was to seize major cities and spark a civilian uprising that would overthrow the U.S.-backed South Vietnamese regime. As its principle architect, Giap planned the operation to coincide with Tet – the three-day Vietnamese holiday celebrating the new year. North Vietnam had called for a holiday cease-fire, and just prior to the offensive Giap used diversionary raids to pin down U.S. forces in the northern border regions and central highlands. By the start of the campaign Giap had moved some one hundred thousand soldiers and tons of supplies undetected into South Vietnamese cities. On 30 January communist forces at-tacked over forty provincial capitals and major cities, including an unsuccessful but stunning assault on the American embassy in Saigon, as well as the presidential palace. U.S. and South Vietnamese forces were quickly able to repel the communist offensive, although fighting continued for weeks in Hue. The Tet Offensive was a military disaster for Giap and the communist forces, which suffered losses of nearly forty to one. Politically, however, the Tet Offensive had a devastating impact on public opinion in the United States, undermining U.S. resolve to deepen or even sustain its military commitment to South Vietnam. The Tet Offensive also played an indirect role in causing the downfall of U.S. president Lyndon B. Johnson, who, after Tet, performed poorly in the New Hampshire primaries and chose not to seek reelection.

The Tet Offensive left the NLF decimated, and the burden of fighting the war now fell entirely on Giap's forces. In 1972 Giap convinced the DRV politburo to commit the entire PANV to the fighting. He organized the Eastertide Offensive, which ended disastrously – his forces suffering heavy casualties. Having suffered successive military defeats in the Second Indochina War, Giap was replaced as commander in chief by his protégé and chief of staff, Van Tien Dung. In 1980 he was replaced as defense minister by Dung.

Books by Giap

People's War, People's Army (New York: Praeger, 1962);

The Military Art of People's War, Selected Writings (New York: Monthly Review Press, 1971);

Unforgettable Days (Hanoi: Foreign Languages Publishing House, 1974).

To Arm the Revolutionary Masses, to Build the People's Army (Hanoi: Foreign Languages Publishing House, 1975);

The People's War for the Defense of the Homeland in the New Era (Hanoi: Foreign Languages Publishing House, 1981);

Dien Bien Phu (Hanoi: Foreign Languages Publishing House, 1984).

Books about Giap

Peter Macdonald, *Giap: The Victor in Vietnam* (New York and London: Norton, 1992);

Robert O'Neill, *General Giap: Politician and Strategist* (New York: Praeger, 1969).

–J.R.-S.

SEE ALSO THESE RELATED ENTRIES
Ho Chi Minh, 2; Lyndon B. Johnson, 1; Ngo Dinh Diem, 2.

Edward Gierek

First Secretary, Polish United Workers Party, 1970–1980
Born Porabka, Poland, 6 January 1913

Edward Gierek, Polish political leader and first secretary of the Polish United Workers party (PUWP) from 1970 to 1980, was born into a miner's family in the Polish village of Porabka in the industrial region of Silesia. His father's death in a mine disaster in 1923 led Gierek and his mother to immigrate to France. He lived in France from 1923 to 1934 and at the age of thirteen started working in French coal mines where he came under strong communist influence. Gierek joined the French Communist party in the early 1930s but was deported from the country in 1934 for helping to organize an illegal miners' strike. He returned to Poland for a brief time and then immigrated to Belgium. In 1937 he joined the Belgian Communist party, and during World War II he reportedly became a leader of a group of Polish partisans fighting in the anti-Nazi underground in Belgium.

Early Career in the PUWP

In 1948 Gierek returned to Poland and joined the PUWP. He established his political base in the important mining city of Katowice in upper Silesia. By 1951 he had become party first secretary in the city. He worked to improve living standards among the Silesian miners and won local support for his efforts. He was also well respected within the party for his accomplishments in organizing communist control over the coal mines and industrial plants and for boosting productivity in the region. In 1954 he graduated as an engineer from the Academy of Mining and Metallurgy in Kraków and was named director of Poland's heavy industry department. He also rose quickly through the ranks of the PUWP. In 1956 he was made a member of the Politburo, and in 1957 he became first secretary of the party organization in Katowice.

First Secretary of the PUWP

As PUWP chief in Katowice, Gierek acquired a reputation as an efficient administrator and was popular with the technocrats in the party and government. He succeeded Wladyslaw Gomulka as first secretary of the PUWP on 20 December 1970, during a major national crisis. Gomulka's downfall was the result of the outcry arising from a police massacre of several dozen workers in the Baltic shipyards who were protesting against a substantial and sudden rise in food prices. Gierek promised to improve the material situation of working families and reevaluate the government's economic policies, as a result gaining some measure of trust among the work force.

Economic Reforms

Once in office, Gierek made a series of changes in the party and in the management of the economy. He purged most of the Gomulka supporters from the PUWP leadership, rebuilt the entire party organization to promote members with better educational and managerial qualifications, and lowered the emphasis on ideological fidelity. In 1971 the government embarked on a program of economic recovery, which brought positive results for a few years and helped to satisfy growing consumer demands.

Poland's industrialization advanced rapidly in the next ten years, fueled largely by massive loans from the Western bankers and other creditors. The West believed that Warsaw was embarking on major structural reforms and that Polish industry would therefore become efficient and competitive. But as the country's hard-currency debt mounted, it became evident that Western credits had been mismanaged in large, unprofitable projects and that Polish industry remained under the control of a self-perpetuating communist management structure.

Deteriorating Economic Conditions

The few years of relative prosperity under Gierek in the early 1970s also raised popular expectations at a time when the economy began to nosedive. Deteriorating conditions and the sudden raising of food prices triggered strikes and demonstrations in several cities in June 1976, which were brutally suppressed by militia units. Repression against protesting workers led to the birth of several opposition groups, including the Workers Defense Committee, which began to pressure the regime to respect its own laws and abide by the Helsinki Final Act on human rights, signed by most European states in 1975.

The Birth of Solidarity

The government tried to suppress the growing political opposition but found itself increasingly unable to control the situation, particularly after Pope John Paul II's visit to Poland in 1979. The papal pilgrimage helped to

Chris Niedenthal

Edward Gierek

breach the barrier of popular fear erected by the Warsaw regime. In the summer of 1980 massive strikes erupted around the country after the Gierek government arbitrarily raised food prices to protect its collapsing economic program. The government eschewed the use of violence and instead opted to enter into negotiations with striking workers. This led to the historic Gdansk, Szczecin, and Jastrzebie agreements at the end of August, which paved the way for the birth of Solidarity, the first free trade union in the communist world.

Resignation

Gierek resigned as first secretary in September 1980, politically discredited after the nationwide protests. Under pressure from Moscow and the PUWP Politburo, Gierek was expelled from the party in July 1981. He had been accused of gross economic mismanagement and corruption. He was briefly detained during the imposition of martial law in December 1981, as the regime of General Wojciech Jaruzelski sought to distance itself from any association with the pre-Solidarity period. Gierek then slipped out of the public eye

and focused on writing his memoirs while continuing to live in a suburb of Katowice.

Books about Gierek

Adam Bromke and John W. Strong, eds., *Gierek's Poland* (New York: Praeger, 1973);

Keith John Lepak, *Prelude to Solidarity: Poland and the Politics of the Gierek Regime* (New York: Columbia University Press, 1988).

General References

J. F. Brown, *Eastern Europe and Communist Rule* (Durham, N.C. and London: Duke University Press, 1988);

Robert L. Hutchings, *Soviet-East European Relations: Consolidation and Conflict, 1968–1980* (Madison: University of Wisconsin Press, 1983);

Christopher D. Jones, *Soviet Influence in Eastern Europe: Political Autonomy and the Warsaw Pact* (New York: Praeger, 1981);

Joseph Rothschild, *Return to Diversity: A Political History of East Central Europe since World War II* (New York: Oxford University Press, 1989);

Sarah M. Terry, ed., *Soviet Policy in Eastern Europe* (New Haven: Yale University Press, 1984);

Adam Ulam, *Expansion and Coexistence* (New York: Praeger, 1968);

J. B. de Weydenthal, *The Communists of Poland* (Stanford, Cal.: Hoover Institution Press, 1986).

—J. B. and A. B.

SEE ALSO THESE RELATED ENTRIES

Wladyslaw Gomulka, 2; Wojciech Jaruzelski, 2; Lech Walesa, 2.

Wladyslaw Gomulka

First Secretary, Polish United Workers Party, 1956–1970
Born 6 February 1905, Krosno, Poland
Died 1 September 1982 Warsaw, Poland

Wladyslaw Gomulka, Polish political leader and first secretary of the Polish United Workers party (PUWP) from 1956 to 1970, was born in Krosno, Poland. Before his birth his parents had immigrated to the United States but had returned to Poland, reportedly disillusioned by their experience. His father became an oil worker and a socialist activist. Gomulka finished primary school and was trained as a locksmith but at the age of fourteen became an apprentice mechanic.

Early Training in Moscow

In his late teens, after Poland had regained its independence in the aftermath of World War I, Gomulka joined the socialist youth movement and, soon after, the illegal Polish Communist party. He began organizing communist labor groups and became a leading party activist. He was arrested in 1926 for his revolutionary activities, but his prison sentence was suspended. In the late 1920s Gomulka was dispatched by his party superiors to Moscow, where he received ideological and organizational training. He subsequently returned to Poland to become a trade union organizer. In 1930 he was elected national secretary of the militantly socialist Chemical Workers Union. He helped organize strikes around the country and suffered a serious leg injury during a textile strike in Lodz in 1932 that left him with a permanent limp.

Gale International Portrait Gallery
Wladyslaw Gomulka

World War II

From 1934 to 1935 Gomulka studied in Moscow at the International Lenin School. He returned to Poland to continue his political work and to organize industrial protests among unionized workers in demand of higher wages and improved working conditions. In 1936 Gomulka was arrested and sentenced to seven years in prison. He was released when the Germans and Russians invaded Poland in September 1939 and according to communist historians took part in the defense of Warsaw against the German assault. After the Polish surrender he returned to Krosno and began to organize the Communist underground movement against the Nazi occupation. In July 1942 he moved to Warsaw, where he became a district secretary and member of the Central Committee of the newly formed Polish Workers' party (PPR). He continued to work in the underground against the Nazi regime, and in November 1943, after his predecessor was arrested by the Gestapo, Gomulka became secretary general of the PPR.

Communist Takeover of Poland

In 1944 Gomulka joined the Polish National Liberation Committee, which was formed under Stalin's orders as the Red Army swept westward driving the Germans out of Polish territories. After the liberation by Russian forces in 1945, he returned to Warsaw as the deputy premier of the new puppet administration and helped the Soviets to install a communist system throughout the country. He displayed great zeal in the suppression of rival political parties and presided over the fraudulent postwar referendum of 1946 and the rigged elections in 1947 which capped the Communist party takeover.

Ouster and Rehabilitation

Gomulka was ruthless in eliminating all opposition to communist rule. He led the struggle to crush the Polish Peasant party and was responsible for the enforced merger of some elements of the Polish Socialist party (PPS) with the PPR, which resulted in the formation of the PUWP in 1948. Gomulka, however, did not strictly abide by every tenet of the official Stalinist line. He opposed the rapid or coercive collectivization of agriculture, in which private farming was outlawed, and expressed reservations about the formation of the Moscow-directed Cominform (Communist Information Bureau) in September 1947. His independent attitude cost him his prominent position, and he was removed from power, ousted from the party, and replaced by Boleslaw Bierut as the party chief in 1948.

In August 1951 Gomulka was arrested and imprisoned, as the PUWP under Moscow's direction conducted a purge of both "national communists" and suspected followers of Yugoslavia's Marshal Tito, who had broken with Stalin three years earlier. In 1954, a year after Stalin's death, Gomulka was released, and in 1956 he was politically rehabilitated. Party leader Bierut was ousted and died in March of that year. In April the new party first secretary, Edward Ochab, admitted that Gomulka should not have been arrested. The party leadership managed to avert both a major national crisis and the possibility of a Red Army crackdown when it persuaded Soviet leader Nikita S. Khrushchev that some reforms were essential to preserve communist rule in Poland.

Gomulka had achieved relative public popularity due to the persecution he had endured and the high expectations engendered during the liberalizing "Polish October," when restrictions on intellectual life were somewhat loosened. In October 1956 he was appointed first secretary of the PUWP and reinstated as Poland's top leader. After the years of Stalinist terror, wide sectors of the population, including intellectuals and workers' leaders, believed that Gomulka's government would undertake significant reforms and gain a large margin of Polish independence from the Soviet Union.

The 1968 Crisis

In the first few years of his rule, Gomulka dissolved most of the unproductive collective and state farms and restored private agriculture in Poland, a country where small-scale family farming had a strong tradition. He also arranged a modus vivendi with the persecuted Roman Catholic church and allowed more freedom of cultural expression. However, personal liberties remained restricted, and no major economic or political reforms were undertaken. By the late 1960s Gomulka had come under increasing criticism by the intelligentsia for the maintenance of censorship and for bureaucratic interference in academic and cultural life. In a major crackdown on intellectual opposition, the government, in March 1968, orchestrated an anti-Semitic campaign in Poland's universities and ordered militia units to attack student demonstrators. The extensive purges of the intelligentsia were depicted by the communists as an "anti-Zionist" campaign to rid the universities of "foreign agents" and "Zionist sympathizers" who were seeking to undermine Polish-Soviet policies in the Middle East and to overthrow the socialist system. Thousands of intellectuals fled the country, and the universities were placed more firmly under party control.

Gomulka survived the 1968 crisis but had clearly lost his public credibility. His political support in the party also began to shrink as he faced successive challenges to his leadership. He tried to save his position by adopting some novel policies. For example, in 1970 he helped to normalize relations with West Germany, an initiative launched by German chancellor Willy Brandt under his Ostpolitik policy, which went a long way toward sanctioning Poland's western border. Relations between the two states had began to improve in the mid 1960s, when Poland's Catholic bishop had issued a letter calling for reconciliation between Germany and Poland. Gomulka also initiated some economic reforms, but by then it was too late to improve the ailing economy or to avert workers' protests.

The Gdansk Massacre and Resignation

As part of the new economic plan to raise money for imported technology, the government announced a drastic increase in the prices of food and fuel just before the Christmas holidays in 1970. This move resulted in a week of demonstrations by workers in the Baltic Coast shipyards in several Polish cities. After police and army units opened fire and massacred several dozen protesting workers in Gdansk, Gomulka was forced to resign in December and was replaced as PUWP leader by Edward Gierek. Gomulka subsequently slipped completely out of public eye and died in Warsaw on 1 September 1982.

Book by Gomulka
On the German Problem: Articles and Speeches (Warsaw: Ksiàzka i Wiedza, 1969).

Books about Gomulka
Nicholas Bethell, *Gomulka: His Poland, His Communism* (Harmondsworth, England: Penguin, 1970);

Peter Raina, *Wladyslaw Gomulka* (London: Polonia, 1969).

General References
J. F. Brown, *Eastern Europe and Communist Rule* (Durham, N.C. and London: Duke University Press, 1988);

Robert L. Hutchings, *Soviet-East European Relations: Consolidation and Conflict, 1968–1980* (Madison: University of Wisconsin Press, 1983);

Christopher D. Jones, *Soviet Influence in Eastern Europe: Political Autonomy and the Warsaw Pact* (New York: Praeger, 1981);

Krystyna Kersten, *The Establishment of Communist Rule in Poland, 1943–1948* (Berkeley: University of California Press, 1991);

Joseph Rothschild, *Return to Diversity: A Political History of East Central Europe since World War II* (New York: Oxford University Press, 1989);

Sarah M. Terry, ed., *Soviet Policy in Eastern Europe* (New Haven: Yale University Press, 1984);

Adam Ulam, *Expansion and Coexistence* (New York: Praeger, 1968);

J. B. de Weydenthal, *The Communists of Poland* (Stanford, Cal.: Hoover Institution Press, 1986).

–J. B. and A. B.

SEE ALSO THESE RELATED ENTRIES

Boleslaw Bierut, 2; Edward Gierek, 2; Lech Walesa, 2.

Mikhail Gorbachev

General Secretary, Soviet Communist Party, 1985–1991
Born Privolnoye, Soviet Union, 2 March 1931

Mikhail Gorbachev, the most influential Soviet leader in the second half of the twentieth century, will have a place in history as one of the great reformers of Russia. On becoming general secretary of the Communist party in March 1985, he faced a daunting array of problems inherited by the Soviet Union after decades of misrule and abuse, problems most apparent in the corruption of the party bureaucracy and the stagnation of the economy. Gorbachev immediately introduced a program of economic and political reforms that came to be known by the overarching terms *perestroika* and *glasnost*, reforms that became more and more daring with each passing year. His initiatives in foreign policy were as bold: he ceded independence to Eastern Europe and embarked on efforts to repair relations with the West, efforts that resulted in the end of the Cold War.

Mikhail Sergeyevich Gorbachev was born in the village of Privolnoye in the Stavropol region of Russia. The village lies between the Don and Volga rivers in the fertile steppes of the northern Caucasus. Predominantly rural, the region has historically produced large amounts of grain. Both Gorbachev's parents were peasants, and his father worked as a machine operator in a local tractor station.

Mikhail Gorbachev

Collectivization

Gorbachev's birth coincided with the peak year of collectivization, Joseph Stalin's ruthless program to nationalize the Soviet peasantry, and Stavropol suffered along with the rest of the Soviet Union. His parents were among the first assigned to the new collective farm in Privolnoye, and his grandfather, Andrei, was arrested one night. After being charged with hoarding forty pounds of grain, he was sentenced to nine years in a labor camp. The winter of 1932–1933 saw famine strike Stavropol, and some fifty thousand peasants starved to death.

In World War II Gorbachev's father and brother were called up to fight. His father came back from the war, but his brother was killed in the battle for Kursk in 1943. The war interrupted Gorbachev's education, but he resumed his normal schooling in September 1943. He spent summers working on the col-

lective, only going back to school after the autumn harvest. The first postwar harvests were poor, but 1949 was a very good year, and Privolnoye overfulfilled its quota. For his work Gorbachev won the Order of the Red Banner of Labor.

In 1950 he entered Moscow University, the most prestigious university in the Soviet Union, to study law. His attraction to law was unusual: it was a profession that in Stalin's era had fallen into low repute, especially among the peasantry, who had come to associate it with the repressive and coercive tactics of collectivization.

Working for the Komsomol

At the university Gorbachev performed propaganda activities for the Komsomol (Communist

Youth League) and in 1952 became a Communist party member. One of his roommates was Zdenek Mlynar, a prominent member of the 1968 Czech reform movement known as the Prague Spring. He described Gorbachev as loyal and honest without being arrogant and said that he showed a tendency not to accept the party's position blindly. Before leaving the university Gorbachev married Raisa Titorenko, a philosophy student.

Gorbachev returned to Stavropol in 1955 and joined the city Komsomol committee to work in propaganda, an undemanding job for a Moscow graduate. He never actually practiced law. The main benefit he appears to have received from his legal education was a formal training in oratory.

Propaganda work in the Komsomol aimed to inspire the young with a sense of purpose, and here Gorbachev displayed a natural talent. His contemporaries have remarked on his ability to take a complicated topic, such as an agricultural directive from Moscow, and translate its complexities for the residents of rural Stavropol, using a sense of humor and a love of language to drive home simple points.

By 1960 he had quickly risen to first secretary of the Stavropol regional Komsomol committee. At about this time he became a protégé of Fyodor Kulakov, a promising agronomist who had been sent from Moscow to take charge of the regional party committee. Kulakov would keep an eye on Gorbachev for the next eighteen years and ensure his political rise.

Soviet Agricultural Policy

In March 1962 Gorbachev was unexpectedly appointed to a position organizing agricultural production in a rural part of the district. This marked his departure from the Komsomol and the beginning of his career in the party. It is probable that Kulakov had a say in this transfer. To remedy his lack of formal training in agronomy, Gorbachev enrolled in a correspondence course. But immediately after the 1962 harvest he was promoted to head the regional party organs, placing him in control of promotions and demotions of party cadres in the region. This was a desk job with some travel to the outlying districts. Stavropol, with its benign climate and warm springs, was home to hundreds of holiday resorts and spas. All of the upper-level ministries and party organs had their own spas and sanatoriums, and legions of high-level party officials came to Stavropol. Gorbachev is sure to have come into contact with them.

He occupied this regional post for four years. During this time Raisa began a sociological study on the Stavropol peasantry, for which she received a doctorate in 1967. Gorbachev earned his second degree in 1967 after completing his correspondence studies, making him eligible for promotion to second secretary of the regional committee responsible for agriculture. In 1970 he became first secretary, a fairly high position which included membership in the Communist party's Central Committee.

Gorbachev's career was undistinguished during this period until Kulakov, who had become the secretary for agriculture in the Central Committee, devised a scheme in 1976 to increase the yields of Soviet agriculture. In the past, up to 30 percent of the Soviet grain harvest had been lost because of delays in harvesting. Kulakov hoped to eliminate these delays through better organization and logistics, and he decided to test his plan during the 1977 harvest in the Ipatovsky district of Stavropol.

Gorbachev, as Kulakov's protégé and first secretary of Stavropol, also had his career tied to the scheme, and he was entrusted by Kulakov with its execution. As it happened, the harvest was a complete success. Ending on 14 July 1977 it had taken only nine days instead of the usual three or four weeks. Ipatovsky delivered to the state not just the promised 120,000 tons of wheat, but an additional 80,000. Stavropol basked in its newfound glory, and Gorbachev received the Order of the October Revolution for his work.

Kulakov's method was used again the following year in Ipatovsky, and again it was successful, helping to yield a record Soviet crop. Kulakov by now looked to be almost certainly Leonid Brezhnev's heir apparent. But on 17 July 1978 Kulakov suddenly died, leaving vacant his position of agricultural secretary in the Central Committee. In November 1978 Gorbachev was named to fill it.

For various reasons the four harvests between 1979 and 1982 were failures. Gorbachev managed to avoid blame and continued his political ascent, becoming a candidate member of the Politburo in 1979 and a full member in 1980.

Agricultural Secretary

The 1981 harvest was a disaster, the worst since 1975. Realizing the grave danger facing the Soviet Union, Brezhnev in May 1982 unveiled his "Food Program," which promised to make the Soviet Union self-reliant in its food supply within ten years. Despite the fanfare with which the plan was introduced, it included no real reforms, serving instead as a highly detailed ten-year timetable. The harvest for 1982 was above the previous year's level but was a failure nevertheless. By now Gorbachev's career was bound up with the fortunes of Soviet agriculture. At the regular plenary meeting of the Central Committee, it was expected that Gorbachev would be called to account. The meeting had been scheduled for 16 November. On 10 November, however, Brezhnev died, an occurrence that probably saved Gorbachev's career.

Serving under Andropov

In the battle for succession that followed, Yuri Andropov prevailed over Brezhnev's former aide and own favorite, Konstantin Chernenko. Andropov immediately began to tackle the Soviet Union's accumulated economic problems, announcing a new emphasis on discipline, hard work, and initiative. He found a strong ally in Gorbachev and saw to it that the younger man received an exposure to Soviet domestic and foreign policy not traditionally seen by a secretary of agriculture in the Central Committee. He assigned Gorbachev to oversee a nonviolent purge of Brezhnev-appointed apparatchiks in an attempt to bring a younger, more imaginative generation to the forefront of the party leadership. It was apparent by this time that the seventy-one-year-old Andropov was preparing his younger protégé for eventual succession to general secretary.

Andropov died in February 1984. His fifteen-month tenure had not been sufficient to implement any truly effective reforms. Gorbachev, his protégé, was considered too young and inexperienced by the Politburo and was passed over for general secretary in favor of Chernenko, who represented the older Brezhnev faction. Chernenko promised to continue Andropov's reforms, but he lacked his predecessor's firm commitment and vigor. In any case, Chernenko was gravely ill and held the top position for only thirteen months. In his last six months he began to disappear from view, and during this time Gorbachev assumed greater control over the prestigious functions of ideology and foreign affairs.

General Secretary

At Chernenko's death in March 1985 the struggle for succession among Gorbachev, Moscow party chief Victor Grishin, and Gregory Romanov, secretary for military and industrial affairs, was short but intense. What ultimately decided the matter in Gorbachev's favor was the support of two elder and respected members of the Politburo, Foreign Minister Andrei Gromyko and Yegor

Ligachev. Speaking extempore to the Central Committee, Gromyko reportedly said of Gorbachev: "He has a nice smile, but teeth of iron."

Perestroika

When he assumed the post of general secretary on 14 March 1985, Gorbachev inherited a stagnant economy whose average annual gross national product (GNP) for the past ten years had languished at around 1.8 percent. He immediately put into effect a program of economic reforms, a "revolution from above" that has since become known as perestroika. The reforms began modestly with Gorbachev resuming the widespread personnel changes begun under Andropov and exhorting the workers and officials to strive for greater discipline and initiative. By 1986 Gorbachev had replaced roughly one-fifth of the *nomenklatura* – the top 450,000 of the 19-million-strong Soviet Communist party. Among the notable changes in the top leadership, Gromyko – the veteran cold warrior – was replaced as foreign minister by Eduard Shevardnadze, a reformist Georgian leader whom Gorbachev had known from his days in the Komsomol. Two other Gorbachev allies, Anatoly Dobrynin and Alexander Yakovlev, were appointed to the Secretariat.

In May 1985 Gorbachev unveiled an antialcohol campaign in an effort to reduce absenteeism as well as drunkenness on the job and to raise workers' productivity. The campaign was highly unpopular and not particularly effective, and it was abandoned in September 1988.

By spring of 1987 Gorbachev realized that the Soviet economy required further, more drastic reform. At its June plenary meeting the Central Committee approved measures that would introduce market forces into the economy, especially in setting prices. The "Law on Socialist Enterprise" brought the Western practice of cost-accounting to the Soviet Union, forcing all enterprises to match expenses with revenues so as to weed out the economically inefficient. And for the first time ever the Soviet economy entertained the possibility of bankruptcy.

In May 1988 Gorbachev went further: his "Law on Cooperatives," approved that month, established the right of three or more persons to form a cooperative business. Initially these businesses were limited to the service economy and the production of consumer goods, but by 1990 the cooperatives generated roughly 5 percent of the Soviet GNP and were perestroika's only real success to that date.

In March 1990 Gorbachev announced his intent to develop a market economy for the Soviet Union. That month he authorized limited ownership of farms and businesses, and the way was prepared for the creation of a stock market.

Glasnost

By the spring of 1986 Gorbachev's economic reforms had met enough resistance from the entrenched party elite that he decided to take his case to the masses in the hope of mobilizing public opinion against bureaucratic inertia. At the June Plenum of the Central Committee he formally announced a new campaign of openness and candor between the party and the citizens – and borrowed a term from Lenin's lexicon to name it: glasnost. Glasnost opened the media to present differences of opinion and a plurality of views, cultural freedoms hitherto never permitted in the Soviet Union. Books and films that had been banned for political reasons appeared openly in the Soviet Union for the first time. *Doctor Zhivago*, by Boris Pasternak; *The Gulag Archipelago*, by Aleksandr Solzhenitsyn; and *Children of the Arbat*, by Anatoly Rybakov, were among the more prominent works that finally saw the light of day in Soviet society.

Glasnost, however, went further: in December 1986, Gorbachev personally telephoned dissident physicist Andrei Sakharov, in exile in the closed city of Gorki (now Nizhni Novgorod) to tell him that he was free to return to Moscow. Sakharov did so, in time becoming one of Gorbachev's most influential supporters.

The premiere of *Repentance*, a film by Georgian director Tengiz Abuladze, in January 1987 marked the beginning of Gorbachev's anti-Stalinist campaign, which encouraged a public reappraisal of the former dictator and his legacy. The role of Stalin's more prominent opponents, notably Leon Trotsky and Nikolay Bukharin, "non-persons" since their demise in the 1930s, was reexamined in a more impartial, even sympathetic, light.

In a dramatic gesture that represented a partial conciliation with the Russian Orthodox church, Gorbachev permitted national television coverage of Easter services from Moscow's Yelokhovsky Cathedral in 1988. Later that year the church primate, Patriarch Pimen, was invited to the Kremlin, signaling a greater official tolerance for open religious practices.

Taking advantage of glasnost to continue her intellectual pursuits, Raisa Gorbachev sat on the board of the Soviet Cultural Foundation to publicize the literary and artistic heritage of Russia. She had in the meanwhile assumed a public profile higher than was traditional for the wife of a Soviet leader, accompanying her husband abroad on his official visits and projecting a very un-Soviet aura of glamour and sophistication. There had been some criticism within the Soviet Union for her elegant dress and supposed haughtiness, but this appeared not to deter her.

Demokratizatiia

By early 1988 Gorbachev decided to effect institutional reforms that went beyond the cultural liberalization provided by glasnost and sought to change the Soviet political apparatus. To this end he began a policy of reform known as *demokratizatiia*, or "democratization," which would be his lasting legacy to the Soviet Union. In introducing this policy his goal was nothing less than a constitutional change involving a transfer of power away from the party to an elected parliament and an executive presidency.

At the Nineteenth Party Conference in June 1988 Gorbachev pushed through his plan that called for the abolishment of the current Supreme Soviet, a shadow parliament of 1,500, in favor of a 2,250-member Congress of People's Deputies, which would meet once a year to elect a radically different Supreme Soviet. Its 400 members would act as a sitting parliament with legislative powers. According to the timetable set that June, elections for the Congress of People's Deputies were to be held in March 1989, and it was expected that Gorbachev would assume in April the office of chairman of the Presidium of the Supreme Soviet, hitherto a largely ceremonial position corresponding to head of the Soviet state and at that time occupied by Andrei Gromyko.

Gorbachev and his allies still formed a minority in the ruling Politburo, a situation that limited the scope and effectiveness of perestroika. Consequently, after the 1988 Party Conference he acted to increase his power within the state – as opposed to party – apparatus and to reduce the party's ability to obstruct his reforms. Moving quickly in the fall of 1988, Gorbachev forced Gromyko into retirement and named himself to head the Supreme Soviet. Simultaneously he restructured and weakened the Central Committee of the Communist party and its two centers of power, the Politburo and the Secretariat. In the shake-up the large number of Central Committee departments that had run particular industries disappeared, removing the party bureaucracy from detailed economic decision making. Gorbachev also used the occasion to appoint five new members to the Politburo, replacing those whose thinking he considered anachronistic. Several thousand government workers also lost their jobs, representing a 40-percent cut in the bureaucracy. And the next year Gorbachev strengthened the office of chairman of the Supreme Soviet. Finally, in March 1990, at Gorbachev's behest, the Congress of People's Deputies voted to rename the position of Chairman of the Supreme Soviet the Presidency and to give it a five-year term. Gorbachev at that time was named to occupy the office until 1995, when it would be filled by popular vote.

Foreign Policy

Bold and decisive initiatives marked Gorbachev's foreign policy regarding the West, leading to the warmest relations between the Soviet Union and the United States since the onset of the Cold War. In a series of summits between 1985 and 1990, Gorbachev met each year with the incumbent American president, first Ronald Reagan and then George Bush. At their December 1987 meeting in Washington, Gorbachev and Reagan reached agreement on the Intermediate-range Nuclear Forces Treaty (INF), intended to remove and destroy an entire class of nuclear weapons – medium-range missiles. The agreement was made possible largely because of Gorbachev's worry about the ambitious American plan to develop an antiballistic-missile defense system that would sit in outer space – the Strategic Defense Initiative [SDI], or "Star Wars." Gorbachev painfully realized that any attempt to match SDI would come at the expense of his domestic reforms. He therefore dropped a long-standing Soviet demand to include British and French nuclear forces in the scope of any agreement with the United States.

When Eastern European countries, in the spirit of perestroika, began to take tentative steps towards political liberalization, Gorbachev made no move to stop them. In 1989 Poland, Hungary, Czechoslovakia, and Bulgaria moved, at varying speeds, to assert independence from Moscow and abandon communism. The extent to which Eastern Europe freed itself of Soviet control went beyond what Moscow had expected and desired: in all these countries the communist dictatorships fell and were replaced by multiparty governments.

The most striking example of the Soviet Union's new attitude toward its former satellites was Gorbachev's decision to allow, even to encourage, radical change in East Germany. On 7 October 1989, amid growing demonstrations throughout the country, Gorbachev warned Erich Honecker's government that it could not count on Soviet support to quell the civil unrest, and he advised the communist leadership to begin its own version of perestroika: "Life itself punishes those who delay." It was, however, too late. On 3 December 1989 the East German Communist party's Politburo and Central Committee resigned en masse, and on 3 October 1990 East Germany was formally incorporated into West Germany. What was most remarkable about these revolutions in Eastern Europe was Moscow's role as initiator: in direct contrast to Hungary in 1956, Czechoslovakia in 1968, Poland in 1980–1981, the Soviet Union urged unwilling national Communist parties to undertake reforms. This radical turnaround of Soviet policy regarding Eastern Europe and the idea of a united Germany in the Western sphere of influence probably more than anything else signaled the end of the Cold War.

Gorbachev's foreign policy offered other surprises as well. He made a series of unilateral moves to extricate the Soviet Union from some of its embarrassing and costly foreign entanglements left over from the Brezhnev era. He began to withdraw Soviet troops from Afghanistan in May 1988, where they had been ensnarled in a war with the mujahedin guerrillas since December 1979. Soviet pressure facilitated the beginning of a Cuban pullout from Angola in 1988, which was completed by mid 1991, and a Vietnamese withdrawal from Kampuchea, which was completed by October 1989.

Gorbachev made attempts to repair the longstanding Sino-Soviet rift by signing in June 1985 a five-year trade agreement with Beijing. The Chinese, however, had informally set three conditions as a prerequisite to any real improvement in relations with the Soviet Union. Two of these had been met by Gorbachev's new policies toward Afghanistan and Kampuchea. The third was satisfied in December 1988 at the United Nations (UN) when Gorbachev dramatically unveiled a plan whereby he would unilaterally cut Soviet armed forces by half a million troops before the end of 1990 and destroy a sizeable quantity of tanks and aircraft. The destruction of equipment was of dubious significance, since most of it was obsolete. But 250,000 troops would be taken from the Sino-Soviet border in an attempt to demilitarize the frontier.

Gorbachev reputedly made the UN offer without extensively consulting with the Soviet high command. That he was able to do so was a consequence of having worked to reduce the independent power of the military since becoming general secretary. His new defense minister, Marshal Sergei Sokolov, had been kept from full Politburo membership. In May 1985 Gorbachev forced the retirement of more than a dozen top officers, holdovers from the Brezhnev era like Admiral Sergei Gorshkov. He forced more cuts in May 1987 after a nineteen-year-old German named Mattias Rust landed a small aircraft in Moscow's Red Square after having successfully (and unwittingly) bypassed Soviet air defenses. Gorbachev used this as an excuse to sack Sokolov and over a hundred other high-ranking officers. Apart from the obvious political benefits of a more compliant military, it was necessary to the success of perestroika that the military's privileged status in economic planning be reduced.

Unrest in the Soviet Republics

Gorbachev's tolerance for national autonomy did not extend to the Soviet republics, as witnessed by his treatment of Lithuania and Latvia. Both Baltic states had declared independence in 1990, Lithuania in March and Latvia in May. The Soviet Union conducted an economic blockade of Lithuania between April and June and in August drafted a memorandum that called for a drastic crackdown.

Gorbachev's policy of openness had the unintended effect of releasing interethnic tensions within the Soviet Union itself — tensions that had been kept contained in the less-benign political climate of his predecessors. On at least five occasions since December 1986 Soviet troops intervened in the smaller republics to break up fighting among the ethnic minorities: in Kazakhstan in December 1986, in Georgia in April 1989, in Uzbekistan in June 1989, in Azerbaijan in January 1990, and in Tadzhikistan in February 1990.

By the end of 1990 the pace of reform appeared to have slackened, concurrent with a reassertion of state authority under an apparently more conservative President Gorbachev. In the economic sphere he had still not approved an ambitious five-hundred-day plan devised by Stanislav S. Shatalin that would have given the Soviet Union a free-market system, doubtless aware that to do so might mean an initial surge in prices that would fuel unrest among the populace. Politically, Gorbachev was granted stronger powers by the Supreme Soviet in October, powers that he used to appoint conservatives to important positions and to secure greater control over the increasingly rebellious republics.

Political Opposition

He faced continued opposition from both ends of the political spectrum: on the left the proposals of Boris Yeltsin, the hugely popular president of the Russian Republic, tended to obscure the truly revolutionary achievements of Gorbachev. Yeltsin demanded reforms more radical than those that had already been implemented, calling for a true multiparty democracy. Gorbachev realized that this would effectively end the preeminence of the Communist party in the Soviet Union, and he was unwilling to take this last, drastic step.

From the political right Gorbachev was still faced by the entrenched interests of the domestic triad of Soviet power: the party, the military, and the KGB. Despite his strenuous efforts to neutralize or weaken these groups, they still had the power to obstruct his most far-reaching reforms — forms that threatened the very basis of their existence. An August 1991 coup attempt against Gorbachev by conservative elements in the Soviet leadership weakened Gorbachev's hold on power. In December 1991 the Soviet Union was dissolved, and Gorbachev found himself without a job. Boris Yeltsin, the president of the Russian Federation, became the dominant political force. Subsequent attempts by Gorbachev to reenter Russian politics failed, and he has been occupying himself since by traveling, speaking, and writing.

Gorbachev altered Soviet society and government to an extent inconceivable when he first came to power. The terms *perestroika* and *glasnost* will be irrevocably associated with his name, and to his foreign policy must be credited the end of the Cold War.

Books by Gorbachev

Perestroika: New Thinking for our Country and the World (London: Collins, 1987);

The August Coup (London: HarperCollins, 1991).

Books about Gorbachev

Michael Beschloss, *At the Highest Levels: The Inside Story of the End of the Cold War* (Boston: Little, Brown, 1993);

Seweryn Bialer, *Politics, Society and Nationality inside Gorbachev's Russia* (Boulder, Colo.: Westview Press, 1989);

Seweryn Bialer, *The Soviet Paradox: External Expansion, Internal Decline* (New York: Knopf, 1986);

Susan L. Clark, ed., *Gorbachev's Agenda: Changes in Soviet Domestic and Foreign Policy* (Boulder, Colo.: Westview Press, 1989);

Martin Crouch, *Revolution and Evolution: Gorbachev and Soviet Politics* (New York: Prentice Hall, 1990);

Dusko Doder and Louise Branson, *Gorbachev: Heretic in the Kremlin* (New York: Penguin, 1991);

Neil Felshman, *Gorbachev, Yeltsin, and the Last Days of the Soviet Empire* (New York: St. Martin's Press, 1992);

Jerry F. Hough, *Russia and the West: Gorbachev and the Politics of Reform* (New York: Touchstone Press, 1990);

Robert G. Kaiser, *Why Gorbachev Happened: His Triumphs and His Failure* (New York: Simon & Schuster, 1991);

Martin McCauley, ed., *The Soviet Union under Gorbachev* (New York: St. Martin's Press, 1987);

Zhores A. Medvedev, *Gorbachev* (New York: Norton, 1986);

John Miller, *Mikhail Gorbachev and the End of Soviet Power* (New York: St. Martin's Press, 1992);

Gerd Ruge, *Gorbachev: A Biography* (London: Chatto & Windus, 1991);

Richard Sakwa, *Gorbachev and His Reforms, 1985–1990* (New York: Prentice-Hall, 1991);

Stephen White, *Gorbachev and After,* updated and expanded edition (New York: Cambridge University Press, 1991).

General References

Anders Aslund, *Gorbachev's Struggle for Economic Reform,* updated and expanded edition (Ithaca, N.Y.: Cornell University Press, 1991);

Arnold Beichman and Mikhail S. Bernstam, *Andropov, New Challenge to the West: A Political Biography* (New York: Stein & Day, 1983);

Seweryn Bialer, *The Soviet Paradox: External Expansion, Internal Decline* (New York: Knopf, 1986);

Zbigniew Brzezinski, *The Grand Failure: The Birth and Death of Communism in the Twentieth Century* (New York: Scribners, 1989);

Timothy J. Colton, *The Dilemma of Reform in the Soviet Union* (New York: Council on Foreign Relations, 1986);

Karen Dawisha, *Eastern Europe, Gorbachev, and Reform: The Great Challenge* (New York: Cambridge University Press, 1988);

Marshall I. Goldman, *What Went Wrong with Perestroika* (New York: Norton, 1991);

Ed A. Hewett, *Reform in the Soviet Economy: Equality versus Efficiency* (Washington, D.C.: Brookings Institution, 1988);

Zhores A. Medvedev, *Andropov* (New York: Penguin, 1984);

John W. Parker, *Kremlin in Transition* (Boston: Unwin, 1991);

Jonathan Steel and Eric Abraham, *Andropov in Power: From Komsomol to Kremlin* (Garden City, N.Y.: Anchor Press / Doubleday, 1983);

Ilya Zemtsov, *Chernenko, the Last Bolshevik: The Soviet Union on the Eve of Perestroika* (New Brunswick: Transaction Books, 1989).

– M. B.

SEE ALSO THESE RELATED ENTRIES
Leonid Brezhnev, 2; Perestroika, 3; Ronald Reagan, 1; Reykjavik Summit, 3.

Sergei Gorshkov

Commander in Chief, Soviet Navy, 1956–1985
Born Kamenets-Podolski, Ukraine, Russia, 26 February 1910
Died Moscow, Soviet Union, 13 May 1988

Sergei Georgievich Gorshkov, commander in chief of the Soviet Navy from 1956 to 1985, presided over the transformation of the Soviet Union into a global seapower during the 1960s and 1970s. Born of Russian nationality in the Ukraine, he joined the navy in 1927 to attend the Frunze Naval Academy. Like many of his generation who were not objects of Joseph Stalin's purge of the Communist party in the 1930s, he advanced quickly through the thinned ranks of the army. Before World War II he commanded detachments in the Black Sea and the Far East, gaining expertise in minelaying and minesweeping. During the war he served largely in the Black Sea, with one temporary assignment commanding army troops in the Caucasus. He joined the Communist party in 1942 and was promoted to rear admiral that same year. After the war he returned to the Black Sea Fleet, becoming its commander in chief. He remained there until 1955, when party secretary general Nikita Khrushchev named him first deputy commander in chief of the navy. In January 1956 he was given command of the Soviet Navy.

The Soviet Navy under Khrushchev

As a result of Khrushchev's "single-variant strategy," which accorded nuclear missile forces the prime role in Soviet military planning, Gorshkov initially watched the navy's share of the budget shrink. Construction of warships was reduced by 60 percent, the savings allocated to the domestic economy.

By 1961, however, senior military officers had forced a reevaluation of the doctrine of nuclear deterrence, and, in view of the Western lead in technology and the new theories of limited nuclear war then in vogue, they emphasized a more balanced Soviet military structure, with special regard for combined arms operations. Within the navy, nuclear submarines were expected to play two roles: operate against Western ships in waters far from the Soviet coast and match the West's "strategic reserves." The holder of strategic reserves would not use these weapons in the early stages of a nuclear war but save them for a second strike.

Sergei Gorshkov

Gorshkov clearly favored submarines and accorded them the chief position in his navy. But in a series of articles published in the navy's journal in the early 1970s, he argued for a larger, more balanced navy. This navy would not only be necessary for supporting long-range submarine operations; it also could be used to extend Soviet conventional power, especially in combined arms operations. Navy ships and planes would inter alia conduct antisubmarine warfare, transport amphibious troops, and project Soviet power to the Third World. To a large extent Gorshkov received the ships he wanted, and by the 1970s Soviet vessels were patrolling the world's oceans.

119

Sea Power of the State

In 1976 he published *The Sea Power of the State*, which has since become a classic work of maritime strategy. The book, however, went beyond strategy and was part of Gorshkov's continuing efforts to gain a greater, more independent voice for the navy by almost intentionally reducing the importance of the other Soviet services. When Marshal Nikolai Ogarkov became chief of the general staff in 1977, one of his first tasks was to restrain Gorshkov and remind him of the need for combined arms operations.

In late 1985 Gorshkov retired from active duty, having suddenly been replaced by a submariner, his former chief of staff Admiral Vladimir N. Chernavin. He died on 13 May 1988.

Book by Gorshkov

The Sea Power of the State (New York: Pergamon Press, 1979).

Books about Gorshkov

Robert W. Herrick, *Soviet Naval Theory and Policy: Gorshkov's Inheritance* (Newport, R.I.: Naval War College Press, 1988);

Dale R. Herspring, *The Soviet High Command, 1967–1989: Personalities and Politics* (Princeton, N.J.: Princeton University Press, 1990);

Michael McGuire, "Soviet Naval Doctrine and Strategy" in *Soviet Military Thinking*, edited by Derek Leebaert (London: Allen & Unwin, 1981).

– M. B.

SEE ALSO THESE ENTRIES
Andrei Grechko, 2; Nikita S. Khrushchev, 2; Nikolai Ogarkov, 2.

Klement Gottwald

President of Czechoslovakia, 1948–1953
Born Dedice u Vyskova, Moravia, 23 November 1896
Died Moscow, Soviet Union, 14 March 1953

Klement Gottwald, Czechoslovak communist politician and journalist who was successively deputy premier, premier, and president of Czechoslovakia during the 1940s and 1950s, was born into a peasant family in Dedice u Vyskova in Moravia. He was drafted into the Austro-Hungarian army in 1915 and fought in Russia and Italy during World War I. He deserted near the end of the war to serve with the Czechoslovak army, which was established as the Austrian military disintegrated during 1918.

Czechoslovak Politics after World War I

Gottwald was discharged from the army in 1920 and soon afterward became an active member of the Czechoslovak Social Democratic party. In 1921 he took part in the formation of the Czechoslovak Communist party (CCP), which was promptly admitted into the Moscow-controlled Comintern (Communist International). Gottwald worked as an editor for numerous communist periodicals and served as a party functionary in Slovakia, and he helped steadily to build up the CCP membership in the country. Unlike those in other East European states, the CCP received significant indigenous support, particularly in the industrialized regions of Bohemia where a large working class had been in existence since before the achievement of Czech independence.

In 1925 Gottwald was elected to the CCP's Central Committee and its Politburo. He directed the Agitation and Propaganda Division from 1926 to 1929 and became CCP general secretary in 1929, when the process of Bolshevization, or "democratic centralism," in the party was completed. From 1929 forward Gottwald also served as a deputy in the Czechoslovak National Assembly. He was considered an instigator and a troublemaker by the police, and in 1934, despite his prior election to the National Assembly, he was forced to leave the country. He fled to the Soviet Union, where he stayed for the next two years, but returned to Czechoslovakia in 1936. At the start of World War II in 1938, he left again for Moscow, where he helped to organize the Stalin-sponsored National Front of Czechoslovak Communist Exiles. Moscow intended to use this nucleus of activists to install a communist regime after the war.

Klement Gottwald

The Elections of 1946

When the war ended, Gottwald went back to Czechoslovakia. He became deputy premier of the new Czechoslovak government formed in April 1945 in Kostice in Slovakia when the Red Army crossed into Czechoslovak territory. Gottwald was named the prime minister of a coalition government after the relatively free parliamentary elections in May 1946, in which the communists gained a narrow majority of the vote. Stalin delayed the imposition of a communist monopoly of power in Czechoslovakia until 1948, partly because he considered the local Communist party to have some measure of indigenous support and legitimacy, and partly because he did not wish to antagonize unduly the West at a time when the Sovietization of other East European states, including Poland, was being intensified.

121

The Coup of 1948

The Communist party's relative popularity declined sharply under the new government as it began to implement its socialist agenda. Gottwald became chairman of the CCP in 1947 and played a major role in the bloodless communist coup d'état of February 1948, designed to forestall an election defeat. The CCP pressured President Edvard Beneš to form a new government containing a communist majority in order to give the new regime a veneer of legitimacy. Meanwhile, several prominent noncommunist Czechoslovak leaders fled to the West or were arrested by the security police. In February 1948 the noncommunist foreign minister Jan Masaryk mysteriously fell from a window to his death while under police custody; he was believed to have been murdered by the communist police. Beneš resigned in June 1948, in protest against the unconstitutional takeover, and one month later Gottwald was appointed the country's new president.

Imposition of Stalinism

Under Moscow's direction Gottwald imposed a Stalinist political and economic model on the country, and the party extended its control over all state bodies, bureaucracies, social organizations, and cultural institutions. During the national elections in May 1948, which were closely supervised by Communist party activists, the single list of procommunist candidates received almost 90 percent of the vote, and parliament was transformed into a pliant instrument of one-party rule. Having secured its monopoly, the party launched a program of agricultural collectivization designed to subordinate peasant production to state control. Heavy industrialization was also promoted in imitation of the Soviet economic model. Private enterprises, aside from some small-scale manufacturing, were outlawed, and the state assumed control over all banking and commerce. In the cultural field the Soviet-backed regime imposed a rigid form of artistic and literary expression known as "socialist realism," in which the construction of socialism was idealized. Under this doctrine intellectuals and artists were expected to reflect the objectives of the Communist party and the Soviet state.

Slánsky and the Terror Campaign

At the height of the Stalinist terror campaign from 1949 to 1953, all "bourgeois elements," including about one hundred thousand political dissidents, were incarcerated to root out political opposition. The former CCP general secretary Rudolf Slánsky was hanged in 1952 for being a nationalist and a supporter of Yugoslavia's ruler Josip Broz Tito, who was expelled from the Soviet alliance in 1948 for challenging Stalin's policies. Numerous other trials and executions were staged under Gottwald's supervision. Shortly after Stalin's death on 5 March 1953, Gottwald traveled to Moscow for the funeral and contracted a mysterious illness that proved fatal; he died on 14 March 1953.

General References

J. F. Brown, *Eastern Europe and Communist Rule* (Durham, N.C. and London: Duke University Press, 1988);

Christopher D. Jones, *Soviet Influence in Eastern Europe: Political Autonomy and the Warsaw Pact* (New York: Praeger, 1981);

Karel Kaplan, *Report on the Murder of the General Secretary* (Columbus: Ohio State University Press, 1990);

Josef Korbel, *The Communist Subversion of Czechoslovakia, 1938–1948: The Failure of Coexistence* (Princeton, N.J.: Princeton University Press, 1959);

Me'ir Ko'ti'k, *The Prague Trial: The First anti-Zionist Show Trial in the Communist Bloc* (New York: Herzl Press, Cornwall Books, 1987);

Eugene Loebl, *Stalinism in Prague: The Loebl Story* (New York: Grove Press, 1969);

Arthur Gerard London, *The Confession* (New York: Morrow, 1970);

Joseph Rothschild, *Return to Diversity: A Political History of East Central Europe since World War II* (New York: Oxford University Press, 1989);

Joseph Slanska, *Report on My Husband* (New York: Atheneum, 1969);

Marian Slingova, *Truth will Prevail* (London: Merlin, 1968);

Zdenek Suda, *Zealots and Rebels: A History of the Ruling Communist Party of Czechoslovakia* (Stanford, Cal.: Hoover Institution Press, 1980);

Sarah M. Terry, ed., *Soviet Policy in Eastern Europe* (New Haven: Yale University Press, 1984);

Adam Ulam, *Expansion and Coexistence* (New York: Praeger, 1968).

–J. B. and A. B.

SEE ALSO THESE RELATED ENTRIES

Georgi Malenkov, 2; Rudolf Slansky, 2; Joseph Stalin, 2; Josip Broz Tito, 2.

Yakubu Gowon

Head of State, Nigeria, 1966–1975
Born Gram, Nigeria, 19 October 1934

Yakubu Gowon was the head of the federal military government of Nigeria from 1966 to 1975. General Gowon commanded federal military forces during the bloody and protracted Nigerian civil war, also known as the Biafran War.

Gowon was educated at Saint Bartholomew's School, Wusasa, and the Government College in Zaria. In 1954 he joined the army and was sent for officer-training courses to Ghana and England. Gowon served twice in the United Nations peacekeeping force in the Congo during the Congolese civil war (1960–1965), after which he was promoted to major and then to lieutenant colonel.

The Coup of 1966

The civilian political institutions of Nigeria, which gained its independence from Britain on 1 October 1960, were in a state of collapse by 1965. The fragile political system was undermined by ethnic factionalism and regional political imbalances that threatened Nigeria's national unity and territorial integrity. By 1966 Nigeria's civilian government had fallen apart in the face of intensifying struggles for power among the various ethnic-based political leaders as well as corruption and factionalism within the army. On 15 January 1966 junior officers of the Ibo ethnic group staged a violent coup d'état. The takeover exacerbated the fears and resentment of the northern ethnic groups, such as the Hausa and Yoruba, of Ibo domination in the federal government. Gowon, who was out of the country when the coup took place, was named chief of staff by Major General Johnson Aguiyi-Ironsi, an Ibo and the new head of state. Shortly after the coup violent riots and factional violence directed against Ibo peoples broke out in northern Nigeria.

The situation deteriorated rapidly when on 29 July 1966 northern officers staged a countercoup, precipitating talks of secessions by the Ibo-dominated eastern region. In an attempt to placate Ibo fears, Lieutenant Colonel Gowon, who was a northerner from a minority ethnic group, was appointed head of state and supreme commander of the army. Gowon's efforts to restore order failed, as the situation had deteriorated beyond repair after the massacre of Ibos in the northern region by northern factions in the army during September and November. Amid the rapidly spreading, large-scale interethnic violence, Gowon announced on 27 May 1967 the creation of a twelve-state federation in place of the four

Yakubu Gowon

states, in an effort to prevent the country from splintering. Notwithstanding Gowon's efforts to restore Ibo confidence, the ten-million-member Ibo ethnic group, led by Lieutenant Colonel C. Odumegwu-Ojukwu, declared independence for the eastern region of Nigeria as the independent state of Biafra on 30 May 1967. A bloody and violent civil war ensued.

The Biafran War

The Biafran War, which coincided with the June 1967 Arab-Israeli War, captured international attention, but unlike the Six-Day War it lasted much longer and had a deep impact on Western public opinion. The Nigerian civil war, described by Gowon as a "police action," drew the involvement of the superpowers, with Britain and the Soviet Union supporting the federal government (now reconstituted as the Supreme Military Council) and France supporting the Biafrans. Regarding it as an internal problem, the United States remained officially neutral and refused to sell arms to either side, although the so-called Biafran lobby pressed for humanitarian aid for the Biafrans. By December 1969 superior federal manpower and resources had effectively defeated the Biafran forces in a war of attrition in which an estimated two million Biafran civilians were killed, largely by starvation.

Postwar Policies

Gowon emerged from the war with his reputation and status greatly enhanced by his handling of the civil war. Widely seen after the war as a national leader of mature judgment and compassion, Gowon's main objective was to bring Biafra back and keep Nigeria united. He sought to restore Ibo confidence in the federal government and supported postwar policies of reconciliation and national unity. Those policies met with considerable success in the initial steps toward national reconciliation. Gowon, reflecting the army's reluctance to relinquish power, outlined his reconstruction plans in October 1970. He also proposed a return to a civilian government within six years, once the military regime had restored peace and political stability.

Gowon's military government was unable to restore political stability in Nigeria, and Gowon was unable to restore discipline and unity in the military. He was overthrown on 29 July 1975 in a bloodless coup d'état while attending the Organization of African Unity meeting in Kampala, Uganda. Gowon went into voluntary exile in England, where he enrolled at the University of Warwick to study political science. He was implicated in the February 1976 abortive coup, dismissed from the army, and declared a wanted person. He was later pardoned by civilian president Shehu Shegari and allowed to return to Nigeria. In 1984 he received his Ph.D. from Warwick.

Books about Gowon

John Digby Clarke, *Yakubu Gowon: Faith in a United Nigeria* (London: Frank Cass, 1987);

J. Isawa Elaigwu, *Gowon: A Biography of a Soldier-Statesman* (Ibadan: West Publishing, 1986).

General References

Suzanne Cronjé, *The World and Nigeria: A Diplomatic History of the Biafran War, 1967–1970* (London: Sidgwick & Jackson, 1972);

James J. Oluleye, *Military Leadership in Nigeria, 1966–1979* (Ibadan: University Press Ltd., 1985);

John J. Stremlau, *The International Politics of the Nigerian Civil War, 1967–1970* (Princeton: Princeton University Press, 1977);

Auberon Waugh and Suzanne Cronjé, *Biafra: Britain's Shame* (London: M. Joseph, 1969).

–J. R.-S.

Andrei Antonovich Grechko

Soviet Minister of Defense, 1967–1976

Born Golodaenka, Russia, 17 October 1903
Died Moscow, Soviet Union, 26 April 1976

Andrei Antonovich Grechko was a veteran of both the Russian civil war and World War II. A harsh man, he was known to intimidate his subordinates physically. Grechko rose through the ranks of the Red Army to become the Soviet Union's minister of defense in 1967, a post he held for the remainder of his life. Along the way he was promoted to commander of the Soviet forces in Germany, commander in chief of the Soviet land forces, and commander in chief of the Warsaw Pact forces. Under his leadership, the Soviet armed forces increasingly grew in both power and prestige and exercised a degree of influence over foreign policy unmatched in the postwar Soviet Union.

Grechko was born to a peasant family in Golodaenka (now Kuibyshev) in Rostov-na-Dony *gubernia*. Little is known of his family or life before 1919, when Grechko joined the Red Army. He served as a private and later as a noncommissioned officer during the civil war. During the early years of his military service he received a primary education, which enabled him to enroll in Cavalry Military School, from which he graduated in 1926. Grechko continued to further his career by joining the Communist party of the Soviet Union in 1928 and graduating from the Frunze Military Academy in 1936. During Soviet leader Joseph Stalin's purges of the military in the late 1930s, he rose from a regimental cavalry officer to the chief of staff of a division. In 1941, on the eve of World War II, he graduated from the prestigious Voroshilov Academy of the General Staff and was soon sent off to the front.

Andrei Antonovich Grechko

World War II

Grechko saw a variety of commands throughout the Ukraine during World War II, which the Soviets referred to as the Great Patriotic War. In 1941 he was in charge of the Thirty-Fourth Cavalry Division on the southwestern front, and from January to April 1942 Grechko commanded the Fifth Cavalry Corps on the southern front. He was transferred to the Donbas and the North Caucasus regions and from September to December 1942 led the Forty-Seventh and Eighteenth Armies in the Krasnodar offensive. From January through October 1943 Grechko commanded the Fifty-Sixth Army and took part in the capture of the North Caucasus in the successful Novorossisk-Taman campaign. His impressive performance during these battles was rewarded with a promotion to deputy commander of the Voronezh (First Ukrainian) front.

Grechko played an active part in planning the complex Soviet attack to recapture Kiev in the fall of 1943 and in December 1943 became the commander of the First Guards Army, which saw extensive action throughout the Ukraine in the last years of the war. While fighting in the Ukraine, he came to know and work with two future Soviet leaders, Nikita S. Khrushchev and Leonid I. Brezhnev.

Grechko's Rise in the Military

After World War II Grechko was appointed commander of the Kiev Military District, a position which he held until 1953. In 1953 Grechko — after Stalin's death and during Khrushchev's rise to power — was promoted to the key post of commander of the Soviet forces in Germany, where he remained until 1957. He was named marshal of the Soviet Union in 1955.

In 1957 after Rodion Malinovski replaced Georgii K. Zhukov as minister of defense, Grechko was appointed to fill Malinovski's vacated position as first deputy minister of defense and commander in chief of the Soviet land forces. In 1960 he was named commander in chief of the Warsaw Pact forces and served in that position until 1967. During this period Grechko also assumed several important positions within the Soviet government and the party. He was named a full member of the Central Committee in 1961.

When Malinovski died in 1967, many believed that Dmitri Fedorovich Ustinov, the civilian head of the military-industrial complex, would be appointed as the next minister of defense. While Ustinov apparently had the support of the majority of the Politburo members, the Soviet armed forces vigorously lobbied for Grechko. In order to gain the support of the armed forces and improve party-military relations, Soviet leader Brezhnev named Grechko minister of defense some thirteen days after Malinovski's death.

The Czechoslovakian Crisis

Grechko's military experience in Eastern Europe was soon put to use, as he planned and successfully executed the invasion of Czechoslovakia in 1968. He also served as a Soviet emissary during the crisis. In order to secure Alexander Dubcek's removal from the Czech leadership and effect personnel changes in the Czech Politburo, the Kremlin sent Grechko to warn Czech leaders that action might be taken against them personally if they did not fulfill Soviet wishes. The Czechs acquiesced, and Grechko was named a hero of the Czechoslovak Socialist Republic in 1969. The Soviet military benefited from the invasion, for it demonstrated the need for the continued expansion of the ground forces. The result was a dramatic increase in the number of troops facing North Atlantic Treaty Organization (NATO) armies in West Germany.

Soviet Communist Party-Military Relations

In 1973 Grechko acquired more power inside the Kremlin when he was named a full member of the Politburo. Brezhnev brought in the heads of the three key security agencies – the minister of foreign affairs, the chairman of the KGB, and the minister of defense – to garner additional support for his foreign policy. While Andrei Gromyko, Yuri Andropov, and Andrei Grechko all actually opposed Brezhnev's policies of détente, their political fortunes were tied to the general secretary so they did not make public their opposition. Indeed, Grechko reportedly had reached an "agreement" after the 1969 Plenum not to attack détente or Strategic Arms Limitation Talks (SALT) as long as Brezhnev did not reduce the military budget.

This symbiotic relationship between the party leadership and the military lasted until Grechko's death, with Brezhnev using the military's nominal support to bolster his case for détente and Grechko using his position in the Politburo and on the Defense Council to further the military's goals and, in particular, his personal goal of increasing Soviet "internationalism." He pressed for the Soviet Union to use its military power abroad as an instrument of foreign policy. In a keynote speech in 1974 Grechko proclaimed: "At the present stage the historic function of the Soviet armed forces is not restricted merely to their function in defending our Motherland and other socialist countries. In its foreign policy activity, the Soviet state . . . supports the national liberation struggle, and resolutely resists imperialist aggression in whatever distant region of our planet it may appear." The 1970s was a decade of Soviet intervention, or "adventurism," in Angola, Ethiopia, Mozambique, Cambodia, Nicaragua, and Afghanistan. Under Grechko's leadership the armed forces experienced a massive arms buildup. The Soviet Union greatly expanded its navy and increased its Far Eastern ground-forces divisions from eleven to forty-three in the late 1960s in order to meet the new Chinese threat. The Soviet Union also surpassed the United States in the stockpiling of intercontinental ballistic missiles (ICBMs) and in the total megatonnage of its warheads. The buildup resulted in a strategic parity with the United States – the most important accomplishment of the Soviet military since World War II – that enabled Soviet leaders to feel more comfortable in projecting their power abroad.

Grechko died on 26 April 1976 of a heart attack. His ashes are interred in the Kremlin wall.

General References

Harry Gelman, *The Brezhnev Politburo and the Decline of Détente* (Ithaca, N.Y.: Cornell University Press, 1984);

David Holloway, *The Soviet Union and the Arms Race* (New Haven, Conn.: Yale University Press, 1983);

George W. Simmonds, ed., *Soviet Leaders* (New York: Crowell, 1967).

– P. M.

SEE ALSO THESE RELATED ENTRIES

Leonid Brezhnev, 2; Détente, 3; Strategic Arms Limitation Talks, 3.

Andrei Gromyko

Foreign Minister, Soviet Union, 1957–1985
Born Old Gromyki, Russia, 18 July 1909
Died Moscow, Soviet Union, 2 July 1989

Andrei Andreyevich Gromyko, Soviet foreign minister from 1957 to 1985, served every Soviet leader from Joseph Stalin to Mikhail Gorbachev. After his appointment as ambassador to the United States in 1943, Gromyko met with every American president from Franklin D. Roosevelt to George Bush, Gromyko's seemingly permanent scowl an enduring comment on Soviet-American relations. The extent of his actual power within the Soviet leadership has always been a source of debate among Sovietologists, but beyond dispute are his loyalty to the Soviet Union and his faithful execution of the Kremlin's directives.

Gromyko was born in the village of Old Gromyki, which lay in the heavily forested region of Gomel in White Russia, about halfway between Moscow and Kiev. It was the custom of the inhabitants to take the name of the village, and so Andrei Burmakov became Andrei Gromyko in the town and church records. Gromyko's father, Andrei Matveyevich, was a literate peasant who took whatever work he could find around the village. At the age of fourteen Gromyko joined his father in looking for odd jobs at the local Vesuvius Match factory or work cutting timber in the surrounding forests.

He attended a technical college near Minsk, where he joined the Communist party in 1930. The next year he married Lydia Dmitrievna Grinevich, the daughter of a peasant. The couple was close, seen holding hands years later at diplomatic functions. They had two children, Anatoly, who like his father went into the foreign service, and Emilia, who married a diplomat after completing her doctorate in history.

Following graduation from the technical institute, Gromyko was appointed director of a secondary school in the province of Dzerzhinsky, near Minsk. He became more closely involved in party affairs, helping to collectivize the peasantry in Dzerzhinsky.

Academic Career

After a few months at the secondary school, several local party officials encouraged him to continue his university studies, whereupon he and Lydia moved back to Minsk, and Gromyko began postgraduate work in economics and studied English. In his second year he and several other students were transferred to Moscow, where he finished his degree in 1936. He joined the Economics Institute at the USSR Academy of Sciences and

Gale International Portrait Gallery

Andrei Gromyko

prepared for a career in research. As a sideline he worked on a journal, *Problems of Economics*, and occasionally lectured at Moscow's Municipal Construction Engineering Institute. He also taught classes and held study groups for the workers at local factories. By the end of 1938 Gromyko had been appointed academic secretary of the Economics Institute. He tried unsuccessfully to take flying lessons, but his age kept him from joining the "veritable cult of aviation" that had overtaken the Soviet Union in those years.

In 1938 Gromyko was offered the position of academic secretary of the academy's Far Eastern Division, a prestigious post which he declined, claiming that it was better suited for an "eminent scientist."

Foreign Ministry

At about that time the Central Committee (CC) of the Communist party of the Soviet Union (CPSU) was seek-

127

ing young candidates for the foreign service, largely to replace those officials who had perished in Stalin's purge of the party in the 1930s. In early 1939 Gromyko received orders to report to the foreign ministry. The interviews with Vyacheslav Molotov, the foreign minister, and other leading party figures must have gone well, for within a few days Gromyko was called back to the Foreign Ministry and told that he would be transferred to diplomatic work. His first assignment was to the American Department in the Commissariat for Foreign Affairs. Later, Gromyko would credit his party work and his command of English as the deciding factors in his selection.

Stalin himself must have taken an immediate interest in the young man's career. After six months the general secretary summoned Gromyko to his office to tell him he had been picked to become the new counselor at the Soviet embassy in Washington, second only to Ambassador K. A. Umansky. Stalin then inquired about Gromyko's command of English. He suggested that once Gromyko arrived in America he should attend church services. Stalin recounted that when "Russian revolutionaries lived abroad they used this method to improve their knowledge of a foreign language."

Gromyko's first months in the United States were mostly spent touring factories in the Midwest. He then returned to Washington where he assumed his duties at the Soviet embassy. Soon after the German invasion of the Soviet Union on 22 June 1941, Umansky was replaced as ambassador by M. M. Litvinov. Stalin felt that Litvinov's previous association with the League of Nations would appeal to the American president, Franklin D. Roosevelt. But Litvinov evidently did not impress Stalin, and in 1943 Gromyko became the new Soviet ambassador to the United States. Stalin continued, however, to deal directly with Roosevelt on the significant issues facing the Soviet-American alliance, leaving Gromyko to settle the details.

The "Big Three" Meetings

Gromyko was present at the Tehran Conference, the first of several wartime meetings of the "Big Three" – Roosevelt, Stalin, and Winston Churchill, the British prime minister. The atmosphere of the Tehran meeting, held in November and December of 1943, was cordial, but divergences of opinion arose that would widen during the course of the war. Stalin and Roosevelt tentatively agreed on a postwar partition of Germany, but Churchill opposed this idea, accepting only a possible detachment of Prussia from Germany. As to Soviet postwar strategy in Eastern Europe and the Baltic states, Roosevelt proposed that Stalin make a public statement on the inhabitants' right of self-determination. Stalin did not appear to understand Roosevelt's desire not to lose Polish-

American votes and suggested that "some propaganda work be done."

At Dumbarton Oaks, Washington, D.C., Gromyko took part in talks between 21 August and 7 October 1944 that gave rise to the United Nations (UN), an international organization designed to settle disputes among its member nations. A sticking point during the talks was whether a permanent member of the UN Security Council, composed of the United States, the Soviet Union, Great Britain, France, and China and bearing ultimate responsibility for the maintenance of peace, should have the power to veto a decision. Gromyko, head of the Soviet delegation, argued – successfully, as it turned out – for veto power, no doubt keeping in mind Stalin's fear that the other members would join against the Soviet Union. In April 1945 Gromyko headed the Soviet delegation at the San Francisco Conference, where the UN charter was drawn up and approved.

In February 1945 Gromyko attended the last of the "Big Three" meetings, which was held in the former czarist palace at the Crimean resort of Yalta. The Allied leaders discussed several issues, but Poland's future figured in seven of the ten plenary sessions. Ultimately, Churchill and Roosevelt accepted the provisional Polish government supported by Moscow in return for the promise of free elections by the Polish people.

Potsdam Conference

The future of Germany dominated the agenda of the Potsdam Conference, held near Berlin in July 1945. Gromyko was there, arguing for hefty reparations from Germany to help rebuild the Soviet Union. The American delegation, led by the new American president, Harry S Truman, resisted this demand, feeling that if Germany were stripped of its industrial base, the United States government would ultimately have to pay for its rehabilitation. The compromise that was reached strengthened the authority of the commanders of the four allied occupation zones and undermined the principle of a unified Germany.

Gromyko was never fond of Truman, whom he described later as a "pale reflection, like the moon, of his predecessor."

Soviet Representative to the United Nations

In 1946 Gromyko, now a deputy foreign minister under Vyacheslav Molotov, became the first permanent Soviet representative to the United Nations. When in New York for UN sessions, he lived in a suite at the Plaza Hotel. His view of America dating from this time was bleak: "Profit is the pitiless filter through which everything to do with culture and art and the country's spiritual life has to pass."

At the United Nations he quickly became involved in growing tensions between the Soviet Union and the West. He was to use his veto power, which he had argued for at the Dumbarton Oaks Conference, twenty-five times during his tenure at the United Nations.

In March 1946 it appeared as if Soviet troops were moving in support of a possible annexation of the Iranian province of Azerbaijan. The Iranian government, with the tacit approval of the United States, brought the matter up in the UN Security Council. Gromyko, in an attempt to have the matter dropped from UN consideration, stormed out of the chamber on 27 March. A week later, however, the Soviet Union publicly recognized Iranian sovereignty over Azerbaijan.

Later in 1946 Gromyko was involved in a UN debate over the future of nuclear energy. On 14 June, Bernard M. Baruch, on behalf of the United States, proposed the establishment of a UN body that would take control over the world's uranium and thorium deposits in order to prevent the unauthorized use of fissionable materials by any country. Gromyko attacked this proposal as inimical to great-power unity and instead suggested the destruction of all atomic weapons.

First Deputy Minister of Foreign Affairs

In July 1948 Gromyko gave up his post at the United Nations. A year later he was recalled to Moscow, where he became first deputy minister of foreign affairs under Andrei Vyshinsky. During Vyshinsky's occasional absences Gromyko assumed the role of foreign minister. These absences coincided with some of the early episodes of the Cold War: the Berlin blockade of 1948–1949, when the Soviets stopped all land traffic between Berlin and the West; the creation of the Western military alliance, the North Atlantic Treaty Organization (NATO) in 1949; and the invasion of South Korea by the Soviet-supported North in 1950. It was always Gromyko's contention that the United States incited Cold War tensions between the West and the Soviet Union so that American business would profit.

Soviet Ambassador to England

In 1952, when Molotov, the former foreign minister and Gromyko's patron, fell out of favor with Stalin, Gromyko was demoted and sent to London as the new Soviet ambassador. He presented his credentials to Queen Elizabeth at Buckingham Palace, noting later that if the reception hall at the Palace "were a few meters wider and higher" it might compare with St. George's Hall in the Kremlin. In spite of this perceived deficiency, Gromyko was generally impressed with the royal family and their grasp of foreign affairs. While ambassador, he completed his book, *Export of U.S. Capital*, which he published under the pseudonym G. Andreyev and which earned Gromyko a doctorate from Moscow State University. He was to continue his research in economics through the years, publishing two more books on the nature of American capitalism.

He was ambassador only a few months. Stalin's death in March 1953 allowed Molotov to regain his old position as foreign minister, and he called Gromyko back to Moscow and appointed him first deputy minister.

Soviet Foreign Minister

Over the next few years Nikita S. Khrushchev emerged as the new leader of the Soviet Union. In the process Molotov again fell out of favor, and in February 1957 Gromyko succeeded him as foreign minister, a position he would hold for the next twenty-eight years.

Gromyko's figure paled beside that of the colorful and forceful Khrushchev, and his imprint was absent from most of the Soviet Union's major foreign policy decisions of this era. The Soviet leader had scant regard for his foreign minister's abilities. Later, Khrushchev would describe Gromyko as a "good civil servant who always went by the book."

Cuban Missile Crisis

On 17 October 1962, after the United States had released photographs which showed Soviet missile bases inside Cuba, Gromyko went to the White House to meet with President John F. Kennedy. President Kennedy repeated his previous demand that the Soviets remove the missiles. According to observers, though, Gromyko denied that the Soviet Union had placed missiles in Cuba. Later Gromyko claimed in his memoirs that the topic of Soviet rockets in Cuba never arose at the meeting with Kennedy. Whether he really knew of the rockets is debatable: that he loyally defended the actions of his superiors and the intentions of the Soviet Union was characteristic of Gromyko both during and after the Khrushchev era.

The Soviet backdown over Cuba marked the beginning of Khrushchev's fall from power. In a bloodless coup in October 1964 Leonid Brezhnev became first secretary of the CPSU, leaving Gromyko in place as foreign minister.

Shaping Soviet Foreign Policy

Gromyko came into his own under Brezhnev, gradually acquiring power and helping to shape Soviet foreign policy. During the Prague Spring of 1968, when it appeared as if Czechoslovakia might see democratic reforms, Gromyko urged military intervention to restore Soviet control.

Brezhnev entrusted Gromyko with carrying out many of the details and negotiations required for the Soviet policy of détente with the West. With the Cuban missile crisis a recent memory, Brezhnev sought to relax tensions with the West as a means to avoid a direct confrontation and as a way for the Soviets to attain several practical benefits, such as advanced western technology.

Gromyko negotiated the 1970 treaty between the Soviet Union and the Federal Republic of Germany (FRG) by which Germany accepted the postwar division of Europe.

Later he was involved in the Conference on Security and Cooperation in Europe that took place in Helsinki between 1972 and 1975. With the Final Act, signed in Helsinki on 1 August 1975, the Soviet Union achieved European recognition of the postwar status quo in Europe.

SALT I

Gromyko was even more closely involved in the Strategic Arms Limitation Talks (SALT) that resulted in the first major arms-control agreement between the United States and the Soviet Union. The treaty, signed on 26 May 1972 by Brezhnev and President Richard M. Nixon, placed a ceiling on the number of strategic launchers each side could have and virtually eliminated antiballistic missile (ABM) systems.

Gromyko appreciated both Nixon and his secretary of state, Henry A. Kissinger, as practical men with whom the Soviet Union could negotiate.

With each new success of détente Gromyko's stature within the Soviet leadership rose. He was becoming as much an architect as an executor of Soviet foreign policy. On 27 April 1973 in recognition of his increased authority and status the Politburo granted him full membership, making him part of the executive body of the CPSU's Central Committee, the center of power in the Soviet Union.

Gromyko accompanied Brezhnev to Vladivostock, the icy Soviet port city on the Sea of Japan, in November 1974 to meet with American president Gerald R. Ford and set guidelines for a second arms control treaty to take effect after SALT I's expiration in October 1977. Brezhnev was later prepared to sign an accord based on the Vladivostock agreement, but President Jimmy Carter, who took office in January 1977, offered a new American proposal in March which would have sharply reduced the numbers of missiles on both sides.

SALT II

The treaty, SALT II, that was eventually signed on 18 June 1979 in Vienna by Carter and Brezhnev after two years of negotiations, bore closer resemblance to the Vladivostock accords than to Carter's March 1977 proposal. Gromyko had been the chief negotiator for the Soviet Union, meeting with his American counterpart, Secretary of State Cyrus Vance, in Moscow, Washing-

ton, and Geneva during the course of steadily deteriorating Soviet-American relations. The treaty never took effect because President Carter formally asked the United States Senate to discontinue its consideration following the Soviet invasion of Afghanistan on 27 December 1979.

As Brezhnev's health began to fail Gromyko assumed greater control over the course of Soviet foreign policy, a course that was becoming increasingly aggressive. He was critical of President Carter, whose policies he viewed as the cause of worsening Soviet-American relations. Gromyko saw Carter's linkage of Soviet human rights abuses with American foreign policy as meddling in domestic Soviet affairs.

In the mid 1970s the Soviet Union sent equipment and advisers to be used in the civil war in Angola. In the Horn of Africa, Cuban troops operating Soviet equipment intervened to help force Somalian troops from Ethiopia in 1978.

Gromyko championed the invasion of Afghanistan, done to install a puppet government under Babrak Karmal in Kabul. The ensuing war between Soviet troops and Afghan resistance fighters dragged on for more than a decade despite continuing efforts by the United Nations to arrange a Soviet pullout. Gromyko insisted in his memoirs that the war was merely a case of "neighborly assistance" from the Soviet Union.

Following strikes in Poland to protest rising food prices, Gromyko supported Soviet intervention. Martial law was declared in Poland on 13 December 1981, and the independent trade union that had arisen, Solidarity, was banned.

Brezhnev died on 10 November 1982, having chosen his longtime aide Konstantin Chernenko as his successor. The Politburo, however, nominated Yuri Andropov to the top spot of general secretary of the CPSU, a decision encouraged by Gromyko. Gromyko, by supporting Andropov, signaled his recognition, by now common among the Soviet leadership, of the dire need to end the political and economic stagnation that defined Brezhnev's final years. Although any real change would have to wait for the ascendance of Mikhail Gorbachev, the way was being paved for eventual reforms in the Soviet Union.

Andropov died in office on 9 February 1984, and Chernenko took over, selected by the Politburo to be a transitional leader. During Chernenko's short tenure as first secretary, shorter even than Andropov's, Gromyko's power and control over Soviet foreign policy reached its peak, coinciding with an extremely hard line taken by Moscow after the Soviet Union broke off the Intermediate-range Nuclear Force (INF) talks. The talks had been aimed at eliminating Soviet and American medium range weapons from Europe. But on 23 November 1983, after it became a foregone conclusion that the North Atlantic

Treaty Organization (NATO) would go ahead with its 1979 decision to place nuclear-armed Pershing II and ground-launched cruise missiles in Europe, the Soviet delegation walked out of the talks.

By late 1984, however, the Soviets decided to begin to repair relations with the United States. Gromyko came to New York to meet with President Ronald W. Reagan, and early in 1985 he met with Secretary of State George P. Shultz in Geneva to discuss the possibility of beginning new talks on controlling space-based systems and nuclear weapons.

Chernenko died in March 1985. It was already apparent that Gorbachev would become the next secretary general, a succession that Gromyko had unsuccessfully fought, preferring the Central Committee's secretary for military-industrial affairs, Grigori Romanov. With Gorbachev's accession to power inevitable, Gromyko managed to position himself, though, so that he could nominate Gorbachev at a closed session of the Central Committee. Taking the floor, Gromyko praised Gorbachev as "a man of principle [and] strong convictions" and reportedly warned his colleagues, "This man has a nice smile, but he has iron teeth."

Later that year, in July, Gorbachev named Gromyko chairman of the Presidium of the Supreme Soviet, a largely ceremonial post corresponding to president. This honored Gromyko for his years of loyal service to the Soviet Union and simultaneously removed him as a threat to Gorbachev. Romanov, at the same time, was stripped of all his leadership positions. Eduard Shevardnadze, with little diplomatic experience and no power base, became foreign minister.

Gromyko remained chairman of the Presidium until his retirement in 1988. In April 1989 Gorbachev removed him from his place in the Politburo along with several other "dead souls" —those remaining in the Central Committee without any other function — in a sweeping purge to make room for younger, more imaginative leaders in line with Gorbachev's new thinking. On 2 July of that year, Gromyko died of a stroke, two weeks short of his eightieth birthday. He was buried in Moscow's Novodevichy Cemetery.

Book by Gromyko (Selected)
Memories (London: Hutchinson, 1989).

Books about Gromyko
Robin Edmonds, *Soviet Foreign Policy: The Brezhnev Years* (Oxford: Oxford University Press, 1983);

Donald R. Kelley, *Soviet Politics in the Brezhnev Era* (New York: Praeger, 1980).

General References
Vernon Aspaturian, *Process and Power in Soviet Foreign Policy* (Boston: Little, Brown, 1971);

Margoit Light, *The Soviet Theory of International Relations* (New York: St. Martin's Press, 1988);

Carl A. Linden, *Khrushchev and the Soviet leadership, 1957–1964* (Baltimore: Johns Hopkins University Press, 1966);

Allen Lynch, *The Soviet Study of International Relations* (New York: Cambridge University Press, 1987);

Michel Tatu, *Power in the Kremlin, from Khrushchev to Kosygin* (New York: Viking, 1969).

– M. B.

SEE ALSO THESE RELATED ENTRIES
Leonid Brezhnev, 2; Cuban Missile Crisis, 3; Détente, 3; Henry Kissinger, 1; Nikita S. Krushchev, 2; Andrei Vyshinski, 2.

Károly Grósz

Prime Minister of Hungary, 1987–1990

General Secretary, Hungarian Socialist Workers Party, 1988–1989

Born Miskolc, Hungary, 1 August 1930
Died 6 January 1996

Károly Grósz, Hungarian communist leader and prime minister, was born in the industrial city of Miskolc in northeastern Hungary. He started his career as a printer but went on to complete his studies at the Higher Party School and at Loránd Eötvös University, both located in Budapest. He became a teacher and then joined the communist-controlled Hungarian Young People's Federation, later becoming secretary of this organization.

Early Career

In 1954 Grósz became an official of the Borsod County Party Committee of the ruling Hungarian Socialist Workers party (HSWP). He was editor of the Miskolc daily *Eszak Magyarország* from 1958 to 1961. His role during the 1956 Hungarian uprising is not known, but after the revolution he emerged holding prominent posts in the purged and "normalized" party. After 1962 he served as secretary of the HSWP Committee at Hungarian Radio and Television. From 1968 until 1973 he was a deputy department head at the HSWP Central Committee, after which he was named first secretary of the Fejér County Party Committee. In 1974 Grósz returned to Budapest to head the propaganda department of the HSWP Central Committee. He remained in that position until 1979, when he returned to Borsod as first secretary of the party committee in the county.

Prime Minister

In 1985 Grósz was appointed first secretary of the Budapest HSWP Committee. In 1987 he was named prime minister and increasingly gained the reputation of a moderate reformer. He presided over a renewed reform program designed to revive the Hungarian economy and to defuse potential political and social unrest.

Reform Program

From the mid 1980s onward, the HSWP leadership stood at the forefront of the reform process in Eastern Europe. It undertook various steps to open up the political process to noncommunists: for example, allowing for multicandidate local elections, permitting the emergence of distinct factions within the party, and tolerating the emergence of alternative political organizations, including the Hungarian Democratic

Károly Grósz

Forum. The government realized that some degree of political pluralism was needed to gain domestic credibility and to assure success for the accelerated economic reform program, which envisaged the expansion of the private sector and more extensive market mechanisms. The tolerant attitude of the Mikhail Gorbachev regime in the Kremlin also encouraged the Hungarian reforms and allowed for the opening up of the Hungarian economy to Western influence and investment.

General Secretary of the HSWP

Grósz was elected general secretary of the HSWP in May 1988, and in July 1988 he became the first Hungarian leader in forty-two years to visit the United States. But as reformist pressures accelerated within and alongside the communist establishment, Grósz was increasingly perceived as a centrist. Although he remained party leader during the stormy months of 1989, his powers were curtailed by the appointment of key radical reformers to the HSWP Presidium as the party sought to regain public legitimacy. In October 1989 the HSWP transformed itself into the Hungarian Socialist party, which elected a new leadership and devised a new party program based on genuine democratic principles. Grósz did not join the new organization but instead remained linked with the harder-line communists who reestablished the HSWP at the close of 1989. The communists were swept from power during the multiparty democratic election in March 1990, won by the right-of-center Democratic Forum, and Grósz slipped out of the political limelight.

General References

J. F. Brown, *Eastern Europe and Communist Rule* (Durham, N.C. and London: Duke University Press, 1988);

Andrew Felkay, *Hungary and the USSR, 1956–1988: K'ad'ar's Political Leadership* (New York: Greenwood Press, 1989);

Charles Gati, *Hungary and the Soviet Bloc* (Durham, N.C.: Durham University Press, 1986);

Franklin D. Holzman, *The Economics of Soviet Bloc Trade and Finance* (Boulder, Colo.: Westview Press, 1987);

Robert L. Hutchings, *Soviet-East European Relations: Consolidation and Conflict, 1968–1980* (Madison: University of Wisconsin Press, 1983);

Bennett Kovrig, *Communism in Hungary: From Kun to Kadar* (Stanford, Cal.: Hoover Institution Press, 1979);

Joseph Rothschild, *Return to Diversity: A Political History of East Central Europe since World War II* (New York: Oxford University Press, 1989);

William Shawcross, *Crime and Compromise: Janos Kadar and the Politics of Hungary since Revolution* (London: Weidenfeld & Nicolson, 1974);

Sarah M. Terry, ed., *Soviet Policy in Eastern Europe* (New Haven: Yale University Press, 1984);

Adam Ulam, *Expansion and Coexistence* (New York: Praeger, 1968).

—J. B. and A. B.

SEE ALSO THESE RELATED ENTRIES

Ernö Gerö, 2; Mikhail Gorbachev, 2; János Kádár, 2; Mátyás Rákosi, 2.

Ernesto "Che" Guevara de la Serna

Revolutionary, 1955–1967
Born Rosario, Argentina, 14 June 1928
Died La Higuera, Bolivia, 8 October 1967

Ernesto "Che" Guevara de la Serna was a controversial revolutionary figure in the post–World War II period. He was closely linked to the Cuban revolution of 1959, though his writings on guerrilla warfare were his most significant contribution to revolutionary theory and practice. Guevara saw armed guerrilla warfare as the only way to destroy imperialist forces in Third World countries and Marxism-Leninism as the means to create more just and humane societies.

Guevara was the oldest son of middle-class parents active in left-wing politics. He had four brothers and sisters. His interest in politics may have developed from his association with several childhood friends whose parents had been killed or exiled during the Spanish civil war.

As a youth he was intensely idealistic, and his struggle to overcome a chronic asthmatic condition was reflected in his adventurous spirit. At age twenty-four he took a break from medical school at the University of Buenos Aires to motorcycle and hitchhike across the South American continent with a friend. After visits to Chile, Peru, Ecuador, Colombia, and Venezuela, Guevara returned to Argentina, completing his degree in medicine in 1953.

Ernesto "Che" Guevara de la Serna

The Arbenz Coup in Guatemala

Immediately following graduation from medical school, the restless Guevara again set out across South America. The conditions endured by the lower class in several countries that he visited served to reinforce his left-wing views. Eventually his travels led him to Guatemala, where he made his "discovery" of Marxism. Under the influence of his wife Hilda Gadea, who was a member of a revolutionary Peruvian party, and the Alliance of Democratic Youth (the mass organization closely linked to Guatemala's Labor party), which Guevara had joined, he first encountered the writings of Karl Marx and Vladimir I. Lenin. Guevara also witnessed the revolutionary program of the leftist government of Jacobo Arbenz Guzmán and the Central Intelligence Agency (CIA)-sponsored overthrow of that government in late 1954. From his experience in Guatemala, Guevara concluded that armed struggle was necessary to defeat imperialist forces.

Joining Castro

Following the Arbenz overthrow, Guevara managed to cross the border into Mexico, where the following year he joined in Mexico City a group of revolutionary Cuban exiles under Fidel Castro Ruz. There he received secret military training in guerrilla warfare tactics. In December 1956 Castro and some eighty revolutionaries, including Raúl Castro Ruz and Guevara, landed on the coast of Cuba's Oriente province in a dilapidated yacht named "Granma." Their intention was to overthrow Cuban dictator Fulgencio Batista y Saldívar. Guevara was the only foreigner among them. He had never set foot on Cuban soil.

Guevara and the Castro brothers were among the few survivors to escape this ill-fated landing by fleeing into the nearby Sierra Maestra. For the next two years Castro's 26th of July Movement, named for their unsuccessful 26 July 1953 attack on the Moncada army barracks, waged a revolutionary guerrilla struggle against the U.S.-backed Batista regime. During this time Guevara

134

served in the rebel ranks as doctor and military commander with the rank of major. He soon emerged as an influential leader in the movement and a trusted friend to Castro.

Bureaucratic Positions

Castro and his followers assumed full control of the Cuban government in early 1959, and Guevara was given charge in the fields of finance and economic planning. He served as head of the industrial department of the National Institute of Agrarian Reform (1959), head of the National Bank (1959–1961), and minister of industry (1961–1965). In this last post Guevara opposed policies emphasizing sugar production that the Soviet Union encouraged in Cuba in 1963, continuing to favor instead massive industrialization. He also argued in favor of moral rather than material incentives to increase worker productivity. He believed that Marxism would bring about the creation of a new "socialist" man, a man so idealistic that he would no longer need or use money.

Theoretical Writings

Guevara's most significant contributions, however, were his writings on guerrilla warfare, in which he adapted Marxism to his view of the Latin American reality. In *La guerra de guerrillas* (1960; translated as *Guerrilla Warfare*, 1961), Guevara argued that armed struggle would be a more effective means to stimulate revolution among the masses than the long-term political activity advocated by most communists in Latin America. Guevara advocated the Cuban revolutionary experience of the late 1950s, with a "focus" of guerrillas operating in the countryside, as the proper way to transform Latin America through revolution. Several guerrilla bands in South America in the 1960s and early 1970s tried to duplicate the Cuban success in their own countries, but, due in part to U.S. assistance with counterinsurgency methods to Latin American armies, none succeeded.

The Exit from Cuba

In early 1965 Guevara mysteriously dropped out of sight. Rumors began circulating that he had argued with Fidel Castro over Cuban economic policy and had perhaps left Cuba to placate the Soviets. It was also thought that Castro had dispatched Guevara on foreign missions as a kind of punishment because his charisma and popularity with the Cuban people rivaled Castro's own. Castro maintained that Guevara had departed freely to con-

tinue the cause of the socialist revolution abroad. The CIA made learning Guevara's whereabouts a top priority.

The Bolivian Revolution

Castro's explanation was substantiated in late 1966 when Guevara appeared in Bolivia. With Castro's support Guevara had assembled a force of Cuban and Peruvian revolutionaries and traveled to Bolivia to apply his ideas on guerrilla warfare in South America. Some Bolivians joined his forces, and they began their campaign in southeastern Bolivia the following year. The Indian peasants in that area, however, had already benefitted from land reform and were unsympathetic to the foreign revolutionaries. On 8 October 1967 a Bolivian ranger unit, trained by the CIA, wounded and captured Guevara near Vallegrande. He was executed in La Higuera, Bolivia, the next day by an officer of the Bolivian army. He was thirty-nine years old.

Guevara left a theoretical legacy dedicated to interpreting and changing the world. His thought, although based on the experience of Cuba and Latin America, is universal in its appeal and scope. His writings have gained wide recognition among the disaffected peoples of Africa, Asia, and Latin America, and they are the subject of study and discussion in schools and universities. Today he is considered a hero to Cuban socialists and leftists the world over.

Books by Guevara

Guerrilla Warfare (New York: Monthly Review Press, 1961);

Reminiscences of the Cuban Revolutionary War (New York: Monthly Review Press, 1968);

Venceremos! The Speeches and Writings of Ernesto Che Guevara, edited by John Gerassi (New York: Macmillan, 1968);

Che Guevara on Revolution: A Documentary Overview (Coral Gables, Fla.: University of Miami Press, 1969);

Che Guevara and the Cuban Revolution: Writings and Speeches of Ernesto Che Guevara, edited by David Deutschman (New York: Pathfinder, 1987).

Books about Guevara

Richard L. Harris, *Death of a Revolutionary: Che Guevara's Last Mission* (New York: Norton, 1970;

Marvin D. Resnick, *The Black Beret: The Life and Meaning of Che Guevara* (New York: Ballantine, 1970);

Andrew Sinclair, *Che Guevara* (New York: Viking, 1970).
– L. H.

SEE ALSO THESE RELATED ENTRIES

Central Intelligence Agency, 3; Jacobo Arbenz Guzmán, 2; Fidel Castro Ruz, 2; Raúl Castro Ruz, 2.

George Habash

General-Secretary, Popular Front for the Liberation of Palestine, 1967–
Born Lydda, Palestine, 1926

George Habash is the general-secretary of the Popular Front for the Liberation of Palestine (PFLP), a group within the Palestine Liberation Organization (PLO) that is fighting for a leftist, secular Palestinian state. The PFLP is the second largest group within the PLO after Fatah, whose leader, Yasir Arafat, is also leader of the PLO. It is the leading radical critic of the mainstream Fatah PLO policy and has endorsed popular and class warfare to achieve its goals. During the late 1980s and early 1990s, however, the PFLP has accepted the idea of convening an international conference that would lead to the establishment of an independent Palestinian state in the West Bank and Gaza Strip.

Arab Nationalists' Movement

Habash, now married with one daughter, was born in 1926 in Lydda, Palestine (now Lod, Israel), to a middle-income, Greek Orthodox family. He became involved in nationalist politics, following the expulsion of his family from Lydda in 1948 by advancing Jewish forces. Habash, then a medical student at the American University of Beirut (AUB) in Lebanon briefly worked with a group of Egyptian terrorists in Damascus before spearheading the Arab Nationalists' Movement (ANM) from a literary/nationalist group at AUB. In keeping with the ideas of Pan-Arabism, which were extremely popular at the time, the ANM advocated the elimination of Zionism and imperialism and the creation of a united Arab state. It was a strong supporter of Egyptian president Gamal Abdel Nasser.

During the late 1950s Habash used his medical training to open and run clinics for free treatment of the poor in Amman, Jordan, where he was imprisoned for political activities, and then in Damascus, Syria, where he was expelled for his pro-Nasser beliefs.

The NFLP

By the early 1960s, with Arab nationalism proving increasingly elusive, the ANM's internal cohesion began to erode. Helena Cobban describes the process by which the Pan-Arab movement became a Palestinian one: "The Palestinian branch of the ANM had been formed only in 1964. Before that date, the movement's many Palestinian members had been expected to shed any 'Palestinian regionalist' sympathies they might have harbored and to act within the ANM organizations of their place of resi-

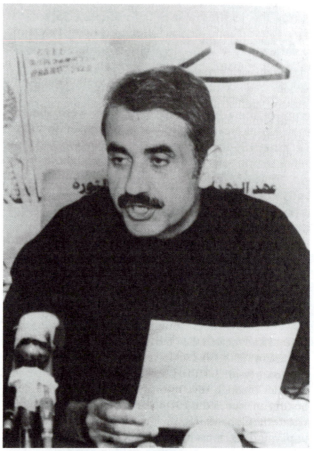

George Habash

dence. However, the establishment of the PLO in 1964, as well as the early organizing activities of Fatah, prompted Habash . . . to start forming a distinct Palestinian grouping within the ANM."

The new grouping, the National Front for the Liberation of Palestine (NFLP), included a military wing called the Vengeance Youth, which launched its first cross-border raids against Israel in November 1964 and continued intermittent sabotage against Israeli targets for the next two and one-half years. In the aftermath of the June 1967 Arab-Israeli war, while Palestinian movements were entering a period of explosive growth, the ANM and its groupings were caught in the throes of internal disunity and change. Habash adopted a Marxist-Leninist model of class struggle to create a revolutionary transformation of the Arab world.

136

The PFLP

In December 1967, following a call from Habash, the NFLP and two other guerrilla groups formed the PFLP. "The only weapon left in the hands of the people," said the PFLP's first public statement, "is revolutionary violence." Yet while Yassir Arafat's Fatah, with its sole focus on Palestinian nationalism, was able to promote itself as the representative of the masses, the leftist PFLP was marginalized within the Palestinian movement. At the crucial stage when Fatah first established control over the PLO, in late 1968 and early 1969, "the PFLP was cast as the chief opponent." It often appealed, writes David McDowell, "to those with more education or to those who felt that only a vision of what was meant to be created gave meaning to their endeavours to recover Palestine."

Israel considers the PFLP a terrorist organization, and in fact Habash has been a leading exponent, within the Palestinian movement, of the acceptability of terrorist means, defined broadly as the use of armed force against civilians to achieve a political goal. Beginning in 1968, for example, the PFLP began a campaign of hijackings directed against Israel, various Western states, and what it considered reactionary Arab regimes. In September 1970, however, a PFLP hijacking of three civilian aircraft provided the pretext for Jordan's King Hussein ibn Talal, in a bloody campaign known as "black September," to expel all Palestinian armed resistance, including less radical groups within the PLO, into Lebanon. In March 1972 Habash acknowledged that hijackings were counterproductive, but Wadi Haddad, who was in charge of the PFLP's external military operations, continued them on his own.

Other Splinter Groups

In the years that have followed, the PFLP has stood in stark contrast to Fatah, as have other radical groups that have broken away from it. These breakaway groups include the Popular Front for the Liberation of Palestine–General Command (PFLP–GC), founded by Ahmad Jibril in October 1968, and the Democratic Front for the Liberation of Palestine (DFLP), founded by Nayif Hawatmeh in February 1969. After the 1973 Arab-Israeli war, for example, Habash's opposition to an international peace conference, reconciliation with Jordan, and the for-

mation of a Palestinian state in the West Bank and Gaza led him to spearhead the Rejection Front, which lasted from 1974 until 1978. In other disagreements with Arafat's ideas, Habash participated in the Palestine National Salvation Front in 1985 and boycotted the PLO executive committee from 1974 to 1981 and again from 1983 to 1987.

The suspension of dialogue between Arafat and King Hussein in 1986 and Arafat's abrogation of their agreement the following year, however, led to a reconciliation between Habash and Arafat. At the eighteenth session of the Palestine National Council (PNC) in Algiers, Habash accepted resolutions calling for creation of an independent West Bank–Gaza state and the convening of an international peace conference. Since the eruption of the *intifadah* (uprising) in the occupied territories in December 1987, Habash's relationship with Arafat has further improved. The uprising's unified leadership is generally assumed to be composed of supporters of Fatah, the PFLP, the DFLP, and other groups.

Book about Habash

Walid Kazziha, *Revolutionary Transformation in the Arab World: Habash and His Comrades from Nationalism to Marxism* (New York: St. Martin's Press, 1975).

General References

Jillian Becker, *The PLO: The Rise and Fall of the Palestine Liberation Organization* (New York: St. Martin's Press, 1984);

Rex Brynen, *Sanctuary and Survival: The PLO in Lebanon* (Boulder, Colo.: Westview Press, 1990);

Helena Cobban, *The Palestinian Liberation Organization: People, Power and Politics* (Cambridge: Cambridge University Press, 1984);

David McDowell, *Palestine and Israel: The Uprising and Beyond* (Berkeley: University of California Press, 1989);

Shaul Mishal, *The PLO under Arafat: Between Gun and Olive Branch* (New Haven, Conn.: Yale University Press, 1986);

Emile F. Sahliyeh, *The PLO After the Lebanon War* (Boulder, Colo.: Westview, 1986).

– A.F.

SEE ALSO THESE RELATED ENTRIES

Yassir Arafat, 2; Gamal Abdul Nasser, 2.

Haile Selassie I

Emperor of Ethiopia, 1930–1974
Born Harar, Ethiopia, 23 July 1892
Died Addis Ababa, Ethiopia, 27 August 1975

Haile Selassie I was the emperor of black Africa's oldest country, Ethiopia, and the last of its feudal rulers. The 225th ruler of Ethiopia, Haile Selassie claimed, and tradition maintained, that he was a descendant of King Solomon and the Queen of Sheba. He was crowned on 2 November 1930 as His Majesty Haile Selassie I, King of Kings, Conquering Lion of the Tribe of Judah, Elect of God.

Born Tafari Makonnen on 23 July 1892 in Harar, in eastern Ethiopia, Haile Selassie (or "Power of the Holy Trinity") was the son of Prince Makonnen, the cousin of Ethiopia's Prince Menelik II. He received his early education from clerical and foreign tutors and at the age of fourteen was named governor of a province. In 1911 he married Waizero Menan, the daughter of the powerful King Mikhael of Wollo. In 1916, when Emperor Menelik's daughter, Princess Zauditu, assumed power, Haile Selassie was proclaimed regent and heir to the throne. However, he dominated Ethiopian politics from behind the scenes throughout Princess Zauditu's reign, engineering, for example, Ethiopia's entrance into the League of Nations in 1923 and passing a decree abolishing slavery a year later. Crowned emperor of Ethiopia in 1930, the new king introduced social and economic reforms, while at the same time centralizing political power and decision making. In 1931 he introduced Ethiopia's first written constitution in its three-thousand-year history, although reforms remained nominal. Haile Selassie's reforms were interrupted in 1935 by the invasion of Ethiopia by Italy. He was forced into exile in Britain when the Ethiopian resistance failed, but, with the help of British troops, he returned triumphantly to reclaim his throne on 5 May 1941 after the defeat of the Italian forces. The brief Italian occupation marked the only break in the three thousand years of Ethiopian independence.

Gale International Portrait Gallery

Haile Selassie I

Leadership in Africa

Haile Selassie continued his modernization program with assistance from the United Nations and Western countries, while facing a mild opposition and an insurrection in the province of Tigre. Haile Selassie, who endeavored to give Ethiopia a major role in developments in Africa, urged the creation of the United Nations Economic Commission for Africa in 1958. During the 1960s, a decade of decolonization, he emerged as a world states-man with his role in helping to found the Organization of African Unity (OAU) in 1963 and as a mediator in intra-African disputes. Both the Economic Commission for Africa and the Secretariat of the OAU were headquartered in Addis Ababa, the capital of Ethiopia. Haile Selassie, who became respected as an elder statesman in Africa, fostered close ties with the United States, which constructed military and surveillance facilities in strategically located Ethiopia. Ethiopia became one of the principal clients of the United States in Africa, which led to criticism of Selassie from other Third World countries.

During the 1970s the power and authority of Haile Selassie, whose legitimacy was popularly believed to be

138

conferred by God and who was considered to possess quasi-divine attributes, were increasingly challenged. He had already faced an attempted coup d'état in 1960 while on a state visit to Brazil. The emperor's base of political support progressively weakened with the defection of close allies and his own resulting alienation, and by the early 1970s the main pillars of his rule had begun to crumble. By 1973 the internal political and military situation had deteriorated to the point of precipitating his downfall. Ethiopia was beset by general strikes, popular demonstrations, attempted coups, and widespread military mutinies. The devastating drought of 1973, for which many people blamed the emperor, gave rise to general discontent, student unrest, strikes, and political instability. The political turmoil generated by the growing secessionist guerrilla wars in the provinces of Eritrea and Tigre was further complicated by an army mutiny in Eritrea which led to mass resignation from the cabinet.

The 1974 Coup

The overthrow of Haile Selassie in 1974 has been described as a "creeping revolution," since the military seized power slowly while eliminating all vestiges of the old regime. Beginning in February 1974, Haile Selassie was unable to govern amid administrative paralysis during months of protests, demonstrations, and famine; the situation turned anarchic with a rise in gasoline prices and subsequent demonstrations. After the cabinet resigned in February 1974, the military stepped into the power vacuum and called for a new constitution to limit the emperor's powers. On 12 September the eighty-two-year-old Haile Selassie was arrested, although the monarchy was retained. By November, however, the coup d'état was completed when the Military Coordinating Committee announced the ouster of Haile Selassie and the formation of the Provisional Military Administrative Council, the military government headed by Lieutenant General Aman M. Andom and Lieutenant Colonel Mengistu Haile Mariam. Emperor Haile Selassie was placed under arrest and confined to a military compound. He died on 27 August 1975 in uncertain circumstances.

Books about Haile Selassie
Christopher S. Clapham, *Haile Selassie's Government* (New York: Praeger, 1969);

Fred Halliday, *The Ethiopian Revolution* (London: Verso, 1981);

Ryszard Kapuscinski, *The Emperor: Downfall of an Autocrat,* (New York: Vintage, 1984);

Harold G. Marcus, *Haile Selassie I: The Formative Years, 1892–1936* (Berkeley: University of California Press, 1987).

–J. R.-S.

SEE ALSO THESE RELATED ENTRIES

Mengistu Haile Mariam, 2.

Václav Havel

President of Czechoslovakia, 1989–1992
Born Prague, Czechoslovakia, 5 October 1936

Václav Havel, Czech playwright, prominent dissident, and president of the Czechoslovak Federal Republic from 1989 to 1992, was born in Prague into a prosperous family. He received his higher education at the drama department of the Academy of Arts in Prague. Havel published his first book at the age of nineteen, and his plays were performed in the 1960s at the Theatre of the Balustrade in Prague, where he was a resident playwright. He became an internationally recognized writer but his plays were not allowed to be performed in Czechoslovakia after the August 1968 Soviet invasion and the crushing of the Prague Spring liberalization. His books were banned, and those already published were removed from public libraries and other institutions.

Charter 77

During the 1970s Havel became a prominent proponent of human rights and one of the three initiators of the human rights movement, Charter 77, created in January 1977. The Charter 77 campaign was launched to expose government abuses of human rights and to pressure the authorities to abide by the principles of the Helsinki Final Act, signed at the Conference for Security and Cooperation in Europe (CSCE) and which Prague had ratified in October 1976. Charter 77 was organized not as an expressly political movement but as a citizens' initiative to campaign for civil liberties and eventually to create a "civil society" not under the control of the communist party-state.

Havel remained at the forefront of the campaign during the 1980s and acted as a spokesman for Charter 77 on several occasions. His prominence and frequent exposure of government abuses led to incessant police harassment and occasional periods of imprisonment. For example, in 1977 he spent four-and-a-half months in "investigative custody" for his involvement with Charter 77 and with the Committee for the Defense of the Unjustly Prosecuted (VONS). VONS monitored and publicized hundreds of cases of political repression in the country.

Imprisonments

In 1977 Havel's civil rights were formally suspended for three years because of his alleged subversive and anti-state activities, and he was kept under house arrest from 1977 until 1979. In October 1979 he was charged with subversion, tried, and sentenced to four-and-a-half years

Václav Havel

imprisonment. He was transferred to a hospital in February 1983, with serious abdominal pains, and was released from jail the following month. Havel was arrested again in January 1989, for incitement and obstruction of a police investigation, and in February 1989 he was sentenced to an additional nine months' incarceration. During his longest term of imprisonment (from 1979 to 1983), he wrote constantly to his wife Olga. *Letters to Olga*, which chronicled his daily life and his philosophical speculations, was published in 1988.

The Velvet Revolution

In November 1989 Czechoslovakia was shaken by a peaceful and popular "velvet revolution," as hundreds of thousands of citizens took to the streets to demand a complete change of the government and the communist system. Havel and his colleagues established the Civic Forum in Prague to negotiate with the communists and pressure them to introduce sweeping political and economic reforms. The regime refrained from using force, as it did not receive Moscow's support to crush the popular revolt. Within weeks the government collapsed, and a provisional coalition administration was created to prepare for free national elections. Havel was the most popular figure throughout the revolution, and his calmness and determination also gained him significant international credibility.

President of Czechoslovakia

On 29 December 1989 Havel was elected by the incumbent Parliament as Czechoslovakia's first noncommunist president since the Communist party takeover in February 1948. During the course of 1990, communist control over the state, the police, the army, and other institutions was curtailed and severed. On 8 June the Civic Forum in Bohemia and Moravia and the Public Against Violence movement in Slovakia comfortably won the federal and republican elections. In July, Havel was reelected president by the new Federal Assembly (or parliament), and the government began to draw up plans for far-reaching reforms to transform the state-controlled command economy into a productive market system.

In the international arena Havel's government offered various initiatives to establish new relations with neighboring states and to draw the Czech and Slovak Federal Republic toward European integration. For example, Prague was offered as the headquarters for a permanent CSCE office, and Czechoslovakia joined the "Pentagonal Group" of central European states (including Austria,

Hungary, Italy and Yugoslavia), which promoted economic cooperation in the region. Havel also faced constitutional problems and a potential rift within the Czech-Slovak federation as calls for Slovak autonomy and independence increased markedly during 1990. Prague miscalculated that, with the introduction of market-oriented economic reforms and far-reaching political decentralization, Slovak aspirations could be satisfied within the federation.

Following the second multiparty general elections in June 1992, the federation moved closer to dissolution. The new Federal Assembly failed to reelect Havel as Czechoslovak president. Havel formally stepped down from the presidency in October 1992, but was elected president of the new Czech Republic in January 1993.

Books by Havel (Selected)

Letters to Olga: June 1979–September 1982, translated by Paul Wilson (New York: Knopf, 1988);

Disturbing the Peace: A Conversation with Karel Hvizdala, translated by Paul Wilson (New York: Knopf, 1990);

Open Letters: Selected Writings, 1965–1990, translated by Paul Wilson (New York: Knopf, 1991);

Summer Meditations, translated by Paul Wilson (New York: Knopf, 1991).

General References

Janusz Bugajski, *Czechoslovakia: Charter 77's Decade of Dissent* (Washington, D.C. & New York: CSIS/Praeger, 1987);

H. Gordon Skilling, *Charter 77 and Human Rights in Czechoslovakia* (London: Allen & Unwin, 1981).

–J.B. and A.B.

SEE ALSO THESE RELATED ENTRIES

Aleksander Dubcek, 2; Klement Gottwald, 2; Gustáv Husák, 2; Milos Jakés, 2; Antonín Novotny, 2.

Ho Chi Minh

President of the Democratic Republic of Vietnam, 1945–1969
Born Kim Lien, Vietnam, 19 May 1890
Died Hanoi, Democratic Republic of Vietnam, 3 September 1969

Ho Chi Minh, one of the most prominent revolutionary leaders of the twentieth century, was the founder of the Vietnamese Communist party and president of the Democratic Republic of Vietnam. His struggle to unify North and South Vietnam under the Communist party led to the single greatest failure in the American foreign policy of global containment.

Born Nguyen Sihn Cung (his name was later changed by his father to Nguyen That Thanh) on 19 May 1890, Ho Chi Minh was the son of peasants in Kim Lien, a small village in the Nghe An province of central Vietnam. Trained in the classical Confucian tradition, Ho was also influenced by the anticolonial, nationalist views of his father, Nguyen Sinh Huy, who had been a scholar and a government official. Ho received his secondary education at the Quoc Hoc, the national academy, in Hue, Vietnam's imperial capital. After completing his education in 1909, he moved south and taught school in several villages. In 1911 in Saigon he signed aboard a French ocean liner as a cook's apprentice. He traveled outside of Vietnam for the next thirty years, visiting Africa, North America – spending one year in the United States working in New York – and Europe.

French Communist Party

He settled in Paris, France, in 1919. During this period he used the pseudonym Nguyen Ai Quoc (Nguyen the Patriot). Inspired by U.S. president Woodrow Wilson's international call for self-determination and democracy, he attempted to meet with President Wilson at the Versailles Conference to present him with proposals for Vietnamese independence, but was turned away before his petition could be acknowledged. Strongly influenced by Marxist literature during his years in Paris, he was a founding member of the French Communist party in 1920. He wrote and spoke widely on Indochina's problems and advocated Vietnamese independence from French colonial rule. In 1923 he traveled to Moscow, where he attended the Fifth Congress of the Communist International (Comintern) and studied at the University of Oriental Workers. In 1924 he traveled to Canton, China, where he spent the next two years training approximately two hundred Vietnamese cadres in revolutionary tactics and Marxism-Leninism. While operating in southern China, Ho briefly joined Chinese communist

Ho Chi Minh

leader Mao Zedong's Eighth Route Army. In 1925, while in Canton, he founded the first Marxist revolutionary organization of Vietnam – the Revolutionary Youth League of Vietnam, or Thanh Nien – which he organized into the leading nationalist movement opposed to French colonial rule. Its principal activity was the publication of an underground nationalist journal, which it distributed throughout Indochina.

Indochinese Communist Party

With the military seizure of power in China by anticommunist general Chiang Kai-shek, Ho Chi Minh fled

142

to Moscow in April 1927, finally ending up in Bangkok, Siam (presently Thailand). Inside Vietnam various nationalist and communist organizations had been formed to challenge French colonial rule, including the first Indochinese Communist party, founded by breakaway radicals of the Thanh Nien in 1929. In the wake of the French repression of communist-led uprisings during 1929 and 1930, the Vietnamese nationalist movement had become fragmented, and the Comintern urged Ho to work to unify it. In February 1930 he presided over the founding of the unified Vietnamese Communist party, later renamed the Indochinese Communist party (ICP), in Hong Kong. At a time when Vietnam was in a state of general unrest due to its worsening economic conditions and a worldwide recession, Ho drafted the party's program — its main points dealing with the overthrow of the French, Vietnamese independence, the establishment of a proletarian government, the confiscation of the means of production, and land and wealth redistribution. After his arrest in Hong Kong by British officials, Ho left for the Soviet Union in 1933 to study and teach at the Lenin Institute in Moscow.

In early 1940 he returned to southern China, where he tried to persuade Allied forces to provide him with arms and assistance to fight the Japanese. Ho was confident that by siding with the Allies, whom he assumed would live up to the principles of the Atlantic Charter, he could afterward secure Vietnamese independence.

Vietminh

After a thirty-year absence Ho returned to Vietnam in February 1941, and later in the year the communist-led League for the Independence of Vietnam (Vietminh) was formed after the Eighth Plenum of the ICP. As its chief architect, Ho hoped to use the Vietminh, a broad national front which would actively cooperate with other nationalist groups, to solidify the various urban and rural revolutionary forces into a single independence movement. The Vietminh, under the leadership of Vo Nguyen Giap, became highly effective in organizing guerrilla and intelligence networks to operate against the French and Japanese, and establishing apparatus whereby local militias could be established in liberated zones. In August 1942 Ho, by now widely recognized as the principal nationalist leader in Vietnam, was arrested in China and imprisoned for thirteen months while on a trip to seek assistance from Chinese leader Chiang Kai-shek.

Ho and his fellow partisans — many of whom were trained by American military personnel in China — worked with the Allied forces in China to rescue downed American and British fliers. Considering the United States a friend to colonized peoples, he frequently wrote to U.S. president Harry S Truman asking for help in securing Vietnamese independence from the French. The ICP sought to have the Vietnamese independence movement recognized as one of the victorious Allied forces under the leadership of the United States.

With the Viet Bac provinces — comprising the northeast region bordering China — under its control, the Vietminh moved to take advantage of the power vacuum, created when the French colonial administration crumbled in the wake of the Japanese occupation, and to prepare for a general uprising. In March 1945 the Japanese declared Vietnam independent under Japanese control. After the Japanese surrender and transfer of power to the Vietminh, the Vietminh National Congress convened on 16 August to elect a National Liberation Committee, which would serve as a provisional government headed by Ho. That same day the congress ratified the ICP central committee decision to call for a general uprising, officially launching the so-called August Revolution. In less than a week most of the provincial capitals north of Hanoi had fallen to the communist revolutionary forces. Before the end of the month, Vietminh forces took Hue, Saigon, and Hanoi, where Ho subsequently moved his headquarters. On 28 August the Vietminh announced the formation of a provisional government of the Democratic Republic of Vietnam (DRV), with Ho as president, Vo Nguyen Giap as minister of the interior, and deposed emperor Bao Dai as "supreme adviser" to the provisional government. On 2 September, before a gathering of a half-million people, Ho read the Vietnamese Declaration of Independence, which was based on the American Declaration of Independence and the French Declaration of the Rights of Man and the Citizen.

First Indochina War

The political situation quickly deteriorated in and around Hanoi and elsewhere, however, as various nationalist groups and the French tried to assert control. Supported by the Truman administration in its efforts to reimpose colonial rule, the French refused to recognize Vietnamese independence and sent some fifteen thousand troops into northern Vietnam, accompanied by Chinese and British expeditionary forces established by the Potsdam Conference. With the collapse of negotiations with the French and escalating violence, Ho and the Vietminh prepared for war. The first Indochina War (1946–1954) broke out after the French naval bombardment of the port city of Haiphong in November 1946. The French retook most of the provincial capitals, while the Vietminh controlled the countryside, where it concentrated on building up its military strength and guerrilla network. The U.S.-backed French forces had succeeded in retaking most of the country by the fall of 1947. The Vietminh, however, rebounded from its losses by late 1948 with a rebuilt force of some 250,000 troops.

The border between the Vietminh-controlled northern half of the country and the southern half was established when in May 1948 the French granted nominal independence to all of Vietnam as the Associated State of Vietnam headed by Emperor Bao Dai and existing within the French Union. Ho and other nationalist leaders – including Ngo Dinh Diem, who refused to join the new government – criticized the agreement. Ho argued that the Democratic Republic of Vietnam was the only legal government in Vietnam. China and the Soviet Union formally recognized the DRV in 1950.

The Chinese communist revolution in October 1949 and the subsequent invasion of South Korea by communist North Korea in June 1950 dramatically affected the DRV's place in international affairs. Ho had been the subject of growing suspicion and discomfort for the United States, and the American policy of containment, initially focused on Europe, was extended to Asia by the Truman administration to protect the region from communist encroachment. The Indochina War quickly turned into a decisive stand against Soviet expansionism, a struggle between "communism and the free world," in the eyes of American policymakers. Aided by the People's Republic of China (PRC), under Chairman Mao Zedong, the Vietminh were orchestrating stunning defeats of the U.S.-backed French forces by late 1950. Even though it had recognized the French hold on Indochina as "tenuous," the American government increased its military aid to the French, which by 1954 had reached an estimated $2 billion.

The turning point in the war came in May 1954 with the French defeat at Dien Bien Phu. That same month multilateral negotiations got under way in Geneva, Switzerland, resulting in a cease-fire in Vietnam, Cambodia, and Laos, and a compromise agreement that provided for the temporary border dividing Vietnam along the 17th parallel between the DRV in the North and the Bao Dai government in the South. The agreement further called for national reunification elections to be held in the summer of 1956. The more militant members of the DRV regime initially opposed the compromise settlement, but were later convinced by Ho of the dangers of American military involvement if the fighting were to continue, and the possibility of achieving an independent, reunified Vietnam through peaceful revolution if a compromise were agreed to.

After years of sacrifice, the Vietminh, however, were unwilling to accept a permanent partition. The Geneva agreements proved a failure when in October 1955 the southern half of Vietnam was proclaimed the Republic of Vietnam, headed by Ngo Dinh Diem as president, and with the backing of the United States, which began to provide direct military aid to South Vietnam. The hardline, anticommunist Diem regime initiated a crackdown on communists and Vietminh remnants in the South. Diem's anticommunist campaign convinced the DRV to adopt a more militant approach to reunification.

Conflict with the Diem Regime

Until 1959 Ho and the Hanoi leadership had discouraged the southern communist movement from engaging in armed conflict with the Diem regime. The DRV was preoccupied with serious domestic problems – both economic and political – and for Ho the priority was first to consolidate the North and wait for a more favorable balance of forces before urging an uprising in the South. Ho began to plan the uprising after 1959, despite the reluctance of senior leaders to become involved militarily in South Vietnam. In December 1960, preceded by communist military advances in the South, the National Front for the Liberation of South Vietnam (NLF), labeled the "Vietcong" by the Diem regime, was founded. The NLF, led by veterans of the Vietminh, was ostensibly a southern movement, although it was widely believed it took its orders from Hanoi. At the same time, the construction of the Ho Chi Minh Trail, an elaborate communist infiltration route into the South through Laos and Cambodia, began. That same year some ninety thousand Vietminh troops had infiltrated South Vietnam and established liberated zones in the lower Mekong Delta region. North Vietnam began to commit regular units to the fighting, and in 1964 alone an estimated ten thousand North Vietnamese advanced into the South. Three years later North Vietnamese regulars were streaming into the South at a rate of twenty thousand per month. As early as 1964 almost half of South Vietnam was under communist control, even though American involvement in the conflict had deepened.

The Vietnam War

For the United States, Vietnam had become a test of American resolve. Alarmed by the perceived threat of communist advances in the rest of Southeast Asia, it mobilized to prevent the collapse of the tottering South Vietnamese regime, whose viability was undermined both by the spreading communist insurgency and internal political unrest. On 6 February 1962 the American Military Assistance Command was formed in South Vietnam, and by midyear American military personnel in Vietnam had increased to an estimated twelve thousand. In early August 1963, after a clash between American and North Vietnamese vessels, U.S. aircraft bombed North Vietnam for the first time.

Anticipating an escalation of the war into North Vietnam, Ho appealed to the DRV's principal patrons, the People's Republic of China and the Soviet Union, for increased economic and military assistance. Even though relations between China and the Soviet Union had soured, he skillfully maintained good relations with both countries. Ho, who headed the nominally pro-Soviet faction in the DRV leadership, exploited the rift between the Soviet Union and China, whose policies toward Vietnam were motivated by their own interests, to secure continued assistance from both. On 7 August 1964 the U.S. Congress passed the Tonkin Gulf resolution, which allowed President Lyndon B. Johnson to take all necessary measures to prevent further aggression. Although reluctant to commit American combat troops, even though the number of American military advisers in Vietnam had reached some sixteen thousand by mid 1964, President Johnson ordered air strikes against targets in North Vietnam in early February. The sustained bombing of North Vietnam, called Operation Rolling Thunder, began on 24 February 1965 – and American commitment in Vietnam deepened. On 8 March 1965 two battalions of U.S. Marines landed in Da Nang, the first American combat troops in Vietnam, and by December an estimated two hundred thousand had been deployed in South Vietnam. By 1968 that number had swelled to over a half-million troops.

After the mid 1960s Ho Chi Minh, aging and in poor health, was less actively involved in the decision-making process and operated mainly from behind the scenes, even though he remained president and general secretary of the party. Drawing on his fervent popular backing and prestige, he continued to mobilize the population by stirring Vietnamese nationalistic sentiment. His essential role was to bridge factional rivalries within the Hanoi leadership and to maintain cooperative relations with North Vietnam's principal backers. Ho Chi Minh died on 3 September 1969 at the age of seventy-nine. Throughout his tenure as the most prominent Vietnamese nationalist leader and long after his death, Ho Chi Minh was revered by his countrymen as the symbol of Vietnamese national unity and independence.

Books by Ho Chi Minh (Selected)
On Revolution: Selected Writings, 1920–1966 (New York: Praeger, 1967);

Patriotism and Proletarian Internationalism (Hanoi: Foreign Languages Publishing House, 1979).

Books about Ho Chi Minh
Jean Lacouture, *Ho Chi Minh: A Political Biography*, translated by Peter Wiles (New York: Random House, 1968);

Milton Osborne, *Ho Chi Minh* (New York: University of Queensland Press, 1982).

General References
David Halberstam, *The Best and the Brightest* (Greenwich, Conn.: Fawcett, 1972);

George Herring, *America's Longest War: The United States and Vietnam, 1950–1975* (New York: Knopf, 1979);

Stanley Karnow, *Vietnam: A History* (New York: Viking, 1984; revised, 1991);

Gabriel Kolko, *Anatomy of a War: Vietnam, the United States, and the Modern Historical Experience* (New York: Pantheon, 1985).

–J. R.-S.

> **SEE ALSO THESE RELATED ENTRIES**
> Chiang Kai-shek, 2; Ngo Dinh Diem, 2; Vo Nguyen Giap, 2; Lyndon B. Johnson, 1; Mao Zedong, 2; Harry S Truman, 1.

Enver Hoxha

First Secretary, Albanian Workers Party, 1954–1985

Prime Minister of Albania, 1944–1954

Born Gjirokastër, Albania, 16 October 1908

Died Tiranë, Albania, 11 April 1985

Enver Hoxha, Albanian Communist party leader and chief of state, was born in Gjirokastër, Albania, near the Greek border to a middle-class Muslim family, where his father was a cloth merchant. He received his secondary education at the French lyceum at Korçë and spent some time at the American Technical School in Tiranë. In 1930 Hoxha went on a state scholarship to the University of Montpellier, France, but he lost his scholarship a year later because of a poor academic record. He left school and moved to Paris, where he joined the French Communist party and began a publishing career for the party newspaper. Many of his articles were attacks against the reign of King Zog I in Albania. From 1934 to 1936 Hoxha was also a secretary at the Albanian consulate general in Brussels. He returned to Albania in 1936 and became a teacher at his old school in Korçë but was dismissed in 1939 for his subversive activities.

World War II

In April 1939 Italy invaded and occupied Albania. Hoxha refused to join the Albanian Fascist party, which supported the new puppet regime. Instead he opened a tobacco store in Tiranë and became active during World War II in Albania's communist partisan forces. After the partition of Albania by Germany and Italy in 1941, Hoxha helped to organize the Albanian (Communist) Party of Labor (APL). He was elected secretary general of the APL Central Committee by the First Party Congress in 1943. After the downfall of the Italian Fascist regime and the withdrawal of German forces, the Albanian guerrilla forces went on the offensive. With the backing of Yugoslav communists, Hoxha's guerrillas captured control of the country by the end of 1944. At the close of World War II, Albania became a communist republic under overall Yugoslav protection.

In 1944 Hoxha became minister of foreign affairs and minister of defense, as well as the prime minister. Despite Yugoslavia's strong political influence over Albania, Hoxha was able to gain full independence for the country by playing upon the growing rift between Yugoslavia and the Soviet Union. Albania strongly backed Soviet leader Joseph Stalin against Yugoslavia's Marshal Josip Broz Tito when the latter opposed the creation of the Comin-

Enver Hoxha

form (Communist Information Bureau) under Moscow's direction. The Tiranë regime attacked the Yugoslavs for "revisionism" and nationalism, and supported Yugoslavia's expulsion from all Soviet bloc alliances in 1948.

Stalinist Policies

During the late 1940s and early 1950s Hoxha's hard-line Marxist-Leninist regime eliminated its nationalist and royalist opponents and imposed a reign of police terror in order to collectivize agriculture, suppress organized religion, and regiment all social, cultural, and educational activities. After the break between Tito and Stalin, Albania adopted a strong pro-Soviet position and used its alliance with Moscow as a counterweight to potential pressure from Belgrade. Hoxha built up an elaborate personality cult based on the Stalin model, and maintained it even after Stalin's death. Unlike the other East European states, de-Stalinization, or the easing of the most repressive features of the communist system, made little progress in Albania. The various political and economic reforms in the Soviet Union and other East European states did not penetrate Albania. The hard-line regime maintained an orthodox Marxist-Leninist system that began to look increasingly anachronistic in post-Stalin Europe.

Hoxha's relations with the Soviet Union deteriorated in the late 1950s. The new Kremlin leadership toned down its support for communist takeovers in the Third World and pursued some domestic reforms, which the Albanians condemned as "revisionist" or backtracking on the communist dogmas of the "dictatorship of the proletariat" and "world revolution." In 1960 Albanian-Soviet relations were severed and Tiranë withdrew from all the Soviet-sponsored alliances. The Soviets were in no position to intervene in Albania as the two countries did not share a common border and there was no history of Soviet influence over Albania.

Relations with China

At the same time Hoxha sought to strengthen Albania's ties with Maoist China, which was seen as the bulwark of authentic Marxism-Leninism. But this alignment did not last much beyond Mao Zedong's death in 1976. As the Beijing regime improved its relations with the United States and other capitalist powers, and introduced economic reforms which seemed to depart from Marxist-Leninist collectivism, all military and most eco-

nomic aid to Albania was stopped. Albania was left almost completely isolated on the international arena, but maintained some contact with hard-line communist regimes such as North Korea and Cuba, as well as vehemently anti-American but noncommunist governments in the Third World with which it conducted economic transactions.

Hoxha died on 11 April 1985 in Tiranë and was replaced by his protégé Ramiz Alia, who initiated more reformist policies and allowed for an opening to some West European states.

Books by Hoxha (Selected)

Selected Works, 6 volumes (Tiranë, Albania: "8 Nentori" Publishing House, 1974–1987);

Imperialism and the Revolution (Chicago: World View Publications, 1979);

Eurocommunism is Anti-Communism (Toronto: Norman Bethune Institute, 1980);

With Stalin: Memoirs (Toronto: Norman Bethune Institute, 1980).

General References

Anton Logoreci, *The Albanians: Europe's Forgotten Survivors* (Boulder, Colo.: Westview, 1977);

Nicholas C. Pano, *The People's Republic of Albania* (Baltimore: Johns Hopkins University Press, 1968);

Peter R. Prifti, *Socialist Albania Since 1944: Domestic and Foreign Developments* (Cambridge, Mass.: MIT Press, 1978);

Tom Winnifrith, ed., *Perspectives on Albania* (New York: St. Martin's Press, 1992).

–J. B. and A. B.

SEE ALSO THESE RELATED ENTRIES
Ramiz Alia, 2; Mao Zedong, 2; Josip Broz Tito, 2.

Hua Guofeng

Chairman of the Chinese Communist Party, 1976–1977
Born Liuyang City, Shanxi Province, China, 1921

Hua Guofeng was Mao Zedong's handpicked successor to lead the People's Republic of China (PRC). After Mao's death and armed with Mao's personally written cryptic endorsement "with you in charge, I am at ease," Hua began a short reign which could be described as a transition period between Mao Zedong and Deng Xiaoping. Hua's cautious politics illustrated both his tenuous position and his foreign relations inexperience. Because he lacked a solid base of support, Hua's descent from high-level politics into obscurity was rapid.

Hua Guofeng was born in the industry-rich Shanxi province. Little is known about his parents, only that they were poor peasants. Hua completed two years of middle school before joining the communist guerrilla forces fighting against Japan in 1938. He officially entered the Chinese Communist party (CCP) in 1940.

Hua's speciality was teaching guerrilla tactics. The Chinese army was in short supply of weapons during the war with Japan, so Hua trained soldiers to construct "homemade" mines and grenades. He also took his talents to peasants, teaching them the finer techniques of mine laying. Hua was an expert in sabotage. He infiltrated Japanese encampments while disguised as a villager and contaminated Japanese water supplies. He continued to train communist guerrillas during the Chinese civil war (1946–1949), earning praise for his skill.

In 1949 Hua became a party secretary in Hunan, Mao Zedong's home province. He spent the next twenty-two years in Hunan working his way up from training cadres as a county secretary to managing provincial affairs as the top official in Hunan. Although his area of expertise was agriculture, he was responsible for improving literacy rates and overseeing Hunan's finance and trade.

The Cultural Revolution

Hua was the second secretary in Hunan in 1967, when he met the same fate as so many other longtime party members: he was stripped of power during the Cultural Revolution (1966-1976), Mao's plan to reexpose China to revolutionary struggle. Unlike the others, however, Hua was quickly rehabilitated and was made first secretary of Hunan in 1970, the most powerful provincial rank.

In 1973, in what was a symbol of the unpredictability of the Cultural Revolution, Hua Guofeng was elected to the twenty-one-member Politburo, the second highest po-

litical decision-making body in the party. The appointment baffled Western observers because Hua was seldom heard of and had little experience in national politics.

Hua's ascension to party chairman came in 1976. The year saw the deaths of the PRC's two most dominant forces, Premier Zhou Enlai and Mao Zedong; the purge of a third, Deng Xiaoping; massive demonstrations violently repressed by the army; and a gigantic earthquake which killed a quarter-million people. The unexpected and tragic became commonplace in China. In choosing his successor just prior to his death in September, Mao sought a compromise choice between the moderate and radical factions of the party and opted for the man in the middle, Hua Guofeng.

"Gang of Four"

Mao's wife, Jiang Qing, leader of the radical faction and propaganda queen of the Cultural Revolution, plotted to assume leadership after Mao's death. She and her accomplices, later called the "gang of four," outlined a scheme which included a military takeover. Hua, however, undermined Jiang's efforts by planning his own ascension. With the help of other party leaders and the military, Hua had the "gang of four" arrested on 6 October. Four days later he was named party chairman.

Foreign Policy under Hua

Although he physically resembled Mao in his height, square face, and large, penetrating eyes, Hua, unlike Mao and other Chinese leaders, was modest and uncharismatic. He also had only a hazy knowledge of global politics. Before his election as chairman he had never even been abroad. It is this lack of experience coupled with unstable domestic politics which helped distinguish the Hua era for its caution.

Hua chose to continue the foreign policy of Mao and Zhou Enlai. Hua denounced the Soviet Union as the "worst" hegemonic superpower and courted the United States as a partner in the U.S.-Soviet-Chinese strategic triangle. Fears of Soviet "adventurism" after Mao's death made the Sino-U.S. rapprochement all the more appealing to Hua.

Although his overtures to the United States helped create an opportunity ripe for normalization, Hua was hindered by his lack of authority within the party. He chose not to risk being charged with being soft on the

Hua Guofeng

United States and ended his conciliatory gesturing. Despite diligent efforts by the Soviets to moderate Sino-Soviet relations, Hua rejected all overtures. Again, the domestic constraints stifled him. The domestic political risk of altering a policy of Mao's would have been critically damaging.

In May 1977 Deng Xiaoping returned to the leadership despite efforts by Hua to keep him purged. Deng seized control of the foreign policy mechanism and left Hua Guofeng to a largely figurehead role. By 1979 Hua Guofeng had little power in the party and, after he was stripped of his leadership position and disgraced in 1980, became inactive in politics.

Hua virtually disappeared after 1982, having been relegated to a footnote in modern Chinese history.

Book about Hua
Wang Ting, *Chairman Hua, Leader of the Chinese Communists* (London: C. Hurst, 1980).

General References
Jonathan D. Spence, *The Gate of Heavenly Peace: The Chinese and Their Revolution, 1895–1980* (New York: Viking, 1981).

– K. W. M.

SEE ALSO THESE RELATED ENTRIES

Deng Xiaoping, 2; Mao Zedong, 2; Zhou Enlai, 2.

Huang Hua

People's Republic of China Ambassador to the United Nations, 1971–1976

Minister of Foreign Affairs, 1976–1982

Born Kiangsu, Hebei Province, 1913

Huang Hua was China's preeminent diplomat during the Cold War. The man whom Western diplomats called a "tough negotiator" was a principal player in Chinese foreign relations from the early 1950s through the 1980s. His accomplishments include helping negotiate the end of the Korean War, serving as the People's Republic of China's representative to the United Nations, and helping pave the way for Sino-U.S. normalization.

Huang Hua was born Wang Rumei in Kiangsu in Hebei province. He attended the American Yanjing University in Beijing, where he was a left-wing student activist and class president. In the mid 1930s Huang was an interpreter for Edgar Snow, an American journalist whose classic book, *Red Star over China* (1937), documents the early days of the communist movement in China. During the war against the Japanese (1937–1945) Huang remained in Yanan, the communist capital, serving as a secretary to Red Army commander Zhu De.

Huang served as the communists' interpreter in the peace talks between the communists and the nationalist government in January 1946. With U.S. envoy General George C. Marshall acting as mediator, the talks resulted in a short-lived cease-fire agreement. After the establishment of the People's Republic of China (PRC) in 1949, Huang worked with communist youth. He was transferred to Beijing in 1953 to work in the Ministry of Foreign Affairs.

In fall 1953 Huang received his first major assignment. He was the PRC chief delegate to low-level talks held in Panmunjom, South Korea. The negotiations were designed to settle the questions of foreign troop withdrawal and peaceful unification of Korea. His American counterpart was Arthur H. Dean, who respected Huang's negotiating skills and his fluency in English. The talks effectively ended in mid December when Dean walked out, apparently frustrated by Huang's persistent denunciations of Dean's personal authority, reliability, and sincerity. Negotiations moved to a higher level in Geneva, where Huang served Premier Zhou Enlai as an adviser in April 1954.

For the remainder of the decade Huang was one of the most respected foreign relations experts in China. He was an adviser to Zhou in 1955 at the historic Bandung Conference, where Afro-Asian relations were discussed.

Huang Hua

In 1958 Huang went to Warsaw to participate in the Sino-American ambassadorial talks at the time of the second Taiwan Straits Crisis. Huang traveled extensively and gained a reputation for being a tough negotiator. But, when away from the negotiating table, he was said to be sociable and an interesting conversationalist.

Huang served as ambassador to Ghana from 1960 to 1965 and to Egypt from 1965 to 1970. He was the only Chinese diplomat not recalled to Beijing for self-criticism during the Cultural Revolution (1966–1976), Mao Zedong's effort to rerevolutionize Chinese society.

Huang was ambassador to Canada for about five months in 1971 before being named China's permanent representative to the United Nations (UN). He served in the UN for five years. Huang became China's minister of foreign affairs, the top diplomatic position in the country, in December 1976.

His greatest achievement during his six years as foreign minister was participating in the Sino-U.S. normalization talks in 1978. With his mastery of English, Huang was a natural to help Deng Xiaoping begin a new age of relations between the PRC and the United States. Huang accompanied Deng on a tour of the United States in January 1979 to help generate U.S. interest in China. Huang impressed his hosts with his ability to speak on a wide array of nonpolitical topics.

Huang was a tireless worker who traveled widely. After he was replaced as minister in November 1982, he continued to lead delegations abroad. He retired from his last full-time post as Central Committee member in September 1985. He is still a member of the National People's Congress, which meets infrequently to vote on leadership positions.

Book about Huang Hua

Byron S. J. Weng, *Peking's UN Policy* (New York: Praeger, 1972).

General Reference

Edgar Snow, *Red Star over China* (London: Gollancz, 1937).

– K. W. M.

SEE ALSO THESE RELATED ENTRIES

Deng Xiaoping, 2; Zhou Enlai, 2.

Gustáv Husák

President of Czechoslovakia, 1975–1989
General Secretary, Czechoslovak Communist Party, 1971–1987

Born Dúbravka, Slovakia, 10 January 1913
Died Bratislava, Slovak Republic, 18 November 1991

Gustáv Husák, Czechoslovak Communist leader, was born in Dúbravka, near the Slovak capital of Bratislava. He studied law and practiced as a lawyer in Bratislava. In 1933 he joined the Czechoslovak Communist party (CCP) and was active in various party cells in Slovakia. During World War II Husák was arrested several times for his involvement in the leadership of the then illegal CCP, and in 1944 he became a leader of the Slovak uprising against the pro-Nazi Fascist government in Slovakia.

Purged by Stalin

After the liberation and takeover of Czechoslovakia by the Soviets, Husák became a member of the Central Committee of both the CCP and the Slovak Communist party. In addition, he held several posts in the regional government of Slovakia, including chairman of the Slovak National Council. In 1951 Husák was ousted from the party as part of the Stalinist purges of "native" communists who had spent the war years outside of the Soviet Union and were considered potentially disloyal by Joseph Stalin. He was arrested in 1954 and sentenced to life imprisonment for allegedly advocating Slovak bourgeois nationalism.

Husák was released under a general amnesty in May 1960 and fully rehabilitated three years later. He returned to political life in August 1968, as deputy premier of Czechoslovakia and first secretary of the Slovak Communist party. His return was made possible only after Aleksander Dubcek had become first secretary of the CCP during the liberalizing Prague Spring. Husák's major accomplishments during the reform period were moves to establish a more equitable federation between the Czech lands (Bohemia and Moravia) and Slovakia, in which power was significantly decentralized to the republican level. Although the decentralized republican system was retained after the Prague Spring was thwarted, the reimposition of Communist party control effectively curtailed any degree of local political independence.

Invasion by the Soviets

In August 1968, when Warsaw Pact troops under

Gustáv Husák

Soviet control invaded and occupied Czechoslovakia to crush the reform movement, Husák was a chief voice for compromise. He was selected by Soviet leaders as the replacement for Dubcek because he urged cooperation with the Kremlin but was not tainted with any major role in the Stalinist repression. Dubcek was removed from office, and in April 1969 Husák was appointed first secretary of the CCP under Soviet supervision. He subsequently extinguished most of the reforms that the Dubcek government had implemented. Husák was appointed general secretary of the CCP in 1971, and in 1975 he was also elected president of Czechoslovakia.

During Husák's normalization program in 1969–1970 thousands of CCP members were expelled, internal party discipline ("democratic centralism") was re-imposed, and the CCP restored its monopoly over all political and social activities. The Husák government did not introduce the kind of decentralizing economic reforms then under way in Hungary. It feared surrendering any ground to the Prague Spring reformers who had urged extensive marketization of the economy. During the 1970s the population was kept pacified through a combination of direct police repression, administrative control, and a slow but steady growth in living standards. But in the 1980s the political rigidity of the regime came under increasing criticism, particularly as the economy began to stagnate and as dissent remained strictly prohibited.

Replacement by Jakeš

In December 1987 Husák was replaced as party chief by the younger Miloš Jakeš but retained the largely ceremonial position of head of state. The Jakeš regime, like its predecessor, opposed any liberalization of the political system and criticized the Polish and Hungarian regimes for introducing elements of political pluralism. Together with East Germany, Romania, and Bulgaria, the Czechoslovak government paid only lip service to Mikhail Gorbachev's glasnost campaign, in which the mass media were liberalized in the Soviet Union and restrictions were lifted on intellectual activities. The regime also refrained from criticizing the 1968 Soviet invasion, as any positive reassessment of the Prague Spring would have undermined its own political legitimacy.

When democratic revolutions swept across Eastern Europe in the fall of 1989, the Prague government initially attempted to crack down and contain public protests. But in November 1989 mass demonstrations forced the regime to grant unprecedented political concessions to the newly formed Civic Forum democratic opposition. At the end of November the entire party and government leadership resigned and Husák stepped down from the presidency. Václav Havel, the popular playwright and opposition activist, was appointed interim president in December 1989, in preparation for democratic elections in the spring of 1990. Husák disappeared from the political scene.

General References

J. F. Brown, *Eastern Europe and Communist Rule* (Durham, N.C. and London: Duke University Press, 1988);

Robert L. Hutchings, *Soviet-East European Relations: Consolidation and Conflict, 1968–1980* (Madison: University of Wisconsin Press, 1983);

Christopher D. Jones, *Soviet Influence in Eastern Europe: Political Autonomy and the Warsaw Pact* (New York: Praeger, 1981);

Vladimir Kusin, *From Dubcek to Charter 77: A Study of "Normalization" in Czechoslovakia, 1968–1978* (New York: St. Martin's Press, 1978);

Joseph Rothschild, *Return to Diversity: A Political History of East Central Europe since World War II* (New York: Oxford University Press, 1989);

H. Gordon Skilling, *Czechoslovakia's Interrupted Revolution* (Princeton, N.J.: Princeton University Press, 1976);

Zdenek Suda, *Zealots and Rebels: A History of the Ruling Communist Party of Czechoslovakia* (Stanford, Cal.: Hoover Institution Press, 1980);

Sarah M. Terry, ed., *Soviet Policy in Eastern Europe* (New Haven: Yale University Press, 1984).

—J. B. and A. B.

SEE ALSO THESE RELATED ENTRIES

Aleksander Dubcek, 2; Klement Gottwald, 2; Václav Havel, 2; Miloš Jakeš, 2; Antonín Novotny, 2.

Saddam Hussein

President of Iraq, 1979–
Born Tikrit, Iraq, 28 April 1937

Saddam Hussein, president of Iraq since 1979, has been a leading figure within the Ba'ath party and Iraqi politics since the mid 1960s. Under his leadership Iraq started the war with Iran in 1980 and a decade later occupied Kuwait. With this last invasion Western sentiment turned against him, and U.S. leaders changed the support they had had for him during the previous invasion of Iran and called for his overthrow.

Hussein was born on 28 April 1937 to Sabha Tulfah al-Massallat and her husband, who died just before the baby's birth, in Tikrit, a village three hundred miles north of Baghdad on the Tigris River. Since Hussein assumed the presidency in 1979, the official version of his family history claims that his mother was related to the family of the prophet Muhammad. While Hussein was a baby, his mother married her brother-in-law, al-Hajj Ibrahim al-Hasan, and the family moved to his mud hut in the village of Uja near Tikrit. In his first act of rebellion, at age ten, Hussein decided to attend school. When his family tried to dissuade him, he ran back to Tikrit, to the home of his maternal uncle, Khayr Alla Tulfah.

Hussein began his secondary studies in Baghdad in 1955 and within a year had participated in his first anti-government demonstration. In 1957, at age twenty, Hussein joined the underground Ba'ath party as a low-ranking member. The Ba'ath (Renaissance) party is based on an ideology of pan-Arab, secular socialism in which the party assumes dominance in all aspects of public life; in its Iraqi strain, although the party used the military to gain and consolidate power, for example, it has since stripped the army of its authority.

On 14 July 1958 General Abd al-Qarim Qasim led the army in a coup against the monarchy of King Faisal II. For a few months the Ba'ath was allowed to operate legally, but it soon clashed with General Qasim. While the Ba'ath sought unity with Egypt and Syria in the United Arab Republic, Qasim was intent on preserving Iraqi independence. Not long after the coup, Hussein was jailed for the murder of a Tikriti official.

Attempted Assassination of Qasim

In autumn 1959 the party chose Hussein, then twenty-two, to be among a small group of party loyalists who would assassinate General Qasim. Although Hussein claims to have led the tank assault on the presidential palace in a military uniform, he was not, in fact, an army

Saddam Hussein

officer until he became ex-officio commander in chief of the armed forces. When the assassination attempt failed, Hussein, wounded by a bullet, fled to Syria. In Damascus the Ba'ath leadership gave him a hero's welcome and he met personally with Michel Aflaq, the Syrian Christian who founded the Ba'ath in the 1940s and remained its chief ideologue. Although Aflaq's reputation in Syria later declined, he remained extremely influential in the Ba'ath's Iraqi faction. Aflaq had promoted Hussein to full party membership in the late 1950s and in the mid 1960s had him appointed to the Regional Command, the highest decision-making body of the Iraqi branch of the Ba'ath.

As Edward Mortimer writes about the relationship between Saddam Hussein and Michel Aflaq, who lived in Iraq until his death in 1989, "Saddam continued to attach great importance to Aflaq, and to his own links to him, as a major source of legitimacy for his own leadership. It is comparable to the use that Stalin made of Lenin's name, and of a carefully doctored version of Lenin's heritage, in legitimizing his own absolute power in the Soviet Union."

Overthrow of Qasim

On 8 February 1963 a coalition of Ba'ath loyalists and Nasserist military officers overthrew General Qasim. Hussein returned immediately from Cairo, where he had finished high school and begun dabbling at law school. In Baghdad he became involved in internal security. At this time he also married his maternal cousin, Sajida, daughter of Khayr Alla Tulfah and sister of Adnan Khayr Alla, Iraqi minister of defense from 1977 until his death in 1989. The two have five children: Uday, Qusay, Ghard, Rana, and Hala.

Soon after the Ba'ath came to power, however, it split among rightists, leftists, and a centrist group, which was headed by then–prime minister (and Hussein's relative from Tikrit) Brigadier General Ahmad Hassan al-Bakr. Hussein joined al-Bakr's faction. By late 1963 that rift had extended to a regional ideological rift between the al Bakr-Hussein faction in Iraq and the Hafez al-Assad group in Syria.

Arrest and Imprisonment

In late 1963 the Nasserist president Abd al-Salam Arif, who until then had been no more than a figurehead presiding over an essentially Ba'ath regime, removed the Ba'ath from power. In autumn 1964 the Ba'ath planned a coup against President Arif, but the plan was exposed and the police rounded up the culprits. According to the official version, when Hussein was tracked down in Baghdad that October, he fought off the police with a pistol until he ran out of ammunition and was arrested. Until his escape from prison in July 1966, Hussein passed the time by reading Lenin and contemplating the reasons for the party's failure to stay in power.

Overthrow of Arif

On 17 July 1968 the Ba'ath ousted President Abd al-Rahman Arif (who had succeeded his younger brother after the latter was killed in a helicopter crash in April 1966). Later that month the civilian Hussein was the key figure in removing the two more ambitious and dangerous of the four officers who helped topple Arif. The second coup within less than a fortnight placed power squarely in the hands of the Ba'ath party under President al-Bakr, a career army officer whose family was closely connected with Hussein's. In November 1968 Hussein became assistant secretary general of the party and deputy chairman of the highest decision-making institution, the Revolutionary Command Council (RCC), of which al-Bakr was then chair.

President

Between 1969 and 1971 Hussein outmaneuvered and ousted his and al-Bakr's most formidable opponents in the party and the RCC. Even though Hussein could not control the army with al-Bakr and lacked popular support, he became the main influence in all political and economic decisions from the early 1970s. On 16 July 1979 Hussein pushed out al-Bakr (who was honorably retired, ostensibly at his own request on grounds of ill health), purged his enemies, executed his party rivals, and took over the positions of president and RCC chair. By 1 August 1979 some five hundred high-ranking Ba'athists had been executed and Hussein was firmly in charge.

Methods of Rule

Since then, Hussein has ruled through a cult of personality, a network of family members and others from his home village of Tikrit, a propaganda machine that has churned out some 250 booklets in his name, and a mass of competing internal security services. Hussein's cousin Adnan Khayr Alla, for example, was defense minister from 1977 until his death in a helicopter crash in May 1989, suspiciously soon after a falling-out with Hussein when the latter had an indiscreet affair. Two other leading figures in internal security also are relatives: Saddam's son Uday is married to the daughter of Izzat Ibrahim, his most faithful lieutenant. Uday also headed the Iraqi Olympic Committee until the ruler tried his son for murdering his food taster and bodyguard in 1988.

Through such repression and connections Hussein has held power in Iraq, despite numerous coup attempts over the years. "All of them know that if they don't defend him, they will fall with him," says Sahib al-Hakim, an Iraqi dissident, "because he has made sure that they have shared in the killings." At a 1982 cabinet meeting, for example, when health minister Riyadh Ibrahim suggested that Hussein temporarily step down as a way of ending the war with Iran, he was taken to a side room and executed.

Hussein's seizure of power, however, reversed the process of militarization in Iraq that had defined that country's politics since the 1958 coup. After the Ba'ath took power, for example, some two thousand to three thousand army officers, who were regarded as dangerous to party rule, were purged. Among the deposed was Abd al-Razzaq Nayif, the senior non-Ba'ath participant in the coup, who was deposed and exiled thirteen days after becoming prime minister in 1968. At the time of the coup the highest policy-making body, the RCC, was composed of army officers; two decades later all but one of its nine members were civilians. At the same time the party's ranks have swelled; in 1968 there were probably no more than one thousand full members and between five thousand and ten thousand lower members; by 1987 the party comprised some 1.5 million people, or nearly 10 percent of Iraq's total population of 17 million people.

The Iran-Iraq War

In spring 1969, not long after the Ba'ath party had seized power, Iran and Iraq clashed over sovereignty rights to the Shatt-al-Arab waterway. The border was then agreed upon in the 1975 Algiers agreement, under which, as quid pro quo for getting its way on the dispute, Iran (and, covertly, the United States) agreed to stop funding the Kurdish rebellion in Iraq. When Ayatollah Ruhollah Khomeini came to power in Iran in 1979, Hussein declared the Algiers accord null and void. Iraq's political struggle, he declared after a 1980 coup attempt, was a "revolution which aims to destroy the bases of imperialism, to shine over the whole Arab world, to make it a new power on the world scene." A few months later, on 22 September 1980, Iraqi aircraft invaded Iran, followed the next day by ground forces.

The Gulf states lent Iraq some $35 billion to pay for "Hussein's Qasidiya" and, along with Jordan, provided that country with badly needed logistical routes. In November 1984 Hussein also reestablished full diplomatic relations with the United States. While the Soviet Union supplied Iraq with arms the United States gave it credit guarantees, interest-free loans, and subsidized food deliveries. The United States also reportedly gave Iraq access to intelligence on the Iranian military, and U.S. firms have reportedly helped Iraq develop missile production capability; it imposed an effective arms embargo on Iran (until the Iran-contra scandal) and sent its navy into the Gulf, which seriously hampered the Iranian war effort. During the war Iraq lost around 1 percent of its total population and accumulated debts of somewhere between $60 billion and $100 billion. Since the war, Iraqis have confronted rapidly rising prices, underemployment, and continuing political repression.

In August 1990 Iraq invaded its neighbor Kuwait, a small, rich sheikhdom with large supplies of oil. Iraqis had long regarded Kuwait as rightfully part of their country, in much the same way many Syrians view Lebanon as part of "Greater Syria." In 1961, for example, General Qasim sent the Iraqi army to Kuwait's frontier after declaring that Britain had "declared an oil well a state"; but Britain forced him to back off, and the newly proclaimed emirate stood. This time U.S. troops, supported by a coalition of Europeans and pro–U.S. Arab states, launched a massive air war, followed by a quick ground war, and evicted Iraq from Kuwait while inflicting heavy damage on Iraq's military capability. Since 1991, Iraq has been subjected to UN-led economic sanctions, and close inspections of its weapon-making facilities.

Books and Articles about Hussein

Amazia Baram, "Saddam Hussein: A Political Profile," *Jerusalem Quarterly*, 17 (Fall 1980): 115–144;

Amir Iskander, *Saddam Hussein: the Fighter, the Thinker and the Man* (Paris: Hachette Realities, 1980);

Fuad Matar, *Saddam Hussein: A Biography* (Beirut: Highlight, 1981).

General References

Hanna Batatu, *The Old Social Classes and the Revolutionary Movements of Iraq* (Princeton, N.J.: Princeton University Press, 1978);

Marion Farouk-Sluglett and Peter Sluglett, *Iraq Since 1958: From Revolution to Dictatorship* (London: Routledge & Kegan Paul, 1987);

Lawrence Freedman and Efraim Karsh, *The Gulf Conflict, 1990–1991: Diplomacy and War in the New World Order* (Princeton: Princeton University Press, 1993);

Majid Khadduri, *Socialist Iraq: A Study in Iraqi Politics Since 1968* (Washington, D.C.: Middle East Institute, 1978);

Samir al-Khalil, *Republic of Fear: The Politics of Modern Iraq* (Berkeley: University of California Press, 1990);

Phoebe Marr, *The Modern History of Iraq* (Boulder, Colo.: Westview Press, 1985);

Middle East Watch/Human Rights Watch, *Human Rights in Iraq* (New Haven, Conn.: Yale University Press, 1990);

Stephen C. Pelletiere, Douglas V. Johnson II, and Leif R. Rosenberger, *Iraqi Power and U.S. Security in the Middle East* (Washington, D.C.: Strategic Studies Institute, U.S. Army War College, 1990);

The United Nations and the Iran-Iraq War (New York: Ford Foundation, 1987).

– A. F.

SEE ALSO THESE RELATED ENTRIES
Michel Aflaq, 2; Hafez al-Assad, 2; George Bush, 1.

Hu Yaobang

General Secretary, Chinese Communist Party, 1980–1987
Born Hunan Province, China, 20 November 1915
Died Beijing, People's Republic of China, 15 April 1989

As general secretary of the Chinese Communist party (CCP) from 1980 to 1987, Hu Yaobang was the voice of radical economic reform in the People's Republic of China (PRC). More than any other leader of his generation, Hu championed change to an increasingly youthful and open China. More of a promoter than a designer of policies, his dynamic speaking style was ideal for soliciting support for Chinese leader Deng Xiaoping's programs. Preferring Western suits and ties over the customary Mao jacket, Hu endeared himself to China's youth by sometimes eschewing CCP conventions. Hu also alienated Communist party hard-liners, and in 1987, at the height of his powers, was struck down by conservative elements in the party. He was subsequently made a political martyr by Chinese university students. Hu's death in 1989 triggered China's greatest political crisis in decades.

Hu Yaobang was born in the southern province of Hunan. Hu's family worked together growing flax that his mother wove into cloth for selling. Hu's parents strongly emphasized education, so he was tutored for two years before entering elementary school. When he was eleven his father sent him to an elementary school in a nearby village. One of his teachers taught him the virtues of the communist movement. In Hu's childhood, China was a poverty-stricken country divided and ruled by warlords. Communism seemed an appealing alternative to the existing system, so Hu and some of his classmates established their own branch of the New Democratic Youth League (NDYL). The NDYL was an organization for training prospective party candidates before they entered the CCP.

Hu left Hunan at age fifteen to join the communist guerrilla base in Jiangxi province. He became one of the "the little red devils" that figured so prominently in Edgar Snow's classic account of the Chinese Revolution, *Red Star over China* (1937). The little red devils were youths, between eleven and sixteen years of age, who worked as orderlies, water carriers, spies, and propagandists in the base. Hu was appointed bugler in the Chinese Red Army, but his superiors noticed him because he was educated, and made him responsible for general and political education of children. At the time, 80 percent of communist youth were illiterate and 95 percent of Chinese people in general could not recognize the simplest words.

In late 1933 Hu was admitted to the Chinese Communist party and was named general secretary of the Communist Youth Central Bureau. The position carried power and

Hu Yaobang

prestige because he was responsible for overseeing the educational development of potential party members.

The Long March

In the fall of 1934 Chiang Kai-shek, leader of China's nationalist government, and his army were closing in on the Jiangxi base to root out the communists. The CCP decided to break out of the nationalists' grip by undertaking an orderly retreat that came to be called the Long March. The communists averaged more than twenty-two miles a day in this last-ditch effort to elude the nationalists, who resolutely pursued them. Hu's passionate style was displayed on the battlefield. Before marching into battle, he would bellow inspirational speeches to motivate the soldiers. His harangues were often punctuated with derisive comments about leaders of the opposing side. When the fighting finally began, Hu was at the front of the charge, leading the way.

His active duty was interrupted on 27 February 1935, when he was wounded by a nationalist bomb and had to be carried on a stretcher for days.

In the spring of 1937 Hu was one of more than twenty-seven hundred trainees to enter the newly established Chinese People's Anti-Japanese Military and Political University. The purpose of the school was to train cadres in the strategy and tactics of fighting the Japanese and in the political ideology of Mao Zedong, the CCP's revered leader. Hu was one of the university's finest students and continued in advanced studies after graduation.

Hu's World War II activities involved molding youthful intellectuals into party members and acting as a liaison between CCP leaders and high-level military officers. His work in recruiting new members greatly increased the size of the Communist party.

Hu returned to the battlefield during the Chinese civil war as a political commissar for a thirty-thousand-man army in the Shansi-Hopeh region. He built guerrilla units and taught tactics and ideology.

His Rise in the Party

After the war and the ascendancy of the communists under Mao, Hu spent two years in Szechwan province overseeing land reform efforts and suppressing undercover nationalist guerrillas. His superior was future party leader Deng Xiaoping, political commissar of Szechwan. Hu was named first secretary of the NDYL (renamed the Communist Youth League in 1957), placing him in control of the direction of recruitment and publications. He was the central figure in all Youth League functions, dominating League affairs in a manner unrivaled in any other important body in Chinese politics. He also was elected to the ninety-seven-member Central Committee, giving him decision-making power at the national level.

The first signs of Hu's liberal policy stances could be detected in the early 1960s. Through the 1950s Hu had been an ardent proponent of so-called Maoism. In 1958 he advocated Mao Zedong's "Great Leap Forward" economic plan to enlarge work units and drive the human spirit in order to raise China's economic status to the level of Great Britain in fifteen years. But with the abandonment of the Great Leap Forward after China's economic collapse in the early 1960s, Hu moved toward President Liu Shaoqi and General Secretary Deng Xiaoping's more pragmatic line, emphasizing efficiency over ideology. In 1961 he told anguished peasants in Hebei province that "free markets must be started," and encouraged more freedom of production.

The Cultural Revolution

As the Cultural Revolution began to unfold in early 1966, the Youth League was experiencing increasing pressures to radicalize. Part of Mao's scheme to reobtain control of the CCP was to create a corps of radical Mao-worshipping "groupies," called Red Guards, to "remold" China and defend its revered leader. Hu resisted the imposition of the radicals, prompting a reprimand from Mao, and in December 1966 Hu was arrested by the Red Guards. He disappeared from the CCP for almost nine years, until July 1975, when he was brought back by his friend Deng Xiaoping to rebuild the Chinese Academy of Sciences. Hu thereafter continued to ascend within the party ranks, following on the coattails of Deng, who became China's most powerful leader in 1978. In January 1979 Hu was elected general secretary in charge of day-to-day operations of the Central Committee, and in February 1980 he was elected to the seven-member Politburo Standing Committee, the most powerful organ in the CCP. Hu was now heir-apparent to Deng.

Chinese Foreign Policy

Hu had little foreign-policy experience prior to 1980, but he learned quickly and asserted himself. His philosophy of foreign relations was an offshoot of his ideas for developing China's domestic economy. In order to liberalize the economy, he was willing to create friendships with noncommunist as well as communist nations. In June 1986 Hu went to Great Britain, West Germany, Italy, and France to enhance China's business image abroad. Hu was also instrumental in improving relations with Japan, a country with which China had erratic relations in the past.

Hu was cautious in dealing with the United States and Soviet Union because of growing pressures from the conservatives in the CCP. To show that he was not leaning too close to the United States, Hu stated in 1982 that China would always be a Third World country and would never attach itself to the "big powers." He put forward the concept of a Chinese "independent foreign policy," a departure from the outdated "strategic triangle" formula of Mao. Chinese policy would no longer be based on the quality and tone of U.S.-Soviet relations, but on the independent value of each country's friendship with China.

Hu was also realistic in his views on Third World aid, citing Mao's attempts to export revolution as provoking a "few mistakes and lessons." Hu sounded more like a leader of a status quo nation than a revolutionary, a stark contrast with the radical statements made by PRC leaders in the 1950s and 1960s.

Hu was above all the promoter of Deng's policies. Gregarious and excitable, he was well liked personally. His patriarchal relationship with China's youth made him popular with the masses. But Hu was probably never a serious candidate for Deng's position. Even his supporters recognized that he was not a seminal thinker and that he did not exude the stately presence of a leader.

Hu often took the brunt of disapproval from Deng's opponents. On 5 December 1986 a prodemocracy protest by more than one thousand students at the Chinese National University of Science and Technology in Anhui province set off a wave of activism in cities such as Beijing and Shanghai. The demonstrations split China's leadership. Hu sided with the students, arguing with his colleagues for a greater emphasis on young leadership, better treatment of intellectuals, and a continuance of economic liberalization. Deng joined party conservatives in lashing out at Hu for releasing a "bourgeois liberal flood." It was felt by many party leaders that Western-style economic liberalization brought with it the peril of democracy. Unable to evade this explosion of criticism, Hu resigned as general secretary on 16 January 1987, signaling a brief resurgence of conservative party leadership. In the meantime, Hu became symbol for China's democracy movement.

Tiananmen Square

Hu Yaobang died on 15 April 1989, seven days after suffering a heart attack during a Politburo meeting in Beijing. His death provided an immediate catalyst for prodemocracy demonstrators, who saw Hu as a scapegoat for party incompetence. On April 23, one hundred thousand students marched in Beijing to honor Hu on the day of his funeral. The students won considerable support from intellectuals and the populace, who were disenchanted with government corruption and high inflation.

After a brief cooling-off period in late April, the movement suddenly revived when three thousand students initiated a hunger strike in mid May, just days before the historic first meeting between Soviet president Mikhail S. Gorbachev and Deng Xiaoping. The Western press, in Beijing to record the Sino-Soviet summit, found itself documenting the poignant hunger strike and democracy protests for all the world to see.

The movement culminated on May 17–18 with the largest mass protest ever staged in Beijing, involving more than one million Chinese who occupied the city's Tiananmen Square. After issuing repeated admonishments to the students to evacuate the square, soldiers charged in on the evening of June 3–4 to remove them. Intense violence occurred on both sides, as the protestors resisted the force. Remarkably, the soldiers were not

equipped with riot-control devices such as tear gas or rubber bullets. Several soldiers were beaten or stoned to death, and sixty military vehicles were destroyed by Molotov cocktails. The number of civilian casualties remains uncertain, but at least seven hundred protestors were killed, and some Western observers estimate that perhaps thousands perished.

China's foreign relations deteriorated after the Tiananmen Square massacre. International condemnation was followed by swift, if inconsistent, sanctions, including the suspension of contracts and the freezing of foreign aid programs. The violent upheaval caused the Chinese government to declare martial law and launch a massive propaganda campaign aimed at Western countries, which the Chinese accused of interference in China's internal affairs. The crackdown also reversed many of the economic advances made during the Deng era. One casualty was purged general secretary Zhao Ziyang, successor to Hu and also a strong proponent of the liberal economic reforms of the 1980s.

Sino-American relations plummeted to their lowest point since before the visit of American president Richard M. Nixon to Beijing in 1972. In response to the crackdown, the United States suspended military and high-level technology sales and allowed Chinese students in America to extend their visas for human rights reasons. Even with American president George Bush's efforts to maintain a dialogue and stabilize the relationship, China's semipariah status continued because it did not make a symbolic gesture of compunction. Scholars suggested this inability to act decisively was due to furtive maneuvering among CCP leaders planning to replace Deng Xiaoping after he leaves office.

Book about Hu

Yang Zhongmei, *Hu Yaobang* (Armonk, N.Y.: M. E. Sharpe, 1988).

General References

Harry Harding, *China's Second Revolution* (Washington, D.C.: Brookings Institution, 1987);

Edgar Snow, *Red Star over China* (London: Gollancz, 1937).
— K. W. M.

Miloš Jakeš

General Secretary, Czechoslovak Communist Party, 1987–1989
Born Ceské Chalupy, Czechoslovakia, 12 August 1922

Miloš Jakeš, Czechoslovak politician and Communist party leader, was born to a poor peasant family. During the 1930s he studied electrical engineering at the Higher School of Industry. He was also employed from 1944 to 1950 as an installation worker and an industrial designer at the Svit factory in Gottwaldov in Bohemia.

In June 1945, shortly after Czechoslovakia was liberated from Nazi occupation by the Red Army, he joined the Czechoslovak Communist party (CCP) and became a leader at the local level. He occupied leadership positions on the Central Committee of the communist-controlled Czechoslovak Union of Youth from 1947 to 1956. He also carried out party functions at the Svit factory and served on the CCP district and regional committees in Gottwaldov. During the 1950s he studied at the Higher Party School in Moscow, where he received intensive political and ideological training.

Crushing the Prague Spring

After graduating from the Moscow academy, Jakeš was appointed department head in the CCP's Central Committee. In 1961 he was named secretary of the Government Commission for National Affairs. In 1965 and 1966 he worked as the deputy chairman of the Central Office for Local Economic Development. He also served as deputy minister of the interior in charge of civil administration from 1966 to 1968 and as chairman of the party's Central Auditing Commission from 1968 to 1977. Jakeš achieved greater prominence after the Soviet invasion in August 1968 and the crushing of the reformist Prague Spring. After the invasion Jakeš participated in the purge of party members who had supported the liberalization program. The CCP control committee under his direction expelled five hundred thousand party members in 1969 and 1970.

General Secretary of the CCP

In 1977 Jakeš became a secretary of the CCP Central Committee and chairman of the Committee on Agriculture and Food. Through the introduction of some incentive schemes for farmers, he helped to increase food production without ending central planning and cooperative agriculture. He was also appointed a member of the party's ruling Presidium and chairman of the CCP Central Committee Commission on the National Economy from 1981 to 1987. He held positions in the state structure

Gustáv Husák and Miloš Jakeš

as a member of the Czechoslovak National Assembly after 1971 and was a Presidium member of the Assembly after 1981. On 17 December 1987 Jakeš was elected general secretary of the CCP after Gustáv Husák was given the state presidency. He gained the reputation of a moderate reformer, who sought to preserve the communist monopoly of power without surrendering any significant ground to the political opposition.

Revolution of 1989

As public protests escalated in November 1989, the entire Communist party leadership resigned, and Jakeš was replaced by Karel Urbanek. This peaceful revolution changed the structure of power in the country, as communist controls over all public institutions were dismantled and free elections were held in June 1990, relegating the communists to a marginal political role. Jakeš himself disappeared from the political scene.

General References

Vladimir Kusin, *From Dubcek to Charter 77: A Study of "Normalization" in Czechoslovakia, 1968–1978* (New York: St. Martin's Press, 1978);

Zdenek Suda, *Zealots and Rebels: A History of the Ruling Communist Party of Czechoslovakia* (Stanford, Cal.: Hoover Institution Press, 1980).

                                                    —J. B. and A. B.

SEE ALSO THESE RELATED ENTRIES

Aleksander Dubcek, 2; Václav Havel, 2; Gustáv Husák, 2; Antonín Novotny, 2.

Wojciech Jaruzelski

President of Poland, 1989–1990

First Secretary, Polish United Workers Party, 1981–1989

Born Kurów, Poland, 6 July 1923

Wojciech Jaruzelski, Polish political and military leader, prime minister from 1981 to 1985, first secretary of the Polish United Workers party (PUWP) during the 1980s, and president of Poland from 1989 to 1990, was born to a family of the small-landed gentry. His father was a cavalry officer who became administrator of an estate in the Lublin area. During the late 1930s Jaruzelski attended a boarding school run by the Catholic order of Marian Fathers at Bielany, a Warsaw suburb.

After the German-Soviet invasion and partition of Poland in September 1939, Jaruzelski and his family were captured by the Red Army and deported to the Soviet Union. His father died in exile in Siberia during the war, while his mother and sister survived the war and returned to Poland. Jaruzelski himself was forced to work as a laborer at the Karaganda coal mines in Kazakhstan before being recruited to a Soviet cadet school in Ryazan. After graduating from Ryazan, he joined the First Polish Army, a Soviet-sponsored army corps under the leadership of General Zygmunt Berling. As the Soviets pushed westward and captured Polish territory, he fought in battles on the Vistula River and at the Magnuszewo bridgehead.

Political and Military Careers

At the close of the war Jaruzelski was active in combating the anticommunist Polish Home Army partisans. He repeatedly distinguished himself in his duties and was dispatched by his commanders to the Higher Infantry School and the General Staff Academy for higher officer training. He graduated with honors in 1955 and became the youngest general in the Polish army the following year. His military and political careers developed swiftly and in tandem. He was appointed brigadier general in 1956, division general in 1960, head of the Armed Forces Main Political Board in 1960, deputy minister of defense in 1962, army chief of staff in 1965, and minister of defense in 1968, the last shortly before the invasion of Czechoslovakia by Warsaw Pact forces, which included a Polish contingent.

The 1970 Protests

In December 1970 strikes broke out in Polish shipyards along the Baltic Coast, with workers protesting against sudden price rises and intolerable economic conditions. According to government sources, Jaruzelski refused to order the army to shoot at striking workers. The official media subsequently tried to downplay the involvement of high government officials in the massacre of several dozen shipyard workers by security forces, but the episode served to bring down party leader Wladyslaw Gomulka.

Jaruzelski also rose steadily through the ranks of the Communist party, which he joined in 1947. He was appointed to the PUWP Central Committee in 1964, became a candidate Politburo member in December 1970, and a full Politburo member in 1971. Jaruzelski was also a parliamentary deputy after 1961, as well as deputy

General Wojciech Jaruzelski (center) with Generals Kulikov of the Soviet Union (left) and Hoffman of East Germany (right)

chairman of the communist-sponsored veterans organization, ZBOWID.

Prime Minister

After the summer of 1980, as the PUWP began to lose control and came under increasing challenge from the free-trade union Solidarity, Jaruzelski was promoted to the highest state and party positions. He was appointed prime minister in February 1981 and first secretary of the PUWP in October 1981. Jaruzelski won Moscow's confidence and was considered to be the only credible leader strong enough to hold the Polish party together and to reverse the movement of Polish society toward democratization. While engaging in negotiations with the Solidarity leadership, he was secretly planning with full Soviet approval a violent showdown with the labor union.

Martial Law

On 13 December 1981 Jaruzelski imposed martial law and formed under his chairmanship a Military Council of National Salvation to run the country. Thousands of Solidarity and other opposition activists were arrested, and strikes were violently suppressed throughout the country with some casualties recorded. Solidarity was formally outlawed in October 1982, and the government proceeded to set up its own trade unions and other associations under communist and military supervision. Jaruzelski's position was further strengthened when in November 1983 he was named the supreme commander of the armed forces and chairman of the National Defense Committee, which now assumed the role of a supra-governmental agency.

Although he lifted martial law in July 1983, Jaruzelski remained in full charge of the Polish government and the Communist party. But his efforts to revitalize the PUWP and reform the economy all but failed, as the political and economic crisis deepened during the 1980s. In 1985 Jaruzelski stepped down as prime minister, but maintained his positions in the party and the military. When strikes flared up again in the spring and summer of 1988, Jaruzelski initially tried to suppress them. But he realized that the country faced a dangerous spiral of social revolt as economic conditions deteriorated. The massive use of force to put down unrest would have proved counterproductive and could have further depressed economic conditions. It would also have jeopardized steadily improving East-West relations and contradicted the policies of the Gorbachev leadership in the Kremlin, which supported peaceful reforms in Eastern Europe.

In February 1989 Jaruzelski agreed to begin roundtable negotiations with leaders of Solidarity and the political opposition in order to devise some new power-sharing arrangement and pacify mounting public discontent. The negotiations led to the relegalization of Solidarity and to partially democratic parliamentary elections in June 1989, in which independent candidates were assured of one-third of the seats in the lower house of Parliament. After further negotiations and the inability of the communists to form a governing alliance, a Solidarity-led coalition government was established in August 1989.

In order to preserve political stability at a time when Poland stood at the forefront of political reform in Eastern Europe, Jaruzelski was appointed state president. But as the political and economic reforms overturned communist control over various public institutions and the democratic revolutions snowballed throughout the East European region, pressures mounted for early presidential and parliamentary elections in Poland. Jaruzelski's position looked increasingly vulnerable as he lacked public support and his record in suppressing political dissent undermined his credibility as head of state. Presidential elections were held in November and December 1990, after Jaruzelski signaled that he was prepared to vacate the office; Solidarity leader Lech Walesa was elected president. In a parting public gesture, Jaruzelski apologized to the Polish people for his role during the years of communist repression.

Book about Jaruzelski

Leo Labedz, *Poland Under Jaruzelski* (New York: Scribners, 1984).

General References

G. C. Malcher, *Poland's Politicized Army: Communists in Uniform* (New York: Praeger, 1984);

George Sanford, *Military Rule in Poland: The Rebuilding of Communist Power, 1981–1983* (London: Croom Helm, 1986);

Andrew Michta, *Red Eagle: The Army in Polish Politics, 1944–1988* (Stanford, Cal.: Hoover Institution Press, 1990).

–J. B. and A. B.

SEE ALSO THESE RELATED ENTRIES

Wladyslaw Gomulka, 2; Jacek Kuron, 2; Adam Michnik, 2; Lech Walesa, 2.

Pope John Paul II

Bishop of Rome, 1978–
Born Wadowice, Poland, 18 May 1920

Pope John Paul II, the first Polish pope and the first non-Italian pope in 455 years, was born Karol Wojtyla to a working-class family. His mother died when he was nine years old, and his father died during World War II. In 1938 Wojtyla enrolled in the Jagiellonian University in Kraków to study poetry and drama. In 1939 German troops closed the university, and he was forced to work in a stone quarry. At the same time he started to study secretly for the priesthood at an underground seminary in Kraków and was ordained a priest in November 1946.

Wojtyla's Rise in the Church

After the war Wojtyla studied at the Angelicum University in Rome and at the Catholic University of Lublin, where he earned doctorates in ethics. His first doctoral dissertation was on the question of faith in the writings of the mystic Saint John of the Cross. His second thesis concerned the compatibility of the German phenomenologist Max Scheler's ethical system with traditional Christian ethics. In 1954 Wojtyla joined the Department of Philosophy at the Catholic University of Lublin, the only independent university in communist Eastern Europe. He published several books and many articles and became fluent in English, French, German, and Italian. He was appointed auxiliary bishop of Kraków in 1958 and became vicarcapitular (administrator) of the See in 1962, archbishop of Kraków in 1964, and cardinal in 1967.

The Church and Resistance

Catholicism in Poland was a crucial factor in maintaining national resistance to communist rule. Poland is the most religiously homogeneous country in Eastern Europe, with over 90 percent of the population declaring themselves as Catholics, and with a close historical link between religion and nationalism. The church managed to retain a high degree of independence, particularly after the replacement of the Stalinist regime in the mid 1950s, as the new government tried to gain some credibility by courting the church hierarchy. The church leadership itself avoided collaborating too closely with the regime and sheltered various independent educational and cultural endeavors. Under the leadership of Stefan Cardinal Wyszynski and activist bishops such as Wojtyla, the church expanded its church-building program, steadily increased recruitment into the clergy, and maintained a high degree of political influence in the country.

Felici

Pope John Paul II

Elected as Pope

On 6 October 1978 Wojtyla was elected pope and formally invested on 22 October, becoming the first Polish pope in the history of the Roman Catholic church. He took the name John Paul II to honor his predecessor, John Paul, who had died after only a few weeks in office. His relative youth and language abilities allowed him to become a roving international ambassador for the church. He undertook extensive travels to Latin America, the United States, Canada, Africa, Europe, and the Far East. His pilgrimage to Poland in June 1979 profoundly affected political developments in the country. It brought millions of people together at rallies and open-air masses, helped to break the barrier of fear erected by the communist regime to forestall independent social activities, and reaffirmed noncommunist values. The visit displayed the vulnerability and unpopularity of the regime and acted as a catalyst for the birth of the Solidarity free labor union a year later.

Assassination Attempt

On 13 May 1981, at a general audience in Vatican City, Pope John Paul II was shot and seriously wounded by Mehmet Ali Agca, a Turkish national believed to have been hired by the Bulgarian secret service at the behest of the Soviet KGB. Three Bulgarians and three other Turks were also suspected of conspiring against the pope, and the Kremlin was widely believed to have masterminded the plot. Their motivation was thought to be John Paul II's outspoken support of the Solidarity movement in Poland and of religious rights throughout Eastern Europe and the Soviet Union.

John Paul II has been a critic of many materialistic and inhumane aspects of modern life. He has expressed support for democracy and economic justice among poorer nations as well as political freedom in dictatorial states. But he has opposed the participation of priests in politics in the Third World, even while championing greater cler-ical involvement in various social and humanistic activities on behalf of the poor. Pope John Paul II has also proved theologically orthodox, and the Vatican has upheld a conservative position on the issues of abortion, birth control, women clergy, and sex education.

During Poland's political crisis in the early 1980s, after the introduction of martial law, Pope John Paul II consistently criticized the Polish government for its repressive policies. He paid a second visit to Poland in the summer of 1983 to give solace and comfort to the traumatized population. The Catholic church played an important role during the 1989 East European revolutions, particularly in Poland, where it helped to mediate in the political agreements arranged between the communist regime and the Solidarity opposition movement. In December 1989 John Paul II was the first pope to meet with a Soviet leader when Mikhail Gorbachev paid a visit to the Vatican, and in April 1990 he became the first pope to visit Czechoslovakia since World War II.

–J. B. and A. B.

SEE ALSO THESE RELATED ENTRIES

Wojciech Jaruzelski, 2; Lech Walesa, 2; Stefan Cardinal Wyszynski, 2.

János Kádár

First Secretary, Hungarian Socialist Workers Party 1956–1988

Prime Minister of Hungary, 1956–1958, 1961–1968

Born Fiema, Hungary, 12 May 1912
Died Budapest, Hungary, 6 July 1989

János Kádár, Hungarian communist leader from 1956 to 1988, was born Laszio Csermanek into a working-class family in Fiema, Hungary, now Rijeka, Yugoslavia. His family was abandoned by his father, and he settled with his mother in Budapest, where he worked as a machinist. When he was seventeen Kádár joined the illegal Hungarian Communist party (HCP) and became an organizer in the HCP youth movement. He was arrested many times by the Hungarian police and jailed twice. In 1940, after the quasi-fascist Hungarian government formed an alliance with Nazi Germany, he went underground, adopted the name of János Kádár, and began to help reconstruct the HCP. During the next few years he rose quickly through the party ranks, and by the end of World War II he was secretary of the party's underground home organization.

When the communists were placed in power by the Red Army, in a provisional coalition government in 1945, Kádár became a member of the Politburo of the renamed Hungarian Socialist Workers party (HSWP). In May of 1945 he also became deputy chief of the Budapest police force. He was appointed minister of the interior in 1949 but came into conflict with the staunchly Stalinist leadership. As part of the Stalinists' purges against "native" communists, whose loyalties to Moscow were suspect, Kádár was arrested in April 1951 on charges of treason and sentenced to four years in prison. He was released in July 1954, after pressure from Nikita S. Khrushchev and the post-Stalin Kremlin leadership, who tried to build a more legitimate Hungarian government from among the "native" communists not implicated in the worst of the Stalinist crimes.

The 1956 Revolt

Kádár rejoined the HSWP Politburo and became party secretary in Budapest in July 1956, on the eve of the Hungarian revolution. In October 1956 he became minister of state in the reformist government formed by Prime Minister Imre Nagy, who tried to forestall the tide of popular discontent against communist rule by offering various concessions to the political opposition. But government concessions, such as promises of free elections, failed to stop the escalation of protests and political de-

János Kádár

mands among various social groups and the creation of new political parties and independent workers councils. Mass demonstrations in Budapest on 23 October 1956 triggered the revolt after the security forces fired on unarmed demonstrators. But the shootings failed to quell the protests, which swiftly spread when units of the Hungarian army and police force joined the insurgency or supplied the rebels with arms.

Kádár had first sided with the revolutionaries but quickly changed his allegiance when Soviet troops began to mass on Hungary's border and the Nagy government was condemned by Moscow for aiding and abetting the insurgents. After the Red Army invasion in November 1956, the revolt was swiftly crushed, and Nagy's reformist administration was dissolved by the Soviet authorities.

A group of loyal pro-Moscow Hungarian communists was assembled and formed a new government under Kádár's leadership.

First Secretary and Prime Minister

Kádár became first secretary of the HSWP and served as the country's prime minister from 1956 to 1958, and again from 1961 until 1968. Upon his assumption of power, Kádár imposed a program of "normalization" in which all autonomous organizations were banned and central controls were reestablished in all areas of public life. A wave of mass arrests and dismissals swept the country, and about five thousand people were executed by the regime, including the deposed Hungarian leader Nagy, who was charged with "counterrevolutionary activities."

Kádár maintained close ties with the Soviet Union, but at home he tried to regain the trust of the people. Once all overt resistance had been crushed, Kádár attempted to forge with the people a new "social contract," embodied in his famous phrase "whoever is not against us is with us." Society was to forsake political activism in exchange for a measure of economic security and steadily rising living standards. Kádár's solution did not envisage a return to strict Stalinist methods, but it precluded any repeat of Nagy's liberalization program. He did not reestablish a police state and even reached an accord with the Roman Catholic church. Kádár launched a mass HSWP recruitment drive in 1957, and in November 1962 the party congress declared Hungary to be embarked upon the construction of a fully socialist society.

New Economic Mechanism

In 1968 the Kádár government launched a more liberal economic program styled as the New Economic Mechanism. It combined some market elements with decentralized planning and greater autonomy. These policies loosened state control over the economy and allowed for some private enterprise. But the economic reform program did not overturn the communist political monopoly as the operation of independent pressure groups and other organizations remained prohibited.

Despite some marked economic improvements during the 1970s and a significant economic opening to the West, the Hungarian economy began to stagnate in the early 1980s. The government was unwilling to release its grip on the most vital economic sectors and implement a broad program of privatization. As economic conditions deteriorated, pressures began to mount in society and within the party to introduce more meaningful political and economic reforms. A reformist faction led by Karoly Grosz and Imre Pozsgay took over the HSWP leadership, and Kádár was removed from power in 1988 and given the largely ceremonial position of party president. Shortly before his death on 6 July 1989, he was removed from all his posts. The new leadership attempted to disassociate itself from its Kádárist past, and thus gain some degree of popular legitimacy in preparation for multiparty elections in the spring of 1990.

Book by Kádár

Selected Speeches and Interviews (Oxford, New York: Pergamon, 1985).

Books about Kádár

Andrew Felkay, *Hungary and the USSR, 1956-1988: K'ad'ar's Political Leadership* (New York: Greenwood Press, 1989);

William Shawcross, *Crime and Compromise: Janos Kadar and the Politics of Hungary since Revolution* (New York: Dutton, 1974).

General References

J. F. Brown, *Eastern Europe and Communist Rule* (Durham, N.C.,: Duke University Press, 1988);

Charles Gati, *Hungary and the Soviet Bloc* (Durham, N.C.: Duke University Press, 1986);

Franklyn D. Holzman, *The Economics of Soviet Bloc Trade and Finance* (Boulder, Colo.: Westview Press, 1987);

Robert L. Hutchings, *Soviet-East European Relations: Consolidation and Conflict, 1968–1980* (Madison: University of Wisconsin Press, 1983);

Bennet Kovrig, *Communism in Hungary: From Kun to Kadar* (Stanford, Cal.: Hoover Institution Press, 1979);

William F. Robinson, *The Pattern of Reform in Hungary: A Political, Economic, and Cultural Analysis* (New York: Praeger, 1973);

Joseph Rothschild, *Return to Diversity: A Political History of East Central Europe since World War II* (New York: Oxford University Press, 1989);

Sarah M. Terry, ed., *Soviet Policy in Eastern Europe* (New Haven: Yale University Press, 1984);

Adam Ulam, *Expansion and Coexistence* (New York: Praeger, 1968).

–J. B. and A. B.

SEE ALSO THESE RELATED ENTRIES

Karoly Grosz, 2; Imre Nagy, 2; Imre Pozsgay, 2.

Kenneth Kaunda

President of Zambia, 1964 – 1991
Born Lubwa, Northern Rhodesia, 28 April 1924

As the founder of modern Zambia and its first president, Kenneth David Kaunda was one of Africa's elder statesmen and was widely regarded as a key player in southern African politics.

Kaunda was born in Lubwa, Northern Rhodesia (now Zambia). His father, David, was a Christian evangelist in the Livingston Mission in Lubwa. Kaunda's education began at the local mission school, and he received his secondary education in Lusaka. He was trained as a teacher and in 1943 returned to his native village to teach, serving as headmaster of the mission school from 1944 to 1947. In 1946 he married Betty Banda, with whom he has nine children. After teaching briefly in Tanganyika (present-day Tanzania), he returned to Northern Rhodesia in 1948 to continue teaching at the mission school, serving also as a social worker.

Northern Rhodesia African National Congress

In 1950 Kaunda was elected secretary of the Chinsali African Welfare Association, the local branch of the Northern Rhodesia African National Congress (NRANC), at the time one of the leading nationalist organizations in the British colony. African nationalism in the British settler colonies – such as Northern Rhodesia, Southern Rhodesia (Zimbabwe), and Nyasaland (Malawi) – revolved around the loosely organized "congress" movements, which initially functioned as mouthpieces for native grievances. The NRANC was agitating against racial discrimination and inequality in the British settler colony. A skilled organizer, Kaunda was elected general secretary of the NRANC in 1953 and became editor of *Congress News*. Kaunda and other nationalist leaders organized mass demonstrations and stressed civil disobedience in protesting the 1953 territorial merger of Northern Rhodesia, Southern Rhodesia, and Nyasaland into the settler-controlled Central African Federation. The creation of the federation, viewed by the Africans as a further attempt by the white settlers to consolidate power, proved to be a turning point in the evolution of African nationalism in the territories. The NRANC, which had been complaining of the white political and economic monopoly in the territories, began to demand full independence. As strikes, boycotts, and demonstrations intensified, the colonial administration arrested and jailed Kaunda and the other leaders of the NRANC in November 1953. Kaunda was arrested again on 6 January 1955 and sentenced to two months imprisonment for possession of banned literature.

Kenneth Kaunda

Zambian African National Congress

In 1957 Kaunda traveled to England as a guest of the Labour party – which was sympathetic to NRANC demands – to study the British political system. Upon his return in 1958, the NRANC split when a faction led by Kaunda refused to participate in the colonial elections and broke away to form the Zambian African National Congress (ZANC), with Kaunda as president. The new party quickly became the rallying point for nationalists pressing for independence. In December 1958 Kaunda attended the All-African People's Conference convened by Kwame Nkrumah in Accra, Ghana. Amid growing social and political unrest he was arrested on 12 March 1959 and imprisoned for nine months, and the ZANC was banned under a state of emergency.

Zambian Independence

Already a leader of international stature, he was elected prime minister in January 1964, following political reforms that resulted in internal self-government. On 24 October Zambia became independent, with Kaunda – who ran on the slogan, "One Zambia, One Nation" – elected as its first president. A believer in centralized economic planning, he introduced his "Zambianization" socialist economic policies, which have had limited success.

Kaunda has been a major player in southern African politics. A leading spokesman for black majority rule in the region, he has provided political support and matériel for regional liberation movements, many of which use the capital, Lusaka, as sanctuary and headquarters. During the Rhodesian war of independence, Zambia was the base for one group of Rhodesian guerrillas, the Zimbabwean African People's Union (ZAPU) led by Joshua Nkomo, fighting the white minority regime. Rhodesia retaliated by launching several air raids into Zambian territory, causing considerable economic disruption. The South African nationalist liberation organization, the African National Congress (ANC), used Lusaka as its headquarters. The first foreign visit of South African nationalist leader Nelson Mandela, who was released in December 1989 after spending twenty-seven years in prison, was to Kaunda.

Zambian Diplomacy

In addition to being a counselor to and international spokesman for national liberation movements in southern Africa, Kaunda has been active in regional and international diplomatic efforts to achieve peaceful resolutions to regional problems. As a leader of the Front Line States (Angola, Botswana, Mozambique, Tanzania, Zambia), he played a major role during years of negotiations aimed at bringing an end to the war in neighborhing Rhodesia (now Zimbabwe). In addition to cooperating with U.S. secretary of state Henry A. Kissinger during his 1976 shuttle-diplomacy mission in the region, Kaunda launched an unprecedented but short-lived détente with the white minority regime in South Africa in 1975. As the home of the ANC and a leading proponent of economic sanctions leveled against South Africa, Zambia has been the target of occasional South African military raids and South African–sponsored internal subversion during the late 1970s and 1980s. Several times in the late 1980s Kaunda accused South Africa of plotting his government's overthrow.

Political and Social Unrest

In addition to regional problems and violence, Zambia's political stability has also been upset by deteriorating economic conditions since the mid 1970s that have sparked recurrent social and political unrest. Faltering economic performance in early 1976, in part caused by the war

in neighboring Rhodesia, led to widespread unrest, which forced Kaunda to declare a state of emergency in January. Again in early 1981 there were new riots and strikes, as the price of copper, Zambia's principal export, dropped and its terms of trade slumped. The combination of deteriorating economic conditions and austerity measures produced angry demonstrations and riots in October 1985 and again in July 1989. The July riots and the angry calls for the longtime president to step down led many people to question whether the aging Kaunda had outlived his role as the nation's leader.

The mid and late 1980s continued to be a period of unrest for Kaunda, who was now facing internal security problems, a growing economic crisis, and unprecedented challenges to his authority from within the regime, including an attempted coup by junior officers in the army.

As many parts of the continent moved toward political reforms and multiparty democracy in the early 1990s, Kaunda and his ruling party resisted nationwide calls for a multiparty democratic system. As the opposition, headed by the movement for multiparty democracy (MMD), grew in strength and general dissatisfaction spread, Kaunda finally agreed to reforms. The 31 October 1991 national elections were nothing short of a total repudiation of Kaunda and the ruling party. Kaunda lost the presidential race to MMD leader Frederick Chiluba by a 76 percent to 24 percent margin, and the MMD won four-fifths of the parliamentary seats. After the elections, Kaunda faced allegations that corruption had taken place under his rule.

Book by Kaunda (Selected)
Zambia Shall Be Free: An Autobiography (London: Heinemann, 1962).

Books about Kaunda

John Hatch, *Two African Statesman: Kaunda of Zambia and Nyerere of Tanzania* (London: Secker & Warburg, 1976);

Fergus Macpherson, *Kenneth Kaunda of Zambia: The Times and The Man* (Lusaka: Oxford University Press, 1974).

General References

Douglas Anglin and Timothy M. Shaw, *Zambia's Foreign Policy: Studies in Diplomacy and Dependence* (Boulder, Colo.: Westview Press, 1979);

Timothy M. Shaw, *Dependence and Underdevelopment: The Development and Foreign Policies of Zambia* (Athens: Ohio University Center for International Studies, 1976).

–J. R.-S.

SEE ALSO THESE RELATED ENTRIES
Henry Kissinger, 1; Robert Mugabe, 2; Kwame Nkrumah, 2; Julius Nyerere, 2; Jonas Savimbi, 2.

Jomo Kenyatta

President of Kenya, 1963–1978

Born Kiambu region, Kenya, circa 1893
Died Mombasa, Kenya, 22 August 1978

Regarded as the father of Kenyan independence, Jomo Kenyatta, having served as Kenya's first prime minister and president (1963–1978), was also widely recognized as one of the fathers of African nationalism and a respected African elder statesman.

Although Kenyatta's exact date of birth is unknown, it is believed by most historians that he was born sometime around 1893 into the Kikuyu ethnic group in the Kiambu region of central Kenya. Born Kamau Ngeni, he was given the Christian name of Johnstone and attended local Christian mission schools and the Church of Scotland Mission school in Nairobi, the capital of British-controlled Kenya. He worked for the colonial administration in Nairobi from 1921 to 1926, a period of emerging political activism centered around land grievances. In 1922 Kenyatta joined the East African Association – the precursor of the Kikuyu Central Association (KCA) – of which he was elected general secretary in 1924. The KCA, at the time a leading cultural-nationalist political organization, voiced the political demands of the Kikuyu, Kenya's dominant ethnic group. The principal grievances of the Kikuyu centered around the dispossession of traditional land by Kenya's large white settler population. Kenyatta also became the editor of the KCA newspaper, *Muigwithania*, in 1928.

In February 1929 Kenyatta was appointed to head a delegation – primarily representing Kikuyu interests – sent to England to press the British government for reforms. Kenyatta remained in Europe for the next fifteen years, traveling extensively in England and the rest of Europe. Assisted by communist-directed organizations, Kenyatta became associated with other activists, such as George Padmore, the West Indian nationalist. He visited the Soviet Union in 1929, and took courses at Moscow University. In late 1930 Kenyatta attended the International Negro Worker's Conference in Hamburg, Germany, where he met leading members of communist organizations. In England he studied at the London School of Economics, where he enrolled in 1936 to study anthropology, and Selly Oak College.

The Kenyan Nationalist Movement

By this time considered to be the leading spokesman for Kenyans, Kenyatta attended the Pan-African Congress in Manchester, England, in 1945, where he came

Gale International Portrait Gallery

Jomo Kenyatta

into contact with other leading African nationalists, such as Kwame Nkrumah of Ghana. He returned to Kenya in September 1946 at a time when the nationalist movement was disintegrating. The following year he was elected president of the newly formed Kenya African Union (KAU), which replaced the banned KCA. The nationalist movement was reinvigorated by the liberalizing principles emerging out of World War II and the Atlantic Charter. Over the next several years Kenyatta sought to increase membership and mobilize broad popular support for the KAU, which never had a strong appeal to groups outside of the Kikuyu tribe. Recognized as the leader of the nationalist movement, Kenyatta was arrested by British colonial authorities in late October 1952 and sentenced on 8 April 1953 for allegedly masterminding the so-called Mau Mau rebellion. The Mau Mau, a predominantly Kikuyu clandestine group, carried out terrorist activities against white farmers and Africans involved in the colonial administration. Kenyatta's precise involvement with the Mau Mau has never been clarified, although he clearly was the spiritual leader of the entire nationalist movement. The banned KAU reconstituted itself as the Kenya African National Union (KANU). By 1960 the British colonial administration had implemented reforms aimed at creating a limited self-government and in February 1961 held legislative elections which were won by KANU. However, KANU and other nationalist parties refused to form a government until Kenyatta was released to assume his role as the country's political leader. Kenyatta was released by the British on 21 August 1961. In January 1962 he was elected to the legislative council, and several months later was appointed minister of state for constitutional affairs and economic planning in the transitional coalition government.

Kenyan Independence

Preaching ethnic and racial unity, Kenyatta became Kenya's first prime minister in the internal self-government as KANU emerged victorious in the June 1963 pre-independence elections. When Kenya became independent on 12 December 1963, he continued as prime minister and as minister of security and defense. After Kenya was transformed into a one-party unitary state, Kenyatta was elected first president of the republic in December 1964, and was again reappointed president in 1966. He would serve three more terms until his death in 1978.

Kenya's political and economic successes in the post-independence era were largely attributed to Kenyatta's pragmatic leadership. After surviving a mild power struggle in the government, he directed economic development in accordance with a capitalist philosophy that differed sharply from that of most postcolonial African states. While his Kenyanization policy stressed equal opportunity for all Africans, Kenyatta's economic policies emphasized the primacy of the market. The white settler-controlled private sector remained dominant in Kenya, and the government's liberal investment policies attracted substantial foreign investments.

Foreign Policy under Kenyatta

In contrast to his earlier flirtation with European communism, Kenyatta's foreign policy beliefs were based on Western-oriented nonalignment, characterized by moderation and close association with Western countries, in particular Great Britain and the United States, which provided the bulk of Kenya's foreign economic and military aid. Kenya, recognized as one of the most influential states in sub-Saharan Africa and located in the militarily strategic and politically unstable Horn of Africa, became an important associate of the United States, even though its foreign policy stances were often made independent of U.S. influence. Kenya experienced uneasy relations with its neighbors, primarily Soviet-backed Somalia, which had historic territorial claims on Kenya, and socialist Tanzania, which denounced Kenya's capitalist economy. Kenyatta's long history as the spokesman of Kenyan independence and his charisma gave him wide personal prestige and popular support. He maintained absolute control over the political machine and patronage system, and his rule became increasingly autocratic. Kenyatta died on 22 August 1978 and was succeeded by his protégé, Daniel Arap Moi.

Books by Kenyatta

Facing Mount Kenya: The Tribal Life of the Gikuyu (London: Secker & Warburg, 1938);

The Challenge of Uhuru: The Progress of Kenya, 1968 to 1970 (Nairobi: East African Publishing House, 1971).

Books about Kenyatta

Gay Arnold, *Kenyatta and the Politics of Kenya* (London: Dent, 1974);

Rowland Mans, *Kenyatta's Middle Road In A Changing Africa: A Model For The Future?* (London: Institute for the Study of Conflict, 1977);

Jeremy Murray-Brown, *Kenyatta* (London: Allen & Unwin, 1972);

Dennis Wepman, *Jomo Kenyatta* (New York: Chelsea House Publishers, 1985).

General Reference

Cherry J. Gertzel, *The Politics of Independent Kenya, 1963–8* (Evanston, Ill.: Northwestern University Press, 1970).

—J. R.-S.

SEE ALSO THESE RELATED ENTRIES

Kwame Nkrumah, 2.

Ruholla Musavi Khomeini

Supreme Leader of Iran, 1979–1989
Born Khomein, Iran, 24 September 1902
Died Tehran, Iran, 3 June 1989

Ayatollah Ruholla Musavi Khomeini was the Islamic spiritual leader who sparked the Iranian revolution in 1979 and led the country for a decade until his death in 1989.

Khomeini was born on 24 September 1902 in the town of Khomein, about two hundred miles south of Tehran. His father, Mustafa Musavi, a leading cleric, was murdered five months after Ruholla's birth; both his mother, Hajar, and his aunt, Sahabeh, who raised him, died when he was fifteen. In 1928 he married a high-ranking cleric's daughter, with whom he had three daughters and two sons, one of whom was allegedly killed by Shah Mohammad Reza Pahlevi's security agents.

Khomeini learned to read the Quran at age six, studied Islamic jurisprudence from his brother, Ayatollah Murteza Pasandideh, and later studied with Ayatollah Abdul Karim Haeri-e Yazdi, the model for many devout Shi'as. Khomeini's title, ayatollah (sign of God), denotes the highest scholarly religious standing a Shi'a cleric can achieve.

Opposition to the Shah

Khomeini had written in opposition to secular authority in the early 1940s and began his outspoken opposition to Mohammad Reza Pahlevi in 1961. He was one of the early critics of the shah's White Revolution, a program for Western-style economic and political development that was announced in 1963. In particular he opposed the call for woman suffrage, which he viewed as antithetical to Islam, and the land-reform program, which threatened the clerics' vested interest in revenues from lands they held and used for religious educational purposes. The shah belittled the opposition ayatollahs by calling them hojatolislam, a lower religious rank, and Khomeini responded by calling the king "Mr. Shah"; the shah then had him arrested.

The Riots of 1963

In June 1963, during the religious holidays of Muharram (in memory of the martyrdom of Imam Hussein, grandson of the prophet Muhammad), pictures of Khomeini covered the bazaars, and crowds of pro-Khomeini protesters formed there. Rioting spread throughout the country for three days until the army's "shoot-to-kill" response quelled the protests. After four

Ruholla Musavi Khomeini

such clashes, Khomeini was exiled to Turkey in October 1964. From Turkey he traveled on to Iraq and remained in exile there until 1978, when he moved to Paris. But Khomeini continued to oppose the imperial regime from exile, covertly distributing cassettes with his revolutionary Islamic message.

The United States, which had reinstalled the shah on the Peacock Throne in 1953 and considered him a pillar of U.S. policy in the region, was oblivious to the growing upheaval. On New Year's Eve 1977, U.S. president Jimmy Carter termed Iran "an island of stability in one of the more troubled areas of the world." A few days later, strikes began to spread throughout the country. From then on, as each mourning period of the previous violence approached at forty-day intervals, new anti-imperial rioting spread throughout the country. By late 1978 striking oil workers had brought petroleum production, on which Iran's economy depended, to a twenty-seven-year low, and antigovernment protesters were burning trucks and cars on the streets of Teheran.

Return from Exile

In January 1979 the shah finally fled the country, and in February the revolutionary militia seized control. But the forces that had coalesced to oust the shah had a variety of political and religious ideologies. Upon his return to Tehran on 1 February 1979, Khomeini consolidated his power by taking advantage of these factions. The three main groups included the religious and secular nationalists who formed the core of the Provisional Revolutionary Government (PRG) under the leadership of Prime Minister Mehdi Bazargan; the religious and secular socialists such as the Mujahedin-e Khalq and the Tudeh (communist) party; and the Shi'a fundamentalists represented by the Islamic Republican party (IRP).

The Islamic Republic

In spite of political opposition, Khomeini formally established the Islamic Republic of Iran on 1 April 1979. It was, he told the *New York Times*, "the first day of a government of God." Khomeini's concept of an Islamic state, under the rulership of the jurisprudent (*velayat-e faqih*), had been outlined in lectures that were published in 1970 as a book, *Hokumat-e Islam* (Islamic Government). Although the concept of the faqih was not new for Shi'a Islam, Khomeini was the first to put it into practice. Iran's new constitution stated in article five that the faqih was to exercise divine authority in the absence of the Twelfth Imam, who, it is believed, will ultimately reappear to establish just and equitable rule. The faqih's political power in such a system is near absolute.

By calling for such a government, which was ultimately supposed to lead to a world Islamic government, Khomeini rejected "the very idea of the nation-state." As R. K. Ramazani writes: "In Khomeini's ideal Islamic world order there would be no room for the modern secular post-Westphalia conception of the international system. The present international system must be transformed into the abode of humankind and, above all, the home of the 'oppressed masses of the people.'"

But while Khomeini called for rights for the masses, he continued to consolidate his own power. He first threw his weight behind the secular and religious nationalists. During this stage Iran left CENTO (Central Treaty Organization), the U.S.-created alliance that included Pakistan and Turkey, but maintained diplomatic relations with the United States, avoided conflict with the Soviet Union, and continued to trade with the rest of the world.

Only in November 1979, with the PRG's collapse, did Khomeini back the Shi'a fundamentalists, hailing the seizure of the U.S. embassy and taking of hostages as the beginning of the "second revolution." With his backing of the IRP, Khomeini effectively appropriated the power of the revolutionary courts, Revolutionary Guards, and *komitehs*, the local autonomous committees. At this stage Iran's foreign policy became increasingly radical and removed from the rest of the world. In September 1980 Iraq invaded Iran, beginning the lengthy and bloody war.

Internally, while he had assailed the shah's extensive powers after taking over Iran, Khomeini sought to expand the state's powers. On 22 June 1981, for example, Khomeini and the fundamentalists seized complete control of the government by ousting President Abul Hassan Bani-Sadr. And on 1 June 1988, a year before his death, the ayatollah called for "absolute rule by the faqih."

Khomeini died in Tehran on 3 June 1989 and was buried amid millions of mourners. With Khomeini's death President Hojatolislam Sayyed Ali Khamenei was chosen as Iran's supreme leader, while Hojatolislam Ali Akbar Hashemi Rafsanjani was elected president.

Book by Khomeini

Islam and Revolution: Writings and Declarations of Imam Khomeini, translated and annotated by Hamid Algar (Berkeley, Cal.: Mizan Press, 1981).

General References

Said Amir Arjomand, *The Turban for the Crown: The Islamic Revolution in Iran* (New York: Oxford University Press, 1988);

Shaul Bakhash, *The Reign of the Ayatollahs: Iran and the Islamic Revolution* (New York: Basic Books, 1984);

Fred Halliday, "Iranian Foreign Policy Since 1979: Internationalism and Nationalism in the Islamic Revolution," in *Shi'ism and Social Protest,* edited by Juan R. I. Cole and Nikki R. Keddie (New Haven, Conn.: Yale University Press, 1986): pp. 88–107;

Dilip Hiro, *Iran Under the Ayatollahs* (London: Routledge & Kegan Paul, 1985);

Roy Mottahedeh, *The Mantle of the Prophet: Religion and Politics in Iran* (New York: Pantheon, 1985);

R. K. Ramazani, *Revolutionary Iran: Challenge and Response in the Middle East* (Baltimore, Md.: Johns Hopkins University Press, 1986);

Edward W. Said, *Covering Islam: How the Media and the Experts Determine How We See the Rest of the World* (New York: Pantheon, 1981);

Gary Sick, *All Fall Down: America's Tragic Encounter with Iran* (New York: Penguin, 1986);

Thomas Walton, "Economic Development and Revolutionary Upheavals in Iran," *Cambridge Journal of Economics* (1980), pp. 271–292.

– A. F

Nikita S. Khrushchev

First Secretary, Soviet Communist Party, 1953–1964
Born Kalinovka, Russia, 17 April 1894
Died Petrovo-Dalneye, Soviet Union, 11 September 1971

Nikita Sergeyevich Khrushchev was born in the small Russian village of Kalinovka. His father, Sergei Khrushchev, was a poor peasant farmer who had to supplement the family's meager income by working in the winter in the coal mines of the Donbas region, three hundred miles southwest of Kalinovka in the Ukraine. Nikita began working at an early age as a shepherd and as a watchman. He learned to read and write at the village school, which he sporadically attended between the ages of seven and twelve.

Peasant revolts in 1905 began in Khrushchev's province and spread throughout Russia. The revolts facilitated the Revolution of 1905, which resulted in Czar Nicholas II's creating a legislative body, the Duma, and decreasing the payments the peasants had been making on their land. But even with fewer payments to the government the Khrushchevs could not survive as farmers. In 1908 they moved from their native village to the Uspenovsky mines near the industrial center of Yuzovka, Ukraine.

In 1909 Khrushchev, at the age of fifteen, began working as a fitter in the German-owned Bosse Engineering factory. To Khrushchev the wretched conditions in the factory were indicative of the exploitation of Russian workers by foreign capitalists. In the spring of 1912 the workers in the Bosse factory went on strike, and Khrushchev acted as a messenger for the strike committee. He was fired by the Bosse company and found another job at the French-owned Rutchenkovo mines.

Because he was an industrial worker, Khrushchev was exempted from military service when World War I began in 1914. In that year Khrushchev married Galina Yefronsinya, with whom he had a son, Leonid, in 1916

Gale International Portrait Gallery

Nikita S. Khrushchev

and a daughter, Yulia, in 1918. While the war dragged on, revolutionary activity in Russia increased. In 1915 and again in 1916 Khrushchev helped organize strikes at the Rutchenkovo mines.

Russian Revolution of 1917

The Russian Revolution of February 1917 resulted in the czar's removal from power and in the creation of a governing national legislative body known as the General Assembly and various local councils, or soviets. Khrushchev was a member of the Donbas Soviet, which was dominated by the Social Revolutionaries and Mensheviks. The Social Revolutionaries were best known for their use of terror to overthrow the state. The Mensheviks were opposed to the Bolsheviks – the two competing factions of the Russian Social Democratic Workers' party – in advocating a more broadly-based party membership. The November 1917 revolution, however, established the dominance of the Bolshevik party. Khrushchev's membership in the Donbas Soviet indicates that he was probably not yet a Bolshevik.

Russian Civil War

By the fall of 1917, however, Khrushchev was active in the Bolshevik Military Revolutionary Committee (RevKom). In December the Donbas region was attacked by the cossack general Aleksei Kaledin, who was leading an offensive for the White forces against areas controlled by the Bolsheviks. Khrushchev joined the Red Army and fought the Whites for the next several months.

In the spring of 1918 Khrushchev returned to the Rutchenkovo mines. Within weeks the area was occupied by the Germans, who had installed a nationalist government in the Ukraine. Khrushchev returned to his native village in Russia, where he officially joined the Bolshevik party sometime between April and the fall of 1918. Khrushchev was assigned to the political department of the Ninth Army. His work consisted of agitating and motivating the soldiers who were fighting General Anton Denikin's army north of the Donbas region.

In the spring of 1920 Denikin's army was defeated, and Khrushchev returned to the mines. The Bolsheviks, however, faced severe problems with industrial production following the civil war. Production at the Rutchenkovo mines, which were now owned by the Soviet government, fell to half the output of 1913. Khrushchev helped to rebuild industrial capacity in the area and in 1921 was put in charge of political affairs.

New Economic Policy

In 1921 the Soviet Union experienced widespread famine. During this period the party replaced its policy of War Communism – which had virtually abolished private enterprise – with the New Economic Policy (NEP), which actually encouraged certain features of a free market. Khrushchev spent a good deal of 1921 explaining the NEP to the miners in his region. His wife died in that year, leaving him with a son of five and a daughter of three.

In 1922 Khrushchev was selected for the Workers' Faculty of the Donbas Technical College in Yuzovka while still a student at the school. He was appointed the school's party secretary. He also received his first formal training in Marxism. In 1924 Khrushchev married Nina Petrovna Kukharchuk, a local schoolteacher. They would have two daughters, Rada and Yelena, and a son, Sergei. After his graduation from the technical college in the spring of 1925, Khrushchev was appointed secretary of the Petrovsko-Mariinsky district party committee (*raikom*), which oversaw an area that included the village of Maryinsk and the Petrovsk mine near Yuzovka, which had been renamed Stalino.

At the same time that Khrushchev was appointed head of the Petrovsko-Mariinsky raikom, Lazar Kaganovich was appointed general secretary of the Ukrainian Communist party. Kaganovich had tied his fortunes to those of Joseph Stalin, and from the moment Khrushchev linked his own to those of Kaganovich, he began to rise rapidly within the party hierarchy.

The Purges and Khrushchev's Rapid Rise

In December 1925 the Fourteenth Party Congress was held, and Khrushchev attended as a nonvoting representative from Stalino. At the party congress Khrushchev witnessed Stalin's campaign against Leon Trotsky, Grigory Zinoviev, and Lev Kamenev, three intellectuals who represented the old Bolshevik leadership, largely responsible for the revolution, and who now presented an obstacle to Stalin's consolidation of power. In October 1926 the first Ukrainian Party Conference was held and Khrushchev made his first important speech in which he too called for repression of the "Trotsky oppositionists." Khrushchev was promoted in 1927 to head the organizational department of the party in Stalino. In early 1928 he was appointed to head the Kharkov then the Kiev party committee. When the Second Ukrainian Party Congress was held in April 1929, Khrushchev spoke in support of Stalin's campaign against Nikolai Bukharin and the "rightists." The campaign, which involved removal of those leaders who had been his allies against Trotsky and the "oppositionists," resulted in Stalin's gaining complete control of the party.

In the fall of 1929 Khrushchev entered the newly founded Academy of Heavy Industry in Moscow. When the academy was reorganized because of the expulsion of "rightists," Khrushchev was rewarded for his loyalty to Stalin by being appointed head of the academy's party bureau in May 1930. During this time he became friends with Nadezhda Alliluyeva, Stalin's wife. It is possible that this friendship was responsible for Khrushchev's rapid rise to power in Moscow. More likely, Kaganovich, who had become head of the Moscow party in April 1930, was rewarding his protégé from the Ukraine.

In January 1931 Khrushchev was made head of the Bauman district, in which the academy was located. Within a few months Khrushchev became first secretary of Krasnaya Presnya, one of Moscow's most important industrial centers. In 1933 Khrushchev was elected second secretary of the Moscow party. In early 1934 he became first secretary and was elected to the Soviet Central Committee at the Seventeenth Party Congress. In March 1935, at the age of forty, he succeeded Kaganovich as head of the Moscow region. Khrushchev's main concern as Moscow's party leader was the construction of the Moscow metro system, which was to become one of the finest in the world.

Khrushchev was participating in Soviet leadership at the time of Stalin's bloodiest purges. At first the purges were directed against those within the party leadership who were perceived to be in opposition to Stalin. By 1935, however, Stalin's reign of terror had begun. Many people who were considered members of undesirable ethnic groups were being moved to Siberia, and by early 1937 tens of thousands had been arrested. Later in the year, show trials were held in Moscow, and many of Khrushchev's colleagues were publicly condemned for having committed crimes against the state and sentenced to death. Of the nine Moscow regional party secretaries who were appointed with Khrushchev in March 1931, he alone survived the purges.

Although Khrushchev did not initiate any of the purges, there is no evidence that he ever opposed any of Stalin's policies. For his loyalty to Stalin, Khrushchev was nominated as a candidate to the Supreme Soviet, to which he was elected in the fall of 1937. In January 1938 he was elected to the Presidium and as a candidate (nonvoting) member of the Politburo. Khrushchev, who now held important posts in both the state and the party, had become one of the most influential people in the country.

First Secretary of the Ukrainian Party

Party members in the Ukraine fell victim to a particularly brutal purge. In 1937 alone, 150,000 Ukrainian party members were arrested by the NKVD (predecessor of the KGB) in Stalin's attempt to create a completely new leadership in the republic. Stalin then chose Khrushchev to act as first secretary of the Ukrainian party. His appointment was announced in the Soviet press on 29 January 1938.

Evidence suggests Khrushchev had little control over the terror which devastated the Ukrainian party. In August 1937, however, Khrushchev had traveled to Kiev with Prime Minister Vyacheslav M. Molotov and NKVD head Nikolai Yezhov, along with NKVD troops loyal to Moscow. Molotov demanded that the Ukrainian party dismiss S.V. Kossior and replace him with Khrushchev. When the Ukrainians refused, Kossior was brought to Moscow where he was arrested, tortured, and killed. By the time Khrushchev was "elected" first secretary of the republic, the majority of its Central Committee members had been arrested.

While in charge in the Ukraine, Khrushchev concentrated less on party purges and more on agriculture. After overseeing several good harvests, he gained a reputation as an agricultural expert. In the summer of 1939 Khrushchev oversaw the incorporation of the Western Ukraine into the Soviet Union. The Soviets received this territory through a secret agreement with the Nazis as part of the Molotov-Ribbentrop Treaty of 1939. Khrushchev also oversaw the incorporation of Bessarabia – which was taken from Romania – into the Soviet Union. He was a devout "russianizer" and chose to suppress any expression of nationalism in the areas which he ruled.

World War II

On 22 June 1941 the Nazis invaded the Soviet Union, and within four months they occupied the entire Ukraine. In July, Khrushchev was made a member of the War Council of the Southwest Directorate under Marshal Semyon Budenny. In September, Kiev was completely surrounded by the Nazis. Khrushchev and Budenny recommended retreat, but Moscow vetoed this decision and replaced Budenny with Semyon Timoshenko. Timoshenko and Khrushchev ordered a retreat on 11 September, but Moscow did not give its agreement to the order until the 17th. Khrushchev witnessed six hundred thousand Soviet troops being captured and many of the senior officers killed. This was the first time he had come into direct conflict with Stalin. A similar conflict arose in the early spring of 1942, over the taking of the Ukrainian city of Kharkov. This time Khrushchev saw two hundred thousand Soviet troops captured.

Khrushchev then went to Stalingrad (later renamed Volgograd) to serve as the political representative on the Military Council. Although a Soviet victory, the battle for Stalingrad was a brutal one in which eight hundred thousand of the city's one million inhabitants were killed. The strategic importance of the city as a gateway to the country's oil fields and the symbolic importance of the battle as the turning point of the war led to Khrushchev's being rewarded with the title of lieutenant general for his participation.

Khrushchev then went to the Military Council of Voronezh, where he helped lead Soviet troops in successfully defending the Ukraine in the battle of the Kursk Bulge. In August 1943 he helped with the liberation of Kharkov, and then Kiev a few months later. On 6 February 1944 Khrushchev was appointed head of state in the Ukraine but he retained his position as first secretary of the Ukrainian party. His main task then was to reconstruct the republic's economy.

Reconstruction

The Ukrainian republic was still reeling from the damage inflicted on it by the war when it was hit by a drought, which led to a famine in 1946. The Ukraine was expected to supply much of the food for the entire country, and Khrushchev was severely criticized for the shortage. At a Central Committee meeting in February of 1947 he advocated the planting of winter wheat over spring wheat. Stalin was opposed to this plan and in March replaced him as first secretary of the Ukrainian party with Khrushchev's former mentor Kaganovich. Kaganovich only ruled the Ukraine until the end of the year, when he returned to Moscow. Khrushchev was again elected to head the party, although D. S. Korotchenko became the head of the Ukrainian government. Khrushchev continued to occupy himself with the republic's agricultural problems until he was called back to Moscow to become first secretary of the Moscow region.

Return to Moscow

Stalin had brought Khrushchev back to act as a counterbalance to Georgi M. Malenkov, who in Stalin's view had gained too much power. Khrushchev quickly became involved in the agriculture of the Moscow region. He soon began to propose the creation of "agrotowns" — large units, composed of several collective farms, that would provide some of the amenities of urban life for the farmworkers. In March 1951 *Pravda* published an article by Khrushchev outlining his plan. Malenkov, who was responsible for agriculture, was extremely critical of the article and the plan, as was Stalin. At the Nineteenth Party Congress in October 1952 Malenkov continued to criticize Khrushchev's approach to agriculture.

Despite this setback, Khrushchev managed to remain in Stalin's favor. At the party congress he was made a member of the newly created Bureau of the Presidium, which included Stalin. Khrushchev continued to be one of Stalin's top advisers, regularly dining with the aging dictator. On 6 March 1953, Stalin died. Khrushchev, like so many Soviets, wept.

Stalin's Heirs

Stalin's control of the Soviet Union had been so complete that at first it was not clear who, if anyone, was in charge after his death. Malenkov, who was made prime minister within days of Stalin's death, and Lavrenti Beria quickly joined forces, while Khrushchev and Nikolai Bulganin opposed Beria's reappointment as head of state security. Khrushchev lost his own position as head of the Moscow region but retained his position on the Secretariat. Khrushchev was now in charge of the party. The party, however, had lost most of its authority during Stalin's reign, and Khrushchev realized that his first task was to restore its power.

Beria presented the most formidable obstacle to the restoration of the party. His power over the state security organs gave him control in almost every sphere of government, and he was apparently using his power to stage a coup d'état. Khrushchev, however, worked together with Bulganin, Kliment E. Voroshilov, who headed the armed forces, and Molotov, who was directing the country's foreign affairs, in opposing Beria. In July 1953 Beria was placed under arrest and brought to a special session of the Presidium during which his indictment was read. After several days of dismantling Beria's power by arresting, and in some cases shooting, the top officers in the state security organs, Beria was executed.

With Beria out of the way, Khrushchev could concentrate on strengthening the party. At a Central Committee meeting in September, Khrushchev made a speech that called for increasing the party's role in attempting to solve the country's agricultural problems. In January 1954 Khrushchev sent a secret memorandum to the Presidium that criticized Malenkov's handling of agriculture and suggested utilization of western Siberia's virgin lands and the introduction of corn as two possible methods for increasing production of food.

In February, Khrushchev made his virgin-lands plan public at a Central Committee plenum. However, neither the powerful ministries nor Gosplan, which was in charge of planning the economy, supported him. By the summer of 1954 Khrushchev's popularity had declined, and Malenkov seemed to be the most powerful man in the country.

Malenkov began to emphasize consumer over military spending, which he claimed was less necessary since the Soviets now possessed nuclear weapons. Khrushchev, who would later pursue similar policies, allied himself with Bulganin, Molotov, Voroshilov, and Kaganovich in order to prevent changing the government's priorities.

Together these men were strong enough to challenge Malenkov's authority. In October, Malenkov was conspicuously absent when a delegation of Soviet leaders, including Khrushchev, went to Beijing. At a Central Committee meeting in January 1955, Khrushchev criticized Malenkov's emphasis on light industry, comparing it to Bukharin's "rightist" policies of the late 1920s. On 8 February, Malenkov resigned his position as head of state ostensibly because of the agricultural crisis, although he himself had little to do with agricultural policies. Bulganin replaced Malenkov as prime minister.

Consolidation of Power

Khrushchev's personal control over Bulganin and increasing control over the party allowed him to reorganize the organs of state security, transforming the NKVD into the KGB and appointing Ivan Serov, a loyal friend, as its head. As a consequence Khrushchev had de facto control of the Soviet government.

One of the first policy changes Khrushchev and Bulganin effected was in Soviet foreign affairs. In 1955 the Soviets gave up an occupied zone in Austria and a military base in Finland, and Khrushchev and Bulganin made three trips abroad to sell their new foreign policy. In the spring they went to Yugoslavia. Relations between the Yugoslav leader Josip Broz Tito and Stalin had been tense, and Khrushchev unsuccessfully attempted to create new ties. In the summer they attended a "Big Four" conference in Geneva. Although Bulganin was still prime minister, both U.S. president Dwight D. Eisenhower and British prime minister Anthony Eden noted Khrushchev's dominant role in representing Soviet interests. The conference failed to provide an agreement on nuclear weapons and the German question, but the leaders did stress the idea of "peaceful coexistence" between East and West — a new initiative in Soviet foreign policy which, only days before the conference, had gained acceptance in the Central Committee after Khrushchev had defeated Molotov's opposition to it. In the winter of 1955 Khrushchev traveled to India, where he supported Jawaharlal Nehru and his policy of neutrality.

At the Twentieth Party Congress held in February 1956, Khrushchev outlined his vision of a new Soviet foreign policy. He emphasized peaceful coexistence between East and West and the avoidability of war, and encouraged the recognition of the existence of various paths to socialism, warning that no one path should be imposed on all countries. Khrushchev concluded that the victory of communism over capitalism would come through economic, not military, strength.

De-Stalinization

All of these dramatic breaks with previous Soviet policy were overshadowed by the "secret speech" Khrushchev delivered on 24 February, the day of the final session of the Twentieth Party Congress. It was announced that the final session would be open only to Soviet communists. Khrushchev's three-hour speech attacked Stalin for his role in the murder of thousands of innocent communists, his refusal to heed warnings of Adolf Hitler's plan to attack the Soviet Union, and his cultivation of his own glorification, which Khrushchev called a "cult of personality."

Special party meetings were held throughout the country to explain Khrushchev's speech. Soon after, news of this dramatic break with the past had spread throughout the communist world. Khrushchev had taken a big risk in making the speech. He had attacked Stalin but had also placed the entire Soviet leadership, which had come to

power under Stalin, in a more critical light. Khrushchev decided to lessen the political threat he faced as a consequence of the speech by removing Molotov and Kaganovich — both adamant Stalinists — from power in early June.

By the end of June there was unrest in Eastern Europe. Workers' revolts in Poland were spreading. Marshal Konstantin Rokossovsky was removed from power in the Polish government and replaced by Vladislaw Gomulka, a Polish nationalist who had been imprisoned by Stalin. In the second half of September, Khrushchev traveled to Yugoslavia to convince Tito that if Khrushchev's government fell, Stalinists would return to power. The next month he traveled to Poland along with Anastas Mikoyan, Kaganovich, and Molotov to convince the leadership there to contain the crisis.

The uninvited delegation were sidetracked from their tasks in Poland by a mounting revolt in Hungary. In early November, Imre Nagy announced that Hungary was leaving the Warsaw Pact. There is little doubt that Khrushchev supported the Soviet invasion of Hungary. His own career was in crisis, as signaled by Molotov's and Kaganovich's return to power. On 4 November Soviet troops swept through the city of Budapest, where nearly the entire population was engaged in anticommunist resistance. Many soldiers and civilians were killed before the fighting subsided, and Nagy was replaced with János Kádár. Although at the time he probably would not have been able to stop the invasion, Khrushchev became known as the "Butcher of Hungary."

The "Anti-Party Group"

Khrushchev's power was far from secure. At the February 1957 Central Committee plenum he fought against the increasing power of the state by pushing through economic reforms that decentralized the control of the Moscow ministries and placed more responsibility on the Sovnorkhoz — the local economic bodies. All of these reforms were adopted by the Supreme Soviet in May.

Khrushchev's enemies decided to strike back at a meeting of the Presidium on 18 June. A majority of the Presidium, including Malenkov, Molotov, Kaganovich, and Dmitri Shepilov, informed Khrushchev of his dismissal. Khrushchev insisted that only the Central Committee could make such a decision. With the help of the military he managed to convene a full meeting of the Central Committee, which voted to keep him in power.

Malenkov, Molotov, Kaganovich, and Shepilov were publicly denounced as the "Anti-Party Group." Except for Bulganin, all seven of the members of the Presidium who voted for Khrushchev's dismissal were themselves dismissed. The resulting shake-up of the top leadership was not complete until October, when even Georgi Zhukov, who as head of the armed forces had apparently helped Khrushchev stay in power, was dismissed for fostering his own "cult of personality."

Khrushchevism

The dismissal of Zhukov and the launching of the satellite Sputnik the same month signaled Khrushchev's firm grip on power. Khrushchev continued to emphasize "peaceful coexistence" with the West and economic growth at home. There was, however, an increasingly noticeable rift between the Soviets and the Chinese. In dealings between the communist world and Western countries, Mao Zedong was advocating increased use of military force, while Khrushchev emphasized economic competition. In the summer of 1958 a crisis in the Middle East prompted Khrushchev to call for a "Big Four" summit that also included India. China was not invited to participate.

In November of 1958 Khrushchev faced another crisis, this time, one of his own making. Khrushchev summoned Western journalists to a press conference at which he insinuated that the problem of West Berlin must be solved within six months or the Soviet Union would take unilateral action. The announcement immediately put the Western powers on the defensive. In February 1959 British prime minister Harold Macmillan arrived in Moscow in an effort to lessen East-West tensions. In March, U.S. vice-president Richard M. Nixon visited the Soviet Union. Despite the obvious tension between Khrushchev and the vice-president, it was announced in August that the leaders of the two superpowers would exchange visits. It is possible that this was exactly what Khrushchev had envisioned when he created the Berlin crisis.

On 15 September 1959 Khrushchev became the first head of the Soviet Union to visit the United States. His reception was less than hospitable. In 1957 Khrushchev had told an American television company that their grandchildren would live under communist rule. He had on another occasion claimed that the Soviet Union would "bury" the United States. These remarks, coupled with the "red scares" which had swept across the United States in the 1950s, meant that Khrushchev would face a skeptical American audience in his attempt to demonstrate that the Soviet Union wanted peace.

The highlight of Khrushchev's visit to the United States came on 25–26 September when he and Eisenhower met for talks at Camp David. No concrete agreements were reached during the meeting. Khrushchev's emphasis on domestic policy, however, demanded a relaxed atmosphere between the two countries, and in January 1960 the Soviet Union announced that it would cut its armed forces by 1.2 million troops in the next eighteen months.

U-2 Crisis

Relations between the United States and the Soviet Union were once again strained when on 1 May 1960 the Soviets shot down an American U-2 plane over Soviet territory. The pilot of the plane, Francis Gary Powers, survived and confessed that the purpose of his mission was espionage. When Khrushchev arrived at the Paris summit meeting two weeks later, he demanded an apology from Eisenhower. The United States was not aware that Powers was still alive and insisted that the plane was not being used for espionage. Khrushchev stormed out of the summit. Clearly he needed to convince his critics at home that he was not too weak to handle the West.

Sino-Soviet relations had also reached an impasse. The Chinese were now openly competing with the Soviet Union for influence in the Third World. Khrushchev's attacks against the Chinese became increasingly vehement. In August 1960 the Soviets withdrew all of their technicians and specialists from China.

In September 1960 Khrushchev further infuriated the United States by heading the Soviet delegation to the United Nations (UN) for the fifteenth session of the General Assembly. The Eisenhower administration did not want press attention taken away from the presidential race between Nixon and John F. Kennedy and did not appreciate the Soviet leader coming to the United States uninvited.

During the UN meetings in New York, Khrushchev met with Cuban leader Fidel Castro and advocated China's rights in the United Nations. In an outburst that displayed Khrushchev's intention to make his presence felt at the United Nations, he took off his shoe and began to bang it on the table, having been enraged by a speech delivered by a Western delegate. The Soviet Union was fined ten thousand dollars for this breach of protocol.

The Berlin Wall

Khrushchev struggled to transfer resources from the Soviet military to the civilian economy. In the United States the new Kennedy administration had announced its budget in March 1961, which included increased spending on nuclear and conventional weapons. A June summit between the two leaders did not ease tensions, and the Soviets increased their military spending and nuclear testing in August. That same month the Berlin Wall was erected. Khrushchev had insisted that the problem of a divided Germany be solved by the end of the year or the Soviets would sign a separate peace treaty with the German Democratic Republic (GDR). On 12 August the GDR began to build a wall around all of West Berlin. Soviet and U.S. tanks lined up on opposite sides of the wall. It seemed the world was once again perched on the edge of war, but eventually the West resigned itself to the wall's existence.

The Cuban Missile Crisis

In the summer of 1962 Raúl Castro, Cuban defense minister and brother of Cuban leader Fidel Castro, traveled to Moscow, where he outlined a plan to Khrushchev for sending Soviet nuclear missiles to Cuba. Since the Soviets did not possess any intercontinental ballistic missiles (ICBMs), the plan suited Khrushchev, for it would place the United States within target range of Soviet missiles. The next month the Soviets began shipping the missiles to Cuba under the condition that the missiles remain under Soviet control at all times.

On 19 October President Kennedy was informed of the Soviet missiles, and he placed U.S. troops at combat readiness. Khrushchev, apparently surprised that the Americans would fear Soviet use of nuclear weapons, backed down almost immediately. By 26 October Khrushchev sent a letter to Kennedy offering to withdraw the missiles in exchange for a guarantee that the United States would not invade Cuba.

Cultural Thaw and the Ideological Campaign

That same month saw a loosening of artistic control within the Soviet Union. *Stalin's Heirs,* a critical poem by Yevgeny Yevtushenko, was published in *Pravda.* Soviet artists had begun testing the cultural boundaries in which the state had confined them after Khrushchev had delivered his secret speech at the Twentieth Party Congress in 1956, and they were now receiving some official recognition. At the November Plenum, Khrushchev gave his approval to Aleksandr Solzhenitsyn's *One Day in the Life of Ivan Denisovich,* a semiautobiographical portrayal of the terror of Stalin's prison camps.

Khrushchev's conservative opponents began to criticize this relative openness. On 1 December they arranged a special viewing of abstract painters and sculptors for Khrushchev. Taken aback by the abstract works, Khrushchev vehemently criticized the artists. Afterward he was forced to spend more time emphasizing ideology and its role in the arts.

Khrushchev's Fall

At an earlier Central Committee meeting, Khrushchev had pushed through a plan for splitting the party into industrial and agriculture spheres. The plan isolated the local party bosses – who had previously been a source of Khrushchev's power – from the decision-making processes. His emphasis on nuclear deterrence over conventional military power had already infuriated the military, and many government officials felt their power threatened by Khrushchev's policies.

In the summer of 1963 Khrushchev faced an encouraging international atmosphere and a disastrous domestic one. The East-West détente had established the "hot line" between Washington and Moscow and negotiations for a nuclear test-ban treaty. At home, however, Khrushchev had to contend with a bad harvest, which meant the Soviet government had to purchase millions of tons of grain from the West and ration flour and bread.

Khrushchev managed to stay in power for another year. He showed an increasing reliance on his own personal apparatus, bypassing his colleagues. In September 1964 Khrushchev outlined his proposals for the next five-year plan, due to begin in 1966. The proposals gave priority to light industry over heavy industry. Heavy industry was the sacred cow of the Soviet economy, and Khrushchev had openly attacked it.

On 13 October 1964 Khrushchev was summoned back to Moscow from his vacation villa on the Black Sea to attend a Presidium meeting, where he was removed from power. Khrushchev demanded a Central Committee vote, but this time he lost. When he returned home that evening Khrushchev exclaimed, "Well, that's it. I'm retired now. Perhaps the most important thing I did was just this – that they were able to get rid of me simply by voting, whereas Stalin would have had them all arrested."

Khrushchev moved to a small dacha in Petrovo-Dalneye, Russia, where he and his family enjoyed gardening on their own plot of land. Although there were MVD-KGB troops guarding him, they did not interfere in his life. In the fall of 1970 Khrushchev's memoirs were published in the West. Because Moscow had not given its authorization, he was forced to sign an apology for their publication. On 11 September 1971 Khrushchev died. He was buried in the Novo-Dyevichy cemetery.

Books by Khrushchev

Khrushchev Remembers: The Last Testament (Boston: Little, Brown, 1974);

Khrushchev Remembers: The Glasnost Tapes (Boston: Little, Brown, 1990).

Books about Khrushchev

Edward Crankshaw, *Khrushchev: A Career* (New York: Viking, 1966);

Mark Frankland, *Khrushchev* (New York: Stein & Day, 1979);

Carl A. Linden, *Khrushchev and the Soviet leadership, 1957–1964* (Baltimore: Johns Hopkins University Press, 1966);

Roy Medvedev, *Khrushchev* (Oxford: Basil Blackwell, 1982);

Roy Medvedev and Zhores Medvedev, *Khrushchev: The Years in Power* (New York: Columbia University Press, 1976);

Michel Tatu, *Power in the Kremlin: from Khrushchev to Kosygin* (New York: Viking, 1969).

General References

Vernon Aspaturain, *Process and Power in Soviet Foreign Policy* (Boston: Little, Brown, 1971);

Jack M. Schick, *The Berlin Crisis, 1958–1962* (Philadelphia: University of Pennsylvania Press, 1971);

Robert Slusser, *The Berlin Crisis of 1961: Soviet-American Relations and the Struggle for Power in the Kremlin, June–November 1961* (Baltimore: Johns Hopkins University Press, 1973).

— M.B.

SEE ALSO THESE RELATED ENTRIES

Nikolai Bulganin, 2; Fidel Castro, 2; Cuban Missile Crisis, 3; Anthony Eden, 1; Dwight D. Eisenhower, 1; Georgi M. Malenkov, 2; Anastas Mikoyan, 2; Vyacheslav M. Molotov, 2; Richard M. Nixon, 1; Aleksandr Solzhenitsyn, 2; Joseph Stalin, 2; Josip Broz Tito, 2; Kliment E. Voroshilov, 2.

Kim Il-Sung

President of North Korea, 1948–

Born Mangyondae, Korea, 15 April 1912
Died P'yongyang, N. Korea, 8 July 1994

President of North Korea, Kim Il-Sung is the longest-serving leader of any communist regime. An almost mythical figure in official North Korean political and social history, and an enigma to the outside world, Kim has been the center of the country's closed political system since the partition of the Korean peninsula in 1948.

Kim Il-Sung was born in the village of Mangyondae, southwest of Pyongyang, the current capital of North Korea, into a peasant family. The eldest of three sons, his original name was Kim Song Ju. He later adopted Kim Il-Sung, the name of a legendary hero of the Korean independence movement in Manchuria, China. When he was seven his family left Korea, which had been annexed by the Japanese in 1910, and immigrated to Manchuria, where he attended primary and secondary Chinese schools. There is much uncertainty surrounding Kim Il-Sung's early political activities and participation in anti-Japanese guerrilla movements – further compounded by official state propaganda and the idolization of Kim and his family. It appears that in 1929 he was expelled from school and briefly jailed for his political activities directed against Japanese colonial expansion into northeastern China. After his parents died, he joined various anti-Japanese guerrilla bands operating in Manchuria. At the age of nineteen Kim joined the underground Chinese Communist Youth League, beginning his early association with Chinese communist groups. According to many sources, in 1932 he became the leader of a small band of Korean partisans within the Chi-

Kim Il-Sung

nese communist guerrilla army in Manchuria. He led small bands of partisans into Korea to attack Japanese outposts in remote northern villages. By 1940, however, the Japanese had effectively eliminated all guerrilla activities in the region, and Kim with his remaining comrades fled into Far Eastern Siberia in the Soviet Union in 1941. There he rejoined the Chinese guerrilla movement near Vladivostok, where he married a fellow partisan member of his group. While very little factual information is known about Kim's consequent involvement with Soviet authorities during his four years in Siberia, it is known that he and the other Korean partisans received Soviet military training.

After Soviet forces liberated the northern half of the Korean peninsula from the Japanese in August 1945, Kim returned to Korea as a major in the Soviet Red Army. Although the United States, which liberated the southern half of the peninsula, and the Soviet Union had earlier agreed at the February 1945 Yalta Conference to place Korea under international trusteeship until independence could be granted, no formula had been worked out regarding the governing of the country in the wake of the Japanese surrender. Fearing the possibility of Soviet occupation of the entire peninsula, U.S. president Harry S Truman on 15 August proposed to Soviet leader Joseph Stalin the temporary partition of Korea along the 38th parallel. Immediately after the Japanese surrender the first steps toward the creation of a separate, pro-Soviet state in the north were taken. Having emerged from World War II a nationalist leader, Kim was designated by the Soviet occupation forces to head the formation of a provisional administrative system in the north. Politics in the northern half of the peninsula at the time, however, were in a confused state as numerous local communist and nationalist groups vied for power. After the elimination of both communist and nationalist opponents by the Soviet-backed partisan faction led by Kim, a North Korea Provisional People's Committee was established by the Soviets in February 1946, and in July the North Korean Worker's party was organized with Kim Tu Bong as its chairman and Kim Il-Sung, with whom the real power of government rested, as vice-chairman. With full Soviet backing, Kim organized a Korean People's Army.

With Soviet assistance and supervision, Kim's government began to establish an economic, political, and administrative structure and to initiate sweeping social and economic reforms as part of its communization of the northern half of the peninsula. By late 1946 people's committees had been established at local, county, and provincial levels. In February 1947 the North Korean People's Assembly was established in place of the People's Committee as the highest legislative authority in North Korea, and the assembly in turn elected the Central People's Committee, the executive branch headed by Kim.

Meanwhile the American-Soviet commission on Korea, which had been charged with organizing a single, provisional Korean government and which had been meeting intermittently since March 1946, proved incapable of reaching an agreement on the future of Korea. The temporary division of Korea along the 38th parallel quickly turned permanent as the two superpowers each sought to define the postwar international order in its own irreconcilable image. Unable to reach a workable compromise with the Soviet Union, the United States in September 1948 submitted the Korean question to the United Nations (UN) – despite Soviet objections – and a temporary UN commission was formed to supervise nationwide free elections. The Soviet Union and North Korean leaders, however, refused to accept UN supervised elections, which were held only in the southern half of the country on 10 May 1948. On 17 July the southern half was proclaimed the Republic of Korea, and in December it was recognized by the United Nations General Assembly as the only legitimate government on the peninsula.

North Korean leaders held their own elections in August 1948 for the new Supreme People's Assembly, which ratified a constitution on 8 September. On 9 September the Supreme People's Assembly proclaimed the Democratic People's Republic of Korea as an independent sovereign state, claiming authority over the entire peninsula. Elected premier by the assembly, Kim moved to consolidate his power by eliminating rival groups and political opponents and began advocating the violent overthrow of the South Korean government. Kim regarded military reunification under one communist regime as the only viable solution to the partitioning of the country. With substantial Soviet military assistance, Kim's first priority after coming to power was to assemble a formidable military machine and simultaneously to begin sponsoring communist guerrilla activities in South Korea, which by the spring of 1949 was facing a full-scale guerrilla war. By early 1950 the North Korean strategy of reunification through subversion had failed due to the South's counterinsurgency campaign. With full Soviet backing, bolstered by the communist victory in the People's Republic of China in October 1949 and encouraged by U.S. secretary of state Dean Acheson's declaration that Korea lay outside the American strategic and defense perimeter in Asia, Kim ordered his Soviet-equipped armed forces to cross the 38th parallel into South Korea on 25 June 1950.

Kim Il-Sung regarded the Korean War, known as the "Fatherland Liberation War" in North Korea, as a national war of liberation, and, with South Korea in political and military disarray, Kim's forces were able to reach Seoul within three days of the invasion. The United States, which viewed the North Korean invasion as the Soviet Union's latest bold move to achieve its global ambitions, responded quickly to the North Korean invasion by dispatching American air and naval forces. On 27 June an emergency session of the UN Security Council, which the Soviet delegate boycotted, approved collective military action under American command. On 15 September UN forces commanded by U.S. General Douglas A. MacArthur landed in Inchon and began to push North Korean forces north of the 38th parallel and toward the Yalu River border with the People's Republic of China. This action provoked a massive military intervention by communist China, whose "volunteers" had been infiltrating Korea in large numbers since the Inchon landing. The combined communist forces, assisted by the Soviet Union, which dispatched air force divisions to China and furnished arms and matériel, recaptured the northern half of the peninsula, and by early 1953 a stalemate developed along the 38th parallel. On 27 July 1953 a ceasefire agreement was signed between the UN and communist forces at Panmunjom. Even though a formal peace treaty was never signed, the 155-mile-long Demilitarized Zone (DMZ) became the de facto boundary line.

The war proved destructive for North Korea – which continued to be occupied by Chinese forces until 1958 – and intensified the ideological and political rivalry of the Cold War, effectively precluding any possibility of a peaceful reunification of the two Koreas. For the next decade Kim concentrated on consolidating power and rebuilding North Korea's devastated economy and military with Soviet and Chinese aid. He launched an economic plan based on heavy industrialization and purged North Korean communists and other opponents, many of whom were executed, imprisoned, or forced into exile. Over the next decade and a half his Stalinist regime remained largely closed and isolated internationally, with relations maintained only with Communist bloc countries.

Following the war North Korean foreign policy was directed mainly toward South Korea, with the ultimate goal of reunification of the peninsula under communist control. Kim called for the withdrawal of American troops and advocated the destruction of the anticommunist southern regime, sending terrorists and agents to infiltrate South Korea. His belligerent, anti-American posture led to sporadic incidents along the unstable DMZ, which paradoxically has one of the highest concentrations of weapons and soldiers in the world. Weeks following the January 1968 North Korean–sponsored assassination attempt on South Korean president Park Chung Hee, North Korean forces seized the USS *Pueblo* in international waters. During this period Kim also found his regime caught in the rift between his two major supporters, the Soviet Union and China, which in 1960 had begun to drift apart. Strained relations developed with both countries, even though Kim attempted to maintain a neutral stand by urging solidarity within the international communist movement. The increasingly bitter and often violent Sino-Soviet split posed serious dilemmas for

North Korea, which found itself in a position of having to choose sides even though it could not afford to alienate either of its sponsors for political, economic, and military reasons. An orthodox Marxist-Leninist, Kim was disturbed by the revisionism emanating out of the Soviet Union during the de-Stalinization campaign of Soviet premier Nikita S. Khrushchev. His subsequent tilt toward China, with whom North Korea had closer cultural and geographic proximity, caused a strain in Soviet-Korean relations and a drop in Soviet economic and military assistance during 1963–1964. By 1967, however, Kim found himself under severe Chinese criticism during Mao Zedong's so-called Cultural Revolution. He was denounced for his efforts to repair damaged relations with the Soviets. His fallout with the Chinese led to a brief border dispute between the two countries. The continued Sino-Soviet split, however, enhanced North Korea's independence of movement, and as a result Kim began to espouse an increasingly independent, self-reliant foreign policy.

After two decades of isolation North Korea in the early 1970s moved to join the wider community of nations and garner international legitimacy. With Soviet-U.S. and Sino-U.S. relations serving as a backdrop, Kim Il-Sung's belligerent foreign policies regarding reunification modified and a mild rapprochement between the North and the South began to develop. In addition to conducting low-level secret meetings with the South, Kim also launched a diplomatic and cultural campaign to bring North Korea out of isolation. In 1973 North Korea was granted observer status in the United Nations as relations improved with South Korea, the United States, and Japan – even though it continued to push for the international isolation of South Korea.

During the first half of the 1970s North Korea made feverish efforts to cultivate ties with the Third World and the so-called Non-Alignment Movement as a major part of its search for international legitimacy. North Korea's diplomatic offensive in the Third World proved successful, and by 1976 it had established diplomatic relations with over 130 countries. North Korea, which had been one of the most important Third World small-arms producers in the 1950s, became a major supplier of arms to the Third World, both to governments and to guerrilla groups in Africa, Asia, and Latin America.

Its improved international image was brief, however, as its militant foreign policy stance and unconventional diplomatic practices alienated other states. North Korea resumed its bellicose posturing toward the South and revived its anti-American policies. Amid the renewed Sino-Soviet hostilities during the mid 1970s, North Korea's foreign policy became more self-reliant and independent. In a measure to demonstrate its foreign policy independence in Communist bloc affairs, North Korea officially disapproved of the December 1979 Soviet invasion of Afghanistan.

The situation remained tense along the DMZ throughout the latter part of the 1970s. The situation nearly broke out into full-scale armed confrontation in July 1977, when North Korean forces shot down an unarmed American army helicopter a year after North Korean soldiers killed two American officers at Panmunjom. Kim continued to insist on the withdrawal of American forces from South Korea as a precondition to normalization talks. In addition, North Korean support for subversive activities against the South continued unchecked during the late 1970s and into the early 1980s, and several North Korean spy rings and underground groups were uncovered. Following the discovery by Canadian officials in April 1982 of a North Korean conspiracy to assassinate the South Korean President Chun Doo Hwan, the South Korean navy destroyed a North Korean vessel which had been dispatched to destroy a nuclear power plant in the South. Relations between the North and the South grew tense after another assassination attempt on Chun Doo Hwan in Rangoon, Burma, on 9 October 1983. The bombing attack, which was attributed to North Korean terrorists, killed seventeen high-ranking South Korean officials. In May 1984 the UN command discovered a series of "invasion tunnels" being constructed by North Korea under the DMZ.

North Korean anti-Western foreign policy has been a major source of tension for the United States, which has not lifted its diplomatic and economic embargo of the country. North Korea was a major arms supplier to Iran during the Iran-Iraq Gulf War during 1980–1988, as well as a supplier of arms to Libya and Syria. Kim Il-Sung's regime has also been implicated as an active supporter of international terrorism. Evidence of its responsibility for the November 1987 destruction of a South Korean airliner, resulting in the deaths of 115 people, led to an abrupt deterioration of relations with the South. As early as 1986 North Korea had threatened to disrupt the 1988 International Olympic Games to be held in Seoul, the capital of South Korea. In late 1986 North Korea announced plans to build a dam north of the DMZ capable of flooding much of central Korea and Seoul.

Toward the close of the 1980s relations between North and South Korea relaxed somewhat. In September 1990, after several stalled preliminary talks, the prime ministers of North and South Korea met, the first high-level talks between the two sides since the end of the Korean War. The talks and subsequent developments not only improved the prospects for some form of accommodation, but for national reunification as well.

While Kim Il-Sung remains an enigma to the outside world, official North Korean propaganda and revisionism have turned him into a demigod. Kim set in motion a cult of personality – a self-deification campaign – to further consolidate his powers as "Supreme Leader." In addition to political mythmaking, Kim constructed a pervasive internal security apparatus. Embodying both state and party, Kim's monocracy has controlled all aspects of North Korean life. Kim formulated his own political philosophy, Chuch'e, which he hoped would become the guiding ideology in the Third World. While there is an ambiguous relationship between it and Marxism-Leninism, Chuch'e stresses self-reliance. It was hoped that its emphasis on independence and nonalignment in foreign policy would make it appealing to the Third World. In August 1984 it was announced that Kim's son, Kim Jong Il, would succeed Kim Il-Sung as president. It appeared that by the late 1980s Kim Il-Sung had turned over the effective daily operation of the government to his handpicked heir and retreated into semi-retirement.

Selected Books by Kim Il-Sung

Kim Il Sung, Selected Works (Pyongyang: Foreign Languages Publishing House, 1965);

On the Building of the People's Government (Pyongyang: Foreign Languages Publishing House, 1978);

On the Non-Aligned Movement (Pyongyang: Foreign Languages Publishing House, 1982).

Books about Kim Il-Sung

Dae-Sook Suh, Kim Il Sung: The North Korean Leader (New York: Columbia University Press, 1988);

Tae-sok O, The Benevolent Sun (Pyongyang: Foreign Languages Publishing House, 1980).

General References

Byung Chul Koh, ed., The Foreign Policy Systems of North and South Korea (Berkeley: University of California Press, 1984);

Kong Dan Oh, Leadership Change in North Korean Politics: The Succession to Kim Il-Sung (Santa Monica, Cal.: Rand, 1988);

Peter Lowe, The Origins of the Korean War (London: Longman, 1986);

Alan D. Romberg, The United States, the Soviet Union, and Korea: Beyond Confrontation (New York: Council on Foreign Relations, 1989);

Tai Sung An, North Korea in Transition: From Dictatorship to Dynasty (Westport, Conn.: Greenwood, 1983).

–J. R.-S.

SEE ALSO THESE RELATED ENTRIES
Dean Acheson, 1; Douglas MacArthur, 1; Mao Zedong, 2; Joseph Stalin, 2; Harry S Truman, 1.

Alexsei Nikolaevich Kosygin

Prime Minister of the Soviet Union, 1964–1980
Born Saint Petersburg, Russia, 21 February 1904
Died Moscow, Soviet Union, 18 December 1980

Alexsei Nikolaevich Kosygin was born into a poor, working-class family in Saint Petersburg, Russia. His father, Nikolai Kosygin, was a lathe operator in a nearby factory.

As a teenager Kosygin was captivated by the Bolsheviks and the revolution they had successfully brought to his country. At the age of fifteen, Kosygin volunteered to serve in the Red Army when the civil war between the Bolsheviks and the Whites broke out in 1919.

Having distinguished himself as a brave and dedicated soldier, he was released from military service after the civil war ended in 1921. He returned to Saint Petersburg (renamed Leningrad after the revolution) and attended the Leningrad Cooperative Technicrum, a trade school where he was trained to serve as a manager of a cooperative. The cooperative movement was growing in popularity in Russia after the revolution, and, after graduating in 1924, Kosygin found employment in Siberia as an instructor in the Irkutsk oblast (regional) cooperative. Soon afterward Kosygin became the head of the Siberian Association of Cooperatives. While working in Siberia, he married. He and his wife, Klavidia, would have two children. He also was admitted to the Communist party in 1927, after having been a member of the Komsomol, the Communist party youth organization. Kosygin, however, would not be noted as a party ideologue. He rarely referred to Marxism or Leninism in his writings and speeches and never wrote anything that contributed to the body of communist theory.

The Purges

In 1929, after spending five years in Siberia, Kosygin returned home and entered the Leningrad Kirov Textile Institute. Shortly before Kosygin graduated in 1934, Sergei M. Kirov, the party leader in Leningrad, was assassinated. Although Kirov's murder is believed to have been carried out under the orders of Soviet leader Joseph Stalin, the incident was used by Stalin to initiate massive

Gale International Portrait Gallery
Alexsei Nikolaevich Kosygin

purges – under the leadership of Kirov's replacement, Andrei A. Zhdanov – of party leaders. As a consequence of the purges, many high posts in Leningrad's party organization became vacant in the 1930s, making advancement in the party less difficult for young and ambitious members, such as Kosygin.

After graduating from the institute, Kosygin was employed as the foreman of a textile plant in Leningrad and was made director of the Oktyabr spinning plant two years later. Meanwhile, Kosygin's party work continued. At the height of the purges in the mid 1930s, Kosygin sat on the party committee of the city's Vybourg region.

Rise in the Party Ranks

Zhdanov quickly brought the promising young communist into the party's top hierarchy. In June 1938 Kosygin became the head of the Industrial Transportation Department of Leningrad's party committee, and four months later he was appointed mayor of Leningrad. At the same time Kosygin was climbing his way to the top of the city's party hierarchy, he was also moving up within the Communist party's national structure. In 1938 Kosygin was elected to the Supreme Soviet, the Soviet Union's legislative body, and in January 1939 he became a people's commissar of the textile industry.

In March 1939, at the Eighteenth Party Congress, Kosygin delivered a speech in which he sharply criticized the policies of other textile ministers and recommended that the entire textile industry be reorganized using the American industry as a model. During the congress Kosygin, whose speech was supported by Stalin, was elected to the seventy-one-member Central Committee of the Communist party.

World War II

In April 1940 Kosygin was made deputy prime minister, a position in the upper levels of the Soviet government, and worked directly under Vyacheslav M. Molotov, who headed the Ekonomsovet, the Soviet economic council. Molotov worked directly under Stalin. When World War II began in 1941, Kosygin remained in Leningrad. In January 1942 he led the evacuation of five hundred thousand people from Leningrad across the frozen Lake Ladoga to safety. The city was under siege by the Nazis and the Finns. Kosygin spent six months in Leningrad during the siege.

As the war continued, Kosygin occupied himself with the Soviet Union's war-torn economy and helped raise the Soviet defense industry's level of productivity. For his efforts he was rewarded in 1943 with an appointment as prime minister of the Russian Republic, the largest of any of the Soviet republics. After the war Kosygin helped to restore the Soviet Union's devastated industrial base, and in March 1946 Stalin made him a candidate (nonvoting) member of the Politburo.

Full Member of the Politburo

In February 1948, at the age of forty-four, Kosygin was made a full member of the Politburo and was appointed minister of finance. The appointment came on the heels of an economic panic in the Soviet Union, resulting from a devaluation of the currency. Kosygin managed to restore calm and order to the country's finances,

and in December 1949 he was made minister of light industry.

Death of Stalin

While Kosygin was climbing to the top of the party hierarchy, massive purges were taking place. In Leningrad – where the purges were particularly brutal – Georgi M. Malenkov had nearly all the party leaders arrested after Zhdanov's mysterious death in 1948. But Kosygin managed to survive all of these purges unscathed. In the fall of 1952, however, it appeared that Kosygin, too, would be purged when, during the Nineteenth Party Congress, Stalin himself criticized Kosygin and reduced him to an alternate member of the Politburo. It is unknown whether or not Kosygin would have been purged from the party leadership had Stalin not died a few months later in March 1953.

After Stalin's death the Politburo was reduced from twenty-five to ten members. Although Kosygin was dropped from its membership, he remained minister of food and light industry.

At first the triumvirate of Malenkov, Molotov, and Lavrenti P. Beria continued to rule in the Stalinist tradition. It soon became clear, however, that Nikita S. Khrushchev, who was made first secretary of the party within weeks of Stalin's death, was consolidating his power. Kosygin supported him and was rewarded with an appointment as a deputy prime minister in the fall of 1953. In December 1956 Khrushchev decided to put to use Kosygin's talent for economics and transferred him to Gosplan – the state planning commission, where he served as deputy chairman.

Anti-Party Group

In June 1957 Khrushchev's leadership was challenged by the "anti-party" group, led by two of Stalin's closest advisers, Malenkov and Molotov. They arranged for a Presidium vote to dismiss Khrushchev as first secretary of the party. Khrushchev, however, insisted that only a full session of the Central Committee could decide these matters and managed to assemble such a session, in which Kosygin sided with Khrushchev against the anti-party group. For his loyalty, Kosygin was rewarded with candidate membership to the Politburo and once again became deputy prime minister.

From this moment on, Kosygin rapidly gained power in the Soviet government. He became chief of the economic planning commission in March 1959 and in May 1960 was made a full member of the Politburo and first deputy prime minister.

Khrushchev's Fall from Power

As the 1960s wore on, party elites became increasingly dissatisfied with Khrushchev's leadership. Several failures in Soviet foreign policy – such as the Cuban Missile Crisis and the decaying relations with China – exacerbated Khrushchev's problems in domestic affairs. Khrushchev had attempted to implement agricultural reforms, including placing restrictions on the use of private plots and livestock and attempting to reverse the country's chronic food shortages by planting corn. The harvest of 1963, however, was so poor that the Soviets had to use some of their emergency stocks of grain – and, worse, had to undergo the embarrassment of importing grain from the West – to avoid disaster. In October 1964 Khrushchev was removed from power.

Collective Leadership

Kosygin moved into Khrushchev's office in the Kremlin. But it soon became clear that the new Soviet leadership would be a collective one. Kosygin took over the economic policies and assumed leadership of the government as chairman of the Council of Ministers. Leonid I. Brezhnev, who was elected general secretary, led the party and handled relations with other communist powers, and Nikolai V. Podgorny performed the ceremonial functions of the state as chairman of the Presidium.

Kosygin's diplomatic work involved traveling to many countries, including France, Britain, and the United States. When he first came to power he expressed his desire to improve U.S.-Soviet relations, but, after the United States bombed North Vietnam while a Soviet delegation was there, his attitude toward the United States became more hostile. Although he attempted to negotiate a cease-fire in Vietnam in 1967, Kosygin believed that U.S. involvement in Southeast Asia made normal relations between the superpowers an impossibility. In an interview that appeared in *Life* magazine in 1968, Kosygin warned that "in the light of American aggression, we cannot have normal relations with the United States as long as it continues the war."

Still, Kosygin was above all a pragmatist. Although he had earlier refused an invitation from U.S. president Lyndon B. Johnson, he visited the United States in 1967 as part of the Soviet delegation to the United Nations General Assembly meeting on the Arab-Israeli War, and twice he met with President Johnson at Glassboro State College, in Glassboro, New Jersey. The Glassboro Talks helped create a personal relationship between the two leaders that led to a more cooperative atmosphere. A year later the United States and the Soviet Union signed a treaty on the nonproliferation of nuclear weapons. Despite his importance as a leader in the international arena, however, Kosygin will be most remembered as an economic reformer.

The Kosygin Reforms

Soviet decline in economic performance at the end of Khrushchev's reign forced a relatively open debate on how to improve the situation. In September 1962 Evsei Liberman of Karkhov University published an article in *Pravda* calling for a complete overhaul of the incentive system. At the Plenum of the Central Committee in September 1965, Kosygin announced economic reforms that closely paralleled the suggestions of Professor Liberman. The reforms had three objectives. First, reinstitute the ministerial system that Khrushchev had decentralized. In 1966 twenty-three industrial ministries were created, and greater authority was given to Gosplan and other centralized planning organs. Second, restructure the incentive system. Largely the implementation of Liberman's suggestions, more responsibility was given to enterprise managers – who would in turn benefit directly from increased profits – starting in 1967. A system of self-financing, known as *khozraschet*, was instituted, although no bankruptcy was allowed. Third, reform the method of pricing. Also put into place in 1967, these reforms called for Goskomtsen, the government organ responsible for pricing, to set prices at levels that more realistically reflected the costs of production and supply and demand.

The Failure of the Reforms

Despite Kosygin's reforms, the economic situation did not improve. The Soviet Union's gross national product fell from a 3.7 percent growth rate during the Ninth Five Year Plan (1971–1975) to 2.7 percent during the Tenth Five Year Plan (1976–1980). According to the Central Intelligence Agency estimates of another significant economic indicator – the output per unit of combined factor inputs – the Soviet Union's economy showed a steady decline during the 1960s and 1970s.

There are many reasons why Kosygin's reforms were not successful. Various groups entrenched within the Soviet bureaucracy blocked all attempts at change for fear they would lose their power as a consequence of reform. For similar reasons many Soviet officials only half-heartedly implemented the changes, dooming them to failure. There was also an increase in military spending during the period of the Kosygin-Brezhnev leadership, leaving less money to invest in the country's industrial base. The Soviet leadership was also not dynamic enough to implement radical change.

The Kosygin reforms also failed due to basic flaws in their structure. The reforms lessened ministerial interference in enterprise management but never actually lessened the ministries' responsibility for these enterprises, and as a result many ministries decided it would be better to continue their close supervision of enterprises. Kosygin, in short, tried to build a healthy economy on top of an unhealthy one. Because he did not allow enterprises to go bankrupt, he never solved the problem of unnecessary and unwanted production. Poor quality goods continued to be produced in large quantities with no end in sight.

Breakup of the Collective Leadership

Kosygin began to lose some of his power as the economy continued its decline. The first sign of a break in the collective leadership came in 1968. The Soviet leaders met with the rest of the Communist-bloc leaders in July of that year to discuss the popular movement, taking place in Czechoslovakia, which sought to create "socialism with a human face." Kosygin did not agree with Brezhnev's call for the use of force against Czechoslovakia. The Warsaw Pact's invasion of Czechoslovakia one month later signaled Brezhnev's increased power within the leadership.

In the early 1970s Brezhnev completed his rise to the top, moving Kosygin out of the way. He took over Kosygin's work in foreign policy, negotiating with U.S. president Richard M. Nixon in Moscow in May 1972. Unlike his predecessors, Brezhnev saw no need to remove Kosygin completely from the leadership. Kosygin remained in charge of the economy and retained his position as chairman of the Council of Ministers, or prime minister.

Although his reforms were a failure by the early 1970s, Kosygin continued to try to improve the economy. He was highly critical of management and agricultural policies and stressed intensive rather than extensive growth. However, Kosygin, who had watched the Soviet bureaucracy undermine his reforms, did not advocate drastic change of the economic system. When Kosygin met with Josip Broz Tito in Yugoslavia in 1973, he expressed his disapproval of Yugoslavia's implementation of certain aspects of a market economy.

Economic and Political Stagnation

Throughout the 1970s, both the Soviet economy and the Soviet leadership became gradually less dynamic. Ko-

sygin exemplified the aging bureaucrats who were "muddling through" the decade. He suffered from hardening of the arteries, which resulted in two heart attacks, and by 1979 his poor health had severely limited his ability to fulfill his duties. Kosygin resigned his post as prime minister on 23 October 1980. Brezhnev paid no tribute to Kosygin when he retired, creating speculation in the West that Kosygin was leaving for political reasons. Many thought Brezhnev was making Kosygin a scapegoat for the economy's poor performance.

Kosygin died on 18 December 1980, but there was no immediate mention of his death in the Soviet press. It has been suggested that either the Soviet leadership was slow to react because it was not sure how to treat Kosygin's death or it was preoccupied with paying tribute to Brezhnev, who was celebrating his seventy-fourth birthday. The Kremlin did not release the news of Kosygin's death until 20 December.

At Kosygin's funeral Brezhnev and all the available members of the Politburo took great pains to eulogize him. Brezhnev called him a "true son of the Communist party and the Soviet people" and announced that Kosygin's ashes would be buried at the wall of the Kremlin, alongside other respected leaders. The party bused in thousands of workers from nearby factories to ensure that the funeral was well attended. In a sense the funeral was a fitting end to Kosygin's life. Like him, it was straightforward, austere, and devoid of any overt ideological or emotional expressions.

General References

Ed A. Hewett, *Reforming the Soviet Economy: Equality versus Efficiency* (Washington, D.C.: Brookings Institution, 1988);

Michel Tatu, *Power in the Kremlin* (London: Collins, 1969).
– L. E.

SEE ALSO THESE RELATED ENTRIES
Leonid Brezhnev, 2; Nikita S. Khrushchev, 2; Georgi Malenkov, 2; Vyacheslav Molotov, 2; Joseph Stalin, 2; Andrei A. Zhdanov, 2.

Jacek Kuron

Member of Polish Parliament, 1989–
Adviser, Solidarity Trade Union, 1980–1989
Born Lwów, Poland, 3 March 1934

Jacek Kuron is a Polish political activist, writer, and a member of parliament. Kuron was born in Lwów, Poland, into a professional family. In 1949, after the imposition of a Stalinist dictatorship, he joined the communist-led Polish Youth Union and in March 1953, the ruling Polish United Workers party (PUWP). He was thrown out of the party in November of that year for refusing to confess to alleged ideological deviations and for not writing a self-criticism of his activities. In 1954 he helped to found a communist-led scouting organization, the General Walter Teams. He was readmitted to the party in October 1956, during the "Polish October" upheaval that witnessed some temporary liberalization of cultural, educational, and religious life. At the same time, Kuron began to study history at the University of Warsaw.

Early Dissent

In 1957 Kuron helped to establish an independent political debating club which was soon suppressed, as the regime of Wladyslaw Gomulka began to clamp down on dissident activity in general and the critical intelligentsia in particular. But Kuron maintained his oppositionist stance, and in 1964 he cowrote, with fellow political dissident Karol Modzelewski, an open letter addressed to the communist party leadership. In the letter they criticized the dictatorial policies of the PUWP and proposed a redefinition of Marxist socialism and a restructuring of the political system to allow for the operation of alternative political groups. Both men were thrown out of the party, charged with sedition, and sentenced to three years in prison. They served their terms but both were arrested again on 8 March 1968 for helping to organize a mass demonstration of students on the Warsaw University campus. The protest was staged against state censorship and called for a comprehensive democratization of public life. Both dissidents received three-and-a-half-year prison terms.

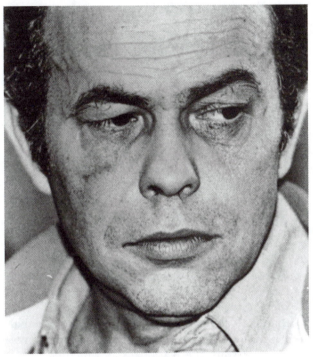

Jacek Kuron

Committee for Defense of Workers

In 1975 Kuron was one of the authors of a manifesto signed by fifty-nine intellectuals protesting the new Polish constitutional amendments that would have imposed further restrictions on civil liberties and bound Poland more closely to the Soviet Union. In June 1976 strikes broke out among industrial workers in several cities in protest against drastic and sudden food price increases. In September of that year Kuron, together with other intellectuals, set up the Committee for Defense of Workers (KOR) to provide legal, medical, and financial assistance to workers imprisoned or tortured by the police after the June turmoil. KOR also engaged in independent publishing, disseminated uncensored information in Poland and abroad, and organized meetings and educational programs for interested workers.

In 1979 KOR was renamed the Committee for Social Self-Defence (KSS-KOR) and broadened its independent activities to trying to limit the powers of the Communist party-state. Together with other dissident groups, KSS-KOR helped to set up small cells of independent labor unions in several industrial centers. Its leaders operated on the premise that instead of attacking and destroying party committees, workers and other social sectors should focus their activities on establishing their own independent bodies. This strategy laid the groundwork for the Solidarity movement.

Solidarity

During the birth of the free trade union Solidarity in the summer of 1980, Kuron became active in coordinating and supplying information on strike actions around the country. He was appointed as one of the chief advisers to Solidarity leader Lech Walesa during protracted negotiations with the government in August 1980. The Polish and Soviet governments were taken by surprise by the scale of the protests and the organizational skills of strike leaders and their advisers. Unwilling to sanction the use of force to quell the work stoppages, the regime acceded to most of the strikers' demands. But it secretly calculated that Solidarity could be undermined, and the communist monopoly over the workers movement restored, without the employment of Soviet troops and massive bloodshed.

After Solidarity was officially registered, Kuron became an adviser to the Solidarity regional branch in Gdansk and to the free trade union's national leadership, the National Coordinating Commission.

Martial Law

In December 1981, when martial law was declared by General Wojciech Jaruzelski to crush the Solidarity movement, Kuron was arrested together with several hundred other political activists. He was placed on trial nine months later on charges of attempting to overthrow the state. His wife died during the martial law while he was still imprisoned. Kuron was released under the 1984 amnesty and then acted as an adviser to Solidarity's underground leadership, the Interim Coordinating Commission, while continuing his independent writing and publishing.

Transition to Democracy

After strikes broke out again in the summer of 1988, over intolerable political and economic conditions, Kuron became a member of the Solidarity Citizens Committee formed under the leadership of Lech Walesa. He took part in roundtable negotiations with government representatives beginning in February 1989, as the authorities began to make important concessions to avoid a social explosion. During the partially free national elections in June 1989, Kuron was elected to the lower house of parliament and two months later was appointed minister of labor and social policy by the new Solidarity-led government. Under the premiership of Tadeusz Mazowiecki, the new government launched a program of far-reaching economic reforms to transform the commercial economy into a productive market system. In addition to his political activism, Kuron has also been a prominent publicist and essayist.

Books by Kuron

and others, *Revolutionary Marxist Students in Poland Speak Out, 1964–1968* (New York: Merit Publishers, 1968);

and Karol Modzelewski, *An Open Letter to the Party* (London: Pluto Press, 1972).

General References

Keith John Lepak, *Prelude to Solidarity: Poland and the Politics of the Gierek Regime* (New York: Columbia University Press, 1988);

Jan Joseph Lipski, *KOR: A History of the Workers Defence Committee* (Berkeley: University of California Press, 1985);

Jadwiga Staniszkis, *Poland's Self-Limiting Revolution* (Princeton: Princeton University Press, 1984).

– J. B. and A. B.

SEE ALSO THESE RELATED ENTRIES
Wojciech Jaruzelski, 2; Adam Michnik, 2; Lech Walesa, 2.

Li Xiannian

President of the People's Republic of China, 1983–1988

Born Hubei Province, China, 1909

Li Xiannian, currently one of the elder leaders of the Chinese Communist party (CCP), is the conservative voice in Chinese foreign policy. Known as an economic specialist through the 1950s and 1960s, he influenced China's foreign affairs during his tenure as president of the People's Republic of China (PRC) from 1983 to 1989.

Li Xiannian's parents were poor peasants. Li joined the CCP in 1927 and spent a brief period in the united forces of the Kuomintang (KMT), or Nationalist party, fighting on the Northern Expedition (1926–1928) – KMT leader Chiang Kai-shek's military campaign to defeat China's warlords and unify the country. Li left in April 1927 after Chiang declared war on the communists.

In 1934–1935 Li was a military commander on the Long March retreat designed to elude the extermination campaigns that the KMT was conducting against the communists. After receiving a military education at the communists' Chinese People's Anti-Japanese Military and Political University in 1937, Li led guerrilla bands in China's war against the Japanese (1937–1945). By 1941 he was in command of sixty thousand troops. During the Chinese civil war (1946–1949) Li was a deputy in the communists' best fighting unit, the Liu-Deng army, led by Liu Bocheng and Deng Xiaoping.

Li was called to Beijing in September 1956 to be part of the seventeen-member Politburo, a high decision-making organ in the CCP. The next year he was appointed minister of finance, and he held this position for the next two decades. Li's position allowed him to travel extensively abroad, giving him foreign relations experience.

In October 1976 Li was one of three CCP leaders – along with Chairman Hua Guofeng and Vice-chairman Ye Jianying – who conspired to arrest the "gang of four." The gang of four, led by Mao Zedong's wife Jiang Qing, was the most radical fringe of the CCP during the Cultural Revolution (1966–1976) and had been planning to take over the leadership of the PRC.

Li was an active participant in Chinese foreign relations during the 1980s. Unlike PRC leader Deng Xiaoping or General Secretary Hu Yaobang, however, Li was not reform minded. He advocated a conservative foreign policy with regard to the superpowers. In 1982 Li publicly criticized Deng's efforts to normalize relations with the United States and suggested China should instead concentrate on easing tensions between it and the Soviet Union. Shortly after this criticism was made party general

Li Xiannian

secretary Hu Yaobang issued the "independent foreign policy" of China, which stated that the PRC would pursue a foreign policy no longer based on the dynamics of a Sino-Soviet-U.S. strategic triangle.

Li was elected state president of China in 1983, further broadening his foreign relations role. Although his new position was largely ceremonial, he received international dignitaries in addition to heading delegations going overseas. Li was not a day-to-day manager of foreign policy, as Hu Yaobang and Premier Zhao Ziyang were. His influence in policy-making, however, was nevertheless felt, as he presided over the Foreign Affairs Small Group, a gathering of high-level party members who discuss foreign relations and provide input to China's foreign-policy makers. It was said by Zhao Ziyang that he and Hu Yaobang consulted Li when they had foreign-policy queries.

Li retired from active party duty in 1988, but did not leave the political scene. He is the chairman of the Chinese People's Political Consultative Committee, an advisory body to the CCP. In the spring of 1989 Li was a harsh critic of Zhao Ziyang and other liberals in the party for sympathizing with students demonstrating for democracy in Beijing's Tiananmen Square. Li trumpeted the conservative opinion – which, in the end, prevailed – that a rigid stance against the protests ought to be taken.

He continues to press for the implementation of traditional communist-planned economic policies.

General Reference

A. Doak Barnett, *The Making of Foreign Policy in China* (London: IBTaurus, 1985).

– K. W. M.

SEE ALSO THESE RELATED ENTRIES

Hu Yaobang, 2; Hua Guofeng, 2; Zhao Ziyang, 2.

Lin Biao

Minister of Defense, People's Republic of China, 1959–1971
Born Huangang, China, 5 December 1907
Died unclear circumstances, 12 September 1971

Lin Biao, who emerged as Mao Zedong's heir apparent in the late 1960s, will long be remembered for his failed coup attempt rather than for his lengthy career as a brilliant military leader and politician. Lin's military career was impressive. He was described even by his enemies as a brilliant tactician, capable of using guerrilla and conventional strategies to defeat his opponents' forces, which sometimes outnumbered his own troops by as many as ten to one. He was an ambitious politician whose vitriolic speeches against Mao's opponents ensured his rise to power during the first half of the People's Republic of China's most tragic decade (1966–1976). But Lin's thirst for power eventually made Mao suspicious of him. Lin's legacy will be the infamous "Project 571" – his plan to assassinate Mao. The attempted coup had profound effects on the Chinese people. For the first time the masses began to question the strength of Mao's leadership.

Lin Biao was born Lin Yuyong in Huangang County in the central province of Hubei. Although Lin's landowning father was, in accordance with Chinese tradition, considered fortunate to have four sons, his small handicraft business went bankrupt, forcing him to become a purser on a riverboat on the Yangtze. Lin went to middle school in the city of Wuchang. While there, he was introduced to Marxism. From 1921 to 1925 he was a student activist and a member of the Social Welfare Society, a group dedicated to promoting government reforms in China. During this period Lin joined the Kuomintang

(KMT). The KMT, or Nationalist party – which traced its origins to the revolutionaries who fought and eventually defeated the Manchu Dynasty in 1911– drew on ardently nationalistic political and cultural themes in its pursuit of a united China.

After finishing middle school in 1925, Lin went to Shanghai to attend a conference of student leaders. While there, he joined the Communist Youth League. His membership helped him gain entry to the prestigious Whampoa Military Academy of Canton in October 1925. The Whampoa Academy was the most successful military school in China's history. Under the leadership of commandant Chiang Kai-shek, future president of the Chinese Nationalist government, the academy employed a staff which included Zhou Enlai, the future Communist party premier; Nie Rongzhen, future coordinator of China's nuclear weapons project; and Ye Jianying, future party leader.

Before Lin graduated in October 1926, he left the KMT. Chiang Kai-shek had issued an order in 1925 for all cadets holding membership in both the Nationalist and Communist parties to renounce one or the other. Lin chose to remain a communist, but he was still allowed to fight in Chiang's nationalist army. Lin was placed in the Fourth Army on the Northern Expedition – Chiang's plan to drive north to conquer the warlords and unite China. Lin immediately displayed his military skill and rapidly ascended in the ranks of the Fourth Army. He rose from deputy platoon leader to platoon leader to company commander, and then to battalion commander in a single year.

Lin Biao

The Nanchang Uprising

In August 1927, when nineteen-year-old Lin was a junior officer, he took part in the Nanchang Uprising — the communist backlash in the city of Nanchang — led by, among others, Zhou Enlai. The uprising was a response to Chiang's bloody anticommunist coup on 12 April 1927, in which hundreds of Communist party members were killed, leaving the party in disarray. The Nanchang attack was initially successful. The rebels occupied the city for several days and set up a revolutionary committee. But the city was recaptured by Chiang's forces, and the communists, including Lin, fled. The uprising, however, is regarded as the birth of the Chinese Red Army. For the first time communists were fighting in their own units led by their own commanders.

From 1930 to 1934 Chiang Kai-shek, having successfully completed his Northern Expedition, focused his attentions on destroying the remaining communist enclaves in what came to be called the "five extermination campaigns." The campaigns were brutal. Lin Biao, who

by this time was a commander of a regiment in the Fourth Red Army, was a leader of the communist defense. He enhanced his reputation as a military prodigy by using a technique called "quick-attack." Lin was able to surprise Chiang's KMT forces while minimizing his own casualties. He was promoted to commander of the First Army Corps in January 1932. It is said that this twenty-thousand-man corps never lost a battle under Lin.

The Long March

Still, the KMT's superiority in numbers took its toll on Chinese Red Army troops. In October 1934, at the end of the fifth extermination campaign, the communists were forced to embark on the legendary Long March retreat. More than eighty-five thousand communists left their base in Jiangxi province, traveling a horseshoe-shaped escape route to Shaanxi province. They arrived in Shaanxi one year later; only nine thousand had survived. Lin Biao emerged from the fighting with a military reputation so great, American journalist Edgar Snow wrote in his account of the Chinese revolution, *Red Star over China*, that the mention of his corps' name would "sometimes put a Nanking (KMT) army to rout." Chiang Kai-shek despised Lin so much he placed a one-hundred-thousand-dollar bounty on his head.

The Japanese occupation of Manchuria in 1935 brought the warring factions together, and the KMT and communists fought on the same side again from 1937 to 1945 in the "War of Resistance" against Japan. Lin commanded the 115th Division, one of three communist divisions in the united Chinese army. His active duty ended in the spring of 1938, when he was wounded in west Shanxi province. Lin went to Moscow in either late 1938 or early 1939 for medical care. He stayed for three years, acting as a CCP representative to the Soviet Union.

After World War II the truce between the KMT and CCP proved weak. Chiang immediately positioned his forces against the communists. At the urging of the United States, both sides began negotiations for a settlement to put China at peace. U.S. ambassador Patrick Hurley, an anticommunist Oklahoman with startlingly little knowledge of Chinese affairs, represented American political interests in mediating the negotiations, but the talks reached a dead end in the fall of 1945. The United States sent another representative, General George C. Marshall, in December 1945, but he, too, failed to negotiate an agreement. Taking into account the years of bloody feuding between the two camps, there was never really much of a chance for success.

The Chinese Civil War

When the Chinese civil war began in mid 1946, Lin was already in control of two hundred fifty thousand troops. He had spent months prior to the war's outbreak

193

amassing an army –the Northeast Democratic Allied Army (NEDAA) – in Manchuria. The NEDAA soldiers were equipped with Japanese weapons seized in World War II. Lin's strategy called for "tactical withdrawal and mobile warfare, abandoning the towns for the country." After initial failure against the much larger KMT army, Lin started a counteroffensive in early 1947, which succeeded in pushing the KMT forces south by winter. During a one-month period in early 1948, the NEDAA captured Liaoyang, Anshan, Jilin, and Sipingkai. Beginning in September 1948, the NEDAA fought in the war's fiercest battle, known as the Liaoxi-Shenyang campaign. Lin's troops prevailed in fighting that lasted almost two months. Lin now controlled all of Manchuria. In January 1949 he had eight hundred thousand men. A communist victory in the civil war appeared inevitable.

The communists took over China in October 1949. The KMT loss was a shock to American politicians, and many of them blamed the "China hands" in the State Department – those who supported the communist cause. But the reasons for the loss were more likely that the Japanese war bought the Chinese Red Army enough time and space to grow, while the poorly led KMT forces suffered from corruption and morale problems in their ranks. The KMT loss would prompt the United States to reconsider its Asian strategy, for it was determined to go to great lengths in the future to avoid "abandoning" other Asian anticommunist regimes again. The "loss of China" had also confirmed America's fears that the Soviets were expanding communism beyond their borders.

Although Lin's political career was often put on hold in the 1950s because of an extended illness, reported to be tuberculosis, he emerged in 1955 as one of the thirteen top leaders in the People's Republic of China (PRC) when he was elected a member of the Communist party Politburo. Lin's physical condition improved in 1958, and he was subsequently elected a member of the seven-member Standing Committee, the highest decision-making organ in the party. Lin now sat beside the most powerful leaders in China – Chairman Mao, Premier Zhou, General Secretary Deng, Zhu De, Chen Yun, and Liu Shaoqi.

Minister of Defense

Lin's military promotion came in September 1959. Mao purged Defense Minister Peng Dehuai, following Peng's scathing attack on Mao's economic policy at a party plenum. Lin was named to replace Peng as minister of defense and de facto head of the Military Affairs Commission. It became his responsibility to shape the PRC's army.

Lin was a loyal follower of Mao and felt it was his duty to implement Mao's policies. Throughout the 1960s he asserted China's support for revolutionary movements abroad. This support, however, usually did not consist of more than a few statements. The Chinese rarely

backed communist movements in Africa or South America with more than token matériel. Lin Biao's essay, "Long Live the Victory of People's War," articulated Chinese foreign policy. Although he proclaimed China's encouragement for revolutionary war movements overseas, he provided a rationale for China to limit, or even avoid, direct involvement with these movements by advising foreign revolutionaries to rely on their own resources to fight. Lin's essay appeared at a time when China's foreign policy in Latin America and Africa had experienced only limited success.

Lin's attitude toward the United States and the Soviet Union was one of hostility. He opposed having any relations with the United States, "an imperialist country exploiting the Vietnamese people." He also rejected relations with the Soviets, whom he called "revisionists," a particularly biting epithet in the communist lexicon. The relationship between the Soviets and Chinese had been deteriorating rapidly since 1960, when the Soviets withdrew more than a thousand advisers, including nuclear-weapons specialists, from China. Lin used his influence to strengthen the People's Liberation Army (PLA) for a possible Sino-Soviet military conflict. It came in March 1969 in east Asia near a disputed island in the Ussuri River, which constitutes part of the border between China and the Soviet Union. The border skirmishes persisted until May. About a thousand soldiers died, mostly Chinese. During the fighting the Soviets threatened nuclear warfare, giving China the dubious distinction of being the only country to be threatened with nuclear destruction by both superpowers–the United States having used the threat during the Korean War and the Taiwan Straits crises of 1955 and 1958.

The Cultural Revolution

Lin was known more for implementing rather than making policy. With Mao as his personal guide, Lin used his position to put into effect the policies of the Cultural Revolution, a brainchild of Mao designed to reexpose the country to revolutionary struggle. The plan was to purge the existing party leaders who had become too bureaucratized. Young radical leaders, called Red Guards, would be sent to destroy the existing establishment of bourgeois liberals. It also meant that Mao would resume leadership of the party, which he voluntarily relinquished in 1959.

Lin assured complete PLA loyalty to Mao and propagated the "cult of Mao." Statues and portraits of Mao were distributed throughout the country, and his sayings were plastered on all available boards. Lin also ordered the publication of the compendium *Quotations from Chairman Mao Zedong*. Millions of Chinese children carried the book with them everywhere they went.

Red Guards caused countrywide turmoil. National leaders were arrested and paraded through the streets wearing dunce caps and placards listing their counterrevolutionary acts. Schools were closed, families torn apart, and hundreds of thousands of people – known in China as the "lost generation" – were persecuted or killed. Among the leadership arrested were Deng, Liu Shaoqi, and Peng Dehuai. These arrests, coupled with demotions of other leaders, allowed Lin to become Mao's heir.

The cult of Mao continued at the Party Congress in April 1969. In a speech delivered to the congress, Lin mentioned Mao by name 148 times. Reference to the philosophy of Mao Zedong was restored to the constitution after a thirteen-year absence. Lin Biao's name was then included in the constitution with a paragraph concluding "Comrade Lin Biao is Comrade Mao Zedong's close comrade in arms and successor."

Lin's position as Mao's heir did not go unchallenged. Two factions had developed within the leadership. One faction was led by Lin. Mao's wife, Jiang Qing, a former Chinese B-movie actress, was the leader of the radical faction – an especially ruthless and ambitious group of ideologues later known as the "Gang of Four." She controlled the cultural propaganda in China and specialized in a curious entertainment genre called "revolutionary ballet." Jiang was such an abrasive radical that she managed to alienate every party leader, including her husband Mao, who was estranged from her. Jiang, as did Lin, diligently maneuvered to become Mao's successor.

In 1970 Mao became aware of Lin's quest to replace him. At a party plenum in the northern resort area of Lushan, Lin and propaganda expert Chen Boda were supposed to have raised the issue of amending the constitution to include the position of head of state. The plan was to nominate Mao as the new president and then have Lin automatically voted in as vice-president. Mao became suspicious and rejected the proposal. Chen was consequently disgraced, but Lin kept his position.

The Lin Biao Affair
According to official Chinese sources, Lin began planning a coup immediately after his failure at Lushan. The plot included a bold assassination attempt on Mao and a takeover of the military. It was called "Project 571" for its Chinese homonym, "wuqiyi" (armed uprising). Mao, a master of sensing danger, took precautionary steps and thwarted Lin. When Lin realized his plot had crumbled, he tried to escape. On 12 September 1971 Lin Biao, his wife Ye Qun, and his son Lin Liguo boarded a plane for the Soviet Union. Two hours after takeoff, the plane crashed in a desolate area in Mongolia. Eight badly burned bodies were recovered – there were no survivors.

The "Lin Biao Affair" has been surrounded by much speculation and intrigue. Another version of his death alleges that Lin's son Liguo, an officer in the air force, and Lin's wife were coconspirators. After having become privy to the plot, Mao and Zhou set a trap for Lin and his wife. On 12 September Lin was invited to Mao's home for dinner. That evening they ate and engaged in pleasant conversation. As Lin's black limousine rolled down the driveway to leave, a group of Mao's henchmen ambushed the vehicle with 40-mm rockets. The only identifiable feature left of Lin was his intact right eye and bushy eyebrow. Mongolian authorities seemed to support this version. They had found the plane in which Lin reputedly had died and in early 1990 reported that Lin Biao's remains were not in the wreckage. Lin's death was a symbolic end to a five-year period in which the PRC led an isolationist existence. No progress was made in foreign relations. The leaders who had supported the development of relations with the West, such as Liu and Deng, were all under arrest. Those in leadership positions, such as Lin Biao, wanted little to do with either superpower. Lin's death cleared the way for more serious discussions between the United States and China.

The Lin Biao Affair had a tumultuous effect on the Chinese people. It is cited by scholars as the event which changed the Chinese people's belief in the infallibility of the chairman and in the harmony of the leadership. The heir to Mao had been killed in a coup attempt only one year after he had sat next to Mao in overseeing the "Great Proletarian Cultural Revolution."

Books about Lin:

Jaap Van Ginneken, *The Rise and Fall of Lin Piao* (New York: Penguin, 1972);

Wu Tien-wei, *Lin Biao and the Gang of Four* (Carbondale and Edwardsville: Southern Illinois Press, 1983);

Yao Ming-le, *The Conspiracy and Murder of Mao's Heir* (London: Collins, 1983).

General Reference

Edgar Snow, *Red Star over China* (London: Gollancz, 1937).

– K. W. M.

SEE ALSO THESE RELATED ENTRIES
Mao Zedong, 2; Peng Dehuai, 2; Zhou Enlai, 2.

Liu Shaoqi

President of the People's Republic of China, 1958-1966
Born Huaminglou, Hunan Province, China, 1898
Died Kaifeng, People's Republic of China, 13 November 1969

Liu Shaoqi was the second most powerful man in the People's Republic of China (PRC) from its inception in 1949 to the beginning of the Cultural Revolution in 1966. Although he lacked the flamboyance of Chairman Mao Zedong, Liu managed to gain universal admiration for his theoretical writings. His body of work concerning communist ideology and organization is only matched in stature and potency by Mao's. Liu Shaoqi took over leadership of the Chinese Communist party's (CCP) day-to-day operations in 1959 and proceeded to implement an economically efficient system that rescued China from years of famine. In foreign affairs Liu was an orthodox Marxist in advocating – and actively seeking – a unified socialist world fighting against imperialist aggressors. Liu, however, was purged during the Cultural Revolution when his policies of economic efficiency and technocracy clashed with Mao Zedong's principles of broad revolutionary struggle.

Liu was born in 1898 in Huaminglou in Hunan Province, near Mao Zedong's birthplace. Liu's parents, like Mao's, were wealthy peasants. As a middle-school student in 1914, Liu was already embracing radical politics. In 1920 Liu joined the Socialist Youth League, an organization set up by the Russians to prepare young Chinese for the Communist party, which was eventually established in China in 1921. In 1920 Liu went to Moscow to study at the Communist University of the Toilers of the East. He joined the CCP while in Moscow in 1921.

Liu returned to Hunan the following year and became a labor union organizer. He showed the first signs of his organizational genius in September 1922 when he helped assemble a strike involving as many as twenty thousand miners and fifteen hundred railway workers. The strike was eventually suppressed and the union destroyed.

Liu was one of the CCP's leaders in the early days of the party. He was general secretary of the powerful All-China Federation of Labor. In the spring of 1927, after Chiang Kai-shek launched his bloody purge of the communists who had been assisting him on his military campaign to unite China, Liu spent a few months working underground as a party organizer in the city of Wuhan.

In October 1934 Liu accompanied the communists on the Long March, a calculated retreat from Chiang Kai-shek's troops who were poised to annihilate the communist base in Jiangxi Province. Liu marched for the first

Liu Shaoqi

three months before being sent to Manchuria to help organize a communist base in the Northeast. He spent the next two years in Beijing, mainly concentrating on recruiting the "white areas" – the intellectuals, students, and professionals.

During the war of resistance against the Japanese (1937–1945), Liu worked on building the communist support base behind enemy lines. He also developed friendships with the communist military leaders when he was named a political commissar of the Chinese Red Army in 1941. Liu's theories about communist organization and ideology first appeared at this time. His most famous exegesis, entitled *How to Be a Good Communist*, appeared in 1939 and blended an interpretation of classic Marxist and Confucian texts to form an argument for overcoming individualistic and bureaucratic tendencies and for maintaining absolute loyalty to the party. It was a major work, often cited for its restatement of Leninist principles.

In the spring of 1945 Liu delivered a speech to the CCP, entitled "On the Party." Its message was far-reaching, dealing with many areas of party organization, leadership, and discipline, and it became one of the key documents in the study of the history of communist China.

Liu's influence was widely felt in the party. He was a master of organization, a military man, and a theorist. By the time the CCP came to power in China in the fall of 1949, Liu was second only to Mao in the party hierarchy. He was placed on the PRC's Central People's Government Council, at that time the leading political organ in the central government.

Liu was Mao's right-hand man during the 1950s, serving as a supervisor for routine management of domestic affairs. In early 1958 the PRC launched Mao's plan to expedite China's transformation to communism. With the implementation of the Great Leap Forward (GLF) Mao planned to "catch up to Great Britain's economy in 15 years" by enlarging the communist work units and driving the people to exert a herculean effort to increase China's productivity. The plan failed miserably, causing Mao to hand over voluntarily the day-to-day operations to a new president – Liu Shaoqi.

Liu's foreign-policy views originated from the Marxist concept of "international proletarianism." Liu saw the world in terms of a broad communist movement in which "bourgeois nationalist" aggression among nations could not be tolerated. He believed countries should unite in opposition to imperialism, and any defection from this union, such as through aggression, was a betrayal of communism.

Liu became an important figure in China's foreign affairs during the late 1950s and early 1960s – a period when tensions between China and the Soviet Union were increasing. After the Soviets withdrew scientific and technological advisers from China in 1960, Liu joined secretary-general Deng Xiaoping as part of a Chinese delegation attending an international conference, which in-

tended to bring together eighty-one communist leaders to discuss the world communist movement. The Chinese, however, were preoccupied with the Sino-Soviet hostilities. The most volatile of the contingent was Deng Xiaoping, who showed little tact in his harangues against the Soviets. Liu Shaoqi tried to ease tensions, declaring to the Soviet delegation on 7 December, "as you will not see the sun rising from the west, you will never see a rift between the great parties, nations, and peoples of China and Soviet Russia." Less than six years later the two countries formally ended relations.

The Chinese tried to unite all "oppressed" nations under the PRC wing during Liu's years of leadership, actively lobbying foreign communists to choose their camp over the Soviets. Liu entertained emissaries from South America and Africa, as well as from within the Asia-Pacific region. In 1963 he made trips to Indonesia, Burma, Cambodia, North Vietnam, and North Korea to denounce the Soviet Union. Liu lashed out at the Soviet Union, claiming that its "peaceful coexistence" with the United States "may not be used to negate the obligation of a socialist country to support the revolutionary struggle of an oppressed nation and its people" – in effect, accusing the Soviets of having forsaken their responsibility to a united communist world fighting imperialist aggression.

Liu promoted China as a protector of Third World countries. After the Chinese detonated their first nuclear weapon in October 1964, he declared that "all oppressed nations and peoples . . . too, have nuclear weapons." The PRC, however, did reiterate its pre-nuclear-bomb doctrine, which declared the bomb to be a "paper tiger."

Liu had mixed success in attracting foreign countries to the Chinese side. He failed in persuading Indonesia's and Vietnam's communists to choose the CCP over the Soviets. One reason for this failure was China's tendency to support foreign revolutions with spirited language rather than with money and weapons – matériel that mattered most to Third World countries seeking assistance. Still, the Chinese trumpeted their intention to export communist revolution throughout the world, causing many Western nations to perceive China as at least as great a threat as the Soviet Union.

Liu's greatest achievement as president was his program to remedy the Chinese economy following the abysmal failure of the GLF. He and Deng along with other economic leaders, such as Chen Yun, instituted a liberal plan that called for private plots and free rural markets to get the economy running again. The success of the program, however, marked the beginning of the end for Liu Shaoqi. His growing prominence and liberal economic success enraged Mao. In 1966 Mao began to engineer a plan known as the Cultural Revolution (1966–1976) that would swing China away from liberal policies and toward radical fundamentalism. The plan included criticism of those – such as Liu and Deng – who had called for reforming Chinese economic policy.

Liu was accused in mid 1966 of "bourgeois" crimes and demoted. If he were a man of lesser stature in the CCP, he certainly would have been quickly eliminated from the party hierarchy. But because of his legions of strong and loyal followers, he did not succumb to the pressure of the Cultural Revolution until a year later. The reason why Liu did not resist his downfall in 1967 is a point of speculation. One view holds that he sacrificed himself out of fear that a leadership struggle would cripple China. Another view portrays him as the unsuspecting victim of the Cultural Revolution – having no idea he was its central target.

Liu was toppled in a movement which led to ten years of mayhem in China, years during which Chinese foreign relations came to a standstill. Liu's movement toward a more open economy was seen by China's radicals as the embodiment of sinful bourgeois thought, and Liu paid for this with his life.

Liu Shaoqi died in a Kaifeng prison on 13 November 1969. His death certificate lists the cause of death as "illness," but he was known to have diabetes and was not treated for it. Liu was posthumously rehabilitated in 1980 and is now hailed as one of the "heroes of the revolution" in China.

Book by Liu:
Selected Works of Liu Shaoqi (Oxford: Pergamon, 1984).

Book about Liu:
Tien-min Li, *Liu Shao-ch'i* (Stanford: Hoover Institute Press, 1975).

General Reference
Stanley Karnow, *Mao and China* (New York: Penguin, 1990);

Edgar Snow, *The Other Side of the River* (London: Gollancz, 1963).

–K. W. M.

SEE ALSO THESE RELATED ENTRIES
Deng Xiaoping, 2; Mao Zedong, 2.

György Lukács

Hungarian Philosopher

Hungarian Minister of Culture, 1956

Born Budapest, Hungary, 13 April 1885
Died Budapest, Hungary, 4 June 1971

György Lukács, a Hungarian Marxist philosopher, writer, and literary critic who influenced the mainstream of European communist thought during the first half of the twentieth century, was born into a wealthy Jewish family. He was educated at the Universities of Budapest, Heidelberg, and Berlin. During World War I Lukács became a Marxist ideologue, and in 1918 he joined the Hungarian Communist party (HCP).

The Belá Kun Government

Lukács served as commissar for culture and education in the short-lived Hungarian communist regime of Béla Kun in 1919. Kun's Soviet republic was established by Hungarian Bolsheviks seeking to emulate Lenin's success in Russia at a time of political turmoil in Budapest at the end of World War I. But the new government lacked any worker support, its repressive policies provoked resistance and opposition, and the embryonic Soviet state was unable to provide substantive assistance.

After the collapse of the Kun regime, Lukács moved to Vienna. He remained there for the next ten years, writing, lecturing, and helping to reorganize the HCP in exile. He moved to Berlin in 1929, and except for a year spent studying at the Marx-Engels Institute in Moscow, he stayed in the German capital until 1933. He then left Berlin for Moscow where he attended and taught at the Institute of Philosophy. After the 1945 communist takeover in Hungary, Lukács moved back to Budapest and became a member of parliament and a professor of aesthetics and the philosophy of culture at the University of Budapest.

The 1956 Revolt

During the 1950s Lukács became increasingly disillusioned with the Stalinist regime, and by the time of the 1956 Hungarian uprising he had acknowledged the bankruptcy of the prevailing communist doctrine with its emphasis on control over all economic activities. He called for freedom of philosophical enquiry and stressed the importance of a cultural revolution if socialism were to have a solid social foundation. He served as the minister of culture in the reformist government of Imre Nagy, but after the Soviet invasion in November 1956, he was ar-

György Lukács

rested and deported to Romania. Lukács was allowed to return to Budapest in 1957, as the new communist government wanted to benefit from his popularity and international renown among Western Marxists, including the influential "Frankfurt School." When he refused publicly to condemn the 1956 revolution, he was formally criticized and condemned by party ideologists and expelled from the party.

Lukács withdrew into scholarly seclusion and was not allowed to publish in Hungary until 1964. As the government of János Kádár began to introduce a program of economic reforms in 1967, Lukács was readmitted into the Communist party. He remained openly critical of the

East European Marxist-Leninist systems, which he considered to have betrayed the principles of socialism. Lukács died in Budapest on 4 June 1971. He wrote more than thirty books and hundreds of essays and lectures. Among his major philosophical works are books and articles on G. W. F. Hegel, existentialism, and aesthetics.

Books by Lukács (Selected)

The Historical Novel (London: Merlin, 1962);

Lenin (London: New Left Books, 1970);

History and Class Conciousness (London: Merlin, 1971);

Georg Lukács: Political Writings 1919–29 (London: New Left Books, 1972);

The Young Hegel (London: Merlin, 1975).

Book about Lukács

Victor Zitta, *Georg Lukács' Marxism* (The Hague: Nijhoff, 1964).

General Reference

Bennett Kovrig, *Communism in Hungary: From Kun to Kadar* (Stanford, Cal.: Hoover Institution Press, 1979).

–J. B. and A. B.

SEE ALSO THESE RELATED ENTRIES

János Kádár, 2; Imre Nagy, 2.

Patrice Lumumba

Prime Minister of Congo, 1960
Born Onalua, Belgian Congo, 2 July 1925
Died Katanga Province, Congo, 17 January 1961

Patrice Lumumba was a Congolese militant nationalist leader and served as the first prime minister of Congo (now Zaire) during the tumultuous first few months following its independence from Belgium.

Patrice Lumumba was born on 2 July 1925 in the village of Onalua in the Kasai province. After his primary education at a local mission school, he attended secondary school in Leopoldville (now Kinshasa), the capital of Belgian Congo. He left school at the age of eighteen to work as a postal clerk in Orientale province. Having settled in Stanleyville, Lumumba became the president of the local *évolués* (educated and Westernized natives) club and a columnist. Teaching himself a wide range of subjects, including law and philosophy, he wrote a book, *Congo, My Country* (published, 1962), in 1956 and 1957. Lumumba, who was active in the cultural and political life of the province, was elected provincial president of the Association of Native Personnel (APIC), an association of native civil servants that voiced African demands for advancement and fair play. After a brief prison term in 1956 for embezzlement, he moved to Leopoldville to work for a brewery in 1957 and to continue his political activities. The following year he attended the All-African People's Conference in Accra, Ghana, convened by Kwame Nkrumah, the Ghanaian president and prominent African revolutionary leader. The conference, and

Patrice Lumumba

the Pan-Africanist, socialist revolutionary thinking of Nkrumah, impressed and inspired Lumumba, who returned to Belgian Congo to press for independence from Belgian rule.

The Congolese National Movement

In December 1958 Lumumba, the first Congolese nationalist leader to call for independence, founded the Congolese National Movement (MNC). Although 1959–1960 was a time of growing nationalist political activism, nationalist politics in the Belgian Congo was both fragmented and fraught with ideological differences. Lumumba, who by this time had emerged as a dynamic political organizer and fiery orator, was arrested in October 1959 after MNC-led protests and riots in the capital. He was released a few months later in order to attend the Round Table Conference, the independence talks held in Brussels, Belgium, in January–February 1960, attended by forty-five African delegates from different political groups. An agreement between the African delegates and the Belgian colonial administration set 30 June 1960 as the date of independence following provincial and national elections. Over one hundred political parties, most of which were regionally based, participated in the 21–22 May elections. The MNC, however, failed to win an absolute majority in the inconclusive elections, although Lumumba succeeded in forging an ill-fated and short-lived compromise coalition government, with him as prime minister and Joseph Kasavubu, leader of the Alliance of the Bakongo party, as president. In addition to personal, ethnic, and ideological differences within and among the fragmented, ethnic-regional based parties, political unity was further hampered by strong regionalist interests and disagreements over the form of government. The militant, left-leaning Lumumba favored a strongly unitary system, while Kasavubu and Katangese leader Moise Tshombe, as well as the white European settlers, favored a federation. The preindependence dispute between the federalists, who feared the domination of a central government over the provinces, and the unitarians, who were influenced by mainstream African nationalist thinking at the time, undermined both the fragile coalition and national unity. In the ensuing political turmoil the central government's authority progressively deteriorated.

The Congolese Civil War

The Congolese civil war began a week after the Congo became independent, starting with the 5 July 1960 army mutiny against Belgian officers. The mutiny touched off riots and violence that quickly spread outside the capital city. The several instances of violence against Europeans, which led to panic and the evacuation of foreign nationals, captured international headlines. The weakened, al-

most paralyzed central government was unable to assert its authority beyond the capital city limits. Belgium intervened in the crisis on 10 July by sending paratroops into Luluabourg and Elisabethville, ostensibly to protect Belgian citizens and restore order. Lumumba and Kasavubu, concerned that Belgium was trying to reoccupy the country, strongly opposed the Belgian intervention and called for the immediate withdrawal of Belgian troops. On 11 July, Tshombe declared the mineral-rich Katanga (now Shaba) province an independent state with the tacit backing of the Belgian troops. The following day Lumumba and Kasavubu appealed to the United Nations (UN) for military and administrative assistance, after having originally asked American president Dwight D. Eisenhower for help. A few days later, on 14 July, the first contingent of the UN police force was airlifted by the United States to the Congo, thus heralding the United Nations' first "police action" in Africa. Coming at the heels of the Cuban revolution in 1959, the Congo crisis inaugurated superpower involvement in sub-Saharan Africa. Both the United States, alarmed by Lumumba's radicalism, and the Soviet Union, which sought to court left-leaning clients in the emerging nations, maneuvered to establish influence in the strategically located, mineral-rich country.

After the declaration of martial law and the arrest of various political rivals, Lumumba hoped to use the UN forces to crush the Katangese secessionist forces, who had the de facto backing of Belgian paratroops. Angered by UN secretary-general Dag Hammarskjöld's refusal to use UN troops to put down the secession, he requested the withdrawal of UN troops. Lumumba, who had initially sought U.S. assistance, then appealed to the Soviet Union and East bloc countries for military aid to quell the secession, but received only token assistance from the Soviet Union. Lumumba's actions heightened U.S. concerns that he was a communist, and the United States stepped up clandestine efforts to support anti-Lumumba factions and to find ways to undermine his position. Meanwhile a constitutional crisis emerged between the moderate, conservative Kasavubu and Lumumba, whose fragile relationship was clouded by ideological differences. On 5 September, as the country approached anarchy, Kasavubu dismissed Lumumba, causing a split in the already paralyzed government. In the ensuing political deadlock and anarchic situation, Lumumba responded by dismissing Kasavubu. On 14 September, Colonel Joseph D. Mobutu, originally appointed army chief of staff by Lumumba, stepped into the vacuum to "neutralize" the government, dissolving parliament and placing Lumumba under house arrest. While fleeing to Stanleyville to join his supporters, Lumumba was arrested in December by Mobutu's troops and handed over to Katangese forces. On 17 January 1961 Lumumba was killed while in custody. The U.S. Central Intelligence Agency was subsequently implicated in his death.

Branded a communist by his opponents, Lumumba's militant, left-of-center nationalism clashed with competing domestic and international interests during the Congo crisis. Even though his sincere objective may have been an independent, unified Congo free of outside involvement, he found himself involved in superpower competition for ideological and political control of the incipient decolonization process in Africa. The Soviet Union built the Patrice Lumumba University in Moscow in his honor.

Books by Lumumba

Congo, My Country (London: Pall Mall, 1962);

Lumumba Speaks (Boston: Little, Brown, 1972).

Book about Lumumba

Thomas Kanza, *The Rise and Fall of Patrice Lumumba* (Boston: G. K. Hall, 1979).

General References

Georges Abi-Saab, *The United Nations Operation in the Congo, 1960–1964* (Oxford: Oxford University Press, 1978);

Madeline Kalb, *The Congo Cables: The Cold War in Africa* (New York: Macmillan, 1982);

W. A. E. Skurnik, ed., *African Political Thought: Lumumba, Nkrumah, Toure* (Denver: University of Denver Press, 1968);

Crawford Young, *Politics in the Congo: Decolonization and Independence* (Princeton: Princeton University Press, 1965).

−J. R.-S.

SEE ALSO THESE RELATED ENTRIES

Dwight D. Eisenhower, 1; Dag Hammarskjöld, 1; Mobutu Sese Seko, 2; Kwame Nkrumah, 2; Moise Tshombe-Kapenda, 2.

Georgi Malenkov

Prime Minister of the Soviet Union, 1953–1955
Born Orenburg, Russia, 8 January 1902
Died Soviet Union, 14 January 1988.

Georgi Malenkov headed the collective leadership of the Soviet Union after the death of Joseph Stalin. He served as prime minister for two years, but was removed from power in the purges that consolidated power in the hands of Nikita S. Khrushchev.

Although Malenkov issued from peasant stock, it is unlikely that his parents belonged to the working class. Most of the "peasants" of Orenburg were involved in the city's thriving commercial activities. Malenkov volunteered to serve in the Red Army in late 1919 or early 1920. He joined the Bolshevik party in 1920 at the age of eighteen, apparently waiting until the Bolshevik victory had become certain. One of his first party positions was as a "political worker" in the political administration of the Turkestan front. Primarily involved in combating anticommunist activity behind the lines, he also sought to weed out disloyal elements inside the Red Army and was involved in confiscating peasants' grain stocks. After the civil war, Malenkov studied at the Moscow High Technology School (MVTU), serving there as secretary of the school's party cell. During the rivalry between Stalinists and Trotskyists – raging in MVTU as elsewhere – Malenkov carefully avoided strong association with either side, managing nonetheless to win the favor of the Stalin-dominated party elite by the time of V. I. Lenin's death on 21 January 1924. From 1925 to 1930 Malenkov served in the Central Committee (CC) apparatus. Unlike the old Bolsheviks who had participated in the October Revolution, Malenkov was not viewed by Stalin as a serious political threat and therefore emerged from the worst period of the terror (1934–1938) unscathed. Indeed, Malenkov actively participated in the purge of Stalin's opponents. By the time of Adolf Hitler's invasion of the Soviet Union in June 1941, Malenkov was sufficiently trusted by Stalin to work within the group of Stalin's closest associates. He became a candidate member of the Politburo in 1941 and served on the State Defense Committee, the small group which oversaw the Soviet war effort. After the war Malenkov became a full member of the Politburo (1946) as well as second secretary of the Central Committee.

During the Zhdanovshchina, the cultural regime under Stalin of Andrei Zhdanov, when the Soviet Union's most creative artists were silenced, Malenkov had favored production of a set of deluxe editions of Rus-

Georgi Malenkov

sian literature from antiquity to modern times, including the then highly controversial work of Soviet artists Mikhail Zoshchenko and Anna Akhmatova. Zhdanov's efforts to exclude Zoshchenko and Akhmatova by portraying them as representatives of "decadent bourgeois" culture were successful. Had Malenkov's views prevailed, the Soviet climate of cultural ultraorthodoxy – contributing to East-West tensions – might not have been sustainable.

Though Malenkov initially lost one of his party posts in the course of the feud with Zhdanov, he emerged as the leading contender to succeed Stalin when Zhdanov died in 1948. When Stalin died in 1953, Malenkov occu-

203

pied the posts of first secretary as well as chairman of the Council of Ministers (prime minister).

Eugene Varga

In the decade following World War II, Malenkov became associated with the controversial views of Eugene S. Varga, director of the Institute for Western Economics and Western Politics. Varga argued in his major work, *Changes in the Economy of Capitalism as a Result of the Second World War*, that a cautious Soviet foreign policy was most appropriate because the long-awaited "general crisis of world capitalism" had been delayed due to the development of labor productivity, technology, and state economic regulation mechanisms in the West. Moreover, Varga downplayed the importance of the extension of the Soviet system into Eastern Europe, categorizing the Soviet satellites as "state capitalist."

Views on the East-West Rivalry

Malenkov believed that Western hostility toward the Soviet Union was not absolute and that a Soviet strategy of defense was optimal. Like Varga, Malenkov believed the United States was no longer inherently aggressive, due to the increased control of the American government over reckless capitalists. Atomic weapons would deter the imperialists, according to Malenkov, and through a conciliatory policy on Western Europe the Soviets could hope to split the West and reestablish a Soviet-German partnership.

Malenkov's constituency was the Soviet white-collar workers, who were chafing under the increasingly anachronistic system of command from above and sought greater independence from the party. This technical intelligentsia, was, however, divided in its loyalties, owing to the fact that it had benefited more than other sectors of the population from Stalinism and stood to lose its limited perks and privileges in the event of deviation from the dominant Stalinist foreign-policy line.

Of four general foreign-policy stands discernible within the Soviet political elite during the 1950s, Malenkov's was the most pacific toward the West. The other three positions held that 1): Western hostility toward the Soviet Union was unconditional, and that offense had the advantage, a position advocated by Zhdanov; 2): Western hostility was unconditional, but defense had the advantage, a position associated with Vyacheslav Molotov; and 3): Western hostility was conditional, but offense had the advantage, a position pushed by Khruschev.

Early Foreign Policy Statements

Prior to becoming chairman of the Council of Ministers, or prime minister, in 1953, Malenkov made few important foreign policy pronouncements. During the

founding meeting of the Cominform (Communist Information Bureau) in 1947, in fact, Malenkov played a subservient role to Zhdanov. The Cominform held its first meeting in September 1947 in Szlarka Poreba, Poland. Officially designed to disseminate information to member communist parties regarding the current common party line, the Cominform, like its predecessor, the Comintern (Communist International), served as a tool of Soviet policy. The Comintern was disbanded during World War II in order to promote harmony among members of the anti-Hitler coalition but reappeared in the form of the Cominform once the Nazi danger subsided. Whereas Zhdanov delivered the major address of the founding meeting, calling for militant revolutionary activity abroad, including disruption of the U.S.-sponsored Marshall Plan to rebuild Europe, Malenkov spoke only on domestic Soviet questions, lauding the achievements of the Zhdanovshchina (though he had once actively opposed the extreme cultural repression). Malenkov's relatively dovish foreign-policy views found no expression within the context of the Cominform.

Malenkov was eventually forced to surrender the post of first secretary to Khrushchev, but remained prime minister until forced to resign in February, 1955. From 1953 to 1955 Malenkov advocated radical economic reforms, including reduction of the defense budget, increased production of consumer goods, and more incentives for collective farmers. Indeed, though Khrushchev later gained a reputation in the West as a relatively liberal Soviet leader largely as a result of his de-Stalinization campaign, Malenkov was far more willing to challenge established Soviet interests. Malenkov was more Western-oriented than Khrushchev, who later adopted some of Malenkov's reform proposals.

On 13 March 1954 Malenkov delivered a speech to the Supreme Soviet declaring that nuclear war would result in the destruction of world civilization. The implication was that Soviet defense spending could be reduced without loss of security since a stockpile of atomic bombs was sufficient protection. This view was attacked by Molotov, who claimed atomic war would only destroy capitalism, and by the official party journal, *Kommunist*: "Such an argument (that atomic war would ruin civilization) serves the cause of American imperialism, whether willingly or not." Military leaders such as Georgi Zhukov tended to support Molotov, but disagreed with the latter's dismissal of the dangers of atomic war for the Soviet Union.

Resignation as Prime Minister

Khrushchev's political maneuvers in the struggle to succeed Stalin as supreme leader forced Malenkov to resign from the position of prime minister on 8 February 1955. Following Malenkov's resignation, Khrushchev sought further to isolate and discredit him. For instance when, in February 1956, Khrushchev denounced Stalin's policies in a secret session of the Twentieth Party Congress, he portrayed Malenkov as a simple tool of Stalin. Khrushchev's "secret speech," which launched a wide-ranging de-Stalinization campaign, was probably motivated in part by Khrushchev's sincere abhorrence of Stalin's extreme criminality. But political considerations almost certainly played a role as well. Khrushchev, after all, had been no less subservient to Stalin during Stalin's lifetime than Malenkov.

During early June 1957 Malenkov became involved in a plot to remove Khrushchev from power. Along with a majority of his colleagues on the Presidium, the party's ruling body, Malenkov voted for Khrushchev's ouster. However, Khrushchev managed to overturn the Presidium's decision in the larger Central Committee, which he called into emergency session. Marshal Zhukov made special military planes available to Khrushchev in order to speed Central Committee delegates to Moscow. Khrushchev's opponents were labeled the "antiparty group" and expelled from the Presidium in late June 1957.

After his political disgrace, Malenkov confined himself to work in the industrial-administrative sector of the Soviet economy, serving from 1957 to 1961 first as director of a hydroelectric power station and then as director of a heat and electric power plant, both in Kazakhstan. Upon retirement in 1961, Malenkov was virtually a "nonperson" in the Soviet Union, though still a party member. In 1964 his party membership was revoked as well.

A moderating influence upon the generally hawkish Soviet political elite, Malenkov lost out in the end to people who were more subservient to the established interests. Ironically, in 1964 Khrushchev found himself in a position similar to Malenkov's position in 1953–1955, seeking to achieve new goals such as increased economic efficiency and consumer satisfaction, without violating traditional values such as the priority of heavy industry and defense. Like Malenkov, Khrushchev lost his political struggle to people who were perceived as less threat-

ening to the traditional values. A close ally of Stalin, deeply involved in the purges and terror, Malenkov nonetheless possessed enough intellectual independence to perceive the opportunities for a reduction in superpower tensions during the early stages of the Cold War. His swift fall from influence, when Stalin's protection was removed, is testimony to the relative strength of proponents of a more antagonistic relation with the United States during the 1950s.

Book about Malenkov
Martin Ebon, *Malenkov* (New York: McGraw-Hill, 1953).

General References
David J. Dallin, *Soviet Foreign Policy after Stalin* (Philadelphia: Lippincott, 1961);

Timothy Dunmore, *Soviet Politics, 1945–1953* (New York: St. Martin's Press, 1984);

Carl A. Linden, *Khrushchev and the Soviet leadership, 1957-1964* (Baltimore: Johns Hopkins University Press, 1966);

Susan J. Linz, ed., *The Impact of World War Two on the Soviet Union* (Totowa, N. J.: Rowman & Allenhead, 1985);

Charles S. Maier, *The Origins of the Cold War and Contemporary Europe* (New York: New Viewpoints, 1978);

Bruce Parrott, *Politics and Technology in the Soviet Union* (Cambridge, Mass.: M.I.T. Press, 1985);

Ann Phillips, *Soviet Policy Toward East Germany Reconsidered* (Westport, Conn.: Greenwood, 1986);

Myron Rush, *The International Situation and Soviet Foreign Policy* (Columbus, Ohio: Merrill, 1969);

Marshall Shulman, *Soviet Foreign Policy Reappraised* (New York: Atheneum, 1969);

Jack Snyder, "The Gorbachev Revolution: A Waning of Soviet Expansionism?," in *International Security,* 12 (Winter 1987/88): pp. 93–132;

Michel Tatu, *Power in the Kremlin, from Khrushchev to Kosygin* (New York: Viking, 1969).

–J. W.

SEE ALSO THESE RELATED ENTRIES
Nikita S. Khrushchev, 2, Joseph Stalin, 2; Georgi Zhukov, 2.

Rodion Malinovsky

Marshal of the Soviet Union, 1944–1967

Minister of Defense, Soviet Union, 1957–1967

Born Odessa, Ukraine, Russia, 23 November 1898
Died Moscow, Soviet Union, 31 March 1967

Rodion Yakovlevich Malinovsky, marshal of the Soviet Union from 1944 to 1967 and minister of defense from 1957 to 1967, was born in the port city of Odessa to poor Ukrainian parents. During World War I he was conscripted and sent to fight in France with the Russian Expeditionary Corps in 1916. In France he spread propaganda among his fellow soldiers after the Russian Revolution of 1917, urging Russian disengagement from the war. For this the French sent Malinovsky, now a corporal, to North Africa with the Foreign Legion. After his return to Russia in 1919 he volunteered for the Red Army, fighting for the communists in the Russian civil war. A junior commander at the close of the civil war, Malinovsky decided to make the army a career.

Spanish Civil War

During the Spanish civil war (1936–1939) the Soviet Union supported the Republican forces, which represented the elected government, against the Loyalists, led by General Francisco Franco. Malinovsky was seconded to the Republican Army, serving under the nom de guerre of Colonel Malino. The end of his first tour of duty coincided with the Great Terror of 1936–1938, General Secretary Joseph Stalin's massive purge of the Communist party and Soviet society. Malinovsky prudently extended his tour in Spain twice. He was finally ordered back to the Soviet Union in 1938, threatened with a charge of defection. This threat, he wrote later, made his "flesh creep."

World War II

During World War II Malinovsky led the Second Guards Army at the Battle of Stalingrad, which was followed by his promotion to marshal of the Soviet Union in 1944. In 1945 he commanded the Soviet armies on the Trans-Baikal Front against the Japanese in fighting that saw the only instance of the Red Army using the German strategy of blitzkrieg, or "lightning war." Although his performance then and later was not brilliant, he occupies sixth place in the official list of "outstanding [Soviet] leaders and commanders" of World War II.

Rodion Malinovsky

Minister of Defense

When Nikita S. Khrushchev, Stalin's successor, was looking to replace Marshal Georgy Zhukov in October 1957 as minister of defense, he picked Malinovsky, with whom he had been associated on and off since 1942. Khrushchev feared that Zhukov possessed too much fame, popularity, and authority to be politically reliable at a time when Khrushchev's hold on power was not entirely secure.

Single Variant Strategy

It soon became apparent that Malinovsky did not entirely agree with Khrushchev's war-fighting strategy – the so-called single variant strategy – which placed heavy reliance on nuclear weapons. Khrushchev outlined this strategy in a speech, in January 1960, in which he talked of the increasing obsolescence of military aviation and naval surface ships, both of which he felt would eventually be replaced by nuclear rockets. In response to the advantages to be gained from nuclear "firepower," the army and the navy would suffer correspondingly large cuts in manpower. In short, conventional arms and mass armies did not belong in Khrushchev's vision of future warfare.

On the very day that Khrushchev addressed the Supreme Soviet, the government's legislative body, Malinovsky also spoke and reassured the military that all branches of the armed forces would be maintained in "relevant and sound" proportions. This was to be Malinovsky's approach to handling Khrushchev: not to refute his ideas directly but to temper them by degree.

Malinovsky continued to propound military views that departed from those held by Khrushchev. At the Twenty-first Party Congress in October 1961, he assigned nuclear forces primary importance in the initial stages of a future war but maintained that victory would only come as a "result of combined action by all the arms of the Armed Forces." In 1964 he urged greater military readiness, a high state of morale, and adequate conventional forces.

Military Buildup under Brezhnev

Leonid I. Brezhnev deposed Khrushchev in October 1964 and within a year began a massive buildup of Soviet forces, which coincided with the renewed influence of the military. Malinovsky presided over the initial stages of the buildup, which, in addition to qualitative improvements made in the Soviet strategic missile forces, included a greatly increased role for the conventional forces.

When his chief of staff, Marshal Sergei Biriuzov, was killed in an aircraft crash in November 1964, Malinovsky was able to return Marshal Matvei Zakharov to the post – after Khrushchev had removed Zakharov in 1963 – a sign that the new leadership approved Malinovsky's broad-based plan for military expansion.

In his last public comment on the Soviet military, made on 23 February 1967, Malinovsky emphasized the importance of submarine-launched ballistic missiles (SLBMs) and intercontinental ballistic missiles (ICBMs).

He died on 31 March 1967, and his ashes were placed in the Kremlin Wall facing Red Square, a high honor for Soviet military leaders.

Article about Malinovsky
Seweryn Bailer, "Rodion Yakovlevich Malinovsky," in *Soviet Leaders,* edited by George W. Simmons (New York: Cromwell, 1967), pp. 126–137.

General References
Dale R. Herspring, *The Soviet High Command, 1967–1989: Personalities and Politics* (Princeton, N.J.: Princeton University Press, 1990);

Edward L. Warner, *The Military in Contemporary Soviet Politics: An Institutional Analysis* (New York: Praeger, 1977).

– M. B.

SEE ALSO THESE RELATED ENTRIES

Leonid Brezhnev, 2; Sergei Gorshkov, 2; Nikita Khrushchev, 2; Georgi Zhukov, 2.

Mao Zedong

Chairman of the Chinese Communist Party, 1949–1959, 1966–1976

Born Shaoshan, China, 26 December 1893
Died Beijing, People's Republic of China, 9 September 1976

Chairman Mao Zedong was one of the most significant political figures of the twentieth century. As the driving force behind the People's Republic of China (PRC) from its inception in 1949 to his death in September 1976, Mao dominated every area of Chinese politics. He was the PRC's chief strategist, statesman, and political philosopher. Mao was influenced by the writings of Karl Marx and V. I. Lenin but was also inescapably a Chinese nationalist. He believed that the communist revolution in China was distinct from all others because of the weight of its history and culture.

Even if Mao had not lived to lead China for three decades, his pre-1949 achievements would have guaranteed his place in Chinese history. His greatest feat was directing the Chinese communists to a stunning victory over Chiang Kai-shek's nationalists, finally uniting the most populous nation in the world and putting it at peace. Still, due to the Cold War chill, he was shunned by the United States, which did not meet with him until 1972. In his years as leader Mao transformed every aspect of China. His commitment to revolutionize China through struggle, however, led to a series of regrettable programs in the 1950s and 1960s which attempted political, economic, and social change.

Mao Zedong was born in the village of Shaoshan in Hunan province. His mother was a devout Buddhist and his father, as described by Mao, a rich peasant. As a child Mao was bright, sensitive, but impudent, often clashing, sometimes physically, with his demanding father. He left school at the age of thirteen to assist his father on the family farm, but by that time was already well versed in the *Analects of Confucius* and other Chinese literary classics. Young Mao was a voracious reader, who once became so involved in a book he let an ox roam off and eat a neighbor's vegetables, enraging his father. When Mao was fourteen his parents arranged his marriage to a twenty-year-old. He would later claim that the marriage was never consummated. A restless adolescent, he left his father's farm for good at sixteen and entered Hsianghsiang Middle School in Changsha, the capital of Hunan province.

In October 1911 Mao, yearning to help strengthen his native land, joined the Hunan revolutionary army, one of many regional armies that revolted against the Qing Dynasty and forced its downfall in late 1911. Mao left

Mao Zedong

the army the next year and entered the First Teachers Training School, a Hunan college where he excelled in literature and social science. He also was an activist who was threatened with expulsion after he attempted to organize a student strike protesting the raising of tuition fees.

After graduating in 1918, Mao went north to Beijing University, where he worked in the periodical room of the library. It was there he first read – with only rudimentary understanding – translations of the works of Marx and Lenin. He returned to Hunan in April 1919 and participated in the May Fourth Movement, the enormously influential event that united Chinese youth and intellectuals in their denunciation of foreign imperialism and native weakness.

Chinese Communist Party

Beginning in 1920, after having read Marx and Friedrich Engels's *Communist Manifesto* (1848) and seeing in it the inspiration for a Chinese revolt similar to the Russian Revolution, Mao embraced Marxism as a window to China's future. In July 1921 the Chinese Communist party (CCP) was founded when Mao joined twelve other Chinese and two Comintern envoys on a Shanghai tourist boat to take part in the First Congress of the Communist party in China. Mao was married that year to Yang Kai-hui, a daughter of one of his professors.

In the early 1920s Mao was a respected organizer for the communists in Hunan province and Shanghai. He heartily supported Sun Yat-sen, the patriarch of the Kuomintang (KMT) or Nationalist party, who had been for years planning revolutions to take control of China. Sun allowed the communists to join the nationalist coalition. In 1926 Mao was for a short time in control of the nationalists' propaganda department. His association with the nationalists ended in April 1927 when rabid anticommunist Chiang Kai-shek, who after Sun's death had taken over leadership of the nationalists in 1925, ordered his troops to wipe out the communists in Shanghai. The "Shanghai Massacre" was the start of fighting between the communists and nationalists that would last for more than two decades.

In the autumn of 1927 Mao led a failed communist uprising in Hunan and was captured. Just before meeting the firing squad, he made a dash for it. Mao hid for hours in tall grass, barely escaping his executioners. Yet, despite his bravery, he was demoted for his frequent spats with communist leaders, such as his nemesis Li Li-san. The future chairman argued for a revolution focused on peasants, while most others, such as Li, stressed a revolution of the urban proletariat.

The early 1930s were tragic and frustrating for Mao. His wife was executed by the nationalists in 1930 (he remarried later that year to eighteen-year-old He Zizhen). The new communist leaders, called the 28 Bolsheviks for their schooling in the Soviet Union and adherence to Russian-style principles of revolution, rejected Mao's theories on building a peasant base for revolt and initiating guerrilla warfare. Although he was made the titular leader of the communist government, he was cast aside as a policymaker.

The Long March

In October 1934, as Chiang Kai-shek's army prepared to levy the final crushing defeat on the communists, Mao joined his cohorts in the epic Long March retreat. When the communists left their base in Jiangxi province, Mao was a subordinate without allies among the leadership. His fortunes changed in February 1935, when the communists made camp at Zunyi. Mao's trenchant criticisms of the CCP leaders' sloppy military tactics garnered vocal support from most party members, including chairman of the Military Council Zhou Enlai. After the Zunyi Conference, Mao was effectively the leader of the CCP, a role he would not relinquish until his death.

Mao and the approximately nine thousand communists who survived the year-long march settled in Yenan in Shanxi province. Yenan became the capital of the communists, the place where Mao the philosopher, and Mao the leader, came of age.

The Xian Incident

In December 1936, as he was planning his sixth extermination campaign against the communists, Chiang Kai-shek was captured in the city of Xian by his own troops, who thought it was more prudent to fight the Japanese, who had invaded China's northeastern provinces (Manchuria), rather than the CCP. Although some question remains as to the relationship between nationalist renegade Marshal Zhang Xueliang and the CCP, most scholars believe the kidnapping — which came to be known as the Xian incident — was at least a mild surprise to the communists. After some debate by CCP leaders over their response to the kidnapping, Mao chose to take the lenient route and sent Zhou Enlai to negotiate for Chiang's release. The successful negotiations had two monumental effects. First, after Chiang was freed, he turned his attention to fighting the Japanese, which allowed the communists a respite from the bloody extermination campaigns. Second, Zhou's bargaining convinced many skeptical Chinese that the CCP was sincerely fighting to strengthen China.

The Cult of Mao

Mao's years in Yenan further enhanced the future chairman's image, which began to take shape on the Long March, when his almost "superhuman" ability to block out physical suffering awed his comrades. After the march, in Yenan, a kind of hero worship — which would come to be known as the cult of Mao — began with portraits of Mao being displayed and his calligraphy exhibited in public. Mao took on the aura of a demigod. Other party members began to refer to him as a "genius" and "our savior."

His output at Yenan only served to enhance his standing among the communists. Many of Mao's early philosophical and military tracts were completed while he sat inside his cave dwelling in the Yenan hills. His classic treatise on China's perspective of World War II, "On Protracted War," was written in nine days, during which time Mao was so focused on his work that he refused to eat and sleep. After each page was completed and tossed into a stack, Mao squeezed a rock to relax his numb fingers. On the eighth day Mao felt faint and had to be treated by a doctor who pleaded with him to rest. On the next day Mao finished the text, which would fill eighty printed pages.

Mao's military writings are lively, descriptive, and nationalistic. In "Problems of Strategy in the Anti-Japanese Guerrilla War," he outlines what came to be the Chinese revolutionary military doctrine – the People's War, in which China's greatest strength – its enormous population – would be used to defeat the opposition: trading space for time with an invading force, China's large populace would lure and eventually surround the enemy.

Maoism

Mao also formulated his theories on Chinese-style communism – or Maoism – between 1936 and 1945 in Shanxi province. He used Karl Marx's radical philosophy as a foundation, but believed the CCP must adapt communism to the pragmatism inherent to Chinese culture. He believed true communism must be learned through experience. He often railed at party members who accepted Marxist doctrine without "investigating" it. Mao differed from Marx in some critical areas of socialist philosophy. Mao believed that the slave society could jump directly into socialism, as opposed to Marx, who saw as necessary the existence of feudal and capitalist phases prior to socialism. Moreover, whereas Marx foresaw an urban-led revolution, Mao emphasized the importance of peasants as the "main force" behind a revolution.

Before the end of World War II, Mao divorced He Zizhen and married Lan Ping. Lan, who later renamed herself Jiang Qing, was an attractive and ambitious actress – whose film career had not been very successful – and a radical, who had served in the communist underground. She caught the roving eye of Mao after a speech he gave at the Academy of Art. There is no known date for the marriage, but by 1939 they were living together and by early 1941 had had a daughter.

Negotiations Between the Nationalists and the Communists

In 1944 the United States tried to help negotiate peace between Chiang and Mao by sending Ambassador Patrick Hurley – an anticommunist with little knowledge of Chinese affairs – to act as mediator. Hurley was ill-prepared for his task, which would have been herculean for the finest diplomat. As he got off the plane in Yenan in late 1944, he addressed Mao Zedong by either "Moose Dung" or "Mouse Tongue," depending on which of Hurley's aides is to be believed. Mao later said to one of his generals, "this fellow's a clown." From then on, in communist circles, Hurley was known as "the Clown."

Mao's feelings toward the United States during the mid 1940s were not hostile. Much of his understanding

of the United States derived from his reading of accounts of its colonial army's defeat of the "imperialist" British in the American Revolution. Mao tried to pass a secret message to President Franklin D. Roosevelt in January 1945 proposing a visit to Washington, but the note was intercepted by the pro-Chiang Hurley and promptly destroyed. It would be another twenty-seven years before Mao met a U.S. president.

Negotiations between the two sides having failed, fighting between the communists and nationalists resumed in mid 1946. Mao now felt contempt for the United States, which was funneling millions of dollars into Chiang's government and supplying his troops with arms. By March 1947 the nationalists appeared on the verge of destroying the communists. They had captured the communist enclave in Yenan and held a three-to-one troop advantage and five-to-one weapons advantage. Chiang predicted the war would last only three months more.

Yet, as was the case in the fall of 1934, Mao's men would not be destroyed. Mao's Yenan forces, which numbered only 20,000, faced a nationalist army of 230,000. Mao's general, Peng Dehuai, however, was able to lure the nationalists to the north. The tactic caused Chiang's army to overextend itself, and by November 1948 the nationalists were being outnumbered. The shocking communist victory came less than a year later. Just months before, both the Soviet Union and the United States had supported a seemingly invincible Chiang. Now Mao sat on the throne. The Dwight D. Eisenhower administration was so miffed at the "loss of China" that it purged the China experts – labeled CCP sympathizers – from the U.S. State Department.

In the early 1950s Mao stressed domestic restructuring. In rural China wealthy landowners gradually disappeared, and their land was redistributed to those who formerly owned little or nothing. For many it was liberating to confiscate property from the often-tyrannical landowners. The cities began to stress small neighborhood industries instead of large factories which had relied on foreigners. Mao intended to transform the cities into centers of "production" rather than "consumption." The government also instituted communist thought reform. The hundreds of thousands who refused to comply were either executed or placed in labor camps.

The Korean War

Mao, "The Great Helmsman," made his first major foreign policy decision in October 1950, committing some 250,000 troops to fight against United Nations (UN) forces in Korea. His decision was based on the maintenance of Chinese security, and most scholars feel that Soviet leader Joseph Stalin played a significant role in convincing Mao that if he did not attack, General

Douglas MacArthur's troops would strike China. The conflict in Korea provided a perfect scenario for Stalin: the Soviet army would stay at home, leaving the Chinese to protect Korea's fledgling communists. The Soviets monetarily profited from China's involvement in the war. China paid full market prices for all of the Soviet arms used in Korea and, more incredibly, the room and board for Soviet journalists who went to cover the war.

China's military – the People's Liberation Army (PLA) – met with mixed success during the 1950s. The PLA would try twice and fail to dislodge Chiang Kai-shek from Taiwan in 1955 and 1958. Mao lost his best opportunity to finish off the nationalists and lost his son, Anying, who was killed by a bomb blast in the Korean hills.

"Hundred Flowers Campaign"

The luster of Mao began to dull in 1956 when a series of speeches he gave encouraging free speech evolved into the "Hundred Flowers Campaign." By releasing the party's reins on the press and granting freedoms to activists, Mao hoped to create mass enthusiasm for his economic programs. Instead, he received sharp criticism from liberal intellectuals who questioned the CCP's single-party rule. Mao was forced to dump the program in early 1957.

"Great Leap Forward"

In the following year Mao introduced the ambitious "Great Leap Forward" (GLF) economic plan. The PRC economy had shown growth in the early 1950s, but it was unremarkable by Mao's standards. He sought to overcome China's deficiencies with raw energy and emotional fervor. The GLF which was more of an intellectual concept than an economic plan, sought to bypass capitalism and take China directly into socialism. The plan projected industrial output to equal that of Great Britain's in less than two decades. To accomplish this task the CCP organized labor into larger units called "people's communes," where mass euphoria would enhance China's production. Mao succeeded in driving Chinese society to its limits, but before the end of 1958 he was already admitting the GLF's failures. The GLF would cause catastrophic famine in the early 1960s.

The "Hundred Flowers" and the GLF diminished Mao's status within the party. The first challenge to his authority came from Defense Minister Peng Dehuai at the CCP plenum in Lushan in July and August 1959. Peng, who was incapable of subtlety, lashed out at the GLF's unsophisticated economic planning and demanded Mao share the blame for the travesty. Mao was hurt and threatened to abandon the CCP and "build a new Red Army, starting over," unless Peng was removed. Peng was sacked before the end of the plenum, but the voting was close. Peng's strong showing, especially among military men, illustrated just how far Mao's crown had slipped.

Mao's domestic policies were met with derision from the Soviet Union. It was not the first time he had clashed with the Soviets. Mao first went to the Soviet Union in December 1949 to ask Stalin for aid to the new communist nation. Stalin kept Mao waiting for days at a time, and when he did see the chairman, he treated him as a student rather than an equal. After two frustrating months, Mao left with a scant agreement.

Relations with the Soviets

The relationship between Mao and Stalin's successor, Nikita S. Khrushchev, was even more strained. When Khrushchev went to Beijing in late 1954 to visit with Mao, he was shocked to hear the Great Helmsman's views on nuclear weapons. Mao failed to grasp the meaning of the nuclear revolution in its early days. He dismissed the atom bomb as a "paper tiger." Mao knew of the destructive capabilities of the bomb from the razing of Hiroshima and Nagasaki, but his military philosophy would not allow him to perceive the bomb as the ultimate weapon. Nuclear weapons, Mao believed, could not alone defeat China, for men were still more powerful than any weapon. Khrushchev later said, "I tried to explain to him that one or two missiles would turn all the divisions in China to dust."

Mao felt he was the heir to Stalin as leader of the communist world. When Khrushchev blasted Stalin in 1956, Mao felt threatened. Even though he did not get along with Stalin, he had too much respect for the Russian to carp publicly. That the Soviets did not inform Mao before the de-Stalinization speech was delivered further infuriated Mao. When Khrushchev went to China in October 1959 for the tenth anniversary of the PRC, he insulted Mao by flying into Beijing directly from the United States. He also upset Mao by commending President Eisenhower for his peaceful actions and referred to the Soviet Union and the United States as the world's policemen.

The Sino-Soviet relationship became openly hostile in mid 1960 when, almost overnight, the Soviets withdrew all of their advisers from China, including assistance to China's nuclear bomb project. After two more years of public bickering, during which time each side took its turn raising the volume of excoriations, Mao delivered the communist version of a low blow by announcing that the Soviet leadership was "usurped by revisionists." In the winter of 1964–1965 Mao declared the Soviets to be worse than the Americans, reasoning that both were "bastards" but the Russians were also "liars." Relations between China and the Soviet Union did not improve until long after Mao's death.

In 1959, as a result of the GLF debacle, Mao withdrew from the day-to-day operations of the party and government, allowing President Liu Xiaoqi and General Secretary Deng Xiaoping to assume power. He withdrew to his home province of Hunan to do his three favorite things — read, think, and write poetry. During this period Mao appeared to be an unchanged man. He was earthy and simple in needs. He spoke obliquely, always suggesting he was uttering the profound. He had, however, lost his customary spark: the expert on "struggle" began to talk about mortality. His most satisfying moments during his absence from government came in 1964 when Khrushchev was ousted in favor of Leonid Brezhnev and the PRC detonated its first nuclear device.

Although he rarely attended party functions, the chairman maintained his influence in Chinese foreign policy. Mao believed that China should attempt to "export" its communist revolution to Africa. Instead of playing the "younger brother" to the Soviet Union, China would act as "older brother" to the newly independent African nations. But, despite success in convincing foreign communist movements of its good intentions, China rarely was able to assist with money or arms.

The Cultural Revolution

While Liu and Deng turned to market mechanisms to correct China's shattered economy, Mao seethed. Not only had his role in the party been diminished, but the CCP had become too bureaucratized. Liu had steered the communists toward pragmatism. Beginning in 1965 Mao began to construct an elaborate scheme to reintroduce struggle to Chinese society. "The Great Proletarian Cultural Revolution" began with a seemingly innocent doctrinal debate resulting in the ouster of the vice-mayor of Beijing, Peng Zhen. But within months Chinese society was tearing apart at the seams.

Mao recruited young Chinese, called Red Guards, to "struggle against the party." The chairman viewed children as untainted by old ideas, therefore able to rebel effectively against the system. The Red Guards took to the streets, destroying whatever they perceived as "bourgeois." Their central target was the CCP. Armed with their ideological daggers, *Quotations of Chairman Mao Tsetung* (1966) — also known as "The Little Red Book" — the Red Guards harassed provincial and national leaders, placing them under arrest and parading them through the streets. By the end of 1968 Liu and Deng were under arrest. Red Guard violence was commonplace. Hundreds of thousands of Chinese were either killed or maimed by the rampaging youths.

Mao's main cohorts during the Cultural Revolution were his wife Jiang Qing and Defense Minister Lin Biao. Jiang was the culture minister in charge of "politically correct" art. Lin Biao was the architect for the resurgence

of the "Cult of Mao." He oversaw the public display of statues, portraits, and posters of Mao which adorned the streets of every town in China. He also put into publication the Little Red Book.

Mao realized the Red Guards had become virtually uncontrollable in 1968 and sent most of them to "struggle" in the countryside. He also had to cope with an increasingly ambitious Lin Biao, who in 1969 was written into the PRC constitution as Mao's successor. As the CCP's "official" version of the story is told, after Lin failed to manipulate the government structure so as to assure himself of ultimate power after Mao died, he schemed to assassinate the Great Helmsman. When his plan collapsed in the summer of 1971, he and his family attempted to escape to the Soviet Union. He died when his plane ran out of fuel and crashed in Mongolia.

Improved Relations with the United States

Mao's final great moment occurred on the heels of a near border war with the Soviets over a disputed island in the Ussuri River in March 1969. The brief scuffle confirmed Mao's opinion that the Soviets were China's greatest threat. Mao wanted to use the United States, which he felt was a declining power, as a buffer against the Soviet Union, a rising one. In February 1972 he met with President Richard M. Nixon in Beijing in a visit that captivated the world. The meeting was ironic for Nixon, who was vice-president in the administration that had threatened China with nuclear attack three times — during the Korean War and the Taiwan Straits crises in 1955 and 1958.

In a single trip Nixon had thawed the Cold War freeze that had lasted for two decades between the two countries. Mao relished playing the part of emperor receiving foreign dignitaries. He joked and mingled with his guests, especially National Security Adviser Henry Kissinger. The summit produced the Shanghai Communiqué in which the United States stated that it did not challenge the PRC view that Taiwan was a part of China and that it hoped the two would settle their differences peacefully. Although both sides agreed to disagree on certain philosophical issues, the pact was a phenomenal success for both Mao and Nixon.

Mao became less active in government affairs during the 1970s. He was forced to recall many of those purged, such as Deng Xiaoping, to fill positions that required experience the cultural revolutionary sycophants simply did not possess. During the last year of his life, suffering from Parkinson's disease, Mao tried to balance the party factions that were positioning to succeed him. He could not bear to see Jiang Qing and her "Gang of Four" radicals assume power, but he also rejected the pragmatic bloc built by Zhou Enlai. The Great Helmsman, with his typical unpredictability, chose little-known Hua Guofeng to ascend to chairman. Mao Zedong died on 9 September 1976.

Books by Mao

Selected Works of Mao Tse-tung, volumes 1 and 2 (Beijing: People's Publishing Company, 1951, 1952, 1953, 1960);

Quotations of Chairman Mao Tse-tung (Beijing: Foreign Language Press, 1966);

Selected Works of Mao Tse-tung, volume 5 (Beijing: Foreign Language Press, 1977).

Books about Mao

Jerome Ch'en, *Mao and the Chinese Revolution* (London: Oxford University Press, 1965);

Samuel B. Griffith, *Mao Tse-tung on Guerrilla Warfare* (New York: Praeger, 1961);

Roderick MacFarquhar, *The Origins of the Cultural Revolution*, volumes 1 and 2 (Oxford: Oxford University Press, 1974–1988);

Stuart Schram, *Mao Talks to the People* (New York: Pantheon, 1974);

Stuart Schram, *Mao Tse-tung* (New York: Simon & Schuster, 1966);

Ross Terrill, *Mao* (New York: Harper & Row, 1980).

General References

Edgar Snow, *Random Notes on Red China, 1936–1945* (Cambridge: Chinese Economic and Political Studies, Harvard University; distributed by Harvard University Press, 1957);

Edgar Snow, *Red Star over China* (London: Gollancz, 1937);

Roxane Witke, *Comrade Chiang Ch'ing* (Boston: Little, Brown, 1977).

– K. W. M.

SEE ALSO THESE RELATED ENTRIES

Chiang Kai-shek, 2; Deng Xiaoping, 2; Hua Guofeng, 2; Nikita Khrushchev, 2; Henry Kissinger, 1; Lin Biao, 2; Liu Shaoqi, 2; Richard M. Nixon, 1; Peng Dehuai, 2; Joseph Stalin, 2; Zhou Enlai, 2.

Tadeusz Mazowiecki

Prime Minister of Poland, 1989–1990
Born Plock, Poland, 18 April 1927

Tadeusz Mazowiecki, lay Catholic activist and the first noncommunist prime minister of Poland since the communist takeover, was born to a family of the intelligentsia. Trained as a lawyer and journalist, after World War II he became chairman of the Academic Publishing Cooperative in Warsaw. In 1948 he was dismissed by Poland's Stalinist authorities and charged with promoting "clericalism" because of his Catholic sympathies. Mazowiecki became a member of PAX, the Roman Catholic Association, which was tolerated by the communists in an attempt to break the unity of the church. He was a regular contributor to its various publications and then chief editor of a PAX publication, the *Wroclaw Catholic Weekly*. He was dismissed in 1955, under pressure from the regime, and suspended as a PAX member because of his criticisms of the Communist party.

Dissent in the 1960s

After a period of unemployment in the 1950s, Mazowiecki became active in the Young Intelligentsia Club movement during the 1960s and was cofounder and chief editor of the Catholic monthly *Wiez* (Bond) in 1968. During a period of relative tolerance under Wladyslaw Gomulka's regime, Mazowiecki was also a Catholic deputy to the Polish parliament. As a member of the parliamentary Catholic association *Znak* (Sign), he was elected leader of a small opposition group seeking to soften and change the communist dictatorship from within the parliamentary structures. He campaigned in particular for educational pluralism and the autonomy of Polish universities.

During the 1968 crackdown on the intelligentsia by the Gomulka government, Mazowiecki coauthored a letter sent by Catholic deputies to the prime minister protesting the banning of the patriotic play *Dziady* (Forefathers) and the brutal militia attacks on student demonstrators. He became involved in workers' issues in December 1970, when he tried to organize a parliamentary commission to investigate the killing of several dozen shipyard workers by security forces in Gdansk and Szczecin. During the 1970s he experienced periods of official tolerance and repression and was sharply criticized by government representatives for speaking out in 1976 about the need for free trade unions.

Juliusz Sokolowski / Delta

Tadeusz Mazowiecki

Solidarity

Mazowiecki became increasingly involved in extraparliamentary intellectual dissident activities in the late 1970s, and was cofounder of the Program Council of the Society for Academic Courses (the independent "Flying University"). When mass strikes broke out around the country in the summer of 1980, Mazowiecki, together with other intellectuals, went to the Gdansk shipyards to lend his support and advice to striking workers. He became head of the Experts Team in the shipyards and a close adviser to Solidarity leader Lech Walesa. Mazowiecki was also coeditor of the Solidarity statutes and a top adviser to the union's National Consultative Commission. He took part in all negotiations with the government and was appointed chief editor of the official Solidarity weekly, *Tygodnik Solidarnosc.*

214

Martial Law

After the declaration of martial law by General Wojciech Jaruzelski in December 1981, Mazowiecki was interned with several hundred other dissident intellectuals and trade union leaders and released a year later. He continued to be active in opposition and church intelligentsia circles and became an adviser to the Polish primate, Jozef Cardinal Glemp. He served as chairman of the primate's Social Council, which aided the victims of martial law, and he became intensely involved in the church-related Catholic Intelligentsia Clubs (KIK).

Prime Minister

In February 1989 Mazowiecki was a leading participant in the roundtable negotiations with the regime which led to the formation of a Solidarity-led government. In August 1989 he was appointed prime minister in an astute compromise arrangement between Solidarity, the church, and the wavering communist party. Benefiting from substantial public trust, Mazowiecki's government launched a drastic program of economic restructuring in January 1990 to transform the ossified command economy into a workable market system.

Increasing friction between Mazowiecki and Walesa over the pace of political reform led to a government reshuffle in July 1990, in which three communist ministers were ousted from the cabinet. Continuous tensions within the Solidarity leadership over the pace of political reform led to presidential elections in November and December 1990, in which Mazowiecki stood as a candidate. During the first round of balloting, Mazowiecki received a disappointing proportion of votes and eventually lost the presidency to Walesa.

On the eve of the elections Mazowiecki signed a historic treaty with West Germany, in which the Bonn government formally accepted the validity of the Polish-German border along the Oder and Neisse rivers. This unresolved issue had exacerbated tensions between the two states during the reunification of Germany, and it led the Mazowiecki government to hesitate over the departure of Soviet troops from Polish soil. Mazowiecki's administration also pursued closer ties with other West European countries and the United States. This policy was designed to bring Poland closer toward the European Common Market and other pan-European institutions and to encourage Western investment in the country.

General Reference

Jadwiga Staniszkis, *Poland's Self-Limiting Revolution* (Princeton, N.J.: Princeton University Press, 1984).

—J. B. and A. B.

SEE ALSO THESE RELATED ENTRIES

Wladyslaw Gomulka, 2; Wojciech Jaruzelski, 2; Helmut Kohl, 1; Lech Walesa, 2.

Golda Meir

Prime Minister of Israel, 1969–1974
Born Kiev, Russia, 3 May 1898
Died Jerusalem, Israel, 8 December 1978

Golda Meir was Israel's fourth prime minister, serving from 1969 until her resignation in 1974, after the release of the Agranat Commission report on her government's conduct on the eve of the 1973 Arab-Israeli war. She was the only woman to head the state of Israel and one of a handful to have led modern nations. When people would ask Meir, who had a reputation for toughness, if she felt handicapped at being a woman minister, she would reply: "I don't know. I've never tried to be a man."

Golda Mabovitch was born in Kiev, Russia, to a dirt-poor Jewish family. The family emigrated to the United States in 1906. During her teens, while living with her parents in Milwaukee, Wisconsin, and her sister, Sheyna, in Denver, Colorado, she came into contact with numerous socialist Zionists and joined Poalei Zion (Workers of Zion) in 1915. With the November 1917 passage of the Balfour Declaration, in which Sir Arthur Balfour committed the British to the support of the creation of a Jewish homeland in Palestine, she decided to emigrate to Palestine, persuading her new husband, Morris Meyerson, with whom she later had two children, to join her.

The Labor Party

For the next decade Golda Meyerson (later Meir) worked for the Histadrut, the Zionist federation of trade unions. When the Labor party was formed in 1930, she became a leading figure in it. Meir opposed partition of Palestine into two states, one Arab and one Jewish, and throughout her political life perpetuated the idea that the Palestinians were a potential fifth column for Israel. When the British arrested Zionist leaders in Palestine in 1946, after a series of bombings of British military installations, Meir was one of the few left free, a circumstance that helped her to gain political importance.

Labor Minister

After the formation of the state of Israel in 1948, Meir became Israel's first ambassador to Moscow but was called back to join the Knesset (parliament) after seven months. During her tenure as labor minister from 1949 to 1956, Meir's main responsibility was overseeing the absorption of Jewish immigrants, tens of thousands of whom were then living in tent cities.

Gale International Portrait Gallery

Golda Meir

In 1956 she became foreign minister. David Ben-Gurion, who was then prime minister, persuaded her to take on the Hebrew-sounding name Meir. She was among the three top Israelis to coordinate with France and Britain the 1956 attack on Egypt, after it nationalized the Suez Canal and closed the Strait of Tiran. The straits, linking the Gulf of 'Aqaba and the Red Sea, were Israel's only southern maritime outlet. During her decade-long tenure as foreign minister, Meir pursued a close relationship with the United States and gained significant quantities of arms from it. She also set up technical assistance programs with African states, a policy that persisted until the early 1970s. After leaving the government in 1966, Meir served until July 1968 as secretary-general of the Labor party.

Prime Minister

In March 1969, following the death of Levi Eshkol, Meir became prime minister. Again, she focused on keeping arms flowing from the United States and resisting initiatives to negotiate with the Palestinians. During this time numerous Jewish settlements were set up on the newly occupied West Bank and Gaza Strip.

When war was about to break out in October 1973, Meir opted against a preemptive attack against the massing forces of Egypt and Syria, in part because of warnings from the United States. Israel came close to losing the war before it mobilized and fought to an inconclusive end, which both sides would claim as victories. Despite the war, Meir won the December 1973 election. Although the Agranat Commission's report cleared her government of responsibility for the Israeli military's lack of preparedness for the war, she announced her resignation and was succeeded by Yitzhak Rabin the following April.

Meir, an unassuming and down-to-earth politician, was accused by her opponents as being stubborn and unsophisticated. Her supporters cherished her warmth and simplicity (during cabinet meetings at her home, she would don an apron and serve home-baked cookies.) A chain-smoker, she was also known for her sharp tongue and self-effacing wit ("anyone who wants to be the prime minister – deserves it," she once said.) She died in Jerusalem on 8 December 1978.

Book by Meir

My Life (New York: Putnam's, 1975).

General Reference

Simha Flapan, *The Birth of Israel: Myths and Realities* (New York: Pantheon, 1987).

– A. F.

SEE ALSO THESE RELATED ENTRIES
David Ben-Gurion, 2; Yitzhak Rabin, 2.

Mengistu Haile Mariam

Head of State of Ethiopia, 1977–1991
Born Wallamo, Ethiopia, 1937

Mengistu Haile Mariam was the Ethiopian head of state from 1977 to 1991, when he was ousted from power by Tigrean and Eritrean rebels. He had first risen to prominence in the 1974 coup that removed Emperor Haile Selassie I from power.

Although very little is known about his exact birthplace, birth date, and early background, Mengistu was raised in the house of a provincial governor and later entered the Holeta Military Academy. Although of obscure origins, Mengistu rose quickly through the ranks after he joined the army.

Lieutenant Colonel Mengistu was a dominant figure during the military's gradual seizure of power, the so-called creeping revolution, that ousted pro-West emperor Haile Selassie I, who was unable to deal with the country's worsening problems, including a devastating drought and secessionist guerrilla wars. By February 1974 the country was hurled into a full-fledged political crisis, precipitated by the monarchy's unpopular war against secessionist rebels in the provinces of Eritrea and Tigre. The secessionist wars and political unrest had politicized the junior and senior officers in the military and undermined the military's morale. Trained and equipped by the United States, the Ethiopian military was one of the largest in Africa. Junior officers organized the Dergue, or DERG, the clandestine military coordinating committee that progressively undermined the monarchy and eliminated political opposition at large. Lieutenant Colonel Mengistu Haile Mariam was regarded as a key figure in the Dergue.

Political Instability

The military consummated its drawn-out coup d'état on 12 September 1974 with the official ouster of Emperor Selassie from power and the announcement of a provisional military government. After the coup Mengistu was named first vice-chairman of the Provisional Military Administrative Council (PMAC), commonly referred to as the DERG, which declared Ethiopia a socialist state in December. The DERG, however, assumed power without any real internal ideological cohesion or political program aside from a vague commitment to socialism. The DERG's provisional military government was headed by Lieutenant General Aman Mikael Andom, but the junta was immediately consumed by an intense power struggle initiated by Mengistu and his supporters. Mengistu re-

Mengistu Haile Mariam

portedly orchestrated the November 1974 assassination of General Andom, who was replaced with a new figurehead chairman, Brigadier General Teferi Bante. The assassination of Andom and his supporters within the DERG was also followed with the execution of several members of the old regime.

Although he did not have full control of the DERG, Mengistu was regarded as the real power behind the figurehead leadership. In December 1976 he was reassigned to the Council of Ministers as chairman in an attempt to limit the power of individual members. Mengistu retaliated on 3 February 1977 by orchestrating a countercoup in which his followers, the so-called Flame Brigade, assassinated DERG chairman Bante and his supporters during an emergency meeting. After Mengistu's pro-Soviet faction had seized control of the DERG, Mengistu announced that he had foiled an attempted counterrevolutionary coup, and he subsequently proceeded to execute systematically his opponents within and outside the regime. To broaden his support base he briefly associated with the pro-Soviet All-Ethiopian Socialist movement Mei'son, but when violence broke out between the Mei'son and its rival communist organization, the Ethiopian People's Revolutionary party (EPRP), Mengistu eliminated both organizations, along with his opponents, in a bloody campaign during 1977 and 1978 that came to be known as the red terror. Mengistu resorted frequently to red terror tactics to eliminate personal enemies and opponents of the regime.

The Tigrean and Eritrean Rebels

The precarious internal security of Ethiopia, a longstanding American client, was further aggravated by the escalating secessionist war in Eritrea and Tigre provinces. Unable to secure military assistance from the United States, which in February 1977 announced aid cutbacks to Ethiopia because of its human rights violations, Mengistu turned to the Soviet Union, which had already agreed to provide substantial military assistance in December 1976. After the announcement of the expulsion of American personnel and the closing of the American military installations in Ethiopia in April 1977, Mengistu moved Ethiopia closer to the Soviet Union, which at the time backed Ethiopia's historic rival, Somalia. Having claimed sovereignty over the Ogaden region of western Ethiopia, Somalia actively supported antigovernment, secessionist guerrilla movements in the predominantly Somali-speaking region. In May 1977 the Ogaden war began after Somalia sent its Soviet-equipped army into the Ogaden region to aid secessionist rebels of the Western Somali Liberation Front. The Ogaden war precipitated a superpower confrontation in the strategic Horn of Africa, as Ethiopia and Somalia each switched alignment to the other superpower in the quest for greater military assistance. On 13 November the Mohamed Siad Barre regime in Somalia, which had been the target of Western efforts to wean it away from the Soviet Union, expelled Soviet military personnel and abrogated its treaty of friendship with the Soviet Union and appealed to the United States for assistance. While the administration of President Jimmy Carter tried to avoid direct confrontation with the Soviets, by November the Soviet Union had launched a decisive intervention on behalf of Mengistu's forces with the introduction of an estimated sixteen thousand Cuban combat troops and over one thousand Soviet military personnel over the following months. Mengistu's Soviet/Cuban-led counteroffensive pushed back the Somali forces, which eventually withdrew from the Ogaden region under American pressure.

Internal stability and economic development eluded Mengistu's military dictatorship. Ethiopia's predominantly agricultural economy suffered considerable disruption since the beginning of the 1970s through the combination of failed socialist policies, severe drought, and spreading secessionist wars. The regime was widely criticized for its role in the 1983–1984 catastrophic famine which captured international headlines. The famine, in which an estimated five hundred thousand to 1 million people perished, was exacerbated by the effects of the war as well as the regime's collectivization and resettlement policies. By 1986 approximately 6 million people in the countryside had been resettled in government-constructed villages as part of the regime's counterinsurgency strategy to weaken the rebel's support.

While his regime was implicated for supporting guerrilla movements in neighboring Somalia and the Sudan, Mengistu ruled over a country which itself was threatened with disintegration. Plagued by long-standing ethnic divisions, Ethiopia was home to Africa's longest civil war. The military regime, which inherited secessionist guerrilla movements in the provinces of Eritrea, Tigre, and Oromo, was unable to resolve these protracted secessionist wars either politically or militarily. Rebel advances in Eritrea, which were spearheaded by the Eritrean People's Liberation Front (EPLF), and in Tigre, by the Tigre People's Liberation Front (TPLF), in the late 1980s placed visible strains on the Mengistu regime. His Soviet/Cuban-backed and -equipped military became demoralized and disgruntled as the rebels took control of Eritrea and Tigre. Supplied with advanced weapons by the Soviet-bloc countries, Mengistu assembled the largest army in Africa, with over three hundred thousand men under arms. Relations with the Soviet Union, however, changed after Premier Mikhail S. Gorbachev came to power in March 1985. The new Soviet leadership, no longer willing to finance the costly wars and policies of its Third World clients, began to put pressure on the Mengistu regime to bring the secessionist wars to an end. The long-standing hostility and tense relations between Ethiopia and Somalia continued unabated, resulting in frequent border clashes between the two sides. During the late 1980s, however, the two countries moved toward accommodation, and in 1988 they agreed to cease support for secessionist movements in each other's territory.

In May 1989 Mengistu survived an abortive coup staged by senior military officers, but doubts emerged regarding his hold on power and the future stability of his regime. As the rebel groups advanced on Addis Ababa in early 1991, Mengistu resigned and fled to Zimbabwe on 21 May 1991.

General References

Glen Bailey, *An Analysis of the Ethiopian Revolution* (Athens: Ohio University, 1980);

Fred Halliday, *The Ethiopian Revolution* (London: Verso, 1981);

David Korn, *Ethiopia, the United States, and the Soviet Union* (Carbondale: Southern Illinois University Press, 1986);

Mulatu Wubneh, *Ethiopia: Transition and Development in the Horn of Africa* (Boulder, Colo.: Westview, 1988).

—J. R.-S.

SEE ALSO THESE RELATED ENTRIES

Mikhail Gorbachev, 2; Haile Selassie I, 2.

Adam Michnik

Member of Polish Parliament, 1989–

Adviser to Solidarity Trade Union, 1980–1981

Dissident, 1965–1989

Born Warsaw, Poland, 17 October 1946

Adam Michnik, Polish dissident, intellectual, and parliamentary deputy, was born to a family of the intelligentsia. As a history student at Warsaw University in the 1960s, he was twice suspended by the authorities for dissident activities, and in 1965 he was arrested and held for two months. Michnik was thrown out of the university in 1968 for protesting against the communist government ban on the patriotic play *Dziady* (Forefather's Eve, 1828) by Adam Mickiewicz, and was sentenced to three years in prison. He received amnesty in 1969, but thereafter managed to obtain work only as a welder.

Workers Defense Committee

Michnik was one of the leading members of the Workers Defense Committee (KOR), established in September 1976 to assist workers who had been arrested and beaten up by police following antigovernment protests in several Polish towns three months earlier. He was also a co-organizer and lecturer in the clandestine Society for Academic Courses, or the "Flying University," established in order to bypass official censorship. From 1977 onward Michnik was a chief editor of several samizdat, or underground, publications and a member of the executive board of the newly created Independent Publishing House.

Solidarity and Martial Law

During 1980 and 1981 Michnik was a key adviser to the free trade union Solidarity in the Warsaw region and an adviser to the Steelyard Workers' Commission in the

industrial city of Nowa Huta. He was arrested along with hundreds of union activists and dissident intellectuals during the imposition of martial law by General Wojciech Jaruzelski in December 1981. Nine months later he was accused of trying to overthrow the communist regime by force, even though he consistently advocated peaceful, evolutionary methods for ending totalitarian rule. Although released in 1984, he was arrested again in early 1985, publicly tried along with three of his colleagues, and sentenced to three years in prison. He was given amnesty once again in the summer of 1986, when the government released most of the remaining political prisoners.

1989 Elections

Michnik continued to be an adviser to Solidarity's underground leadership, the Interim Coordinating Commission. He participated in the roundtable negotiations with the regime in February 1989, which set the stage for far-reaching political reforms including the relegalization of Solidarity and the partially democratic parliamentary elections. Michnik became chief editor of the independent daily *Gazeta Wyborcza* (Election Gazette) and was elected to the lower house of parliament (Sejm) in June 1989.

Throughout his long dissident career, Michnik has been a prominent political essayist and a winner of several international awards for his literary work and human rights endeavors. Together with his close associates from the disbanded KOR, Michnik has been critical of Lech

Adam Michnik

Walesa for his alleged dictatorial tendencies after he dismissed several former advisers from leading positions in the Solidarity movement. In turn, Michnik and his intellectual colleagues have been attacked by the Walesa side for trying to create a new political monopoly in the wake of the collapse of communist rule. Michnik became closely associated with the Tadeusz Mazowiecki government which pursued a radical program of economic reform while trying to preserve the Solidarity political coalition. It was criticized for delaying the holding of fully democratic parliamentary elections, for maintaining communists in the government, and for blocking the emergence of a multiparty system in Poland.

Book by Michnik

Letters From Prison and Other Essays (Berkeley: University of California Press, 1985).

General References

Jan Jozef Lipski, *KOR: A History of the Workers Defense Committee* (Berkeley: University of California Press, 1985);

Peter Raina, *Independent Movements in Poland* (London: London School of Economics, 1981).

–J. B. and A. B.

SEE ALSO THESE RELATED ENTRIES
Jacek Kuron, 2; Tadeusz Mazowiecki, 2; Lech Walesa, 2.

Anastas Mikoyan

President of the Soviet Union, 1964–1965

Born Sanain, Russia, 25 November 1895
Died Moscow, Soviet Union, 1978

Anastas Ivanovich Mikoyan, president of the Soviet Union in 1964–1965, was a prominent figure in the Soviet Communist party for half a century. Probably the most widely traveled party official of his time, the "wily Armenian" was best known in the West as a shrewd trade negotiator, diplomatic emissary, and long-term survivor of the vicissitudes of Soviet politics.

Mikoyan was born in the Armenian village of Sanain. Little is known about his early life except that he was graduated from the Armenian Theological Seminary in Tiflis. Instead of entering the priesthood, however, he became interested in politics, lending his support initially to the liberal Kadet party. In 1915 he joined the Bolshevik wing of the Social Democratic party, the faction led by V. I. Lenin that would go on to become the Communist party of the Soviet Union (CPSU).

Russian Civil War

After the Bolsheviks seized power during the October 1917 revolution, Mikoyan remained in the Caucasus, working as a journalist and party organizer but seeing some duty as a squad leader during the initial fighting of the Russian civil war (1917–1920). In September 1918 he escaped from the Caspian seaport of Baku along with many of the local party commissars when Turkish troops took the town. Their boat, however, was captured by rival Socialist Revolutionaries, and most of the Bolsheviks were shot. Mikoyan's escape of this fate has since become a party legend. After serving several months in prison he was released in early 1919.

Early Career in the Soviet Communist Party

During the early 1920s he continued his party work and was increasingly seen as a supporter of Joseph Stalin, a rising contender in the struggle to succeed Lenin. By 1926 Mikoyan had simultaneously become a candidate member of the Politburo, the Communist party's ruling elite, and commissar of foreign and domestic trade. He presided over a 50 percent increase in foreign trade in four years, a feat for which he was named commissar of supply in 1930. He subsequently became commissar of food industry, serving from 1934 to 1938 before returning to oversee foreign trade, which he did until 1949.

During the 1930s, as Stalin maneuvered to attain complete dominance over the party, Mikoyan was one of his

Anastas Mikoyan

most ardent public supporters. This to a large extent ensured his survival during the purge years, when Stalin did away with his rivals. After Stalin's death Mikoyan would become one of his harshest critics, but it is doubtful that during Stalin's lifetime he openly resisted any of the dictator's policies. In 1935, in recognition of his loyalty, Mikoyan was made a full member of the Politburo, a position he would hold until 1966.

Soviet Diplomacy under Stalin

In 1936 he traveled to the United States to observe firsthand the manufacturing methods that he had ad-

222

mired for so long. He had by this time become the Soviet Union's chief negotiator for industry and trade. But as time went on his diplomatic and bargaining skills would often be used by a succession of party general secretaries in areas unrelated to trade.

Mikoyan took part in the negotiations that resulted in the nonaggression pact between the Soviet Union and Germany in 1939. This pact temporarily eased Hitler's worries about a military threat from the Soviet Union and cleared the way for the German invasion of Poland on 1 September.

During World War II Mikoyan strenuously worked to ensure that steady supplies of food and clothing reached the Red Army, efforts for which in 1943 he was awarded the first of four Orders of Lenin. In 1945 he recommended that Stalin drop his demand for direct reparations from Germany and instead establish Soviet-run corporations in occupied Germany to manufacture goods for export to the Soviet Union. Stalin subsequently approved this plan.

In 1949 Mikoyan resigned as minister of foreign trade but continued to advise Soviet leaders on trade matters. The following year he played a key role in the negotiations that led to the Sino-Soviet treaty of 14 February, a pact that helped to keep alive for a time the facade of worldwide communist unity.

It has been speculated that Mikoyan fell out of Stalin's favor in the early 1950s, even though he continued publicly to support the general secretary. Nikita S. Khrushchev, the Soviet leader between 1955 and 1964, claimed that only Stalin's death on 5 March 1953 kept Mikoyan from meeting a "disastrous end."

Soviet Diplomacy under Khrushchev

In the political struggle that followed Stalin's death, Mikoyan bet on the right horse, adroitly putting his full support behind Khrushchev in 1954. One of Khrushchev's strongest supporters, he often acted as the general secretary's emissary abroad.

In 1955 he went with Nikolai Bulganin and Khrushchev – referred to by the Western press as the "team of B and K." – to Yugoslavia in an attempt to mend fences with Marshal Josep Broz Tito, who had been expelled from the world communist movement after a power struggle with Stalin.

At the party's Twentieth Congress in 1956, best remembered for Khrushchev's "secret speech" – his long denunciation of the excesses of Stalinism – Mikoyan was actually the first speaker to attack Stalin publicly. Speaking on 16 February, he also announced his support for "peaceful coexistence" with the West, a central goal of Khrushchev's foreign policy. Mikoyan spoke nine days before Khrushchev, and the whys and wherefores of this

arrangement – if indeed there was one – have never been fully explained.

In 1956 Mikoyan and party ideologist Mikhail Suslov went to Budapest to negotiate with Imre Nagy, whose reformist government threatened to undermine Soviet control of the country. During four tense days in October, the Soviet emissaries assured Nagy that the Soviet Union would not interfere in Hungary's affairs. A week later, however, Soviet troops entered the country to crush the Hungarian revolt.

The Anti-Party Group

The next year Mikoyan was again forced to make a quick political decision when seven of the eleven-member Presidium – as the Politburo was called between 1952 and 1966 – voted to strip Khrushchev of his powers. Mikoyan voted against the conspirators, the "antiparty group," a typically astute move that saved his career after the Central Committee unanimously reversed the Presidium's vote. Afterward, at the party Congress in 1959, Mikoyan would urge clemency for the conspirators in an attempt to limit reprisals by Khrushchev and others.

Foreign Policy Adviser

Mikoyan soon became Khrushchev's principal foreign policy adviser, traveling to Romania and East Germany in 1957 and West Germany, Belgium, and Poland in 1958.

In 1959 he visited the United States to prepare the way for Khrushchev's visit eight months later. He met with President Dwight D. Eisenhower and many government and business leaders, speaking on the need for peaceful coexistence and increased Soviet-American trade. Encountering several hostile demonstrations while in the United States, Mikoyan used his ever-present charm, wit, and sense of humor to project an image that differed from what many Americans had come to expect of a high-level Communist official.

Cuban Missile Crisis

In February 1960 he was in Cuba to negotiate a package of economic aid, which included an agreement whereby the Soviet Union would buy five years' production of Cuban sugar.

Mikoyan returned to the island during the missile crisis in the fall of 1962, a particularly tense time when President John F. Kennedy confronted the Soviet Union over missile bases that it was constructing in Cuba. Khrushchev ultimately backed down in the face of an American naval blockade and a threat to use military force, and he sent Mikoyan to defend the Soviet "compromise" to Cuba's leader, Fidel Castro. Mikoyan later claimed that he was chosen for this duty because he had advised Khrushchev all along against placing missiles in

Cuba. His wife and former childhood sweetheart, Ashkhen, had been terminally ill when Mikoyan left for Cuba. She died on 3 November, but the urgency of his mission kept Mikoyan in Cuba until 26 November, and he sent his son, Sergo, to the funeral in his place.

When Kennedy was assassinated on 22 November 1963 Mikoyan returned to the United States where he represented the Soviet Union at the funeral. In 1964 he went to Japan, where in a speech delivered in May he warned the United States against attacking Cuba.

President of the Soviet Union

Mikoyan became president of the Soviet Union, a largely ceremonial position, on 15 July 1964, succeeding Leonid I. Brezhnev. Later that year Brezhnev deposed Khrushchev to become the party's new general secretary on 14 October. It is unclear what part Mikoyan played in the coup, but afterward his political activities slowed and he stopped traveling abroad. His official activities as president mostly involved receiving foreign visitors to the Soviet Union. He retired on 9 December 1965 and lost his post in the Politburo in April 1966, effectively ending his political career. He had been the last of the "Old Bolsheviks" – those who had known Lenin – and one of the first high-ranking party members allowed to retire peacefully.

Book by Mikoyan
The Memoirs of Anastas Mikoyan (Madison, Conn.: Sphinx Press, 1988).

General Reference
Roy A. Medvedev, *All Stalin's Men* (Garden City, N.Y.: Anchor/Doubleday, 1984).

– M. B.

SEE ALSO THESE RELATED ENTRIES

Fidel Castro Ruz, 2; Cuban Missile Crisis, 3; Nikita S. Khrushchev, 2; Joseph Stalin, 2; 20th Congress of CPUSSR, 3.

József, Cardinal Mindszenty

Primate of Hungary, 1945–1974
Born Csehimindszent, Austria-Hungary, 29 March 1892
Died Vienna, Austria, 6 May 1975

József, Cardinal Mindszenty, a Hungarian Roman Catholic cardinal imprisoned after World War II for his opposition to the communist government, was born into a peasant family in Csehimindszent, in Austria-Hungary. He was politically active from the time he was ordained in June 1915, and was arrested twice and charged with being an enemy of the Austrian-Hapsburg government.

Bishop of Veszprém

In 1944 Mindszenty was consecrated bishop of Veszprém. In November of that year he was arrested by Hungary's Arrow Cross Fascist government for opposing the persecution of Hungarian Jews. He was released from custody at the close of the war and appointed cardinal, primate of Hungary, and archbishop of Esztergom.

Opposition to Communism

Mindszenty strongly opposed the communist takeover of Hungary and protested in particular against the policy of secularizing the Catholic schools. His outspoken views and defense of religious freedoms resulted in accusations of treason and espionage by Hungary's Stalinist regime, and he was arrested in December 1948. His show trial began in February 1949, and the cardinal made a surprising confession of guilt. It was widely believed that he had been drugged, humiliated, and beaten by his jailers before the trial. He was given a life sentence for his alleged crimes, and the government stepped up its religious persecution through the mass arrests of priests and the closing down of monasteries and convents. The State Office of Church Affairs assumed control over all organized religious activities in the country.

The 1956 Revolt

Mindszenty was set free during the Hungarian uprising against communist rule in October 1956. The reformist government of Imre Nagy declared that the charges made against the primate in 1948 "lacked all legal foundations." When the Red Army crushed the revolution in November 1956, the cardinal sought asylum in the United States embassy in Budapest, where he remained until 1971. During his "internal exile" the Soviet-spon-

John Sadovy

József, Cardinal Mindszenty

sored regime reimposed state control over all religious life and launched a campaign to discourage religious practice.

The deadlock between Budapest and the Vatican over Mindszenty's status was not resolved until 1971, when he was recalled by Rome and allowed to leave the country. He settled in Vienna and became a critic of the Vatican's policy of accommodation with Hungary's communist government. He was retired from his posts as archbishop and primate of Hungary in 1974. He died in Vienna on 6 May 1975.

Book by Mindszenty

Memoirs (New York: Macmillan, 1974).

General References
Wilfred Daim, *The Vatican and Eastern Europe* (New York: Ungar, 1970);

Bennett Kovrig, *Communism in Hungary: From Kun to Kadar* (Stanford, Cal.: Hoover Institution Press, 1979).
—J. B. and A. B.

SEE ALSO THESE RELATED ENTRIES
János Kádár, 2; Imre Nagy, 2.

Mobutu Sese Seko
President of Zaire, 1965–1997

Born Lisala, Belgian Congo, 14 October 1930
Died Rabat, Morocco, 7 September 1997

Mobutu Sese Seko was a Zairian military officer and the president of the Republic of Zaire. Pro-Western and autocratic, Mobutu has been one of Africa's longest serving heads of state.

Born Joseph Désiré Mobutu in the village of Lisala, Belgian Congo, Mobutu attended primary and secondary school in the town of Mbandaka. After completing his education he entered the Force Publique, the colonial army of the Belgian Congo (present-day Zaire) in 1950. He left the army in 1956 to work as a journalist until he left for Brussels, Belgium, to study at the Superior Institute of Social Studies. After meeting nationalist leader Patrice Lumumba, Mobutu joined his Congolese National Movement (MNC) in 1958, and became a personal associate of the militant Lumumba. Mobutu was present as an MNC delegate at the Round Table independence talks during January–February 1960 in Brussels, attended by Lumumba and several dozen other nationalist leaders.

Independence and Civil War
After the Congo gained independence on 30 June 1960, Mobutu was named senior aide to Prime Minister Lumumba. The Congo's fragile political coalition and internal stability were violently upset weeks after independence, when on 5 July an army mutiny touched off widespread violence and riots. After the mutiny against Belgian officers, Lumumba appointed Colonel Mobutu chief of staff and sent him around the country to restore order in the army. The army mutiny and the ensuing violence created a chaotic situation in the Congo, which was further complicated when a week later the mineral-rich province of Katanga (now Shaba) seceded under the leadership of Moise-Kapenda Tshombe. The Katanga secession hurled the

Mobutu Sese Seko

Congo into an anarchical situation which quickly drew international (superpower) involvement, including the intervention of United Nations peacekeeping troops. The Congo crisis strained the fragile compromise in the weak central government as differences between the radical Lumumba and the conservative president Joseph Kasavubu resulted in a constitutional breakdown.

With the situation deteriorating progressively, and the central government paralyzed by the political standoff between Lumumba and Kasavubu, on 14 September 1960 Mobutu seized power in what he described as a measure to "neutralize" the civilian leadership. He ordered the arrest of Lumumba, who was later assassinated on 17 January 1961 after Mobutu's troops, with the complicity of American intelligence agents, turned him over to rebel forces. Mobutu ordered the departure of all Soviet-bloc diplomats and personnel. He later formed the College of Commissioners, composed largely of university graduates, to govern the country during the following six months. In January 1961 he returned Kasavubu to power. Over the next five years the Congo crisis continued to border on anarchy with violent uprisings, secessions, rebellions, and the collapse of the central government.

Authenticity and Zairanization

On 24 November 1965 Mobutu and the national army finally seized power during another constitutional crisis, transferring the presidency to himself. Declaring that he would rule for only five years under emergency measures before holding elections, Mobutu suspended parliament, gradually dismantled the political system, and concentrated power in the presidency during the transitional period, which ran from 1965 to 1970. Together with systematically eliminating all possible opposition to his power, he centralized executive and legislative power in his own hands and imposed one-party rule under the 1967 constitution. In 1971 Mobutu introduced his concept of "authenticity," an ill-defined nation-building ideology which stressed the reassertion of tradition and African identity. In addition to changing his own name to Mobutu Sese Seko, the country was renamed Zaire along with other changes of place names. Authenticity was accompanied by "Zairanization," the nationalization of the economy and the transfer of economic resources to African control. Unorganized and haphazard, the Zairanization program met with limited success.

Independent political activity gradually ceased under Mobutu's personal rule through the systematic physical elimination and suppression of opponents. Mobutu fostered close relations with the United States, to which he granted basing and transit rights. Zaire's relations with other African countries, principally Angola, remained tense. Marxist Angola was the base of anti-Mobutu forces consisting of the exiled remnants of the Katangese secessionist rebel forces during the Congo civil war. In March 1977 the Zairian rebels launched an invasion from Angola into mineral-rich Shaba province in an attempt to depose Mobutu. The invading forces were turned back with the assistance of Moroccan troops and military supplies

airlifted by the United States, France, and the United Kingdom. Relations between the conservative, pro-West regime in Zaire and the Marxist-Leninist regime in Angola remained strained and acrimonious following the invasion. In May 1978 the anti-Mobutu paramilitary force based in Angola launched a second invasion into the Shaba province. Accusing the Soviet Union, Cuba, and Angola of orchestrating the invasion, Mobutu appealed to the United States for military assistance. French, Moroccan, and Belgian troops, assisted by an American airlift, helped Mobutu's beleaguered troops repel the invasion. A Pan-African peacekeeping force was installed in the province to monitor activities along the border with Angola.

Mobutu's efforts to play a major role in the Organization of African Unity (OAU) and the Non-Aligned Movement have been only partially successful as a result of his conservative regime's estrangement in Third World politics. His regime was widely criticized for its staunchly pro-Western stance and its normalized relations with South Africa. Zaire became a primary conduit of covert American military aid to the antigovernment rebel forces of the National Union for the Total Liberation of Angola (UNITA) fighting the Marxist Angolan government. During the second half of the 1980s, Mobutu played an important role in international efforts aimed at a regional settlement involving Namibian independence and the Angolan civil war. After the December 1988 American-sponsored tripartite regional accords were signed by Angola, South Africa, and Cuba, Mobutu and other African heads of state sponsored reconciliation talks between the Angolan government and UNITA rebels. On 21 June 1989 President Mobutu mediated a conference between Angolan president José Eduardo dos Santos and rebel leader Jonas Savimbi in Gbadolite, which produced a cease-fire. Mobutu's efforts to recast himself as an African peacebroker, however, did not result in concrete agreements between the warring parties.

The Mobutu regime is regarded as authoritarian and corrupt. Mobutu, who is reported to have billions of dollars in personal wealth, has successfully combined external backing and ruthlessness at home to sustain his rule. In addition to overseeing a rigidly centralized political system in one of Africa's largest and most populous countries, Mobutu has set in motion an elaborate political myth-making campaign. The high degree of official corruption, patrimonialism, and concentration of economic and political power in few hands have led many observers to term the Zairian political system "kleptocratic." Since 1991 Mobutu has faced a growing amount of organized political opposition to his rule. The opposition, which consists of a disparate collection of organizations and parties united under a "National Conference," has pressed for free elections and a multiparty democracy. Mobutu has responded with a measure of restraint and cooperation as well as with outright repression. Faced with a country and continent undergoing an unprecedented movement toward greater political pluralism and democracy, in late 1992 Mobutu signaled his willingness to enter negotiations for political change.

General References

Madeline Kalb, *The Congo Cables: The Cold War in Africa* (New York: Macmillan, 1982);

Crawford Young, *Politics in the Congo: Decolonization and Independence* (Princeton: Princeton University Press, 1965);

Crawford Young, *The Rise and Decline of the Zairian State* (Madison: University of Wisconsin Press, 1985).

–J. R.-S.

SEE ALSO THESE RELATED ENTRIES

Patrice Lumumba, 2; Moise-Kapenda Tshombe, 2.

Mohammad Reza Pahlevi

Shah of Iran, 1941–1979
Born Tehran, Iran, 26 October 1919
Died Cairo, Egypt, 27 July 1980

Mohammad Reza Pahlevi was the shah of Iran from his father's forced abdication in 1941 until the Islamic revolution of 1979.

Considered a bulwark of U.S. foreign policy in the region, the shah acquired weapons for billions of dollars from the United States and tried to modernize Iran along a Western model at a rapid pace. But his rule was authoritarian, his economic policies divisive, and his ties to the United States despised. The combined forces of Iran's Islamic clerics and bazaar merchants ended the self-proclaimed Pahlevi dynasty in 1979 and brought to power the Islamic regime of Ayatollah Ruholla Khomeini.

Mohammad Reza Pahlevi was the first son of Reza Khan, the Iranian army officer who had seized power from the old Qajar dynasty in a 1921 coup, crowned himself Reza Shah Pahlevi, and named himself the first in a line of hereditary kings. Young Mohammad was named crown prince at age six and separated from the women of his family, his mother, elder sister, and twin sister, Princess Ashraf. The boy had a sickly childhood and came close to death at least once, but always managed to recover.

Childhood Experiences

Reza Shah did everything possible to make his boy into a future king. He sent Mohammad to Switzerland for five years where he attended an elegant boarding school and then enrolled him in Tehran's Military Officers' School, from which he was graduated in 1938

Gale International Portrait Gallery
Mohammad Reza Pahlevi

with the rank of second lieutenant. In 1939 Mohammad was married to the daughter of Egypt's King Farouk, Queen Fawzia, with whom he had a daughter before they were divorced. His second marriage, to Soraya Bakhtiar, also ended in divorce because of the shah's unsuccessful attempts to father a son whom he could name crown prince. With his third wife, Farah Diba (Empress Farah Pahlevi), the shah had two sons and two daughters.

Mohammad Reza Pahlevi came to the throne on 10 September 1941 at age twenty-one when his father was forced to abdicate by British and Soviet forces occupying Iran in an invasion designed to keep supply routes open during the war. (Reza Shah died in exile in South Africa three years later.) Despite his pompous title, His Imperial Majesty, Mohammad Reza Pahlevi, King of Kings, Light of the Aryans (Shahanshah, Aryemehr), the shah was a weak ruler, and his support was tenuous. Propped up by the occupying powers as a source of stability in the region, the new shah attempted to get rid of all of his internal enemies.

Mossadegh and Oil Policy

Not long after Mohammad Pahlevi became shah, his father's nemesis, National Front leader Mohammad Mossadegh, gained reelection to the Majlis (parliament). In the late 1940s Mossadegh began a drive to nationalize Iran's oil, the country's main resource and source of income, which had been controlled by the Anglo-Iranian Oil Company (AIOC) under concessionary agreements since 1901. At this time most of the oil-exporting states were attempting to end foreign domination of their resources or at least to change the terms of trade with the major oil companies.

In 1951, after much dispute concerning a new royalty agreement that had been negotiated between the Majlis and the AIOC, Mossadegh was able to push through a bill nationalizing the oil industry. In April 1951 the shah succumbed to popular pressure and appointed Mossadegh prime minister, and by July the new cabinet had drawn up a charter for the new state oil company, the National Iranian Oil Company (NIOC). Not surprisingly, the British were infuriated and began garnering U.S. support to depose Mossadegh.

The 1953 Coup

An international boycott of Iranian oil effectively strangled the Iranian economy. Iran's oil exports plummeted from more than $400 million to less than $2 million during the remainder of Mossadegh's rule. When a confrontation with Mossadegh led the shah to flee the country on 15 August 1953, the Central Intelligence Agency (CIA) and the British intelligence agency, MI6, organized street demonstrations in his support. The shah returned to Tehran on 22 August 1953 and was propped up with

a $45 million grant from the United States, while Mossadegh was put on trial, jailed, and then exiled to the Iranian countryside.

The CIA-sponsored coup that returned the shah to the Peacock Throne marked the beginning of extensive U.S. support for Iran, which was viewed by U.S. policymakers as synonymous with the shah. Between August 1953 and December 1956, for example, the United States sent Iran $414 million of military and economic aid. With the help of the CIA and later the Israeli intelligence agency, Mossad, the shah established SAVAK, the secret police force responsible for internal security and foreign intelligence and known for its brutal methods. Richard Nixon, who was to develop a close relationship with the shah during his presidency, first met the shah during the U.S. intervention of the early 1950s.

The Nixon Doctrine

The Nixon Doctrine was articulated in 1969, and the so-called two-pillar policy — the use of Saudi Arabia and especially Iran to protect U.S. interests (particularly oil) in the region — was implemented in 1971. The United States implemented this policy of using Iran as a military proxy in the Gulf, and against the Soviet Union, during a trip that President Nixon and National Security Adviser Henry Kissinger made to Tehran in May 1972. Nixon and Kissinger promised the shah the unlimited right to buy any nonnuclear weaponry, including F-15 fighter planes, without congressional or Pentagon review, a bypass of the arms acquisition procedure required of all other foreign states. The shah, who dreamed of propelling Iran to the status of regional military superpower, and who now had the oil revenues to do so, seized on the opportunity and began ordering fancy and expensive arms. Between 1972 and mid 1976, for example, the United States sold Iran some $10 billion of military equipment.

The Algiers Accord

Iran's U.S. ties also helped the country reach an agreement, the Algiers Accord of 1975, on a long-standing dispute with Iraq about the border at the Shatt al-Arab waterway. In exchange for Iraq accepting the border, the shah agreed to stop funding Iraq's Kurds, who were fomenting a nationalist rebellion; the covert role of the United States in funneling money through the shah to the Kurds, which began with Nixon's 1972 visit, was later detailed in the Pike Report (1979).

The White Revolution

Domestically, the country was following the path of the White Revolution, which the shah had proclaimed in January 1963. This western-style economic modernization program included six main points: land reform, woman suffrage, forest conservation, rural literacy, denationalization of state-owned industries, and profit sharing for industrial workers.

While he achieved some of these goals, the gap between rich and poor continued to widen and his opposition grew. In 1971, in one of the most remembered excesses, the shah hosted a lavish celebration at Persepolis, replete with silken tents and imported food, in honor of twenty-five hundred years of Persian monarchy. Other excesses, from the billions of dollars of military imports to the grandiose construction projects, however, were common. This spending was entirely dependent on the continued influx of oil revenues at the levels of the boom years after the 1973 price hikes. As the *Economist* notes, the country's history of economic development is "largely an analysis of the utilization of oil revenues and any revenues that could be raised for the creation of new assets."

Iran, the world's second-largest oil exporter (after Saudi Arabia), relied on oil exports in the 1970s for more than 75 percent of government revenues. Within the first year of the boom, government spending had spiraled by 140 percent, and when estimates of oil revenues for the Fifth Plan for economic development (1973–1978) were again raised, the shah doubled projected expenditures, despite warnings that this revised plan could create infrastructural bottlenecks, labor shortages, and inflation.

When oil revenues dropped 12 percent in 1975, the worst fears about that economic plan came true. The infrastructure could not cope with the expansion, labor shortages had forced wages up significantly, and inflation was rampant. The shah, more interested in building a "Great Civilization" and consolidating his own power, increased the budget again and began bartering oil for military goods.

The combination of economic distress and political repression proved to be the shah's downfall. Increasingly isolated and protected by SAVAK, the shah ignored the masses' growing discontent. He traversed the crowded and dirty capital city in a helicopter, far above the daily realities of Tehran's inhabitants.

In the fall of 1977, more than fifty well-known Iranians, some of them National Front leaders, signed an open letter to the shah, calling for a more open political system and the release of all political prisoners, but the shah paid no heed. And that New Year's Eve, President Jimmy Carter toasted the shah at a party at Niavaran Palace outside Tehran: "Iran, because of the great leadership of the shah," said Carter, oblivious to the irony, "is an island of stability in one of the more troubled areas of the world." Only a few days later, strikes began to spread through the country. From then on, as each forty-day mourning period of the previous violence approached, new anti-imperial rioting spread throughout

the country in a cycle that came to be known as "doing the 40-40."

The main voice of the growing rebellion was that of Ayatollah Ruholla Khomeini, an exiled antishah cleric whose message was spreading through Iran on underground cassettes. Khomeini had begun his outspoken opposition to the shah's rule in 1961 and had criticized the tenets of the White Revolution, particularly woman suffrage, since its proclamation. In June 1963, during the religious holidays of Muharram (in memory of the martyrdom of Imam Hussein, grandson of the prophet Mohammad), pictures of Khomeini covered the bazaars; the state, angered, arrested the ayatollah. In response, crowds of pro-Khomeini protesters formed in the bazaars, and government troops began shooting. Rioting spread throughout the country for three days, until the government's violent response quelled the protests. After four such clashes, Khomeini was exiled to Turkey in October 1964, from which he traveled on to Iraq and remained in exile until 1978.

But the coalition that opposed the shah included National Front supporters, students, merchants, and intellectuals, as well as religious Muslims who supported Khomeini's ideas of an Islamic state. In November 1978, after the shah formed an ineffectual military government, Khomeini said from Paris that he would call for civil war if the shah did not step down. At the same time striking oil workers brought petroleum production to a twenty-seven-year low, and antigovernment demonstrators burned trucks and cars on the streets of Teheran; soldiers fired on rioters, bringing the year's death toll into the thousands. In January 1979 the shah finally left the country, bringing much of his billion-dollar fortune with him.

In the fall of 1979, Jimmy Carter granted the shah asylum, and he was flown to New York for medical treatment for cancer. On 27 July 1980 the shah died in a Cairo hospital, where he had been undergoing a final operation. His remains are interred in Cairo's al-Rifai mosque, reportedly awaiting their return to Iran.

During his thirty-eight-year rule, the shah had a profound effect on both Iranian politics and U.S. foreign policy in the Gulf. Internally, numerous antishah forces coalesced during the Iranian revolution, but divisions among the groups quickly appeared. Now, more than a decade after the revolution, under the rule of Hashemi Rafsanjani the ideological divisions are still being played out.

For the United States, the fall of the main "pillar," as the shah's overthrow was viewed in Washington, was a major setback. The weakening of Iran and the preoccupation of its rulers with domestic affairs led to increasing instability in the Gulf region.

Book by Mohammad Reza Pahlevi

Answer to History (Briarcliff Manor, N.Y.: Stein & Day, 1980).

General References

Ervand Abrahamian, *Iran Between Two Revolutions* (Princeton, N.J.: Princeton University Press, 1982);

Said Amir Arjomand, *The Turban for the Crown: The Islamic Revolution in Iran* (New York: Oxford University Press, 1988);

Jahangir Amuzegar, *Iran: An Economic Profile* (Washington, D.C.: Middle East Institute, 1977);

Richard Cottam, "The Iranian Revolution," in *Shi'ism and Social Protest*, edited by Juan R. I. Cole and Nikki R. Keddie (New Haven, Conn.: Yale University Press, 1986);

The Economist Intelligence Unit, *Country Profile: Iran* (London: The Economist Publications, 1986);

Robert Graham, *Iran: The Illusion of Power*, revised edition (New York: St. Martin's Press, 1980);

Edward W. Said, *Covering Islam: How the Media and the Experts Determine How We See the Rest of the World* (New York: Pantheon Books, 1981);

Gary Sick, *All Fall Down: America's Tragic Encounter with Iran* (New York: Penguin Books, 1986);

Thomas Walton, "Economic Development and Revolutionary Upheavals in Iran," *Cambridge Journal of Economics* (1980): 271–292.

                                      – A. F.

SEE ALSO THESE RELATED ENTRIES

Jimmy Carter, 1; Ruholla Musavi Khomeini, 2; Mohammad Mossadegh, 2.

Vyacheslav Michailovich Molotov

Soviet Foreign Minister, 1939–1949, 1953–1956

Born Kukara, Russia, 9 March 1890
Died Moscow, Soviet Union, 8 November 1986

Vyacheslav Michailovich Molotov played an extremely important role in the creation of both Stalinist Russia and the Cold War world. As Joseph Stalin's right-hand man, he helped shape much of Soviet foreign and domestic policy during the Cold War. Indeed, Stalin once said that "if Molotov did not exist, it would be necessary to invent him."

Molotov was born Vyacheslav Michailovich Scriabine in 1890 in Kukara, a small town in central Russia, into a family of relatively well-off peasants. The family provided Vyacheslav with an education and training in music, and by the age of fourteen he had mastered the violin. The family planned on sending Vyacheslav to a conservatory to study music. Russia's defeat at the hands of the Japanese in 1905 and the ensuing revolution, however, politicized the Scriabines. The 1905 Revolution was the culmination of peasant and worker unrest in Russia. In Moscow and Saint Petersburg attempts were made to create an alternative form of government in the form of the soviet – local councils led by the socialists. The revolutionary activity of 1905 convinced Vyacheslav to pursue a more practical education, and with the approval of his family he moved to the city of Kazan. The night before Vyacheslav left for his new home he witnessed a scene that further radicalized him: several peasants were burning one of the local landlords, who had been especially cruel to them.

In Kazan, Vyacheslav took part in the 1905 workers' uprising and began his study of Marxism. He became a member of the Social Democratic party, a Marxist coalition which had split into two factions – the Mensheviks and the Bolsheviks – at a party congress in Brussels in 1903. Within Russia, however, this split was generally ignored since there were too few party members in the country to create factions. By June 1906 Vyacheslav, now working under his chosen pseudonym of Molotov, was expelled from school. He began to spend all his time working on revolutionary activities and spent the summer of 1906 agitating among political exiles in Nolinsk. In the fall he returned to Kazan and continued his work among the Social Democrats.

Exile

Molotov was arrested in April 1909 for his political activism. He was sentenced to two years in internal exile,

Vyacheslav Michailovich Molotov

a relatively mild sentence since the state considered him young enough to be "redeemable." After spending the first year of exile in two isolated hamlets, he was allowed to move to Vologda, not far from Saint Petersburg. While in exile he continued to work for the revolution, agitating among the railroad workers.

After his term of exile ended, Molotov moved to the capital and enrolled in the Saint Petersburg Polytechnic Institute. In the spring of 1912 he met Joseph Stalin. Molotov's aunt provided Stalin, who was constantly being pursued by the police, with a room, and the two men began their lifelong friendship.

Molotov helped found *Pravda*, the party newspaper, in 1912. When Yakov M. Sverdlov, the editor of *Pravda*, and Stalin were exiled to Siberia in 1914 Molotov took over the operation of the paper. After Molotov himself was arrested and confined to a small town outside of Saint Petersburg, he managed to continue his work with *Pravda*, until it was closed in early summer of 1914.

When World War I began Molotov traveled to Moscow where he worked to increase the antiwar sentiment among the workers and teach the techniques of agitation and propaganda. He was arrested again for his revolutionary activities and exiled to Irkutsk in the spring of 1915.

By June of 1916 Molotov managed to escape from his exile in Siberia and return to Saint Petersburg, where he headed *Pravda* until Stalin returned from his exile. Molotov worked by Stalin's side during the Revolution of 1917, in which the provisional government – set up after the 1905 Revolution – was overthrown, and the Soviet state was born.

Russian Civil War

Almost immediately after the communists took power in November of 1917, the civil war broke out between the communists – Reds – and Whites, the anti-Bolshevik forces. During this test of the new regime, Molotov proved himself an extremely competent administrator. In 1918 he oversaw the nationalization of industry in northern Russia. In 1919 Molotov traveled by special train to oversee the establishment of local governing committees in areas controlled by the Red Army. As a military administrator, Molotov came to believe that any deviation from the Bolshevik party line was dangerous and, hence, sought to institutionalize a communist dictatorship within the local committees he established.

During the civil war he also participated in a propaganda tour on the river steamer *The Red Star*. Molotov, along with Soviet leader Vladimir I. Lenin's wife, Nadezhda Krupskaya, and several other party workers, made their way down the Volga, explaining Marxism and the new regime to peasants in Perm, Nizhni Novgorod, and Kazan.

By November 1920 Molotov had been made secretary of the Ukrainian Communist party. On his first official trip to the Ukraine, Molotov met Paulina Semionova Carpovskaya, a young party worker on a sugar beet farm. The two were married with Stalin acting as best man.

During the Tenth Party Congress, held in March 1921, Molotov was made a member of the Central Committee. He continued his party work in Moscow throughout the 1920s, linking his political fortunes to Stalin's. By the spring of 1922, with Lenin in ill health, Molotov – with Valerian Kuibyshev – was second in command of the Central Committee, with Stalin filling the post of general secretary.

Serving Under Stalin

After Lenin's death in January 1924, Stalin, with Molotov by his side, continued to consolidate his power. In December 1925, Stalin brought Molotov, Kliment E. Voroshilov, and Mikhail I. Kalinin into the Politburo in an attempt to create a coalition against Grigory Y. Zinoviev, Lev B. Kamenev, and Leon Trotsky – the trio, known as the "oppositionists," who were attempting to oust Stalin from power. In November 1928 Trotsky was expelled from the party, and the oppositionists were thoroughly defeated. Stalin then began to work against Nikolai Bukharin and the "rightists." By the end of the year Stalin removed Bukharin from the Politburo and replaced Aleksei I. Rykov with Molotov as chairman of the Council of People's Commissars, a position equivalent to head of state.

Stalin successfully managed to bring the entire Soviet government under his control, and Molotov was riding on his coattails. The two worked closely together, even moving into the same living quarters in the Kremlin. Stalin gave him unparalleled access to his decision-making process, allowing Molotov to influence and shape his policies during briefing sessions held every morning.

When Stalin began the collectivization of agriculture in 1928, it was Molotov who led the fight against the kulaks, the wealthier peasants who were accused of working against the government's policy. Molotov also led the way in helping to create a system of surveillance of party members and ordinary citizens alike. According to Molotov, "eternal vigilance" was the price of progress.

As Stalin continued his purge of the party during the 1930s, Molotov was among the few who remained unscathed, due in part to Molotov's ability to serve without challenging Stalin's authority. By 3 May 1939 Stalin had replaced Maxim Litvinov with Molotov as commissar of foreign affairs.

The Ribbentrop-Molotov Pact

With the rise of fascist Germany and the world on the brink of war, Molotov began negotiations with the West and simultaneously secret talks with the Nazis. The Nazis, anxious to reach an agreement with the Soviets so they could concentrate on other war efforts, were more amenable to Soviet demands than were the British and French. On 23 August 1939 Count Joachim von Ribbentrop, the German foreign minister, concluded a treaty of nonaggression with Stalin in Moscow.

Known as the Ribbentrop-Molotov Pact, the treaty's secret protocols, confirmed by Soviet officials in 1989, divided much of Europe into Soviet and Nazi spheres of influence. The Soviets received a large portion of eastern Poland, Finland, and the Baltic states.

Despite the treaty and a visit by Molotov to Berlin in December 1940, Adolf Hitler launched an invasion of the Soviet Union on 21 June 1941. Although Stalin had been warned of the invasion by Soviet intelligence, he was taken by surprise and was unable to mount a response to the attack for several days. A committee of defense was formed, with Molotov serving directly under Stalin. Voroshilov was placed in charge of the military, Lavrenty P. Beria headed the secret police, and Georgi M. Malenkov headed the party.

In May 1942 Molotov traveled to London where he concluded a treaty with Britain on mutual economic and military aid. From London, he traveled to the United States where he met with U.S. president Franklin D. Roosevelt and received what Molotov perceived to be an agreement for the creation of an Allied-led second front in Europe, which the Soviets hoped would divert some of the Nazi forces which were concentrating their attack on the Soviet Union.

In October 1943 Molotov met with British foreign minister Anthony Eden and U.S. secretary of state Cordell Hull in Moscow and paved the way for the first meeting of the Allied leaders, which took place one month later in Tehran. Molotov took part in this conference, as he did in every major conference thereafter.

Yalta Conference

As World War II drew to a close and the configuration of the new world order was being worked out, it was Molotov who played a leading role in dividing the world into two camps. At the Yalta Conference in 1945 Molotov was even more unwilling than Stalin to reach an agreement with British prime minister Winston Churchill and Roosevelt. During the San Francisco Conference in April, at which the United Nations (UN) was created, Molotov spoke vehemently of two worlds, the capitalist and the socialist. He refused to recognize U.S. secretary of state Edward Stettinius as the UN permanent chair and objected to France and China having a veto power. He objected to the participation by Holland and Australia in the Paris Peace Conference.

By the time the Paris Peace Conference took place in the fall of 1946, Molotov's tactics were even more inflammatory. He continued to exacerbate East-West tensions by giving speeches such as the one in November 1947 entitled "All Roads Lead to Communism" and helped create the Soviet foreign policy that increased the tensions of the Cold War. Molotov supported the aggressive Berlin blockade and the various "national liberation" movements, such as those in Indonesia, Malaya, and Burma.

Beginning in March 1949 Molotov was mysteriously absent from Soviet politics. Five months later it was announced that Molotov and Foreign Trade Minister Anastas Mikoyan had been relieved of their posts, although they remained members of the Politburo. Whether or not Stalin was planning on purging Molotov from party leadership is not clear. However, Molotov did emerge again to play a visible role in the Politburo until Stalin's death in March 1953. Indeed, at Stalin's funeral, Molotov was the only speaker to show any emotion.

As Nikita S. Khrushchev slowly consolidated power after Stalin's death, Molotov maintained his position in the Soviet leadership. It soon became clear, however, that Khrushchev had no intention of sharing power with any of Stalin's men. When Khrushchev traveled to Yugoslavia in June 1955, Molotov, who was foreign minister, was conspicuously absent. On 22 September 1955 Molotov was publicly criticized for suggesting that socialism did not yet exist in the Soviet Union. One month later, Molotov publicly confessed in the newspaper *Trud* that his statements about socialism had been "theoretically mistaken and politically harmful." In the spring of 1956, Dmitry T. Shepilov replaced Molotov as foreign minister.

Molotov eventually formed a coalition with Malenkov and Lazar M. Kaganovich to challenge Khrushchev's position of power. At a meeting of the Presidium in June 1957, the three joined with others to have Khrushchev dismissed. Khrushchev insisted that only the full Central Committee of the Communist party could dismiss him, and, with the help of the military, managed to convene a session which firmly entrenched him in power. Molotov and six others, known as the antiparty group, were removed from power. Like many other defeated Soviet leaders, Molotov slipped into obscurity. He was rehabilitated in the 1980, but his death on 8 November 1986 received little notice in the Soviet press.

Book about Molotov

Bernard Bromage, *Molotov: The Story of an Era* (London: Peter Owen, Ltd., 1956).

General References

Seweryn Bialer, *The Soviet Paradox: External Expansion, Internal Decline* (New York: Knopf, 1986);

Alan Clark, *Barbarosa: The Russian-German Conflict* (New York: Morrow, 1964);

Robert Conquest, *The Great Terror: Stalin's Purge of the Thirties* (New York: Macmillan, 1968);

Isaac Deutscher, *Stalin: A Political Biography* (London & New York: Oxford University Press, 1949);

Milovan Djilas, *Conversations with Stalin* (New York: Harcourt, Brace & World, 1962);

Charles Gati, *The Bloc That Failed: Soviet–East European Relations in Transition* (Bloomington: Indiana University Press, 1990);

Nikita S. Khrushchev, *Khrushchev Remembers,* edited by Strobe Talbott (Boston: Little, Brown, 1970);

William H. McNeill, *America, Britain, and Russia: Their Cooperation and Conflict, 1941–46* (New York: Oxford University Press, 1964);

Robert C. Tucker, *Stalin in Power: The Revolution from Above 1929–1941* (New York: Norton, 1990);

Adam Ulam, *A History of Soviet Russia* (New York: Holt, Rinehart & Winston, 1976);

Adam Ulam, *Stalin: The Man and his Era* (New York: Viking, 1973).

– L. L. E.

SEE ALSO THESE RELATED ENTRIES

Nikita S. Khrushchev, 2; Georgi Malenkov, 2; Joseph Stalin, 2; Leon Trotsky, 2.

Mohammad Mossadegh

Prime Minister of Iran, 1951–1953
Born Tehran, Iran, 16 June 1882
Died Tehran, Iran, 5 March 1967

Mohammad Mossadegh was prime minister of Iran from April 1951 to August 1953, during which time he took power from the shah, set up a constitutional government, and nationalized the oil companies. He was ousted in a coup supported by the Central Intelligence Agency (CIA).

Mossadegh was born to a prominent family in Tehran; his father was a financial administrator in Khurasan province under the Qajar dynasty and his mother the granddaughter of a reformist Qajar prince. When Mossadegh was sixteen his father died, and Mossadegh took over his government post. After a decade he resigned to continue his education, first at l'Ecole des Sciences Politiques in Paris and later at the University of Neuchâtel in Switzerland, from which he became the first Iranian to receive a doctorate of law degree, in 1914. Mossadegh returned to Iran that year, joined the School of Political Sciences in Tehran, and wrote several books on legal subjects.

Mossadegh's rise as a nationalist leader and head of the Jibheh–i Milli (National Front) political movement began with the 1921 coup by Reza Khan, an illiterate army officer who "decided to become first in a new line of hereditary kings." As a deputy to the fifth Majlis (parliament) in 1925, Mossadegh voted against Reza Khan's decision to crown himself Reza Shah Pahlevi, arguing that such an act was a subversion of the 1906 Iranian constitution, a belief that he held through the end of his career. But the Majlis voted over Mossadegh's objections to legitimize the new dynasty. In Mossadegh's first round of power struggles with the first Pahlevi shah, Mossadegh lost. He was not elected to the seventh Majlis in 1928, was arrested twice, and was exiled to his home village of Ahmadabad near Tehran.

Following Reza Shah's forced abdication and departure from Iran in 1941 and the accession of his son, Mohammad Reza Pahlevi, however, Mossadegh was again elected to the

Mohammad Mossadegh

Majlis. In the fourteenth Majlis (1944) Mossadegh gained national attention by questioning the credentials of Sayyed Zia al-Din Tabatabai, a pro-British politician and cohort of Reza Khan's in the 1921 coup. And he began his battle against the foreign oil companies.

Oil Policy

Not surprisingly, Mossadegh's policy on oil brought him into confrontation with the United States and Britain, which wanted to retain their control over Iran's natural resource. The Anglo-Iranian Oil Company (AIOC) controlled Iran's oil under a sixty-year concession granted by a previous shah in 1901, which had been revised and renewed for another sixty years in 1933. About half of the stock of Anglo-Iranian (later British Petroleum) was held by the British government and half by Shell Oil and individuals. The company also had extensive marketing agreements with the Mobil and Exxon corporations. In the elections for the fifteenth Majlis in 1947, Mossadegh ran on a platform that emphasized oil's importance for the country's national independence, garnering support of a wide range of forces.

The Supplemental Agreement

In 1947 Iran negotiated the Supplemental Agreement with AIOC, which increased Iran's royalties. After opposition from the National Front, the Majlis sent this pact to its Committee on Oil, chaired by Mossadegh, for review. The committee raised the issue of nationalization. By the early 1950s, British-Iranian relations were at a low and Iran was polarized on the issue of nationalization. In 1951, only days after Prime Minister Ali Razmara expressed his support for the agreement to the Majlis, he was assassinated. The Majlis quickly passed a bill nationalizing the oil industry, and Mossadegh, as the prime mover behind that bill, became the most popular politician in Iran. In April 1953 the shah appointed Mossadegh prime minister.

Prime Minister

Mossadegh introduced his cabinet in May 1951 and by July had drawn up a charter for the new state oil company, the National Iranian Oil Company (NIOC). In response to British arguments that the 1933 revised concession remained in effect because of its acceptance by the previous cabinet, Mossadegh replied, "Neither the Iranian Majlis nor any other parliament in the world can restrict the right of its successors to legislate." But the conservative British government scuttled any possible agreement, and when Dwight Eisenhower assumed the U.S. presidency, Britain found the help it wanted to get rid of Mossadegh.

The Coup

An international boycott of Iranian oil effectively strangled the Iranian economy. Iran's oil exports plummeted from more than $400 million in 1950 to less than $2 million during the remainder of Mossadegh's rule. The United States cut off aid and found an unscrupulous anti-Mossadegh leader within the army, General Fazlollah Zahedi, to pull off a coup. And when a confrontation with Mossadegh led the shah to flee Iran on 15 August 1953, the CIA and the British intelligence agency MI6 organized street demonstrations in his support.

While that coup has often been described in the United States as an attempt to stop a communist takeover in Iran, that explanation is not credible in light of Mossadegh's record of anticommunism, which included outlawing the Tudeh (communist) party during his first year in office. Rather, Mossadegh was "a prudent secular reformist" who both admired western secular values and adhered to a rationalist jurisprudential position.

The shah returned to Teheran on 22 August 1953 and was propped up with a $45 million grant from the United States. Mossadegh was arrested, put on trial in November, and given a three-year jail sentence after which he was exiled to his home village. He died in Tehran on 5 March 1967.

The end of the Mossadegh era marked the beginning of extensive U.S. support for the shah, which lasted until the revolution of 1979.

Book by Mossadegh

Memoirs, translated by Homa Katouzian (London: Jebhe, 1988).

Books about Mossadegh

James A. Bill and William Roger Louis, *Mossadegh, Iranian Nationalism and Oil* (Austin: University of Texas Press, 1988);

Farhad Diba, *Mohammad Mossadegh: A Political Biography* (London: Croom Helm, 1986);

Sepehr Zahib, *The Mossadegh Era: Roots of the Iranian Revolution* (Chicago: Lake View Press, 1982);

General References

Ervand Abrahamian, *Iran Between Two Revolutions* (Princeton, N.J.: Princeton University Press, 1982);

Jonathan Kwitny, *Endless Enemies: The Making of an Unfriendly World* (New York: Penguin, 1984).

— A. F.

SEE ALSO THESE RELATED ENTRIES
Mohammad Reza Pahlevi, 2; Ruholla Musaui Khomeini, 2.

Robert Mugabe

President of Zimbabwe, 1987–
Prime Minister of Zimbabwe, 1980–1987
Born Kutama, Southern Rhodesia, 21 February 1924

Robert Mugabe was a major figure in the struggle to free Rhodesia and served as prime minister of Zimbabwe from 1980 to 1987. He is currently president.

The son of a village carpenter and a member of the dominant Shona ethnic group, Mugabe was born on 21 February 1924 in the small village of Kutama in the British settler colony of Southern Rhodesia (present-day Zimbabwe). After a Roman Catholic mission school education, Mugabe attended Fort Hare College, a training ground for black political leaders, in South Africa in 1950. After he graduated in 1952, Mugabe became a schoolteacher in Southern Rhodesia, Northern Rhodesia (present-day Zambia), and Ghana, where he taught from 1956 to 1960.

He returned to Southern Rhodesia in 1960 with his Ghanaian wife to join the nationalist movement as an officer in the National Democratic party (NDP), headed by the prominent veteran nationalist leader Joshua Nkomo. After the NDP was banned on 9 December 1961, Mugabe became the secretary-general of the successor organization to the NDP, the Zimbabwean African People's Union (ZAPU), which was founded in Tanzania under Nkomo's leadership. Mugabe was arrested by the white Southern Rhodesian government after ZAPU itself was banned in September 1962, but he managed to escape in April 1963 to Dar es Salaam, the capital of Tanzania, where he rejoined ZAPU. However, growing personal and ideological differences with the moderate Nkomo led to his break from ZAPU in July 1963 to join the newly formed Zimbabwean African National Union (ZANU) as secretary-general. Mugabe, who remained relatively obscure in the nationalist movement, returned to Rhodesia in 1964 but was arrested again in August and jailed until 1974. While in jail he completed university degrees in law, administration, and education by correspondence.

Release from Prison

Mugabe, who all but disappeared from nationalist politics as a result of his detainment, was released in early December 1974 as part of a general amnesty issued by the Rhodesian prime minister Ian Smith; the amnesty was declared at the urging of South African prime minister John B. Vorster and Zambian president Kenneth

Robert Mugabe

Kaunda. Zambia, a principal African sponsor of the Rhodesian liberation movements, and South Africa, Rhodesia's closest ally, had engaged in a short-lived détente diplomacy to bring the warring sides to a negotiated settlement to the conflict.

The regional power balance, however, was suddenly altered in April 1974 when the Portuguese military staged a coup d'état in Portugal, thereby setting in motion the independence of the Portuguese colonies of Angola and

Mozambique. The fall of neighboring white-ruled territories left Rhodesia exposed politically and militarily. Mozambique's September 1974 independence gave ZANU a secure base of operation and support. Mugabe, who managed to gain control of ZANU and its Mozambique-based Zimbabwean African National Liberation Army (ZANLA), developed a close relationship with Mozambican president Samora Machel. By 1976 Mugabe was recognized as the head of ZANLA, and emerged as a leading contender for the top leadership position within the fragmented nationalist movement. The militant Chinese-backed ZANU, which had a socialist, Pan-Africanist program, became the leading guerrilla force facing the white minority regime and was responsible for the bulk of the fighting.

The escalating Rhodesian war gave rise to sustained regional and international attempts to secure a negotiated settlement between the Smith regime and the two main nationalist groups, ZANU and the Zambia-based ZAPU. At the same time, Smith unsuccessfully tried to reach a viable internal accommodation with moderate black leaders inside Rhodesia, including separate negotiations with Nkomo begun in late October 1975.

U.S. and Soviet Involvement

By mid 1975 southern Africa was beset by violent conflict, revolutionary upheavals, and superpower confrontation, particularly in Angola, which during the second half of the year went through a large-scale Soviet-Cuban military intervention and a South African invasion. The United States secretary of state Henry Kissinger, alarmed by the unprecedented Soviet-Cuban intervention in the Angolan civil war and concerned that a radicalization of the Rhodesian war would provide more opportunities for Soviet involvement, declared on 27 April 1976 in Lusaka, Zambia, that the United States supported black majority rule in southern Africa. Kissinger's diplomatic initiative achieved a partial breakthrough agreement on majority rule within a time frame acceptable to the various sides, although subsequent negotiations were derailed by disagreements over constitutional arrangements. As subsequent regional negotiations collapsed, the presidents of the Front Line States (Angola, Botswana, Mozambique, Tanzania, and Zambia), the principal supporters of the liberation groups, sponsored the creation of the Patriotic Front (PF), a powerful, albeit uneasy, alliance between Mugabe of ZANU and Nkomo of ZAPU. The PF refused to participate in Smith's internal arrangements with moderate black leaders in the country, which in June 1979 led to the creation of "Zimbabwe-Rhodesia" with a nominal black prime minister, although real power remained entrenched in white hands. The Front Line States, themselves the targets of repeated and destructive armed re-

taliation by Smith's forces, pressured the PF to accept a negotiated settlement to the war.

The avowedly Marxist Mugabe, who regarded armed struggle as the only viable means to defeat the intransigent white regime, was at the center of intense diplomatic maneuvering during the Lancaster House negotiations in London, England, between the PF and Ian Smith (with the participation of the American, British, and Front Line governments) during the second half of 1979. Mugabe was persuaded by the leaders of the Front Line States, principally Samora Machel, to accept the terms of the Lancaster House agreements of 21 December 1979. In addition to a cease-fire and the renunciation of independence by Zimbabwe-Rhodesia, the Lancaster House agreements scheduled parliamentary elections for February 1980, with twenty of the one hundred seats reserved for whites. Unable to resolve long-standing factional and ideological differences with Nkomo, Mugabe's ZANU wing of the PF decided to run as an independent party (ZANU-PF) in the February national elections. On 18 April 1980 Zimbabwe declared its independence. Mugabe, whom whites in both Rhodesia and South Africa had long hoped to keep out of power because of his alleged radicalism, was elected prime minister as ZANU won fifty-seven of the eighty African seats in the parliament.

Policies as Prime Minister

The transition to black majority rule in Zimbabwe was relatively stable; there was no mass exodus of white settlers or factional warfare. Mugabe, however, faced difficult policy questions, and the inheritance of a settler-colonial economy constrained his options. Mugabe, faced with the constraints imposed by white control of the economy and the uncertainty of neighboring South Africa's reaction to the new government's policies, retreated from his initial promises to embark Zimbabwe on a road toward socialist transformation. Already under extreme pressures from the historically disadvantaged black population to redistribute wealth, Mugabe adopted a conciliatory stance, stressing political and racial reconciliation, the need to restore stability, and a nonaligned foreign policy. He was careful not to alienate the substantial white population, which controlled the modern sectors of the Zimbabwean economy, both industrial and agricultural. To placate white concerns further, Mugabe announced that he would not pursue rapid transformations toward a socialist state. In September 1987, however, the provision reserving twenty seats in the house and ten in the senate for whites was abolished.

Widely regarded as politically astute and pragmatic, Mugabe moved quickly to abolish racial discrimination and inequality, while at the same time turning Zimbabwe into one of Africa's few economic success stories during the decade, particularly in agriculture. Despite the rhetoric of socialist transformation, the government pursued market-oriented policies, and the economy remained mixed and moderately open.

During the first few years after independence Zimbabwe briefly experienced mild political instability, capped by the January 1981 falling-out with Nkomo, a junior partner in Mugabe's government. Throughout the early half of the 1980s, instability and violence, including charges of human rights abuses, plagued the Matabeleland provinces, which were Nkomo's ZAPU strongholds. The situation finally improved after an amnesty issued to armed renegades in the wake of November 1987 massacre. An April 1988 reconciliation agreement between the two men created a political union between the two parties, even though Mugabe's ZANU, which had swept the 1985 elections, retained its political dominance. From the time he assumed power, Mugabe had made public his preference to turn Zimbabwe into a one-party state, and the union with Nkomo appeared to cement the move toward a de facto one-party system. In late 1988 the Mugabe government was faced with another serious political crisis as a result of a major corruption scandal in the government. In the wake of the scandal, a new political party, the Zimbabwean Union Movement, was formed by a former cabinet official but appeared to pose no threat to political domination by ZANU.

Policies toward South Africa

Independent Zimbabwe, the dominant regional economic and military power outside South Africa, has played a pivotal role in southern African politics, the principal area of concern for Mugabe's foreign policy. Zimbabwe's foreign policy has been largely shaped by the problems besetting the troubled region and the unequal distribution of economic and military power between the majority-ruled states and South Africa. In the wake of the emergence of black-ruled states (and their international affiliations) in the region, South Africa pursued a dual-track policy of destabilizing neighboring regimes economically and militarily, both overtly and through proxies, as part of its grand strategy of establishing a constellation of regional states based on South African primacy. Since independence Zimbabwe has faced a series of South African destabilization attempts, including direct military strikes ostensibly in retaliation for its support of the African National Congress (ANC), the South African liberation organization, which had offices in Zimbabwe. Vulnerable to South African military reprisals, Zimbabwe, however, refused to allow the ANC to establish training camps in the country. In the early 1980s reports surfaced that South Africa was arming bands of dissidents in the province of Matabeleland.

Mozambique

In addition to the threat posed by South Africa, Zimbabwe's security has also been undermined by the brutal civil war in neighboring Mozambique. Mugabe, by 1988, committed over fourteen thousand Zimbabwean troops to Mozambique, principally to protect the so-called Beira Corridor, the rail network running across Mozambique to the port of Beira and Zimbabwe's principal access route to the sea, against the South African-backed Mozambican National Resistance (MNR). By the late 1980s Zimbabwean troops were engaged in direct fighting with the MNR, which carried out repeated incursions across the border into Zimbabwe. In addition to Zimbabwe, the Mozambican government also received military assistance from Tanzania, which also deployed several thousand troops in Mozambique, and some Western countries, principally Great Britain.

Relations with the superpowers were somewhat cool, and Mugabe has displayed independence and nonalignment in the area of foreign affairs. Even though his political thinking has Marxist orientations, Mugabe's regime did not develop close ties with the Soviet Union, which had supported the rival guerrilla group during the war. Relations with the United States, which had provided economic aid, have been periodically strained, as when, for example, Zimbabwe strongly condemned the American military action in Grenada in 1983. Another source of tension between Zimbabwe and the United States was the issue of international economic sanctions against South Africa, and the former's criticisms of the latter's reluctance to impose sanctions. Relations erupted abruptly in July 1986 after a senior Zimbabwean official denounced American foreign policy during 4 July ceremonies at the U.S. embassy in Harare, the Zimbabwean capital. As a result of the official's comment, the American government cut off economic aid, but relations gradually normalized.

A major priority in Mugabe's foreign and domestic policies has been to lessen landlocked Zimbabwe's dependence on South Africa in the areas of trade and transport, and he has advocated rebuilding alternate transport routes through Angola and Mozambique. The strongest of the Front Line States and a major mineral exporter, Zimbabwe played a prominent part in the formation of the Southern African Development Co-ordination Conference (SADCC), a regional organization aimed at lessening economic dependence on South Africa. Founded in April 1980, SADCC seeks to promote economic development and regional integration among its member states (Angola, Botswana, Lesotho, Malawi, Mozambique, Swaziland, Tanzania, and Zambia) and their consequent economic liberation from South Africa. Mugabe was a leading spokesman in Africa for the imposition of economic sanctions against South Africa and a supporter of the ANC. Mugabe has also been active in the Non-Aligned Movement, which he chaired from 1986 to 1989, following its 1986 annual heads-of-states meeting in Harare.

Book about Mugabe

David Smith, *Mugabe* (London: Sphere, 1981).

General References

Gwendolyn M. Carter and Patrick O'Meara, eds., *International Politics in Southern Africa* (Bloomington: Indiana University Press, 1982);

Michael Clough, ed., *Changing Realities in Southern Africa: Implications for American Policy* (Berkeley: University of California Press, 1982);

Jeffrey Herbst, *State Politics in Zimbabwe* (Berkeley: University of California Press, 1990);

David Martin and Phyllis Johnson, *The Struggle for Zimbabwe: The Chimurenga War* (London: Faber & Faber, 1981).

—J. R.-S.

SEE ALSO THESE RELATED ENTRIES

Kenneth Kaunda, 2; Henry Kissinger, 1; Kwame Nkrumah, 2; Ian Smith, 2.

Imre Nagy

Prime Minister of Hungary, 1953–1955, 1956

Born Kaposvár, Hungary, 7 June 1896
Died Budapest, Hungary, 16 June 1958

Imre Nagy was born into a family of poor peasants. He was due to become an apprentice to a locksmith but was drafted into the Austro-Hungarian army at the start of World War I. He was captured and taken to Russia as a prisoner of war, and there he became a communist and subsequently was recruited into the Red Army. He returned to Hungary soon after the war, but, when the short-lived communist regime of Béla Kun collapsed in 1919, he fled back to the Soviet Union to try to rebuild the party organization.

Training in Moscow

Nagy spent brief periods in Hungary during the 1920s, but in 1929 he settled in Moscow. His interests were primarily in agriculture and economics, and he became a member of the Institute for Agrarian Sciences in Moscow, where he remained until late 1944. The Soviet army occupied Hungary in 1945, after the Nazi withdrawal, and Nagy was able to return to the country to become minister of agriculture in the interim coalition government. He helped to establish a Stalinist communist system and held several ministerial posts between 1944 and 1948. But Nagy was not a blind follower of Stalin, and he became increasingly critical of those Hungarian communist leaders who followed orders from the Kremlin without question. He was reportedly distressed about Soviet exploitation of Hungary's economic resources, and in 1949 he was dismissed from the government because of his strong support for the welfare of the peasantry. This was demonstrated by his opposition to forced collectivization and the compulsory sale to the state of farmers' crops at low prices.

Prime Minister

After Stalin's death in 1953, Moscow loosened its grip on its Eastern European satellites and tolerated some liberalizing measures. Nagy was appointed prime minister in June 1953, replacing the hard-line Stalinist Mátyás Rákosi. He initiated a policy of liberalization, especially in agriculture, where he curtailed the program of enforced collectivization of the peasantry. These measures were popular with the rural people, but his attitude was considered to be too radical and independent by Moscow. The Kremlin feared that Hungary would follow Yugoslavia's path in breaking free of Soviet control. In February 1955 Nagy was forced out of office by his more orthodox rival Rákosi, who took over his position of head of the government. Nagy was accused of "right-wing deviation" and expelled from the party.

The 1956 Revolt

Nagy had a teaching position until the beginning of the October revolt. He was called back to the premiership in mid October 1956, as the authorities hoped his reappearance would stop the growing public clamor for radical reform. A mass demonstration in Budapest on 23 October triggered the revolution, when the Hungarian security police opened fire on unarmed protesters. The rebellion swiftly spread as the revolutionaries were joined by units of the Hungarian army and some sympathetic policemen. During the uprising, the insurgents put forward a program for extensive political, economic, and social change, including a full multiparty system, free elections, independent labor unions, the abolition of the secret police, and the restoration of a mixed economy. Their demands exceeded the policy of communist reformers such as Nagy, who was swept along in the popular tide and acceded to the protesters' demands.

Demands for Change

Nagy bowed to increasing public pressure for the termination of the Leninist dictatorship and declared his opposition to Russian pressures to reestablish communism by force. He made sweeping political changes in the country by announcing the abolition of the one-party state and promising free elections, an authentic coalition government, and the legalization of other parties.

The Soviet Crackdown

The Kremlin increasingly feared that the local communists would permanently lose power if free elections were allowed to take place. Moscow was also concerned that the overthrow of communism in Hungary would set a precedent for other Eastern European countries and could signal the disintegration of the Warsaw Pact alliance. The Soviet army forcefully intervened against the revolt on 4 November 1956. During the fighting, ten thousand to twenty thousand Hungarian insurgents were estimated to have died, more than two hundred thousand people fled the country, and several thousand people

Imre Nagy

were arrested, imprisoned, executed, or deported to Soviet labor camps.

Immediately after the Red Army intervention and before the revolt was crushed, Nagy declared that Hungary would withdraw from the Warsaw Pact. He announced the country's neutrality and appealed in vain to the West for assistance. The Western powers gave some verbal support to the Hungarians and the Nagy government, but they declined provision of material assistance or armed intervention, wary of provoking a major East-West confrontation. They were also preoccupied with the Suez crisis. The independent labor unions proclaimed a general strike after the invasion, but most armed resistance was violently subdued by mid November.

Imprisonment and Execution

Nagy took refuge in the Yugoslav embassy, but on 22 November he was lured out by a guarantee from the Soviet authorities that he would obtain safe passage out of Hungary and avoid arrest. Instead, he was captured, deported, imprisoned in Romania, and never directly heard from again. On 17 June 1958 the new communist government in Budapest announced that Nagy had been returned to Hungary for trial and charged with plotting the "counterrevolution" and organizing the 1956 uprising. Although he never confessed to any of these charges, he was found guilty and executed on 16 June 1958.

Throughout the rule of Nagy's successor, János Kádár, communist authorities censored debate about Nagy, and his place of burial was not revealed. In an attempt to gain popular legitimacy for the reformist party leadership after Kádár's ouster, Nagy was ceremoniously reburied with full state honors in June 1989 and officially depicted as a national hero. The 1956 uprising was no longer condemned as a "counterrevolution" by the communists but redefined as a "popular uprising." Despite their efforts to benefit from the popularity of the Nagy government, the reform communists lost Hungary's first free elections in March 1990.

Book by Nagy

On Communism: In Defense of the New Course (London: Thames & Hudson, 1957).

General References

Andrew Felkay, *Hungary and the USSR, 1956-1988: Kadar's Political Leadership* (New York: Greenwood, 1989);

Charles Gati, *Hungary and the Soviet Bloc* (Durham, N.C.: Duke University Press, 1986);

Bennett Kovrig, *Communism in Hungary: From Kun to Kadar* (Stanford, Cal.: Hoover Institution Press, 1979);

Bill Lomax, *Hungary 1956* (New York: St. Martin's Press, 1976);

Miklos Molnar, *Budapest 1956: A History of the Hungarian Revolution* (London: Allen & Unwin, 1971).

William Shawcross, *Crime and Compromise: János Kadar and the Politics of Hungary since Revolution* (London: Weidenfeld & Nicolson, 1974).

– J. B. and A. B.

SEE ALSO THESE RELATED ENTRIES
János Kádár, 2; Mátyás Rákosi, 2.

Gamal Abdul Nasser

President of Egypt, 1956–1970

Prime Minister of Egypt, 1954–1956

Born Bani Morr, Egypt, 16 January 1918
Died Cairo, Egypt, 28 September 1970

Gamal Nasser was the most important and influential Arab leader of the mid twentieth century. One of the founders of the Non-Aligned Movement and the leading spokesman of Arab nationalism, Nasser played a unique role in modern Egyptian history and Arab politics in the postwar period.

The son of a postal clerk, Gamal Abdul Nasser was born in a small farming village of Bani Morr in the Asyut province of northern Egypt. He attended primary school in Alexandria and secondary school in Cairo, Egypt's capital. During secondary school he participated in student demonstrations and other nationalist activities against the Egyptian monarchy. After completing his secondary education, Nasser entered the Egyptian Military Academy in 1937. His entry into the military came at a time of growing political unrest and military involvement in Egyptian national politics. Even though Egypt had been formally independent from British colonial rule since 28 February 1922, Great Britain, which retained the legal right to occupy the Suez Canal zone, continued to exercise a preponderant role in national political life. Nasser graduated with the rank of second lieutenant and was assigned to Upper Egypt along with other members of his class, notably Anwar al-Sadat. Promoted to the rank of captain, he served as an instructor at the Egyptian Military Academy and later graduated from the General Staff College. During the 1948–1949 Arab-Israeli war he served as a battalion commander and was briefly held as a prisoner of war in Israel.

After he returned to Egypt in late 1949, Nasser began to organize the so-called Free Officers Committee, a clan-

Gale International Portrait Gallery

Gamal Abdul Nasser

destine association of young officers from lower- and middle-class backgrounds who, like himself, were disenchanted with the foreign domination of Egypt and the social inequalities that persisted under the monarchy. The political program of the Free Officers movement called for the elimination of British presence and influence in Egypt, the abolition of feudalism and capitalism, and the establishment of a democratic government. Nasser remained the dominant figure in the secret society of military conspirators.

During the first few years of the 1950s Egypt was beset by social and political unrest, sparked by the growing resentment toward foreign presence and the deteriorating socio-economic conditions. By mid January 1952 Egypt became almost ungovernable as a wave of political unrest, violence, and riots broke out in Cairo, parts of which were burned down. In the wake of the crisis, which had been precipitated by a confrontation between British troops and Egyptian police in the city of Ismailia in the canal zone, the old political order crumbled beyond repair. On 23 July 1952 the Free Officers movement seized power in a bloodless coup d'état that ousted King Farouk I from power. After a brief phase of civilian government, on 7 September the military officially took command of the government. General Muhammad Neguib, a member of the Free Officers movement, was appointed commander in chief of the armed forces and head of the military government – constituted as the Revolutionary Command Council (RCC). Neguib was regarded as a figurehead, however, with real power resting in the Free Officers executive under Nasser's leadership. After assuming power the military government initiated reformist social and economic policies, including an extensive land reform program that altered the traditional distribution of power and wealth in the country. On 23 January 1953 all political parties were dissolved, with the constitution suspended on 10 February, and on 18 June the monarchy was abolished and Egypt declared a republic. Neguib was appointed president and prime minister, and Colonel Nasser, who had hitherto remained in the background, was appointed deputy prime minister and minister of the interior.

What began as a nonideological military coup soon turned into a revolution. Yet the revolutionary leadership remained ill-defined, and it was not clear whether the Free Officers had come to power with any program other than the desire to restore Egyptian national pride and power, which had been eclipsed for almost a millennium. In addition, the Free Officers movement had a mixed ideological makeup, ranging from Marxism to Islamic fundamentalism. A power struggle surfaced between Neguib, whose political tendencies were conservative and Islamic, and Nasser, who replaced Neguib as prime minister and chairman of the RCC on 25 February 1954. Within a few days, however, Neguib was restored to his former posts, although the underlying sources of disagreements remained unresolved. In April, Nasser was appointed prime minister in place of Neguib, who retained the nominal post of president. By late 1954 Nasser had become the supreme political authority in Egypt, and on 14 November Neguib was finally ousted from the leadership and placed under house arrest following allegations of his involvement in an antiregime conspiracy, including an assassination attempt on Nasser by the Muslim Brotherhood, an influential fundamentalist group.

Nasser came to power with the ambitious goals of not only ridding the country of Western influence and domination, but also of turning Egypt into a modern, powerful state and the leader of the Arab world. His regime, however, was not guided by any coherent ideology but used his charisma and nationalist rhetoric to appeal directly to the people. A key part of transforming Egypt, a poor country with a large, illiterate rural population, into a modern, industrialized socialist state was the construction of the Aswan High Dam, which was to be financed by international agencies and foreign governments. Nasser's domestic and international standing, which had already been elevated by his successful negotiation of the Anglo-Egyptian Suez agreement of 19 October 1954, which had provided for the withdrawal of British troops, was further enhanced by his outspoken criticism and opposition to the so-called Baghdad Pact (later to become the Central Treaty Organization), a Western-initiated defense pact between Iraq and Turkey signed on 24 February 1955. Nasser, who opposed the pact on grounds that the Arab states should avoid alliances with foreign powers, concluded his own defense agreement with Syria and Saudi Arabia in October. Despite his militant, nationalist rhetoric, Nasser's early foreign policy toward Israel was marked by moderation, partly out of his preoccupation with building the revolution at home.

Nasser emerged as one of the leading spokesmen and founding members of the Nonalignment movement in the Third World. He became an advocate of "positive neutralism," which called on Third World states to take a position of neutrality vis-à-vis the East-West rivalry while maintaining positive relations with both sides. Nasser was the key figure at the Bandung Conference, the first major gathering of Third World countries, in Bandung, Indonesia, on 18–25 April 1955. Attended by prominent Third World leaders such as Bung Sukarno of Indonesia, Chou Enlai of China, Josip Broz Tito of Yugoslavia, Kwame Nkrumah of Ghana, and Jawaharlal Nehru of India, the conference gave birth to the Non-Aligned Movement, a loose union of diverse Third World countries that espoused an ostensibly neutral foreign policy with respect to the superpowers.

The conference came at a time when Egypt's relations with Western countries had cooled as a result of Nasser's opposition to the Baghdad Pact and his active support for the National Liberation Front in Algeria, the guerrilla movement fighting against French colonial rule. Relations with the United States, whose secretary of state, John Foster Dulles, considered neutrality to be a de facto alignment with the Soviet Union, had deteriorated, even though both the United States and Britain had agreed in principle to finance the Aswan project. Nasser, who was unwilling to accept Western conditions on the technical and financial assistance for the project, unsuccessfully sought military assistance from the United States following violent border clashes with Israeli forces in mid 1955. Unable to obtain Western arms, he concluded an arms agreement in September with Czechoslovakia, a Soviet-bloc country, and with one stroke ended the Western monopoly on arms transfers to the Middle East. The arms agreement, which provided Egypt with advanced Soviet weapons, was a point of departure in the super-power competition in the Middle East and further strained Egypt's relations with the West. On 20 July 1956 the United States and Britain formally withdrew their offers to finance the Aswan project and moved to block multilateral financing through the International Bank for Reconstruction and Development. Over Western protest, Nasser responded by nationalizing the Suez Canal Company, a French-British Concern, on 26 July, and announced that the revenues from the canal would be used to finance the construction of the Aswan.

In the background of growing Western concerns over Soviet expansionism in the Middle East and displeasure over Nasser's independence of action, on 29 October Israeli forces, in a joint military action with Britain and France, invaded Egypt and advanced toward the Suez Canal. The attack, which allowed Britain and France to reoccupy the canal zone, drew immediate international opposition. Under pressures from the American presidential administration of Dwight D. Eisenhower and the United Nations (UN), Britain and France withdrew their forces, which along with Israel's had occupied the entire Sinai Peninsula, following a UN cease-fire agreement that put in place a UN peacekeeping force in the Sinai. While the fiasco ended French-British influence in the Middle East, Nasser emerged from the Suez crisis as an Arab hero, and Egypt was once again considered the center of the Arab world. For the first time a leader of a small Third World country had successfully withstood "Western imperialist aggression." Nasser's defiance of the great powers had stirred an emotional response in the Arab world, and he was widely seen as the leader of all Arab peoples. The Suez crisis helped to create an image of Nasser in the Arab Middle East as a strong nationalist leader under attack from the West and the Arabs' implacable enemy, Israel, which for the first time since its founding in 1948 was forced to withdraw from Arab territory.

The period between 1956 and 1967 was the peak of the Nasserist era, and Nasser became the symbolic representative of the Arab people – the bearer of its aspirations, hopes, and pride. Nasserist political parties and sympathizers emerged all over the Middle East, and his Pan-Arab nationalism was diffused through a "Voice of the Arabs" radio broadcast in Cairo. By the year following his political triumph in the Suez crisis, Nasser, who began to use his newly found stature to advocate Arab unity, concentrated on events and developments in the Middle East. The first serious attempt to implement his Pan-Arab philosophy came on 1 February 1958, when Egypt and pro-Soviet Syria entered into a political union known as the United Arab Republic (UAR), with the charismatic Egyptian leader as president, although it was only in mid 1960 that a national assembly was opened in Cairo. To the resentment of the Syrians, the nominal federation was dominated by Egypt, and Nasser took the credit of making the first step toward the creation of the "Arab Nation," involving the sentimental longing for the unification of all Arab peoples under one flag. Nasser invited other Arab states to join the union, and in March 1958 Yemen joined the loose federation. Regional tensions heightened when American and British troops were dispatched to Lebanon and Jordan following the 14 July 1958 pro-Egyptian military coup in Iraq, which overthrew the staunchly pro-Western regime there. Nasser, who strongly criticized the Western action, met with the coup leaders and announced that Iraq and the UAR would join forces to repel any outside aggression. Relations with the pro-Soviet, nationalist regime in Iraq, however, soon gave way to an Egyptian-Iraqi rivalry.

Even though there were no indications in his political thinking to suggest an ideological commitment to Marxist-Leninism or that he was a particular admirer of the Soviet Union (and in fact the Egyptian Communist party remained banned under his regime), Nasser drifted ideologically and politically closer to the Soviet Union following the rupture in relations with the West. In addition to Soviet funding for the Aswan High Dam, the UAR received military and industrial assistance from the Soviet-bloc countries. Despite Soviet efforts to lure his regime into the Communist bloc, Nasser's relationship with the Soviet Union remained ambiguous, motivated mostly by a desire to counterbalance the Western presence in the region and its backing of Israel. By late 1958, however, relations with the Soviet Union had degenerated, partly out of Nasser's belligerent posture toward Arab Communist parties as well as the Soviet Union's enthusiastic support for Iraq.

By mid 1961 Syrian dissatisfaction with the union began to surface, and on 28 September 1961 Syria withdrew from the UAR after a military coup. Nasser, president of Egypt since 1956, reorganized the government of

Egypt, which retained the official title of the United Arab Republic, with an elected national assembly whose members were all from the Arab Socialist Union (ASU), a new political party founded and controlled by Nasser himself. Through his political and administrative engineering he assumed a thorough and direct control of the government and every facet of executive power save the army, which retained a measure of autonomy. The administrative and political reorganization was accompanied by a renewal of revolutionary fervor in domestic and foreign policy and a deepening commitment to socialism, state capitalism, and Arab nationalism. While he pursued social and economic reforms, Nasser maintained a restrictive political system, with politics limited to the ASU.

Regionally, however, Nasser's revolutionary fervor, policies, and hypnotic hold on the Arab masses were alienating the conservative Arab states. In what came to be called "Nasser's Vietnam," the Nasserist regime intervened in the Yemeni civil war, which was sparked after pro-Nasserist military officers overthrew the Yemeni royal family on 27 September 1962. Nasser moved quickly to support the shaky republican regime against the Saudi Arabian–backed royalist rebel forces by dispatching an estimated fifteen thousand troops to Yemen during September and October. Nasser's entanglement in the Yemeni civil war, to which he would eventually commit more than fifty thousand troops, proved costly not only in terms of men and money, but also in terms of relations with other Arab states, particularly Saudi Arabia, which was weary of his heavy-handed meddling. Efforts toward political union between Egypt, Syria, and Iraq were renewed, but progress proved to be slow as a result of domestic political differences in all three countries. Not all Arab states were receptive to Nasser's Pan-Arab ideology and his calls for an Arab union, which provided Nasser with the means to export Egypt's revolution as well as to ensure Egyptian primacy in the Arab world. Despite Nasser's mass popular appeal and bid for the dominant leadership role in the Arab world, inter-Arab relations in the late 1950s and early 1960s continued to be marked by mutual animosity and rivalry. Egyptian relations with Syria and Iraq regularly alternated between détente and traditional rivalry, generated partly out of the adversarial competition for dominance in Arab politics between Nasser and the Ba'athist regimes in both Syria and Iraq. Due to deep ideological and personal differences, attempts at an Arab union remained hollow exercises.

Internationally, Egypt's relations with the West continued to deteriorate while relations improved with the Soviet Union, whose premier, Nikita S. Khrushchev, made a sixteen-day state visit to Egypt in May 1964. Relations with the United States reached their nadir over Nasser's involvement in the Congolese civil war (1960–

1965). Although he had previously disengaged from the civil war, Nasser renewed his backing of rebel forces who had supported Patrice Lumumba, the Congolese nationalist leader assassinated in 1961.

By early 1967 a perilous confrontation had developed between the Arab states and Israel, partly as a result of the guerrilla attacks carried out by the Palestine Liberation Organization (PLO) and Israeli reprisal raids into Arab territories. The Arab-Israeli confrontation had emerged as the defining current of Middle Eastern politics, and the events of 1967 dramatically transformed the regional political horizon. Precipitated by the growing Syrian-backed guerrilla activities in Israel, a violent border clash between Syrian and Israeli forces, in which six Syrian aircraft were shot down, took place on 7 April. Nasser, who had been warning against a military confrontation with Israel occurring before the Arab states had sufficient military power, was widely criticized for not assisting Syria despite a mutual defense agreement declared in 1966. However, in early May, after Israeli warnings of severe reprisals if guerrilla activities were not brought under control, Nasser massed troops on the border with Israel after he secured the withdrawal of the UN peacekeeping force, and he sought to consolidate Arab solidarity in the growing confrontation with Israel. On 23 May he closed the Strait of Tiran to Israeli shipping, a move Israel considered an act of war. Nasser's bold moves brought his prestige in the Arab world to its peak, and as tensions mounted he concluded a mutual defense agreement with Jordan and Iraq. On 5 June, Israel launched a large-scale preemptive attack against Egypt, Jordan, Iraq, and Syria. Israel's spectacular simultaneous air and land assaults destroyed the bulk of the Arab air and ground forces, and by the time of the cease-fire agreement on 11 June the American-backed Israeli forces had occupied Egypt's Sinai Peninsula up to the Suez Canal and also the Gaza Strip, the West Bank of Jordan, and the Golan Heights of Syria. Despite their close ties with the countries involved in the conflict, the United States and the Soviet Union took little direct action.

The 1967 Six-Day War was a major turning point in Middle Eastern politics, and Nasser's standing and prestige had suddenly been eclipsed by the stunning Arab defeat. On 9 June Nasser, who claimed personal responsibility for the debacle, had announced his resignation on Egyptian television, but after spontaneous, widespread popular demonstrations of support he withdrew the resignation. Domestically the aftermath of the war exacerbated Egypt's daunting economic problems and fueled mild political unrest. The war proved financially burdensome, and the costs of rebuilding the armed forces strained resources in spite of financial aid from the other Arab states.

Regionally Nasser moved to strengthen Egypt's position in the Arab world and improve relations with individual Arab states. In December 1967 he reached a reconciliation agreement with the royal house of Saudi Arabia, with whom relations had been poisoned by Egypt's involvement in the Yemeni civil war. Nasser, who had been designated by the August 1967 Arab summit meeting in Khartoum, Sudan, to pursue a political solution to the Arab-Israeli conflict, gave his preliminary support for the November 1967 United Nations Resolution 242, which laid the basis for settlement on the principle of land in exchange for peace. He pursued a brief détente with the United States in the hopes of putting pressure on Israel to withdraw from the occupied territories. Multilateral diplomatic efforts to bring the two sides together had yielded little success by late 1968, however, and tensions remained high between Israel and the Arab states. Throughout 1969 sporadic fighting, including artillery fire, commando raids, and aerial clashes, took place between Egypt and Israel during the so-called War of Attrition. Nasser's efforts to promote Arab unity in the wake of the 1967 war proved as frustrating as efforts to obtain increased Arab contributions during the war of attrition.

Egypt's vulnerability to Israeli attacks, and its crushing defeat in the Six-Day War, forced Nasser to seek increased Soviet military assistance. In addition to replacing half of the lost Egyptian aircraft and other military weapons, the Soviet Union, which was granted basing rights by the Nasser regime, supplied Egypt with modern air defense systems and military advisers. By early 1970 there were an estimated fifteen thousand to twenty thousand Soviet troops and military personnel stationed in Egypt. Generally supportive of multilateral attempts at reaching an Arab-Israeli settlement, Nasser backed a peace plan put forth by the American secretary of state, William P. Rogers, on 25 June 1970, which brought a cease-fire in the War of Attrition. Nasser's acceptance of the Rogers Plan was widely criticized in the Arab world.

Nasser, who remained the dominant Arab leader through the strength of his personality, rhetoric, and charisma, played a major role in mediating the Jordanian civil war between King Hussein ibn Talal I and Jordanian-based Palestinian guerrillas in September 1970, even though a subsequent agreement mediated by Nasser on September 27 collapsed. On 28 September Nasser died of a severe heart attack in Cairo and was succeeded by Vice-president Anwar al-Sadat, a close associate and member of the Free Officers movement.

Even though his successor would reverse many of the domestic and foreign policies of his regime, Gamal Nasser's political legacy continued to wield a powerful influence throughout the Middle East. He had come to symbolize not only popular aspirations and Arab unity, but also the awakening of the Arab world through his transformation of Egypt from a weak, peripheral country into the leader of the Arab world and a major actor in international affairs. Long after his death, he remained the embodiment of the widely felt, albeit elusive, sentimental attachment to the unification of all Arab peoples into one Arab nation and an enduring source of inspiration for ordinary Arabs, nationalists, and radicals alike.

Book by Nasser
The Philosophy of the Revolution: Egypt's Liberation (Washington, D.C.: Public Affairs Press, 1955).

Books about Nasser
Abdel M. Farid, *Nasser: A Reassessment* (London: Arab Research Center, 1981);

Jean Lacoutre, *Nasser: A Biography* (New York: Knopf, 1973);

Robert H. Stephens, *Nasser: A Political Biography* (New York: Simon & Schuster, 1972).

General References
Raymond Baker, *Egypt's Uncertain Revolution under Nasser and Sadat* (Cambridge, Mass.: Harvard University Press, 1978);

Twafig Y. Hasou, *The Struggle for the Arab World: Egypt's Nasser and the Arab League* (London: Routledge & Kegan Paul, 1985);

Malcom Kerr, *The Arab Cold War: Gamal Abdul-Nasser and His Rivals* (London: Oxford University Press, 1971);

Walter Laqueur, *Nasser's Egypt* (London: Weidenfeld & Nicolson, 1957);

P. J. Vatikiotis, *Nasser and His Generation* (New York: St. Martin's Press, 1978).

– J. R.-S.

SEE ALSO THESE RELATED ENTRIES

Arab-Israeli War, 3; John Foster Dulles, 1; Dwight Eisenhower, 1; Nikita S. Khrushchev, 2.

Antonio Agostinho Neto

President of Angola, 1975–1979
Born Katete, Portuguese West Africa, 17 September 1922
Died Moscow, Soviet Union, 10 September 1979

Antonio Agostinho Neto was an Angolan nationalist revolutionary leader, poet, doctor, and first president of independent Angola. Neto was born in the town of Katete, a Mbundu village outside Luanda, the capital city of Portuguese West Africa, now Angola, on 17 September 1922. The son of a Methodist pastor, he was one of the few black Angolans to graduate from Luanda's prestigious Liceu Salvador Correia secondary school. After his secondary education he worked in the colonial health services from 1944 to 1947. Neto received a scholarship from the American Methodist mission in 1947 to study medicine in Portugal, where he attended the universities of Lisbon and Coimbra.

Neto became deeply involved in nationalist politics and the cultural nationalism movement during his university years. A secret member of the Portuguese Communist party and organizations against the fascist regime of Antonio Salazar, Neto was in and out of prison for his political activities, opposition politics, and radical writing. Prominent in the nationalist movement among the African students studying in Europe, Neto's revolutionary writings and political activism gained international recognition. Neto became a close associate of other nationalist leaders from the Portuguese colonies, including fellow Angolan Jonas Savimbi and Amilcar Cabral of Cape Verde. Neto's association with Cabral formed the basis for a common program and close ties among the liberation movements in the Portuguese colonies. Arrested again in February 1955, he was finally freed in June 1956 by Portuguese authorities, who were under international pressure from artists, intellectuals, and liberal politicians to release him.

The MPLA

After completing his medical studies in 1958, Neto returned to Angola with his white Portuguese wife. He ostensibly was to begin his medical practice, but the practice provided him with a cover for his nationalist political activities. He was elected president of the Popular Movement for the Liberation of Angola (MPLA). In 1960 he was arrested by the Portuguese secret police and sent into exile in Portugal. He was later placed only under house arrest because of international pressure on Portugal. In 1962 he escaped from house arrest in Portugal and fled to Leopoldville (present-day Kinshasa) in the Congo

Antonio Agostinho Neto (right) and Deloloa, Director of the MPLA Center for Revolutionary Instruction

(Zaire), where the MPLA was based. The MPLA, founded in 1956, was at the time suffering from internal factionalism. From its new headquarters in Brazzaville, Congo, Neto directed the MPLA liberation struggle as its president, traveling to the Soviet bloc countries and African states to solicit aid. He continued to publish his revolutionary poetry throughout the independence war.

The Angolan independence struggle was characterized by disunity and internecine fighting among the three liberation movements – the Marxist-Leninist-oriented MPLA, the National Front for the Liberation of Angola (FNLA), and the National Union for the Total Independence of Angola (UNITA) – as well as considerable disunity within each of the movements, especially the MPLA. The MPLA was particularly hampered by a lack of internal cohesion, although Neto and his faction were able to withstand challenges from other factions and splits, including the violent May 1974 split in which the breakaway faction joined the FNLA. Furthermore, the three liberation movements were based on ethnic divisions; the *mestico* (people of mixed blood)-led MPLA had its base of support among the Mbundu, the second-largest ethnic group.

Independence and Civil War

The 24 April 1974 military coup d'état in Portugal set in motion the process of freeing the colonies. Neto was the chief spokesman for the MPLA during the independence talks with the Portuguese. The talks were also attended by the other two liberation groups and culminated in the Alvor Accords of January 1975. The Alvor Accords, which established 11 November 1975 as the date for independence, provided for a transitional government headed by the Portuguese commissioner with representatives from the MPLA, the FNLA, and the UNITA, and provisions for elections for a constituent assembly. Within days of the agreement internecine warfare flared up between the MPLA and the FNLA as the three movements jockeyed for control of the capital, Luanda, which was the MPLA stronghold and base of support. By July, after several failed attempts by outside African leaders to reconcile the three movements, Neto's Soviet-backed MPLA had driven out the United States–backed FNLA from the Luanda region while pushing the UNITA forces out of the capital. By September 1975 the MPLA controlled most of the provinces and major urban centers.

The Angolan independence struggle and subsequent civil war saw an unprecedented level of superpower intervention for the decolonization period. While the United States, the Soviet Union, and China had been actively sponsoring the three liberation movements since the 1960s, it was not until 1974 and 1975 that their involvement escalated into large-scale intervention and confrontation. Even though Soviet arms had ceased flowing to Neto's group a year before, as a result of a Soviet-MPLA rift, the Soviet Union and Cuba, supporter of the MPLA since the 1960s, began to increase weapons shipments to the MPLA throughout 1974. Beginning in March 1975 weapons deliveries, in addition to Soviet and Cuban military personnel, were reaching Angola through ports in MPLA-controlled Luanda. From November 1974 to September 1975 there were an estimated three thousand to five thousand Soviet and Cuban military personnel in Angola to support Neto's organization. Neto, who had a poor working relationship with the Soviet Union, had developed a close association with Fidel Castro Ruz, the Cuban revolutionary leader, since the early phases of the Angolan war.

With the number of Cuban combat troops and Warsaw Pact military personnel in Angola to support the MPLA increasing rapidly, on 23 October 1975 overt foreign intervention in Angola's internationalized civil war began. South Africa, with the collaboration of both the FNLA and the UNITA, undertook a limited invasion of Angola, and within days the Soviet Union responded with a massive airlift of Cuban combat troops and equipment to the MPLA. By early February 1976 over twelve thousand Cuban troops had been airlifted to Angola, in addition to additional Soviet military personnel. The sequence of events leading up to the South African invasion remains controversial, but the Cuban and Soviet-led MPLA offensive enabled the MPLA to establish its dominant position in the country. On 11 November 1975 the MPLA declared the People's Republic of Angola, with Agostinho Neto as president. The UNITA and remnants of the FNLA declared the independence of the Democratic People's Republic of Angola independent days later in the southern city of Huambo. With the South African withdrawal in late 1975, however, the rival coalition government proved abortive, although the anti-MPLA forces vowed to keep fighting.

Following Angola's violent transition to independence, Neto's Soviet-installed MPLA government not only faced the formidable task of national reconstruction after years of warfare and destruction, but also had to contend with an ongoing civil war against UNITA rebels, led by veteran nationalist leader Jonas Savimbi. The MPLA was committed to the Marxist-Leninist scientific socialist road to development, but preoccupations with power consolidation and the civil war hampered any real national development efforts. Neto's Angola, which remained heavily dependent on the thousands of Cuban troops stationed in the country, was at the center of the region's volatile political and security situation.

The 1977 Coup Attempt of the MPLA

The frail political cohesion of the MPLA, eroded by ethnic and ideological differences, erupted into the most serious challenge to Neto's leadership on 27 May 1977, when a predominantly African faction, led by Nito Alves, the minister of the interior, attempted to seize power. After suppressing the attempted coup d'état, the Neto faction formulated its own orthodox Marxist-Leninist course for organizing Angolan society and economy. Relations with the Soviet Union, which reportedly gave its implicit support for the attempted coup by Alves, remained cool, even though it was Angola's principal provider of military and economic aid.

Neto died of leukemia on 10 September 1979 in Moscow and was succeeded by José Eduardo dos Santos, the Angolan foreign minister. Neto was regarded as reserved, cautious, and moderate, even though his MPLA had a militant Marxist-Leninist outlook. Neto died before he could carry out his hopes of building a socialist state.

Books by Neto

Sacred Hope (Dar es Salaam: Tanzania Publishing House, 1974);

On Literature and National Culture (Luanda: U.E.A., 1979).

General References

David Birmingham, "The 27th of May: An Historical Note on the Abortive Coup of 1977 in Angola," *African Affairs*, 77 (October 1978): 554–564;

John Marcus, *The Angolan Revolution* (Cambridge, Mass.: M.I.T. Press, 1979);

John Stockwell, *In Search of Enemies: A C.I.A. Story* (New York: Norton, 1978).

—J. R.-S.

SEE ALSO THESE RELATED ENTRIES

Amílcar Cabral, 2; Fidel Castro Ruz, 2; José Eduardo dos Santos, 2; Jonas Savimbi, 2.

Nguyen Van Thieu

President of the Republic of Vietnam, 1967–1975
Born Trithuy, Vietnam, 5 April 1923

A Vietnamese military officer and anticommunist leader, Nguyen Van Thieu served as president of South Vietnam from 1967 to 1975.

Thieu was born in Trithuy village in central Vietnam. His father was a small landowner and a fisherman. Thieu received his primary education at the Roman Catholic Pellerin School in Hue, the imperial capital. After World War II he joined the Vietminh communist forces fighting against French colonial rule, serving as a youth leader and district chief. He soon became disillusioned with the Vietminh, however, and abandoned the revolutionary movement to attend the Merchant Marine Academy. In 1948 he transferred to the Vienamese National Military Academy, which was established to train officers to serve in the army of the Associated State of Vietnam, created by the French as a nominally independent country in the French union. He graduated in 1949 with a second-lieutenant commission. After serving as a combat officer during the first Indochina War (1945–1954), Thieu was appointed superintendent of the National Military Academy in Dalat in 1956 and was promoted to commander of the Fifth Infantry Division of the Army of the Republic of Vietnam (ARVN). In 1957 he was sent to the United States to take a five-month course at the Command and General Staff College.

U.S. Military Assistance

After the French defeat by the Vietminh forces led by Ho Chi Minh at Dien Bien Phu on 7 May 1954, Vietnam had effectively become a nation divided between the communist-ruled North and the American-backed South, led by the staunchly anticommunist Ngo Dinh Diem. Vietnam had become a source of growing concern for the United States, which began direct military aid to South Vietnam in early 1955. To policymakers in the United States, the defense of South Vietnam became a test of American resolve to contain communist advances worldwide. After the American Military Assistance Command was set up in South Vietnam in February 1962, the number of American military personnel swelled to twelve thousand, but the effectiveness of the South's anticommunist war effort was undermined by internal political instability.

Overthrow of Civilian Government

General Thieu became involved in national politics following the bloody overthrow of the Ngo Dinh Diem regime on 1 November 1963. Thieu was appointed to several posts, including chief of staff of the army, vice-minister of defense, general secretary of the Armed Forces Council, and commander of the Fourth Army Corps. In June 1965 he was one of the so-called Young

Nguyen Van Thieu

Turks in the Armed Forces Council who overthrew the civilian government and was named chairman of the military junta's National Leadership Committee, becoming the de facto head of state. Thieu, who had been reluctantly sharing power with his rival, General Nguyen Cao Ky, was elected president in September 1967, following the election of a new constituent assembly and the drafting of a new constitution.

By 1967 American troop strength in Vietnam had approached a half million, but victory over the communist forces proved elusive. Over the next four years Thieu attempted with limited success to bring stability to South Vietnam and win popular support for the war against the Vietcong. He implemented a wide-ranging land reform program to redress inequalities in landholdings. In 1971 Thieu was elected to a second four-year term amid charges that the United States mission in Saigon, the South Vietnamese capital, had persuaded other candidates not to run against him. Although plagued by corruption and administrative incompetence, Thieu's regime was politically more stable than its predecessors.

Having converted to Christianity after his marriage into a prominent Vietnamese Catholic family in an overwhelmingly Buddhist nation, Thieu was never able to attract broad popular support. Indicative of South Vietnam's inability to build a viable government since

1955, his regime depended on American military and economic aid to stay afloat. Relations with the United States, however, were often marked by mutual ambivalence and mistrust.

"Vietnamization"

Nguyen Van Thieu's two terms in office corresponded to the intensification of the Vietnam War, from which the United States began to extricate itself in the early 1970s. The war in Southeast Asia had expanded into Cambodia and Laos, but American commitment to the war ebbed as U.S. president Richard M. Nixon and Henry A. Kissinger, U.S. national security adviser and later secretary of state, searched for a negotiated end to the conflict. The Nixon administration proposed to reduce American forces in Vietnam, who had carried the brunt of the fighting, through a policy of "Vietnamization," the withdrawal of American troops and their replacement by South Vietnamese troops. Thieu, who adamantly opposed any settlement with the communist forces and North Vietnam, unsuccessfully resisted the American decision to sign the Paris Agreements of 27 January 1973. The agreements had provided for a ceasefire, but communist forces continued to advance. By March the northern provinces had fallen to the communists, and by early April Vietcong and North Vietnamese regular forces had surrounded Saigon. Despite President Nixon's promise of adequate military aid for the defense of South Vietnam, Nixon's successor, Gerald R. Ford, was unable to persuade the United States Congress to increase military aid to the Saigon regime.

Dependent on American military assistance for its survival, the Thieu regime rapidly disintegrated in the face of the communist forces' final offensive in early 1975, and Thieu decided to abandon the entire northern half of the country to the North Vietnamese forces. The decision signaled the collapse of South Vietnam. On 20 April 1975, a few days before the North Vietnamese entered Saigon, Thieu resigned and days later fled to Taiwan. He currently resides in England.

General References

Alan Dawson, *55 Days: The Fall of South Vietnam* (Englewood Cliffs, N.J.: Prentice-Hall, 1977);

Anthony J. Joes, *The War for South Vietnam, 1945–1975* (New York: Praeger, 1989);

Stanley Karnow, *Vietnam: A History* (New York: Viking, 1983);

Douglas Welsh, *The History of the Vietnam War* (London: Hamlyn, 1981).

—J. R.-S.

SEE ALSO THESE RELATED ENTRIES

Ngo Dinh Diem, 2; Gerald R. Ford, 1; Ho Chi Minh, 2; Henry Kissinger, 1; Richard M. Nixon, 1; William C. Westmoreland, 1.

Kwame Nkrumah

President of Ghana, 1960–1966

Prime Minister of Ghana, 1952–1960

Born Nkrofu, British Gold Coast, 21 September 1909
Died Bucharest, Romania, 27 April 1972

Kwame Nkrumah was an African statesman and socialist, a revolutionary leader who was the architect of Ghanaian independence and the country's first prime minister. Nkrumah was the leading proponent of Pan-Africanism and a fervent spokesman for African independence and political unification.

Nkrumah was born on 21 September 1909 in Nkrofu, a small village in the southwestern region of the British Gold Coast (present-day Ghana). After completing primary schooling at a Catholic mission school, he attended secondary school in Achimota. From 1930 to 1935 he taught at the Government Training College in Accra, the capital of the Gold Coast. In 1935 Nkrumah left for the United States to study at Lincoln University in Pennsylvania, a black university attended by many African students. He was politically active on campus, graduated in 1939 with bachelor's degrees in economics and sociology, and decided to continue to study philosophy and education at Lincoln's Theological Seminary and the University of Pennsylvania.

Nkrumah's Pan-Africanist thinking evolved during his years in the United States, where he came under the influence of figures such as George Padmore, West Indian nationalist leader and activist, and Marcus Garvey, Jamaican black leader. Pan-Africanists espoused the ideas of racial, cultural, and political solidarity in the African diaspora. Nkrumah made his political debut at the Pan-Africanist Conference in New York City in 1944 and the following year left for London to study at the London School of Economics. At the time African nationalism and political activity were taking form outside of Africa among the politically aroused African students abroad. Nkrumah's own militant nationalism and revolutionary ideas were molded during his years in the United States and England, where he became involved with the British Communist party. In England he became the vice-president of the West African Student Union in London and served in 1945 with Jomo Kenyatta, Kenyan nationalist leader, as the cosecretary of the Fifth Pan-Africanist Conference held in Manchester, England. Nkrumah also became editor of the *New African*, a militant publication put out by African students in England.

Kwame Nkrumah

The CPP

In 1947 Nkrumah returned to the Gold Coast at a time of social and political ferment in the British colony. Already known in the country for his leadership skills and political activism, Nkrumah was invited to become the secretary of the United Gold Coast Convention (UGCC), the leading nationalist organization in the colony. He set out to transform the UGCC into a mass political party to press for independence, but his relationship with the more conservative leadership of the organization was stormy. The growing differences between Nkrumah and the moderate, gradualist leadership of the UGCC caused Nkrumah to break away and form the Convention People's party (CPP), the first party to emerge in black Africa with a truly mass appeal. Organized by Nkrumah into a modern, radical political party, the slogan of the CPP was "Self Government Now!" Armed with a fiery oratory that aroused popular passions, Nkrumah's simple message and militant nationalism turned him into the leading figure of the Ghanaian independence movement.

The Coussey Report

In response to growing political unrest and disturbances, the British Government issued the Coussey Report in 1949, outlining political reforms for limited internal self-government. Nkrumah, who strongly opposed the report, toured the country calling for "positive action," his policy of nonviolent civil disobedience, noncooperation, boycotts, and strikes. After a state of emergency was declared by the colonial administration in late 1949, Nkrumah was arrested and sentenced to three years in prison. Preparations for limited self-government went ahead, and in February 1951 national elections were held for an all-African national assembly.

Released from prison after the popular CPP won the elections, Nkrumah, who agreed to abandon his cry for "Self Government Now," set out on a historic partnership with the colonial governor, Sir Charles Arden-Clarke, to bring about full independence under a new constitution. The Gold Coast, renamed Ghana, became independent on 6 March 1957, the first country in black Africa to achieve independence. Ghana's independence thrust Nkrumah onto the world stage and made him a symbolic, inspirational figure in Africa.

Nkrumah's domestic and foreign policies were guided by his ambitious, idealistic goals. In addition to his economic experimentation, he also embarked Ghana on the road to personal rule under a one-party system. A proponent of an ill-defined "African socialism," he favored nationalization and heavy industrialization based on the Soviet model. Ghana's first major development project, the Volta River hydroelectric project, however, was to be financed by Western (American and British) capital, in spite of his anti-imperialist, socialist rhetoric.

President for Life

In addition to economic centralization, the period of Nkrumah's rule witnessed an increasingly centralized and autocratic political system. After a brief honeymoon period popular dissatisfaction and political unrest began to mount, largely as a result of deteriorating socio-economic conditions and the closing of the political system. In August 1962 he was the target of an assassination attempt by political dissidents, the first of several such attempts on his life. Nkrumah, a proponent of a one-party system, responded to political dissent and agitation by adopting draconian measures to suppress opposition. In 1962 the nominal national assembly elected Nkrumah president-for-life. By early 1964 Ghana had become a one-party state as his rule became more repressive, corrupt, and dictatorial.

Nkrumah's activist foreign policy was motivated by his ambitions to become the prime architect of African political unity. He used his newly found international stature to press for the immediate independence of other African colonies, and became an active supporter of African liberation movements. Even though the notion of an all-African political union remained vague, Nkrumah became the leading advocate of continental solidarity and cooperation, as well as solidarity in the Third World. In a manner similar to the calls for Pan-Arab political unity by Egyptian president Gamal Abdul Nasser, Nkrumah advocated the creation of a federation of African states which would shield the continent from a hostile international environment and facilitate economic development. He denounced the West's relations with the newly independent states as "neo-colonialism." He argued that despite the granting of formal independence, the former colonial powers maintained dominance over the new states through various economic and political devices aimed at exploiting their resources and retarding their development.

The All-Africa Peoples Conference

In April 1958 Nkrumah convened a conference of independent African states, attended by Egypt, Ethiopia, Liberia, Libya, Morocco, Sudan, and Tunisia, and later that same year called for the All-Africa Peoples Conference, precursor to the Organization of African Unity (OAU). In 1959 Nkrumah pushed for a political union with neighboring Guinea-Conakry, which was later expanded into a federation including Mali. At the Casablanca Conference of January 1961 he joined other heads of state in drawing up a charter which was to form the basis of a union of African states. Up to the founding of the OAU in 1963, Nkrumah was the leader of the so-called Casablanca Group of states, among them Ghana, Guinea, Morocco, and Libya. All favored continental political unity. However, his forceful advocacy for political unity met considerable resistance from other African countries, the so-called Monrovia Group, which included Nigeria, Tunisia, and Liberia. Frustrated by the lack of enthusiasm and revolutionary fervor of his more conservative neighbors, Nkrumah began to call for their overthrow. His support for the overthrow of more conservative governments in the region alienated his African neighbors and led to his growing international isolation. The OAU, founded on 15 May 1963, while an essential compromise between the two groups of states, put an effective end to Nkrumah's vision of continental union.

Relations with the United States

The first country in black Africa to become independent, Ghana attracted overtures from the superpowers, both of whom sought to capitalize on the decolonization process in Africa and Asia. Although relations with the United States, which was providing economic and technical aid to Ghana, were cordial initially, they became strained during the Congolese civil war in 1960 (in which Nkrumah supported Patrice Lumumba, the militant prime minister). President John F. Kennedy, who viewed Ghana as the key to American policy in Africa, sought to strengthen the relations between the two countries, which came under growing strain with Nkrumah's ideological drift toward the Soviet Union.

Nkrumah pursued his distant, lofty goals at the expense of the day-to-day running of the government. Increasingly isolated abroad, Nkrumah's own domestic support and popularity began to erode as a result of deteriorating economic conditions and an increasingly repressive rule. In addition to basing his rule on a cult of personality, Nkrumah actively sought to give rise to an new ideology, "Nkrumahism," an ambiguous blend of Pan-Africanist and African-socialist ideas. In addition to clamping down on political opposition, he alienated the

army which he sought to control and weaken as a separate institution. Amid growing unrest and alarmed by his ties with the Soviet Union, young military officers, led by General Joseph Ankrah, overthrew the Nkrumah government on 24 February 1966 while Nkrumah was on a state visit to the People's Republic of China. He went into exile in Guinea-Conakry, where he was given the title of "co-president" by Guinean leader Ahmed Sekou Toure. Nkrumah died of natural causes on 27 April 1972 in Bucharest, Romania. His Egyptian wife, Fatiah, and three children returned to Egypt.

Books by Nkrumah

The Autobiography of Kwame Nkrumah (Edinburgh: Thomas Nelson, 1957);

Africa Must Unite (New York: International Publishers, 1963);

Revolutionary Path (New York: International Publishers, 1973).

Books about Nkrumah

Henry L. Bretton, *The Rise and Fall of Kwame Nkrumah* (London: Pall Mall, 1966);

C. L. R. James, *Nkrumah and the Ghana Revolution* (London: Allison & Busby, 1977);

Charles Jarmon, *The Nkrumah Regime: An Evaluation of the Role of Charismatic Authority* (Lawrenceville, Va.: Brunswick Publishing, 1981);

David Rooney, *Kwame Nkrumah: The Political Kingdom in the Third World* (New York: St. Martin's Press, 1988);

W. A. E. Skurnik, *African Political Thought: Lumumba, Nkrumah, Toure* (Denver, Colo.: University of Denver Press, 1968).

–J. R.-S.

SEE ALSO THESE RELATED ENTRIES
John F. Kennedy, 1; Patrice Lumumba, 2; Gamal Abdul Nasser, 2.

Manuel Antonio Noriega Moreno

Commander, Panama Defense Forces, 1983–1989

Chief of Intelligence, Panama, 1970–1983

Born Panama City, Panama, 11 February 1936

Manuel Antonio Noriega Moreno was Panama's chief of intelligence from 1970 to 1983, commander of the Panama Defense Forces from 1983 to 1989, and Panamanian chief of state from 15 December 1989 to 20 December 1989. Beginning in the mid 1970s he became increasingly involved in drug trafficking, money laundering, gunrunning, and intelligence gathering for both the United States and Cuba. The use of massive military force by the United States in December 1989 brought about his surrender to U.S. military authorities on 10 January 1990 in Panama City. He was arrested, tried, and found guilty in 1992 on drug trafficking charges in the United States. He was subsequently sentenced to forty years in prison.

Noriega was born on 11 February 1936 in an impoverished bayside neighborhood of Panama City, Panama. His mother, María Moreno, was a cook and a laundress. His father was said to have been Ricuarte Noriega, an accountant. Noriega was raised as an orphan by his godmother, "Mama Luisa." As a young boy he sold newspapers and read avidly.

From 1952 to 1955 Noriega attended the National Institute, considered the best public high school in Panama. As a member of the Socialist party's youth wing he provided U.S. intelligence agencies with inside information on the activities of his left-wing associates, beginning the double-dealing which was to characterize much of his military career.

After studying military engineering in Lima, Peru, from 1958 to 1962, Noriega was commissioned in Panama's National Guard. His heavy drinking and brutality toward prisoners and prostitutes alike earned him a reputation as a thug. By 1966, however, he was given his first full-time assignment as an intelligence officer, and he met Felicidad Sieiro, a young high school teacher, the daughter of Spanish immigrants. They were married and had the first of their three daughters in 1967. He also attended a series of American seminars in 1967 to study intelligence, counterintelligence, and psychological operations.

In 1970 Noriega was given command of the newly expanded intelligence unit of the National Guard. It was in this position that he began his official liaison with intelligence agencies of the United States and was given

© *Don Goode*

Manuel Antonio Noriega Moreno

access to large sums of Central Intelligence Agency (CIA) contingency funds.

Panama Defense Forces

By 1983 Noriega had worked his way to the head of the National Guard, which he transformed from a corrupt and loosely held organization into a tightly run business, renaming it the Panama Defense Forces (PDF). From this position of power he was able to install a series of puppet presidents until declaring himself maximum leader on 15 December 1989.

Throughout his career Noriega had not been able to resist the opportunity to increase his profits and power through criminal activities, activities of which U.S. intelligence agencies were well aware. The Richard Nixon administration in the early 1970s had learned that Noriega was involved in trafficking marijuana, heroin, and cocaine through Panama. The Gerald Ford administration discovered that Noriega was buying the services of its own intelligence agents. The Jimmy Carter administration caught Noriega illegally sending arms to Nicaraguan resistance forces. And the Ronald Reagan administration knew Noriega was a drug trafficker, that he had stolen elections, and that he had sanctioned the murder of a political opponent.

His crimes, however, were overlooked by the CIA and the Pentagon. In the early 1970s the arrest of the chief of intelligence of a friendly nation was out of the question. After the Watergate scandal broke in 1972–1974, Noriega's dealings were concealed by the CIA, seeking to avoid further scandals. Eager for passage of the Panama Canal Treaties in 1977, U.S. officials played down Noriega's crimes. And by the early 1980s U.S. support for Nicaragua's contras depended on Noriega's intelligence on the Sandinistas. For nearly two decades Noriega provided American agencies, including the CIA, the Pentagon, the Drug Enforcement Administration, and the Federal Bureau of Investigation, with exactly what they wanted, all the time serving his own agenda, which included selling intelligence and high technology to the Cubans, money laundering, gunrunning, and transferring arms to guerrilla movements throughout the region.

In February 1988 two grand juries in Miami returned indictments charging Noriega with violation of U.S. drug laws and racketeering, transforming him into a domestic policy issue. Two years of inconsistent and halfhearted economic sanctions coupled with unfulfilled threats ensued.

Invasion by the United States

Following a failed coup attempt on 3 October 1989, Noriega's rhetoric escalated quickly. On 15 December 1989 he declared himself maximum leader of Panama and announced that the country was in a state of war with the United States. In the tense atmosphere that resulted, Panamanian troops shot and killed a U.S. marine, provoking the U.S. invasion on 19 December. Noriega took refuge in the Vatican embassy, but within two weeks his support in Panama had completely eroded. He surrendered to U.S. authorities in Panama City and was taken into maximum security confinement in the United States. Although the U.S. show of force was denounced by many Latin Americans, Panamanians jubilantly celebrated his fall. Guillermo Endara was sworn in as the new president of Panama.

Books about Noriega

John Dinges, *Our Man in Panama* (New York: Random House, 1990);

Frederick Kempe, *Divorcing the Dictator: America's Bungled Affair with Noriega* (New York: Putnam's, 1990).

– L. H.

SEE ALSO THESE RELATED ENTRIES

George Bush, 1; Jimmy Carter, 1; Central Intelligence Agency, 3; Colin Powell, 1.

Antonín Novotny

President of Czechoslovakia, 1957–1968
Born Letnany, Bohemia, 12 October 1904
Died Prague, Czechoslovakia, 28 January 1975

In his youth Antonín Novotny was a journeyman machinist. He was one of the founding members in 1921 of the Czechoslovak Communist party (CCP) and thereafter rose steadily through the party ranks. During World War II and the Nazi occupation of Czechoslovakia, he was arrested for helping to organize the anti-Nazi resistance and was imprisoned in the Mauthausen concentration camp from 1941 to 1945.

First Secretary of the CCP

In 1946 Novotny was elected to the CCP's Central Committee and in February 1948 took a leading role in the communist takeover of the Czechoslovak government. Known as a loyal Stalinist, Novotny was admitted to the CCP Politburo in 1951 and became first secretary of the Communist party in 1953, after the Stalinist political and economic system was already in place. After the death of Czechoslovak president Antonín Zápotocky on 13 November 1957, he was also appointed president of the Czechoslovak Republic and reelected to a five-year term in 1964.

Opposing De-Stalinization

Novotny resisted pressures for political and cultural liberalization and managed to delay the shock waves of de-Stalinization which were sweeping across Eastern Europe. He tightened party discipline in the late 1950s and early 1960s and ousted any suspected reformist elements. A new constitution was adopted in 1960, that declared Czechoslovakia to be a Socialist Republic, and some economic reforms were implemented to raise living standards and pacify the working class. Despite Novotny's repressive policies, by the mid 1960s the forces of reform both inside and outside the party had gathered momentum. Novotny was forced to resign from the CCP leadership in January 1968 and was replaced by the reformer Alexander Dubcek. In March 1968 General Ludvik Svoboda replaced Novotny as the country's president. The neo-Stalinist faction was purged from the CCP and the communist system began to be gradually dismantled during the Prague Spring reform movement.

During the period of liberalization, Novotny lost his remaining party positions, and his membership in the

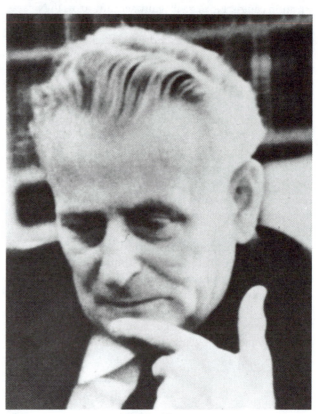

Antonín Novotny

CCP was withdrawn at the end of 1968. But after the Soviet intervention and the installment of a more orthodox communist regime in Prague, he was restored to party membership in 1971. This was depicted as a compromise arrangement in which some leniency was shown toward the ousted Dubcek by the Soviet authorities. Novotny did not regain any important party or state positions and died in Prague on 28 January 1975.

General References

J. F. Brown, *Eastern Europe and Communist Rule* (Durham, N.C. and London: Duke University Press, 1988);

Francois Fejto, *A History of the People's Democracies: Eastern Europe Since Stalin* (Harmondsworth, U.K.: Penguin, 1974);

Christopher D. Jones, *Soviet Influence in Eastern Europe: Political Autonomy and the Warsaw Pact* (New York: Praeger, 1981);

Robert L. Hutchings, *Soviet–East European Relations: Consolidation and Conflict, 1968–1980* (Madison: University of Wisconsin Press, 1983);

Joseph Rothschild, *Return to Diversity: A Political History of East Central Europe since World War II* (New York: Oxford University Press, 1989)

Zdenek Suda, *Zealots and Rebels: A History of the Ruling Communist Party of Czechoslovakia* (Stanford, Cal.: Hoover Institution Press, 1980);

Sarah M. Terry, ed., *Soviet Policy in Eastern Europe* (New Haven, Conn.: Yale University Press, 1984);

Adam Ulam, *Expansion and Coexistence* (New York: Praeger, 1968).

–J.B. and A.B.

SEE ALSO THESE RELATED ENTRIES

Alexander Dubcek, 2; Klement Gottwald, 2; Gustav Husák, 2.

Julius Nyerere

President of Tanzania, 1962–1985
Born Butiama, Tanganyika, April 1922

Julius Nyerere was the president of Tanzania from 1962 to 1985. Nyerere, popularly referred to as "Mwalimu" (teacher), is generally regarded as one of Africa's elder statesmen. His political thinking on government, society, and economic development is internationally recognized.

The son of the eighteenth wife of a minor local chief, Nyerere was born in Butiama, a small village near Lake Victoria. There is some uncertainty about his exact date of birth, although most sources cite April 1922. He grew up in traditional village life, and at the age of eight he entered a nearby middle school before enrolling at the Tabora Government Training School in 1934. In 1943 he won a scholarship to study at the prestigious Makerere University College in Kampala, Uganda, where he received a degree in education in 1945. After he graduated, Nyerere, a Catholic, was given a teaching position at a Catholic mission school in Tabora. In 1949 he was awarded another scholarship to study at the University of Edinburgh, Great Britain, from which he graduated in 1952 with an M.A. in history. He was the first Tanganyikan student both to attend a British university and to be awarded an M.A. It was during his years at Edinburgh that Nyerere began to develop his political thinking. After he returned from England he married Maria Gabriel.

Gale International Portrait Gallery

Julius Nyerere

TANU

Nyerere returned to colonial Tanganyika in 1952 and began teaching history at St. Francis College near Dar es Salaam, the capital. A year later he assumed the presidency of the Tanganyikan African Association (TAA), which subsequently was transformed into the Tanganyika African National Union (TANU). In May 1954 Nyerere was appointed a temporary member of the colonial legislative council, and in July he was elected president of the newly created TANU. The new party's political program called for democratic self-government, nationalism, and an end to racial discrimination. Under his able leadership TANU became one of the best-organized mass parties in colonial Africa.

The transition to independence in Tanganyika was peaceful and was preceded by progressive political reforms introduced by the British colonial administration. TANU emerged victorious in the restricted general elections of September 1958 and February 1959, followed by further steps toward self-government. Appointed chief minister after the August 1960 national elections, Nyerere conducted talks with the British colonial authorities leading to internal self-government in May 1961, followed by full independence on 9 December. TANU, which had dominated nationalist politics leading up to independence, emerged as the dominant political force, and the newly independent country emerged as a virtually one-party state. In April 1964 Tanganyika forged a political union with Zanzibar after a coup d'état in that island republic. The growing socio-economic problems faced by the United Republic of Tanzania, as the new country became known, pushed Nyerere and the rest of the TANU leadership toward a socialist path of development.

The Arusha Declaration

Nyerere, who achieved international recognition for the egalitarian themes in his political thinking, became one of Africa's leading advocates of state socialism. In early 1967 Nyerere launched his own version of African socialism in the Arusha Declaration, which outlined his policy of political, social, and economic development. The Arusha Declaration, which stressed socialism, self-reliance, and democratic participation, posited that economic development would have to come from Tanzania's own resources, and gave agricultural development priority over industrialization. Arguing that rural development must come through community villages, he pursued policies that made widely scattered rural villages into planned villages and cooperative and familylike farming communities, or ujamaa. The goal of Nyerere's ambitious villagization program was to raise agricultural output through collective agriculture. Nyerere's bold political experimentation was based on his concerns that the

country had drifted from its egalitarian objectives, and it sought administrative reforms aimed at greater decentralization. Aside from advances in the areas of education and health care, Nyerere's blueprint for development, together with drastic cutbacks in foreign aid and deteriorating external terms of trade, retarded real economic growth, which declined during the 1967–1985 period. Nyerere resisted the economic restructuring and austerity measures proposed by the International Monetary Fund and the International Bank for Reconstruction and Development (World Bank) in exchange for loans.

Relations with neighboring countries, principally Uganda and Kenya, were strained during the 1970s, leading to the disintegration by 1977 of the East African Community (EAC), the economic cooperation grouping of Tanzania, Kenya, and Uganda.

Deteriorating relations between Tanzania and the regime of General Idi Amin of Uganda worsened in late 1978 after renewed border fighting. After Amin's forces annexed the Kagera salient of Tanzania in November 1978, Nyerere, a strong critic of Amin's erratic and brutal rule, launched direct military intervention in Uganda by Tanzanian troops and exiled Ugandan rebels. Even though the invasion succeeded in removing Amin from power, Tanzania's intervention became a source of controversy with the Organization of African Unity.

Diplomacy in Southern Africa

Tanzania, an active supporter of black majority rule in southern Africa, became a major player in regional politics and international diplomatic efforts to secure negotiated settlements to regional problems. A member of the so-called Front Line States (the informal forum including Angola, Botswana, Mozambique, Tanzania, and Zambia), Tanzania offered military training facilities and assistance to the nationalist guerrilla forces fighting the white minority government in Rhodesia (present-day Zimbabwe). Tanzania was also one of the principal sponsors of the Front for the Liberation of Mozambique, the nationalist movement fighting Portuguese colonial rule in neighboring Mozambique. Nyerere, a personal friend of Zambian president Kenneth Kaunda, and the other front-line presidents sponsored the uneasy alliance between the two major Rhodesian guerrilla groups led by Robert Mugabe and Joshua Nkomo. Nyerere, a key intermediary during the brief 1976 shuttle diplomacy of U.S. secretary of state Henry Kissinger during the Rhodesian war, was an important factor during Rhodesian settlement talks in London in late 1979. Tanzania became one of the founding members of the Southern Africa Development Co-Ordination Conference (SADCC), which seeks to reduce member state economic dependence on South Africa.

Nyerere's political philosophy emphasized the primacy of the moral approach to political problems. He toured the country to articulate his vision of a just and prosperous society. Nyerere has been responsible for a measure of political stability uncommon in postindependence African states, and he became one of the leading proponents of African socialism and the one-party state system. Although not an autocrat, Nyerere's personal authority, prestige, and popular backing enabled him to impose his own vision of Tanzanian national life. While his ujamaa villagization and socialist policies failed, he instilled a sense of national identity in Tanzania, promoted Swahili as the national language, and improved the basic human services for his people. Even though he presided over one of the poorest countries in the world, Nyerere became an internationally respected statesman.

Although he faced no serious challenges to his power, in March 1984 Nyerere announced his intention to leave office after the end of his term in 1985. Nyerere became one of the few African leaders voluntarily to step down from power. He was succeeded by Vice-president Ali Hassan Mwinyi on 27 October 1985. He remained chairman of the ruling party, the Chama Cha Mapinduzi (CCM), which he sought to strengthen, and continued to wield considerable influence on national politics and de-cision making. Nyerere openly criticized the Mwinyi government for its retreat from the socialist policies of the past. In August 1990 the sixty-eight-year-old Nyerere resigned as party chairman.

Book by Nyerere (Selected)

Crusade for Liberation (New York: Oxford University Press, 1978).

Books about Nyerere

William R. Duggan, *Tanzania and Nyerere: A Study of Ujamaa and Nationhood* (Maryknoll, N.Y.: Orbis Books, 1976);

John C. Hatch, *Two African Statesmen: Kaunda of Zambia and Nyerere of Tanzania* (London: Secker & Warburg, 1976);

Cranford Pratt, *The Critical Phase in Tanzania, 1945–1968: Nyerere and the Emergence of a Socialist Strategy* (Cambridge: Cambridge University Press, 1976);

William E. Smith, *We Must Run While They Walk: A Portrait of Africa's Julius Nyerere* (New York: Random House, 1972).

–J. R.-S.

SEE ALSO THESE RELATED ENTRIES

Idi Dada Amin Oumee, 2; Kenneth Kaunda, 2; Henry Kissinger, 1; Robert Mugabe, 2.

Nikolai Ogarkov

Chief of the Soviet General Staff, 1977–1984
Born Kalinin District, Soviet Union, 30 October 1917

Nikolai Vasilevich Ogarkov, chief of the Soviet general staff between 1977 and 1984, was born in Kalinin district. He joined the Red Army in 1938 and was sent to the Kuibyshev Military Engineering Academy, from which he graduated in 1941. During World War II he served on the Karelian and Baltic fronts as an engineering officer. Credited with a keen sense of military operations and engineering knowledge, he advanced quickly through the ranks. In 1953 he was named deputy chief of staff for the Far Eastern Military District, where his superior officer was Marshal Rodion Malinovsky, a future defense minister (1957–1967).

In 1959 he attended the Voroshilov General Staff Academy, requisite training for an up-and-coming officer, followed by command of a motorized rifle division in Germany. Between 1965 and 1968 he commanded the Volga Military District.

SALT I

Because of his proficiency in scientific and technical issues, Ogarkov in 1969 was appointed number two negotiator and chief military representative to the Soviet delegation at the Strategic Arms Limitation Talks (SALT) with the United States. An American delegate at the talks described him as a "forceful" negotiator with a finely honed analytic mind, possessing a seemingly inexhaustible knowledge of Soviet and Western military systems.

On 8 January 1977 Ogarkov, with Leonid I. Brezhnev's endorsement, succeeded Viktor Kulikov as chief of the general staff. Brehnev, general secretary of the Communist party of the Soviet Union (CPSU), wanted to control increases in military spending and saw Ogarkov as a prospective ally. Both men initially agreed on the implementation of a defense policy in which Ogarkov would oversee structural and operational reforms within the military, while Brezhnev would seek further arms control agreements with the West.

As chief of staff, Ogarkov argued that a war between the superpowers would not necessarily involve nuclear weapons. Accordingly, he sought to reduce the prominence of the Strategic Rocket Forces (SRF), the independent nuclear missile service created by former general secretary Nikita Khrushchev in 1959. Ogarkov felt that the SRF's importance during a conventional war only extended as far as deterring a Western first strike. Furthermore, he publicly endorsed Brezhnev's Tula speech

Nikolai Ogarkov

of January 1977, in which the Soviet Union formally renounced the goal of strategic superiority. In 1978 Ogarkov began to refer to all three of the services with nuclear weapons – the SRF, air force, and navy – as the "strategic nuclear forces."

Reorganization of the Soviet Military

In an important contribution to Soviet military strategy, Ogarkov reorganized the structure of the armed forces, combining interservice forces under one autonomous commander. In a future war this commander would concentrate a highly flexible Soviet triad of air power, air defense, and ground forces at certain points to break through enemy lines. Mobile second and third echelon forces would then exploit the breakthrough to drive deep into enemy territory. This strategy would effectively deter escalation to nuclear weapons; Warsaw Pact forces would overrun North Atlantic Treaty Organization (NATO) forces and seize their nuclear assets before a decision could be made to use them. In carrying out this reorganization, Ogarkov was particularly concerned to integrate the Warsaw Pact forces more closely into the Soviet command structure.

Ogarkov realized that high technology would enlarge the scale and scope of conventional warfare. He called for an officer corps trained in science and technology and upbraided those officers who appeared resistant to change. In 1983 and 1984 he pushed for the introduction of a series of new highly sophisticated weapons systems based on "new physical principles," – armaments of near-nuclear destructive capability. These weapons, however, would be expensive, and Ogarkov was finding the Soviet political leadership increasingly reluctant to support the level of spending he felt was necessary to keep the Soviet Union militarily competitive with the West.

Decrease in Defense Spending

Economic forecasts for the Soviet Union had been uniformly pessimistic for the past decade and were borne out by poor harvests and unfulfilled production quotas. Civil unrest in Poland in 1980–1981 brought into sharper focus the need for more spending on the consumer-goods sector. The Eleventh Five-Year Plan, approved in May 1982, reflected a gradual shift away from the increases in defense spending that had marked much of the Brezhnev era.

Ogarkov continued, however, to press the politicians for a larger military budget. His immediate superior, Defense Minister Dmitry Ustinov, was of little help: caught between his chief of staff and Brezhnev, Ustinov would support the policies of the latter. Consequently, Ogarkov's machinations assumed a higher profile. In two articles published in 1981 he called for an increased state of military readiness, implying that the military would require more money.

On 2 October 1982 in *Pravda*, the Central Committee's newspaper, he urged a closer relationship between the military and civilian economies. Ogarkov apparently felt that if the military were denied a larger share of the budget, it at least should have more control over economic planning. A rapid and efficient changeover from a peacetime to a wartime economy would be of critical importance during the early stages of a conflict.

Ogarkov increasingly voiced his opposition to arms control after about 1981. His initial enthusiasm for détente had waned following the 1978 NATO decision to introduce 572 Pershing II and ground-launched cruise missiles into Europe. The breakdown of the SALT II negotiations after the Soviet invasion of Afghanistan in 1979 and the American military buildup begun under President Jimmy Carter further contributed to Ogarkov's opinion that arms control was not in the Soviet Union's interest. Brezhnev, however, continued to signal his willingness to seek accommodation with the West.

In a May 1981 article Ogarkov drew a comparison between the 1930s and 1980s to show the "aggressive, unchanging face of imperialism." In a 1982 book he urged a higher state of military preparedness to bolster Soviet security. By the time Brezhnev died, in November 1982, Ogarkov had gone from being a staunch advocate to a harsh public critic of the general secretary's defense policies.

Ogarkov found Yuri Andropov and Konstantin Chernenko, Brezhnev's successors, unwilling to alter the basic course of military spending or the Soviet commitment to arms control. Ogarkov in turn reiterated his support for greater military expenditures. In an interview on 9 May 1984 he called for an increased reliance on high-technology conventional weapons.

On 6 September 1984 Ogarkov was replaced by Sergei Akhromeyev as chief of staff, presumably because of Ogarkov's tendency to confront the political leadership over military spending and arms control. In a larger sense Ogarkov's confrontation with arms-control–minded party officials marked an attempt by the military to wrest control over that aspect of national security that had traditionally been in the party's domain: the authority to formulate military doctrine.

It has also been argued that by emphasizing the need for high-technology weapons at a time of shrinking military budgets, Ogarkov had become a threat to those members of the military-industrial complex who had a vested interest in conventional heavy armaments.

Ogarkov had also by this time acquired a high public profile, unusual for a Soviet military officer and all the more threatening in view of his disagreements with the politicians. At a press conference shortly after the Soviet Union had shot down a Korean airliner on 31 August 1983, Ogarkov was there to defend the Soviet action. He dominated the event, coming across to observers as overbearing and disrespectful of the civilian officials present. His behavior revealed the high degree of autonomy that the military had achieved.

Ogarkov's last assignment was command of the Western Military Theater, a position he held until 1988. Thereafter, he was transferred to the Main Inspectorate, synonymous with retirement from active duty.

General References

Timothy J. Colton and Thane Gustafson, eds., *Soldiers and the Soviet State: Civil-Military Relations from Brezhnev to Gorbachev* (Princeton, N.J.: Princeton University Press, 1990).

Dale Herspring, *The Soviet High Command: 1967–1989* (Princeton, N.J.: Princeton University Press, 1990).
— M. B.

SEE ALSO THESE RELATED ENTRIES
Leonid Brezhnev; North Atlantic Treaty Organization, 3; Strategic Arms Limitations Talks, 3; Dmitry Ustinov, 2.

Daniel Ortega Saavedra

President of Nicaragua, 1985–1990

Chairman of the Council of Government of Nicaragua, 1979–1984
Born La Libertad, Nicaragua, 11 November 1945

Daniel Ortega Saavedra was a leader of the Sandinista revolutionaries in Nicaragua and served as head of state and president of Nicaragua from 1979 to 1990.

Ortega joined the nationalist movement at an early age, during the time when it was trying to overthrow the dictatorship of Luiz Somoza Debayle. He was arrested for the first time in 1959, when he was only fourteen. Ortega enrolled in the Jesuit-run Central American University in Managua, but dropped out soon thereafter and fled to Cuba in 1963 to join the Sandinista Front for National Liberation (FSLN), which had been founded in 1961. The FSLN, or Sandinistas, used as their movement's inspiration the legendary Nicaraguan revolutionary, Augusto César Sandino, who had fought against U.S. occupation in the early 1930s.

While in Cuba, at the time home to many Latin American revolutionaries, Ortega and the other Nicaraguan nationalists received military and ideological training. He returned to Nicaragua to help organize urban guerrilla cells and to head the FSLN's student-movement wing, but he was captured in 1964 and jailed until late 1974. After his release he returned to Cuba for further training. By the early 1970s the FSLN had about thirty to fifty guerrillas and on the eve of the revolution in 1978 had about three hundred.

By this time, however, the entire nationalist movement had grown, along with mounting popular opposition to Anastasio Somoza Debayle, another member of the ruling dynasty. Opposition to Somoza's regime had intensified and consolidated following Central America's December 1972 earthquake, when Somoza had embezzled the international funds earmarked for earthquake relief. In addition to the Cuban-backed Sandinistas, op-

Daniel Ortega Saavedra

position to the regime was also present in aboveground organizations, notably the broad, middle-class-based Democratic Union for Liberation (UDEL), which was founded and led by Pedro Joaquin Chamorro, owner of Nicaragua's only independent newspaper, *La prensa*. The

FSLN itself suffered from infighting and organizational disunity. It was split into three factions: two more-radical, Marxist, urban and rural factions and a third, more pragmatic faction, the *Terceristas*, led by Ortega and which included his brother Humberto and Eden Pastora.

By mid 1978, however, the FSLN had regained some internal cohesion and unity through the mediation and pressure of Cuba's Fidel Castro. In the wake of the January 1978 assassination of Chamorro by Somoza's National Guard, the opposition coalesced into a broad-based national movement marked by continual mass protests, civil unrest, and insurrection. Ortega's pro-Cuban *Tercerista* faction formed tactical alliances with the above-ground opposition, and the regime's position further eroded with the stunning August 1978 takeover of the National Palace by Pastora and other guerrillas. By September the FSLN had begun coordinated attacks on major cities that touched off general uprisings among the local populations. The Cuban-backed and equipped Sandinistas were also joined by Cuban military personnel in their operations against Somoza's forces. Ortega commanded the southern front from 1977 to 1979.

The Overthrow of Somoza

U.S. policy was inconsistent as a result of an unwillingness to back either Somoza or the Sandinistas. Sanctions were imposed on Nicaragua in February 1979, but efforts to find a moderate alternative to the Sandinistas continued. Somoza, however, remained intransigent to U.S. and multilateral diplomatic efforts to bring about a negotiated settlement. By midyear, however, his regime had begun to crumble rapidly amid defections and military setbacks. In June 1979 the opposition formed a provisional government-in-exile in Costa Rica, among whose five members were Ortega, Violeta Barrios de Chamorro – the widow of the assassinated Pedro – and Alfonso Robelo. In the wake of a stillborn last-minute U.S. attempt to bring about the mediation and intervention of the Organization of American States, Somoza finally fled Nicaragua on 17 July 1979. Two days later the Sandinistas marched triumphantly into Managua. Ortega, who had been a member of the FSLN's nine-member national directorate, was given the rank of commander of the revolution.

Provisional Government of National Reconstruction

In addition to the vast social and economic costs of the civil war, the new Provisional Government of National Reconstruction also faced internal problems. Ortega became chairman of the ruling Junta of National Reconstruction and the council of government, but within a short period of time moderate members, such as Violeta Chamorro, Robelo, and Arturo Cruz, resigned from the Sandinista-dominated regime. Moderates and veteran anti-Somoza political leaders became wary of the socialist policies, Marxist rhetoric, and pro-Soviet orientation of the Sandinistas. Faced with growing internal and external opposition, the Sandinistas began to clamp down on opponents and close off political space. Elections were finally held in November 1984, but the opposition withdrew amid charges that Ortega's regime was not permitting free and fair elections.

Ortega's regime faced immediate external crises and challenges, aside from the domestic policies and deteriorating conditions which had begun to spawn local opposition soon after the revolution. Ortega's greatest challenge was hostility to Sandinista rule on the part of the United States, whose policy had turned more aggressive by 1981. The regime quickly found itself caught in the midst of an intensifying superpower confrontation in Central America, which for most of the 1980s was gripped by spreading internal and interstate violence. Ortega was committed to breaking Nicaragua's traditional dependency on the United States and in July 1980 signed economic treaties with Cuba, the Soviet Union, and many Eastern European countries. Nicaragua turned to the Soviet-bloc countries for the bulk of its trade and military assistance. Soviet economic and military aid to the Sandinistas reached an estimated $3 billion during 1979–1989. In addition to military and economic aid, the Soviet Union, Cuba, and East Germany provided state security and intelligence assistance and supervision. The Sandinista regime was also committed to aiding revolutionary movements in the rest of Central America, especially the guerrilla movement in neighboring El Salvador.

Nicaragua's relations with the United States were initially amicable, and despite lingering mutual suspicion the lame-duck administration of Jimmy Carter extended economic aid to the new regime. Relations began to deteriorate precipitantly as a result of Nicaragua's growing pro-Soviet orientation, its support for guerrillas in neighboring El Salvador, and a change in U.S. policy under the administration of Ronald Reagan. The Reagan administration defined the internal and interstate violence and instability in Central America as products of Cuban and Soviet involvement, with Nicaragua as a conduit of arms to guerrillas in other parts of the region. It accused Nicaragua of undermining regional stability and denounced its close ties to the Soviet Union as a threat to U.S. security. Cutting off economic aid in early 1981, the new administration turned to multilateral economic, political, and paramilitary pressures on Ortega's regime. In late 1981 the administration approved covert operations against the regime and, with Argentine help, began to organize, train, and fund paramilitary rebels that came to be called "contras" (or counterrevolutionaries). The contras initially consisted mainly of former National Guard members who had begun to organize themselves soon after the revolution. The original justification used by the administration for the contras was to prevent the flow of arms from Nicaragua into El Salvador. The objective soon turned to the destabilization and overthrow of the Sandinista regime. Despite the August 1982 Boland Amendment, which prohibited the use of funds to overthrow the Nicaraguan government, the administration sought to apply ever-increasing pressure on the Sandinistas, including soliciting third-country assistance, the mining of Nicaraguan harbors in 1984, and the imposition of a total embargo in 1985.

The Iran-Contra Affair

U.S. aid and supervision of the contras touched off one of the most intense and divisive political debates in post-Vietnam American politics. The issue of covert lethal aid to the contras ignited frequent clashes between the administration and Congress, which by mid 1985 had succeeded in blocking military aid. The first U.S. military aid ($19 million) to the contras was approved by Congress in November 1981, but in February 1984 aid was suspended by Congress. After the 1986 military and non-lethal-aid package, the administration was unable to get additional congressional support for aid to the contras. The policy struggle brought in its wake institutionally damaging consequences, capped off by the administration's illegal transfers of aid to the contras through clandestine arms sales to Iran. The Iran-contra scandal resulted in the successful prosecution of several top government officials (many of whom were later pardoned by President George Bush in December 1992).

Entangled in a costly war against the U.S.-backed rebels and unable to secure more substantial Soviet-bloc aid, the Ortega regime continued to face daunting economic problems and growing popular disillusionment. As the war escalated, Ortega declared a state of emergency in March 1982. The Sandinista regime became the focal point of regional and international diplomatic initiatives to bring about a negotiated settlement both in the region as a whole and in Nicaragua. One of the more notable initiatives was undertaken by the Contadora Group (Colombia, Mexico, Panama, Venezuela), which presented a peace plan in September 1984. The Contadora effort met with limited success, however, as a result of disagreements by the United States and Nicaragua with the plan. In August 1987 President Oscar Arias Sánchez of Costa Rica presented a peace plan which called for a suspension of contra aid, a cease-fire, and free elections in Nicaragua.

National elections were finally held on 25 February 1990. Ortega and the Sandinistas suffered a stunning electoral loss, with Violeta Chamorro and the National Opposition Union receiving 55 percent of the vote. Ortega continued to be involved in opposition politics and to head the Sandinista party, which maintained significant influence within the bureaucracy and military. He devoted most of his attention to reforming the FSLN party.

Book about Ortega

Roger Miranda Gomez, *War and Peace in Nicaragua* (New Brunswick, N.J.: Transaction, 1992).

–J. R.-S.

SEE ALSO THESE RELATED ENTRIES

George Bush, 1; Jimmy Carter, 1; Fidel Castro Ruz, 2; Violeta Barrios de Chamorro, 2; Ronald Reagan, 1.

Peng Dehuai

Minister of Defense, People's Republic of China, 1954–1959
Born Shixiang, Hunan Province, China, 24 October 1898.
Died China, 29 November 1974

As the People's Republic of China's (PRC) minister of defense from 1954 to 1959, Peng Dehuai led the Chinese army at a time when China was readying itself for an anticipated invasion by foreign forces. Peng was a career soldier whose aggressive – almost reckless – military strategies led to impressive victories and demoralizing defeats. He led Chinese forces in the Korean War and the Taiwan Straits crises.

Peng Dehuai was born Peng Dehua in the village of Shixiang in the southern province of Hunan. His home was not far from the birthplace of Mao Zedong. Peng lived his early years in poverty. After the death of his mother in 1904 and the subsequent failure of the family's business, Peng and one of his brothers were forced to beg for food in their neighborhood.

Peng left his home in 1915 to join the Hunan warlord army – one of several regional military forces controlling sections of China. Peng distinguished himself as an excellent soldier and chose to further his military career by entering the Hunan Military Academy in September 1922.

After his graduation, Peng served in several armies fighting to unify China, including Chiang Kai-shek's nationalist forces. While a major in Chiang's army, he became impressed with the communists' sympathy for the common man and began to align himself with the communist faction within the nationalist forces. Peng joined the Chinese Communist party (CCP) in February 1928, breaking his association with Chiang.

Peng Dehuai

The Long March

Peng immediately became a leader in the CCP's Red Army, commanding a unit of eighteen thousand men when the communists embarked on the Long March in October 1934. The Long March was a desperate attempt by the communists to elude Chiang Kai-shek's forces, which were conducting extermination campaigns against them. Only three thousand of Peng's men survived the one-year trek, but Peng, a burly man with a flair for the dramatic, emerged from the Long March a hero of the CCP.

Peng was a general in the "united front" army – composed of communist and nationalist forces – during World War II. The communists deployed three divisions in the war against the Japanese occupiers. He occasionally led guerrilla forces on surprise attacks on the Japanese.

Chinese Civil War

During the Chinese civil war (1946–1949), Peng commanded the 175,000-man Northwest Field Army. He was given the difficult task of protecting the communist capital of Yenan. The opposing general, Hu Tsungnan, was one of Chiang Kai-shek's best strategists. In March 1947 Hu launched a 260,000-man offensive that pushed Peng's forces back toward the Inner Mongolian border in northwest China. Peng's troops were able to save Mao Zedong from being captured in one of the battles, and Mao honored his general's courage and skill by dedicating a poem to him. Peng's troops recaptured Yenan in April 1948. Hu evacuated his troops to Taiwan in the fall of 1949, signaling the communist victory.

Korean War

The reasons why the PRC entered the Korean War remain unknown, but the current accepted wisdom is that Soviet leader Joseph Stalin persuaded the Chinese to do so. Stalin believed the United Nations (UN) forces, led by General Douglas MacArthur, were going to rout the communist North Koreans, thereby uniting Korea under the South Korean leader Syngman Rhee. Stalin, it is believed, convinced Mao that the Korean War could be used as a guise for starting another Chinese civil war, and Mao coaxed the skeptical PRC leadership to agree to enter the war. On 5 October 1950 Peng was named commander in chief of the Chinese forces assigned to save North Korea. Peng commanded the Chinese People's Volunteers (CPV), an army of 380,000 men.

The CPV crossed the Yalu River into North Korea on 18 October and seven days later engaged the U.S. First Corps at Unsan. In three major campaigns between October 1950 and January 1951, the CPV attacked the UN army on the east and west coasts of North Korea. The CPV forced MacArthur's troops to retreat below the 38th parallel. On 31 December 1950 Peng's men captured Seoul, South Korea's capital city. It was Peng's greatest victory. He later lost Seoul when the CPV engaged UN forces led by General Matthew B. Ridgway, who had taken over battlefield control of MacArthur's thoroughly demoralized forces. Peng's ambition was to capture all of South Korea, but instead he was pushed back above the 38th parallel where the war stalemated. Peng personally signed the armistice agreement at Panmunjom on 27 July 1953. North Korean president Kim Il Sung hailed him as a Korean national hero.

Peng's strategy during the Korean War was to use the CPV's only real advantage – numerical superiority. He applied "human wave" tactics to overwhelm UN forces. Swarms of soldiers using bayonets advanced – with little to no artillery, tank, or air support – into the teeth of concentrated UN fire. Chinese losses during the war were appallingly high. No official statistics have been reported, but conservative Western estimates place the losses at 450,000.

Minister of Defense

In the spring of 1954 Peng was named China's minister of defense, becoming, in effect, the supreme commander of China's army, the People's Liberation Army (PLA). On 18 January 1955 Peng used his new position to lead twelve thousand soldiers on an attack of the Dachen Islands. Chiang Kai-shek, who escaped to Taiwan in December 1949, was in possession of the islands and had been using them as a base from which he could launch commando raids into mainland China. The United States persuaded Chiang to evacuate his ten thousand soldiers from the Dachens by promising U.S. congressional approval of the Taiwan Straits Resolution, which gave the U.S. president authority to use force to protect Taiwan. In addition to the Dachens assault, the PRC was shelling two other strategic islands, Quemoy and Matsu, just off the mainland. Quemoy received the brunt of the assault. After China and the United States engaged in several acts of brinkmanship – including U.S. secretary of state John Foster Dulles's thinly veiled nuclear threat against China – the shelling subsided in the summer of 1955.

Peng's forces shelled Quemoy again in August 1958, using as many as sixty thousand artillery shells a day. Peng's navy blockaded the island, hoping to "starve" Quemoy into a surrender. The United States intervened, protecting Chiang's supply lines from Taiwan to Quemoy with its Seventh Fleet. Peng's air force sustained heavy losses while engaging Taiwan's fighter planes. Thirty-seven of Peng's planes were shot down. The Chinese eventually ended the blockade and shelling in October 1958 after more brinkmanship by the United States. Peng's mission was a failure.

In the late 1950s Peng tried to use his influence to upgrade the PLA. His objective was to revamp the military with modern weapons and disciplined training. He did not achieve his goal because he was purged by Mao Zedong in August 1959, after challenging Mao's economic policy, the Great Leap Forward (GLF), presented in 1958. Peng died in prison on 29 November 1974, a victim of the radical politics of the Cultural Revolution (1966–1976).

Peng was posthumously rehabilitated in 1978. He is now regarded as a hero in China.

Book about Peng

Jurgen Domes, *Peng Te-huai: The Man and the Image* (Stanford, Cal.: Stanford University Press, 1987).

General References

Russell Spurr, *Enter the Dragon* (New York: Newmarket, 1988);

Allen Whiting, *China Crosses the Yalu* (Stanford, Cal.: Stanford University Press, 1960).

– K.W.M.

SEE ALSO THESE RELATED ENTRIES

Chiang Kai-shek, 2; Lin Biao, 2; Douglas MacArthur, 1; Mao Zedong, 2; Matthew B. Ridgway, 1.

Augusto Pinochet Ugarte

President of Chile, 1974–1990

Born Valparaíso, Chile, 25 November 1915

Augusto Pinochet Ugarte was the Chilean army general who led the right-wing military coup that overthrew socialist president Salvador Allende Gossens on 11 September 1973. As president of Chile from 1974 to 1990, Pinochet instituted conservative economic policies and presided over human- and civil-rights violations in an attempt to suppress dissent.

Pinochet graduated from military school in 1938 and continued his studies at the Infantry School, the War Academy, and the National Defense Academy. He served in several infantry regiments and taught in the War Academy as a junior officer. Following several overseas assignments, Pinochet served as subdirector of the War Academy, regimental commander, division commander, and commanding general of the garrison of Santiago. He also wrote several books on geopolitics, geography, and the war of the Pacific. He and his wife, Lucía Hiriart Rodríguez, have three daughters and two sons.

Augusto Pinochet Ugarte

The 1973 Coup

In the early 1970s Pinochet was second-in-command of the Chilean army under General Carlos Prats, who led those in the armed forces who insisted on a constitutional apolitical role for the military. When a 29 June 1973 army revolt in Santiago was crushed and General Prats was forced to resign, General Pinochet succeeded him as commander of the armed forces and led the bloody military coup that ousted Allende. Thousands of Chileans were wounded or killed during the military attacks on major industrial centers, where worker support for Allende's government was strong. A ruling four-man junta named Pinochet president and suspended congress indefinitely.

The ousted Allende had been the first Marxist to be elected president of a Latin American nation. During his three years in power, from 1970 to 1973, he nationalized private banks, copper mines, and many other industries. Agrarian reform was accelerated, and diplomatic relations were established with China, Cuba, and other communist countries.

But from the beginning the Allende government was besieged by a series of political and economic problems. Allende faced open hostility from the Nixon administration, which intensified Chile's economic problems by cutting off U.S. aid. The Central Intelligence Agency (CIA), which had failed in its attempts to prevent Allende from taking power, began spending large sums of money to destabilize and subvert the new government. By 1972 there were widespread demonstrations by the members of the middle class, who opposed Allende's plans for a socialist Chile.

General Pinochet's military dictatorship set out to reverse the Marxist social and economic programs instituted by Allende. Nationalized industries

269

were sold back to private investors. Social welfare programs were suspended. Political parties, labor unions, and strikes were also outlawed. The military took control of all the universities, and strict censorship was imposed on the press. Thousands of Allende supporters were imprisoned and tortured, and many were driven into exile or disappeared without a trace. Pinochet had ended a long democratic tradition in Chile and instituted harsh repression, but his government in general benefited from strong U.S. support.

The 1981 Plebiscite

Pinochet proved to be an adept military politician, transforming the regime, centered originally on his leadership of the armed forces, into a personal dictatorship. An outward show of legality was given to this arrangement in 1981 with the drafting of a new constitution, approved by plebiscite. The new constitution guaranteed, among other things, Pinochet's continuance in power until at least 1989.

Pinochet's economic advisers, many of whom received their advanced degrees in economics from the free-market–oriented University of Chicago, implemented "shock treatment" policies to combat a 1,000 percent inflation rate in the first year of the regime. The policies triggered an economic depression almost as severe as that of the 1930s. Tariffs and other protectionist devices were subsequently dismantled, resulting in the destruction of a major

segment of the country's uncompetitive manufacturing sector. By the late 1980s, however, the economy showed strong signs of recovery and growth, and Pinochet's free trade economic policies became a model for other Latin American policymakers.

On 5 October 1988 the military held the long-awaited presidential plebiscite. Pinochet lost by a decisive margin. The victor in presidential elections held 4 December 1989 was Christian Democrat Patricio Aylwin, who was inaugurated the following spring. Pinochet retained control of the Chilean armed forces until early spring 1998, when he retired to become senator for life, a position bestowed on him by the Chilean parliament.

Books by Pinochet

The Crucial Day, September 11, 1973, translated by Maria Teresa Escobar (Santiago de Chile: Editorial Renacimiento, 1982);

A Journey through Life, translated by Mabel Nettle de Couyoumdjian (Santiago de Chile, 1991–).

Books about Pinochet

Genaro Arriagada, *Pinochet: The Politics of Power* (Boulder, Colo.: Westview Press, 1991).

Pamela Constable and Arturo Valenzuela, *By Reason or by Force: The Pinochet Years in Chile* (New York: Norton, 1991).

–L. H.

SEE ALSO THESE RELATED ENTRIES
Salvador Allende Gossens, 2; Fidel Castro Ruz, 2; Central Intelligence Agency, 3; Henry Kissinger, 1; Richard M. Nixon, 1.

Pol Pot

Prime Minister of the Democratic Republic of Kampuchea, 1975–1997

Born Prek Sbau, Cambodia, 19 May 1928
Died Cambodia, 15 April 1998

In post–World War II history no other ruler has butchered more of his own people than did Pol Pot. He controlled Cambodia from 1975 to 1979, during which between one and two million citizens of that country – the exact figures may never be known – were murdered, tortured, overworked, or starved to death.

Pol Pot was born Saloth Sar on 19 May 1928 in Prek Sbau, a hamlet in Kompong Thom province, where traditional customs were still widely practiced. His parents were wealthy by peasant standards, owning about thirty acres of land and six buffalo. The family also had royal connections. A cousin of Pol Pot became one of the principal wives of the king of Cambodia, and his sister was chosen to be a royal consort.

At the age of six, Pol Pot spent a year at a Buddhist monastery, followed by six years in an elite Roman Catholic school. As a twenty-year-old carpentry student in Phnom Penh, the capital of Cambodia, he received a scholarship to study radio and electronic technology in France. In Paris he joined the Cambodian section of the French Communist party and became acquainted with future party leaders Khieu Samphan and Ieng Sary, who would later be among his closest comrades in the Cambodian Communist party. During this period he met his future wife, Khieu Ponnary, Khieu Samphan's sister. She would later act as leader of the women's movement in the Cambodian Communist party. While in France, Pol Pot wrote a series of articles for Cambodian leftist magazines under the pseudonym "Original Khmer," an early indication of his nationalist fervor.

He returned home in January 1953 and was introduced to the communist movement – the Khmer People's Revolutionary party (KPRP) – by his brother, Saloth Chhay. The KPRP had been formed just two years before out of the Indo-Chinese Communist party (ICP). The leadership of the KPRP was handpicked, trained, and controlled by the Vietnamese. They put Pol Pot to work organizing party branches at the village level, work which Pol Pot resented, believing his foreign experience enti-

Pol Pot

tled him to more important responsibilities within the party. He was also sharply critical of what he perceived to be a Vietnamese intent within the KPRP on using the Cambodians to further Vietnam's struggle, rather than to help the Cambodians in their revolution. After the French left Cambodia in 1954, Pol Pot, described by many of his former associates as charismatic, advanced within the party.

Increasing dissatisfaction with the Vietnamese leadership prompted Pol Pot, Tou Samouth, who had been Pol Pot's mentor in the KPRP, and Ieng Sary to create the Workers party of Kampuchea (WPK) in 1960. Pol Pot became the party's general secretary in 1963, and in 1966 he changed the name of the party to the Communist party of Kampuchea (CPK), which became popularly known as the Khmer Rouge.

Two factors contributed to the rapid rise in popularity of the Khmer Rouge among Cambodians: the U.S. bombing of Cambodia and the overthrow of Norodom Sihanouk, who had ruled Cambodia since it received its independence from the French in 1954. U.S. president Richard M. Nixon ordered the "secret" bombardment of Cambodia, which began in 1969 and ended in 1973, during which 540,000 tons of bombs were dropped on Cambodia, devastating the countryside, killing approximately 150,000 people, and destroying millions of dollars worth of private and public property, including Pol Pot's father's house. Tens of thousands left their homes and farms and fled to Phnom Penh, doubling the population of the capital. Many others joined the swelling ranks of the CPK. In 1970 Norodom Sihanouk, the prime minister of Cambodia, was overthrown by his former defense minister, Lieutenant General Lon Nol. Sihanouk, who was made king of Cambodia by the French colonial administration in 1941, had enjoyed popular support even though he ruled in the style of a feudal potentate. He worked to keep Cambodia neutral during the war in Vietnam, attempting to simultaneously maintain diplomatic relations with the United States, Soviet Union, and China. But the United States badly needed Cambodian support to defeat the Vietcong, and this Sihanouk had been reluctant to give. As a consequence, the Nixon administration backed right-wing factions of the Cambodian military, who deposed Sihanouk in March 1970. Lon Nol and his generals were more intent on making money than ruling the country.

Sihanouk fled to Beijing after the coup and struck an alliance with Pol Pot – even though the Khmer Rouge had previously fought against him – and sent recorded messages to the Cambodian peasantry asking them to unite under the banner of the Rouge. On 17 April 1975 the Khmer Rouge took over Phnom Penh, just thirteen days before Saigon fell to the Vietcong. Pol Pot renamed Cambodia the Democratic Republic of Kampuchea.

The Khmer Rouge immediately began to depopulate the capital. Nearly the entire population of hnom Penh – approximately one million people – was forcibly marched to communal farms set up in villages, some of which were hundreds of miles outside the capital. All those suspected of having been associated with the previous regime, or considered tainted for having associated with foreigners, were executed. All those considered to be intellectuals were also killed. It was sometimes enough merely to speak a foreign language, or to wear spectacles, to receive a death sentence. The purges were part of

Pol Pot's plan to cleanse the existing Khmer race and to preside over a glorious new revolutionary civilization that would surpass in greatness Cambodia's ancient civilization.

Despite having benefited from the early support of Vietnamese communists in building a Cambodian revolutionary movement, Pol Pot resurrected a historic, nationalistic hatred of Vietnam. All friendly mention of Vietnam and its help to Cambodia was forbidden and was erased from Cambodian history books.

In Pol Pot's Cambodia all property was communally owned, from farms and factories to household utensils. There were only three categories of citizens: workers, peasants, and soldiers. Parents were separated from their children, husbands from their wives. All citizens had one duty only, to defend the country. Mostly, this duty consisted of working hard and increasing production. To this end all citizens not in the Khmer Rouge militia were put into cooperatives. Once there, all undesirables were weeded out and killed. Men and women slept in separate communal quarters. They worked from daybreak until sunset and, in the evenings, attended classes of ideological indoctrination. Food and medicines were scarce, and informants were rampant, with people being driven by desperation to inform upon relatives and friends in order to receive increased rations. Death was usually the penalty for breaching the strict Khmer disciplinary code. Many among those who survived the long marches to the cooperatives, as well as the weeding-out process, and even managed to keep on the good side of the Khmer Rouge cadre starved to death. The bodies were dumped in mass graves. It has been estimated that no less than one-fifth of the population of Cambodia was eliminated by the Khmer Rouge.

More than 100,000 ethnic Vietnamese, 225,000 ethnic Chinese, 100,000 Cham (Muslims), and 12,000 Thais were also killed as part of Pol Pot's program of ethnic cleansing in Cambodia. Those who survived were not allowed to practice their religion or the customs of their culture. Pol Pot also sought to rid Cambodia of its Buddhist influence. At the beginning of his rule there were some 2,680 Buddhist monks in Cambodia; at the end, 70. Not spared either were members of the CPK who had dissented. In 1974 Pol Pot had purged the party of all those trained by, or suspected of being loyal to, Vietnam. After he came to power, all who had been purged were killed. Also killed were any members of the party who deviated, even in the slightest, from Pol Pot's party line. Among the hundreds of party workers killed was Saloth Chhay, Pol Pot's brother. Throughout his rule Pol Pot kept his family background a close secret. Saloth Chhay had presented a risk because he could have revealed the family's aristocratic connections.

In 1977 Pol Pot launched a series of raids into Vietnam, claiming parts of Vietnamese territory as historically Cambodian. Backed by China, which had its own scores to settle with Vietnam resulting from the Sino-Soviet split in the early 1960s, Pol Pot was confident that the Vietnamese would not offer much resistance. The Vietnamese government tried to persuade Pol Pot to negotiate, then lobbied China to apply diplomatic pressure to Phnom Penh. When diplomacy failed, Vietnam began organizing Khmer Rouge defectors, including senior figures Heng Samrin and Hun Sen, and established an anti-CPK communist resistance force loyal to Vietnam. In January 1979 the Vietnamese army moved into Cambodia and drove the Khmer Rouge out of power. Pol Pot and other leaders took refuge in China. Unhappy with Vietnam, China provided military backing for the Khmer Rouge, which set up camps along Thailand's border with Cambodia and began a guerrilla war against the Vietnam-backed Heng Samrin regime.

The Vietnamese invasion of Cambodia brought the atrocities of Pol Pot to the attention of the international community. In exile Pol Pot reunited with Sihanouk, whom he had kept under house arrest for several years. The two, along with the noncommunist Kampuchean People's National Liberation Front (KPNLF), led by Son Sann, formed a new resistance coalition. Backed by China, the United States, and the countries of the Association of Southeast Asian Nations, it was recognized as the legitimate government of Cambodia by the United Nations (UN). As the Cold War escalated in the 1980s, following the Soviet invasion of Afghanistan, the Heng Samrin regime was increasingly isolated internationally. It received support from few nations other than those in the Soviet bloc. Aided by the Chinese, the Khmer Rouge attacked the Heng Samrin government, which only managed to survive due to the large number of Vietnamese troops that helped it fight the Khmer Rouge. After Gorbachev came to power and changed the foreign policy of the Soviet Union, Vietnam pulled its troops out of Cambodia in 1989. New diplomatic efforts were made to resolve the Cambodian conflict. The United States

supported Sihanouk and the KPNLF but came under increasing domestic pressure for doing so — many fearing that U.S. support of the KPNLF would strengthen the Khmer Rouge and result in Pol Pot's return to power in Cambodia. In 1985, mainly in order to defuse international criticism, the Khmer Rouge announced that Pol Pot had retired from politics and would no longer play an active role in the resistance coalition. The announcement was met by skepticism among most political analysts, for Pol Pot's replacement, Khieu Samphan, was one of his closest friends and associates. In late 1990 the United States decided to halt aid to those fighting Cambodia's pro-Vietnamese government in order to help bring a stop to the fighting in Cambodia. In fall 1997 a rebellious faction of the Khmer Rouge staged a show trial of Pol Pot, witnessed by Western journalists, in which he was sentenced to house arrest for life. In mid-April 1998, the Khmer Rouge anounced that Pol Pot died in his sleep of a heart attack. Requests by the Cambodian and Western government to have an autopsy performed on the body were rebuffed, and he was cremated.

Books about Pol Pot

David P. Chandler, Ben Kiernan, and Chanthou Boua, eds., *Pol Pot Plans the Future* (New Haven, Conn.: Yale University Press, 1988);

Ben Kiernan, *How Pol Pot Came to Power* (London: Verso, 1985).

General References

Elizabeth Becker, *When the War Was Over: The Voices of Cambodia's Revolution and its People* (New York: Simon & Schuster, 1986);

Wilfred Burchett, *The China Cambodia Vietnam Triangle* (Chicago: Vanguard, 1981);

Nayan Chanda, *Brother Enemy: The War after the War* (San Diego: Harcourt Brace Jovanovich, 1986);

François Ponchaud, *Cambodia Year Zero* (New York: Holt, Rinehart & Winston 1977);

William Shawcross, *The Quality of Mercy: Cambodia, Holocaust, and Modern Conscience* (New York: Simon and Schuster, 1984);

William Shawcross, *Sideshow: Kissinger, Nixon, and the Destruction of Cambodia* (New York: Simon & Schuster, 1979).

—Q. I.

SEE ALSO THESE RELATED ENTRIES
Henry Kissinger, 1; Richard Nixon, 1; Heng Samrin, 2; Norodom Sihanouk, 2.

Imre Pozsgay

Hungarian Politician and Reformer
Born Konyi, Hungary, 26 November 1933

Imre Pozsgay, Hungarian communist reformer, studied at the Lenin Institute in Budapest after World War II and graduated as a secondary-school teacher qualified in history and Marxism-Leninism. Pozsgay also obtained in philosophy the second highest postgraduate academic degree awarded in Hungary.

Early Career in HSWP

Pozsgay became a member of the ruling Hungarian Socialist Workers party (HSWP) in 1950. He did not play a prominent role in the 1956 national revolt. But his rise through the party hierarchy after Soviet forces crushed the uprising indicates that he was not involved on the side of the rebels or implicated by the government of Janos Kádár in "counter-revolutionary" activities. In 1957 Pozsgay was appointed director of the Marxism-Leninism Evening School of the Bács-Kiskun County Party Committee. From 1965 to 1968 he was head of the Propaganda and Culture Department of the county HSWP committee, and in 1968 and 1969 he served as the HSWP secretary in Kiskun county. In 1970 he became sub-department head of the HSWP's Agitation and Propaganda Department, and in 1971 he was appointed deputy editor in chief of the party publication *Társadalmi Szemle* (Social Review).

Patriotic People's Front

Pozsgay rose steadily through the party-state hierarchy during the 1970s. From 1975 to 1976 he served as the deputy minister of culture, and between 1976 and 1980 as the minister of culture and education. From 1982 to June 1988 he was general secretary of the National Council of the Patriotic People's Front, the HSWP's umbrella body for various social organizations. He was also elected a member of parliament in January 1983. Pozsgay was awarded various honors by the communist authorities, including both the Order of Labor and the Order of Merit for Socialist Hungary. Under his leadership the Patriotic Front began to speak out more forcefully in favor of major political reforms. Pozsgay himself gave guarded approval to the formation in 1987 of the noncommunist organization, the Hungarian Democratic Forum.

During 1988 and 1989 Pozsgay increasingly supported far-reaching political reforms and an end to the communist monopoly of power as a means to avert social unrest and to

Imre Pozsgay

help implement essential market reforms. At this time, Hungary stood at the forefront of peaceful, democratic change in Eastern Europe as it began to open up the political system to noncommunist organizations. In addition, in August 1989 the government decided to allow thousands of East Germans, who had sought asylum in the West German embassy in Budapest, to cross without hindrance into Austria. This helped to stir massive protests in East Berlin and other East German cities, where citizens demanded a lifting of travel restrictions and a respect for other human rights in the hard-line communist state.

Hungarian Socialist Party

Pozsgay remained a member of the HSWP Politburo until October 1989, when together with three other young reformers he was elected a member of the Presidium of the newly established and democratized Hungarian Socialist party (HSP). In September 1989, under the leadership of Pozsgay and other reformers, the party reached agreement with opposition forces on a multiparty system and on new laws for pluralistic national elections. But, despite the party's new image and democratic initiatives, in the March 1990 parliamentary elections the reformed HSP received less than 10 percent of the vote. Pozsgay himself was elected to the new democratic parliament, evidently benefiting from some measure of personal popularity. But he failed to obtain the post of state president to which he had aspired, as the reform-communists were swept out of all important offices.

General References

J. F. Brown, *Eastern Europe and Communist Rule* (Durham, N.C. and London: Duke University Press, 1988);

Charles Gati, *Hungary and the Soviet Bloc* (Durham, N.C.: Duke University Press, 1986);

Franklyn D. Holzman, *The Economics of Soviet Bloc Trade and Finance* (Boulder, Colo.: Westview, 1987);

Robert L. Hutchings, *Soviet–East European Relations: Consolidation and Conflict, 1968–1980* (Madison: University of Wisconsin Press, 1983);

Bennett Kovrig, *Communism in Hungary: From Kun to Kadar* (Stanford, Cal.: Hoover Institution Press, 1979);

Joseph Rothschild, *Return to Diversity: A Political History of East Central Europe since World War II* (New York: Oxford University Press, 1989);

Sarah M. Terry, ed., *Soviet Policy in Eastern Europe* (New Haven, Conn.: Yale University Press, 1984);

Adam Ulam, *Expansion and Coexistence* (New York: Praeger, 1968).

–J.B. and A.B.

SEE ALSO THESE RELATED ENTRIES
Károly Grosz, 2; János Kádár, 2.

Mu'ammar al-Qaddafi

Head of State, Libya, 1970–
Born, Region of Sirte, Libya, 1942

Mu'ammar Muhammad al-Qaddafi is the head of state of Libya and a militant revolutionary leader. Qaddafi rejects all formal titles of leadership.

Mu'ammar al-Qaddafi was born in the region of Sirte in early 1942 (the exact date of birth is unknown) into a nomadic, Bedouin peasant family. The youngest child of a family belonging to the Qadhdhadhifa, an Arabized Berber tribe, he received a traditional religious primary education, and from 1956 to 1961 he attended the Sebha preparatory school in Sidra. He was influenced by the dramatic, revolutionary changes taking place in neighboring Egypt under Gamal Abdul Nasser, whose fervent appeals to Arab unity and condemnation of Western influence inspired young Arabs. The charismatic, nationalist young Qaddafi excelled in school and was politically active. The Sebha preparatory school, regarded as the birthplace of the Libyan revolution, was where Qaddafi and a small group of friends formed a nucleus of militant revolutionary leaders who would eventually take power in 1969. Qaddafi, an early admirer of Nasser and an Islamic fundamentalist, was expelled from school in 1961 for his militant political activities and views.

In 1963 he decided to follow Nasser's example by entering the Military Academy in Benghazi, where he and a few of his fellow militants organized a secret corps of "Free Unionist Officers," whose explicit aim was the overthrow of the moribund, pro-Western monarchy. He also organized a popular committee to attract young nationalists committed to a revolution and to his vision of a Libya free of foreign domination. After graduating from the academy in 1965, he was sent to Britain for further training, returning a year later as a commissioned officer in the Signal Corps.

On 1 September 1969 Colonel Qaddafi and young officers from the Free Unionist movement staged a bloodless, unopposed coup d'état in Tripoli, the capital, overthrowing King Idris Senussi I and gaining complete control of the country within a few days. While the coup leaders initially remained anonymous, the Revolutionary Command Council (RCC), chaired by Qaddafi, assumed power and proclaimed the Libyan Arab Republic. A mild power struggle soon surfaced between Qaddafi and the young officers on one side and the older senior officers and civilians who had participated in the coup on the other. By January 1970 Qaddafi, whose faction re-

Gale International Portrait Gallery

Mu'ammar al-Qaddafi

ceived support from Egypt, had assumed complete control after eliminating his opponents.

The principal ideological thrust of the new regime was a combination of Pan-Arabism, religious reformism, and what came to be called "Islamic socialism." Since coming to power, the Qaddafi regime has sought not only to rid Libya of Western presence and influence but also to undermine Western, particularly American, interests in the region. British military installations in the country were expelled in March 1970, followed by the much larger American presence in June, and Western specialists and technicians were replaced by Arabs. The regime's early foreign policy sought to foster closer ties with Egypt and other Arab states. Qaddafi espoused Nasser's conception of Pan-Arabism, becoming a fervent advocate of the unity of all Arab states into one Arab nation. He also became an advocate of Pan-Islamism, the notion of a loose union of all Islamic countries and peoples. After Nasser died on

28 September 1970, Qaddafi tried to assume his mantle of the ideological, revolutionary leader of Arab nationalism and the leading proponent for Arab unity. The Federation of Arab Republics (Libya, Egypt, and Syria) was officially proclaimed on 1 January 1972, but the loose arrangement soon proved impossible to bring to fruition when the three countries failed to agree on the specific terms of merger. For Qaddafi, federation was the first step toward the creation of his "Arab Nation," with Egypt as the key element in any possible unification. He urged Egyptian president Anwar Sadat, who was unenthusiastic about a merger with Qaddafi, to agree to further measures on unification, organizing a "holy march" of thirty thousand Libyans to Cairo to demonstrate Libyan support. Qaddafi, who had an uncompromising attitude toward Israel, also became a strong supporter of the Palestine Liberation Organization (PLO), often putting him at odds with other Arab states he criticized for the lack of total commitment to the Palestinian cause.

On the domestic front Qaddafi sought to restore national control over Libya's economy and resources as well as to implement his vision of direct, popular democracy based on an entirely new political order. In April 1971 an agreement was reached with foreign oil companies operating in Libya for higher oil prices. By December the process of nationalizing foreign oil companies and other foreign businesses began with the nationalization of the assets of British Petroleum.

Cultural Revolution

In April 1973 Qaddafi launched a "cultural revolution," outlining a blueprint for the transformation of Libyan society and politics. The new social and political order was based on the tenets of the Koran and the rejection of foreign ideologies. In May he presented his "Third International Theory," which he hoped would serve as an alternative to "capitalist materialism and communist atheism." When strains and splits developed within the RCC in early 1974, Qaddafi relinquished his administrative duties and posts on 5 April to concentrate on ideological and popular mobilization revolving around his Islamic socialism. After reemerging in late 1974, he engineered the political and administrative reforms that established the so-called people's congresses, which were to be responsible for local and regional administration. Legislative power, previously held by the RCC, was turned over to the General People's Congress, with Qaddafi serving as secretary-general. This new political order was in effect a horizontal reorganization of society, which in theory would lead to the eventual withering of the state. The people themselves would become the authority; they would become the instruments of government, and their participation would be assured at all levels.

Qaddafi outlined his political philosophy undergirding the new political order in his *Green Book*, published in 1976. After changing the country's name to the "Socialist People's Libyan Arab Jamahiriya," Qaddafi became the "leader, theoretician and symbol of the revolution" in 1978, while the people theoretically exercised all power. While in theory the power of the people was to be exercised by the people's congresses established at various levels of society, participation in decision making and de facto power remained limited. Although Qaddafi has not faced any known serious challenges to his power, there is some domestic opposition to his rule, and during the 1980s there were several reported attempts to overthrow him. Qaddafi has responded to domestic and external opposition through violence, and in February 1980 his revolutionary committees called for the "physical liquidation" of Libyan dissidents living abroad, after which "hit squads" were sent abroad to silence opponents of the regime. On 17 April 1984, for example, Libyan representatives in the Libyan People's Bureau in London fired shots at Libyan dissidents during a demonstration, killing a British policewoman.

Relations with the Soviet Union

Qaddafi's international prominence has been based more on his aggressive, anti-Western, and unconventional foreign policies than on his domestic experimentation. The young regime set out to accomplish the ambitious goal of transforming the political landscape of North Africa and the Middle East. Qaddafi, a leading exponent of Arab nationalism following Nasser's death, sought to create for Libya a major role in North African and Middle Eastern politics based on Soviet-supported Libyan military strength and oil wealth. Despite an initial coolness, by the mid 1970s Libya had developed closer ties with the Soviet Union at a time when Egypt was drifting closer to the West. Libyan-Soviet relations were based more on a coincidence of geopolitical and military interests than ideology or shared objectives. Despite the lack of any formal treaties, by 1978 Libya had become the first country outside of the Soviet bloc countries to receive the supersonic MIG-25 combat fighters, signing new arms agreements in 1980 totaling $8 billion. Relations with the Soviet Union remained somewhat distant, however, as a result of Qaddafi's mercurial temperament and unpredictability.

Qaddafi's views and policies, however, alienated most of his neighbors and other Arab states in the Middle East. He openly criticized other Arab leaders who opposed his Pan-Arabic initiatives for union and publicly offered aid for the overthrow of moderate, pro-Western leaders in Chad, Egypt, Jordan, Saudi Arabia, and the Sudan. His relations with neighboring Egypt deteriorated after he boycotted the October 1974 Arab summit in Rabat, Morocco, which recognized the PLO, under Yassir Arafat, as the sole representative of Palestinians. He subsequently began actively to support splinter factions within the PLO, the so-called rejectionist front, which rejected the possibility of a negotiated settlement with Israel. Relations between Libya and Egypt worsened precipitously, leading to a brief shooting war along the border in 1977. A major break between the two countries occurred after Sadat concluded his separate peace with Israel in March 1979. Libya became the leader of the "rejectionist states," the Arab states that opposed any type of settlement of the Arab-Israeli conflict short of the destruction of Israel, and Qaddafi called for the total political and economic isolation of Egypt.

Throughout the 1970s Qaddafi's regime was implicated in subversive and terrorist activities in both Arabic and non-Arabic countries. As did other the Arab countries, Libya also became a major supplier of financial and military assistance to terrorist groups as well as revolutionary and secessionist movements throughout the world, including North Africa, Zaire, New Caledonia, Northern Ireland, and Nicaragua. Qaddafi also sought to increase Libyan influence in sub-Saharan Africa, especially in states with an Islamic population. He called for the creation of a Saharan Islamic state and gave military support to antigovernment forces in Mali, Sudan, Niger, and Chad. In 1973 Libyan forces invaded Chad and annexed the mineral-rich Aozou Strip, the territory along Libya's southern border. Qaddafi's armed involvement in Chad continued into the 1980s, increasing support to secessionist rebels in the civil war, including the introduction of Libyan troops, which enabled rebel forces to capture the capital city in December 1980. Soon after the Libyan-installed rebel leader and Qaddafi announced plans for a merger of the two countries, which brought international outcry and opposition, especially in West Africa. Under international pressure, Libya's estimated fifteen thousand troops were forced to withdraw back to the Aozou Strip. The forces of Hissein Habre ousted the rebel government in 1983, retaking the southern half of Chad and inflicting heavy losses on the Libyan-backed rebels. In response to a new Libyan-backed rebel offensive, France responded to a request by the Chad government by deploying three thousand troops in Chad. Despite a September 1984 Libyan-French agreement to withdraw foreign troops from Chad, Libya continued to keep nearly seven thousand troops in the northern region to assist rebel offensives. By March 1987 government forces had succeeded in driving back the rebels and forcing Libyan forces to withdraw toward the Aozou Strip, killing an estimated four thousand Libyan soldiers in three months of fighting. Following an 11 September 1987 cease-fire agreement, efforts were made by both sides and third parties to reach a settlement, and on 3

October 1988 the two countries announced the resumption of diplomatic ties, even though no progress had been made on the status of the Aozou.

In January 1980 a brief crisis erupted between Libya and Tunisia after an alleged Libyan-backed raid on a Tunisian mining town, prompting France to send military assistance to Tunisia in the event of a Libyan attack. Following the burning of the French embassy and consulate in Libya, Qaddafi vowed to counter France's interests and intervention in Africa by any means. In early 1980 a more serious rift developed between Libya and Arafat's al-Fatah, the largest faction in the PLO. After relations were formally broken with al-Fatah, Qaddafi openly supported the revolt against Arafat's leadership and increased Libyan political and material support for Palestinian splinter groups, many of whom were based in Libya. Libyan-Sudanese relations deteriorated over the Chadian invasion and Libya's involvement in antigovernment subversive activities. Libya was implicated in the 1988 overthrow of Jafar Mohammed Nimeiri in the Sudan. Qaddafi had also supported Ugandan leader Idi Amin, unsuccessfully airlifting Libyan troops to Amin's rescue during the 1979 civil war. In spite of his denunciations of moderate Arab leaders and support for subversive activities, he has frequently changed course in his relations with countries in the region. On 13 August 1984 Libya and Morocco unexpectedly announced a political union treaty, abrogated by Morocco's King Hassan in August 1986. In October 1987 Libya and Algeria agreed in principle to a political union, and in April 1988 Libya and Tunisia, with which Libya had formed a short-lived union in 1974, signed a cooperation pact. Qaddafi sees himself both as a leader of the Arab and Islamic world as well as the Third World and has attempted several times to become the chairman of the Organization of African Unity (OAU).

Qaddafi's militant foreign policy and active support for revolutionary movements and terrorist organizations, from various Palestinian terrorist groups to the Irish Republican Army (IRA) and the Japanese Red Army, have placed Libya in open conflict with the Western countries, principally the United States. Strained relations with the United states since 1969 gave way to mutual hostility following the sacking of the American embassy in Tripoli. In May 1980 Qaddafi, angered by the American arms embargo and export limitations, demanded billions of dollars in compensation from the United States, Britain, and Italy for the damages Libya sustained during Allied campaigns in World War II.

Libya became a principal target of the aggressive antiterrorist policy and tough stance towards radical Third World states adopted by the new U.S. administration of Ronald Reagan, which took economic and political measures to isolate Libya and to try to bring about the downfall of Qaddafi. Tense relations flared into armed conflict in 1981 when two American jet fighters shot down two approaching Libyan fighters during American naval maneuvers in the Gulf of Sidra. The United States accused Libya of promoting international terrorism and producing chemical and biological weapons. Relations between Libya and the United States, which also accused Libya of seeking to acquire nuclear weapons, degenerated to their lowest point toward the end of 1985, following terrorist bombings in the Rome and Vienna airports by the Abu Nidal terrorist group based in Libya. A dispute over navigational rights in the Gulf of Sidra, all of which Libya claimed constituted its territorial waters, led to another armed clash on 24–25 March 1986 when American fighter aircraft bombed missile and radar installations in the coastal town of Sirte after Libya had fired ground-to-air missiles at American aircraft flying inside the gulf. The Reagan administration, which accused Libya of sponsoring the 5 April terrorist bombing of a West Berlin discotheque, which killed an American soldier, ordered air raids against military installations, airports, suspected terrorist training camps, and government buildings, including Qaddafi's residential compound, in Tripoli and Benghazi. Although the administration had hoped the raids would lead to his ouster, Qaddafi managed to turn the American attack to his advantage domestically and internationally. Another clash came in January 1989, when two Libyan fighter aircraft were shot down by American fighters in international waters amid new tensions produced by American accusations that Libya was producing chemical and biological weapons with West German and Japanese assistance.

Qaddafi's international prominence throughout the 1970s and 1980s attests as much to his controversial figure as Libya's strongman as it does to his fundamental disagreement with established international rules of conduct. Flamboyant and eccentric, he has been depicted by the international mass media as a madman and dangerous terrorist. Unlike any other Third World leader, Qaddafi has relied extensively on unconventional methods, principally state-sponsored terrorism, to pursue goals that go beyond Libya's narrowly defined interests, displaying a lack of inhibition in the use of terror and violence both in support of radical causes and in opposition to his enemies. His strident rhetoric, revolutionary foreign policy, and anti-Western stance have brought him prestige in the Arab world. At the same time, his interventionist policies in and around the Middle East, his sponsorship of terrorist organizations, and support for Iran in the Iran-Iraq war have made him more feared than admired. Throughout he has remained a colorful personality, always dressed in his traditional ancestral robes and living in a tent. Qaddafi's populist revolutionary ideology has given rise to a certain degree of a personality cult inside Libya. For most of the outside world he remains an unpredictable, volatile leader.

Book by Qaddafi

The Green Book (London: Martin Brian and O'Keefe, 1976–1977).

Books about Qaddafi

Mirella Bianco, *Gadafi: Voice From The Desert* (London: Longman, 1975);

David Blundy, *Qaddaffi and the Libyan Revolution* (Boston: Little, Brown, 1987);

Mohamed A. El-Khawas, *Qaddafi: His Ideology in Theory and Practice* (Brattleboro, Ver.: Amana Books, 1986).

General References

Mary-Jane Deeb, *Libya's Foreign Policy in North Africa* (Boulder, Colo.: Westview, 1989);

L. C. Harris, *Libya: Qadhafi's Revolution and the Modern State* (Boulder, Colo.: Westview, 1986);

Bruce St. John, *Qaddafi's World Design: Libya's Foreign Policy, 1969–1987* (London: Saqi Books, 1987);

Martin Sicker, *The Making of a Pariah State: The Adventurist Policies of Muammar Qaddafi* (New York: Praeger, 1987).

–J. R.-S.

SEE ALSO THESE RELATED ENTRIES

Yassir Arafat, 2; Gamal Abdul Nasser, 2; Ronald Reagan, 1.

Yitzhak Rabin

Prime Minister of Israel, 1974–1977, 1992–1995
Israeli Defense Minister, 1984–1990

Born Jerusalem, Palestine, 1 March 1922
Died Tel Aviv, Israel, 4 November 1995

Yitzhak Rabin was one of Israel's most prominent military strategists, but his political career was hampered by a long-standing feud with former Labor party leader Shimon Peres and by a political scandal that forced Rabin's resignation as prime minister in 1977. A hard-liner within the Labor party, Rabin, as defense minister, initiated an ironfisted policy to quell the Palestinian uprising (intifada), which began in the Israeli-occupied West Bank and Gaza Strip in December 1987.

Yitzhak Rabin was born in Jerusalem to Russian immigrants. Both his father, Nehemiah, a tailor and labor organizer, and his mother, Rosa, a leftist political activist, were active in Labor politics. The young Rabin, in keeping with early Zionist dreams of reclaiming the land, entered the Kadouri Agricultural School in Galilee and moved to Kibbutz Ramat Yohanan, near Haifa, after graduation in 1940. His military career began there, when he stopped to talk with local Haganah (Jewish underground army) leader, Moshe Dayan, in the communal dining hall; Dayan invited Rabin to volunteer for the elite strike-force (Palmach) unit.

Rabin joined the Haganah in May 1941, starting his military career by cutting telephone wires behind French lines in Lebanon. He was arrested during a British sweep in 1946, but the following year Palmach commander Yigal Allon appointed Rabin his deputy. A month before Israeli independence, declared on 15 May 1948, Rabin was put in charge of the Palmach's operations to break Arab strongholds along the Tel Aviv–Jerusalem road, which included expelling more than fifty thousand Arabs from the towns of Lydda (now Lod) and Ramle.

Early Military Career

During the state of Israel's early years, Rabin held a variety of military positions: head of the army's tactical operations division from 1950 to 1952, head of the training branch from 1954 to 1956, and commanding officer of the northern command from 1956 to 1959. During this time Rabin married Leah Schlossberg, with whom he had two children, Dalia and Yuval.

In 1959 he became army chief of operations, rising to chief of staff in January 1964. As chief of staff, Ra-

Yitzhak Rabin

bin restructured the army and acquired more advanced weaponry, which were crucial to Israel's military victory in the June 1967 Six Day War. In the period preceding the war, Rabin suffered a thirty-four-hour nervous breakdown, which he blamed on fatigue and nicotine poisoning. The breakdown has dogged him throughout his later political career.

In February 1968 Rabin was named ambassador to the United States. During his five years in that job, Rabin became in some senses Israel's de facto foreign minister and guaranteed that arms and military aid kept flowing from the United States. After the October 1973 Yom Kippur war and subsequent Knesset (parliament) elections, prime minister–elect Golda Meir invited him to become defense minister because of Moshe Dayan's refusal to serve in the government. But when Dayan changed his mind, Rabin got shifted to the labor ministry – a post he once claimed was less than he hoped for but more than some of his colleagues wanted for him.

Prime Minister

Meir quickly resigned following publication of the Agranat Commission's interim report on her government's unpreparedness for the 1973 war, and the choice for a new prime minister focused on two Labor party stalwarts: Peres, the civilian politician, and Rabin, the lieutenant general and military careerist. But Rabin and Peres had been feuding since the days when Rabin had been army chief of operations and Peres had been deputy defense minister, almost twenty years before. The conflict originated with a disagreement about who had the power to set priorities in the acquisition and manufacture of arms; Rabin wanted military control, while Peres wanted defense-ministry control. On 22 April 1974 Rabin was chosen by a narrow vote of the Labor party central committee to become prime minister, partly because of his military background, partly because of his ties to Washington, and partly because of his being one of the few Labor party leaders "untainted" from service to Meir's government. Peres's strong showing, however, earned him the cabinet's second-ranking post, that of defense minister, from which he tried to undermine Rabin's authority.

Much of Rabin's focus as prime minister, as throughout his career, was military. He concentrated on rebuilding the Israeli army after the 1973 war, purchasing increasingly sophisticated weaponry. With U.S. help he negotiated a second disengagement of forces with Egypt. And he invested an estimated $150 million in building up the Christian militias that were fighting for dominance in Lebanon.

Domestically, Rabin's rule was rocked by a troubled economy, strikes, and charges of corruption. In January 1977 his housing minister, Avraham Ofer, under investigation for alleged abuses as director general of the Histadrut's housing company, committed suicide on a Tel Aviv beach. The next month, Asher Yadlin, governor of the Bank of Israel, was sentenced to five-years imprisonment for evading taxes and taking bribes, $20,000 of which he claimed to have given to the Labor party.

In March revelations that the Rabins had an illegal bank account in Washington, D.C., with a $23,000 balance, forced Rabin to step down only a month before the elections that he had engineered in an attempt to outmaneuver his opponent, Peres. The fall of the Rabin government in 1977 helped the Likud to seize power during the elections in May 1977. In the interim Rabin was required to retain the titles of his office but to operate under the shadow of Peres, who was given the position "chairman of the Cabinet meetings" as if Rabin were merely on leave.

National Unity Government

In 1984 Rabin staged a political comeback and became defense minister in the National Unity Government (NUG) between Labor and Likud that was formed following the July 1984 election. A longtime opponent of Palestinian nationalism and a believer in a peace solution that involves Jordan, Rabin adopted an ironfisted policy toward the intifada, under which the Palestinian death toll rose daily.

When hard-liner Ariel Sharon caused the national unity government to collapse in the spring of 1990 and the new government formed by Prime Minister Yitzhak Shamir veered further to the right, Rabin lost his defense portfolio. "This government," he told the *New York Times*, "is a Sharon government under the name of a Shamir government."

In February 1992 Rabin defeated Peres in the Labor party's primaries to become party leader. In the June 1992 elections Labor defeated Likud, and Rabin became prime minister for the second time.

In his 1974–1977 tenure Rabin led Israel to sign the historic peace agreements with the Palestinians and with Jordan, and began the process of normalizing Israel's relations with other Arab states. On 4 November 1995, after speaking at a mass rally for peace in Tel Aviv, Rabin was assassinated by a Jewish religious fanatic who opposed his peace policies toward the Palestinians.

Book by Rabin

The Rabin Memoirs (Boston: Little, Brown, 1970).

Book about Rabin

Robert Slater, *Rabin of Israel: A Biography* (London: Robinson Books, 1977).

General References

Conor Cruise O'Brien, *The Siege: The Sage of Israel and Zionism* (New York: Simon & Schuster, 1986);

David McDowell, *Palestine and Israel: the Uprising and Beyond* (Berkeley: University of California Press, 1989);

Bernard Reich and Gershon R. Kieval, eds., *Israel Faces the Future* (New York: Praeger, 1986).

— A. F.

SEE ALSO THESE RELATED ENTRIES
David Ben-Gurion, 2; Levi Eshkol, 2; Golda Meir, 2; Ariel Sharon, 2.

Mátyás Rákosi

General Secretary, Hungarian Socialist Workers Party, 1945–1956
Born Ada, Serbia, 14 March 1892
Died Gorki, Soviet Union, 5 February 1971

Mátyás Rákosi, communist ruler of Hungary from 1945 to 1956, was a socialist activist in his youth and became a Communist party member in 1918. He served in the Austrian army during World War I and was held as a prisoner of war in Russia. After the Bolsheviks seized power in Russia in 1917, he was released and underwent political and ideological training. He became a committed communist.

Between the Wars

At the close of the war in late 1918, Rákosi returned to Hungary. He served as commissar for socialist production in the short-lived communist regime of Béla Kun during 1919, which unsuccessfully tried to emulate V. I. Lenin by imposing a Marxist dictatorship in Hungary. When the Kun regime collapsed because of lack of internal and external support, Rákosi went again to Moscow for further political training. He returned to Hungary in 1924, to try to reorganize the Hungarian Communist party (HCP) and to infiltrate the trade unions and other organizations with communist cells and sympathizers. As general secretary–elect of the HCP, he was also a delegate to various conferences and meetings organized by the Kremlin-controlled Comintern (Communist International). During the early 1920s he was also responsible for Italian communist affairs in the Comintern.

Rákosi was arrested by the Hungarian security forces in 1926, and was charged with conducting subversive activities and plans to overthrow the Hungarian government. During the ensuing police interrogations, Rákosi reportedly denounced some of his comrades to save himself and his party membership and as a result was suspended by the Comintern for betraying his colleagues. Collaboration with the police, however, was of little help, and he was sentenced to eight years in prison. Shortly after his term expired in 1935, he was rearrested and sentenced to life imprisonment for his complicity in the 1919 "red terror" in which dozens of government opponents were executed and hundreds arrested during the efforts to establish Kun's Soviet-style regime.

Rákosi's long spell in jail improved his standing within the party, and Soviet leader Joseph Stalin agreed that he should be reinstated to the HCP. A massive propaganda campaign was launched by Moscow on his behalf which gained substantial support for Rákosi in his future bid for

John Hillelson

Mátyás Rákosi

party leadership. He was released from prison in November 1940, and allowed to travel to the Soviet capital to meet with his exiled colleagues. He became a Stalin loyalist and was favored by the Soviet dictator to assume leadership of the Hungarian communists in March 1942.

The Coalition Government

During World War II Rákosi became a Soviet citizen, but he returned to Hungary with the victorious Soviet army in 1944. A provisional coalition government was established in Budapest in December 1944, but the communists took command of the most important instruments of power including the army, security service, police, and civil service. The party also penetrated and assumed control over various mass organizations and labor unions and began to undercut the position of rival political parties.

Repression of the Opposition

Under Rákosi's leadership, and with Soviet assistance, "people's courts" were established in February 1945 to eliminate "reactionaries," or those who wanted to restore the prewar system. About 150,000 people were summarily arrested, imprisoned, tortured, or deported to Siberia. Although the HCP lost the elections in October 1945, it retained its preeminent position and expanded its powers. Similar to his tactics in the rest of Eastern Europe, Stalin did not immediately impose a full communist dictatorship in Hungary. Instead the takeover was accomplished in stages with a period of collaboration with other "progressive" though noncommunist forces. The objective was to lull the West, prevent concerted opposition, and gain some indigenous support for the socialist program.

The Communist Takeover

Under Rákosi's supervision, the "Muscovite" and "Native" factions within the Communist party were merged, nationalism itself was outlawed, and Leninist discipline was enforced. In January 1946 Hungary was proclaimed a "People's Republic," a term invented by Moscow to signal progress toward a fully socialist state. Rákosi began to apply his infamous "salami tactics" to sow dissension within and between other parties and weaken their influence. Various repressive administration and police measures were also employed to eliminate the opposition, and a program of economic socialization was launched in which all industry and trade were placed under state control and agriculture was collectivized. Despite these measures, the HCP lost the next national elections in August 1947. Fearing a delay in the creation of a communist monopoly because of too much emphasis on legalistic means to gain power, Rákosi now stepped up the pressure on the opposition. Prime Minister Ferenc Nagy was exiled, and other government leaders were imprisoned or executed. The major noncommunist party, the Smallholders, was forcibly disbanded, and in June 1948 Rákosi presided over the forced merger of the HCP and the Social Democrats to form the Hungarian Socialist Workers party (HSWP) under firm Leninist control.

The Fraudulent Elections of 1949

The HSWP won the fraudulent elections of May 1949, and the country's new constitution formalized the party subordination to Moscow. Rákosi now launched a program of full-scale Stalinization and conducted a major purge of the party to remove unreliable elements. Between 1949 and 1953, more than 350,000 "revisionists" and "national deviationists" were expelled amid massive police terror and the threat of imprisonment or execution. Hundreds of communists were liquidated to ensure absolute loyalty to Stalin and the Rákosi leadership. They included Interior Minister Lázló Rajk, who was suspected of being sympathetic to Yugoslavia's Marshal Josip Broz Tito, who had stood up to Stalin and was expelled from the communist bloc. Under Rákosi's leadership the Soviet economic model was imposed in Hungary, with the full-scale collectivization of agriculture and the nationalization of all industrial and manufacturing enterprises aside from some marginal private production. Recognized as a committed follower of Stalin, Rákosi served as party chief from 1949 to 1953, and as prime minister in 1952 and 1953.

De-Stalinization

After Stalin's death in 1953, Moscow sought to remove his closest henchmen and jettison some of the worst features of the "cult of personality" which had terrorized party officials as well as ordinary citizens. Rákosi was forced to relinquish the premiership to Imre Nagy, who attempted to liberalize domestic conditions. However, Rákosi stayed on as party general secretary and was able to dismiss Nagy from office in February 1955, charging him with "right-wing deviation." Rákosi's return to government in early 1955 reversed the Nagy liberalization process but failed to stem rising aspirations for democratization, particularly among Hungarian intellectuals and students.

Under pressure from the Kremlin, which feared widespread social unrest and a loss of communist control, Rákosi was removed from power and replaced as party first secretary in July 1956 by the reformist Erno Gerö. By this time, Hungarian intellectuals had become emboldened in their campaign to restore democracy in the country: in fact, they had become more radicalized by Rákosi's dogmatism. But the new Gerö leadership was unable to forestall mounting discontent by granting partial concessions to the opposition, and a full-scale popular revolution was under way by October 1956. After the revolution was crushed by Soviet tanks in November 1956, Rákosi fled to the Soviet Union. He was too discredited by this time to assume any important offices in the Soviet-installed government as Moscow sought out younger leaders not linked with the years of Stalinist dictatorship. Rákosi reportedly died in Gorki, Soviet Union, on 5 February 1971.

General References

J. F. Brown, *Eastern Europe and Communist Rule* (Durham, N.C. & London: Duke University Press, 1988);

Charles Gati, *Hungary and the Soviet Bloc* (Durham, N.C.: Duke University Press, 1986);

Franklyn D. Holzman, *The Economics of Soviet Bloc Trade and Finance* (Boulder, Colo.: Westview Press, 1987);

Robert L. Hutchings, *Soviet–East European Relations: Consolidation and Conflict, 1968–1980* (Madison: University of Wisconsin Press, 1983);

Bennett Kovrig, *Communism in Hungary: From Kun to Kadar* (Stanford, Cal.: Hoover Institution Press, 1979);

Miklós Molnár, *Budapest 1956: A History of the Hungarian Revolution* (London: Allen & Unwin, 1971);

Joseph Rothschild, *Return to Diversity: A Political History of East Central Europe since World War II* (New York: Oxford University Press, 1989);

Sarah M. Terry, ed., *Soviet Policy in Eastern Europe* (New Haven: Yale University Press, 1984);

Adam Ulam, *Expansion and Coexistence* (New York: Praeger, 1968).

–J. B. and A. B.

SEE ALSO THESE RELATED ENTRIES

Ernö Gerö, 2; János Kádár, 2; Imre Nagy, 2; Joseph Stalin, 2.

Syngman Rhee

President of the Republic of Korea, 1948–1960
Born Whanghai Province, Korea, 26 April 1875
Died Honolulu, Hawaii, 19 July 1965

Syngman Rhee was born into a Buddhist family in Whanghai province, Korea. He attended an American mission school in Seoul. At an early age he became active in the Independence Club, a broad-based nationalist organization that pressed for democratic reforms. He was imprisoned in 1897 for leading student demonstrations against the Korean monarchy. While in prison he converted to Christianity, translated English works into Korean, and wrote *The Spirit of Independence*, in which he called for a democratic Korean state. After he was released in 1904, Rhee traveled to the United States, where he received his bachelor's degree from George Washington University, a master's degree from Harvard University, and a doctorate in theology from Princeton University.

In 1910 Rhee returned to Korea and worked as an organizer of the Young Men's Christian Association (YMCA). Harassed by the Japanese – who had occupied Korea – for his political views and activities, Rhee fled to Hawaii in 1912, where he lobbied for Korean independence. In 1919, while still in exile, he was elected president of the Korean provisional government. In August 1945, after the defeat of Japan by the Allied forces and the liberation of the Korean peninsula from Japanese colonial rule, Rhee returned to Korea recognized as the country's most prominent political leader.

An agreement reached at the Potsdam Conference in August 1945 created a temporary division of the Korean

peninsula along the 38th parallel, separating U.S.-occupied southern Korea from Soviet-occupied northern Korea. Subsequent U.S.-Soviet talks to establish a unified Korean government collapsed in the face of the growing tensions between the two superpowers. In contrast to southern Korea — where efforts at forming a government were slow and unorganized — northern Korea, with the creation of the North Korean Provisional People's Committee headed by Kim Il-Sung, had been making great strides in establishing a political system.

In December 1946 an interim legislative assembly was created for South Korea amid political fragmentation and rivalry between leftists and conservatives. Unable to reach a compromise with the Soviet Union, the United States submitted the question of Korean unification to the United Nations (UN), which called for UN-supervised elections in the southern half of the Korean peninsula to be held in May 1948. In July 1948 the Republic of Korea was established in the south, with Rhee elected its president by the national assembly. Two months later the north proclaimed itself the Democratic People's Republic of Korea, under the communist regime of Kim Il-Sung.

Syngman Rhee's government faced immediate economic problems, army mutiny, and small-scale communist guerrilla insurgency. In addition to North Korean–sponsored communist agitation, a power struggle in the government quickly emerged, further undermining Rhee's regime. On 25 June 1950 North Korean forces invaded South Korea, reaching the capital city of Seoul within a few days of the invasion. A UN multinational force, under U.S. command, joined South Korean forces in pushing back the communists to the Chinese border, provoking the entry of Chinese forces into the war. By early 1953 the fighting had reached a stalemate along the 38th parallel, and on 27 July a cease-fire agreement, which Rhee strongly opposed, was signed between the UN and the communist forces of North Korea and China.

The North Korean invasion had merely postponed the political struggle between Rhee and his opponents at home. Soon after the close of the war in 1953, the struggle between Rhee, who favored a presidential form of government, and members of the National Assembly, who favored a parliamentary form of government, was re-sumed. After he declared martial law in May 1952, Rhee called for the popular election of the president. His arbitrary manipulations of the Korean constitution, however, led to growing popular discontent, with his support quickly declining in major urban centers.

Although the Rhee regime laid the foundations for modern South Korea's development, its political stability proved elusive. Rhee, who depended on a small circle of advisers, became increasingly alienated politically amid charges of administrative corruption. In May 1956 the eighty-one-year-old Rhee was reelected president with only a 55 percent voter turnout. His rule grew more autocratic and repressive, and he took measures to purge leftist political opponents. Rhee won a fourth term in office in March 1960, but his reelection was tainted by political unrest and accusations of electoral fraud. Widespread antigovernment demonstrations and civil disorder gave way to the so-called April 1960 Student Revolution, which forced Rhee to resign on 26 April. Rhee, who went into voluntary exile in Hawaii, was succeeded by an interim government, which was subsequently overthrown in a military coup d'état by General Park Chung Hee in 1961. Rhee died 19 July 1965.

Books about Rhee

Robert T. Oliver, *Syngman Rhee and American Involvement in Korea, 1942-1960* (Seoul: Panmun Books, 1978);

Quee-Young Kim, *The Fall of Syngman Rhee* (Berkeley: University of California Press, 1983).

General References

Peter Lowe, *The Origins of the Korean War* (London: Longman, 1986);

Pak Chi-Young, *Political Opposition in Korea, 1945-1960* (Seoul: Seoul National University Press, 1980);

Alan Romberg, *The United States, the Soviet Union, and Korea: Beyond Confrontation* (New York: Council on Foreign Relations, 1989);

Dae-sook Suh and Chae-Jin Lee, eds., *Political Leadership in Korea* (Seattle: University of Washington Press, 1976).

–J. R.-S.

SEE ALSO THESE RELATED ENTRIES
Kim Il-Sung, 2; Douglas MacArthur, 1.

Konstantin Rokossovski

Soviet Deputy Minister of Defense, 1957–1968

Polish Minister of Defense, 1949–1956

Born Velikiye Luki, Russia, 21 December 1896
Died Moscow, Soviet Union, 3 August 1968

Konstantin Rokossovski, Soviet military commander and Polish minister of defense after World War II, was born on 21 December 1896 in Velikiye Luki, Russia; his father was a railroad mechanic of Polish origin. Rokossovski served in the Czarist army during World War I as the youngest noncommissioned officer. In 1917 he enlisted in the Red Army and fought for the Bolshevik side in the civil war. In 1917 he also joined the Russian Communist party and was sent to Frunze Military Academy where he specialized in tank warfare.

The Purges and World War II

Rokossovski was imprisoned during Joseph Stalin's extensive purges of the Soviet officer corps in 1937 and 1938, but was subsequently released and reinstated. During World War II, he participated in campaigns against the Germans during the siege of Moscow in 1941, and he directed six Soviet battalions at the crucial battle of Stalingrad (1942–1943), where his forces trapped and then annihilated twenty-two divisions of the German Sixth Army.

The Capture of Eastern Europe

In 1943 he led the Soviet western offensive on the central front and played a major role in the liberation of Belorussia and eastern Poland. When Stalin set up a Polish communist regime at the close of the war, Rokossovski was empowered to take over the Polish armed forces and ensure their loyalty and obedience to Moscow. In 1949 he was appointed Poland's minister of defense and deputy premier and given the rank of Polish marshal. He also became a member of the Communist party Politburo. Rokossovski's mission was to ensure that the Polish army become a replica of the Red Army. He was also to act as Stalin's personal representative in Warsaw because the Soviet leader remained deeply suspicious about the reliability of the Polish forces.

The Remaking of the Polish Army

Rokossovski purged the Polish officer corps and replaced them with his own appointees. According to some estimates, by the early 1950s Soviet officers formed about

Konstantin Rokossovski

50 percent of the entire Polish officer corps and they dominated the Defense Ministry. Between 1949 and 1956 the Polish army became part of the Moscow-controlled East European armed forces directly subordinate to the Soviet high command. This was formalized by the creation of the Warsaw Treaty Organization (or Warsaw Pact) in May 1955. The communist regime in Warsaw had little or no say in the running of its armed forces, as Rokossovski took his orders directly from the Soviet army general staff.

De-Stalinization

After Stalin's death in 1953, reformist factions in the Warsaw government sought to limit Soviet control over the Polish military. Following the Poznan riots in June 1956, when troops fired on protesting workers and caused heavy civilian casualties, the hard-line party leadership was replaced and the army underwent sweeping changes. Wladyslaw Gomulka, who had been imprisoned by the Stalinist leadership, was appointed to be the new party chief, and Rokossovski was dropped from the party Politburo in October 1956.

Gomulka managed to reassure the Kremlin leadership of Nikita S. Khrushchev that Poland would remain a loyal Soviet ally and would not deviate from its communist course. In return, one of Gomulka's key demands to the Russians was the transfer of direct control of the army back into Polish hands, to which Moscow agreed. The majority of Soviet officers were sent home, and the Soviet military presence in Poland was limited to two divisions, largely acting as logistical and communications support for the large Russian force in East Germany. Rokossovski was sent back to Moscow and replaced as Polish army commander by Gomulka's confidant General Marian Spychalski. Back in the Soviet Union, Rokossovski was appointed deputy defense minister in November 1957, and enrolled as commander of the Transcaucasian military district. He was repeatedly decorated and twice nominated a hero of the Soviet Union. Rokossovski died in Moscow on 3 August 1968.

General References

George C. Malcher, *Poland's Politicized Army: Communists in Uniform* (New York: Praeger, 1984);

Andrew Michta, *Red Eagle: The Army in Polish Politics, 1944–1988* (Stanford, Cal.: Hoover Institution Press, 1990).

—J. B. and A. B.

SEE ALSO THESE RELATED ENTRIES
Boleslaw Bierut, 2; Wladyslaw Gomulka, 2.

Andrei Sakharov

Soviet Physicist and Dissident
Born Moscow, Soviet Union, 21 May 1921
Died Moscow, Soviet Union, 14 December 1989

Andrei Sakharov's relationship to the Soviet regime was both as an "insider" and an "outsider." Once a member of the Soviet Union's ruling elite, he became one of its foremost dissidents and critics.

During Joseph Stalin's brutally repressive reign, Sakharov was isolated within the world of his work in physics. But as social and political restraints within the Soviet Union eased, and relations with Western countries became increasingly "normal," Sakharov found he could no longer be silent and, like many before him, looked to the West to provide the antidote to the excesses of the Soviet state. Sakharov's tendency to use the West in order to reform his own country made him an important figure in East-West relations during the Cold War.

Born in Moscow to a family of intellectuals, Sakharov spent his early years in relative privilege and luxury. His father, who was a professor of physics, made sure young Andrei had a governess who could teach him German.

In 1938, after graduating from high school with honors, Sakharov entered Moscow State University. He was an exceptional student of physics and as a result was excused from military service in World War II.

Upon graduating with honors from the university in 1942, Sakharov moved first to Kovrov, then to Melekess, where he worked in a logging operation. The work in the remote settlement provided the young physicist with his first impressions of peasants and workers.

In September 1942 Sakharov began work as an engineer in an armament plant on the Volga River. Two years later, in 1944, he wrote several articles on theoretical physics. Although these articles were never published, they gave him enough confidence in his abilities to begin graduate studies at the P. N. Lebedev Physics Institute of the Soviet Union Academy of Sciences in Moscow.

While at Lebedev, Sakharov worked with the theoretical physicist Igor Tamm, and in 1948, after having successfully defended his thesis the previous year, began working with Tamm's research group. This group would develop the Soviet Union's first thermonuclear weapons.

In August 1953 the Soviets tested their first hydrogen bomb. The same year, Sakharov, widely considered the father of this generation of weapons, was the youngest scientist to be elected to the Soviet Academy of Sciences. At that time, Sakharov believed he was "working for

peace, that (his) work would foster a balance of power and that it would be useful to the Soviet people and even to some extent, humankind as a whole."

The Path to Dissent

In 1958 Sakharov found himself at odds with the Soviet leadership over atmospheric tests of nuclear weapons. Sakharov believed these tests were unnecessary and posed serious health risks to the population. Although he was successful in helping to place a moratorium on testing that year, he was unable to prevent the resumption of testing in 1961, despite a personal appeal to Soviet Premier Nikita S. Khrushchev. This experience left Sakharov with a feeling of powerlessness that would profoundly alter his perception of the Soviet Union's social and political systems.

Sakharov began to reexamine the policies of the Soviet regime. In 1963 he participated with Zhores Medvedev in a campaign against "Lysenkoism," a theory of plant genetics based on the teachings of Trofim Lysenko, an agronomist. Under Stalin, Lysenko's theories – such as refrigerating seeds so that when they sprouted they could withstand cold weather – were embraced by the state and considered proven facts. Although much of Lysenko's work had been discredited by Soviet biologists after Stalin's death, Khrushchev showed interest in renewing Lysenkoism. Sakharov and his colleagues, however, were successful in, once again, repudiating Lysenkoism, and as a consequence Russian scientists gained greater freedom from Soviet political control.

In 1966 Sakharov again struck out against Stalinism. In that year, he signed two open letters, one protesting any rehabilitation of Stalin, the other criticizing two new articles to the Criminal Code. These articles, 190-1 and 190-3, were correctly perceived as being potential weapons against any forms of organized dissent.

On the Outside

In the 22 July 1968 issue of the *New York Times* Sakharov published an essay that signified his break with the establishment. Entitled "Progress, Coexistence, and Intellectual Freedom," it called for combining the best of socialism with the best of capitalism, and was repeatedly broadcast on Voice of America. When Sakharov refused

Andrei Sakharov, 1975

to sign a denunciation of his essay, he was stripped of his security clearance and his job.

In 1969 Sakharov returned to the Lebedev Institute to work as a researcher. His first wife, Klavdiva, with whom he had three children, died the same year. By 1971, when Sakharov married Elena Bonner, whom he met at a dissident rally, he had already become an active critic of the Soviet state.

In 1970 Sakharov and two other Russian physicists – Valery Chalidze and Andrei Tverdokhlebov – founded the Moscow Committee for Human Rights. Stressing the creation and implementation of "guarantees of human rights" within the Soviet Union, the committee members tried to work as "constructive consultants" to the Soviet government. Soviet officialdom, however, did not appreciate the group's help, and in 1972 forced Chalidze to emigrate.

In the summer of 1973 Sakharov held his first interviews with Western correspondents, in which he urged the United States not to ignore human rights in order to pursue the new policy of détente. To this end, Sakharov even went so far as to enter the fray of a U.S. congressional debate when he supported the Jackson-Vanik amendment to a trade bill, linking U.S trade concessions to the Soviet Union to the Soviet policy on emigration. Sakharov's willingness to support Western critics of the

Soviet Union led to the campaign against him in the Soviet press in the fall of that year.

Sakharov gained further prominence in the West – and experienced increasing isolation in the Soviet Union – when he won the Nobel Peace Prize in 1975. Because he was at the trial of human rights activist Sergei Kovalov in Vilnius, Sakharov did not attend the prize ceremony held on 11 December at the Swedish Academy of Science in Stockholm, Sweden. His wife, acting as his proxy at the ceremony, read his speech, "Peace, Progress, and Human Rights," which, in linking the three concepts, asserted that it was impossible to achieve one if the other two were ignored. The message was directed not only at his own government, but at the governments of the West, as well. The West was attempting to promote both peace and progress through détente, but Sakharov feared it was ignoring the violations of human rights being perpetrated by the Soviet state.

Sakharov's tireless work in the dissident movement continued for the rest of the decade. In 1976 he was elected vice-president of the International League for Human Rights. In 1977 his appeal to U.S. President Jimmy Carter concerning a fellow dissident led to correspondence between the two. In the same year Sakharov wrote "Alarm and Hope," and a year later, "The Human Rights Movement in the U.S.S.R. and Eastern Europe: Its Goals, Significance, and Difficulties, " both of which appeared in the Western press. He also wrote appeals to Leonid Brezhnev and world leaders. The appeals covered a wide range of issues, from the right of Crimean Tartars to return to their homeland, to the protection of Charter 77 in Czechoslovakia, to ending the persecution of individual dissidents. All the while, Sakharov continued his work in theoretical physics, publishing his ideas on elementary particles and "The Baryon Asymmetry of the Universe" in several articles.

Sakharov's political work did not go unnoticed by the KGB, which continued to harass him and his family. But, as a member of the Academy of Sciences, Sakharov retained use of a chauffeured car, which was sometimes used to attend dissident meetings and press conferences.

Internal Exile

The invasion of Afghanistan by Soviet troops in December 1979 ushered in a decade of heightened tensions between the superpowers and increased suppression of dissent within the Soviet Union. After criticizing Soviet policy in Afghanistan in an interview with Western correspondents, Sakharov was arrested. While in custody, Sakharov was notified that two weeks earlier, on 8 January 1980, the Supreme Soviet had stripped him of all his government awards and prizes. Immediately after their arrest, Sakharov and Elena Bonner were transported to the closed city of Gorky, about 250 miles southwest of Moscow.

Sakharov and his wife were moved into a four-room apartment, complete with a resident presumed to be a spy. Sakharov, however, was allowed to meet with colleagues, friends, and even some local students who wanted to discuss science and human rights. Elena Bonner, who was allowed to travel to Moscow, immediately issued an appeal on Sakharov's behalf. Many, including some prominent Soviets, expressed outrage at Sakharov's banishment, particularly since no trial was held.

What relative freedom Sakharov initially enjoyed in Gorky was quickly ended by the KGB. The KGB began to monitor all conversations, censor correspondence, block radio signals, and even steal. Twice the KGB stole the autobiography on which Sakharov was working: in March of 1981, while Sakharov was at the dentist, his bag containing the manuscript was stolen, and in October 1982 the reconstructed manuscript was taken from Sakharov while he was sitting in a parked car. A few months later, KGB agents openly confiscated Sakharov's work from Bonner while she was in a train returning from Moscow.

Despite the harassment, Sakharov continued to publish articles in the Western press. On 4 June 1980, an essay appeared in the *New York Times Magazine*. A year later, *Parade* published "What Should the U.S. and U.S.S.R. Do to Preserve Peace." In June 1982 Sakharov

published an article in *Nature* criticizing Soviet scientists for not supporting one another as Western scientists have supported them. The summer of 1983 brought an article in *Foreign Affairs* on the danger of thermonuclear war. In this controversial article, written as an open letter to Sidney Drell, deputy director of the Stanford Linear Acceleration Center, Sakharov warned against a nuclear freeze and supported Ronald Reagan's plan for one hundred MX missiles. Sakharov's autobiography was published in 1990, having been secretly smuggled out of Gorky during his exile. As always, Sakharov continued his scientific work as well.

While in Gorky Sakharov and Bonner twice decided to embark on hunger strikes. The first began on 22 November 1981. A few days earlier, Bonner had played a tape to several Western correspondents explaining the reason: Bonner's son, Alexei Semyonov, had emigrated to the United States in 1978, but his wife, Liza Alexeyevna, had been denied permission to join him. On the thirteenth day of the strike, Sakharov and Bonner were forcibly removed to separate hospitals. Five days later, Liza received permission to emigrate.

The second hunger strike was not as successful. It began in May of 1984 to protest the government's refusal to allow Bonner, who was not in exile, to receive medical treatment in Italy. Bonner was suffering from a chronic eye condition and had had two, possibly three, heart attacks. It was planned that Sakharov would begin the strike alone, while Bonner sought refuge in the U.S. embassy. The authorities caught wind of the couple's plan, and charged Bonner with "anti-Soviet slander" and "anti-Soviet agitation and propaganda." Sakharov continued his strike, although he was moved to a hospital. After being force-fed through a nasal tube, he ended the strike in early July and was allowed to rejoin Bonner, who had received a sentence of five years of exile.

On the Outside Looking In

Sakharov and Bonner remained in Gorky until Soviet president Mikhail Gorbachev invited them back to Moscow in December 1986. Gorbachev's policies of glasnost (openness) and perestroika (restructuring) ended Sakharov's exile since his presence was needed to both legitimize Gorbachev's rule and to help in the creation of a new Russian society.

It was a role Sakharov gladly embraced. In 1989 Sakharov became a deputy to the newly formed Congress of People's Deputies. From his sixth-row seat, Sakharov provided support for the leadership of Gorbachev while simultaneously urging the leadership not to be satisfied with social and political reforms until a truly just society had been forced. Together with other leading reformers, such as Yuri N. Afanasyev, Sakharov helped form the Interregional Group, which served as an opposition caucus to help move perestroika forward.

On 14 December 1989 Sakharov stood up in congress and vehemently denounced the Communist party's constitutional monopoly on power and demanded a multiparty system. Gorbachev, who was chairing the congress, cut Sakharov's speech short and continued the meeting. While returning home to his study, Andrei Sakharov suffered a heart attack and died. The next day, the Soviet press, which had not so long ago considered Sakharov an enemy of the people, offered warm praise for him as an advocate of human rights. Gorbachev described him as a "man of conviction and sincerity." Outside his apartment, thousands of Soviet citizens stood to mourn the loss of their "conscience."

Although many were skeptical of Sakharov's often uncritical support of Western leaders, few doubted his motives. Sakharov wanted to make the Soviet Union a better society, one which would respect the rights of its citizens. Sakharov believed that only when his country had achieved that goal could it possibly help create a more lasting peace with the West.

Books by Sakharov (Selected)

Progress, Coexistence, and Intellectual Freedom, edited by Harrison E. Salisbury (New York: Norton, 1968);

Sakharov Speaks, edited by Harrison E. Salisbury (New York: Knopf, 1974);

My Country and the World, translated by Guy Daniels (New York: Knopf, 1975);

Alarm and Hope, edited by Efrem Yankelevich and Alfred Friendly, Jr. (New York: Knopf, 1978);

Andrei Sakharov and Peace, edited by Edward D. Lozansky (New York: Avon, 1985);

Memoirs, translated by Richard Lourie (New York: Knopf, 1990);

Moscow and Beyond, 1986 to 1989, translated by Antonina Bouis (New York: Knopf, 1991).

Books about Sakharov

Alexander Babyonyshev, ed., *On Sakharov*, translated by Guy Daniels (New York: Knopf, 1982);

Elena Bonner, *Alone Together*, translated by Alexander Cook (New York: Knopf, 1986).

– L. L. E.

SEE ALSO THESE RELATED ENTRIES

Jimmy Carter, 1; Mikhail Gorbachev, 2; Perestroika, 3; Ronald Reagan, 1; Joseph Stalin, 2.

Heng Samrin

President of the People's Republic of Kampuchea, 1979–
Born Prey Veng Province, Cambodia, 25 May 1934

Like many other leaders of the Khmer Rouge, details of the early period of Heng Samrin's life are hard to come by. According to a 1979 Vietnamese broadcast at the time Heng Samrin became president of Cambodia following the Vietnamese invasion of that country in 1978, he was born to a large family of poor peasants from the Prey Veng province in eastern Cambodia. The official statement claimed he began "revolutionary activities" in 1959 with the Khmer People's Revolutionary party (KPRP), the forerunner of the Khmer Rouge. He was a trusted political commissar and a military leader under Pol Pot from 1976 till his defection to Vietnam in 1978.

Under Pol Pot

After the 24 September 1977 massacre of Vietnamese civilians by Khmer Rouge troops in Tay Ninh, Heng Samrin was promoted to deputy chairman of the Eastern Region military staff, in the provinces of Cambodia bordering Vietnam. His exact role in the massacre, a watershed event in Vietnamese-Cambodian relations, is not known. What is known is that Pol Pot planned the attack as early as May 1977 to shock Vietnam. From the beginning of that year Cambodian troops had launched incursions into Vietnamese territory to bolster Pol Pot's claims that parts of Vietnam on the border with Cambodia actually belonged to Cambodia. After being repulsed by Vietnam every time, the Khmer Rouge leader wanted to escalate the fighting. Several of his commanders, however, refused to kill Vietnamese civilians and were themselves executed. Others escaped to Vietnam, including a senior Khmer Rouge leader.

Samrin defected to Vietnam in September 1978. By then, many Vietnamese diplomatic efforts to implore China – the Khmer Rouge's most influential international backer – to restrain Pol Pot had failed. Vietnam successfully launched several attacks of its own into Cambodia. Pol Pot reacted to these defeats by carrying out a purge of Khmer Rouge officers in the area, killing dozens, including a brother of Heng Samrin. Fearing for his life, Samrin hid in the jungles with a couple of thousand of his soldiers. More than 350,000 Cambodians fleeing the excesses of Pol Pot had now become refugees in Vietnam. Some of them were trained and organized by the Vietnamese into an army, the first brigade of which was formally commissioned in April 1978. Another of Heng

Heng Samrin

Samrin's brothers who had fled to Vietnam and Hun Sen, a former senior Khmer Rouge leader, both leaders of this army, persuaded the Vietnamese to send troops into Cambodia to rescue Samrin.

President of the KNUFNS

On 2 December 1978 the National Front for the National Liberation of Kampuchea (KNUFNS) was formally launched by Vietnam two miles inside the Cambodian border, with Heng Samrin as its president and Hun Sen as foreign minister. Of the fourteen members of its central committee, six were ex-leaders of the Khmer Rouge and four were Cambodian communists with long-standing ties to Vietnam. At the same time, Vietnamese forces, aided by KNUFNS troops, moved deeper into Cambodia. Having failed in its diplomatic endeavors to persuade Pol Pot to cease the border raids, and with thousands of refugees streaming into the country, Vietnam decided it had no option but to invade Cambodia. The expected resistance did not materialize. Demoralized by Pol Pot's purges and executions, the Khmer Rouge almost disintegrated in the face of the advancing Vietnamese, and Pnompenh fell on 7 January 1979. A new government was announced in the form of a people's revolutionary council, with Heng Samrin as president. He changed the name of the country to the People's Republic of Kampuchea (PRK) and opened it to foreign visitors, showing a shocked world for the first time details of the "autogenocide" practiced by Pol Pot.

History of Vietnam's Role

Vietnam knew its actions in Cambodia would not be without heavy costs. From the beginning of its existence, the Vietnamese communist government had tried to reduce its dependence on the Soviet Union by improving relations with China and the United States. But both those countries saw Vietnam as a pawn of the Soviet Union. To the Chinese leadership, Pol Pot's Cambodia was a potentially more reliable ally in Indochina. The Chinese, therefore, made only halfhearted attempts to pressure Pol Pot to stop attacking Vietnam and, after it became clear that Pol Pot was adamant in his refusal to stop, increased its arms shipments to the Khmer Rouge.

Cyrus Vance, U.S. secretary of state, had almost persuaded President Jimmy Carter to restore diplomatic ties with Vietnam, broken off at the end of the war in 1975. But in 1978 the United States was about to establish full diplomatic relations with China, and National Security Adviser Zbigniew Brezinski convinced Carter that such a move should be postponed in order not to antagonize China. Following its invasion of Cambodia, Vietnam's relations with the United States deteriorated rapidly, and did not improve until Vietnam pulled its troops out in 1989.

China, too, retaliated against Vietnam. In mid 1978 Vietnam announced that all Vietnamese who continued to engage in capitalist trade would be sentenced to death. This enraged China, since the overwhelming majority of such traders were ethnic Chinese. In June, China announced that it was halting all aid to Vietnam. The Soviet Union, meanwhile, advised Vietnam to "do a Czechoslovakia" in Cambodia. With the Soviet Union being its only international ally, Vietnam finally decided to abandon its attempts at détente with China and formally signaled its alignment with the Soviet Union by joining the Council for Mutual Economic Assistance (COMECON) on 28 June. In August, Vietnam and the Soviet Union signed a friendship treaty, and the Soviet Union began airlifting arms to Vietnam. In reaction to this, China stepped up diplomatic pressure. Finally, after Vietnam took over Cambodia, China attacked Vietnam on 17 February 1979. For a brief period Chinese troops occupied

some parts of northern Vietnam and destroyed all property they came across before leaving the country.

The Heng Samrin Government

Subsequent events in Cambodia were almost totally decided upon by outside powers. Under Chinese auspices, Pol Pot came together with two other resistance groups, including one headed by former head of state Norodom Sihanouk, to form a government in exile. This was recognized as the legitimate government of Cambodia by the United Nations (UN), China, and the United States, and the countries of the Association of South East Asian Nations led the world in keeping Vietnam and Cambodia politically and economically isolated. As a result, Cambodia's economy faltered and was kept alive only by Soviet aid. The Heng Samrin government also came under consistent threat from the forces of the rejuvenated Khmer Rouge, armed by China and operating from bases in neighboring Thailand. Samrin's government managed to hold on, due only to the help of approximately 180,000 Vietnamese troops stationed in the country. As a result of the new fighting, thousands of refugees now fled to refugee camps in Thailand. In 1987 Heng Samrin bowed to international pressure by finally agreeing to negotiate about the future of Cambodia. As the Soviet Union changed under Mikhail Gorbachev, it put pressure on Vietnam to withdraw its troops from Cambodia, which it did in 1989. By then Heng Samrin had lost out in a power struggle to his prime minister, Hun Sen. Though Heng Samrin remained president of the country and leader of the party, effective power was wielded by Hun Sen. Hun Sen, with Vietnamese backing, indicated that he was willing to negotiate the future of Cambodia with China and the United States, but was unwilling to let the Khmer Rouge return to power. UN-sponsored talks on Cambodia were stalled until late 1990, when China indicated a softening of its support for the Khmer Rouge.

General References

Elizabeth Becker, *When the War Was Over: Cambodia's Revolution and the Voices of its People* (New York: Simon & Schuster, 1986);

Wilfred Burchett, *The China Cambodia Vietnam Triangle* (Chicago: Vanguard Books, 1981);

Nayan Chanda, *Brother Enemy: The War After the War, A History of Indochina since the Fall of Saigon* (New York: Harcourt, Brace Jovanovich 1986);

Ben Kiernan, *How Pol Pot Came to Power* (London: Verso, 1985);

François Ponchaud, *Cambodia Year Zero* (New York, 1977);

William Shawcross, *Sideshow: Kissinger, Nixon and the Destruction of Cambodia* (New York: Simon & Schuster, 1979).

– Q. I.

┌───┐
│   SEE ALSO THESE RELATED ENTRIES   │
│ Pol Pot, 2; Norodom Sihanouk, 2.   │
└───┘

José Eduardo dos Santos

President of Angola, 1979–

Born Luanda, Portuguese West Africa, 28 August 1942

José Eduardo dos Santos is the current president of Angola. The son of a stonemason, dos Santos attended the Liceu Salvador Correia secondary school in Luanda. An ardent nationalist during his student years, he joined the banned Popular Movement for the Liberation of Angola (MPLA) at age nineteen, fleeing to Léopoldville, Congo (present-day Zaire), where the MPLA was based. The Marxist-oriented MPLA, founded in 1956 under the leadership of Antonio Agostinho Neto, was one of three main liberation movements fighting Portuguese colonial rule in Angola. As a member of the guerrilla army, he was appointed deputy president of the movement's youth wing.

In 1963 dos Santos was sent to the Soviet Union on an MPLA scholarship to study at the Patrice Lumumba University in Moscow, where he graduated in 1970 with degrees in petroleum engineering and radar telecommunications. He returned to Angola in 1970 to serve in the MPLA army in the oil-rich Cabinda province and became second in command of telecommunications services for the MPLA. Briefly serving as the movement's representative to Yugoslavia, dos Santos quickly rose to the top ranks of the MPLA. One of MPLA leader Neto's closest advisers, he was appointed to the MPLA Central Committee in 1974, ranking fifth in the Political Bureau.

Independence and Civil War

Angola experienced a violent transition to independence as internecine warfare between the three liberation groups – the Soviet-backed MPLA, the American and Chinese-backed National Union for the Total Liberation of Angola (UNITA), led by Jonas Savimbi, and the American-backed National Front for the Liberation of Angola (FNLA) – drew massive superpower intervention in the form of several thousand Cuban combat

José Eduardo dos Santos

troops and a South African military invasion. The Soviet-Cuban intervention proved decisive in installing the MPLA in power.

President

After independence was declared on 11 November 1975, dos Santos was named foreign minister and later first vice-prime minister under President Neto. The fragile internal cohesion of the MPLA, however, was eroded by the resentment of a faction led by the interior minister, Nito Alves, against the white and *mestiço* (people of mixed race) dominance of the upper echelons of the party. This factional infighting erupted into an attempted coup d'état on 27 May 1977. While his precise role in the coup remains unclear, dos Santos was dismissed from his party post during the late 1977 reshuffle and purge of the party and cabinet. He was soon rehabilitated in 1978 with his appointment as minister of national planning and party secretary for economic development and planning. After the death of Neto on 10 September 1979, the ruling Central Committee unanimously elected dos Santos as Angola's second president, secretary-general of the MPLA, and commander in chief of the armed forces. The MPLA had been troubled by a lack of internal cohesion and factional infighting, but dos Santos, considered a moderate, was not identified with any one faction in the party and was generally respected for his administrative experience.

While dos Santos eventually emerged from Neto's shadow, his regime remained saddled with the problems of national reconstruction following a devastating independence struggle and an intensifying and growing civil war which hobbled the national economy. Throughout the latter half of the 1980s the majority of Angola's eight million people faced severe food shortages, malnutrition, and famine caused by the civil war. The antigovernment rebels targeted the country's economic infrastructure, especially the Benguella Railway, an important transport route for the landlocked state in its goal of lessening its economic dependence on South Africa.

The problems dos Santos inherited are of three dimensions: domestic, regional, and international, each reinforcing the other. Pro-Soviet Angola did not cease to be a stage for superpower confrontation after independence, and the dos Santos regime was dependent on the backing of an estimated (in 1985) twenty-five thousand Cuban combat troops, several thousand Soviet military personnel, and an estimated $1 billion in annual Soviet military aid. In addition to anticommunist South Africa's belligerent posture toward Angola, which actively supported the Namibian guerrilla group, the South West African People's Organization (SWAPO) and the African National Congress (ANC), the dos Santos regime faced a growing challenge to its power by the American- and South African–backed UNITA, which claimed that the rule of the MPLA was illegitimate since it was imposed by outside forces. From the time of its invasion to the late 1980s, South Africa made repeated military incursions into Angolan territory, including the occupation of the southern tip of Angola where some three thousand South African troops were deployed in 1988, ostensibly in hot pursuit of SWAPO guerrillas, who had bases in Angola and who were fighting against South African rule in Namibia. South Africa was a major supporter of UNITA, repeatedly intervening militarily to support it during battle engagements with MPLA forces, in addition to providing it with weapons and basing rights in Namibia.

Since 1975 the southern African region became a major trouble spot in the world, but at the same time it became the focus of regional and international diplomatic efforts to reach a negotiated settlement to the interlinked problems facing the region. Angola was at the center of these diplomatic initiatives, particularly during the U.S. administration of Ronald Reagan, which sought to broker nonaggression agreements between South Africa and its neighbors, secure the linked goals of the withdrawal of foreign troops from Angola and the independence of Namibia. For nearly a decade U.S. assistant secretary of state for African affairs Chester A. Crocker launched a series of initiatives to bring the various sides together in a comprehensive regional agreement. In 1983 Angola and South Africa signed the American-mediated Lusaka Accords, a nonaggression pact that called for the withdrawal of South African troops from Angola, for movement toward the implementation of United Nations resolutions regarding Namibian independence, and for Angola to restrain the activities of SWAPO.

By the second half of the 1980s the civil war had wrought considerable cost and damage to Angola, causing enormous social and economic disruption and human displacement and forcing the dos Santos regime to spend upward of 60 percent of the national budget on the war. The MPLA regime, which ironically established a close partnership with American and Western petroleum companies, financed the war and its external debt in part with the revenues generated by the country's substantial oil production capacity. After Soviet leader Mikhail S. Gorbachev came to power in March 1985, it became apparent that Moscow, no longer willing to subsidize its client's costly, drawn-out war, was pressuring dos Santos to seek a negotiated end to the civil war. Accompanied by unprecedented American and Soviet diplomatic cooperation, and after years of stalled progress, in late 1988 Angola, Cuba, and South Africa took tentative steps toward a negotiated peace settlement. The American-mediated talks between Angola, Cuba, and South Africa finally concluded in an agreement, signed in New York City on 22 December 1988. The 1988 accords provided for the withdrawal of both the estimated (1988) fifty thousand Cuban troops as well as the South African troops in southern Angola, Namibian independence, and the dismantling of ANC bases inside Angola.

While the 1988 accords transformed the political and strategic landscape of southern Africa, it did not resolve the internal Angolan conflict. However, faced with a debilitating and stalemated civil war, both dos Santos and Savimbi soon began to make public their willingness to put an end to the war and to seek national reconciliation. Through the mediation of several African heads of state, dos Santos and Savimbi held direct talks in Zaire on 21 June 1989 that produced a cease-fire and general agreements toward the reintegration of UNITA into Angolan political and social life and a plural political system. The cautious steps toward reconciliation, however, failed to produce any concrete agreements between the warring parties, despite the diplomatic intervention of African heads of states, Portugal, and the superpowers. In August 1990 the senior American and Soviet officials tentatively agreed on a joint effort to seek a settlement in the Angolan civil war, although there were no signs that dos Santos and Savimbi were ready to fashion an accommodation. The October 1992 elections, which dos Santos won, ended in a renewed outbreak of violence as Savimbi and UNITA refused to recognize the results of the elections, which they claimed were fraudulent. As Angola neared civil war, and as violence quickly spread beyond the capital city, in late November UNITA agreed to recognize the elections and dos Santos agreed to open negotiations to form a national unity government and to integrate UNITA forces into the Angolan armed forces. As recently as January 1993, however, there was heavy fighting in many parts of the country.

General References

Gerald Bender, "Angola, the Cubans, and American Anxieties," *Foreign Policy*, 31 (Summer 1978): 3–30;

Richard Bloomfield, ed., *Regional Conflict and U.S. Policy: Angola and Mozambique* (Algonac, Mich.: Reference Publications, 1988);

Chester Crocker, "South Africa: A Strategy for Change," *Foreign Affairs*, 59 (Winter 1980–1981): 323–351;

Helen Kitchen, *Angola, Mozambique, and the West* (New York: Praeger, 1987);

Keith Somerville, *Angola: Politics, Economics, and Society* (Boulder, Colo.: L. Rienner Publishers, 1986).

—J. R.-S.

SEE ALSO THESE RELATED ENTRIES

Mikhail Gorbachev, 2; Antonio Agostinho Neto, 2; Ronald Reagan, 1; Jonas Savimbi, 2.

Jonas Savimbi

President, União Nacional para a Independência Total de Angola (UNITA), 1966–
Born Munhango, Portuguese West Africa, 3 August 1934

Jonas Savimbi is an Angolan nationalist and leader of the União Nacional para a Independência Total de Angola (UNITA), the guerrilla group fighting the Marxist regime of Jose Eduardo dos Santos in Angola.

The son of a railroad stationmaster and grandson of a traditional chief, Jonas Malhiero Savimbi attended Protestant primary and secondary mission schools, and had an early association with Angolan nationalists, one of whom was his secondary school teacher. In 1958 he was awarded a scholarship by the United Church of Christ to study medicine at the University of Lisbon, the capital of Portugal. There Savimbi soon became involved in campus cultural-political activities, including a brief participation in a communist-led campaign against the Portuguese regime of Antonio Salazar.

As his interests in the Angolan nationalist movement broadened, Savimbi came into early association with young Angolan nationalists who were also studying in Lisbon, among whom was Antonio Agostinho Neto, the future first president of independent Angola. After being detained by the Portuguese secret police for participating in antigovernment activities, Savimbi fled Portugal in 1960 with the help of European communist organizations. Even though the original plan was for the young nationalist to go to the Soviet Union, he decided to go to Switzerland, where he continued his medical training at Fribourg University with a new scholarship, later transferring to the University of Lausanne to study law and political science. Although he was initially recruited by the Popular Movement for the Liberation of Angola (MPLA), Savimbi joined the moderate Popular Union of Angola (UPA), the precursor to the Front for the National Liberation of Angola (FNLA), headed by Holden Roberto.

Appointed secretary-general of the movement (while he continued with his studies), Savimbi soon developed personal and ideological differences with the FNLA leadership. In 1962, a year after the first nationalist uprisings in Angola, the Congo (Zaire)-based FNLA organized a government-in-exile with Savimbi as foreign minister, even though he opposed the idea of a government-in-exile. Savimbi favored opening the organization to aid from socialist countries, and independently visited China, Ghana, Algeria, and Tanzania, where he met Cuban revolutionary Ernesto "Che" Guevara. In May 1963 he attended the formation of the Organization of

Jonas Savimbi

African Unity (OAU) in Addis Ababa, Ethiopia, as the representative of the FNLA government-in-exile. He was appointed chairman of an advisory committee, which included Kenneth Kaunda, the Zambian nationalist leader, that recommended the creation of an OAU liberation committee.

In 1964 Savimbi, disillusioned with the American-financed FNLA, broke away to form UNITA. He traveled to the Soviet Union, Eastern Europe, China, and North Korea to solicit international support. Savimbi and ten UNITA cadres traveled to China, with which he had established cordial relations, to study guerrilla warfare at the Nanking Military Academy in 1965. After he returned from China in 1966, Savimbi finally crossed the border into Angola after twelve years. After the group's initial failures on the battlefield, Savimbi decided to concentrate on Maoist guerrilla tactics of small-scale hit-and-run operations in the countryside as well as ideological mobilization of the peasantry. The rival guerrilla groups, the MPLA and the FNLA, were largely responsible for the bulk of the fighting, with UNITA confined to the south-central regions of the country, operating on a small scale.

The Alvor Accords

Unrecognized by the OAU, which had been actively supporting the MPLA, UNITA, the smallest of the three guerrilla groups, had its base of support in southeastern Angola among the Ovimbundu, the largest ethnic group in Angola. In the backdrop of a national independence struggle marked by internecine warfare and longstanding personal, ideological, and ethnic rivalry among the three liberation movements, independence talks between the three groups and Portugal began after the watershed April 1974 military coup d'état in Portugal. The January 1975 Alvor Accords, which set 11 November 1975 for independence, also included provisions for a transitional government with representatives from the three groups; national elections were scheduled for October. However, within days of approving the accords, the ineffectual transitional government and tripartite arrangements collapsed as violent fighting broke out between the Soviet and Cuban-backed MPLA and the U.S.-backed FNLA for control of Luanda, the capital city. Savimbi, who opted to keep his forces out of the fighting, unsuccessfully attempted to mediate between the two groups, but fighting also broke out between the Chinese-equipped UNITA and the MPLA. By July 1975 both UNITA and the FNLA (which was crushed during the fighting) had been driven out of the Luanda region by the heavily armed MPLA. Savimbi, who had emerged as a popular nationalist leader during the transition period and whose spellbinding oratory and political moderation attracted national attention, retreated with his UNITA forces into southeastern Angola while the MPLA asserted its control over most of the provinces by September.

Soviet and Cuban Involvement

While the Angolan independence struggle had been marked by superpower involvement since the 1960s, the later half of 1975 witnessed direct and large-scale superpower intervention in the civil war. The American and Chinese involvement had remained relatively marginal, with American assistance initially confined to low levels of financial transfers to the FNLA, but by July 1975 both countries began to channel modest levels of military aid to UNITA and the disintegrating FNLA. Angola became as much of a stage for U.S.-Soviet confrontation as it was a stage for the intensifying Sino-Soviet rivalry, which

spilled over into politics of Third World liberation movements. China's involvement was motivated primarily by a desire to counterbalance what it termed "Soviet imperialism." Soviet and Cuban arms shipments and military personnel began to arrive in Angola at an accelerated pace after November 1974, and by September 1975 there were an estimated three thousand to five thousand Cuban and Soviet military personnel assisting the MPLA. The turning point in the civil war came on 23 October when South Africa, with the tactical collaboration of UNITA and elements of the FNLA, sent a limited invasion force into southern Angola. The Soviet Union and Cuba responded with an unprecedented military intervention on behalf of the MPLA, and by November massive amounts of weapons, including heavy tanks and artillery, and several thousand Cuban combat troops and additional Soviet military personnel were being poured into Angola. By the first week of February 1976 an estimated twelve thousand Cuban troops had been airlifted to Angola, even though there is evidence that there were never more than two thousand South African troops inside Angola. The Soviet-Cuban intervention proved decisive because it both turned back the South African invasion and inflicted heavy losses on UNITA. It also installed in power the MPLA, which declared independent the People's Republic of Angola on 11 November 1975. That same day Savimbi declared the Democratic People's Republic of Angola independent in the southwestern port city of Huambo, but the rival government and UNITA's position crumbled before the Soviet-Cuban-led offensive and South Africa's withdrawal in January 1976. Despite the Soviet-Cuban intervention, the OAU, which had been internally split over the Angolan problem up to the South African invasion, recognized the MPLA government as the only legitimate Angolan government.

The South African invasion marked the beginning of diplomatic and political ostracism of UNITA in the continent and internationally. Isolated as a result of his collaboration with South Africa, Savimbi concentrated on rebuilding UNITA and consolidating its position in the southeastern corner of the country. Savimbi's cooperation with the South African forces continued after the October invasion, and UNITA directly benefited from South Africa's repeated punitive raids into Angola during the late 1970s and first half of the 1980s, as well as from South Africa's military occupation of Angolan territory along the southern border with Namibia. Although South Africa claimed that its military incursions into Angola were in hot pursuit of the Angolan-based South West African People's Liberation Organization (SWAPO), the guerrilla group fighting against South African rule in neighboring Namibia, it became apparent that the South African defense forces were frequently engaging in battles in the defense of UNITA.

Southern Africa remained a region of superpower confrontation, revolutionary upheavals, and violence throughout the next decade, providing Savimbi with ample opportunities to legitimize his movement and seek external backing. After the March 1977 and May 1978 invasions of Zaire's Shaba province by Angolan-based Zairian antigovernment rebels, Savimbi went on an international diplomatic mission to garner support for his struggle against the MPLA government, which was widely believed to be behind the invasion. UNITA subsequently became an important and controversial factor in the superpower competition in the southern African region as well as the complicated, interlocked problems besetting the region. In addition to South Africa and Saudi Arabia, UNITA received aid from other African countries, including Zaire, Zambia, Ivory Coast, and Morocco, the last providing training facilities and transit for arms shipments. As a result of the December 1975 congressional prohibition on U.S. military assistance to southern African groups, U.S. involvement in the region during the presidency of Jimmy Carter was limited, and largely confined to diplomatic initiatives. South Africa allowed UNITA to use the South Africa–controlled territory of Namibia as a transit point. There were frequent clashes between UNITA and SWAPO, the Namibian guerrilla group and erstwhile ally during the Angolan revolution. UNITA became a principal instrument for South Africa's destabilization campaign in Angola, which in turn supported SWAPO in its independence struggle in Namibia. With the two neighboring conflicts interlocked, South Africa's incursions into Angola — ostensibly in pursuit of SWAPO guerrillas — had turned into conventional exchanges with MPLA forces by the early 1980s.

By 1979 Savimbi's rebuilt guerrilla forces had succeeded in forcing the civil war into a stalemate against the forces of the MPLA government, and by late 1980 began to capture larger towns while pushing northward. The civil war proved devastating for the economy as a result of severe disruption and the targeted destruction by UNITA of the infrastructure, including the Benguella Railway, potentially the most viable alternate route to the sea for the landlocked regional countries. Assisted by South African artillery, in August 1983 UNITA scored a decisive victory over the MPLA forces in the battle of Cangamba, which prompted the introduction of additional Cuban combat troops and Soviet advisers. In September 1985 Savimbi's forces were salvaged by South African air support when it came under attack from a large MPLA, Cuban, and Soviet offensive.

In addition to France, Savimbi began to receive military assistance from another important source, the United States, which until July 1985 was prohibited by congressional mandate to provide military aid to groups in southern Africa. Savimbi's struggle against the Marxist Angolan regime emerged from isolation and obscurity as a result of the vigorous ideological support it received from the administration of Ronald Reagan and the so-called Reagan Doctrine, which called for the active support of anticommunist forces. Despite his checkered ideological past and affiliations, Savimbi was received like a head of state during his widely publicized second visit to the United States in January 1986, meeting with President Reagan, senior administration officials, and congressional leaders. The United States subsequently began providing UNITA with $15 million in covert military aid, including the lethal Stinger anti-aircraft missiles. Savimbi's forty-thousand-strong guerrilla army waged a costly civil war, which not only disrupted socioeconomic life in the central-southern provinces but also placed unbearable costs on the Soviet-financed MPLA regime, which was itself coming under growing pressures from the new Soviet leadership to put an end to the war.

During the 1980s multilateral diplomatic initiatives sought to achieve a peaceful settlement to the region's political and security problems, in particular the independence of Namibia. Stalled regional and international diplomatic undertakings were renewed by the Reagan administration with the dual linked objectives of securing the withdrawal of foreign (both Cuban and South African) troops from Angola and the independence of Namibia under the provisions of United Nations Resolution 435. A major stumbling block in the negotiations was continued American and South African military assistance to UNITA which the MPLA government eventually adopted as a precondition to an agreement. UNITA continues to receive American covert military assistance, which by 1990 had reached an estimated $60 million annually.

While not a direct participant in the American-sponsored negotiations between Angola, Cuba, and South Africa, Savimbi was indirectly affected by the 22 December 1988 agreements. The 1988 accords, which included provisions for the withdrawal of Cuban and South African troops from Angola and Namibian independence, did not resolve Angola's internal conflict, however. With both sides left vulnerable after the regional settlement was signed, reconciliation talks between Savimbi and the MPLA government of Jose Eduardo dos Santos got underway after the government announced a twelve-month amnesty to members of the rebel movement in February 1989. In March Savimbi and dos Santos attended a regional summit sponsored by African heads of state, and on 21 June the two leaders held another summit sponsored by President Mobutu Sese Seko of Zaire, which resulted in a cease-fire agreement and general terms for the reintegration of UNITA back into Angolan social and political life. Subsequent negotiations, however, stalled and fighting renewed, with neither side able to agree to some form of mutual accommodation. In late 1992 both sides finally agreed to elections, which Dos Santos and the MPLA won by a narrow margin. Fighting quickly broke out as Savimbi refused to accept the results of the elections, which international observers had deemed reasonably fair despite claims by UNITA to the contrary. Even though he threatened to renew the civil war, violence was limited. Savimbi agreed to recognize the elections results and to enter negotiations to form a national unity government and to integrate UNITA into the Angolan armed forces. Despite indications of its willingness to enter negotiations, UNITA renewed the civil war. Heavy fighting was reported in many parts of the country as recently as January 1993.

Criticized by his opponents for his alliance with South Africa and for being a power-hungry opportunist and hailed by his supporters as nationalist leader and crusader for democracy, Savimbi remains a controversial figure in southern Africa. What is clear, however, is that perhaps no other African guerrilla leader had fought for so long and against such overwhelming odds.

Book about Savimbi

Fred Bridgland, *Savimbi: A Key to Africa* (New York: Paragon House, 1987).

General References

Richard Bloomfield, ed., *Regional Conflicts and U.S. Policy: Angola and Mozambique* (Algonac, Mich.: Reference Publications, 1988);

Michael Clough, *Changing Realities in Southern Africa: Implications for American Policy* (Berkeley: University of California Press, 1982);

Helen Kitchen, ed., *Angola, Mozambique and the West* (New York: Praeger, 1987);

John Marcum, *The Angolan Revolution* (Cambridge, Mass.: M.I.T. Press, 1979);

John Stockwell, *In Search of Enemies: A C.I.A. Story* (New York: Norton, 1978).

–J. R.-S.

Ariel Sharon

Israeli Housing Minister, 1990–1992

Israeli Defense Minister, 1981–1983

Born Kfar Maalal, Palestine, 1928

Ariel "Arik" Sharon is the leader of the hard-line faction of the Likud, one of the two major Israeli political parties. As defense minister from 1981 to 1983 he led Israel into the Lebanon war in 1982. As housing minister from 1990 to 1992, he was responsible for integration of Soviet immigrants and expansion of Jewish settlements in the occupied West Bank and Gaza Strip. Sharon is regarded as a brilliant strategist by his supporters, but his opponents term him a fascist, an egomaniac, and a liar.

Sharon was born in Kfar Maalal, a communal farm in western Palestine, to Russian immigrants Samuel and Vera (Scheinerman) Sharon. The family used mud and cow manure to plaster the walls of their two-room home and his father, a notoriously stubborn man, always seemed to be at odds with the other farmers. Scheinerman armed his son at age six with an oversize club and told him to search for the children who were picking the Scheinermans' fruit. At age ten, when Sharon joined the Labor Youth Movement, he still carried the club, using it to keep the other children quiet, until the group leader ordered him to stop.

Sharon's military career began at fourteen in the paramilitary high school organization, Gadna. After completing a course in the Negev desert, he became a Gadna instructor at the Mossinsohn Agricultural School. While there, he met his first wife, Margalith, a psychiatric nurse, with whom he had a son, Gur. His wife died in an auto accident in 1962 and his son was shot dead in October 1967 while playing with Sharon's rifle with a friend; after his first wife's death, Sharon married her younger sister, Lilly.

Ariel Sharon

The War of 1948

When the British partitioned Palestine into Jewish and Arab states, Sharon dropped agriculture and joined the Haganah's infantry division. When the state was created in May 1948 and war broke out, Sharon's Haganah unit became part of the Alexandroni Brigade of the Israeli Defense Forces (IDF). Sharon was wounded in the battle of Latrun, considered that war's worst military failure. Sharon became a battalion commander and continued to work his way up through the military. Along the way, he pushed his method of quashing the opponent with reprisals and retaliatory raids. As Uri Benzimin writes in his biography of Sharon: "The battlefield was the primary arena of his creativity and it was here that his personality developed. The aggression that had been seething within him since childhood could be legitimately released on the battlefield."

In June 1953, in response to a request by a military leader, Sharon organized a group of seven men to undertake a reprisal against the Arab village of Nebi Samuil without the cooperation of already constituted forces. That group became the nucleus of a small, special forces unit – known as Unit 101 – whose first raid was to force from the Negev desert a group of bedouins in September 1953. Later that year Sharon led retaliatory raids against the al-Burj refugee camp in Gaza, in which fifteen civilians were killed, and against Kibya, in which some fifty houses were blown up and sixty-nine people killed. While Sharon's tactics almost always exceeded original plans and he often cut himself off from communications with the authorities, he was never given more than a slap on the wrist in response. In fact, Moshe Dayan, who would soon become the IDF chief of staff, encouraged Sharon to enlarge his unit and pointed to its audacity as worthy of emulation by all IDF soldiers. Unit 101 quickly became part of the paratroops, and Sharon became the paratroops' commander.

The Suez Crisis

In Israel's 1956 attack on the Suez Canal, Sharon led the paratroops in an assignment in which one battalion was to parachute over the Mitla Pass in the Sinai Peninsula while the rest of the brigade traveled there by land. The goal was to divert the Egyptian military's attention, to cut off its reinforcement and retreat routes, and to signal to France and Great Britain to enter the foray. Sharon, however, refused to accept such a secondary role in the war. Having received permission to set up a patrol, he instead attempted to capture the western entrance of the Mitla Pass. The attempt was successful, but the unit suffered significant losses. For a time after that fiasco, Sharon was relegated to secondary positions in the army. The earthy, overweight general gained a reputation as being violence-prone, "unconcerned with criticism and completely oblivious to facts and orders when this suited his purpose."

The 1967 War

In 1964 Sharon was appointed chief of staff of the southern command headquarters. During the 1967 Arab-Israeli War, Sharon was a commander of the division that fought the Egyptian command at Abu Ageilah. Sharon orchestrated a brilliant combined-force maneuver to capture the Abu Ageilah fortifications. His battle plan and its execution are topics of study in military schools around the world. After the war Sharon returned to his job as commander of the training section. Sharon relocated army training bases to former Jordanian army camps on the West Bank, which became some of the first visible settlements in the occupied territory. From 1969 to 1973 Sharon was in charge of the southern command, from where he focused on responding to cross-border raids with escalating violence and brutality designed to crush Palestinian activity in the Gaza Strip. In one instance, for example, Sharon ordered soldiers to poison the water wells of desert bedouins after deciding these nomads were aiding the Palestine Liberation Organization (PLO) in Gaza.

The Yom Kippur War

In May 1973, as Israel went into a state of alert in preparation for war, Sharon pushed again to become chief of staff. When Defense Minister Dayan told him that not only would he be a candidate, but that he also would not be granted permission to continue as commander of the southern sector, Sharon resigned from the army. Immediately moving from the military to politics, Sharon joined the Liberal party and pushed for a consolidation of the rightist parties. The Likud party was formed as a conglomeration of those parties in September 1973. During the Yom Kippur War in October 1973, Sharon served as a reserve commander. He planned a brilliant crossing of the Suez Canal, encircling the Egyptian forces and trapping them on the eastern bank of the canal. His commission was not renewed after he attempted to use the army to gain votes for his upcoming electoral campaign.

In 1974 Sharon won a seat in the Knesset (parliament) but quit soon after. In June 1975 Prime Minister Yitzhak Rabin appointed Sharon his special adviser, and Sharon held that position for eight months. When Sharon tried to push his way back to the Likud's forefront, however, its leadership told him that Menachem Begin would have the leading role. In 1976 Sharon briefly formed an unsuccessful rightist party of his own, Shlomzion, which was absorbed into Begin's branch of the Likud after the 1977 elections. In Begin's first government, Sharon was agriculture minister, chair of the cabinet committee on new settlements, and a member of the cabinet committee on security. In those positions, while Israel and Egypt were talking peace, Sharon drew up plans for massive Jewish settlements on the West Bank, authorizing a dozen new ones, in an attempt to preclude the possibility of withdrawal.

The War in Lebanon

After the next elections in 1981 Sharon became defense minister and began concrete preparations for war. "From the day he first entered the defense ministry in early August 1981," write Ze'ev Schiff and Ehud Ya'ari, "Sharon strove to eliminate the traditional mechanisms that mitigated or blocked the government's natural propensity toward extremism." While the change in guard was important, the foundations of war can also be seen in the continuing, and increasingly preemptive, line of reprisals. In March 1978, for example, in "Operation Litani," Israel invaded Lebanon, pushing toward the Litani River with heavy air strikes, in response to a Palestinian cross-border bus attack that left thirty-seven dead and seventy-six wounded. By March 1982 the operational plans for war were well advanced and detailed. And by the time that Israeli ambassador Shlomo Argov was attacked on 3 June 1982 in London "the decision not only to react but how to react was a foregone conclusion." Sharon may have misled the government about the scope of the invasion, reaching and bombing Lebanon's capital city, Beirut, far from the border, but the war's objectives were accepted policy, and largely supported by the government.

After the Kahan Commission report in 1983 cited Israel's indirect responsibility for the massacres of Palestinian civilians by the Phalange at the Sabra and Shatila refugee camps during the war, Sharon was forced to resign as defense minister. But while the Shalom Achshav (Peace Now) peace movement began in response to this war, Sharon's power was barely diminished. He remained a member of the new National Unity government, which was formed in 1984, as well as a member of both the inner cabinet and the ministerial committee for national security. The last time Sharon ran for Likud party leadership in 1984, a little more than a year after being forced to resign in disgrace, he won 42.5 percent of the vote. In 1985 he returned in full to political life as minister of commerce and industry.

In the Likud government that fell in 1992, Sharon served as kingpin. "This government," Rabin charged, "is a Sharon government operating under the name of a Shamir government." It was Sharon who forced Yitzhak Shamir to set up the right-wing government, after causing the previous Likud-Labor coalition government to collapse by resigning as trade minister in February 1990. By early summer 1990 Shamir had appointed Sharon to the government's ministerial defense committee, giving him the largest role in security matters since his disgraced resignation. In Benjamin Netanyahu's Likud government, which came to power in May 1996, Sharon has been serving as minister of infrastructure.

Book by Sharon

with David Chanoff, *Warrior: The Autobiography of Ariel Sharon* (New York: Simon & Schuster, 1989).

Book about Sharon

Uri Benzimin, *Sharon: An Israeli Caesar* (New York: Adama Books, 1985).

General References

Yehoshafat Harkabi, *Israel's Fateful Hour,* translated by Lenn Schramm (New York: Harper & Row, 1988);

Ze'ev Schiff and Ehud Ya'ari, *Israel's Lebanon War,* edited and translated by Ina Friedman (London: Allen & Unwin, 1984).

—A. F.

SEE ALSO THESE RELATED ENTRIES

David Ben-Gurion, 2; Levi Eshkol, 2; Golda Meir, 2; Yitzhak Rabin, 2.

Eduard Amvrosiyevich Shevardnadze

Foreign Minister of the Soviet Union, 1985–1990
Born Mamati, Georgia, 25 January 1928

Eduard Amvrosiyevich Shevardnadze, foreign minister of the Soviet Union from 1985 to 1990, was born in Mamati, Georgia. He joined the Communist party twenty years later and, after completing his university training, became a member of the Georgian Supreme Soviet. In 1985 he was named the interior minister for the republic.

During Shevardnadze's tenure as interior minister, Vassily Mzhevandze served as Georgian Communist party chief. At that time corruption flourished at all levels of Georgian society, extending to Mzhevandze himself. With the direct support of Yuri Andropov, who at the time was in charge of the KGB, Shevardnadze's interior ministry launched an aggressive anticorruption campaign that rocked the republic and ultimately brought Mzhevandze down in 1972.

Reform in Georgia

Mzhevandze was replaced by Shevardnadze, who immediately demonstrated to Georgian party members that the anticorruption campaign would continue. During his first eighteen months in office, Shevardnadze purged approximately 75 percent of the local party leadership. As a result, Shevardnadze was not popular in Georgia. While he was the party's boss, he traveled in a bulletproof car and was the target of two assassination attempts. Nonetheless, according to Martin Walker, a former Moscow correspondent for the *Manchester Guardian*, "among the potentially dissident intelligentsia of Moscow and Leningrad, and among those disgusted by the endemic corruption of the Brezhnev era," Shevardnadze became a symbol "of the system's capacity for reform."

Shevardnadze's image as a reformer was further enhanced by his association with the "Abasha Experiment," a campaign designed by Andropov to improve agricultural productivity. Andropov's support and Shevardnadze's own reformist image were sufficient to propel the Georgian party chief to candidate (nonvoting) membership in the Politburo in November 1978.

Foreign Minister under Gorbachev

Following the death of Leonid I. Brezhnev in November 1978, Soviet politics entered a period of flux that ended when Mikhail S. Gorbachev came to power in March 1985. The relationship between Gorbachev and Shevardnadze dates back to December 1982, when

Eduard Amvrosiyevich Shevardnadze

Gorbachev, who at the time was the Central Committee's secretary for agriculture, visited Georgia. As a Politburo member, Shevardnadze was deeply involved in the Kremlin intrigue typical to political successions in the Soviet Union, and in Shevardnadze, Gorbachev had a political ally.

Gorbachev appointed Shevardnadze to serve as foreign minister. Despite his relative youth – he was fifty-seven years old – and lack of experience in foreign affairs, Shevardnadze brought support to Gorbachev's foreign-policy agenda, as well as a wide range of talents that could be put to use in forging a new domestic policy. His background in domestic affairs meant that he could lend Gorbachev strong support in the Politburo on these issues.

Changes in Soviet Foreign Policy

The policies that Gorbachev and Shevardnadze pursued inspired tremendous changes in Soviet international relations. The Intermediate Nuclear Forces (INF) Treaty between the Soviet Union and the United States, signed on 8 December 1987, mandated unprecedented bilateral arms reductions. The accord banned all missiles with ranges between three hundred and thirty-four hundred miles. The Soviet Union dismantled 1,752 missiles to comply with the treaty, while the United States destroyed 859 missiles.

Under Gorbachev and Shevardnadze the Soviets completed their withdrawal from Afghanistan on 15 February 1989, ending nine years of military intervention in that country. The Soviet Union had invaded Afghanistan in December 1979, following a coup within the Marxist government that deposed Hafizullah Amin and brought Babrak Karmal to power. At the height of the fighting in Afghanistan, the Red Army had 115,000 troops in the country. The Soviets lost 13,000 troops, and an additional 22,000 were wounded.

The Soviet withdrawal from Afghanistan served as a precursor to the revolutionary changes that swept Eastern Europe during the last half of 1989 and marked a dramatic shift in Soviet foreign policy. In Poland, General Wojciech Jaruzelski selected Tadeusz Mazowiecki, a high-ranking member of the Solidarity trade union, to be the country's first noncommunist prime minister since the beginning of the postwar era. In Hungary, the Communist party disbanded on 7 October. Ten days later the parliament in Budapest amended the constitution to permit a multiparty system and free elections. In November revolutions also swept through Bulgaria and Czechoslovakia.

East Germany also was the scene of dramatic change. Although Erich Honecker's regime restricted travel to the West, East Germans were permitted to visit other Warsaw Pact nations. Thus, Hungary's decision to open its border on 10 September gave East Germans the opportunity to travel to the West. Within two months two hundred thousand people reached West Germany. Honecker was replaced by Egon Krenz on 18 October, and on 10 November all travel restrictions to the West were abolished. The ensuing sight of jubilant Germans dancing atop the Berlin Wall provided dramatic evidence to the world that the Cold War was indeed over.

Romania was the last of the Eastern-bloc nations to experience a revolution. The overthrow of Stalinist dictator Nicolae Ceausescu on 22 December occurred amid considerable violence. A week before, on 16 December,

Ceausescu had ordered his security forces to fire on unarmed demonstrators in Timisoara, resulting in considerable bloodshed. Ceausescu's brutal suppression, however, failed to quell popular unrest; by 21 December demonstrations had spread to Bucharest. Ceausescu and his wife, Elena, were executed by the insurgents on 25 December. A government composed mostly of former Ceausescu associates seized power and announced that free elections would be held in April 1990. The head of the transition government, Ion Iliescu, was a former Communist party official who fell into disfavor.

During the Romanian uprising Shevardnadze issued a statement that read, "The Soviet Union regards these events as the expression of the will of the Romanian people, which is working for the renovation of its society on the principles of democracy." The statement reflects the "new thinking" foreign policy, shaped by Shevardnadze and Gorbachev, that allowed the democratization of Eastern-bloc countries and signaled an end to the Cold War.

Shevardnadze surprised his collegues when he announced his resignation from his post as foreign minister on 20 December 1990. In a terse statement delivered to the Parliament of Deputies, Shevardnadze cited the growing influence of "reactionaries" within Gorbachev's goverment as a reason for his resignation. When Soviet military hard-liners and party conservatives staged a coup in August 1991, Shevardnadze joined Boris Yeltsin at the Russian Federation's "White House."

After the Soviet Union was dissolved in December 1991, Georgia decided not to join the Commonwealth of Independent States (CIS). A bloody civil war toppled the old regime in Georgia, and on 10 March 1992 Shevardnadze became the chairman of the state council of Georgia.

General References

Christian Schmidt-Häuer, *Gorbachev: The Path to Power* (London: Tauris, 1986);

Vladimir Solovyov and Elena Klepikova, *Yuri Andropov: A Secret Passage into the Kremlin* (New York: Macmillan, 1983).

–J. R.

SEE ALSO THESE RELATED ENTRIES

Yuri Andropov, 2; James A. Baker, 1; Mikhail Gorbachev, 2.

Mohamed Siad Barre

President of Somalia, 1969–1991
Born Lugh, Somalia, 1919

Mohamed Siad Barre was a Somalian military officer and was president from 1969 to January 1991. While there is uncertainty over the exact date of his birth, Siad Barre was born in the town of Lugh in the southern region of Somalia into a pastoralist family. His parents died when he was ten years old. After his primary education in his native town, he received his secondary education in Mogadishu, the capital of Somalia. Siad Barre is a self-made man, rising from shepherd to president. During the British military administration of Somalia, Siad Barre was a member of the colonial police force, rising to the highest possible rank for a native. In 1952, two years after Somalia was administered under Italian authority in the United Nations Trusteeship Administration, he attended the Carabinier police school in Italy for two years. After his return he took courses at the School of Politics and Administration in Mogadishu. By the time Somalia gained independence on 1 July 1960, Siad Barre was a brigadier general in the national police force. After independence he joined the Somalian National Army, rising to the rank of army commander in 1965.

The 1969 Coup

In late 1969 pro-Soviet Somalia descended into a grave political crisis following the October assassination of President Abd al-Rashid Ali Shirmarke and the subsequent chaotic general elections. In the wake of the political instability, as different factions struggled for control of the civilian government, the military staged a bloodless coup d'état (reportedly with Soviet complicity) on 21 October. The new government called itself the Supreme Revolutionary Council (SRC), and Siad Barre soon emerged as one of the principal conspirators. He was named president of the SRC and head of state of the Somali Democratic Republic. Siad Barre, who moved to take personal control of the government, and the other SRC leaders argued that the coup had been motivated by increasing corruption and nepotism in the civilian government and the need to preserve democracy. Members of the civilian government were arrested, and the national assembly was suspended. The SRC then announced

Mohamed Siad Barre

its intention to establish a scientific socialist state and turned to the Soviet Union – to which it granted permission to construct naval and air facilities in the strategically located port of Berbera in the Gulf of Aden – for substantial military aid. The People's Republic of China became a major source of civilian projects. The military regime transformed itself into the Somali Revolutionary Socialist party with the intention of creating a mass-based political party to replace military authority with civilian authority, although the military remained the essential power source. In addition to a nationalization program of land and industry, the new regime's foreign policy emphasized traditional and religious links to the Arab world and in 1974 joined the Arab League.

The Ogaden Conflict

The Siad Barre regime became deeply entangled in the global rivalry between the United States and the Soviet Union, and Somalia itself became an active battleground of the East-West conflict. The long-standing Somalia objective of national reunification of Somali-speaking people in Ethiopia and Kenya under one nation had been a source of discomfort for its neighbors. Somalia, which had claimed sovereignty over the predominantly Somali-speaking Ogaden province of eastern Ethiopia, actively supported antigovernment secessionist guerrilla forces in the region. Even though there is conflicting information regarding the initial sequence of events surrounding the fighting, it is clear that in May–July 1977 the Siad Barre regime sent its Soviet-equipped forces to aid the Ethiopian rebels, the Western Somali Liberation Front (WSLF), and within a few months drove out the American-equipped Ethiopian forces. The Ogaden war, to date the major international conflict in sub-Saharan Africa, quickly drew superpower intervention in the strategic Horn of Africa and caused regional realignment of superpower clients. The Marxist-Leninist regime of Lieutenant Colonel Mengistu Haile Mariam of Ethiopia appealed to the Soviet Union and the Eastern bloc for military aid. The Soviet Union, which opted to support the larger, strategically located Ethiopia, responded with a massive airlift of sixteen thousand Cuban combat troops, weapons, and Soviet military personnel. The Siad Barre regime calculated that it would receive military assistance from the Western countries in view of the massive Soviet-Cuban intervention. On 13 November 1977 the Siad Barre regime renounced its treaty of friendship with the Soviet Union and expelled the six thousand Soviet personnel in the country. However, the American administration of President Jimmy Carter, reluctant to get involved in a superpower confrontation in the Horn, refused to provide military aid until Somalia withdrew its troops from Ethiopian territory. By March 1978 the Soviet- and Cuban-led Ethiopian counteroffensive had reestablished control of the Ogaden, and under American pressures the Siad Barre regime announced its withdrawal from the region.

The Ogaden war, and the continental and international consensus against it, shattered Somalia's hopes for national-ethnic reunification. The internationalized war also turned the Horn of Africa into a major focus of superpower geopolitical competition. Relations between Somalia and Ethiopia remained hostile in the face of the former's continued support for self-determination for Somalis in Ethiopia. The residue of the Ogaden conflict and the long-standing mutual hostility continued to produce frequent border clashes into the mid 1980s. In June 1982 there was fierce fighting between Somalian and Ethiopian forces along the border. Somalia continued to support the WSLF, while Ethiopia channeled support to the Democratic Front for the Salvation of Somalia (DFSS) and the Somali National movement (SNM), the two principal antigovernment groups operating in Somalia. After the 1979 Soviet invasion of Afghanistan, military ties between the United States and Somalia were strengthened even though the United States was initially reluctant to become involved on the Somali side of the conflict, partly out of the fear of upsetting Kenya, one of the United States' major African allies. In mid 1980 the Siad Barre regime allowed the United States to use the Soviet-built Berbera air and naval facilities for the Rapid Deployment Force, but American military aid to Somalia remained modest. Dissatisfied with the levels of American military and economic aid, the Siad Barre regime began to look elsewhere, and in 1984 reports surfaced that Somalia had sought military aid from Israel and South Africa. Relations were resumed with Libya, from which Somalia reportedly received military aid, in April 1985. Somalia's realignment with the West forced the Siad Barre regime to introduce limited modifications in the country's political and economic system in order to appeal to Western aid donors.

Aside from its uneasy alignment with one superpower then another, the Siad Barre regime continued to face political and social instability, including popular unrest and growing challenges to its power throughout the 1980s. The severe famine and human dislocation in Ethiopia during 1984 and 1985 spilled over into Somalia, triggering its own famine and dislocation crisis. The regime was unable to deal effectively with Ethiopian-backed secessionist movements within Somalia, principally the DFSS and the SNM. In April 1988 an agreement was signed between Somalia and Ethiopia, in which each side vowed to refrain from supporting antigovernment and secessionist groups in the other's territory. Irrespective of pronouncements regarding reforms and an opening of the political system by 1989, political stability proved elusive, and in July 1989 disturbance in Mogadishu led to mass arrests and executions.

Despite promises of reform, the main rebel groups stepped up their offensive and announced their intention to coordinate their campaign to overthrow the Siad Barre government. By mid 1990 rebels were operating in the north, south, and central parts of the country, and the war continued unabated despite third-party efforts to broker a settlement. Growing disorder and lawlessness emerged in the capital city of Mogadishu as Siad Barre's hold on power and authority vanished.

By late December 1990 rebel forces of the United Somali Congress (USC), recently created and cofounded by Ali Mahdi Mohamed, entered Mogadishu and established control. In early January 1991, as severe fighting and disorder engulfed the city, foreign nationals were evacuated, including U.S. personnel who were rescued from the beleaguered American embassy by U.S. Marine special forces. On 27 January the USC declared its control of the government and called for a national conference among the various rebel groups. The USC's hold on power was tenuous, however, and the organization itself was violently split between two competing factions, one headed by Ali Mahdi, the other by Mohamed Farah Aidid. Barre fled Somalia the same day, leaving behind a country that immediately found itself ravaged by renewed internecine violence as the rebel groups and regional warlords vied for power. The fighting, which caused great destruction in Mogadishu and touched off mass starvation and death across the country as rebel forces prevented international relief efforts, provoked a U.S.-led multinational military intervention in December 1992 to restore order and assist in the humanitarian relief operations.

Book by Siad Barre

My Country and My People: The Collected Speeches of General Mohamed Siad Barre (Mogadishu: Ministry of Information and National Guidance, 1970).

General References

Tom Farer, *War Clouds on the Horn of Africa: The Widening Storm* (New York: Carnegie Endowment for International Peace, 1979);

David Laitin, *Somalia: Nation in Search of a State* (Boulder, Colo.: Westview, 1987);

I. M. Lewis, *A Modern History of Somalia: Nation and State in the Horn of Africa* (London: Longman, 1980);

Ahmed I. Samatar, *Socialist Somalia: Rhetoric and Reality* (London: Zed Books, 1988);

Bereket H. Selassie, *Conflict and Intervention in the Horn of Africa* (New York: Monthly Review Press, 1980).

                                        —J. R.-S.

SEE ALSO THESE RELATED ENTRIES

Jimmy Carter, 1; Mengistu Haile Mariam, 2.

Norodom Sihanouk

Head of State, Cambodia, 1955–1970, 1975–1976

President of Cambodia, 1991–

King of Cambodia, 1941–1955
Born Phnom Penh, Cambodia, 31 October 1922

Norodom Sihanouk was born in the Cambodian capital of Phnom Penh to Prince Norodom Suramarith and Princess Monivong Kossamak. They brought him up in a modest fashion, sending him to a public school in the capital and later to secondary school in Vietnam, which at that time, like Cambodia, was a part of French Indochina. In 1941, before he could complete his education, he was summoned back to Phnom Penh and enthroned as Cambodia's king by the French. Sihanouk, eighteen years old at the time, had been a carefree student, and the French believed he would be a more compliant ruler than the actual heir to the throne.

Later that year, during the course of World War II, the Japanese took over Cambodia and asked Sihanouk to remain as titular head of state. Throughout the war Sihanouk was more or less a prisoner in his own home. When the war ended in 1945, Sihanouk asked the French to return and continue administering Cambodia. In neighboring Vietnam the powerful communist movement, led by Ho Chi Minh, which had been fighting French rule, declared the country independent. Sihanouk feared that an independence movement would spill over into Cambodia. By the early 1950s, however, he was demanding Cambodian independence from the French. When he was rebuffed by the French in 1953, he went into voluntary exile in Thailand, hoping to force the French to recognize Cambodia's sovereignty. The next year, as a consequence of the Geneva Accords to end the fighting in Indochina between France and Vietnam, France granted Cambodia its freedom.

Under the accords Sihanouk remained head of state, but elections were slated for 1955. Sihanouk, who wanted actual power, abdicated the throne in favor of his father and established his own political party, the Sangkum party, or Subjects Socialist party. The main opposition to his party came from the Left, and in moving to counter the threat Sihanouk demonstrated his diplomatic skills. He persuaded the other parties of the Right and Center to unite under his banner, while simultaneously appropriating the slogans of the Left – modernization, socialism, neutralism, anti-Americanism – and, using tactics of intimidation at the polling booth, won every seat in the

Norodom Sihanouk

parliament. He continued winning elections, which the opposition charged were fixed, until his overthrow in 1970. His welfarist policies made him a popular ruler, but Sihanouk took no chances. After the first election in 1955 he struck against the communists, and by 1959 he had virtually destroyed their rural strongholds.

During his rule Sihanouk achieved an international reputation for successfully walking a diplomatic tightrope. He kept Cambodia neutral during the Vietnam

War through strenuous diplomatic efforts to maintain friendly ties with the United States, the Soviet Union, China, and North and South Vietnam. "The word brinkmanship was perhaps invented for me," he once said.

As the Vietnam War escalated in the late 1960s, Sihanouk was accused by the United States of doing nothing to stop the communists from using Cambodian territory. The Vietcong used what came to be called the Ho Chi Minh Trail to move supplies from North to South Vietnam through Cambodia – to which Sihanouk had turned a blind eye. In return, the government of North Vietnam did not actively encourage revolution in Cambodia. His deal with North Vietnam, however, enraged the United States, which in 1969 began bombing Cambodian territory in order to put a stop to the transport of supplies to the Vietcong. By 1970 his diplomatic efforts, designed to maintain Cambodian neutrality, had begun to fail. He was under pressure from the United States to allow U.S. forces to infiltrate Cambodia in order to confront the Vietcong and break the Ho Chi Minh Trail. When he resisted, the Richard M. Nixon administration began backing his right-wing opponents. On 18 March 1970, while Sihanouk was in Moscow, he was overthrown by his former defense minister, Lon Nol.

Sihanouk went into exile in China. While in Beijing he allied himself with Pol Pot and the Khmer Rouge, his enemy during his rule, and together they formed the National United Front of Kampuchea. In playing an active part in opposing the Lon Nol regime, he used his popularity among the Cambodian peasantry to urge them to revolt under the banner of the Rouge. The massive U.S. bombardment of rural Cambodia, together with the authoritarianism and corruption of Lon Nol, prompted large sections of the Cambodian peasantry to embrace the Khmer Rouge. On 17 April 1975 the Khmer Rouge took over Phnom Penh, and Sihanouk returned to the country to become titular head of state in a government dominated by Pol Pot. He often clashed with Pol Pot and resigned the next year. He was subsequently placed under house arrest and was released a few days before Vietnam took over Cambodia in January 1979.

Following the Vietnamese invasion Sihanouk once more began a period of exile in China. He again struck up an alliance with Pol Pot and became an international spokesman for the Cambodian resistance to the Vietnamese-backed regime led by Heng Samrin in Phnom Penh. With the support of China, the United States, and the countries of the Association of Southeast Asian Nations, he successfully lobbied the United Nations (UN) to recognize his coalition as the legitimate government of Cambodia.

In the next decade Sihanouk's political fortunes seesawed. Though the international community had little sympathy for Heng Samrin, it was repulsed by the evidence of Pol Pot's atrocities against his own people that Samrin's government had brought to light. In 1991 the international community, through the UN Security Council, worked out a peace plan that called for the creation of a coalition, made up of rebel and Vietnamese-backed factions, to govern Cambodia. Sihanouk was named president of Cambodia in November 1991. However, despite UN presence in the country, the coalition has proven unstable.

General References

Elizabeth Becker, *When the War Was Over: The Voices of Cambodia's Revolution and its People* (New York: Simon & Schuster, 1986);

Wilfred Burchett, *The China-Cambodia-Vietnam Triangle* (Chicago: Vanguard Books, 1981);

Nayan Chanda, *Brother Enemy: The War After the War* (San Diego: Harcourt Brace Jovanovich, 1986);

François Ponchaud, *Cambodia Year Zero* (New York: Holt, Rinehart & Winston, 1978);

William Shawcross, *Sideshow: Kissinger, Nixon, and the Destruction of Cambodia* (New York: Simon & Schuster, 1979).

– Q. I.

SEE ALSO THESE RELATED ENTRIES
Pol Pot, 2; Heng Samrin, 2.

Rudolf Slánsky

Deputy Prime Minister of Czechoslovakia, 1948–1951

General Secretary, Czechoslovak Communist Party, 1945–1951

Born Nezvestice, Bohemia, 31 July 1901
Died Prague, Czechoslovakia, 3 December 1952

Rudolf Slánsky, Czechoslovak communist leader who was the central victim in the November 1952 Stalinist show trials, was born into a Jewish family in Nezvestice, Bohemia, in Austria-Hungary. He joined the Czechoslovak Communist party (CCP) in 1921 and became editor of the party's daily organ, *Rude Pravo*, in 1924. He became regional party secretary in Ostrava in 1927 and a member of the CCP Central Committee and Politburo in 1929. In 1935 he was elected to the Czechoslovak National Assembly as a communist candidate. After Stalin's purge of all subordinate Communist parties in the late 1930s, a move designed to remove all suspected Trotskyites, a new CCP Politburo was formed in Moscow in November 1938, and Slánsky became one of its members.

General Secretary of the CCP

During World War II and the subsequent German occupation of Czechoslovakia, Slánsky became prominent in the CCP's exiled leadership in Moscow. He served with Czechoslovak forces under Red Army command on the Ukrainian front and fought with partisans in Slovakia during the anti-Nazi uprising of 1944. Immediately after the war he was named general secretary of the party, second in power only to Chairman Klement Gottwald. He played a major role in the communist coup d'état and takeover of Czechoslovakia in February 1948 and became the country's deputy prime minister.

Slánsky was very active in the reorganization of the Communist party in the late 1940s and helped impose a rigid Stalinist system in the country. During 1951, however, his own political position deteriorated as the party began to purge its ranks to root out any suspected political or ideological deviations. In September 1951 Slánsky was removed from the CCP Secretariat, and in November he was arrested.

The Show Trial

Under strong psychological and physical pressure, Slánsky confessed to the charges that had been prepared against him. He was accused of being a "Zionist agent" and of engaging in espionage for the West as an "enemy of the people." In November 1952 Slánsky and thirteen other officials were tried and eleven of them, including

Rudolf Slánsky

Slánsky, were sentenced to death. On 3 December 1952 he was executed in Prague. The last few years of Stalin's rule were marked by frequent "show trials" of suspected "nationalists" and "cosmopolitans" in all the Eastern bloc states, as Moscow sought to tighten its control over each ruling party, eliminate any internal factionalism, and find scapegoats for its unpopular policies. Slánsky's trial and execution marked the apogee of the Stalinist terror, during which thousands of political activists were imprisoned and all nonconformism was rooted out from inside and outside the party.

Anti-Semitism

The Slánsky trial was also marked by strongly anti-Semitic overtones, particularly as most of the condemned

311

were Jewish communists. It laid the ground for the infamous anti-Semitic "Doctor's Plot" prepared by Stalin in the Soviet Union. Jewish doctors stood accused of plotting to murder the Soviet leader. The campaign had reverberations elsewhere in Eastern Europe, as party leaders echoed Stalin's paranoia about potential disloyalty and sought to expose and punish political scapegoats. The absurdity of the charges against Slánsky and other victims of the trials proved an embarrassment to the party leadership in later years. The Slánsky case was subsequently reviewed, and in 1963 he was posthumously absolved of the fabricated charges of treason and espionage. His party membership was also posthumously restored in 1968 during the short-lived Prague Spring liberalization.

Books about Slánsky

Karel Kaplain, *Report on the Murder of the General Secretary* (Columbus: Ohio State University Press, 1990);

Me'ir 'Ko'ti'k, *The Prague Trial: The First anti-Zionist Show Trial in the Communist Bloc* (New York: Herzl Press, Cornwall Books, 1987);

Rudolfa Slanska, *Report on My Husband* (London: Hutchinson, 1969).

General References

Eugen Loebl, *Stalinism in Prague: The Loebl Story,* edited and with an introduction by Herman Starobin (New York: Grove Press, 1969);

Artur Gerard London, *The Confession* (New York: Morrow, 1970);

Jiri Pelikan, *The Czechoslovak Political Trials, 1950–1954* (Stanford, Cal.: Stanford University Press, 1971);

Marian Slingova, *Truth Will Prevail* (London: Merlin, 1968);

Zdenek Suda, *Zealots and Rebels: A History of the Ruling Communist Party of Czechoslovakia* (Stanford, Cal.: Hoover Institution Press, 1980).

—J. B. and A. B.

SEE ALSO THESE RELATED ENTRIES
Klement Gottwald, 2; Antonín Novotny, 2; Joseph Stalin, 2.

Ian Smith

Prime Minister of Rhodesia, 1964–1978
Born Selukwe, Southern Rhodesia, 8 April 1919

Ian Smith was the prime minister of Rhodesia from 1964 to 1978. For over a decade Smith was at the center of world attention and criticism for his leading role during Rhodesia's unilateral declaration of independence from Britain.

Smith was born in the Selukwe district near Salisbury (present-day Harare), the capital of the British settler colony of Southern Rhodesia (present-day Zimbabwe). He attended the Chaplin School, a local primary school in the town of Gwelo. He joined the British air force in 1939 as a fighter pilot, two years later joining the Southern Rhodesian air force and serving with British forces in Europe during World War II. After the war he attended Rhodes University in South Africa, and in 1948 he married Jane Watt, a South African schoolteacher. That same year he became a representative of the right-wing Liberal party in the legislative assembly of the self-governing Crown colony. Five years later he broke with the Liberal party to join the United Federal party (UFP), winning a seat in the Central African Federation, a British-contrived, Southern Rhodesian–dominated federation with Northern Rhodesia (Zambia) and Nyasaland (Malawi).

The Rhodesian Front

In 1961 Smith gained national exposure for his opposition to the new constitution that gave blacks nominal representation in the colonial government. He and other right-wing politicians broke with the UFP to form the Rhodesian Front (RF). The RF, whose electoral platform pledged to "preserve Rhodesia for the Rhodesians," won the December 1962 elections, and Smith became deputy prime minister. Internal political divisions within the RF erupted in April 1964 in a revolt, led by Smith, of the more conservative wing. Smith became the new prime minister on 13 April. Vowing that there would not be black majority rule "in my lifetime," Smith moved to secure Rhodesian independence from Great Britain under white rule. Alarmed by Great Britain's granting of independence to Malawi and Zambia in July and October, the white regime threatened to declare independence unilaterally and took measures to suppress black nationalist groups and leaders. Smith was convinced that independence from Great Britain was the only guarantee for the continued political and economic domination of Rhodesia's 250,000 whites over the country's 4 million blacks. Negotiations with Great Britain, which continued to de-

Gale International Portrait Gallery

Ian Smith

mand unimpeded progress toward black majority rule, broke down a few months after the RF swept the 7 May 1965 elections. Bolstered by its electoral victory, the Smith regime turned inward for a unilateral solution, and on 11 November Smith announced the Unilateral Declaration of Independence (UDI).

The UDI

Smith's UDI, however, came under immediate international pressure and censure, principally from independent African states and Great Britain, which refused to use military force to quell the rebel regime but imposed economic sanctions. Great Britain, working through the United Nations (UN), responded by pronouncing the declaration illegal and sought to isolate and pressure the Smith regime economically and diplomatically. In addition to its efforts to have the UN impose mandatory comprehensive sanctions in 1966 and 1968, Britain was able to prevent the recognition of the UDI by other governments, including South Africa. Despite the imposition of economic sanctions, Rhodesia managed to remain economically dynamic with the help of South Africa and the neighboring Portuguese-ruled territories. The Smith regime, undeterred by international pressures, began to take more draconian internal security measures to tighten its control over the black population and to roll back black political advancement, while at the same time making three major attempts – in 1966, 1968, and 1971 – to reach a settlement with Great Britain. By late 1972 the war between the white regime and the two main nationalist guerrilla groups, the Zimbabwean African People's Union, led by Joshua Nkomo, and the Zimbabwean African National Union (ZANU), led by Robert Mugabe, had reached a turning point after ZANU opened its offensive in the northeast region. Smith's position deteriorated precipitously after the fall of Portuguese colonial rule in bordering Mozambique, which had provided ZANU with a secure base of operations.

The Rhodesian war prompted several regional and international efforts to secure a negotiated settlement to the widening conflict, including an extraordinary initiative by Zambia and South Africa in August 1975 to sponsor a settlement between Smith, known for his intransigent views and obdurate temperament, and the guerrillas. In April 1976 Henry A. Kissinger, the American secretary of state, intervened in the stalled negotiations process in an effort to prevent further radicalization of the war and to forestall any possibility of another large-scale Soviet-Cuban intervention in the region. Kissinger was able to convince Smith, who was coming under mounting South African pressure to reach a settlement, to agree in principle to black majority rule, but the diplomatic breakthrough was short-lived. The Rhodesian conflict proved costly not just for the Smith regime but also for neighboring Mozambique and Zambia, which were targets of repeated punitive raids by Rhodesian special forces. The intensifying guerrilla war, which by 1977 had spread to all major parts of the country, placed increasing strains on the Smith regime. By 1977 the domestic and international environment had grown unfavorable for the white regime, with the United States (which had circumvented UN sanctions in 1971 by allowing the importation of Rhodesian chrome) and South Africa pressuring Smith to put an end to the conflict.

Zimbabwe-Rhodesia

The Smith regime, abandoned by its closest allies, the United States and South Africa, sought to reach an "internal settlement" with moderate black politicians inside Rhodesia. Despite the collapse of the six-month-long negotiations begun in October 1975 with Nkomo, Smith

continued to place hopes in reaching an internal accommodation that would ensure continued white domination. On 3 March 1978 he struck an agreement with Bishop Abel Muzorewa, a moderate black political leader, providing for a transitional government with an executive council headed by Smith and three black politicians. In January 1979 the white electorate approved a new constitution allowing for nominal majority rule. After the open elections in April, Smith's political engineering gave rise to Zimbabwe-Rhodesia, with Muzorewa as prime minister, but the new republic remained under de facto white control.

Smith's internal arrangements, opposed by the guerrilla movements, did not bring about an end to the conflict or to Rhodesia's international isolation. A new round of talks began in August 1979 in Lusaka, Zambia, and reopened at the Lancaster House in London on 10 September. The Lancaster House Conference, attended by Smith, black nationalist leaders, British and American representatives, and the heads of state of Mozambique, Tanzania, and Zambia, finally produced an agreement on 21 December. They provided for national elections in February 1980, with twenty of the one hundred seats in the house of assembly and ten in the senate reserved for whites. Smith's RF won all twenty reserved seats in the February elections, and on 18 April Zimbabwe became independent, with Robert Mugabe, whose ZANU party swept the elections, as prime minister.

Smith remained active in Zimbabwean national politics, but his position and influence began to erode in the wake of the new government's moderate and conciliatory policies and the political domination by ZANU. Smith, who became a member of parliament, continued to lead the RF, renamed the Republican Front, but in 1983 a faction of the party broke away to join the government party. Prior to the 1985 elections, the front, which continued to dominate white politics, reconstituted itself as the Conservative Alliance of Zimbabwe (CAZ). Smith's hard-line attitudes and obstructionist politics started to lose appeal by the 1985 elections, and the CAZ continued to splinter as the country moved toward a de facto one-party state. In April 1987 Smith was suspended from parliament, ostensibly as a result of his boisterous support for South Africa, and he later resigned as party leader.

General References

Ian Hancock, *White Liberals, Moderates, and Radicals in Rhodesia, 1953–1980* (London: Croom Helm, 1984);

Anthony Lake, *The "Tar Baby" Option: American Policy Toward Southern Rhodesia* (New York: Columbia University Press, 1976);

David Martin, *The Struggle for Zimbabwe: The Chimurenga War* (London: Faber & Faber, 1981);

W. H. Morris-Jones, ed., *From Rhodesia to Zimbabwe: Behind and Beyond Lancaster House* (London: Cass, 1980);

E. Windrich, *Britain and the Politics of Rhodesian Independence* (London: Croom Helm, 1978).

–J. R.-S.

SEE ALSO THESE RELATED ENTRIES
Henry Kissinger, 1; Robert Mugabe, 2.

Aleksandr Solzhenitsyn

Russian Writer
Born Kislovodsk, Soviet Union, 11 December 1918

Aleksandr Solzhenitsyn, Nobel Prize–winning author whose work has dealt with the Stalinist era and the cruelty of Soviet labor camps, holds the distinction of being Russia's most important living writer. Much of his writing is based on his eight-year imprisonment as a political dissident and has won him acclaim both in his homeland and abroad.

Solzhenitsyn was born in Kislovodsk in Northern Caucasia. His father died six months later, and Solzhenitsyn's mother struggled to make ends meet. They moved to Rostov-on-Don when he was a boy. Although poor, his parents were from the Russian intelligentsia, and his mother would impress upon him the notion that, although art exists for its own sake, the artist has an obligation to improve society. Solzhenitsyn's friends were members of Rostov's intellectual elite, and he was encouraged in the pursuit of books, ideas, and stimulating conversation.

From the age of nine Solzhenitsyn wanted to be a writer. At school he was an outstanding student and excelled in mathematics. He won a scholarship to Rostov University, where he received a double degree in mathematics and physics in 1941. The previous year he had married Natalya Alekseyevna Reshetovskaya, a chemistry student at the university.

Solzhenitsyn's years as a student coincided with Joseph Stalin's Great Purges in the 1930s, which marked one of the bloodiest epochs in Russian history. Millions of people "disappeared," presumed to have been either taken to a prison camp or shot by Stalin's secret police.

Aleksandr Solzhenitsyn

Exile

In October 1941 he was inducted into the Red Army and served as an artillery officer during World War II. He was decorated twice for valor. During the war he carried on a correspondence with a friend in which they criticized the Stalinist regime. The letters were intercepted by the secret police, and Solzhenitsyn was arrested in

February 1945. Branded an "enemy of the people," he received eight years imprisonment beginning in 1945, to be followed by permanent internal exile. He was sent to Moscow's Lubyanka prison and was later moved to Marfino, a scientific research institute where imprisoned intellectuals were forced to work on intelligence-related projects for the secret police. In 1950 he was transferred to a hard-labor camp, where he rafted timber, laid bricks, and developed a keen sensitivity to the peasants, who were his fellow prisoners.

In February 1953 Solzhenitsyn was discharged and became a permanent exile in the remote Asian town of Berlik. He developed intestinal cancer and almost died, an event which he chronicled later in *Cancer Ward* (1968).

One Day in the Life of Ivan Denisovich

By 1956, after Stalin had been dead three years, Solzhenitsyn arranged to be released from exile. He began writing again with a new sense of purpose. He also remarried Reshetovskaya, who had divorced him during his imprisonment, and moved to Ryazan. In 1961 he submitted his first manuscript to the Soviet government for scrutiny. In the political climate of anti-Stalinism, Premier Nikita S. Khrushchev permitted publication of the work, *One Day in the Life of Ivan Denisovich* (1963). The novel's narration, from the point of view of an ordinary Russian peasant who had been brutalized in hard-labor camps during the Stalinist era, employs earthy peasant speech, as well as prison jargon. The corruption endemic to life at the labor camp, Solzhenitsyn felt, reflected the larger corruption in Soviet life.

The novel caused an immediate sensation, and Solzhenitsyn became the spearhead of an artistic emancipation movement in the Soviet Union. In the mid 1960s, however, the government became increasingly restrictive, and after January 1966 none of his works was officially published in the Soviet Union.

The First Circle

In spite of these difficulties, Solzhenitsyn continued to write, and his work was surreptitiously read by Russian intellectuals and smuggled abroad for publication. In *The First Circle* (1968) he wrote of captive scientists at a Stalinist research center. The secret police confiscated his notes on the manuscript, and Solzhenitsyn protested to the Soviet Writers' Union, but to no avail. He was ousted from the union in 1969.

A minority of communist critics, both in the Soviet Union and around the world, was quick to denounce his work for its criticisms of Stalinist Russia. Others, however, praised him for exposing Soviet life under Stalin, and, as a consequence, many made appeals for beginning a new era in Soviet society that would be characterized by glasnost, or openness and candor in public affairs.

Jean-Paul Sartre argued that Solzhenitsyn's short story "Matryona's Place," about a stolid Russian peasant who maintains her morality in the face of widespread corruption in her village, is a model for genuine socialist literature. He likened its moral tone to that of Leo Tolstoy's fiction. Like Tolstoy, Solzhenitsyn revealed the psychological profile of his characters by portraying them against their historical backdrop. In addition, he employed a Tolstoyan ethical code based on individual conscience. The comparison to Tolstoy is also telling, for it reveals Solzhenitsyn's nineteenth-century artistic tastes.

As Social Critic

Solzhenitsyn is an intensely Russian writer, critical of Western society. He views the West as overly materialistic and prefers a simple, austere life in the Russian countryside. Expelled by the Soviet government in 1974 on charges of treason, Solzhenitsyn has since resided in Cavendish, Vermont. In mid 1990 the Soviet Union returned his Soviet citizenship.

That same year Solzhenitsyn published a major article criticizing the "noisy" reforms of Soviet prime minister Mikhail Gorbachev. He urged the dissolution of the Soviet Union and its replacement by a Russian state made up of the three Soviet Slavic republics. He also called for the return of private property in these Slavic states and a form of democracy based on locally elected councils.

Solzhenitsyn won the Nobel Prize for literature in 1970, but the Soviet government forced him to accept it in absentia. Other noted titles in his body of work include *The Gulag Archipelago, 1918–1956* (1973–1978), a three-volume historical account of the Russian prison-camp system; *Lenin in Zurich* (1976), a chronicle of the life of the founder of the Soviet state shortly before the Russian Revolution; and *August 1914* (1972), a portrayal of the failed Russian offensive in East Prussia during World War I.

He divorced Reshetovskaya in 1973 and married Natalya Svetlova. They have two sons, Yermolai and Ignati.

Books by Solzhenitsyn (Selected)

One Day in the Life of Ivan Denisovich (New York: Dutton, 1963);

Cancer Ward (New York: Dial, 1968);

The First Circle (New York: Harper & Row, 1968);

Stories and Prose Poems (London: Bodley Head, 1971);

August 1914 (London: Bodley Head, 1972);

The Nobel Lecture on Literature, translated by Thomas P. Whitney (New York: Harper & Row, 1972);

The Gulag Archipelago, 1918–1956: An Experiment in Literary Investigation, I-VII 3 volumes (New York: Harper & Row, 1973–1978);

Lenin in Zurich (Farrar, Straus & Giroux, 1976).

Books about Solzhenitsyn

David Burg, *Solzhenitsyn* (London: Hodder & Stoughton, 1972);

Vladimir Lakshin, *Solzhenitsyn, Tvardovsky and Novy Mir* (Cambridge: Massachusetts Institute of Technology Press, 1980);

Christopher Moody, *Solzhenitsyn* (New York: Barnes & Noble, 1973);

Abraham Rothberg, *Aleksandr Solzhenitsyn: The Major Novels* (Ithaca, N.Y.: Cornell University Press, 1971);

George Saunders, *Rebels and Bureaucrats* (New York: Merit, 1969);

Michael Scammell, *Solzhenitsyn: A Biography* (New York: Norton, 1984).

– M. G.

SEE ALSO THESE RELATED ENTRIES

Mikhail Gorbachev, 2; Joseph Stalin, 2.

Anastasio Somoza Debayle

President and Dictator of Nicaragua, 1967–1979
Born León, Nicaragua, 5 December 1925
Died Asunción, Paraguay, 17 September 1980

Anastasio Somoza Debayle was the third and last member of the Somoza family to lead Nicaragua. Taking over power from his older brother in 1967, Somoza led his country until his government was overthrown in 1979, ending the forty-three years of the Somoza dynasty.

Somoza's father, Anastasio Somoza García, was elected president in 1936, after manipulating the constitution imposed by the American troops that occupied the country from 1927 to 1933. He led the country in a brutal and corrupt manner until he was assassinated in 1956. His oldest son Luis then took power and led until 1967. The second oldest of the three sons, Anastasio was well groomed to take over where his father and older brother had left off. At age eleven, Anastasio, together with his brother Luis, attended LaSalle Military Academy in New York; at age seventeen, already a captain in the Nicaraguan National Guard, he enrolled at West Point. Somoza served as commander of the National Guard in the 1960s. In 1967, as the presidential candidate of the Nationalist Liberal party, he won 71 percent of the vote.

Dissolution of Congress

To avoid having to step down after the completion of one term (as required by the constitution), Somoza, working with his close supporters, arranged for the dissolution of Congress in August 1971 and maneuvered to retain his personal power for the next few years as the dominant member of a ruling triumvirate. In December 1974, under the aegis of a rewritten constitution, Somoza was elected by Congress to a six-year term.

Anastasio Somoza Debayle, 1980

Erosion of Support

Somoza's rule, like that of his father, was characterized by corruption and brutality. This contributed to the erosion of support among important power centers, including the Catholic church, the moneyed elite, and the U.S. government, which under President Jimmy Carter began to scrutinize more carefully the human rights record of many regimes traditionally supported by the United States. Many former supporters became opponents of the regime, and loyal opposition members were willing to support a more revolutionary alternative that worked outside of the debilitated political system.

The FSLN

The most active opponents of Somoza were members of the Sandinista Front of National Liberation (FSLN), a small but effective guerrilla movement. In 1974, after members of the FSLN took thirty-five hostages during a 1974 Christmas celebration honoring U.S. ambassador Turner Shelton, Somoza declared a state of siege. All constitutional rights were suspended, and a counterinsurgency unit was created.

Support for the anti-Somoza movement swelled in 1978, as a disgruntled population rallied in protest of the assassination by Somoza's professional hit men of Pedro Joaquín Chamorro Cardenal, an outspoken critic and editor of the opposition newspaper, La prensa. Riots, strikes, and urban insurrections ensued, and the Broad Opposition Front (FAO) was formed out of a cross section of Nicaraguan political, religious, and business groups.

Victory of the FSLN

As the FSLN gained the support of civilian insurgents, Somoza and his loyal National Guard became increasingly vulnerable. Although Somoza's men were able to regain control of the cities after the FSLN's first major offensive in late 1978, they were less successful in responding to the FSLN's final offensive in June 1979. The FSLN felt confident enough to establish a government-in-exile. During this period the U.S. government, which had ceased all military and economic assistance to Somoza's regime in February 1979, attempted to negotiate a settlement between Somoza and the FSLN. But these talks failed, primarily because of the insistence of the United States on the preservation of the National Guard.

In July 1979 President Carter agreed to allow Somoza to fly to Miami. However, because Carter refused to grant the Nicaraguan dictator political asylum, Somoza went into exile in Asunción, Paraguay, where he was assassinated 17 September 1980.

General References

Richard Millet, *Guardians of the Dynasty: A History of the U.S.-Created Guardia Nacional and the Somoza Family* (Maryknoll, N.Y.: Orbis Books, 1977);

Thomas W. Walker, "Nicaragua: From Dynastic Dictatorship to Social Revolution," in *Latin American Politics and Development* (Boulder, Colo.: Westview, 1985).

– B. D.

SEE ALSO THESE RELATED ENTRIES

Jimmy Carter, 1; Daniel Ortega Saavedra, 2.

Joseph Stalin

General Secretary, Soviet Communist Party, 1929–1953
Born Gori, Georgia, Russia, 21 December 1879
Died Moscow, Soviet Union, 5 March 1953

Joseph Stalin, Soviet dictator from 1929 until his death in 1953, rivals Adolf Hitler as the twentieth century's most infamous political figure. Stalin's influence on the development of the Soviet Union after the 1917 revolution was immense. It has been argued that during the 1930s he carried out the real revolution when he radically transformed Soviet society and created institutions that remained intact through most of the twentieth century and bore testimony to his influence: the all-pervasive role of the secret police and its implied threat of terror; the dominance of the party, especially over economic affairs; and the cult of personality surrounding Soviet leaders. During World War II Stalin maintained an uneasy alliance with the United States and Great Britain, an alliance marked by suspicion and mistrust. His pursuit of Soviet strategic interests during the war and after, particularly in Eastern Europe and Germany, set the stage for a series of moves and countermoves that culminated in the Cold War between the Soviet Union and the West.

Stalin was born Iosif Vissarionovich Dzhugashvili in the Georgian village of Gori. His father, a shoemaker, died in a drunken brawl when Stalin was eleven, leaving his mother, a peasant woman, to bring him up. She worked to ensure his education so that he could enter the Orthodox priesthood. At the Tiflis seminary between 1894 and 1898, however, he began his political activity, writing poems for a nationalist Georgian paper under the pseudonym Koba, derived from a character in a minor Georgian novel.

Stalin's political activities led to his expulsion from the seminary. He joined the fledgling Social Democratic Labor party and organized workers in Transcaucasia. For this activity he was arrested and exiled to Siberia on more than one occasion. He escaped each time, but it has been estimated that between 1902 and 1917 Stalin spent roughly seven years in exile. Sometime between 1902 and 1904 he married Ekaterina Svandize, who bore a son, Yakov, in 1908. She died shortly afterwards, and Stalin gave the child over to her relatives to bring up.

The party split in 1903 into two factions: the Bolsheviks, the radical wing led by V. I. Lenin who called for continuous political agitation, and the more moderate Mensheviks, who believed that communism would follow Russia's natural evolution into a capitalist state. Stalin sided with the Bolshevik wing, which ultimately became

Joseph Stalin

the Communist party of the Soviet Union (CPSU). He caught the attention of Lenin, who made him a member of the Bolshevik Central Committee in 1912 and assigned him to write for *Pravda*, the party newspaper in Saint Petersburg. In 1913 he took for his byline his second and most famous pseudonym, Stalin.

Russian Revolution of 1917

The importance of Stalin's role in the 1917 Russian Revolution is debatable. Eyewitnesses, most notably Leon Trotsky – later Stalin's most important rival – and the American journalist John Reed, accord him little distinction for leadership. During the October seizure of power by the communists Stalin remained behind the scenes, working in the editorial offices of *Pravda*.

From 1917 until 1922 Stalin acted as people's commissar for nationalities, dealing with the thorny problem of Soviet policy toward the ethnic minorities of the former Russian Empire. Stalin envisioned the Soviet Union as a highly centralized, Russian-dominated federal state, in essence an updated version of the old imperial model. But Lenin considered Stalin's ardent Russian nationalism excessive, and this point would become a source of conflict between them.

General Secretary

In 1922 Stalin was named general secretary of the party, a position he would ultimately transform into the center of political authority in the Soviet Union. By this time Lenin, in failing health, had become alarmed at Stalin's methods and intentions. In a letter he wrote shortly before his death, Lenin warned his colleagues of Stalin's intolerance and capriciousness and expressed fears that as general secretary Stalin might abuse his power. He urged that Stalin be removed from his post, but ill health prevented him from doing more. Lenin died in 1924, and by 1929 Stalin had succeeded in neutralizing his most serious rivals.

Collectivization

In 1930 Stalin reversed Lenin's New Economic Policy (NEP), which in a partial retreat from socialism had encouraged free enterprise as a way to rebuild the economy, shattered from the civil war (1917–1920). The NEP allowed private merchants and kulaks (landholding peasants) to coexist with the Bolsheviks and compete with the state cooperatives. Stalin, however, undertook to nationalize agriculture with the ostensible aim of bringing communism to the countryside. But collectivization revealed, if nothing else, the basic hostility of the Bolsheviks toward the peasantry. Peasants who resisted Stalin's decree – and many slaughtered their livestock rather than let them be seized – were summarily executed or sent to prison work camps, the infamous gulags. Estimates vary, but by the time collectivization had run its course in 1933, agricultural output had declined by more than half, and roughly 5 million peasants had been imprisoned in the gulags. Stalin himself admitted later to Winston Churchill to a total of 10 million deaths. Some 3.3 to 3.5 million died of starvation; in his memoirs Nikita S. Khrushchev – Stalin's successor – tells of a train that reached Kiev after a journey through the Ukraine picking up the bodies of those who had starved to death. Differences with his wife over the policy of collectivization aggravated Stalin's already difficult second marriage, and in 1932 his wife Nadezhda committed suicide.

When the first horrors of collectivization could no longer be ignored, Stalin defended his actions to his colleagues, insisting in a speech of 2 March 1930 that local party members, "dizzy with success," had misunderstood his very simple instructions. Later, Stalin would blame the failures of collectivization on his enemies – kulaks, rightists, Trokskyites, and other counterrevolutionaries.

Industrialization

Stalin's other monumental economic task at this time was to industrialize the Soviet Union, with the aim of transforming it into an advanced socialist state. His ambitious plan was to a large extent made possible by the burgeoning population of the gulags, which provided a massive source of slave labor. The expansion of heavy industry, as laid out in the first five-year plan in 1928, was officially called a success in 1932. By the German invasion on 22 June 1941, Soviet industrial production had increased sixfold.

In a series of purges between 1933 and 1939 Stalin imposed his will on the Soviet Union. He transformed the party into an instrument to serve his personal dictatorship, thereby ensuring that it would never again be a revolutionary movement. Approximately half of the 1.2 million members of the party were arrested, and relatively few regained their freedom. Beginning in the summer of 1937 the high command of the Red Army was largely decimated, followed by the liquidation of half of the officer corps.

Many prominent party figures found themselves accused of conspiring to murder Stalin or of working for foreign intelligence services and were given spectacular show trials, found guilty, and sentenced to death. The first show trial took place in August 1936 and ended with the shooting of Stalin's close colleagues, Grigori Zinoviev and Lev Kamenev, along with fourteen others. The third great trial, held in March 1938, featured Nilolai Bukharin, who had opposed collectivization, and Aleksei Rykov, Lenin's successor as prime minister.

A sense of suffocating fear pervaded Soviet society during these years, a reflection of the systematic terror perpetrated by Stalin's secret police, the People's Commissariat of Internal Affairs (NKVD). Millions of citizens were arrested and charged with a variety of offenses – conspiracy, espionage, sabotage. What made the terror so stifling was its secret pervasiveness; no group or individual was immune, and the denunciations, arrests, and sentencings were carried out with little fanfare: the accused simply disappeared, assumed to have been either executed or transported to the work camps.

One story concerns two engineers and their families who were arrested because the first received a package containing shoes, clothes, and toys from an uncle in Poland. The second engineer was arrested and sentenced to ten years because he was a friend of the first.

Contact with foreigners was particularly dangerous. A cook answered a newspaper advertisement for a position, which turned out to be at the Japanese embassy. He got the job, but before he could begin work he was arrested and charged with espionage.

The prison work camps – the gulags – became an integral part of the mass terror. It has been estimated that by 1937–1938 they held as many as eight million prisoners. The most infamous camps were in the Soviet Far East near the goldfields of Kolyma. These camps, each with about ten thousand prisoners, were spread across the Artic tundra in an area four times the size of France. Outside work was compulsory until the temperature reached minus fifty degrees celsius. Mortality rates at the Kolyma camps were particularly high, and most prisoners did not live more than a year or two. In all about twelve million died in Stalin's camps between 1936 and 1950.

Cult of Personality

The purges coincided with the beginning of Stalin's cult of personality, when he was accorded the status of demigod. By 1933 he had become the "Father of the Soviet People" and the "Great Teacher." Poems and songs were written about him; his writings were studied; his dark eyes stared out from prominently displayed pictures. An engineer passing through Moscow counted 101 portraits and busts of Stalin in the Kazan station. Every meeting that took place in the Soviet Union ended with a standing ovation for Stalin, and all details of the meeting – including the exact length of the applause – were reported by the press. The "ungainly dwarf of a man" rarely appeared, however, before the public, preferring to remain behind the walls of his country dacha.

Foreign Policy Before World War II

Stalin's foreign policy before World War II was largely isolationist. He did, however, recognize the growing threat of Hitler's Germany and took steps to counter the rise of fascism. He established relations with the United States in 1933 and joined the League of Nations in 1934. In 1935 he effected the so-called Popular Front strategy by directing foreign Communist parties to join political coalitions that were openly antifascist. During the Spanish civil war (1936–1939) between the Republicans, the legally elected government, and the Loyalists, led by General Francisco Franco and supported by Germany and Italy, Stalin provided military assistance to the Republican forces in the hopes of protracting the war and diverting German attention to the West. When it became apparent to Stalin that the Loyalists would be victorious, he terminated Soviet aid and even helped to purge the Republican forces of Bolshevik elements. The purge was to prevent the existence of communist parties outside Moscow's control.

Non-Aggression Pact

On 28 September 1939, in a secret protocol to the Non-Aggression Pact, Hitler and Stalin claimed those parts of Europe that each considered essential to his country's strategic interests. For Stalin this meant regaining former parts of the Russian Empire that had been lost at the end of World War I: eastern Poland, parts of Romania, the Baltic states of Latvia, Lithuania, and Estonia, and Finland. Finland put up the most resistance, refusing to grant Stalin territory and bases for the Soviet navy. He reacted by invading Finland on 30 November 1940. The Finns fought back valiantly throughout the winter but were forced in March 1941 to sue for peace and cede territory.

German Invasion

Stalin's annexations enlarged the Soviet Union's strategic boundaries. By July 1940 the Soviet Union encompassed an additional 286,000 square miles and had virtually restored the borders of imperial Russia. In November 1940 Stalin hinted at further territorial ambitions: he wanted German recognition of Soviet interests in large parts of Iraq and Iran, so as to gain access to the Persian Gulf and the oil fields of the Middle East. On 22 June 1941 three German army groups crossed the eastern frontier of Poland in a surprise attack on the Soviet Union.

The Red Army suffered tremendous losses that summer and fall: by 26 September 665,000 Soviet soldiers surrendered at Kiev. The Germans continued the push east, hoping to take Moscow by winter and force a Soviet capitulation. Stalin's army narrowly prevented the capture of the city, and the onset of winter halted further offensive operations until the following year.

In the summer of 1942 Hitler continued his drive against the Soviet army, hoping to capture the Ploesti oil fields in the Caucasus. He planned to capture Stalingrad on the way to secure his flank against future Soviet attacks from the interior. But Stalingrad was not taken, and the fighting continued until General Friedrich Paulus surrendered the German forces on 30 January 1943.

Hitler's last offensive on the Soviet front ended with the Soviet victory at Kursk in July 1943. From then on, the Red Army was able to keep the Germans on the defensive until they surrendered on 8 May 1945.

Role as Military Leader

Stalin maintained a high degree of control over the military during the war, but his abilities as a strategist and leader are debatable. In the 1930s he had purged the Red Army of many of its best officers. In the Winter War of 1939–1940 with Finland, the army had performed miserably against the Finns. Stalin repeatedly ignored warnings from foreign governments and his own generals and spies that Hitler was going to invade the Soviet Union, preferring to believe that he could remain on Hitler's good side. Once war did come he made a series of tactical errors that culminated in the surrender of Kiev, the low point of the Soviet war effort. After the Germans renewed their offense in 1942, Stalin convinced himself that Moscow was their goal when actually it was to take the Crimea. But as the war progressed Stalin's reputation grew, especially after the victory at Stalingrad.

Wartime Relations with Allied Leaders

The German invasion immediately put Stalin in the Allied camp alongside Franklin D. Roosevelt and Winston Churchill. For Stalin this was a marriage of convenience. He was firmly convinced that Roosevelt and Churchill intended to let the Soviet Union bear the brunt of the war against Hitler. At Stalin's urging, Roosevelt promised in May 1942 to open a second front in Europe against the Germans by the end of the year, in order to take pressure off the Red Army. Roosevelt, however, opted for a different proposal, put forth by the British, calling for a preliminary attack in North Africa. This action delayed the invasion of the Continent until June 1944. To Stalin, who made the establishment of an early second front a test of Anglo-American intentions, this two-year delay did nothing more than feed his paranoia.

Stalin was convinced throughout the war that his allies would not hesitate to make a separate peace with Hitler at Soviet expense. When German general Karl Wolff arrived in Bern in March 1945 to negotiate the possible surrender of German forces in northern Italy, Stalin demanded to be included. Roosevelt decided against Soviet participation, feeling that it might spook the Germans. Stalin immediately accused Roosevelt of plotting against him and claimed to know of an arrangement whereby the Germans would allow Allied forces to move into Eastern Europe in exchange for more favorable peace terms.

Postwar Relations with Allied Leaders

Stalin's postwar territorial aims played a strong role in his wartime relations with the Allied leaders. As early as July 1941 Stalin announced that he intended to keep those parts of Poland he acquired as a result of the Non-Aggression Pact. In December 1941 he urged Churchill to support his bid for the Baltic states and parts of Finland and Romania. After Benito Mussolini fell in July 1943 and the Italians were negotiating a possible peace, Stalin insisted on being included so as to have a part in the occupation of Italy. At the Tehran Conference in November 1943 Stalin announced that in return for declaring war on Japan he expected certain territorial concessions in the Far East.

In February 1945 Churchill, Stalin, and Roosevelt met at Yalta in the Crimea, where they sealed the fate of Po-

land. Churchill and Roosevelt accepted the provisional Polish government supported by Moscow in return for the promise of free elections for the Polish people.

At the Potsdam Conference in July 1945 the division of Germany into occupation zones, discussed in 1944, was further set. The conference effectively established the western boundary for Soviet military expansion into Europe. It also set the stage for further disputes among the Allies over their postwar policies toward Germany. Stalin wanted to cart off as much of Germany's industrial plant as he could, both to help rebuild the Soviet economy and to prevent Germany's recovery. Reparations figures were agreed upon at Potsdam, but not to Stalin's liking. The other Allied powers by this point sought to rehabilitate Germany economically, knowing that not to do so would mean future, costly Western aid.

Postwar Foreign Policy

Stalin's postwar foreign policy was a continuation of his wartime goals. His most immediate aim was to secure the Soviet Union's strategic periphery. In Eastern Europe this meant gaining political control over the areas that the Soviet army was then occupying. He based his strategy on the assumption that the United States and Great Britain had ceded to the Soviet Union control of the region's political future. The Soviets were aided by the extensive turnover of political parties and leaders during the war — a turnover which left a vacuum of power across central Europe — and by the respect they had earned for their resistance to the Fascist regimes.

The Soviet Bloc

The formation of the Soviet bloc was completed in two steps. The first, satellization, ensured that the Eastern European states became Soviet allies. Stalin accomplished this by initially directing regional communists to cooperate with other parties within the framework of coalition governments. In the second stage the communists came to dominate the coalitions, which included "fellow travelers," picked by Moscow and content to go along with Soviet directives. The presence of fellow travelers gave a thin veneer of legitimacy to the process, largely for the benefit of Western observers. True political rivals with real popular support, especially Social Democrats, were neutralized. The third stage, Sovietization, saw the Soviets effectively in control and ready to begin transforming the various economies and societies into copies of the Soviet model.

The satellization of Eastern Europe was largely completed by 1947–1948, although the timing varied from country to country. The coalition government in Czechoslovakia, for instance, lasted until the communist coup of March 1948. Czechoslovakia had been spared in order to ease Western fears about the fate of Poland. Ensuring

Soviet control of Poland was a prime concern of Stalin, and the pseudocoalition ruled there from the beginning.

Marshall Plan

Stalin's postwar strategy in Western Europe was different. He ordered the European Communist parties to foment workers' strikes so as to cripple the political structures and economies. The resulting economic chaos led to the Marshall Plan, a U.S. offer of financial assistance made to the European countries in June 1947.

In September 1947 Stalin created the Communist Information Bureau (Cominform) in order to consolidate Soviet power over the regional Communist parties that were expected to come to power or already were in power. Stalin's concern was that these parties, once in command, might not show unquestioning obedience to the Soviet Union; this was the case when Poland and Czechoslovakia initially indicated that they would accept U.S Marshall Plan aid. Stalin's foreign minister, Vyacheslav Michailovich Molotov, had already declined the U.S. offer on behalf of the Soviet Union when he walked out of a meeting in Paris in June 1947. The Eastern European foreign ministers were then summoned to Moscow, reprimanded, and ordered not to accept help from the United States.

Relations with Foreign Communist Movements

The Soviet Union supported only those foreign communist movements that Moscow could expect to control. However, almost every communist movement that succeeded on its own merits – without the Soviet Union's direct or indirect support – had a strongly nationalistic component that was incompatible with Soviet hegemony. A case in point was Yugoslavia: Josip Broz Tito continued to pursue his own foreign and economic policy after World War II. He provided aid to the communists during the Greek civil war in 1948, a policy that threatened Great Britain's traditional interest in the region. Feeling no doubt that this might endanger Soviet actions in Eastern Europe, Stalin ordered Tito in early 1948 to stop aiding the Greeks. Tito refused, and Stalin expelled the Yugoslavs from the Cominform in June 1948.

Stalin also had trouble with the Chinese communists. Poor relations had existed since the abortive Chinese communist revolution in the 1920s. After World War II Stalin, underestimating the communists' power, urged Mao Zedong, the Chinese communist leader, to join the nationalist government of Chiang Kai-shek. Mao preferred to fight the nationalists, and the communists eventually came to power on 1 October 1949. Stalin continued to provide economic assistance to the Chinese in the hope of ensuring Chinese dependency, but the relationship continued to be marked by mistrust. The Chinese situation was a foreign-policy defeat for Stalin because he could never be sure that the Soviet Union's eastern border would be secure.

The Berlin Blockade

By 1948 the British and Americans realized the necessity, if not the desirability, of an economically and politically reconstituted Germany. They had merged their occupation zones in anticipation of German statehood, a merger to which Stalin strenuously objected. He challenged Western plans for Germany by taking advantage of Berlin's isolation, eighty miles inside the Soviet zone of occupation. On 18 June 1948, the day a new currency was introduced in the western zones of Germany, the Soviets stopped all surface traffic between the West and Berlin, citing technical problems with the routes. This was followed by a cutoff of electricity, coal, and food to the city. The Anglo-American powers immediately began an airlift of essential supplies to Berlin, which held out until Stalin called off the blockade in May 1949.

The failure of the Berlin blockade was an acute embarrassment to the Soviet government. Berlin had served as an exit from the Soviet occupation zone for 2.6 million Germans. The city's stand was seen to be symbolic of Western determination and competence in the face of ruthless Soviet designs.

Soviet Atomic Weaponry

On 29 August 1949 the Soviets detonated their first atomic device, finally achieving one of Stalin's primary postwar goals: acquisition of the weapon that would allow the Soviets to attain military parity with the United States. Ever since Stalin had been informed about the existence of the bomb on 24 July 1945, he had outwardly appeared quite unimpressed by it. However, he had immediately ordered his scientists and those captured from Nazi Germany to redouble their efforts to develop fission. The American decision in the 1940s to maintain control over the weapon and its technology contributed to Stalin's mistrust of Western intentions.

The Korean War

The Korean War (1950–1953) marked a serious miscalculation in Stalin's foreign policy. Frustrated by Western European economic recovery, the failure of the Berlin blockade, and the U.S. presence in Japan, he strongly encouraged, if not ordered, the communist government of North Korea to invaded the noncommunist South. Stalin foresaw an easy victory because of the apparent lack of importance accorded Korea in official U.S. pronouncements and the withdrawal of U.S. troops from South Korea in June 1950. Secretary of State Dean Acheson, on 12 January 1950, had laid out the boundaries of the American defense perimeter, which ran "along the Aleutians to Japan and then ... to the Ryukyus." Korea, however, was not mentioned and was made conspicuous by its absence, something Stalin was sure to have noted.

North Korea invaded the South on 25 June 1950. Coming close to a quick victory, the North Koreans were met by a hastily formed United Nations (UN) force composed largely of American troops. By October the U.S. forces were counterattacking and advancing to the Yalu River near the Manchurian border. The Chinese, alarmed by the proximity of U.S. forces and fearing a possible invasion, entered the war in November. Eventually a two-year stalemate developed along the 38th parallel until an armistice was reached in July 1953.

Stalin did gain some advantages from the Korean War: the United States had to commit a large number of troops to the peninsula, troops that otherwise could have been used to hinder Soviet moves in Eastern Europe. Further, the Chinese became more dependent on Soviet military equipment and on the Soviet Union itself, thereby delaying the eventual split between the two countries.

But the Korean War fundamentally transformed American opinion towards the U.S.-Soviet rivalry. Henceforth, military considerations would prevail over political ones in Washington. The recently established North Atlantic Treaty Organization (NATO) would be strengthened accordingly, soon to include the military forces of a rearmed West Germany. Stalin's successors began negotiating an end to the war soon after his death.

During his last years Stalin ruled more autocratically than ever. He assigned small groups of advisers – known as sextets or quartets – to study particular problems and then present their recommendations to him. By assigning more than one group to examine the same problem, he was able to play his advisers off one another and prevent the emergence of any coordinated opposition.

Revival of the Purges
The show trials that marked the "Great Purge" were revived, the latest victims being those accused of Titoist affiliations or sympathies. In January 1953 Stalin accused the doctors in the Kremlin of having murdered Andrei

Zhdanov, a high-ranking party official. This charge, undoubtedly false, was to serve as a pretext for another purge to eliminate more colleagues that Stalin had come to regard with suspicion – Anastas Mikoyan, Lavrenty Beria, and Molotov would have been the next to go. However, Stalin's death two months later on 5 March 1953 kept him from conducting this last purge.

His death may have ended an era in Soviet history, but Stalin's influence persisted until the mid 1980s, when a new generation of Soviet leaders emerged that did not owe their early rise to Stalin.

Books about Stalin:
Robert Conquest, *The Great Terror: Stalin's Purge of the Thirties* (New York: Macmillan, 1968);

Isaac Deutscher, *Stalin: A Political Biography* (London & New York: Oxford University Press, 1949);

Milovan Djilas, *Conversations with Stalin* (New York: Harcourt, Brace & World, 1962);

Robert C. Tucker, *Stalin in Power: The Revolution from Above, 1929–1941* (New York: Norton, 1990);

Adam Ulam, *Stalin: The Man and his Era* (New York: Viking, 1973).

General References
Seweryn Bialer, *The Soviet Paradox: External Expansion, Internal Decline* (New York: Knopf, 1986);

Alan Clark, *Barbarosa: The Russian-German Conflict* (New York: Morrow, 1964);

Charles Gati, *The Bloc That Failed: Soviet–East European Relations in Transition* (Bloomington: Indiana University Press, 1990);

Nikita S. Khrushchev, *Khrushchev Remembers*, edited by Strobe Talbott (Boston: Little, Brown, 1970);

William H. McNeill, *America, Britain, and Russia: Their Cooperation and Conflict, 1941–46* (New York: Oxford University Press, 1964);

Adam Ulam, *A History of Soviet Russia* (New York: Holt, Rinehart & Winston, 1976);

– M. B.

SEE ALSO THESE RELATED ENTRIES

Cominform, 3; Vyacheslav Michailovich Molotov, 2; Potsdam Conference (1945), 3; Leon Trotsky, 2; Andrei Vyshinsky, 2; Yalta Conference, 3.

Bung Sukarno

President of the Republic of Indonesia, 1949–1967
Born Surabaja, Java, 6 June 1901
Died Jogjakarta, Republic of Indonesia, 21 June 1970

Indonesian nationalist leader and first president of Indonesia, Bung Sukarno became widely regarded as one of the leading spokesman for the Non-Aligned Movement in the Third World.

Sukarno was born to a poor Javanese schoolteacher in Surabaja, in East Java. He completed his primary education at a Dutch elementary school in Modjakerto in 1914. He enrolled in a Dutch high school in 1916 in Surabaja, where he lived with the Islamic nationalist leader Omar Said Tjokroaminoto. During his high school years Sukarno became more political, coming into contact with prominent Indonesian nationalist leaders, as well as European socialists. In 1921 he entered the Institute of Technology in Bandung to study architecture and continued his close association with Tjokroaminoto and other nationalist figures. As head of the Taman Siswa, a cultural-nationalist movement at the university, he attracted widespread attention as a fiery, flamboyant speaker and organizer and quickly became one of Bandung's leading political activists.

Indonesian Nationalist Party

He graduated in 1926 and a year later became president of the radical Nationalist Study Club in Bandung and set out to unify the various nationalist organizations. In 1927 he became chairman of the newly created Indonesian Nationalist party (PNI), which called for complete Indonesian independence from Dutch rule and unity in the fragmented nationalist movement. Following his arrest in April 1930 for his political activism, Sukarno became a national hero after his widely publicized trial. The PNI all but disintegrated after he was arrested again in 1932 by Dutch colonial authorities and sent into internal exile.

Indonesian Independence

In 1942 Sukarno was released by the Japanese occupation forces in Indonesia and began to cooperate with the Japanese to secure Indonesian independence. In 1945 he was appointed head of the Preparatory Committee for Indonesian Independence. In *Pantjasila* (Five Pillars) he outlined his political thinking based on nationalism, internationalism, democracy, social justice, and belief in God. In August 1945 the committee adopted a draft constitution for a provisional government, with Sukarno as

Bung Sukarno

provisional president. Following the Japanese surrender, Sukarno declared Indonesia independent on 17 August, despite a fragmented nationalist movement and Allied-backed Dutch efforts to reimpose colonial rule. During the war with the Dutch, Sukarno's shaky new republic withstood a communist-led counterrevolution. Fighting continued until 1949 when, under pressure from the

United States and the United Nations (UN), the Dutch granted Indonesia its independence on 27 December. Sukarno became president of the Republic of the United States of Indonesia under a parliamentary form of government.

Sukarno's impatience with and dislike for parliamentary politics soon became evident, and he began to amass political power. His assertive style of leadership and fiery oratory formed the basis of his popular support. Sukarno also enjoyed the support of the national army. His domestic policies placed great emphasis on achieving national unity in Indonesia, which was fragmented geographically, culturally, and ethnically.

The Third World

He became a strong advocate of Third World "neutralism" in the East-West global competition – although, in fostering close ties with China and the Soviet Union, his foreign policy was anti-Western. In April 1955 Sukarno hosted the Bandung Conference, the first major gathering of Third World countries, attended by twenty-nine independent African and Asian countries. In addition to denouncing colonialism, the conference adopted the "Five Principles of Coexistence," sponsored by Chinese foreign minister Zhou Enlai: mutual respect for territorial integrity and sovereignty; nonaggression; noninterference in the internal affairs of other states; equality and mutual benefit; and peaceful coexistence. Attended by prominent figures – such as Jawaharlal Nehru of India, Gamal Abdul Nasser of Egypt, Josip Broz Tito of Yugoslavia, and Kwame Nkrumah of Ghana – the Bandung Conference gave birth to the Nonalignment movement in the Third World, a loose organization of diverse Third World countries that pursue an ostensibly neutral foreign policy regarding East-West politics. Despite his advocacy of nonalignment, Sukarno increasingly sided with communist bloc countries. Indonesia, which assumed a self-appointed role of revolutionary leadership in the region, became involved in an international dispute with the Netherlands over the status of West New Guinea (Irian Barat) in the late 1950s and early 1960s, as well as a political confrontation with Malaysia during 1963–1965. The Sukarno regime's actions in the region heightened tensions between the superpowers. During the Malaysian fiasco Sukarno accused the Western countries of an "imperialist encirclement" of Indonesia. On 20 January 1965 he formally withdrew from the UN and sought to organize his own Third World international forum.

By 1957 parliamentary democracy in Indonesia had given way to authoritarian rule in the guise of "Guided Democracy." During the period of Guided Democracy (1957–1965) Sukarno ruled in a delicate balance of power between the national army and the Indonesian Communist party (PKI), the two most powerful contending factions in the country. The fragile balance erupted into large-scale violence after an abortive military coup d'état on 30 September 1965. The army used the opportunity to eliminate the PKI and other communists in what turned out to be one of the worst single massacres in Southeast Asian history. In March 1966 the military, headed by General Suharto, assumed emergency powers in taking over the government. Over the next several months a political power struggle occurred between Sukarno and the military, although he was in effect only a figurehead president. In February 1967 Sukarno was finally dismissed from the presidency by Suharto, and he placed him under house arrest the following year. He died on 21 June 1970 of chronic kidney ailments.

Book by Sukarno (Selected)
Sukarno: An Autobiography (New York: Bobbs-Merrill, 1965).

Books about Sukarno
Bernhard Dahm, *Sukarno and the Struggle for Indonesian Independence* (Ithaca, N.Y.: Cornell University Press, 1969);

John David Legge, *Sukarno: A Political Biography* (London: John Lane, 1972).

General References
Harold Crouch, *The Army and Politics in Indonesia* (Ithaca, N.Y.: Cornell University Press, 1978);

Herbert Feith, *The Decline of Constitutional Democracy in Indonesia* (Ithaca: Cornell University Press, 1962);

John Hughes, *The End of Sukarno* (London: Angus & Robertson, 1968);

F. B. Weinstein, *Indonesian Foreign Policy and the Dilemma of Dependence: From Sukarno to Soeharto* (Ithaca, N.Y.: Cornell University Press, 1977).

–J. R.-S.

SEE ALSO THESE RELATED ENTRIES

Gamal Abdul Nasser, 2; Kwame Nkrumah, 2; Josip Broz Tito, 2; Zhou Enlai, 2.

Mikhail Suslov

Member of Soviet Politburo, 1955–1982
Born Shakhovskoe, Russia, 21 November 1902
Died Moscow, Soviet Union, 25 January 1982

Mikhail Andreevich Suslov, a prominent member of the Politburo from 1955 to 1982, was for over forty years the chief guardian of communist ideology and doctrine in Soviet domestic and foreign affairs. Western leaders had little, if any, contact with the reclusive Suslov, and virtually nothing was known of his private life, even to many of the Soviet leadership. Tall and thin with hornrimmed glasses, he possessed a formidable intellect that acted to discourage close friendships. It has been remarked that the death of his wife, Yekaterina, in 1972 was the first indication that he had been married.

He was born to peasants in the village of Shakhovskoe in the province of Ulyanovsk. When the Bolsheviks, soon to become the Communist party of the Soviet Union (CPSU), seized power during the October 1917 Revolution, Suslov joined the Komsomol (Communist Youth League). Later, during the Russian civil war, he worked to cajole food for the Red Army from local peasants. In 1921 Suslov became a party member.

Completing his secondary education at a workers' school in Moscow in 1924, he received further training in economic planning at the Plekhanov Institute. Between 1929 and 1937 Suslov did graduate work in economics with a strong emphasis on ideology. During his studies he taught economics at Moscow University and engaged in propaganda work for the party.

His Rise in the Communist Party

In the 1930s Suslov was involved in General Secretary Joseph Stalin's purges, working in the Urals and the Ukraine to eliminate party rivals and peasants who resisted Stalin's policy of collectivization. Between 1937 and the outbreak of World War II he moved higher in the party, working first in Rostov and then in the Caucasus as party chief of Stavropol. During the war he remained in the Caucasus as a political commissar, instructing the anti-German guerrilla forces. In 1941 he was named to the Central Committee, the high-level party apparatus.

In 1944 he was involved in deporting, from the Caucasus to Siberia, thousands of ethnic minorities accused of having collaborated with the Germans. Appar-

Mikhail Suslov

ently having caught Stalin's attention, Suslov was appointed later that year to oversee the incorporation of Lithuania into the Soviet Union, following the defeat of the German occupation forces. Once again Suslov helped to deport thousands to Siberia, this time Lithuanians suspected of anti-Soviet sympathies.

In 1946 Suslov was made head of the Central Committee's Agitation and Propaganda Department, which was responsible for shaping Soviet public opinion on foreign policy. A year later he was named to the Secretariat, which, along with the Central Committee's Politburo, was one of the two centers of supreme power in the Soviet Union.

He attended the 1948 meeting of the Communist Information Bureau (COMINFORM), the Moscow-dominated organization of world communism that he helped found in 1947, when Yugoslavia was expelled for resisting Soviet hegemony. That same year he assumed responsibility within the Secretariat for relations with foreign Communist parties. He was taking an increasingly higher role in the formation of Soviet foreign policy, which was to remain his principal responsibility. For about a year he was editor in chief of *Pravda*, the party newspaper.

By the time Stalin died in March 1953, Suslov had become the highest ranking member of the Secretariat after Nikita S. Khrushchev, Stalin's eventual successor. In 1955 Suslov was reelected to the Presidium — as the Politburo was then called — and until his death was one of its most powerful members.

Political Opposition to Khrushchev

During his tenure as general secretary, Khrushchev had many disagreements with Suslov, the first major one following Khrushchev's denunciation of Stalin at the Twentieth Party Congress in February 1956. Suslov strongly opposed this policy of "de-Stalinization," which he held responsible for the civil unrest that developed in Eastern Europe in the 1950s. The 1956 Hungarian Revolution was the first significant challenge to Soviet rule in the post-Stalin era. Suslov, as one of the conservatives in the Kremlin, urged a strong Soviet stance. He went to Budapest twice in October to negotiate with the government of Imre Nagy, who had promised political reforms. On the night of 31 October, however, Soviet troops entered Hungary to reassert Soviet domination.

Suslov took a dim view of Khrushchev's attempts to effect a reconciliation with Josip Tito of Yugoslavia. Khrushchev reports in his memoirs that Suslov no longer considered Yugoslavia a socialist country after Tito decided to take it on an "independent road to socialism." Suslov also opposed Khrushchev's efforts to reduce the defense budget in favor of greater consumer spending, preferring the traditional Soviet emphasis on heavy industry and military preparedness.

Yet when a group of Politburo members tried in vain to strip the general secretary of his powers in 1957, Suslov apparently opposed the so-called Antiparty Group, despite his opposition to many of

Khrushchev's policies. His reluctance to join the conspirators ensured his political survival.

Between 1957 and 1964 Suslov's power and prestige increased, and he continued to find fault with Khrushchev's domestic and foreign policies. He opposed Khrushchev's reforms that threatened the party's absolute control over economic affairs. In the cultural realm he sought in vain to prevent the publication of *One Day in the Life of Ivan Denisovich*, Alexander Solzhenitsyn's account of life in a Stalinist prison camp.

Support of Brezhnev

Suslov reportedly led the coalition which deposed Khrushchev in 1964 and installed Leonid Brezhnev as general secretary. Subsequently, under Brezhnev, Suslov reached the peak of his power and influence.

During the Prague Spring of 1968, when it appeared as if Czechoslovakia might challenge Soviet controls, Suslov was part of the leadership group that encouraged Soviet military intervention. He almost certainly helped formulate the "Brezhnev Doctrine" afterward, which clearly stated the Soviet Union's intention to use force to maintain order in the socialist world.

The same hard-line faction within the Politburo was wary of Brezhnev's policy of détente, or relaxed tensions, with the West. During the 1970s Suslov was involved with the crackdown of dissident intellectuals in the Soviet Union. He also criticized Soviet youth for copying Western fashions in dress and music.

The Soviet invasion of Afghanistan in 1979 and the imposition of martial law in Poland in 1981, both done with Suslov's encouragement, fueled rising tensions with the West and contributed to Suslov's growing pessimism over the suitability of détente.

On 25 January 1982 Suslov died suddenly of a stroke, his death preceding Brezhnev's by a mere ten months. Given Suslov's role as kingmaker and his strongly conservative bent, it is quite likely that had he outlived Brezhnev, succession to the post of general secretary would have proceeded much differently, and the beginning of Soviet economic and political reform would have had to wait.

Books about Suslov

Seweryn Bialer, *Stalin's Successors: Leadership, Stability and Change in the Soviet Union* (Cambridge, Mass:. Harvard University Press, 1980);

Grey Hodnett, "Mikhail Andreevich Suslov," in *Soviet Leaders,* edited by George Simmonds (New York: Crowell, 1967);

Myron Rush, *Political Succession in the USSR* (New York: Columbia University Press, 1968).

— M. B.

SEE ALSO THESE RELATED ENTRIES

Brezhnev Doctrine, 3; Cominform, 3; Nikita S. Khrushchev, 2; Refusenicks, 3.

U Thant

United Nations Secretary-General, 1961–1971

Born Pantanaw, Burma, 22 January 1909
Died New York, New York, 25 November 1974

U Thant, Burmese educator and statesman, served as secretary-general of the United Nations from 1961 to 1971. He was recognized for practicing a subtle brand of diplomacy in his efforts to mediate international disputes.

Thant was born in Pantanaw, Burma (present-day Myanmar), into a family of public servants. After attending National High School, he enrolled in the University of Rangoon (present-day Yangon). After graduating in 1929 he began a teaching career and became headmaster of the National High School, where he became close friends with another member of the faculty, U Nu, who would become the first prime minister of independent Burma.

Thant's involvement in politics began with his participation in the government of Japanese-occupied Burma during World War II. He joined the Burmese nationalist movement after the war, and when Burma was granted its independence in 1948 he was invited by U Nu to head the Ministry of Information. A close friend and confidant of Nu, Thant was appointed to serve as aide to Nu and soon became an important figure in Burmese politics.

United Nations

Thant's career in the United Nations (UN) began in 1957 when he was appointed by Nu to serve as Burma's permanent UN representative. Burma's activities in the United Nations came to epitomize a neutralist, non-aligned foreign policy. In 1959 Thant was elected president of the UN General Assembly. After UN secretary-general Dag Hammarskjold was killed in a plane crash, Thant was elected acting secretary-general in 1961. His appointment came at a time of crisis in the United Nations, as each superpower sought to mold the organization to its own liking. The Soviet Union, for example, had been critical of Hammarskjöld because it did not be-

U Thant

lieve he was impartial. Thant had acquired a reputation of impartiality and tolerance, and in 1962 he was elected secretary-general. He sought to use the United Nations

of impartiality and tolerance, and in 1962 he was elected secretary-general. He sought to use the United Nations as a forum in which international crises could be more successfully resolved and small countries could enjoy a more effective voice in the world community.

Efforts at Mediation

One of Thant's first efforts at mediation was directed toward ending the lingering Congolese civil war, which had engendered the first UN police action in Africa. In 1961 the UN Security Council gave the United Nations greater authority to put an end to the civil war and to prevent the country's disintegration, and as a result of its stepped-up presence in the region the United Nations was criticized by various sides for interfering. Fighting broke out between UN troops and the Katanga secessionist rebels – many of whom were European mercenaries – headed by Moise-Kapenda Tshombe. In 1963 Thant devised a plan that brought an end to the civil war, negotiating an end to the secessionist movement and the expulsion of mercenary forces.

Thant led a UN mission to Cuba in 1962 in an effort to settle the Cuban Missile Crisis, which had brought the United States and the Soviet Union to the brink of nuclear war. In the end the two superpowers relied more on bilateral negotiations in resolving their dispute.

During the Indo-Pakistani war of 1965, Thant successfully mediated a cease-fire and was able to persuade both sides to permit a UN observation team to supervise it. He also became involved in multilateral attempts to prevent and, failing that, to put an end to the 1967 Arab-Israeli war. In May 1967 Thant was asked by Egyptian president Gamal Abdul Nasser to remove the UN peacekeeping forces that had been stationed in the Sinai. Thant was unable to persuade Nasser to reconsider, and, soon after the UN contingent was removed, war broke out. He was subsequently blamed by many Western countries for the war. Thant had also been involved in repeated efforts to resolve the Vietnam conflict, but his efforts were met with growing intransigence on both sides.

He was reelected in December 1966 to a second term as secretary-general and resigned in 1971. He died on 25 November 1974 in New York City.

Books by U Thant (Selected)

Toward World Peace: Addresses and Public Statements, 1957–1963, edited by Jacob Baal-Teshuva (New York: T. Yoseloff, 1964);

View from the UN (Garden City, N.Y.: Doubleday, 1978).

Book about U Thant

Ramses Nassif, *U Thant in New York, 1961–71: A Portrait of the Third UN Secretary-General* (New York: St. Martin's Press, 1988).

–J. R.-S.

SEE ALSO THESE RELATED ENTRIES

Cuban Missile Crisis, 3; Dag Hammarskjöld, 1; Gamal Abdul Nasser; 2; Moise-Kapenda Tshombe, 2.

Josip Broz Tito

President of Yugoslavia, 1953–1980

General Secretary, Yugoslav Communist Party, 1937–1980

Born Kumrovec, Croatia, 7 May 1892
Died Ljubljana, Yugoslavia, 4 May 1980

Josip Broz Tito, Yugoslav statesman, communist leader, and head of state, was born on 7 May 1892 (official birthday 25 May) in Kumrovec, Croatia. In 1913 Tito was inducted into the Austro-Hungarian army. He was wounded on the Bukovina front and was captured by the Russians there in March 1915. In 1918 Tito joined the Red Army and became a communist. In 1920 he returned home to the newly established state, the Kingdom of Serbs, Croats, and Slovenes, subsequently renamed Yugoslavia. He joined the local Communist party and in 1928 was arrested by the royalist government and sentenced to five years in prison for subversive activities. After his release Tito worked in Moscow for the Comintern (Communist International). In 1936 he traveled to Zagreb and to Paris to recruit volunteers to fight for the Republican side in the Spanish civil war.

General Secretary

In 1937, after a long climb through the party hierarchy, Tito was elected general secretary of the Yugoslav Communist party, a position he assumed on 1 January 1939. Shortly before World War II, he visited Moscow and in 1940 secretly convened the fifth Yugoslav party congress. The congress adhered to a Comintern (Moscow) directive to keep Yugoslavia out of the war between Nazi Germany and the Western democracies.

Partition of Yugoslavia

In April 1941 Germany, Italy, and Bulgaria invaded and partitioned Yugoslavia. After Germany attacked the Soviet Union in June 1941, Moscow ordered Tito to begin armed resistance against the German and Italian invaders. As commander in chief of the communist-controlled partisan units, he began military operations in Serbia and built up a guerrilla organization that numbered some 250,000 troops by 1943. As his armed strength improved, Tito grew increasingly independent of Moscow.

A rival Serbian underground resistance organization, the Chetniks, loyal to Colonel Draza Mihajlovic, fought for the restoration of the Yugoslav kingdom under the exiled Serbian dynasty that had governed the country before the war. Tito and Mihajlovic met twice in 1941 but failed to reach an agreement because Tito wanted the

Josip Broz Tito

former kingdom transformed into a federal socialist state. The Allied powers initially supported Mihajlovic but then turned to Tito because his partisan units appeared to be fighting the German forces much more effectively than were the Chetniks. By 1944, having wrested large parts of Yugoslavia from the retreating Germans, Tito traveled to Moscow, where he met Joseph Stalin for the first time; he later met Winston Churchill in Italy.

After being recognized as the only legitimate power in Yugoslavia by both the West and the Soviets, Tito began

331

organizing Yugoslavia into a federal state ruled by a totalitarian communist regime. In early 1948 a Russian attempt to replace him with a more pliable pro-Soviet leader failed. The historic split between Belgrade and Moscow followed in June of that year, when Yugoslavia was expelled from the Soviet alliance system. Tito was the first head of an East European state to defy openly the Soviet Union, refusing to participate in the Stalin-directed Cominform (Communist Information Bureau) and insisting that Yugoslavia would dominate its own political course without abandoning communism. Stalin feared that Tito's independent stance would have a profound influence on other East European leaders and would lead to serious resistance to Soviet control in the region.

The Titoist Heresy

The Titoist "heresy" encouraged Moscow to hasten the communization process in Eastern Europe after 1948 and to bind the economies of Eastern Europe more closely to the Soviet Union, while eliminating all manifestations of dissent. Stalin discounted the use of military force to bring Tito back into line, as this might have provoked an East-West confrontation, especially as no Soviet troops were stationed on Yugoslav soil. Instead, he tried to isolate Yugoslavia by instituting an economic blockade, inciting border incidents, and threatening the country with some form of military intervention by the Socialist alliance. But by this time Tito's government was firmly entrenched, and Tito was elected president in January 1953.

After Stalin's death in 1953, the Soviet attitude toward Yugoslavia became more conciliatory, as Nikita S. Khrushchev and other Kremlin leaders tried but failed to draw Yugoslavia back into the Soviet camp. In 1961 Tito was host to the first conference of twenty-five nonaligned nations, and he remained a leading member of the Non-Aligned Movement until his death. Even though some states such as Cuba adopted pro-Soviet positions, Yugoslavia itself steered clear of alliances with either the Soviet Union or the Western states.

Power Sharing in the Federal Republic

Tito devised a system of balanced power sharing among the six Yugoslav republics in order to prevent any one ethnic group's achieving a position of dominance in the federation. His government also introduced a system of "workers self-management" and market exchange to decentralize the mechanisms of economic planning and give local managers some stake in enterprise competitiveness and profitability. But in the long term the reforms did not greatly boost production, and the economy began to stagnate during the 1970s.

A few years before his death, Tito planned for a collective leadership to succeed him in the Yugoslav federation. But the political balance he devised proved inadequate to bind the republics together in the absence of a strong, charismatic president. During the late 1980s the federation began to unravel, as economic conditions deteriorated and nationalist demands were lodged by new republican leaders. During 1990 the first democratic multiparty elections in the postwar era were held in each republic as the communist monopoly of power began to disintegrate. While the northern republics of Slovenia and Croatia were seeking a looser confederal arrangement or outright separation, the Serbian government remained intent on preserving the federation and even expanding Serbian influence. Tito died on 4 May 1980 in Ljubljana, Yugoslavia.

Book by Tito

The Essential Tito (Newton Abbot, Devon: David & Charles, 1971).

Books about Tito

Phyllis Auty, *Tito: An Autobiography* (Harmondsworth, U.K.: Penguin, 1974);

Milovan Djilas, *Tito* (London: Weidenfeld & Nicholson, 1981);

Dennison Rusinow, *The Yugoslav Experiment, 1948–1974* (London: Cape, 1977);

Duncan Wilson, *Tito's Yugoslavia* (Cambridge, Mass.: Harvard University Press, 1979).

–J. B. and A. B.

SEE ALSO THESE RELATED ENTRIES
Nikita S. Khrushchev, 2; Joseph Stalin, 2.

Leon Trotsky

Russian Revolutionary
Born Yanovka, Russia, 7 November 1879
Died Mexico City, Mexico, 21 August 1940

As a political theorist and one of the principal architects of the Russian Bolshevik Revolution in 1917, Leon Trotsky considered himself a Marxist who did not stray in any significant way from "scientific Marxism." As such, Trotsky's real contribution to Russia's political evolution was not in creating an ideology that significantly differed from V. I. Lenin's but rather in providing an opposition to Joseph Stalin, who he believed had betrayed the principles behind the revolution.

Leon Trotsky was born Lev Davidovich Bronstein near Yanovka, Russia, on the southern steppes of the Ukraine. His parents, David Leontievich and Anna Bronstein, were middle-class farmers. The future revolutionary spent the first nine years of his life on the family's isolated farm, with a brief interruption at age seven to attend a private Jewish school in Gromolka.

In the spring of 1889 Lev left his rural home for the city of Odessa. Young Bronstein lived with his cousin, Moisei Spenster, and after a year's preparation attended Saint Paul's Realschule, which offered a relatively progressive education. Lev was expelled from the second grade after helping to organize a protest against an unpopular teacher. He later described this experience as his "first political test," since he picked his friends in school solely on the basis of their behavior during this episode.

Lev finished the sixth class at the realschule and then moved to Nikolayev to complete the final class. In Nikolayev, Lev was slowly drawn into revolutionary activity, which was mostly centered around a discussion group led by Franz Shvigovsky, a Czech gardener. While taking part in this group, Lev met his future wife, Alexandra Sokolovskaya, who was a Marxist. In 1897, Lev, by now a Marxist, helped to create the South Russian Workers' Union and published the journal *Nashe Dyelo* (Our Cause).

First Arrest, Exile, and Escape

In February of 1898 there were mass arrests of revolutionaries by the czarist government. After spending time in prisons in Nikolayev, Kherson, and Odessa for his political activity, Lev ended up in a Moscow transfer prison, where he and Sokolovskaya were married before being exiled to Ust-Kut. They settled in Verkholensk, where there was a large population of exiles, most of whom were populists – pre-Marxist socialists who em-

Gale International Portrait Gallery

Leon Trotsky

phasized the peasantry as the class which would best engender the revolution.

In the summer of 1902 Lev received a copy of the Marxist paper *Iskra* (The Spark) and Lenin's polemic *Shto Dyelat* (What is to be Done). After reading these works Lev and Alexandra decided that he should try to escape and continue his work for the revolution, although they already had two daughters. Traveling under the name of Leon Trotsky, he arrived in London at the doorstep of Lenin and his wife, Nadezhda Konstantinovna Krupskaya, in October 1902.

Trotsky shared a house with two of the founders of Russian Marxism, Jules Martov and Vera Zusulich, and began to write for *Iskra*. He spent time that fall in Paris, where he met Natalya Ivanovna Sedova, who would become his second wife.

333

The Second Congress of the Russian Social Democratic Worker's party – predecessor of the Russian Communist party – was held in Brussels in July 1903. The congress split into two factions over the issue of party membership. Lenin led the Bolshevik, or majority, faction, which advocated a more disciplined and more restricted party membership; Trotsky allied himself with the Mensheviks, who desired a broader-based party. He later described Lenin's stand on the issue as politically "right and necessary."

Uprising of October 1905

In early 1905, after the massacre of peaceful demonstrators on "Bloody Sunday" in Saint Petersburg, Russia entered a period of extreme political unrest. Trotsky returned to Saint Petersburg after writing an essay that articulated his theory of "permanent revolution." The theory asserted that the workers would spearhead the inevitable "bourgeois" revolution, which would in turn become a socialist revolution extending beyond Russia.

In May, Sedova was arrested, and Trotsky fled to Finland. He was back in Saint Petersburg in October, heading the newly formed Soviet of Workers' Delegates. During the next two months, Trotsky played a dominant role in organizing revolutionary activity, including massive worker strikes and the formation of an alternative form of government, the Soviet. When the members of the Soviet were finally arrested on 16 December, Trotsky had distinguished himself as the leader of the 1905 uprising – which proved to be the "dress rehearsal" for the Russian Revolution.

After detention in the Peter and Paul Fortress and a long trial, Trotsky and fifteen other defendants were exiled to Siberia for life. In early 1907, while en route to Siberia, Trotsky escaped and made his way to Finland.

Life as an Emigré

Trotsky and Sedova settled in Vienna, where they remained until the outbreak of World War I. During his stay in Vienna, Trotsky wrote for the official Viennese newspaper, for the *Kievskaya Mysl* (Kiev Thought), and began his own émigré paper, *Pravda*, in 1908. In November 1914 Trotsky moved to Paris and began working with Martov at another émigré paper, *Golos* (The Voice).

In September 1914 Trotsky attended the Zimmerwald conference in Switzerland. Trotsky, Lenin, and other socialists opposed any participation in World War I and criticized those socialists who supported the war for patriotic reasons. The Zimmerwald participants believed that the war was representative of the conflicting interests of bourgeois states, and the universal goal of a workers' revolution must outweigh any desires based on nationalistic sentiment. Within a year of the Zimmerwald conference, Trotsky was expelled from France, and he moved

to Spain. When Spain also expelled him, Trotsky and his family went to the United States, landing in New York City in January 1917.

While living in the Bronx, Trotsky learned of the February Revolution in Russia, resulting in the czar's abdication and the creation of a provincial government. On 22 March 1917 Trotsky and his family set sail on a Norwegian ship headed for Russia. He and several other Russians, however, were delayed in Canada by British police and forced to spend a month in a camp for German prisoners of war.

The 1917 Revolution

In May, Trotsky arrived in Petrograd (formerly Saint Petersburg) and worked in an advisory capacity for the Soviet. He started the newspaper *Bperyed* (Forward) and wrote for Maxim Gorky's *Novaya Zhizn* (New Life). He also made numerous public appearances. When he was arrested on 5 August 1917, Trotsky, who had avoided identifying himself with any one party, admitted that he was a Bolshevik.

After his release in September, Trotsky became the chairman of the Petrograd Soviet. With Lenin in hiding, Trotsky played the most active role of any Bolshevik leader in organizing the party in the weeks before the revolution. When the provisional government fell on 7 November, Lenin was claiming that "there is no better Bolshevik than Trotsky."

Commissar for Foreign Affairs

Trotsky was named the people's commissar for foreign affairs in the new Soviet government headed by Lenin. His first assignment was to negotiate a peace treaty with the Germans. The negotiations began in December 1917 in Brest Litovsk. In response to the Germans' harsh conditions for peace, Trotsky pursued a strategy of "no war, no peace." He refused to sign a treaty yet at the same time admitted the Russians would not fight the Germans. The Germans attacked on 3 March 1918, and the Russians were forced to sign an even more unfavorable treaty than the one Trotsky had refused.

Commissar for War

Trotsky resigned as commissar for foreign affairs but was quickly appointed commissar for war. The civil war began in May, and Trotsky was soon in a position to redeem his reputation, tarnished by his handling of the peace negotiations with Germany. During the two years of war between the Reds and the Whites, Trotsky managed to rebuild the Red Army and direct it in a successful campaign. He emerged from the civil war a hero.

The New Economic Policy

At the end of the civil war and the advent of the New Economic Policy (NEP), Trotsky found himself in an increasingly tenuous position within the Soviet government. Lenin had suffered several cerebral strokes and was no longer able to take an active role in party affairs. Stalin, whom Trotsky had always considered a "mediocrity," was quickly forming a coalition with Lev Borisovich Kamenev and Gregori Yevseyevich Zinoviev against Trotsky. In January 1924 Stalin had convinced the party to censure Trotsky and the "oppositionists."

Remarkably enough, Trotsky chose this time to leave for a vacation in the Baltics. He remained absent from the capital and did not return for Lenin's funeral at the end of January. By the time he returned in late May, the War Commission had been reorganized to favor Stalin, and two hundred thousand new party members were recruited under the "Lenin enrollment." These new recruits, mostly workers, further increased Stalin's influence over the party.

In May the Thirteenth Party Congress was held. Lenin's widow, Krupskaya, sent to the congress her husband's "last testament" — Lenin's final attempt to influence the future leadership of the party. In the document, Lenin sharply criticized Stalin for being too arbitrary in his dealings with other leaders and warned the party against giving Stalin too much power. The entire Central Committee, however, including Trotsky, voted their confidence in Stalin.

In September, Trotsky published *The Lessons of October*, in which he sharply criticized Zinoviev's and Kamenev's hesitation in the 1917 revolution. This criticism set off the "literary debate," which further undercut Trotsky's political support from among other Moscow elites.

By the beginning of 1925 Trotsky had been removed from the Executive Committee of the Comintern, the international body of communists, and had lost his post as commissar for war. Despite these political setbacks, Trotsky again went to the Black Sea for a vacation.

After Stalin's attacks on Zinoviev and Kamenev at the Fourteenth Party Congress in December 1925, Trotsky joined them in a coalition against Stalin. Trotsky did not stay in Moscow, however, but instead traveled to Berlin to have his tonsils removed. After an attempt to take their cause to the "masses" failed, Trotsky and Zinoviev admitted defeat and agreed to end their dispute with the party on 16 October 1926. Two days later, however, Trotsky insulted Stalin by referring to him as the "gravedigger of the revolution." On 23 October, Trotsky was removed from the Politburo and within a month was expelled from the party.

Exile

In January 1928 Trotsky, Sedova, and the elder of their two sons, Lyova, were deported to Alma-Ata on the Chinese frontier. After a year of curtailed political activity, Trotsky received an order from Moscow to end all such work. When he refused, the Politburo exiled him to Constantinople (now Istanbul), Turkey.

Trotsky spent the next four years in an isolated villa on one of the Kizil islands in the Sea of Marmara, writing his memoirs, entitled *My Life: An Attempt at an Autobiography*, and his magnum opus, *The History of the Russian Revolution*. He also ran the *Bulletin of the Opposition*.

In July 1933 Trotsky was allowed to reside in France, but by 1935 the French government, under pressure from the Soviet Union, expelled him. Trotsky traveled to Norway, where he wrote *The Revolution Betrayed*. Stalin's attacks against him were increasing in intensity. The "show trials" — which were part of Stalin's plan to publicly purge anyone in the party who might potentially oppose his dictatorship — began in 1936. Zinoviev, Kamenev, and fourteen other Old Bolsheviks were tried, with Trotsky charged in absentia as the head of this "treasonous" circle. Norwegian officials gave in to political pressure from Stalin and arrested Trotsky in the fall of 1936. He was eventually allowed to immigrate to Mexico, where he spent the last years of his life.

Trotsky lived in Mexico City with the painter Diego Rivera from January 1937 until May 1939, when their relationship soured. After leaving Rivera's residence, Trotsky began work on a biography of Stalin, which was released in 1946. Trotsky's work was interrupted by an assassination attempt organized by the NKVD (the precursor to the KGB), involving over twenty men armed with submachine guns and bombs. Trotsky and his wife, however, emerged unscathed. A second assassination attempt on 21 August 1940 was successful: Trotsky died from several blows of an ice ax to the skull, delivered by Ramon Mercador, a Spaniard who would spend twenty years in a Mexican prison for the murder. After his release from prison, Mercador fled to Havana, Cuba, with the help of officials from the Czechoslovakian embassy, then to Prague, and then presumably to his reward in the Soviet Union.

Despite Trotsky's adamant espousal of orthodox Marxism, the Soviet Union never rehabilitated his reputation. When Nikita S. Khrushchev began the process of "de-Stalinization" with his speech at the Twentieth Party Congress in February of 1956, Trotsky's widow appealed to the Soviet authorities for rehabilitation of her husband. She received no reply.

Books by Trotsky (Selected)

My Life (New York: Scribners, 1930);

The History of the Russian Revolution, 3 volumes (New York: Simon & Schuster, 1932);

Lessons of October (New York: Pioneer, 1937);

The Revolution Betrayed (New York: Doubleday, Doran, 1937);

Stalin (New York: Harper, published in 1941; issued in 1946).

Books about Trotsky

Robert Payne, *The Life and Death of Trotsky* (New York: McGraw-Hill, 1977);

Ronald Segal, *Leon Trotsky* (New York: Pantheon Books, 1979);

Victor Serge and Natalia Sedova Trotsky, *The Life and Death of Leon Trotsky* (New York: Basic Books, 1973);

Robert D. Warth, *Leon Trotsky* (Boston: Twayne Publishers, 1977);

Francis Wyndham and David King, *Trotsky: A Documentary.* (Baltimore: Penguin Books, 1972).

–L. E.

SEE ALSO THESE RELATED ENTRIES
Nikita S. Khrushchev, 2; Joseph Stalin, 2.

Rafael Leónidas Trujillo Molina

Dictator of the Dominican Republic, 1930–1961
Born San Cristóbal, Dominican Republic, 24 October 1891
Died Santo Domingo, Dominican Republic, 30 May 1961

Rafael Leónidas Trujillo Molina was the dictator of the Dominican Republic from 1930 until his assassination in 1961. Born in San Cristóbal into a lower-middle-class Dominican family of mulatto background, Trujillo received little formal education. Despite these handicaps in a society dominated by the white, educated, upper class, he was able to advance in the U.S.-created National Guard, and he became its brigadier general in 1927. In 1930, when a revolt toppled the presidency of U.S.-backed oligarch president Horacio Vásques, General Trujillo declared his neutrality. Shortly after, however, Trujillo stepped in to seize power himself. Although he was officially elected president in 1930, the opposition had little chance because of intimidation by Trujillo's forces.

Power and Brutality

Trujillo was a tyrannical leader who held office from 1930 to 1938 and again from 1943 to 1952. When he was not president, he positioned "puppets" as presidents and led through his position as commander of the armed forces. During his period of rule Dominicans witnessed one of the most powerful and brutal dictatorships in Latin American history. The Trujillo regime controlled almost all aspects of Dominican society. In keeping with his iron-

Rafael Leónidas Trujillo Molina

fisted policy, Trujillo maintained tight reign over the church, the economy, labor, education, family, and sex.

The Dominican Party

The Trujillo dictatorship allowed only one legal party, the Dominican party, over which Trujillo maintained absolute power. He also maintained total control over the Congress and other legislative bodies, appointing supporters to positions in both. A secret police force controlled all political activities, and freedom of the press was dissolved. Trujillo went as far as to proclaim himself the "ultimate" authority in all fields of human knowledge.

Modernization

The period of Trujillo's rule was one of accelerated modernization. As a multitude of public projects were commissioned, the nation's infrastructure was gradually built up. A strong central government bureaucracy emerged. Though these actions may have brought a sense of national pride to Dominicans, they were done primarily for Trujillo's personal gain. For example, when Trujillo nationalized the sugar industry upon which the nation's economy was dependent, it came under his personal ownership. Similarly, many of the new factories and industries that developed during this time were owned by either Trujillo or members of his family. Under the Trujillo rule the Dominican Republic enjoyed a rapid rate of development and modernization and an expanded economy.

Dissent

In the late 1950s Trujillo's domestic problems began to mount: the economy suffered from a drop in the world sugar price, provoking labor unrest; certain elements in the military, angered by barriers to advancement, began to lose their sense of loyalty; and the church became a more outspoken critic of the dictatorship. The U.S. government, sensing that Trujillo's days were numbered and worried since Fidel Castro's takeover in Cuba, plotted against Trujillo in an attempt to secure a noncommunist alternative to Trujillo's rule. Trujillo was brutally assassinated 30 May 1961 by colleagues who sought to inherit the Trujillo wealth and power. When the government took over control of Trujillo's assets after his death, the Dominican economy had the second-largest public sector in Latin America, behind Cuba.

Books about Trujillo

Robert D. Crassweller, *Trujillo: The Life and Times of a Caribbean Dictator* (New York: Macmillan, 1966);

Howard J. Wiarda, *Dictatorship and Development: The Methods of Control in Trujillo's Dominican Republic* (Gainesville: University of Florida Press, 1970).

General Reference

Howard J. Wiarda and Michael J. Kryzanek, *The Dominican Republic: Caribbean Crucible* (Boulder, Colo.: Westview, 1982).

– B. D.

SEE ALSO THESE RELATED ENTRIES
Juan Bosch Gavino, 2.

Moise-Kapenda Tshombe

Prime Minister of the Congo Republic, 1964–1965

President of Katanga, 1960–1963

Born Musumba, Belgian Congo, 10 November 1919
Died Algiers, Algeria, 29 June 1969

Moise-Kapenda Tshombe was a Congolese politician, president of the secessionist Republic of Katanga during the Congo (Zairian) civil war, and later prime minister of the Congo from 1964 to 1965.

Tshombe was born in the mineral-rich province of Katanga in the Belgian Congo into a rich business family with ties to the royal house of the Lunda ethnic group. His father, Joseph Kapend, was one of the most successful Congolese businessmen during the colonial period. Educated at American Methodist mission schools, he took over his father's businesses with limited success. With the status of *évolué* (educated and Westernized), he was a member of the Katanga Province Council and the African Chamber of Commerce from 1951 to 1953. Tshombe began his political career when he founded the Lunda Tribal Association in 1956. Two years later he became regional president of the Association of African Middle Classes (ACMAF), an association of *évolué* entrepreneurs engaged in small business and commercial farming. In 1958, during a period of ethnic tensions and economic recession, which the Katangese blamed on migrant workers from outside the province, Tshombe cofounded the Confederation of Tribal Associations of Katanga (CONAKAT). CONAKAT's political agenda essentially called for an autonomous Katanga province within a larger Congolese federation.

With the backing of the powerful Belgian Union Miniere mining company and the local European community, the moderate Tshombe became president of the CONAKAT. He later incorporated the Katanga Union, an association of white colonists who favored Katangese secession, into CONAKAT. Both the white colonists and CONAKAT were apprehensive over the newly formed Congolese National movement (MNC), which was led by the militant Patrice Lumumba, who favored a strong, unitary state.

The Round Table Conference

At the Round Table Conference, the independence talks held in Brussels, Belgium, during January and February 1960 and attended by forty-five African delegates, Tshombe unsuccessfully defended his federalist position. While the conference produced 30 June 1960 as the date

of independence, underlying political differences among the Congolese delegates regarding the nature of the postcolonial government went unresolved. In addition to the bitter dispute between the proponents of "unitarism," led by Lumumba, and "federalism," led by Tshombe and Joseph Kasavubu, leader of the Alliance of the Bakongo, an ethnically based party that supported autonomy for the Bakongo region, political unity was further hampered by the ethnic and political fragmentation that characterized the Congolese National movement on the eve of independence.

The 1960 Elections

While Tshombe's CONAKAT won the provincial elections, with him elected president of the provincial government, the 21–22 May 1960 provincial and national elections, in which over one hundred political parties participated, proved inconclusive. Tshombe withdrew from the subsequent negotiations to form a coalition, although a fragile compromise was struck with Kasavubu as president and Lumumba as prime minister. A week after independence the country descended into chaos after an army mutiny touched off widespread violence, riots, and attacks against white Europeans. On 10 July, Belgium intervened in the crisis by landing troops in Elisabethville, the Katangese provincial capital, and Luluabourg ostensibly to protect the white settlers and European property. The following day, as the country erupted into violence and ungovernability, Tshombe – who had called on the Belgian troops to restore order in Elisabethville – declared the mineral-rich Katanga province an independent country, with the tacit backing of the Belgian forces.

UN Involvement

The Congo crisis rapidly became internationalized, and the United Nations (UN) intervened at the request of the central government by sending peacekeeping troops. Negotiations between the weakened central government, which hoped to use the UN troops to quell the secession, and Katanga collapsed. UN secretary-general Dag Hammarskjöld arrived in the Congo to mediate a peaceful settlement but was unable to get the two sides to

Moise-Kapenda Tshombe

agree. (Hammerskjöld was killed in a plane crash during the Congo crisis.) Backed by Belgian troops and European mercenaries, Tshombe's rebel regime was not recognized by any country, even though it was supported by Belgium. In December 1960 Tshombe was awarded the Grand Cordon of the Order of the Crown by the Belgian king during his visit to Belgium. Tshombe was implicated in the American-sponsored assassination of Lumumba, who had been captured and imprisoned in Elisabethville, on 17 January 1961.

When fighting broke out between Tshombe's forces and UN troops, Tshombe declared that he would wage war against the UN. After the UN Security Council declared his rebel regime illegal, Tshombe threatened to resort to guerrilla warfare if UN troops attempted to put down the secession. Fighting also broke out between his forces and the national army, as well as with pro-Lumumba rebel forces. With his rebel forces defeated by the national army and UN troops, Tshombe on 14 January 1963 suddenly announced an end to Katanga's secession after a reported agreement between the central government and Union Miniere, which had financed his short-lived rebel government. Tshombe agreed to recognize the authority of President Joseph Kasavubu and Prime Minister Joseph Ileo, both of whom were federal-

ist. With the country still in political turmoil, he flew to exile in Madrid, Spain, in June 1963 and spoke of his willingness to serve the central government during his travels in Europe.

Prime Minister

In the meantime, the chaotic situation in the Congo deteriorated as most of the country became consumed with new rebellions. Tshombe, who had reached an agreement with various rebel leaders and the former Katangese mercenaries based in Angola, was invited to return to the Congo in June 1964 as prime minister to form a new transitional government. Unable to put down the rebellions consuming two-thirds of the country, with the departure of UN forces on 30 June 1964 he recruited European mercenaries to supplement the national army in an effort to restore order. His decision drew strong criticism from other African states and the Organization of African Unity (OAU). On 4 August pro-Lumumbist rebel forces, who controlled nearly half the country, captured Stanleyville and declared an independent republic. Later in the year Tshombe again traveled to Europe to enlist foreign support, primarily American, Belgian, and French military assistance, which allowed him to defeat the rebel regime. Another constitutional crisis arose after the 1965 national elections in which Tshombe's coalition won the majority. On 13 October President Kasavubu, fearful that Tshombe was preparing to oust him, dismissed Tshombe, even though the latter was supported by the parliament. In the ensuing confusion and deadlock General Joseph-Désiré Mobutu (later Mobutu Sese Seko), the army commander, seized power on 24 November 1965.

Tshombe, who was charged with treason by the military regime, fled into exile in Europe after the coup d'état. While traveling from Spain his plane was hijacked by a lone gunman and forced to land in Algeria, where Tshombe was placed under house arrest. Algerian president Houari Boumédienne, however, refused to extradite him to the Congo. Tshombe died in Algeria on 29 June 1969 of a heart attack; his wife took his body to Belgium, where it was buried.

Book by Tshombe

My Fifteen Months in Government (Plano, Texas: University of Plano Press, 1967).

Book about Tshombe

Ian Colvin, *The Rise and Fall of Moise-Kapenda Tshombe: A Biography* (London: Leslie Frewin, 1968).

General References

Madeleine Kalb, *The Congo Cables: The Cold War in Africa — From Eisenhower to Kennedy* (New York: Macmillan, 1982);

Crawford Young, *Politics in the Congo: Decolonization and Independence* (Princeton: Princeton University Press, 1965).

–J. R.-S.

SEE ALSO THESE RELATED ENTRIES

Houari Boumédienne, 2; Dag Hammarskjöld, 1; Patrice Lumumba, 2; Mobutu Sese Seko, 2.

Walter Ulbricht

Chairman, Council of State, German Democratic Republic, 1960–1973

First Secretary, Socialist Unity Party, 1953–1971

Born Leipzig, Germany, 30 June 1893
Died East Berlin, German Democratic Republic, 1 August 1973

Walter Ulbricht, East German Communist party leader and head of the German Democratic Republic (GDR), was born into a tailor's family. He was a cabinetmaker by trade and received only eight years of formal education. In 1912 Ulbricht joined the German Socialist party (SPD), and during World War I he served on the Eastern front in the German army, from which he deserted twice.

Communist Party of Germany

In December 1918 Ulbricht left the SPD to become a founding member of the Communist party of Germany (CPG). The CPG staged an unsuccessful attempt in 1919 to establish a Soviet republic in the southern German province of Bavaria. In 1923 Ulbricht was elected a member of the party's Central Committee. He also became a deputy to the Reichstag (Germany's federal lower house) in 1928. By 1929 Ulbricht headed the CPG's Berlin organization, in which he showed his strong support for Stalin and was instrumental in reorganizing the CPG and imposing a Stalinist agenda.

In October 1933, after Adolf Hitler's rise to power, the Nazi takeover of the state, and the beginning of the crackdown on the political opposition, Ulbricht fled Germany for Paris and then went to Spain. He was appointed a political commissar in the International Brigade, which fought on the side of the Republicans during the Spanish civil war from 1936 to 1939. In January 1938 he settled in Moscow with other German communist leaders. As an official of the Comintern (Communist International), Ulbricht followed Stalin's policies faithfully, endorsing the internal party purges, in which suspected Trotskyists and other "deviationists" were eliminated. He also fully supported the controversial August 1939 nonaggression pact with Hitler, which set the stage for World War II. During the war Ulbricht propagandized among German political prisoners of war and analyzed intelligence information from the German army to the Soviet Union.

Walter Ulbricht

The Soviet Zone in Germany

After the entry of the Red Army into German territory at the close of the war, the "Ulbricht group" of German communists arrived from Moscow in April 1945 to implement Soviet policy. Ulbricht helped to reestablish the CPG and was placed in charge of organizing the administration in the Soviet zone of occupation. Germany had been divided into four zones of occupation after its defeat – Soviet, American, British, and French. The Soviets were assigned the eastern part of the country, which their forces had captured. Rival political groups were suppressed and outlawed by the Soviet occupation army and by Ulbricht's security forces. Stalin was initially hesitant to establish a full communist state in the eastern sector, preferring to prepare the groundwork for a neutral and united Germany. In June 1945 the CPG was reorganized and formed a provisional East German coalition government, with three parties established under communist supervision.

The Socialist Unity Party

When Moscow realized that its role in West Germany would be limited and that the Allies intended to keep their troops on German soil, it sped up the communization of East Germany. In April 1946 the CPG and Social Democrats merged to form the Socialist Unity party (SUP) under communist dominance. Ulbricht became the party's deputy chairman at its founding congress. On 7 October 1949 the SUP's people's congress formally established the German Democratic Republic (GDR) as "a socialist state of the German nation."

Stalin's Exploitation of Eastern Europe

Using the pretext of compensation for the enormous material losses sustained by the Soviet Union during World War II, Stalin launched a massive program of reparations and exploitation of all the Eastern European economies. Entire industries and production equipment in Germany and elsewhere were dismantled and moved to the Soviet Union. Even countries such as Poland and Czechoslovakia, whose rulers had not allied themselves with Nazi Germany during the war, were subject to large-scale Russian looting. In addition to these "reparations" the Soviets established "mixed companies," in which they shared control with the local government, as a mechanism for pumping resources out of the satellite states into the Soviet economy. Trade relations were also established which benefited Moscow at the expense of the Eastern European countries.

General Secretary

From July 1950 to July 1953 Ulbricht was general secretary of the SUP, and afterward he became the first secretary. He imposed an austere Stalinist regime overseen by Red Army forces and Soviet political advisers. Most of the regime's political opponents fled to the West during mass migrations in the late 1940s and 1950s. Ulbricht collaborated with the Soviet occupation forces in crushing the workers' revolts which erupted in June 1953 in East Berlin and numerous other East German cities. The workers were protesting against planned cuts in real wages, and they also demanded major

political changes including Ulbricht's dismissal. Nearly four hundred workers were killed in the clashes, and dozens were later executed or sentenced to long prison terms under the cover of martial law.

Opposing De-Stalinization

The communist regime in the GDR put brakes on de-Stalinization during the late 1950s and only introduced limited economic reforms. As party chief, Ulbricht was at the forefront of the "anti-revisionist" campaign among SUP members and the intelligentsia that was intended to root out dissident reformers. Student unrest during 1957 was resolutely suppressed, and in September 1960 Ulbricht became chairman of the Council of State, or de facto head of state. This drive to eliminate capitalism and collectivize agriculture led to a renewed mass exodus of skilled workers, professionals, and technicians. The erection of the Berlin Wall under Ulbricht's supervision in August 1961 helped to stem the flow of refugees, but it created new tensions between the Soviet and American governments.

New Economic System

During 1963 the regime introduced modifications in central planning under the New Economic System (NES). With greater emphasis on economic profitability and personal incentives for managers, the GDR economy made respectable progress during the 1960s. But by 1968 Ulbricht became suspicious of further liberalization. He reemphasized the SUP's "leading role" and reinstated stricter central controls over the economy. Ulbricht was also a leading critic of the Prague Spring reform movement in neighboring Czechoslovakia, and GDR army units participated in crushing the reforms with other Warsaw Pact troops under Soviet direction. He was equally suspicious of the Soviet policies of détente with the United States and opposed too close a rapprochement with West Germany.

Under pressure from the Kremlin, Ulbricht was forced to resign from the leadership of the SUP on 3 May 1971. Soviet leader Leonid Brezhnev had become increasingly irritated by Ulbricht's opposition to détente and the four-power agreement on the status of Berlin, which appeared to seal and restrict communist control to the eastern part of the city. Ulbricht's credibility within the GDR Communist party leadership was also undercut by worsening economic conditions. Ulbricht was replaced by Erich Honecker in May 1971 but remained chairman of the Council of State until his death at his country home near Berlin on 1 August 1973.

Book about Ulbricht

Carola Stern, *Ulbricht: A Political Biography* (London: Pall Mall, 1965).

General References

J. F. Brown, *Eastern Europe and Communist Rule* (Durham, N.C. & London: University Press, 1988);

David Childs, *The GDR: Moscow's German Ally* (London: Allen & Unwin, 1983);

Robert L. Hutchings, *Soviet–East European Relations: Consolidation and Conflict, 1968–1980* (Madison: University of Wisconsin Press, 1983);

Christopher D. Jones, *Soviet Influence in Eastern Europe: Political Autonomy and the Warsaw Pact* (New York: Praeger, 1981);

Henry Krisch, *The German Democratic Republic: The Search for Identity* (Boulder, Colo.: Westview, 1985);

James McAdams, *East Germany and Detente: Building Authority After the Wall* (Cambridge: Cambridge University Press, 1985);

Joseph Rothschild, *Return to Diversity: A Political History of East Central Europe since World War II* (New York: Oxford University Press, 1989);

Jack M. Schick, *The Berlin Crisis, 1958–1962* (Philadelphia: University of Pennsylvania Press, 1971);

Robert Slusser, *The Berlin Crisis of 1961: Soviet-American Relations and the Struggle for Power in the Kremlin, June–November 1961* (Baltimore: Johns Hopkins University Press, 1973);

Jean Edward Smith, *Germany Behind the Wall: People, Politics, and Prosperity* (Boston: Little, Brown, 1969);

Sarah M. Terry, ed., *Soviet Policy in Eastern Europe* (New Haven: Yale University Press, 1984);

Adam Ulam, *Expansion and Coexistence* (New York: Praeger, 1968).

–J. B. and A. B.

SEE ALSO THESE RELATED ENTRIES
Leonid Brezhnev, 2; Nikita S. Khrushchev, 2.

Dmitry Fedorovich Ustinov

Soviet Minister of Defense, 1976–1984
Born Samara, Russia, 30 October 1908
Died Moscow, Soviet Union, 20 December 1984

Trained as an engineer, Dmitry Fedorovich Ustinov helped oversee the development of the Soviet arms industry and served as the Soviet minister of defense for the last eight years of his life. He was responsible for many of the military-industrial advances made in the Soviet Union during World War II and throughout the Cold War, while in addition playing a key role in the highest levels of the Soviet decision-making apparatus.

Ustinov was born in the Russian town of Samara (now Kuybyshev). In 1927 he joined the Communist party and began working as a diesel engineer in factories in the Gorki and Ivanovo oblasts. After graduating from the Military Institute of Mechanics in Leningrad in 1934, Ustinov began working as an engineer at the Naval Artillery Research Institute in Leningrad. In 1937 he moved to the Bolshevik Arms Factory, also located in Leningrad, and worked as a design engineer. He rose through the factory ranks in a quick succession of promotions, from manager of operations and testing to deputy chief designer, and in 1938 was named director of the factory, a position he kept until 1941. His rise through the military-industrial complex was meteoric; within four years he had become the director of one of the most important armaments factories in the Soviet Union. Ustinov's promotions were undoubtedly in part due to Soviet leader Joseph Stalin's mass purges of party members during the 1930s, in which many in the industrial hierarchy were removed from their posts, leaving the way clear for the advancement of younger party members.

World War II

At the beginning of Soviet involvement in World War II – which the Soviets referred to as the Great Patriotic War – in 1941, Stalin appointed Ustinov to serve as the people's commissar of armaments (the title was changed to minister of armaments in 1946), a position he held until 1953. Ustinov's initial task was to organize the transfer of Soviet war industries to sites east of the Urals, out of reach of the invading German army. This effort was crucial to the Soviet military success in World War II, and Ustinov's adept managing of the project did not go unnoticed. He also oversaw the modernization of the weapons fielded by the Red Army during the war and was named a colonel general of the Engineer Troops for his accomplishments.

Ustinov exercised control over the Soviet military-industrial complex from the end of World War II until his death in 1984. In 1946 Ustinov became a deputy of the Council of Nationalities of the Supreme Soviet and was named a full member of the Central Committee in 1952. In the following year he was appointed minister of the defense industry and kept that position until 1957, when he was named deputy chairman of the Council of Ministers, placing him in charge of the entire Soviet arms industry.

With Nikita S. Khrushchev's rise to power in the Soviet Union in 1954, Ustinov's influence over Soviet military affairs became limited, for Khrushchev did not approve of the amount of money that was being spent on defense. As Khrushchev's power ebbed in the Kremlin, however, Ustinov's political future brightened.

Serving under Brezhnev

From 1963 until 1965 Ustinov served as both chairman of the Supreme Sovnarkhoz (the council on national economy) and first deputy chairman of the Council of Ministers. Ustinov's career was furthered when Leonid I. Brezhnev came to power in 1965. Brezhnev and Ustinov had been friends since before World War II, and soon after Brezhnev's ascendance Ustinov was elected secretary of the Central Committee in charge of the military and the defense industry, as well as the security organs. He also became an alternate (nonvoting) member of the Politburo. These positions allowed Ustinov to sit on the Soviet Defense Council. During this period he continued to play a key role in the development of Soviet rocket and space technology, which soon achieved for the Soviets a strategic nuclear parity with the United States. When Soviet defense minister Rodion Malinovsky died in 1967, Ustinov seemed to be the Politburo's most likely choice to replace him, but pressure from the armed forces to have a military man as defense minister persuaded Brezhnev to appoint Andrei Antonovich Grechko instead.

Minister of Defense

With the death of Grechko in 1976, Ustinov was named minister of defense and became a full member of the Politburo. Ustinov had a good working relationship with Brezhnev and was more supportive of détente and

Dmitry Ustinov and Raúl Castro in Moscow, 1969

arms negotiations with the West than Grechko had been. Ustinov believed that it was the Soviet soldier, and not necessarily Soviet weapons, that had to be improved upon.

Brezhnev looked to Ustinov to help him appease the Soviet military – which was concerned about declining defense spending – and stave off the political challenge being mounted by KGB chairman Yuri Andropov. Ustinov, however, along with Andropov and Andrei Gromyko, had been concerned about Brezhnev's deteriorating health and was preparing for the process to choose his successor. When Andropov positioned him-

self to succeed Brezhnev, Ustinov and Gromyko threw their support behind the KGB head. Andropov was named general secretary in 1984 and kept Ustinov as his defense minister. Ustinov died shortly thereafter on 20 December 1984.

General Reference

Harry Gelman, *The Brezhnev Politburo and the Decline of Détente* (Ithaca, N.Y.: Cornell University Press, 1984).

– P. M.

SEE ALSO THESE RELATED ENTRIES

Yuri Andropov, 2; Leonid Brezhnev, 2; Andrei Antonovich Grechko, 2; Andrei Gromyko, 2; Nikita S. Khrushchev, 2; Rodion Malinovsky, 2.

Kliment Efremovich Voroshilov

Chairman of the Presidium, Soviet Union, 1953–1960
Born Verkhnii, Russia, 4 February 1881
Died Moscow, Soviet Union, 2 December 1969

A leading military and political figure in Soviet history, Kliment Efremovich Voroshilov was a member of the Politburo for over three decades, held the Soviet Union's highest military post for fifteen years, and served as the head of state following the death of Soviet leader Joseph Stalin.

Voroshilov was born 4 February 1881 into a working-class family in Verkhnii, in the Ukraine. At the age of fifteen he began working in one of the many steel mills which were being built during Russia's years of industrialization. Three years later he was fired and arrested for organizing a strike at the plant. Voroshilov later moved to Lugansk, where he joined the Russian Social Democratic Labor party and, as head of the local soviet (a workers' council), led a strike in 1905. Two years later he served as a delegate to the Fifth Party Congress of the Communist party in London.

Between 1907 and 1914 Voroshilov was arrested and sent into exile several times. Upon his last release he made his way to the Donbas region, where he continued his revolutionary work until the Russian monarchy was overthrown in 1917 in the October Revolution. After the Bolsheviks took power he was named city commissar of Petrograd and assisted in the creation of the Cheka – the Soviet secret police. In 1918 he was placed in charge of the Red Army in Lugansk, which fought its way through the German lines to reach Tsaritsyn and relieve the Red soldiers with fresh men and supplies. This military victory was called Voroshilov's Campaign, and afterward these forces formed the core of the Tenth Army, which he and Stalin commanded during the Russian civil war.

After taking an active part in crushing the Kronstadt revolt in 1921 and being made a member of the Central Committee, Voroshilov was named commissar for military and naval affairs, the top military post previously held by Mikhail V. Frunze and Leon Trotsky, in 1925. During the 1934 military reforms Voroshilov was named commissar of defense. He became a marshal of the Soviet Union in 1935.

Prior to World War II the Soviet Union began programs to rebuild its economy and military. In the early 1920s the Soviets had practically no tank industry and only minor warship, ammunition, and artillery industries. In 1929, however, the "State of Defence of the USSR" committed the country to equal the number of

Kliment Efremovich Voroshilov

soldiers likely to be fielded by the enemy and to surpass the enemy's number of tanks, aircraft, and artillery. Voroshilov played a key role in directing this buildup.

Voroshilov, however, was also a central figure in the doctrinal debates that accompanied Stalin's purges in the 1930s. He was resolutely in favor of reestablishing the cavalry battalion, a unit similar to that which he commanded in the civil war. His plan was opposed by M. N. Tukhachevskii, who advocated a military strategy that stressed tank warfare and intelligence operations. When Stalin began the purges of the military in 1937,

Voroshilov seized the opportunity to attack his opponents, proclaiming them a "traitorous, counterrevolutionary military fascist organization" in his 12 June 1937 order announcing their executions. He was one of the few high-level military officials who survived the purges.

After the Red Army's poor showing in the Finnish War (1939–1940), Voroshilov was demoted from his position as commissar of defense and appointed commander of the northwest armies which were to defend Leningrad. Despite its efforts, the Red Army was unable to prevent the Germans from encircling and laying siege to the city, and Stalin relieved Voroshilov of this command as well. Nevertheless, Voroshilov continued to serve in several important positions for the remainder of the war. He remained on the Stavka of the Supreme High Command, the body which effectively ruled the Soviet Union during the war, traveled to the Tehran Conference in 1943, and helped plan the Soviet entry into the war with Japan.

After the war Voroshilov was named director of the Allied Control Commission in Hungary and oversaw the organization of that country's new communist government from 1945 to 1947. It was becoming increasingly apparent, however, that Voroshilov was falling out of Stalin's favor, and had it not been for the dictator's death in 1953, he might have fallen victim to the next wave of purges.

Upon Stalin's death Voroshilov was named chairman of the Presidium of the Supreme Soviet, a position equivalent to that of head of state. He continued to play a significant role in the Soviet government until he took part in the attempt of the "anti-party group" to oust Nikita S. Khrushchev in 1957. Voroshilov kept his seat on the Central Committee until 1961 and was later reappointed to the body when Leonid I. Brezhnev came to power. Voroshilov died on 2 December 1969 and was awarded a full state burial.

Book about Voroshilov

Dennis Wheatley, *Red Eagle: The Story of the Russian Revolution and of Klementy Efremovitch Voroshilov, Marshal and Commissar for Defence of the Union of Socialist Soviet Republics* (London: Hutchinson, 1937).

General References

John Erickson, *The Soviet High Command: A Military-Political History, 1918–1941* (New York: St. Martin's Press, 1962);

Leonard Shapiro, *The Communist Party of the Soviet Union*, (New York, 1971);

George W. Simmonds, ed., *Soviet Leaders* (New York: Crowell, 1967).

– P. M.

SEE ALSO THESE RELATED ENTRIES

Nikita S. Krushchev, 2; Joseph Stalin, 2.

Andrei Vyshinsky

Foreign Minister, Soviet Union, 1949–1953
Born Odessa, Ukraine, Russia, 10 December 1883
Died New York, New York, 22 November 1954

Andrei Yanuarievich Vyshinsky, foreign minister of the Soviet Union from 1949 to 1953, was born to Polish parents in the Ukrainian port city of Odessa. An early supporter of the Mensheviks, the moderate faction of the Russian Social Democratic Labor Party, he switched allegiance in 1920 to the Bolsheviks, the more radical faction led by Vladimir I. Lenin. He taught criminal law at Moscow State University, simultaneously serving as a public prosecutor with the Soviet Supreme Court in the 1920s. Long considered the foremost authority on Soviet legal matters, he continued to write prolifically on Soviet law throughout his career as a statesman and diplomat.

The Great Purge

As prosecutor general of the USSR, Vyshinsky was the ranking legal functionary in Joseph Stalin's Great Purge of 1936–1938, which featured the highly publicized show trials of Stalin's enemies and potential rivals. He was infamous for his brutal and sarcastic courtroom manner, demanding the death penalty for those whom he called the "despicable rotten dregs of humanity." His best-known slogan from this time was "Shoot them like the mad dogs that they are."

Deputy Foreign Minister

Between 1940 and 1946 Vyshinsky acted as deputy foreign minister. In 1944 he led a Soviet commission of inquiry set up to demonstrate to foreign journalists that the Germans, not the Soviets, were responsible for the massacre of eight thousand Polish officers, whose bodies had been found in the Katyn forest.

He was a prominent member of the Soviet delegation to the conferences at Yalta (February 1945) and Potsdam (July 1945) where the leaders of the Soviet Union, the United States, and Great Britain met to determine their post–World War II policies regarding the defeated Axis powers.

After the war Vyshinsky represented the Soviet Union at several international conferences where his talents as an aggressive orator were prominently displayed. He spoke at the Foreign Ministers' Conference at Moscow in 1947, arguing against the prospective division of Germany. In August 1948 he was at the Danube Conference, where the Soviets made a stren-

Andrei Vyshinsky

uous effort to replace the leader of Yugoslvia, Josip Broz Tito, with the Soviet puppets.

In 1947 Vyshinsky became the Soviet representative on the Allied Control Commission for Romania. Already in late February 1945 he had delivered Stalin's ultimatum to King Michael: Either replace General Nicolae Radescu with Petra Groza as head of Romania's government or Romania would cease to exist as a sovereign state. He gave King Michael exactly two hours and five minutes to respond. As he left the room, Vyshinsky slammed the door so hard that the plaster on the wall cracked. King Michael did as he was told.

Soviet Representative to the United Nations

From 1947 to 1954 Vyshinsky was the chief Soviet representative at the United Nations (UN). Here he used the same fiery eloquence he had employed during Stalin's purge trials, but this time to attack Western policies and defend Soviet actions. He came to symbolize Soviet intransigence during the height of the Cold War. In the early 1950s he became involved with UN discussions over nuclear energy and atomic weapons.

Foreign Minister

When Stalin demoted several of his top ministers in 1949, Vyshinsky was named foreign minister in order to release Vyacheslav M. Molotov for other work.

In 1950 Vyshinsky became involved in the dispute over West German remilitarization, calling the foreign ministers of the bloc countries to Prague to protest the impending rearmament of Germany.

On 14 February 1950 Vyshinsky signed the Sino-Soviet Treaty on Friendship and Alliance on behalf of the Soviet Union, a treaty which formalized China's position as junior partner to the Soviet Union in the communist world.

After Stalin's death Vyshinsky was demoted to First Deputy Foreign Minister, a position he held until he died of a heart attack at the Soviet UN Mission on Park Avenue in New York on 22 November 1954. His ashes were placed in the Kremlin wall.

Book by Vyshinsky

The Law of the Soviet State, translated by Hugh W. Babb (New York: Macmillan, 1948).

Books about Vyshinsky

Adam Ulam, *Stalin: The Man and his Era* (New York: Vikng Press, 1973);

Arkady Vaksberg, *The Prosecutor and the Prey: Vyshinsky and the 1930s' Moscow Show Trials* (London: Weidenfeld and Nicolson, 1990).

– M. B.

SEE ALSO THESE RELATED ENTRIES
Joseph Stalin, 2; Josip Broz Tito, 2.

Lech Walesa

President of Poland, 1990–

Chairman, Solidarity Trade Union, 1980–1981, 1990

Born Popowo, Poland, 27 September 1943

Lech Walesa, Polish labor leader, chairman of the independent self-governing trade union Solidarity, and Polish president, was born to a poor worker-peasant family. His father spent the war years in a German labor camp. When Walesa was two years old his father returned to Popowo but died shortly thereafter of pneumonia and severe skull injuries inflicted on him by the Gestapo during interrogations while in captivity.

Early Trade Union Activities

The young Walesa received primary and vocational education before leaving home to find work in industry. In 1967 Walesa obtained employment as an electrician at the huge Lenin shipyards in the Baltic port of Gdansk. In the shipyards he became active in the official communist-controlled union movement and campaigned vigorously to defend workers' interests. In December 1970 he witnessed the massacre of scores of shipyard workers by Communist-party militia units. The workers were protesting price rises and intolerable economic conditions. The government saw the protests as challenging its monopoly on power and its control over the labor union movement. This traumatic experience convinced Walesa of the brutality and duplicity of the regime. It also stiffened his determination to honor his slain colleagues by campaigning for the rights of workers to decent job conditions, wages, and independent labor associations.

Walesa gained a reputation among his colleagues for determination, honesty, and obstinacy, and in the mid 1970s he was elected delegate to the shipyard's official trade union. But he was dismissed from the shipyards by a disconcerted management when he drew up and presented a long list of workers' grievances. During the late 1970s he established links with dissident intellectuals in Warsaw and Gdansk and began to campaign for the creation of independent labor unions free of government control. In 1979 he was fired from an electrical engineering plant for participating in a street demonstration in Gdansk and subsequently found it difficult to obtain any other work.

The Lenin Shipyard Strike

During the summer of 1980 mass protests erupted at the Lenin shipyards, and in numerous other Polish fac-

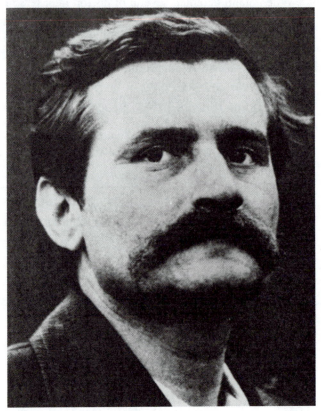

Lech Walesa

tories, over the raising of food prices and the dismissal of popular worker activists. In a dramatic move on 14 August, which changed the course of the strike and ultimately altered the history of Poland, Walesa climbed over the shipyard wall to join colleagues who were about to terminate the protest after having won some promises from management. His forthright arguments convinced the seventeen thousand workers to remain on strike until all of their economic and political demands had been met, including the creation and legalization of free trade unions.

Solidarity

Walesa was elected head of the shipyard strike committee in negotiations with the management. He then became chairman of the Inter-factory Strike Committee, which proclaimed a general work stoppage on the Baltic coast and presented twenty-one conditions to the Warsaw regime. On 31 August 1980 Walesa and Deputy Prime Minister Mieczyslaw Jagielski signed the historic Gdansk Agreement which recognized workers' rights to organize freely and elect representatives to their own labor unions. The Strike Committee was then transformed into Solidarity (Solidarnosc), the first independent labor union in the communist bloc; Walesa was elected chairman. The regime of Edward Gierek acceded to workers' demands once it had discounted the use of massive force to crush the revolt. After the signing of the Gdansk accords, Gierek was replaced, and the new government began to formulate plans to eliminate the Solidarity movement.

Martial Law

During the sixteen months of Solidarity's legal existence, pressures began to mount in Polish society for the dismantling of Communist-party controls over all spheres of public life. Walesa remained at the center of all high-level negotiations with the government, while trying to pacify growing public anger at Warsaw's prevarications and unwillingness to implement major political reforms. Unbeknownst to Solidarity, the party leadership, in collusion with Moscow, was secretly preparing to reverse the rising tide of democratization. In December 1981 General Wojciech Jaruzelski, the first secretary of the Communist party and commander of the armed forces, imposed martial law, arrested thousands of trade union leaders, and violently broke up occupational strikes and street demonstrations around the country. Walesa was arrested and held in solitary confinement for eleven months, but his spirit was not broken, and he refused to collaborate with the ruling Military Council for National Salvation.

Although Solidarity was outlawed and its organizational structure fractured, many of its activists continued in secret. Members built a wide clandestine underground network of opposition to the party/army dictatorship, including a new leadership, the Interim Coordinating Commission, which maintained close contact with Walesa. Martial law was eventually lifted in 1983, but the system of police controls and administrative prohibitions on free expression and free association were kept in place. The regime tried unsuccessfully to discredit Walesa in the eyes of the nation, as well as in international public opinion. But he remained a symbol of opposition and a highly respected international human-rights figure, and was awarded the Nobel Peace Prize in 1983.

The Unrest of 1988

The authorities continued to harass Walesa after he regained work at the Lenin shipyards, but they could not diminish his prestige, authority, and charismatic appeal among the workers. When industrial unrest broke out again during the summer of 1988, Walesa joined his workmates to demand the restoration of Solidarity and dialogue with the regime to introduce essential political and economic reforms. Facing mass turmoil, economic disruption, and the potential for violent revolution, government officials entered into negotiations with Walesa and other Solidarity leaders to try to devise a new power-sharing arrangement.

In June 1989 partially democratic national elections were held, and all candidates who stood with Walesa in the newly established Solidarity Citizens Committee were elected to the Sjem (parliament). After protracted discussions and reassurances to Moscow that Poland would not unilaterally leave the Warsaw Pact or purge the communists from the security forces, a Solidarity-led coalition government was formed in August 1989. Walesa declined any official state position but nominated the lay Catholic activist Tadeusz Mazowiecki as the first noncommunist prime minister since the war. Walesa was reelected chairman of the restored free trade-union movement at Solidarity's second national congress in April 1990.

During 1990 a growing rift became evident between the government of premier Mazowiecki and Walesa's Solidarity leadership. Their disputes revolved around the questions of accelerating political reforms and stimulating economic recovery. The Walesa group argued for early, fully democratic parliamentary and presidential elections, the ousting of the remaining communists from all public institutions, the promotion of political pluralism through appropriate legislation and funding, and adjustments in the economic-reform program to create new jobs for the growing unemployed population. Walesa's critics contended that the Solidarity leader had dictatorial tendencies because he had dismissed several former advisers from key positions in Solidarity's political arm, the Solidarity Citizens Committee, and sought to become a strong president. But both sides agreed that Walesa was one of the few public figures benefiting from widescale support and trust among the work force.

Election as President

As a result of pressure from the Walesa faction, early presidential elections were held in November and December 1990 once General Jaruzelski agreed to step down from the presidency. Walesa won the ballot after the second round, despite a surprise result in the first round when an unknown Polish expatriate, Stanislaw Tyminski, had beaten Mazowiecki to second place. In

December 1990 Walesa was inaugurated as the first non-communist president in postwar Polish history.

Books by Walesa
A Way of Hope (New York: Holt, 1987);

The Struggle and the Triumph (New York: Arcade, 1992).

Book about Walesa
Mary Craig, *Lech Walesa and His Poland* (New York: Continuum, 1986).

General References
Timothy Garton-Ash, *The Polish Revolution: Solidarity 1980–82* (London: Cape, 1983);

Jan B. de Weydenthal, Bruce D. Porter, and Kevin Devlin, *The Polish Drama, 1980–1982* (Lexington, Mass.: Lexington Books, 1983).

–J. B. and A. B.

SEE ALSO THESE RELATED ENTRIES

Wojciech Jaruzelski, 2; Tadeusz Mazowiecki, 2; Adam Michnik, 2.

Stefan, Cardinal Wyszynski

Primate of Poland, 1949–1981
Born Zuzela, Poland, 3 August 1901
Died Warsaw, Poland, 28 May 1981

Stefan, Cardinal Wyszynski, archbishop of Gniezno and Warsaw and primate of Poland, studied in Warsaw, Lomza, and Wloclawek and was ordained a priest at the age of twenty-three in August 1924. Wyszynski was then assigned to the basilica at Wloclawek. He also earned a doctorate in sociology and ecclesiastical law at the Catholic University of Lublin and continued his studies in France, Italy, and Belgium.

When he returned to Poland, Wyszynski founded the Christian Workers University in 1935 and was its director until the start of World War II. Soon after Nazi and Soviet forces invaded Poland in September 1939, he was ordered by the church authorities to leave Wloclawek. Wyszynski was fortunate to elude imprisonment in German concentration camps, where over one thousand Polish priests were murdered by the Nazis during the war.

Primate of Poland
In March 1945, after Poland had been liberated by Soviet forces, Wyszynski returned to Wloclawek to serve as rector of the local seminary. In 1946 he was appointed bishop of Lublin, and on 12 November 1948 Pope Pius XII named him the archbishop of Gniezno and Warsaw and primate of Poland. Although Wyszynski subsequently signed a coexistence agreement with the communist regime, he refused to legitimize the Stalinist persecution of the political opposition and made every effort to preserve the independence of the church from state interference. During the imposition of communist rule in Eastern Europe, the Stalinist regimes sought either to ban all organ-

Eric Lessing/Magnum

Stefan, Cardinal Wyszynski

ized religious activity or to harness all church institutions for the service of the state. The region's Orthodox churches proved more amenable to government control than the Roman Catholic church, which was also highly suspect in the eyes of the communists because of its allegiance to a foreign authority, the Vatican. In Poland in particular, because of the church's strong links with Polish nationalism and its traditional resistance to foreign rule, the post-Stalinist regime needed to reach a modus vivendi with Cardinal Wyszynski in order to gain some measure of public credibility.

Church-State Relations

In 1953 government spokesmen accused the primate of having violated a pledge that the church would punish priests who engaged in antistate activities. He was placed under strict house arrest and only released in October 1956, shortly after the reform communist Wladyslaw Gomulka assumed power. He reached an agreement with Gomulka that allowed religious instruction in state schools, provided that the communist authorities could approve appointments to higher church offices. This compromise, along with others, helped to assuage Soviet fears of Polish "counterrevolution" and contributed to preventing the kind of violent Russian intervention that was then taking place in Hungary.

Wyszynski and Church Autonomy

Throughout Gomulka's rule Wyszynski followed a consistent policy of church autonomy and skillfully countered official attempts to divide, corrupt, and enlist religious leaders in support of government policies. Despite state hindrance Wyszynski organized in 1966 a nationwide religious celebration on the one thousandth anniversary of Christianity in Poland. He also gave his backing to intellectual dissent against state atheism and official censorship. During the government's anti-Semitic campaign against intellectual and student protesters in March 1968, the church spoke out in support of academic freedom and the basic rights of all citizens.

The Gierek Regime

Wyszynski maintained an uneasy accord with the regime of Edward Gierek during the 1970s. In addition to protecting the interests of the Catholic church, he gave verbal and practical support to Polish human-rights movements such as the Workers Defense Committee (KOR), which appeared in the late 1970s to provide assistance to Polish workers persecuted by the regime. He was instrumental in the selection of Karol Wojtyla, the former bishop of Krakow, as Pope John Paul II in October 1978 and in the subsequent papal visit to Poland in June 1979. These events proved to be important ingredients in the creation of the Solidarity free trade-union movement in August 1980.

The Creation of Solidarity

The pope's pilgrimage and sermons helped to stir a national revival and contributed to overcoming public fear and the process of social atomization imposed by the communists. Church leaders under Wyszynski's guidance were closely involved as mediators in negotiations between government officials and striking workers which led to the creation of Solidarity in the summer of 1980. They also played a key role in the formation of the rural Solidarity organization to protect the interests of Poland's farmers.

Cardinal Wyszynski died in Warsaw on 28 May 1981. Enormous crowds gathered for his funeral a few days later in an impressive display of mass mourning. Wyszynski's successor, Józef, Cardinal Glemp, continued to play a key role in protracted negotiations between Solidarity leaders and government officials.

Book about Wyszynski

Andrzej Micewski, *Cardinal Wyszynski: A Biography* (New York: Harcourt Brace Jovanovich, 1984).

General Reference

Hanasjakob Stehle, *The Eastern Policies of the Vatican, 1917–1979* (Athens: Ohio University Press, 1981).

–J. B. and A. B.

SEE ALSO THESE RELATED ENTRIES
Edward Gierek, 2; Wojciech Jaruzelski, 2; Pope John Paul II, 2; Lech Walesa, 2.

Zhao Ziyang

General Secretary, Chinese Communist Party, 1987–1989

Born Hebei Province, China, 17 October 1919

Zhao Ziyang was the liberal economic planner behind China's reform movement in the 1980s. Often overshadowed by Deng Xiaoping, the magnetic helmsman, and General Secretary Hu Yaobang, the charismatic promoter, Premier Zhao was the affable strategist in the leadership triumvirate. Prior to being brought to Beijing by Deng in 1980, Zhao was known for his innovative management of the economies of Sichuan and Guangdong provinces. Although relatively inexperienced in foreign affairs, Zhao worked diligently to open China's economy to the West. After Hu Yaobang resigned as general secretary in January 1987, Zhao succeeded him as Deng's heir. But during the mass demonstrations in Beijing's Tiananmen Square in May–June 1989, conservative leaders forced Zhao's removal because of his support for the student demonstrators.

Zhao Ziyang was born Zhao Xiuye in Hebei province. His father was a landlord in a quiet village, and Zhao's early years were spent comfortably removed from the suffering of most rural Chinese. Still, Zhao became interested in communism while a student. He was admitted to the Communist Youth League – the preparatory body of the Chinese Communist party (CCP) – in 1932 and became a party member in 1938. During the war against Japan (1937–1945), his work in the party varied from distributing propaganda to assisting in agriculture. Zhao was adept at administering land reform in the Hebei-Shandong-Henan border region.

During the Chinese civil war (1946–1949), Zhao again worked on propaganda and organization in central China, impressing his superiors with his enthusiasm. In April 1951 he was transferred south to Guangdong province as part of a group of cadres sent to enforce strict land-reform measures, which often required the execution of landlords prior to property confiscation. Zhao stayed in Guangdong after the land reform, becoming a political generalist. He was capable of engaging in varied tasks including agricultural policy analysis and military organization.

In the early 1960s Zhao advocated the pragmatic economic policies that President Liu Shaoqi and General Secretary Deng Xiaoping preached. Zhao, who became Guangdong's second-highest leader in 1961 when he was made the province's party secretary, emphasized material incentives in agriculture to increase production. Zhao was a prodigy of the CCP. In April 1965 he was pro-

Zhao Ziyang

moted to first secretary – the highest position in the province – at the age of forty-six, making him the youngest first secretary in the country.

The Cultural Revolution

Zhao's quick ascension in the party ranks ended soon after the Cultural Revolution began in 1966. The Cultural Revolution (1966–1976) was Mao Zedong's response to what he saw as an increasingly bureaucratic and nonideological CCP. Mao and his ardent followers in the party sent radical youth, called Red Guards, to purge the CCP of its "capitalist"-minded members. Zhao was arrested on 21 January 1967 by the Red Guards and one month later was paraded through the streets of Guangzhou (Guangdong) wearing a dunce cap and placard around his neck listing his "bourgeois crimes." On 16 October 1967, in Guangzhou, Zhao faced a mob numbering eighty thousand in the Cultural Revolution's bizarre spectacle of degradation called the mass criticism. He did not resurface in the party until April 1971, when he was made party secretary of Inner Mongolia, in charge of agriculture and pasturage.

Zhao returned to Guangdong province in March 1972 and remained there until the fall of 1975. He was renamed first secretary of the province in April 1974. As Guangdong's leader, Zhao stimulated the economy with his agriculture expertise and furthered his influence in foreign affairs and military issues, thus improving his political credentials. Zhao showed a flair for receiving foreign dignitaries. In 1974 he met British prime minister Edward Heath and Danish prime minister Vance Hartling, among others. He also began forming alliances with the People's Liberation Army (PLA) after he was named political commissar, or formal leader, of the Guangdong military district.

Premier Zhou Enlai and Vice-premier Deng Xiaoping thought so highly of Zhao that they plucked him from Guangdong and inserted him as the first secretary of Sichuan province. His objective was to invigorate a moribund economy. Zhao's agrarian reforms brought national attention to the province. Peasants worked on private plots, received pay "according to their work," and began limited sideline productions. The reforms were a forerunner to the national program Zhao later implemented. By the time Zhao was called to Beijing in February 1980, he already was a nationally recognized figure. He gave addresses throughout China and was included in delegations sent to Western Europe.

Pragmatic Policy

Zhao was named the premier of the People's Republic of China (PRC) in September 1980, replacing a foundering Hua Guofeng. Zhao was brought to the capital as a reformer, a man on whom Deng Xiaoping could place the burden of modernizing China. Zhao was different than other Chinese leaders. At the age of sixty he was a young man compared to many of the Chinese leaders who were in their seventies and eighties. He was not a rigid ideologist, but rather a flexible pragmatist. Zhao was also an outsider to the high-level party apparatus, which made him Deng's ideal choice to institute an era of reform.

His objective was to stimulate the Chinese economy through domestic reform and attract foreign business and technology. He was willing to conduct business with virtually all nations that could help China economically. A relationship with the West was crucial to China's economic reform, for the industrialized nations possessed the technology, know-how, capital, and markets required by China in order to stimulate its economy. In cultivating a relationship with the West – a diplomatic process that

came to be known as China's open-door policy – radical changes were made in the PRC's economic sector to facilitate commercial relations with the outside world. China opened fourteen coastal cities as special areas for foreign companies to conduct business. Foreign companies were given tax breaks and free rein to operate. Zhao also favored incentive programs for farmers, giving them freedom to grow cash crops.

By 1984 Zhao and General Secretary Hu Yaobang were in control of the country's day-to-day operations, including foreign policy. Final decisions were still made by party leader Deng Xiaoping, but Zhao and Hu operated with great latitude.

Beginning in 1984, Zhao made regular trips abroad, leading delegations to the Western industrialized countries. In a well-publicized trip, he visited the United States and Canada in January 1984. Zhao also made several visits to Western Europe between 1984 and 1986.

The economic reform had mixed results. Overall development did take place in agriculture and industry, and salaries increased. But these gains were offset in the late 1980s by economic stagnation, as well as high inflation – the result of failed price reform.

General Secretary

Zhao's career reached its pinnacle in January 1987 when he replaced Hu Yaobang as general secretary. Hu had lost his position for siding with students who were holding prodemocracy demonstrations in December 1986. Zhao now appeared to be in line as Deng's successor, although party conservatives were still skeptical of his reform measures. For the next two years Zhao did not improve his party status. His reforms were increasingly checked by the conservatives, who had a resurgence of power in the CCP after Hu's removal. The public was also growing disenchanted with Zhao because of nationwide inflation problems.

Tiananmen Square

Zhao Ziyang's career took a nosedive in the spring of 1989. Hu Yaobang died in April, and an outpouring of grief for the late reformer in Beijing's Tiananmen Square turned into a large prodemocracy demonstration held by students. Zhao openly endorsed what he called the students' "rational demands," implicitly suggesting that criticism and dissent were normal political phenomena.

Three thousand students began a hunger strike in early May which galvanized public support of the protest. The strike coincided with the historic first meeting between Soviet president Mikhail

Gorbachev and Deng Xiaoping. The talks were intended to be the highlight of Deng's career. Instead, Western television journalists, who were in Beijing for the summit, focused on the suffering students, many of whom had to be rushed to the hospital on stretchers.

On 17–18 May more than one million Chinese jammed Tiananmen Square, showing their sympathy for the students and mounting their own protests against government corruption and inflation. The CCP, however, refused to make concessions to the students. Finally, in the early morning hours of 19 May, Zhao Ziyang visited the hunger strikers. He was overcome by emotion. Zhao addressed the protesters, saying, "I came too late, too late. We deserve your criticism, but we are not here to ask for your forgiveness." Zhao's poignant appeal to stop the strike was broadcast on Chinese television. It was the last time he was seen in public until September 1990.

The CCP decided to use the hard-line approach to resolve the problem. On 3–4 June, after repeated warnings to the protesters to leave the square, soldiers charged in. Hundreds and perhaps thousands of Chinese died in the ensuing melee. Controversy remains over the number of fatalities because the CCP ordered a massive cleanup effort following the "massacre," which included removing corpses.

Zhao was formally dismissed as general secretary on 24 June 1990. He lost all of his positions in the party and was severely criticized by the elders in the CCP leadership, including President Yang Shungkun, former President Li Xiannian, and Deng. Zhao was placed under house arrest after the incident, and little was known of his whereabouts until September 1990, when he was seen golfing north of Beijing, accompanied by his wife and over twenty security officials.

Zhao's removal marked China's greatest political crisis in decades. The liberal reformers in the CCP, led by Zhao, who favored continuing economic reforms, relaxing ideological strictures and party controls over intellectual life, and allowing a degree of political pluralism, were the losers in the political upheaval which followed Tiananmen Square. What remains after 4 June 1989 is an isolated China led by a deeply divided CCP. The country has been slow to improve relations with foreign countries, especially with the West. Internally, China appears ambivalent about its economic direction, although elements of Zhao's liberal policies still remain.

Books about Zhao

David Shambaugh, *The Making of a Premier: Zhao Ziyang's Provincial Career* (Boulder, Colo.: Westview, 1984);

Zhao Wei, *The Biography of Zhao Ziyang* (Hong Kong: Education and Cultural Press, 1989).

General Reference

A. Doak Barnett, *The Making of Foreign Policy in China* (London: Tauris, 1985).

– K. W.M.

SEE ALSO THESE RELATED ENTRIES

Deng Xiaoping, 2; Hu Yaobang, 2; Liu Shaoqui, 2; Zhou Enlai, 2.

Andrei A. Zhdanov

Soviet Leader, 1939–1948
Born Tver, Russia, 26 February 1896
Died Moscow, Soviet Union, 31 August 1948

Like Lenin, Andrei A. Zhdanov was the son of a public school inspector. Zhdanov attended the local gymnasium, studied French and German, and became involved in the revolutionary movement in 1912. Zhdanov's rise to political prominence began after he joined the Bolshevik party in 1915. During World War I he carried out propaganda among Russian troops, spreading Lenin's appeal to fraternize with the enemy in the interest of transforming the "imperialist" war of nations into a class war. After World War I Zhdanov worked his way up through party ranks to the position of Central Committee secretary in 1930, becoming a member of the Soviet ruling class.

In 1934 he became secretary of the party machine in Leningrad (the second most important city in the Soviet Union). His predecessor, Sergei Kirov, had been assassinated at Stalin's orders in an incident that became a pretext for the Great Terror. Culminating in a series of three show trials from 1936 to 1938, the Great Terror marked Soviet leader Joseph Stalin's complete liquidation of political opposition. Using the NKVD, the Soviet secret police, Stalin systematically arrested, imprisoned, or executed virtually anyone who questioned his rule. Although the Communist party of the Soviet Union bore the brunt of the terror, no one in the Soviet Union was completely immune from the climate of paranoid distrust and ultraorthodox ideological dogmatism. Criticism of Stalin, his policies, or his interpretation of Marxism-Leninism was once considered tantamount to treason.

In 1939 Zhdanov became a member of the Politburo, the highest party organ. During World War II Zhdanov ledthe defense of Leningrad during the twenty-nine-month siege by Nazi forces. After the war Zhdanov became Stalin's righthand man. The extent of his influence has been debated. By the time of his death in 1948, Zhdanov's only serious rival to succeed Stalin appears to have been Georgi Malenkov, whose power base was in the government.

Repression of Cultural Life

Through Zhdanov, Stalin carried out a massive crackdown on independent cultural life in the Soviet Union after World War II. In the name of socialist realism, the official Soviet art style, Russian artists were severely censored. Socialist-realist art was designed to help propagate

Andrei A. Zhdanov

Marxist-Leninist ideology. By celebrating the supposed joyfulness of labor under communism, socialist realism aimed to create new Soviet men and women, free from traits such as selfishness and greed associated with capitalism.

Two of Russia's greatest poets – Boris Pasternak and Anna Akhmatova – were silenced. Unorthodox culture was attributed to the corrupting influence of the "decadent bourgeois" West.

Zhdanov was put in charge of Soviet ideology after the war, and therefore led the cultural purge. With Stalin's support he generally pushed for a reassertion of Marxist-Leninist values over more scientific and pragmatic values, as represented by Malenkov, the leader of the government. Policy differences between Zhdanov and Malenkov were related to their struggle to become heir apparent to Stalin.

Cominform

Zhdanov also played a key role in the Cominform (Communist Information Bureau), which was founded at a secret meeting in Szklarska Poreba, Poland, in September 1947. Its predecessor, the Comintern (Communist International), had been disbanded in 1943 when international revolutionary activity was being downplayed in the interest of alliance with the West against Hitler. Zhdanov signed the order abolishing the Comintern. However, a "ghost Comintern," performing many of the same functions of the old one, existed during the war. Both the Comintern and the Cominform served primarily as tools of Soviet policy.

Zhdanov appears to have been fully in control of the proceedings at the opening session of the Cominform. He delivered the major address on international affairs, whereas Malenkov was given the humiliating task of speaking on Soviet domestic affairs.

In his speech Zhdanov denounced the U.S. Marshall Plan for promoting the recovery of war-devastated Europe. Portraying the plan as a strategy for rolling back Soviet influence in Europe, Zhdanov called on Western European Communist parties to interfere actively with its implementation. He also led an attack on the French and Italian Communist parties for their policies of participating in the parliamentary systems of their countries. Zhdanov held up Yugoslavia as a model for foreign communists to follow (though the Soviets and Yugoslavs were soon to split, at this time Stalin and Yugoslav leader Josip Broz Tito were still allies, and the headquarters of the Cominform was in Belgrade, Yugoslavia). Zhdanov urged thorough communization of Eastern Europe and emphasized the value of fifth columns in the West, that is, groups of secret sympathizers of communism who were engaged in subversive activity within their nations.

The 2-Camp Theory

It was also in this speech that Zhdanov promulgated his notorious "2-Camp" theory of international relations, according to which the world was split into two irreconcilable forces — communists and capitalists. The capitalist half was especially ripe for revolution, according to Zhdanov, because of division within its ranks between the Western European colonial powers and the United States. Largely as a result of this speech, Zhdanov gained a reputation for unconditional hostility to the West and commitment to militant promotion of global revolution.

In response to Zhdanov's admonitions, the French and Italian communists launched strikes and demonstrations in their countries. But, though highly disruptive, the Cominform was unable to prevent implementation of the Marshall Plan.

Zhdanov's last public appearance was at the June 1948 Cominform meeting, during which the Yugoslavs were officially expelled as a result of Stalin's disapproval of Tito's increasingly independent foreign policy. Yugoslavia's expulsion represented a major political defeat for Zhdanov.

The immediate beneficiary of Zhdanov's death in 1948 was Malenkov, who thus became Stalin's heir apparent (only, however, to lose out to Khrushchev in the end). Though the West may have breathed a collective sigh of relief when Zhdanov died, the influence of his "2-Camp" theory of international relations survived him, especially in the person of Mikhail A. Suslov, who inherited responsibility for ideology until his death in 1982.

Some recent scholarship has suggested that the traditional Western view of Zhdanov as a revolutionary extremist is incorrect. Citing Zhdanov's toleration and encouragement of creativity in fields other than the arts — particularly philosophy and natural science — Werner G. Hahn contends that Zhdanov's ascension to the top post would not have been the unmitigated disaster for the West that was expected. Though hardly a liberal, Hahn argues, Zhdanov held views that were considerably less extreme than those that became official after his death.

General References

David J. Dallin, *Soviet Foreign Policy after Stalin* (Philadelphia: Lippincott, 1961);

Timothy Dunmore, *Soviet Politics, 1945–53* (New York: St. Martin's Press, 1984);

Aleksandr Fadeev, *Leningrad in the Days of the Blockade* (Westport, Conn.: Greenwood Press, 1971);

Werner G. Hahn, *Postwar Soviet Foreign Policy: The Fall of Zhdanov and the Defeat of Moderation* (Ithaca, N.Y.: Cornell University Press, 1982);

Susan J. Linz, ed., *The Impact of World War Two on the Soviet Union* (Totowa, N.J.: Rowman & Allenhead, 1985);

Charles S. Maier, *The Origins of the Cold War and Contemporary Europe* (New York: New Viewpoints, 1978);

Gavriel D. Ra'anan, *International Policy Formation in the USSR: Factional "Debates" During the Zhdanovshchina* (Hamden, Conn.: Archer Books, 1983);

Marshall Shulman, *Soviet Foreign Policy Reappraised* (New York: McGraw-Hill, 1953);

Jack Snyder, "The Gorbachev Revolution: A Waning of Soviet Expansionism?," *International Security*, 3 (Winter 1987/88): 93-132.

—J. W.

SEE ALSO THESE RELATED ENTRIES

Nikita S. Khrushchev, 2; Georgi Malenkov, 2; Joseph Stalin, 2.

Todor Zhivkov

General Secretary, Bulgarian Communist Party, 1981–1989

First Secretary, Bulgarian Communist Party, 1954–1981

Born Pravec, Bulgaria, 7 September 1911

Todor Christov Zhivkov, Bulgarian communist leader and head of state, was born into a poor peasant family. In the late 1920s he moved to Sofia, Bulgaria's capital, where he joined the Youth League of the outlawed Bulgarian Communist party (BCP). In 1937 he became head of the party committee in the Sofia district of Kovyovitsa. During World War II Zhivkov helped to organize a communist resistance movement, known as the People's Liberation Insurgent Army, against the pro-Nazi Bulgarian government.

After the war Zhivkov took command of the People's Militia, which was at the forefront of the Stalinist campaign of repression against the political opposition in Bulgaria. In 1951, in recognition of his services and loyalty to Joseph Stalin, Zhivkov became a full member of the BCP Politburo. After the ouster of Vulko Chervenkov from the BCP leadership, Zhivkov became the youngest Soviet-bloc party leader when he was appointed first secretary of the BCP Central Committee in March 1954. He was a protégé of Soviet leader Nikita S. Khrushchev and came out on top in the internal power struggles in the Communist party in the wake of Stalin's death. Zhivkov also served as premier of Bulgaria from 1962 to 1971.

Gale International Portrait Gallery

Todor Zhivkov

Fall of Khrushchev

The sudden fall of Khrushchev in 1964 removed Zhivkov's most important Soviet patron. Although he maintained himself in power, between 1965 and 1971 the Bulgarian leader had to put down six different coup attempts by military officers and dissident party members. Zhivkov subsequently conducted widespread purges in the security forces and the party apparatus and strengthened his position within the BCP. In 1971 he was also elected president of the State Council, or head of state, a position created by Bulgaria's new constitution.

Economic Reforms

During Zhivkov's long tenure, some agricultural decentralization and other economic reforms (the New Economic Mechanism) were introduced

in the late 1970s, although much more cautiously than the Hungarian economic reforms implemented at the same time. Despite the reforms Bulgaria's economy began to stagnate seriously during the 1980s. In the political arena the ruling party maintained tight control and repressed any manifestations of dissent or organized opposition. Zhivkov's daughter, Lyudmila, played a dominant role in shaping the regime's cultural policies until her death in 1981. She implemented some cultural liberalization during the 1970s, which was reversed in the 1980s by a more conservative-minded government leadership. The regime remained extremely hesitant about imitating Mikhail Gorbachev's glasnost reforms in the Soviet Union.

In the mid 1980s the Zhivkov administration also launched a major campaign of repression against the country's one million citizens of Turkish ancestry. Muslim Turks were forced to Slavicize their names and desist from practicing their faith or using the Turkish language in public. Several dozen Turks who resisted the assimilation campaign were reportedly killed by the security police, while tens of thousands fled the country and sought refuge in Turkey. By launching its drive against the Muslim minority, the Zhivkov regime tried to benefit from Bulgarian nationalism and anti-Turkish sympathies among some sectors of the population in order to preserve its grip on power.

Upheaval and Reform

In November 1989 Zhivkov was forced to resign as party and state leader and expelled from the party as reformist forces within the BCP tried to prevent a repetition of the upheaval in other East European states. The Zhivkov leadership was scapegoated for the years of repression and stagnation, and Zhivkov himself was placed under investigative arrest by the new reform communist government.

Bulgaria held free multiparty elections in June 1990, once political parties were officially allowed to function and the party's "leading role" in the state was formally ended. The BCP dissolved itself and formed the Bulgarian Socialist party (BSP), which managed to win the ballot and regain its hold over the government. But during 1990 economic conditions began to deteriorate seriously, and the government was forced to resign in November 1990, facing growing industrial unrest and political opposition from the increasingly well-organized Bulgarian Democratic Forces. In early 1991 it was announced that Zhivkov would soon stand trial for various abuses committed during his long period in power.

The trial eventually took place, and Zhivkov was sentenced in September 1992 to seven years in prison on charges of embezzlement of state property. He was the first Soviet-bloc leader to be convicted in a court of law.

Book by Zhivkov
Problems of the Construction of an Advanced Socialist Society in Bulgaria (Sofia: Sofia Press, 1969).

Book about Zhivkov
Robert Maxwell, ed., *Todor Zhivkov: Statesman and Builder of New Bulgaria* (London: Pergamon, 1982).

General References
John D. Bell, *The Bulgarian Communist Party from Blagoe to Zhivkov* (Stanford, Cal.: Hoover Institution Press, 1986);

J. F. Brown, *Eastern Europe and Communist Rule* (Durham, N.C. & London: Duke University Press, 1988);

Robert L. Hutchings, *Soviet–East European Relations: Consolidation and Conflict, 1968–1980* (Madison: University of Wisconsin Press, 1983);

Robert J. McIntyre, *Bulgaria: Politics, Economics and Society* (London: Pinter Publishers, 1988);

Joseph Rothschild, *Return to Diversity: A Political History of East Central Europe since World War II* (New York: Oxford University Press, 1989);

Sarah M. Terry, ed., *Soviet Policy in Eastern Europe* (New Haven: Yale University Press, 1984);

Adam Ulam, *Expansion and Coexistence* (New York: Praeger, 1968);

Ivan Volgyes, *The Political Reliability of the Warsaw Pact Armies: The Southern Tier* (Durham, N.C.: Duke University Press, 1982).

–J. B. and A. B.

SEE ALSO THESE RELATED ENTRIES

Georgi Dimitrov, 2; Nikita S. Khrushchev, 2.

Zhou Enlai

Premier of the People's Republic of China
Born Huainan, China, 5 March 1898
Died Beijing, People's Republic of China, 8 January 1976

Zhou Enlai, the premier of the People's Republic of China (PRC), was one of the giants of diplomacy in the twentieth century. One of Chinese Communist party's (CCP) leaders from its early years, Zhou had a distinguished career that covered every foreign-policy success of China's from 1949 to 1976. His negotiating skills were described as masterly and evoked glowing admiration from those who met him at the bargaining table. Away from the diplomatic arena, Zhou was known to be a charming conversationalist with a razor-sharp wit. But he also could be volatile, and never hesitated to denounce an opponent or fellow party member when debating.

Zhou built the PRC foreign ministry virtually by himself. After 1949 he brought to Chinese diplomacy an air of professionalism, which impressed Westerners who had thought of the communists as unsophisticated radicals. In helping to shape and implement China's foreign policy, Zhou combined pragmatism and Marxist radicalism. He supported Mao Zedong's doctrine of exporting revolution but also pursued a relationship with the United States in the early 1970s – a country previously despised by China's party leaders – to counterbalance the military threat posed by the Soviet Union. Zhou was also known for the compassion he showed in advocating moderation and protecting leaders who had been purged during the tumultuous years of Mao's Cultural Revolution.

Zhou Enlai was born in Huainan, a market town near China's eastern seaboard in Kiangsu province. His family had descended from a long line of gentry. He was raised by his aunt until he was ten and lived with two uncles during his teenage years. Zhou was a precocious student who longed to make China prosper: when a teacher asked his class why they were studying, Zhou answered, "so China can rise up."

While at school Zhou became involved in acting and began his training in oratorical skills. Because of a rule forbidding women from appearing onstage with men, he often played female leads. Zhou was a natural actor, whose cinema-idol looks and flamboyant style made him a popular presence on the stage. He even received fan mail for his female roles.

After his graduation from middle school in 1917, he followed many other Chinese students who went to Japan to learn about modernization. Zhou did not attend classes

Gale International Portrait Gallery

Zhou Enlai

but became an avid reader of radical Japanese texts. He remained in Japan until the spring of 1919, when he returned to China to take part in the May Fourth movement, a vociferous and often violent response by Chinese students and intellectuals to their country's acceptance of the terms in the Treaty of Versailles that gave Japan property rights in Manchuria.

In the summer of 1920 Zhou went to France to study but, shortly after arriving, joined the Chinese communist movement. He quickly became one of its leaders and was well known for his inflammatory editorial writing and his organizational skills. He did not spend much time studying or working in France but was a political agitator, encouraging students to strike for more funds.

KMT

Zhou left France in late 1924 to go to Guangdong province, where Nationalist party (also known as the Kuomintang, or KMT) leader Sun Yat-sen was planning a revolution to defeat the despotic warlords who controlled China. Sun allowed communists to join the KMT forces. When the military institution Whampoa Academy was established by Sun, Zhou became the deputy director of its political department.

Zhou accompanied Chiang Kai-shek, who became the leader of the nationalists after Sun's death, on the Northern Expedition, Chiang's drive to the north in 1926 to defeat the warlords and unite China. Zhou barely escaped with his life after Chiang ordered a massacre of the communists in Shanghai on 12 April 1927. When Chiang found that Zhou was not among the five thousand leftists killed, he placed a $200,000 bounty on the future premier's head.

The Nanchang Uprising

In May 1927, at the CCP's Fifth National Congress, Zhou became a member of the five-man politburo, the party's leading organ. He was the mastermind behind a plan to retaliate for the Shanghai purge by taking over the southern city of Nanchang and establishing a communist base there. On 24 July thirty thousand troops led by some of the communists' finest military minds attacked the KMT forces in Nanchang. Five hours after the assault began, the communists held the city and proceeded to create a revolutionary committee. But the communists were in control of Nanchang for only two days before a KMT counterattack scattered them.

Known as the Nanchang Uprising, the communist campaign was ultimately a failure, although it marked the first time the communist army had acted without the KMT leadership. As such, the uprising is considered the birth of the Chinese Red Army.

From 1928 to 1934 Zhou was a prominent player in the communists' effort to rebuild their base. It was a difficult task because the KMT had launched five campaigns to destroy them. During this time the CCP experienced an intraparty struggle between those who believed in an urban-based revolution and a traditional military strategy and those supporting a peasant uprising using guerrilla tactics. Zhou served as a cohesive force in the CCP, positioning himself in the middle and mediating between the two sides. By October 1934 Zhou was one of the party's three most powerful leaders and was responsible for training the military.

The Long March

In mid October 1934 nationalist forces, in what was called the Fifth Extermination Campaign, appeared to be on the verge of wiping out the entire communist camp.

Chiang's men had killed sixty thousand communists and were about to close in on the communist base in the Jiangxi province when Zhou and Mao Zedong, who was at that time a secondary – but well-known – leader, along with other party leaders, decided to embark on the Long March, designed to elude the KMT. The year-long retreat, in becoming a part of the party legend, spawned epic tales of the extreme hardships the communists endured.

Three months into the trek, the caravan stopped in the city of Zunyi to hold a party meeting. Mao criticized the leadership, focusing on strategic mistakes made in Jiangxi province, such as capturing cities instead of villages. Mao's criticisms met with general approval, and he emerged as the party's most influential member. A shake-up in the leadership followed, and Zhou was the only one of the top leaders to survive Mao's coup with his position intact.

The Long March ended in Shanxi province after the group had trudged over eighty-five hundred miles of the world's most forbidding land. Of the over eighty thousand men and women who departed Jiangxi, only about nine thousand survived. Zhou and Mao emerged from the Long March as close associates, even though their personalities clashed. Whereas Zhou was sophisticated and refined, Mao was earthy and volatile. Hence, although Zhou and Mao maintained a strong mutual respect because they needed one another's talents, their friendship was never a close one.

The Xian Incident

In December 1936, with increasing public pressure on the KMT to confront Japanese aggression, Chiang Kai-shek was kidnapped by his own frustrated troops in the city of Xian. When the communists received news of Chiang's seizure, they decided to dispatch Zhou to negotiate with renegade Marshal Zhang Xueliang. Although the communists' motives behind negotiating for the release of Chiang – their most proven enemy – remain unclear, the "Xian Incident" proved to be a public-relations coup for the communists in convincing many skeptics that the communists were sincere in their claims that they stood for the public interest and a stronger China. While the nation nervously awaited news of Chiang's ordeal, Zhou was behind closed doors using his diplomatic skills to free the man who had once placed a bounty on his head. The kidnappers were not easily mollified; they preferred to kill Chiang and answer questions later. Doubt remains over the content of the negotiations, but, after two weeks, Zhou was able to persuade the marshal to free Chiang, who proceeded to make a truce with the CCP and concentrate his efforts on fighting the Japanese.

The Xian Incident is regarded as the turning point in Chinese communist history. It ultimately resulted in a

CCP-KMT "united front" against the Japanese, without which China would have been overrun in a matter of months. The formation of the united front helped sway Chinese public opinion in the communists' favor. Zhou's handling of the Xian Incident showed him to be a calm and resourceful diplomat in an explosive situation.

CCP-Nationalist Negotiations

From 1932 to 1943 Zhou was the chief CCP liaison to the Nationalist government and traveled back and forth between the communist center in Yenan and China's capital in Pahsien. Neither side was comfortable with the collaboration. In 1939 skirmishes broke out between the two parties, provoking anger between Zhou and Chiang.

In November 1944 the United States sent Ambassador Patrick Hurley to help mediate talks between the KMT and the CCP. Hurley was eager to bring the sides together but had little knowledge of China and the nuances of the issues involved. Hurley accompanied Zhou from Yenan to Pahsien for direct talks with Chiang. Little progress, if any, was made, and talks broke off in May 1945.

Zhou went back to the negotiating table in August 1945, only settling with the KMT on some minor issues. In December 1945, as a sign of American eagerness to see the hostilities resolved, Washington sent General George C. Marshall to replace Hurley. Although Marshall and Zhou got along quite well during discussions, the CCP and KMT could not agree to any long-term agreement. Fighting broke out in mid 1946, ending the chance for a peaceful settlement.

Chinese Civil War

Zhou's role during the civil war was mainly administrative, working mostly out of the communist enclave in Yenan. By mid 1948 the war had turned in the communists' favor, and their victory was sealed in the fall of 1949.

After the fall of the KMT, Zhou Enlai was named premier and foreign minister in the new communist government, the People's Republic of China (PRC). Zhou was a highly visible political figure in the early days of the PRC. He attended almost all government and party meetings, writing reports that would fill volumes. He also recruited and trained talented Chinese to serve as diplomats in the foreign ministry.

Korean War

Zhou campaigned against China's entry into the Korean War in 1950. He felt that engaging the superior American forces would detract from China's efforts to rebuild its shattered economy. But after the decision was made in the fall of 1950, Zhou issued innumerable denouncements of the United States and the United Nations

(UN). After initial breakthroughs by both sides, the war came to a stalemate in the spring of 1951. Negotiations would take two more years because of the American insistence on voluntary repatriation of prisoners of war. Zhou thought this was a challenge to Chinese sovereignty and socialist legitimacy.

In April 1954 Zhou was thrust into the international spotlight at the Geneva Conference, where it was hoped that two issues would be settled: the unification of Korea and the Indochina conflict. Zhou's opposite was U.S. secretary of state John Foster Dulles, whose hatred of communism would color Sino-U.S. relations for the next two decades. At the insistence of Dulles, the Chinese were included in the discussions as an "invited" rather than an "inviting" power. Despite the label Zhou's performance was a triumph. His arrival in Geneva was a media sensation. He was accompanied by a staff of two hundred — far more than any other communist nation — and immediately took to portraying the United States as the force responsible for preventing peace in Asia. He contrasted China to the United States, describing China as a country striving for peace and cooperation in a region of great hostility.

In discussions concerning Korea, Zhou dismissed any settlement that would leave the United Nations to supervise Korea. In his view the United Nations, which did not even include the PRC in its membership, was merely an arm of the United States. Zhou's constant parries grated Dulles, who said Zhou was giving the "standard CC boiler plate propaganda line in phraseology as well as in content" and was not using a "sophisticated approach" to diplomacy. Sophisticated or not, Zhou was successful in pitting British and French pragmaticism against the ideological rigidity of Dulles and the containment policy of the United States. He tried to exploit the tensions in the relationships among the British, who were changing from an empire to a commonwealth, the French, who wanted to extricate themselves from a war in Southeast Asia, and the Americans, who viewed regimes such as Chiang Kai-shek's in Taiwan and Syngman Rhee's in South Korea as part of a large scheme to contain communism in Asia.

Dulles's mistrust of the communists prevented him from considering any agreement, and his appearance was meant only to placate U.S. allies. Zhou, on the other hand, believed, perhaps naively, that he could forge an agreement to remove UN influence in Korea through diplomatic compromise. During the month-and-a-half-long session, Zhou repeatedly engaged in sharp exchanges with allied representatives. In mid June Zhou proposed a declaration that the Korean question would be settled at a later date. In a bitter moment for Zhou, the declaration was defeated.

The Indochina question proved less difficult to negotiate than the issues pertaining to Korea. The French, having recently experienced defeat at Dien Bien Phu, had promised its people that it would settle the issue soon, and the British were fearful of U.S. rigidity intensifying the war.

Zhou guided a peace proposal, which a French observer called a "coup de théâtre." It included a cease-fire throughout Indochina and a commission of "neutral" countries to supervise the armistice. Zhou tenaciously pursued an agreement. During a seventeen-day adjournment of the conference, he went to India, Burma, and Vietnam to sell his program. During his trip he and Indian prime minister Jawaharlal Nehru announced to the world the "five principles of peaceful coexistence." This proclamation, which stressed China's respect for the independence and sovereignty of its Asian neighbors, became a cornerstone of Chinese foreign policy.

All of the parties signed Zhou's proposal except the United States. The premier scored many points against the uncompromising Dulles, whose refusal to shake Zhou's hand at the conference embarrassed members of his own staff as well as the delegation's American allies. In a broad sense Zhou was pitting the Chinese policy of peaceful coexistence against America's policy of containment. And although Zhou's stance gained him many admirers in the diplomatic community – including American statesman Dean G. Acheson, who called Zhou "the ablest diplomat of the world not excepting Churchill" – it failed to elicit a compromise from the Americans.

International Diplomacy

In 1955 Zhou scored again at the twenty-nine–nation Afro-Asian Conference in Bandung. Zhou rubbed shoulders with such notables as Egyptian prime minister Gamal Abdul Nasser, Nehru, and Indonesian president Bung Sukarno. The conference resulted in little for China in terms of agreement, but Zhou won over skeptical leaders with his compelling calls for peaceful coexistence and anti-imperialism. Zhou also used the international spotlight to express his willingness to negotiate with the United States on the "question of relaxing tension in the Far East and especially in the Taiwan area." Zhou's proposal, which the United States met with skepticism, is commonly referred to as "Zhou's demarche."

Sino-Soviet Relations

Sino-Soviet relations were the defining feature of China's foreign policy during the 1950s and 1960s. Initially the Soviets played the role of elder brother in the relationship, giving assistance and advice to the CCP. In 1953 Zhou was sent to Moscow as the PRC representative at Joseph Stalin's funeral, where he was the only non-Soviet to stand in the procession.

The relationship, however, began to show strains in 1956 after the Twentieth Party Congress of the Soviet Union, where new leader Nikita S. Khrushchev lashed out at Stalin and his cult of personality. China had not been informed in advance as to the content of Khrushchev's speech, and the Soviet leader's program of de-Stalinization took it by surprise. Although the Chinese voiced little disapproval, Zhou felt that the speech weakened the Soviet's authority as leader of the communist world.

The Soviets began to strengthen their influence in Hungary and Poland in late 1956, and Zhou returned to Moscow in early 1957 to discuss Soviet moves to control Eastern Europe. Although Zhou would eventually play a part in persuading Hungarian leader Imre Nagy to allow the Soviets to "lead world communism" in Eastern Europe, he used his meeting with Khrushchev to criticize the Soviets for taking too much land. According to a story often relayed in communist circles, there occured at this meeting a heated exchange in which Khrushchev, unnerved by Zhou's criticisms, exclaimed, "It is all very well criticizing like this, comrade Zhou. But you must agree that it is I who spring from the working class, whereas you are a bourgeois by birth" – to which Zhou replied, "Yes, comrade Khrushchev. But at least we have one thing in common. We both betrayed our class!"

Zhou returned to Moscow in February 1959 to sign an agreement for Soviet aid in building seventy-eight industrial and power plants. The agreement lasted until July 1960, when the Soviets withdrew all projects and advisers as a result of worsening tensions between the two countries, due to both doctrinal and personality conflicts. Khrushchev believed China had taken a foolish step in launching the Great Leap Forward (GLF) in 1958, which was intended to propel the Chinese economy directly into communism but instead resulted in famine. Khrushchev also felt the Chinese had become haughty in their behavior toward him. The Chinese felt that Khrushchev was attempting to limit their independence from the Soviets and control PRC policies, about which the Soviets, the Chinese believed, had little understanding.

The 1960 withdrawal sparked open hostilities between the two countries that would last the entire decade. During Chinese general secretary Deng Xiaoping and President Liu Shaoqi's visit to Moscow in late 1960, Deng was openly confrontational in his denouncement of Soviet ideology. Zhou arrived in Moscow in October 1961 for the Twenty-second Party Congress of the Soviet Union. The congress turned into mutual finger pointing as a result of Khrushchev's harangue against Albania, a country which China supported. Zhou became so incensed that he walked out of the conference and, in a cruel rebuttal, went to Stalin's grave to lay a wreath. Relations were doomed for the next three decades.

Zhou's relations with Indian prime minister Nehru also became strained at this time. The border between China and India, which Zhou felt was unfavorably drawn by the "British imperialists," was the point of contention that resulted in periodic military scuffles starting in 1959. After failed attempts to compromise in 1962, full-scale conflict erupted, resulting in a humiliating defeat for the Indian army. The misunderstanding and bitterness between Zhou and Nehru never ceased. Zhou would later say that Nehru was the most arrogant man he had ever met.

Zhou's foreign policy during the 1960s focused on exporting the Chinese revolution overseas. In addition to aiding communist movements in Asia, China tried to pry Africa's revolutionary movements away from the Soviet Union. In one of the longest diplomatic sojourns in modern times, Zhou departed China on 11 December 1963 on a seventy-two-day tour, covering thirty-six thousand miles and thirteen Third World countries. He found more differences than similarities in the African revolutions, and eventually China did not substantially assist any of these movements.

The Cultural Revolution

Zhou's most apparent flaw was his unswerving loyalty to Mao Zedong, preventing him from voicing objections to the chairman's errors. This acquiescence was most apparent during the Cultural Revolution (1966–1976), during which Mao and an inner core of radical leaders encouraged the smashing of the "too-bureaucratic" system. Initially, Zhou strongly supported the movement, but when the havoc created by the Red Guards – recruited revolutionary adolescents – began to threaten the institutions Zhou had built, he became skeptical. Still, Zhou did not openly challenge the correctness of the movement but chose to moderate from within the party. Using his political savvy, he continued to speak out in favor of the Cultural Revolution while trying to shield those party members who were attacked, such as Deng Xiaoping and Chen Yi. Zhou himself came under verbal attack by the Red Guards in 1967 and 1968 but, because of his popularity, was able to evade the charges.

Zhou's final great moment as a politician and a diplomat came at the unlikeliest of times. The domestic focus of the Cultural Revolution had forced the foreign ministry into hibernation, and Lin Biao, Mao's chosen successor, was opposed to any rapprochement with the United States. But Zhou, displaying a keen instinct for political opportunism, pressed for renewed relations with the United States. His decision was no doubt influenced by the Soviet threat, which had reached a climax in 1969 in a border scuffle over a disputed island in the Ussuri River. In leaning toward the United States, Zhou proved to be a political realist as well as a Marxist, reasoning that Sino-U.S. comity would give each country a buffer against its most hated adversary – the Soviet Union.

After receiving back-channel gestures of openness from the Chinese in 1970, U.S. president Richard M. Nixon sent National Security Adviser Henry Kissinger on two secret missions to meet with Zhou, in July and October 1971. Rarely have two statesmen gotten along so well. Kissinger would later remark that Zhou had "one of the most acute and unsentimental assessments of reality I have ever encountered." The mission set up Nixon's visit in February 1972: a symbolic end to two decades of belligerence between the two countries. Zhou's move was brilliant. He simultaneously isolated the Soviets in the U.S.-China-USSR strategic triangle and scored with the West. Zhou had finally overcome Dulles's rebuff at Geneva.

Shortly after the visit, Zhou was diagnosed with incurable cancer. In his last years he continued trying to restore the economic health of China and strengthen ties to the West. Although confined to a hospital bed much of the time, Zhou continued to receive some foreign visitors. He died 8 January 1976 in Beijing.

Book by Zhou (Selected)
Selected Works of Zhou Enlai (Beijing: Foreign Languages Press, 1980).

Books about Zhou (Selected)
Kai-yu Hsu, *Chou En-lai, China's Gray Eminence* (Garden City, N.Y.: Doubleday, 1968);

Ronald Keith, *The Diplomacy of Zhou Enlai* (Basingstoke, England: Macmillan, 1989);

Le Tien-ming, *Chou En-lai* (Taipei: Institute of International Relations, 1970);

Dick Wilson, *Zhou Enlai* (New York: Viking, 1984).
– K. W. M.

SEE ALSO THESE RELATED ENTRIES

Chiang Kai-shek, 2; Deng Xiaoping, 2; John Foster Dulles, 1; Henry Kissinger, 1; Nikita S. Khrushchev, 2; Lin Biao, 2; Liu Shaoqi, 2; Richard M. Nixon, 1.

Georgi K. Zhukov

Soviet Minister of Defense, 1955–1957
Born Strelkovka, Russia, 2 December 1896
Died Moscow, Soviet Union, 18 June 1974

The son of Konstantin A. Zhukov, a poor shoemaker, and Ustinya Artemyevna, a farm laborer, Georgi Konstantinovich Zhukov was born in Strelkovka in Kaluga province of Russia. He showed promise as a young student before financial difficulties forced him to abandon his studies. Zhukov's rise to the top military post in the Soviet Union began, ironically, with his enrollment in 1915 as a private in the Imperial Russian Army. By 1917 he had become a sergeant and had been decorated two times with the Cross of Saint George. After the October Revolution of 1917, which brought the Bolsheviks to power, Zhukov decided to join the Red Army. He served as a cavalry officer during the Russian civil war of 1918–1921, when the survival of Lenin's regime was still in doubt. Steadily Zhukov rose through the ranks of the Red Army and participated with Semyon Timoshenko in the development of Soviet armored forces.

Zhukov's career advanced most dramatically during World War II. He was appointed, successively, as chief of staff of Soviet forces in the final stage of the Soviet-Finnish war (January 1940), chief of staff of the Red Army (May 1940), and alternate member of the Politburo (January 1941). Among Zhukov's wartime activities were representation of the high command on the central and Leningrad fronts (June 1941), command of reserve forces around Moscow during the Nazis' unsuccessful efforts to take the Soviet capital, organization of the Stalingrad counteroffensive, guidance of operations leading to the liberation of Leningrad, and command of the Soviet invasion of Germany. Zhukov was personally involved in the major episodes of the German-Soviet conflict and, as deputy commissar of defense under Joseph Stalin, oversaw the entire Soviet war effort. In 1945–1946 Zhukov commanded Soviet occupation forces in Germany, then was recalled to Moscow to serve as deputy minister of defense and commander of ground forces.

Banishment to Obscurity

Promoted to marshal in recognition of his wartime achievements, Zhukov had every reason to expect he would continue to play a key role in Soviet military life, when in 1946 he was suddenly transferred to an obscure command in Odessa. Stalin sought to portray himself as the foremost military genius of World War II and was jealous of Zhukov's reputation. After Stalin's death, Zhukov recalled that Soviet generals had been afraid to warn Stalin of Hitler's impending invasion in June 1941 – despite clear indications of Nazi intentions – because Stalin believed that Hitler would not attack and regarded anyone who disagreed with his views as an opponent. While Stalin displayed tactical genius during the war, his lack of foresight contributed enormously to the large loss of Soviet lives (27 million dead compared to 7 million German dead). By demoting Zhukov, Stalin had hoped both to claim all credit for victory in the war and to remove a potential political opponent.

Though he later gained the reputation in the West as a Soviet hard-liner, at the close of World War II, Zhukov was quite popular in the United States (appearing on the cover of *Time* magazine in December 1947), and he had developed a friendship with Dwight D. Eisenhower from the time of Eisenhower's command of Allied forces in Europe. Zhukov began to reemerge from relative obscurity at the time of the outbreak of the Korean War in June 1950, when North Korean forces invaded South Korea along the 38th parallel. He reportedly attended a Supreme Soviet meeting in the same month as the North Korean invasion, gave military advice to the Chinese forces supporting North Korea during the winter offensive of 1950, and met with Mao Zedong and top North Korean officials in an effort to determine the appropriate level of Soviet involvement in the conflict. By 1952 Zhukov had been reinstated in the posts from which Stalin had earlier removed him.

From his position as deputy minister of defense Zhukov lobbied for the interests of the military. He opposed activities of political officers in the Red Army and argued against the idea, associated with Premier Georgi M. Malenkov, that the Soviet defense budget could be significantly reduced because nuclear weapons would deter both sides from starting a war. Though Zhukov recognized the importance of nuclear weapons, he maintained that ground forces could be a decisive factor in any type of conflict.

Minister of Defense

Soviet communist first secretary Nikita S. Khrushchev depended heavily on support from the military during his struggle with Malenkov to succeed Stalin. In exchange

Georgi K. Zhukov

for his support, Zhukov was named minister of defense in 1955.

During the July 1955 Big Four Summit in Geneva, Switzerland, Zhukov was a member of the Soviet delegation and talked candidly with American president Eisenhower on two occasions, providing, according to Eisenhower, "an amazingly personal briefing on inside Kremlin secrets." The Geneva summit ended inconclusively. The Soviets' apparent eagerness to reduce East-West tensions was not matched by many specific proposals. One exception was the Soviets' treatment of Austria. Zhukov's order to remove forty-four thousand Soviet troops from Austria saved it from the fate of its East European neighbor. The withdrawal of Western and Soviet occupation forces from Austria occurred shortly before the Soviet invasion of Hungary in 1956, in which Zhukov also played a major role.

The 1956 Hungarian Invasion

The Hungarian uprising, which led to the Soviet invasion, was itself triggered by the "secret speech" Khrushchev gave during the Twentieth Party Congress of February 1956 — a speech in which Khrushchev denounced Stalin and, at least by implication, all of the Stalinist regimes that had been imposed on Eastern Europe following World War II.

Unrest first broke out in Poznan, Poland, in October 1956. Zhukov personally directed Soviet forces in Poland to begin moving on Warsaw in an attempt to intimidate the new, relatively independent regime of Wladyslaw Gomulka. This Soviet-Polish confrontation ended in a compromise, once the Soviets realized that the Polish Central Committee would not abandon Gomulka. Certain restrictions on Soviet military power within Poland were instituted, while the country itself remained firmly within the Soviet orbit.

Polish political ferment was a factor contributing to rebellion in Hungary during the same month. But in Hungary events proved to be far less manageable. The political monopoly of the Communist party was challenged. Hungarian nationalist communist leader Imre Nagy formed a government including four noncommunist cabinet ministers. Moreover, Hungarian demonstrators were calling for the removal of Soviet troops from Hungary as well as recognition of Hungarian independence. Khrushchev would not tolerate such defiance and ordered the invasion. Zhukov favored strong action from the beginning of the crisis and probably signed the orders sending Soviet tanks into Budapest on 24 October to crush the uprising. Ten thousand Hungarians and Soviets died in the fighting before the Red Army managed to regain control.

In January 1957 Zhukov made a trip to India, a journey which marked a significant step toward increasing Soviet influence in neutral Asian countries. In March 1957 he delivered the keynote address at the Soviet Armed Forces Conference in Moscow. He reiterated his views regarding the continued relevance of large-scale conventional forces in the nuclear age and also attacked the Eisenhower Doctrine of 1957, according to which the United States pledged to defend the Middle East against communist aggression.

Zhukov reached the height of recognition later in 1957, after helping Khrushchev to survive a major political crisis. A majority of Khrushchev's colleagues on the Presidium had voted to remove Khrushchev from power. Khrushchev appealed the decision to the larger Central Committee. Zhukov ordered Soviet military planes to rush Central Committee delegates to Moscow so as to save Khrushchev from the so-called antiparty group in the Presidium. In appreciation of his support, Khrushchev made Zhukov a full member of the Presidium. Zhukov was the first professional soldier ever to become part of the inner core of the top Soviet political elite but his membership was short-lived. Like Stalin before him, Khrushchev began to fear that Zhukov's reputation might overshadow his own. In October 1957 Zhukov was unceremoniously removed from all of his posts and sent into obscurity for a second time, to be officially pensioned in March 1958. The main charge against Zhukov was trying to restrict Communist party influence within the military. Following Khrushchev's fall from power in 1964, Zhukov was rehabilitated for the second time, but did not regain his earlier power and prestige.

One of the secondary charges against Zhukov in 1957 was "adventurism in foreign policy," a reference to his ultra-hard-line position during the 1956 Hungarian crisis. Zhukov had been a hard-liner from the start of the uprising. But his position soon became Khrushchev's as well. From the early period of Bolshevik power through World War II, Zhukov's foreign-policy views reflected the current priorities of the Soviet regime, at times even before those priorities had crystallized. He was repeatedly disgraced because his achievements threatened to detract from the authority of political leaders, only to be vindicated in the end.

Books by Zhukov (Selected)

Marshal Zhukov's Greatest Battles, edited by Harrison E. Salisbury and translated by Theodore Shabad (New York: Harper & Row, 1969);

The Memoirs of Marshal Zhukov (New York: Delacorte, 1971).

Book about Zhukov

Otto Preston Chaney, Jr., *Zhukov* (Norman: University of Oklahoma Press, 1971).

General References

Seweryn Bialer, *Stalin and His Generals: Soviet Military Memoirs of World War II* (New York: Pegasus, 1969);

John Erickson, *The Soviet High Command: A Military-Political History, 1918–1941* (New York: St. Martin's Press, 1962);

Roman Kolkowicz, *The Soviet Army and the Communist Party: Institutions in Conflict* (Santa Monica, Calif.: Rand, 1966);

Alexander Werth, *Russia at War, 1941–1945* (New York: Dutton, 1964).

– J. W.

SEE ALSO THESE RELATED ENTRIES

Wladyslaw Gomulka, 2; Nikita S. Khrushchev, 2; Imre Nagy, 2; Joseph Stalin, 2.

Mohammad Zia ul-Haq

President of Pakistan, 1978–1988
Born Jullundur, India, 1924
Died Bahawalpur, Pakistan, 17 August 1988

General Mohammad Zia ul-Haq was president of Pakistan from 1978 to 1988. The son of an army clerical officer, Zia joined the British Indian army in 1943 and was commissioned an officer in 1945. He served in Burma, Indonesia, and Malaysia during World War II. Upon the creation of the Pakistani army in 1947, he opted to serve in the Pakistani military. He was sent for military training to the United States and in 1970 served in the army of King Hussein of Jordan during the Jordanian civil war. In 1972 he was promoted to major general in the Pakistani army and given command of an armored division, and he was later promoted to lieutenant general in 1975. In 1976 Zia, who had the reputation of a professional officer with no interest in politics, was appointed chief of staff by Zulfikar Ali Bhutto, the prime minister he would later overthrow in a military seizure of power.

The Overthrow of Bhutto

As the nationwide violence escalated following the contested elections of March 1977, Zia, with the apparent backing and encouragement of other senior military officers, seized power on 5 July 1977. After suspending the constitution, the military justified its actions as necessary for the restoration of conditions for fair elections, but a confrontation erupted between Zia and the ousted prime minister Bhutto. Bhutto was subsequently sentenced to death and eventually executed. Zia, who remained chief of staff and assumed the presidency in September 1978, ruled collectively with an inner circle of the military junta. Decision making is believed to have been collegial. The Zia regime imposed Islamic law, and domestic political life remained closed off under martial law, which was not lifted until late 1985.

Despite the volatility of the domestic situation in Pakistan, Zia maintained a stable foreign policy. He continued efforts to improve relations with Pakistan's traditional rival, India, to remain engaged in Middle Eastern politics, and to promote closer ties with Islamic countries. In his bid to become a leader in the Islamic world, Zia emerged as a key actor in the revival of the Organization of the Islamic Conference, which periodically brought together heads of Islamic states. In 1979 Zia withdrew Pakistan from the U.S.-led Central Asia Treaty Organization and joined the Non-Aligned Movement. Pakistan, whose armed forces are widely recognized for their pro-

Mohammad Zia ul-Haq

fessionalism, training, and discipline, became one of the few Third World countries to have military missions abroad, usually as part of multinational peacekeeping operations.

The one area where Pakistan's foreign policy changed was in relations with the United States. Zia returned Pakistan to a foreign policy of strong ties to the United States, which in turn renewed its security pledge to Pakistan. Despite closer ties with the United States, Zia steered Pakistani foreign policy in a manner sufficient to preclude vulnerability to U.S. pressures, especially in the area of human rights and nuclear technological development.

Soviet Invasion of Afghanistan

In the wake of the Soviet invasion of Afghanistan in December 1979, Pakistan became one of the principal actors in international diplomatic efforts to reach a settlement. Pakistan condemned the invasion, even though its relations with rival Afghanistan traditionally had been poor; it also became the primary host of millions of refugees as well as the main base for Afghan guerrillas, the mujahedin. Zia embarked on an international campaign to garner support for Pakistan's position on Afghanistan and to maintain pressure on the Soviet Union to withdraw its forces. The Soviet invasion drew Pakistan closer to the United States, which renewed large-scale military aid, including a $3.2 billion package in 1981. Pakistan also became the primary conduit of U.S. covert aid to the Afghan guerrilla forces.

Zia ul-Haq's dominance of Pakistani politics continued after the February 1985 elections. The opposition's boycott of the elections allowed Zia to install a nominal civilian government. He remained chief of staff, however. The civilian government was dissolved in May 1988, and new elections were scheduled. Zia ul-Haq died in a suspicious plane crash on 17 August 1988.

General References

Sahid Javed Burki, *Pakistan: A Nation in the Making* (Boulder, Colo.: Westview Press, 1986);

Ayesha Jalal, *The State of Martial Rule: The Origins of Pakistan's Political Economy of Defence* (New York: Cambridge University Press, 1990).

—J. R.-S.

SEE ALSO THESE RELATED ENTRIES
Zulfikar Ali Bhutto, 2.

Contributors

V. A. ....Vera Azar
M. B. ....Michael Brown
J. B. ....Janusz Bugajski
A. B. ....Aimee Breslow
B. D. ....Beth Davis
L. L. E. ....Laurie L. Essig
A. F. ....Amy Feldman
M. G. G. .... Mary G. Gotschall
L. H. ....Linda Hipple
Q. I. ....Qadri Ismail
P. M. ....Peter Macdonald
K. W. M. ....Kin Wah Moy
J. R. ....James C. Raffel
J. R.-S. ....Joao Resende-Santos
G. R. ....Gary Rosen
J. W. ....John Webb

Index

Khmer People's Revolutionary party, 271, 292

Khmer Rouge, 271, 272, 292, 293, 310

Khomeini, Ruholla Musavi, *172–173*, 156, 228, 230

Khrushchev, Nikita S., *174–181*, 11, 33, 44, 45, 51, 52, 58, 59, 72, 80, 110, 119, 125, 129, 183, 186, 187, 203, 204–205, 206, 207, 211, 212, 223, 234, 246, 262, 287, 288, 320, 328, 332, 344, 364, 366, 368

Kikuyu Central Association, 170

Kim Il-Sung, *181–185*, 268

Kim Jong Il, 184

Kirilenko, Andrei, 70

Kirov, Sergei M., 185, 357

Kissinger, Henry A., 20, 47, 98, 130, 169, 229, 238, 251, 260, 314, 365

Komsomol, 11, 69, 112–113, 327

Korea, 150

Korean War, 182–183, 210–211, 268, 323–324, 363, 366

Kosygin, Alexei Nikolaevich, *185–188*, 45, 46

Krenz, Egon, 305

Kulakov, Fyodor, 113

Kulikov, Viktor, 262

Kun, Bela, 199

Kuomintang, 75–76, 78, 79, 192, 194, 209, 362

Kuron, Jacek, *189–191*

Kuusinen, Otto, 11

Kuwait, 16, 23, 156

La prensa, 67, 68, 265

Latvia, 117

Lavon, 29

Lebanese Forces, 99

Lebanese Phalange, 99, 100

Lebanon, 15, 20, 21, 22, 99–100, 302–303

Lenin, Vladimir I., 319, 335

Lenin Peace Prize, 26

Leshi, Haxhi, 5

Liberia, 254

Liberman, Evsei, 186

Libya, 254, 276–279

Ligachev, Yegor, 114

Li Li-san, 209

Li Xiannian, *191–192*, 82

Lin Biao, *192–195*, 212, 365

Lithuania, 117

Litvinov, Maxim M., 128, 233

Liu Bocheng, 79, 191

Liu Shaoqi, *196–198*, 80, 158, 212, 354, 364

Long March, 79, 193, 196, 209, 267, 362

Lon Nol, 272, 310

Luce, Henry, 76

Lukács, György, *199–200*

Lumumba, Patrice, *200–202*, 226, 227, 246, 255, 338, 339

Lusaka Accords, 295

Lysenko, Trofim, 288

MacArthur, Douglas A., 183

Machel, Samora, 238

Macmillan, Harold, 179

Mahdi, Ali, 308

Malawi, 313

Malenkov, Georgi, *203–205*, 51, 177, 186, 186, 234, 357, 358, 366

Malinovsky, Rodion, *206–207*, 125–126

Mandela, Nelson, 169

Mao Zedong, *208–213*, 79, 80, 81, 148, 179, 192, 194, 195, 197–198, 267, 268, 323, 362

Mapai, 28, 93, 94

Marshall, George C., 76, 150, 193, 363

Marshall Plan, 323, 358

Martov, Jules, 333

Masaryk, Jan, 122

Matsu Island, 268

Mau Mau rebellion, 9, 170

Mazowiecki, Tadeusz, *214–215*, 190, 221, 305, 351

McDowell, David, 137

Medvedev, Zhores, 288

Meir, Golda, *216–217*, 94, 280

Mengistu Haile Mariam, *218–220*, 139, 307

Mensheviks, 175, 319, 348

Mercador, Ramon, 335

Michnik, Adam, *220–221*

Mihajlovic, Draza, 331

Mikoyan, Anastas, *222–224*, 45, 234, 324

Military Committee, Syria, 19

Military Council for National Salvation, Poland, 162, 351

Mimeiri, Jafar Mohammed, 278

Mindszenty, József, Cardinal, *225–226*

Mlynar, Zdenek, 113

Mobil Corporation, 235

Mobutu, Joseph D., 201

Modzelewski, Karol, 189

Mohamed, Ali Mahdi, 308

Mohammad Reza Pahlevi, *228–231*, 172, 235

Moi, Daniel Arap, 171

Molotov, Vyacheslav Michailovich, *232–235*, 44, 51, 128, 176, 177, 178, 186, 204, 323, 324

Morales, Machado y, 24

Morocco, 254, 278

Mortimer, Edward, 154

Moscow Committee for Human Rights, 289

Mossadegh, Mohammad, *235–236*, 229

Movement for Assemblies of the People (MAP), Grenada, 34

Movement for the Advancement of Community Effort (MACE), Grenada, 34

Movement for the Triumph of Democratic Liberties, Algeria, 25–26

Mozambican National Resistance, 239

Mozambique, 239, 314

Mugabe, Robert, *237–240*, 260, 314

Muslim Brotherhood, 21, 244

Muzorewa, Abel, 314

Mwinyi, Ali Hassan, 261

Nagy, Imre, *241–243*, 11–12, 101, 166, 223, 225, 283, 328, 364

Nanchang Uprising, 193, 362

Nasser, Gamal Abdul, *243–247*, 3–4, 15, 20, 26, 94, 326, 330

National Council of the Algerian Revolution, 40

National Council of the Homeland, Poland, 32

National Democratic party, Zimbabwe, 237

National Falange party, 95

National Front for the Liberation of Angola (FNLA), 248, 249, 294, 297–298

National Front for the Liberation of Palestine (NFLP), 136

National Front for the Liberation of South Vietnam (NLF), 144

National Front for the National Liberation of Kampuchea, 292

National Front of Czechoslovak Communist Exiles, 121

National Iranian Oil Company, 229, 236

National Liberation Front (FLN), Algeria, 26, 84

National Liberation Movement (NLM), Albania, 5

National Opposition Union, Nicaragua, 68

National Peasant party, Romania, 103

National Revolution Army (NRA), China, 75

National Union for the Total Liberation of Angola (UNITA), 227, 248, 249

National Unity Goverment, Israel, 281, 303

Nayif, Abd al-Razzaq, 155

Nazi-Soviet Non-Aggression Pact, 86

Neguib, Muhammad, 244

Nehru, Jawaharlal, 97, 326, 364, 364–365

Neo-Destour party, Tunisia, 42, 43

Neto, Antonio Agostinho, *248–250*, 53, 60, 295

The New Class (Djilas), 88

New Economic Mechanism, Hungary, 167